New Learning Solutions

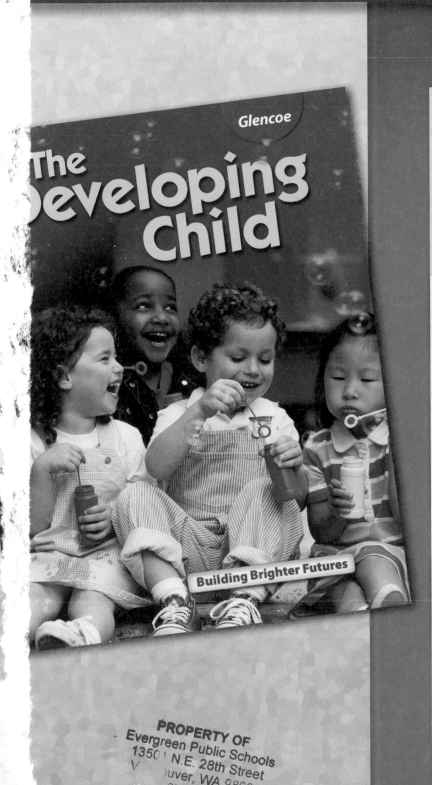

Glencoe

The Developing Child

Building Brighter Futures

Improve Academic Performance
- National Academic Standards
- Academic Vocabulary
- Reading Guides
- Writing Tips and Activities
- Math and Science in Action
- Standardized Test Practice

Connect to the Real World
- Learning Through Play
- Respond to Special Needs
- Culture Matters

Hands-On Learning
- Interpersonal and Collaborative Skills Support FCCLA
- Project-Based Learning
- What Would You Do? Activities
- Unit Thematic Projects

Online Resources
- Online Student Edition
- Graphic Organizers
- Evaluation Rubrics
- Glossary/Spanish Glosario

 Log on to *The Developing Child* Online Learning Center at **glencoe.com**

The Developing Child

Holly E. Brisbane

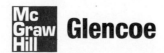

About the Author

Holly Brisbane graduated Magna Cum Laude from Minnesota State University Mankato with a Bachelor of Arts degree in English and Home Economics. She then went on to obtain her Master of Arts degree in English. She taught courses in Family & Consumer Sciences and English. She is also an author and editor who has published numerous articles on teaching and motivation, in addition to textbooks in the field of Family and Consumer Sciences. Holly has appeared in Who's Who in America Among Authors and Writers for her top-selling textbooks, including The Developing Child. Holly was also awarded an Outstanding Alumna Award from Minnesota State University Mankato. She is a current member and past president of American Association of University Women (AAUW), whose mission is to advance the equity for women and girls through advocacy, education, and research.

Glencoe

The *McGraw·Hill* Companies

Send all inquiries to:
Glencoe/McGraw-Hill
4400 Easton Commons
Columbus, OH 43219

ISBN: 978-0-07-888360-6   (Student Edition)
MHID: 0-07-888360-1   (Student Edition)
ISBN: 978-0-07-888432-0   (Teacher Wraparound Edition)
MHID: 0-07-888432-2   (Teacher Wraparound Edition)

6 7 8 9   RJE   14 13 12 11

Reviewers

Teacher Reviewers

Mary Kay Anderson MEd
Family and Consumer Sciences Teacher
Shorewood High Schools
Shorewood, Wisconsin

Linda Brown
Family and Consumer Sciences Teacher
Sanderson High School
Raleigh, North Carolina

Nancy Campbell
Family and Consumer Sciences Teacher
Walker Career Center
Warren Central High School
Indianapolis, Indiana

Mary Beth Carver
Family and Consumer Sciences Teacher
Canadian Valley Technology Center
Chickasha, Oklahoma

Kathryn Cox
Family and Consumer Sciences Teacher
William G. Enloe Magnet High School
Raleigh, North Carolina

Tangela Frost
Family and Consumer Sciences Teacher
Southern Alamance High School
Graham, North Carolina

Christine Bunte Halweg
Family and Consumer Sciences Teacher
Peotone High School
Peotone, Illinois

Janet Hartline
Family and Consumer Sciences Teacher
Fort Payne High School
Fort Payne, Alabama

Vikki Jackson
Family and Consumer Sciences Teacher
Kathleen Middle School
Lakeland, Florida

Tammy Lamparter
Family and Consumer Sciences Teacher
Smyrna High School
Smyrna, Tennessee

Georgia Lash
Family and Consumer Sciences Teacher
Hillcrest High School
Simpsonville, South Carolina

Pheobe McGuire
Family and Consumer Sciences Teacher
James Monroe High School
Lindside, West Virginia

Stephanie Meinke
Vocational Coordinator
Family and Consumer Sciences Teacher
Farmington Public Schools
Farmington, Minnesota

Valerie Morgan
Family and Consumer Sciences Teacher
Water Valley High School
Water Valley, Mississippi

Nancy Plowman
Family and Consumer Sciences Teacher
Davis County High School
Bloomfield, Iowa

Karin Ohr Pyskaty
Department Chair
Family and Consumer Sciences
Lyman Hall High School
Wallingford, Connecticut

Pamela S. Pruett
Family and Consumer Sciences Teacher
Blytheville High School
Blytheville, Arkansas

Shirley Rauh
Department Chair, Family and
   Consumer Sciences
Mehlville High School
St. Louis, Missouri

Becky Roseberry
Family and Consumer Sciences Teacher
Pulaski County High School
Dublin, Virginia

Wendy Whately
Family and Consumer Sciences Teacher
Randleman High School
Randleman, North Carolina

Camille Williams
Family and Consumer Sciences Teacher
Provo High School
Provo, Utah

Kristina Yarborough
Family and Consumer Sciences Teacher
Gray's Creek High School
Hope Mills, North Carolina

Technical Reviewers

Dr. Scott Bledsoe, PsyD
Director, Child and Family
   Development Center
Azusa Pacific University
Azusa, California

Dr. Gayle Mindes EdD
Department Chair
DePaul University
Chicago, Illinois

Gina Montefusco
Pediatric Nurse
Children's Hospital, Los Angeles
Los Angeles, California

Victoria Tennent, M. Ed.
Educational Consultant
Olympia, Washington

Phillip Verhoef, PhD, MD
Departments of Internal Medicine and
   Pediatrics
University of California, Los Angeles
Los Angeles, California

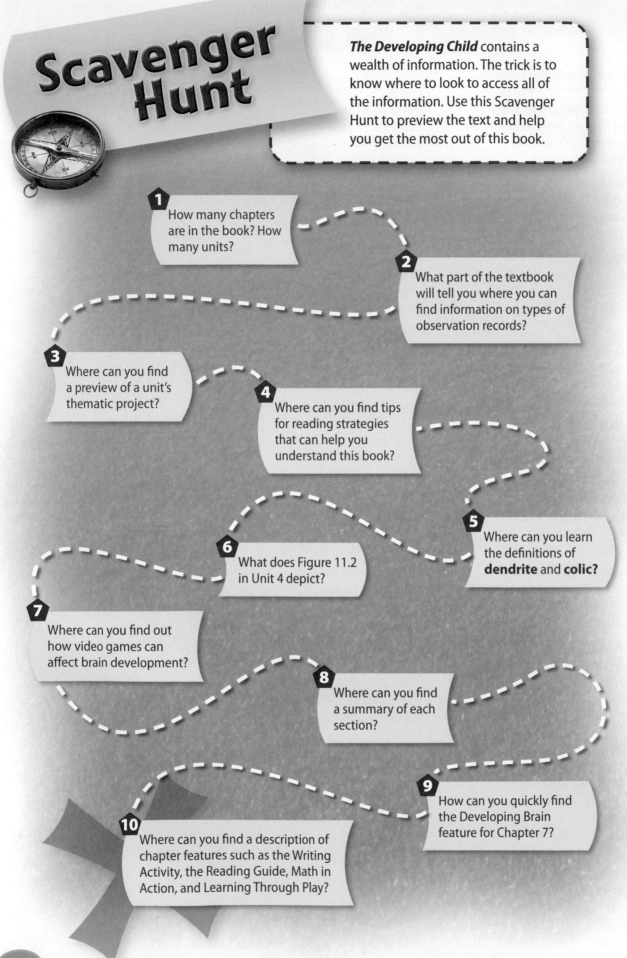

Scavenger Hunt

The Developing Child contains a wealth of information. The trick is to know where to look to access all of the information. Use this Scavenger Hunt to preview the text and help you get the most out of this book.

1 How many chapters are in the book? How many units?

2 What part of the textbook will tell you where you can find information on types of observation records?

3 Where can you find a preview of a unit's thematic project?

4 Where can you find tips for reading strategies that can help you understand this book?

5 Where can you learn the definitions of **dendrite** and **colic?**

6 What does Figure 11.2 in Unit 4 depict?

7 Where can you find out how video games can affect brain development?

8 Where can you find a summary of each section?

9 How can you quickly find the Developing Brain feature for Chapter 7?

10 Where can you find a description of chapter features such as the Writing Activity, the Reading Guide, Math in Action, and Learning Through Play?

Table of Contents

FOCUS ON   **Reading Strategies**
In each section, look for these reading strategies:

- Before You Read
- Graphic Organizer
- As You Read
- Reading Check
- After You Read

Table of Contents

FOCUS ON **Academic Success**
To help you succeed in your
classes and on tests, look
for these academic skills:

- **Reading Guides**
- **Writing Tips**
- **Math Concepts and Hints**
- **Financial Literacy**
- **Science in Action**

Table of Contents

FOCUS ON Visuals
Images help you learn key ideas. Answer the questions for all:

- Unit and Chapter Openers
- Photos and Captions
- Figures and Tables

Table of Contents

FOCUS ON   **Project-Based Learning**
Projects throughout this book can help you use your skills in real-life situations:

- Real-World scenarios
- Step-by-step instructions
- Independent and group activities

Table of Contents

FOCUS ON **Assessment**
Look for review questions and activities to help you remember important topics.

- Reading Checks
- Section Reviews
- Chapter Reviews
- Unit Thematic Projects

Table of Contents

FOCUS ON Online Resources
Look for the online icon and
go to the book's Online Learning
Center at **glencoe.com** for:

- Graphic Organizers
- Evaluation Rubrics
- Career Resources
- Worksheets
- Additional Activities

Table of Contents

Unit 7 **Additional Topics of Study** **516**

Academic Skills for Life!

How much do you think child care will cost? Do you know why someone has brown hair instead of red hair? How does human contact affect brain development? These academic features will help you succeed in school, on tests, and with life!

Math in Action

Science in Action

THE DEVELOPING BRAIN

The Importance of Play

Various forms of play promote learning at each stage of development. It is important to keep children safe while encouraging appropriate play. These features help teach you how!

SAFE CHILD HEALTHY CHILD

Features Table of Contents

Can You Relate?

Put yourself in someone else's shoes and use what you know to offer advice about real-world problems. Be thoughtful and give your informed opinion.

What Would You Do?

Check Out These Skills You Can Use!

Learn basic skills that you can use as a parent, friend, or professional to care for and nurture children. Also learn how special needs can affect child development and child care.

Parenting Skills

RESPOND TO SPECIAL NEEDS

Learn About Children Around the World

Ever wonder how people in other countries are just like you? How are they different? This feature gives you a peek at life in various cultures.

CULTURE MATTERS

What Do You Want to Be?

What career options are open to you? What skills will you need to succeed in your career? Learn how to reach your goals to work with children.

Careers With Children

To the Student

Begin the Unit | Understand the Development of Children

Successful readers first set a purpose for reading. *The Developing Child* teaches skills you need to understand how children grow and develop, physically, socially, emotionally, and intellectually. Think about why you are reading this book. Use the Unit Opener to help you set a reading purpose and understand what you will learn in each unit. Consider how you might be able to use what you learn in your own life.

Read the Chapter Titles to find out what the topics will be.

Preview the Thematic Project at the end of the unit. A preview lets you know what is to come. Use the preview to think about how what you are learning applies to the project.

Unit 3
The Baby's First Year

Chapter **7** — Physical Development of Infants

Chapter **8** — Emotional and Social Development of Infants

Chapter **9** — Intellectual Development of Infants

Unit | Thematic Project Preview

Raise a Healthy Baby
In this unit, you will learn how infants grow and develop during their first twelve months. You will also learn about the important role of parents and caregivers in a baby's physical and mental health. In your unit thematic project, you will explore how caregivers can support a baby's healthy growth and development.

My Journal

Healthy Development Write a journal entry about one of the topics below. This will help you prepare for the project at the end of this unit.
- How can a parent or caregiver help a baby grow up physically healthy?
- How can a parent or caregiver help a baby develop trusting relationships with adults and siblings?
- How can a parent or caregiver help a baby develop language skills?

191

Explore the Photo
Parents play a large role in ensuring their baby's health and well-being. How might a child's early relationships influence his relationships later in life?

190

Use the Photo to Predict what the unit will be about. Answer questions to help focus on unit topics.

Practice Your Writing in a personal journal. Your writing will help you prepare for the project at the end of the unit.

Close the Unit

What Did You Learn About Child Development?

Every unit ends with a Thematic Project that lets you explore an important issue from the unit. To complete each project, you will make decisions, do research, connect to your community, create a visual, and present your project.

Read the Project Assignment and numbered steps. The assignment explains what you will need to do.

Follow the Project Checklist to make sure that you have done everything you need to complete your thematic project.

Unit — Thematic Project

Raise a Healthy Baby

In this unit, you have learned that a child's first year is a time of great change. Parents and caregivers play a very important role in helping the child grow and develop. In this project, you will research a specific area of infant growth and development and explore what parents and caregivers can do to support a baby in this area.

My Journal

If you completed the journal entry from page 193, refer to it to see if your thoughts have changed after reading the unit.

Project Assignment

In this project, you will:
- Choose a feature of infant growth and development that interests you.
- Conduct research about the topic you have chosen.
- Interview a parent or child care professional about your topic.
- Prepare a presentation to share what you have learned with your class.

Child Development Skills Behind the Project

- Evaluate parenting roles and responsibilities.
- Identify a child's physical, emotional, and intellectual needs.
- Describe the growth and development of infants.

Academic Skills

English Language Arts Standards

NCTE 4 Use written language to communicate effectively.

NCTE 7 Conduct research and gather, evaluate, and synthesize data to communicate discoveries.

286 Unit 3 The Baby's First Year

Step 1 Choose and Research Your Topic

The topics below are examples of areas in which infants grow and develop over their first year. Choose one of these topics, or select another topic approved by your teacher. Research its importance to healthy growth and development.
- Language skills
- Motor skills
- Development of emotions
- Vision
- Eating and sleeping
- Attachment to caregivers
- Relating to strangers
- Relating to other children

Write a summary of your research to:
- **Describe** milestones of infant growth and development in the chosen area.
- **Explain** how parents or caregivers can foster an infant's health in this area.
- **Identify** possible problems or disorders that can occur and how caregivers can identify and respond to them.

Step 2 Plan Your Interview

Use the results of your research to write a list of interview questions about your chosen topic to ask a parent or child care professional in your community.

Writing Skills
★ Use complete sentences.
★ Use correct spelling and grammar.
★ Organize your interview questions in the order you want to ask them.

Step 3 Connect with Your Community

Identify a child care professional or parent of a young child in your community who works with infants and toddlers. Conduct your interview using the questions you prepared in Step 2. Take notes during the interview and write a summary of the interview.

Interviewing Skills
★ Record interview responses and take notes.
★ Listen attentively.
★ Write in complete sentences and use correct spelling and grammar when you transcribe your notes.

Step 4 Share What You Have Learned

Use the Unit Thematic Project Checklist to plan and give an oral report to share what you have learned with your classmates.

Speaking Skills
★ Speak clearly and concisely.
★ Be sensitive to the needs of your audience.
★ Use standard English to communicate.

Step 5 Evaluate Your Child Development Skills and Academic Skills

Your project will be evaluated based on:
- Content and organization of your information.
- Proper use of standard English.
- Mechanics—presentation and neatness.
- Speaking and listening skills.

Evaluation Rubric Go to this book's Online Learning Center at glencoe.com for a rubric.

Unit Thematic Project Checklist

Plan	✓ Select and research your topic and summarize your findings.
	✓ Plan and write your interview questions.
	✓ Interview a parent or child care professional and write a summary of what you learned.
Present	✓ Make a presentation to the class to discuss the results of your research and your interview.
	✓ Invite students to ask any questions. Answer these questions.
	✓ When students ask you questions, demonstrate in your answers that you respect their perspectives.
	✓ Turn in the summary of your research, your interview questions, and the summary of the interview to your teacher.
Academic Skills	✓ Communicate effectively.
	✓ Be sensitive to the needs of different audiences.
	✓ Adapt and modify language to suit different purposes.

Unit 3 The Baby's First Year 287

Apply Skills that are behind the project. See what child development and academic skills you will use.

Evaluate Your Work A rubric is a scoring tool that lists the project criteria. You can find the Evaluation Rubric at the book's Online Learning Center at **glencoe.com**.

Begin the Chapter

What Is the Chapter All About?

Use the activities in the opener to help you connect what you already know to chapter topics. Think about the people, places, and events in your own life. Are there any similarities with those in your textbook?

Read the Chapter Objectives to preview the key ideas you will learn. Keep these in mind as you read the chapter.

Section **8.1** Understanding Emotional Development of Infants

Section **8.2** Understanding Social Development of Infants

Chapter **8** Emotional and Social Development of Infants

Chapter Objectives

After completing this chapter, you will be able to:

- **List** six basic emotions that babies experience.
- **Explain** the role of attachment in a baby's emotional development.
- **Describe** how temperament affects a baby's social development.
- **Explain** how the emotional climate of the home can affect a baby's development.
- **Explain** how a baby learns social behavior.
- **Identify** how play and exploration help a baby develop socially.

Writing Activity — Freewriting

Building Relationships From the first moment she is born, a baby begins to develop relationships with her parents or caregivers. Use freewriting to describe your idea of a positive, healthy relationship.

Writing Tips To jumpstart your writing, it can be helpful to write out ideas freely. This is called freewriting. Use these tips to start freewriting:

1. Write everything that comes to mind, in any order.
2. Do not worry about having an introduction or conclusion. You can go back and revise later.
3. Focus on ideas. Correct your grammar and spelling after you are done writing.

Explore the Photo This baby's healthy bond with his caregiver can help him form healthy relationships later in life. *Why do you think a baby's early experiences can affect his self-esteem later in life?*

232

233

Strengthen Your Writing Skills Use the writing tips to continue to develop your writing.

Explore the Photo to jumpstart your thinking about the chapter's main topics.

Review the Chapter

Make Sure You Know and Understand the Concepts

Review what you learned in the chapter and see how this learning applies to your other subjects and other real-world situations.

Read the Chapter Summary to review the most important ideas that you should have learned in this chapter.

Review Vocabulary and Key Concepts to check your recall of important ideas.

Critical Thinking takes your knowledge of the chapter further. If you have difficulty answering these questions, go back and reread the related parts of the chapter.

Practice Academic Skills and connect what you learned to your knowledge of language arts, math, science, and social studies.

Practice Your Observation Skills by completing these activities in real-life scenarios.

Apply Real-World Skills to situations that you might find in your day-to-day life.

Find More Activities Online at this book's Online Learning Center at glencoe.com.

Succeed on Tests with test-taking tips and practice questions.

Begin the Section

Prepare with Reading Guides and Study Tools

Use the reading guide at the beginning of each section to preview what you will learn in the section. See if you can predict events or outcomes by using clues and information that you already know.

Check Vocabulary lists for words you do not know. You can look them up in the glossary before you read the section.

Section 8.1 Understanding Emotional Development of Infants

Reading Guide

Before You Read

Preview Look at each photo in this section and read the photo captions. Write one or two sentences explaining what you think the section will be about.

Use Before You Read Tips to help you understand the section content.

Read to Learn
Key Concepts
- **List** six basic emotions that babies experience.
- **Explain** the role of attachment in a baby's emotional development.
- **Describe** how temperament affects a baby's social development.
- **Explain** how the emotional climate of the home can affect a baby's development.

Main Idea
Caregivers play a large role in babies' emotional development, helping them learn to express feelings and develop a personal identity.

Content Vocabulary
◇ emotional development
◇ emotion
◇ colic
◇ reflux
◇ attachment
◇ failure to thrive
◇ temperament

Academic Vocabulary
You will find these words in your reading and on your tests. Use the glossary to look up their definitions if necessary.
■ crucial
■ hinder

Graphic Organizer
As you read, list things a caregiver can do to promote a baby's healthy emotional development. Use a chart like the one shown to help organize your information.

Healthy Emotional Development
1.
2.
3.
4.

Graphic Organizer Go to this book's Online Learning Center at **glencoe.com** to print out this graphic organizer.

Look for Academic Standards throughout the text. You can apply what you learn to other subjects.

Academic Standards . . . .

🌎 **English Language Arts**
NCTE 4 Use written language to communicate effectively.

🌎 **Social Studies**
NCSS I C Culture Apply an understanding of culture as an integrated whole that explains the functions and interactions of behavior patterns.

NCSS IV C Individual Development and Identity Describe influences that contribute to the development of a sense of self.

NCTE *National Council of Teachers of English*
NCTM *National Council of Teachers of Mathematics*

NSES *National Science Education Standards*
NCSS *National Council for the Social Studies*

234 **Chapter 8** Emotional and Social Development of Infants

Take Notes and Study with graphic organizers. These help you find and identify relationships in the information you read.

Review the Section | Check Your Comprehension with Self-Assessments

After you read, use the section closer to check your understanding. Make sure that you can answer the questions in your own words before moving on in the text.

Emotional Climate of the Home

Babies are very sensitive to the feelings of people around them. Long before they know the meanings of words, they are influenced by adults' emotions, tone of voice, gestures, and facial expressions. Worried or angry caregivers are likely to be tense in handling their babies. Babies sense these feelings and can become irritable and anxious.

Every family has ups and downs, and a baby adapts to them. It is normal for caregivers to feel occasional frustration and anger toward a beloved child. However, a baby needs to feel that affection and caring are the basis of the family's interactions. Feelings of bitterness, mistrust, and anger can **hinder**, or delay, an infant's emotional development.

Handling unwanted feelings, such as anger, frustration, and sadness, is a challenge for every parent and caregiver. It can be an even greater challenge for single parents. Single parents have no other adult to share the work or the worries, and they may feel alone and overwhelmed.

It is important for all parents to find ways of releasing negative feelings away from their children. Dealing with challenging feelings can help parents find the patience to create a caring environment. Every parent needs someone who can give them emotional support.

Section 8.1 — After You Read

Review Key Concepts

1. **List** the most important influences on a child's emotional development.
2. **Explain** ways to build attachment to support a baby's emotional development.
3. **Describe** ways to resolve temperament conflicts.
4. **Explain** why it is important for parents to *not* express negative feelings around their children.

Practice Academic Skills

English Language Arts

5. Describe your temperament using the nine temperament traits described in the section. Now imagine that you are caring for a child whose temperament is very different from yours. Write a letter to a friend describing how this could be challenging and what strategies you might use to handle the challenge.

> **NCTE 4** Use written language to communicate effectively.

Social Studies

6. Temperament, family, culture, and institutions such as schools and churches are important influences on your identity. You are also influenced by your *peers*, or people your same age. Write a report describing the people, places, and things that you think have influenced your identity since you were a baby, and why.

> **NCSS IV C** Describe influences that contribute to the development of a sense of self.

Check Your Answers Check your answers at this book's Online Learning Center at **glencoe.com**.

Section 8.1 Understanding Emotional Development of Infants **243**

Verify Your Understanding of key concepts in the section.

Practice Academic Skills with these cross-curricular activities.

Check Your Answers online at this book's Online Learning Center at **glencoe.com**.

As You Read

Use Reading Strategies and Visuals to Study Effectively

In addition to the reading guide at the beginning of each section, there are lots of reading strategies to help you comprehend the text.

Skim the Headings to help identify the main idea and supporting details.

Emotions and Emotional Development

Emotional and social development begin at birth and continue throughout life. They are as important as physical development to becoming a healthy and happy adult.

Emotional development is the process of learning to recognize and express feelings and to establish a personal identity. A personal identity is a sense of being a unique individual. A child who experiences healthy emotional development will be self-confident. He or she will be able to handle stress and will have empathy for others.

The most important influences on a child's emotional development are the bond between the caregiver and the child, the temperament of the child, and the atmosphere of the home.

Emotions in Infancy

We are all born with the ability to experience emotions. An **emotion** is a feeling response to the world around us. Even newborns can show basic emotions such as contentment and distress. Emotions grow more complex with age. **Figure 8.1** on page 6 shows the development of some basic emotions during a child's first year.

Learning Emotions Through Interaction

Parents and caregivers play a large role in shaping a baby's emotions. Parents can encourage positive emotions. Parents can also help infants cope with negative emotions. Returning a baby's smile, for example, encourages his joyful expression. Rocking a frightened baby teaches her to become calm again after a scary experience.

Babies also learn from their caregivers to learn how to react to situations. A baby whose caregiver is often joyful may learn to approach life with happiness and interest. A baby whose caregiver is often anxious may learn to approach life with fear.

Emotions and Crying

Infants do not have words so they show many of their needs and emotions through crying. At around two months of age, babies start to vary their cries to express different feelings.

Healthy Emotional Development
Touch can help an infant develop healthy emotions. *Why is physical touch important to emotional development?*

Section 8.1 Understanding Emotional Development of Infants **235**

Keep a Vocabulary Journal Write down vocabulary words then find definitions in the text and in the glossary at the back of the book.

Reading Checks let you pause to respond to what you have read.

...perament? ...ns. Is she ...es she love ...the first to ...her eating ...mood. ...ent, you ...ensure a ...nt. Par- ...mind ...y defi- ...need ...idual ...le.

a child's specific traits. A child should not be punished for a temperament trait. If a child is shy, try holding him when you introduce him to someone new. Give him time to warm up to the new person, instead of handing him to the new person right away.

Caregivers have their own temperaments, too. One of a caregiver's responsibilities is to adapt to the temperament of the child, even if they are different. Look for positive ways to adapt to these differences. Suppose that you have a low energy level, but your infant is constantly on the move. You should provide safe opportunities for energetic play. Enjoy a trip to the park or dancing to music. Avoid activities that require the child to sit a lot. Can you think of other strategies you might try?

✓ **Reading Check** **Analyze** Why is it important to understand a baby's temperament?

Examine Visuals to reinforce content. Answer the questions so you can better discuss topics in the section.

Unique Temperaments
Each baby is a unique individual with a different combination of temperament traits. *Why is it useful to know a baby's temperament?*

Section 8.1 Understanding Emotional Development of Infants **241**

Study with Features

Skills You Can Really Use at School and in Life!

As you read, look for feature boxes throughout each chapter. These features build skills that relate to other academic subjects and prepare you for life on your own.

Make Math Simple
You use math every day—even if it is just counting money to buy a snack. Use starting hints to break down math problems and solve them step by step.

Unlock Mysteries of Brain Development These short excerpts on brain development provide additional information at the point of use.

Math in Action

Salary Requirements
Susan earns $8.50 per hour and works 40 hours a week. She is planning for her and Robert's newborn by calculating expected expenses. Her research results in an approximate expense list for one month:

Diapers: $80
Formula: $75
Clothes: $75
Day Care: $400

How much per month does Susan make? What is the total monthly expense of the newborn? What percentage of Susan's salary will go towards the baby?

Math Concept **Rates and Percents** A rate is a ratio of two measurements having different kinds of units, such as dollars per hour. A percent is a ratio that compares a number to 100.

Starting Hint To find Susan's monthly salary, first multiply the rate (8.50) by the hours (40), then by the weeks in a month (4). To find the percentage, divide the total baby expenses by Susan's monthly salary. Multiply the result by 100.

Math For math help, go to the Math Appendix at the back of the book.

NCTM Number and Operations
Understand numbers, ways of representing numbers, relationships among numbers, and number systems.

Science in Action

Technology and the Family
In today's society, we have many technological inventions available for work, home, and entertainment. This includes newer inventions such as cell phones, MP3 players, and video games. Technology also includes older technology such as television and computers. How might these inventions affect a family?

Procedure
Create a survey that lists five technological inventions and asks how much time people feel they spend using these inventions. Ask if they think using these technologies takes away from or adds to their family time. Distribute the survey to at least ten people of various ages.

Analysis
Find the average amount of time each invention is used. Then find the overall average. Chart your findings in a bar graph. Write a summary of your research that explains the results and describes people's opinions about whether these technologies are taking away from family time.

NSES F Develop understanding of science and technology in local, national, and global challenges.

Learn the Secrets of Science
The secret is that it can be easy! You can use scientific principles and concepts in your everyday activities. Investigate and analyze the world around you with these basic skills.

THE DEVELOPING BRAIN

Neural Connections
Babies learn alot in the first three years of life. Newborn babies' brains contain about 100 billion nerve cells, called neurons. Those neurons have about 50 trillion connections. These connections increase rapidly, and by the age of three, a child has twice as many connections as an adult. As a child matures, unused pathways are removed. This means that babies who live in an environment where they learn more will keep more connections.

Science Inquiry A stimulating environment is important for babies' brains to develop to their fullest potential. How would a stimulating environment lead to an increased number of neurological connections?

{ Expert Advice... }

"For infants and toddlers, learning and living are the same thing. If they feel secure, treasured, loved, their own energy and curiosity will bring them new understanding and new skills."

— Amy Laura Dombro and Leah Wallach, early childhood authors, *The Ordinary Is Extraordinary*.

Learn from Professionals
See what child development professionals think about the section's topic.

To the Student

Study with Features (continued)

Learning Through PLAY

From Solo to Social

A child's play changes as she grows and develops. Young babies enjoy play that involves touching, grasping, and using their five senses. Older babies are ready for more challenging forms of object play, such stacking blocks. By age one, babies enjoy parallel play. This means that they play next to each other, but not with each other. They watch and copy one another, and they start to learn how to share. Parallel play helps babies understand that babies have wants and feelings too. By age, children enjoy make-believe play full of complex stories. All these kinds of play help children develop social skills such as feeling comfortable in the world, identifying and expressing feelings, cooperating, and taking turns.

Think About It You are caring for two young toddlers, Maya and Delon, who are playing next to each other. Maya grabs the ball from Delon, and Delon screams. What could you say and do next to help both babies understand how to share?

Play Matters See how to help promote child development with different forms of play for each age and stage.

Parenting Skills

Helping a Baby Develop a Sense of Trust

Meeting a baby's physical and emotional needs helps a baby build a sense of trust. Try these strategies to help a baby develop trust.

- **Follow a predictable routine.** Routine care helps a baby learn to trust a parent or caregiver. Establish regular times for feeding, baths, and naps.
- **Get to know the baby.** Appreciate the baby's uniqueness. Learn about the baby's likes and dislikes. Learn the baby's signs for hunger, tiredness, and boredom.
- **Bond with the baby.** Spend time nurturing and holding the baby. Talk to the baby in a soft, positive tone. Smile and establish eye contact. Enjoy physical closeness.
- **Meet the baby's needs.** Strive to meet a baby's physical, social, and emotional needs. Provide loving care and affection.

Take Charge If you were a caregiver, how could you learn what a baby's different cries mean? Write a one-page journal entry sharing your thoughts.

Be a Positive Influence Learn how to have a positive influence on any children in your life with the tips on encouragement, leadership, and guidance skills.

Happy Children Learn how to keep children safe and healthy while encouraging growth and exploration.

RESPOND TO SPECIAL NEEDS   Autism

Autism is a brain development disorder that affects the way people relate to others. People with severe autism have an impaired ability to interact and communicate with others. Signs of autism usually appear before a child turns three. Autistic children tend to avoid eye contact and cuddling. They often have restricted interests and repetitive behaviors. They do not like changes in routine and they may be very sensitive to lights and sounds. They may not respond to their own names, and they may start talking late. Early diagnosis is important. A child with autism needs a special treatment program.

Therapy and special education help children with autism lead fuller lives. Special diets may also help. Parents can help by showing love and understanding, setting up routines, and praising successes.

Critical Thinking Research the causes of autism. Describe the major theories and explain why some theories are controversial. Summarize your findings in a one-page essay. Cite your sources.

Respond to All Children Learn how special needs can affect child development and child care.

SAFE CHILD HEALTHY CHILD

Exploring Through Taste

Babies' mouths are more sensitive than their hands, so it is no wonder that babies use their mouths to explore tastes, textures, and shapes. *Mouthing* is normal, but it can be dangerous. A baby can choke on small objects or be poisoned by chemicals. Make sure that all toys are too large to fit all the way into a baby's mouth. Keep soaps, medicines, and chemicals out of reach. You can satisfy a baby's need to explore by choosing toys and foods with interesting shapes and textures.

Be Prepared Use the library or the Internet to conduct research on child safety. Make a safety checklist of 20 common choking hazards for babies, including toys and toy parts, household objects, and foods. Share your checklist with the class.

Study with Features (continued)

Think About Your Future
Learn about career options related to children and see what skills you would need to have a similar career.

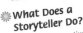

Careers With Children — Storyteller

Before societies had written records, they had storytellers. Storytellers described battles and adventures and told tales of monsters and kings. Today's storytellers educate and entertain as they practice this ancient art. Many traditions are preserved with storytelling.

What Does a Storyteller Do?

Storytellers captivate their audiences with words. Storytellers use their voices the way musicians use instruments. They write and memorize many stories and tell each one with enthusiasm and creativity. Many storytellers add songs and music to their stories, too. Some storytellers focus on certain traditions, such as African folk tales.

Where Do Storytellers Work?

Storytellers perform in many different places, such as schools, libraries, museums, festivals, children's parties, senior centers, prisons, and hospitals. Some storytellers might perform on the radio or on television. Some sell recordings of their performances.

Preparation and Skills

Education and Training
Many storytellers study literature, folklore, music, and drama. Public speaking is also good preparation for storytelling. Look for a Storytellers Guild, or association, in your area to find a mentor or receive tips on developing this career. Some of these groups can help you find jobs to get started.

Aptitudes, Abilities, and Skills
Successful storytellers have imagination, self-motivation, a good memory, acting talent, and communication skills. Storytellers work hard, so they should be motivated and dedicated to their craft.

Academic Skills Required
English Language Arts are used by storytellers in reading and researching stories and ideas, and in writing stories to tell.

Explore Careers

Research other careers that involve performing with children or engaging them through play. Choose one career and ~~~ paragraph describing it. Tell if the career interests you ~~~

Careers Online For more information on caree~~~ Occupational Outlook Handbook Web site thro~~~ on this book's Online Learning Center at **glen**~~~

282 Chapter 9 Intellectual Development in Infants

Find Out More about careers at this book's Online Learning Center at **glencoe.com**.

What Would You Do?

A Healthy Environment

Anne is a pediatric nurse. She has two nine-year-old patients, Ian and Seth, who have asthma. Aside from their age and diagnosis, their situations are different. "Seth has been to the hospital only once for an asthma attack," Anne says. "His mom also has asthma, so they have learned together how to manage their symptoms. They keep emergency medication on hand and clean their house often to reduce dust. Ian, on the other hand, spends a lot of time in the hospital for asthma attacks." Anne continues, "Two conditions in his home can make his asthma worse: his family has a cat and one of his parents smokes." Ian's parents asked how to help reduce his number of attacks.

✎ **Write About It** How might Ian's parents change his environment to reduce the number of his asthma attacks? Write a brief article for the Health section of your local newspaper to offer ideas for Ian's parents.

Solve Real-World Problems
You will encounter disagreements or challenges in your life. Read about real problems and tell how you would resolve the issues.

CULTURE MATTERS

Holding a Baby Close

Carrying babies close to the body is the norm in many cultures. In Somalia, women tie their babies to their backs with long scarves. In Nepal, mothers carry their babies in a garment that also holds money and tools. The Inuit people of the Canadian Arctic can snuggle their babies in the furry linings of their parkas. Baby slings are now growing more popular in North America and Europe. Carrying a baby close provides the baby with a sense of security and lets him feel, see, and smell the parent. It also lets the baby see the world from a different vantage point.

🧍 **Build Connections** What are the advantages of sharing space? What are the disadvantages?

NCSS I C Culture Apply an understanding of culture as an integrated whole that explains the functions and interactions of behavior patterns.

Cultural Diversity
See how cultures around the world address child development needs.

Online Learning Center

Use the Internet to Extend Your Learning

Follow these steps to access the textbook resources at *The Developing Child* Online Learning Center.

Online Learning Center Icon Look for this icon throughout the text that directs you to the book's Online Learning Center for more activities and information.

Graphic Organizer Go to this book's Online Learning Center at **glencoe.com** to print out this graphic organizer.

Step 1
Go to **glencoe.com**.

Step 2
Select **your state** from the pull-down menu.

Step 3
Select **Student/Parent**.

Step 4
Select **Family & Consumer Sciences**.

Step 5
Select **ENTER**.

Step 6
Click **The Developing Child**.

Step 7
Click **Student Center** to access student resources.

Prepare for Academic Success!

By improving your academic skills, you improve your ability to learn and achieve success now and in the future. It also improves your chances of landing a high-skill, high-wage job. The features and assessments in *The Developing Child* provide many opportunities for you to strengthen your academic skills.

Academic Standards Look for this box throughout the text to know what academic skills you are learning.

NCTM Number and Operations Understand numbers, ways of representing numbers, relationships among numbers, and number systems.

National English Language Arts Standards

To help incorporate literacy skills (reading, writing, listening, and speaking) into *The Developing Child,* each section contains a listing of the language arts skills covered. These skills have been developed into standards by the *National Council of Teachers of English and International Reading Association.*

- Read texts to acquire new information.
- Read literature to build an understanding of the human experience.
- Apply strategies to interpret texts.
- Use written language to communicate effectively.
- Use different writing process elements to communicate effectively.
- Conduct research and gather, evaluate, and synthesize data to communicate discoveries.
- Use information resources to gather information and create and communicate knowledge.
- Develop an understanding of diversity in language use across cultures.
- Participate as members of literacy communities.
- Use language to accomplish individual purposes.

National Math Standards

You also have opportunities to practice math skills indicated by standards developed by the *National Council of Teachers of Mathematics.**

- Algebra
- Data Analysis and Probability
- Geometry
- Measurement
- Number and Operations
- Problem Solving

*Standards are listed with permission of the National Council of Teachers of Mathematics (NCTM). NCTM *does not endorse the content or validity of these alignments.*

National Science Standards

The *National Science Education Standards* outline these science skills that you can practice in this text.

- Science as Inquiry
- Physical Science
- Life Science
- Earth and Space Science
- Science and Technology
- Science in Personal and Social Perspectives
- History and Nature of Science

National Social Studies Standards

The *National Council for the Social Studies* is another organization that provides standards to help guide your studies. Activities in this text relate to these standards.

- Culture
- Time, Continuity, and Change
- People, Places, and Environments
- Individual Development and Identity
- Individuals, Groups, and Institutions
- Power, Authority, and Governance
- Production, Distribution, and Consumption
- Science, Technology, and Society
- Global Connections
- Civic Ideals and Practices

Reading Skills Handbook

▶ Reading: What's in It for You?

What role does reading play in your life? The possibilities are countless. Are you on a sports team? Perhaps you like to read about the latest news and statistics in sports or find out about new training techniques. Are you looking for a part-time job? You might be looking for advice about résumé writing, interview techniques, or information about a company. Are you enrolled in an English class, an algebra class, or a business class? Then your assignments require a lot of reading.

Improving or Fine-Tuning Your Reading Skills Will:

- ◆ Improve your grades.
- ◆ Allow you to read faster and more efficiently.
- ◆ Improve your study skills.
- ◆ Help you remember more information accurately.
- ◆ Improve your writing.

▶ The Reading Process

Good reading skills build on one another, overlap, and spiral around in much the same way that a winding staircase goes around and around while leading you to a higher place. This handbook is designed to help you find and use the tools you will need **before, during,** and **after** reading.

Strategies You Can Use

- ◆ Identify, understand, and learn new words.
- ◆ Understand why you read.
- ◆ Take a quick look at the whole text.
- ◆ Try to predict what you are about to read.

- ◆ Take breaks while you read and ask yourself questions about the text.
- ◆ Take notes.
- ◆ Keep thinking about what will come next.
- ◆ Summarize.

▶ Vocabulary Development

Word identification and vocabulary skills are the building blocks of the reading and the writing process. By learning to use a variety of strategies to build your word skills and vocabulary, you will become a stronger reader.

Use Context to Determine Meaning

The best way to expand and extend your vocabulary is to read widely, listen carefully, and participate in a rich variety of discussions. When reading on your own, though, you can often figure out the meanings of new words by looking at their **context,** the other words and sentences that surround them.

Tips for Using Context

Look for clues like these:

◆ A synonym or an explanation of the unknown word in the sentence:
Elise's shop specialized in millinery, or hats for women.

◆ A reference to what the word is or is not like:
An archaeologist, like a historian, deals with the past.

◆ A general topic associated with the word:
The cooking teacher discussed the best way to braise meat.

◆ A description or action associated with the word:
He used the shovel to dig up the garden.

Predict a Possible Meaning

Another way to determine the meaning of a word is to take the word apart. If you understand the meaning of the **base,** or **root,** part of a word, and also know the meanings of key syllables added either to the beginning or end of the base word, you can usually figure out what the word means.

Word Origins Since Latin, Greek, and Anglo-Saxon roots are the basis for much of our English vocabulary, having some background in languages can be a useful vocabulary tool. For example, *astronomy* comes from the Greek root *astro,* which means "relating to the stars." *Stellar* also has a meaning referring to stars, but its origin is Latin. Knowing root words in other languages can help you determine meanings, derivations, and spellings in English.

Prefixes and Suffixes A prefix is a word part that can be added to the beginning of a word. For example, the prefix *semi* means "half" or "partial," so *semicircle* means "half a circle." A suffix is a word part that can be added to the end of a word. Adding a suffix often changes a word from one part of speech to another.

Using Dictionaries A dictionary provides the meaning or meanings of a word. Look at the sample dictionary entry on the next page to see what other information it provides.

Thesauruses and Specialized Reference Books A thesaurus provides synonyms and often antonyms. It is a useful tool to expand your vocabulary. Remember to check the exact definition of the listed words in a dictionary before you use a thesaurus. Specialized dictionaries such as *Barron's Dictionary of Business Terms* or *Black's Law Dictionary* list terms and expressions that are not commonly included in a general dictionary. You can also use online dictionaries.

Glossaries Many textbooks and technical works contain condensed dictionaries that provide an alphabetical listing of words used in the text and their specific definitions.

Dictionary Entry

Forms of the word

Part of speech

Numbered definitions

Example of use

Usage label

help (help) **helped** or *(archaic)* **holp, helped** or *(archaic)* **hol·pen, help·ing**. *v.t.* **1.** to provide with support, as in the performance of a task; be of service to: *He helped his brother paint the room.* ▲ also used elliptically with a preposition or adverb: *He helped the old woman up the stairs.* **2.** to enable (someone or something) to accomplish a goal or achieve a desired effect: *The coach's advice helped the team to win.* **3.** to provide with sustenance or relief, as in time of need or distress; succor: *The Red Cross helped the flood victims.* **4.** to promote or contribute to; further. *The medication helped his recovery.* **5.** to be useful or profitable to; be of advantage to: *It might help you if you read the book.* **6.** to improve or remedy: *Nothing really helped his sinus condition.* **7.** to prevent; stop: *I can't help his rudeness.* **8.** to refrain from; avoid: *I couldn't help smiling when I heard the story.* **9.** to wait on or serve (often with to): *The clerk helped us. The hostess helped him to the dessert.* **10. cannot help but.** *Informal* cannot but. **11. so help me (God).** oath of affirmation. **12. to help oneself to.** to take or appropriate: *The thief helped himself to all the jewels.*—*v.i.* to provide support, as in the performance of a task; be of service. —*n.* **1.** act of providing support, service, or sustenance. **2.** source of support, service, or sustenance. **3.** person or group of persons hired to work for another or others. **4.** means of improving, remedying, or preventing. [Old English *helpan* to aid, succor, benefit.] **Syn.** *v.t.* **1. Help, aid, assist** mean to support in a useful way. Help is the most common word and means to give support in response to a known or expressed need or for a definite purpose: *Everyone helped to make the school fair a success.* **Aid** means to give relief in times of distress or difficulty: *It is the duty of rich nations to aid the poor.* **Assist** means to serve another person in the performance of his task in a secondary capacity: *The secretary assists the officer by taking care of his corresponding.*

Idioms

Origin (etymology)

Synonyms

Recognize Word Meanings Across Subjects Have you learned a new word in one class and then noticed it in your reading for other subjects? The word might not mean exactly the same thing in each class, but you can use the meaning you already know to help you understand what it means in another subject area. For example:

Math Each digit represents a different place **value**.

Health Your **values** can guide you in making healthful decisions.

Economics The **value** of a product is measured in its cost.

▶ Understanding What You Read

Reading comprehension means understanding—deriving meaning from—what you have read. Using a variety of strategies can help you improve your comprehension and make reading more interesting and more fun.

Read for a Reason

To get the greatest benefit from your reading, **establish a purpose for reading.** In school, you have many reasons for reading, such as:

- to learn and understand new information.
- to find specific information.
- to review before a test.
- to complete an assignment.
- to prepare (research) before you write.

As your reading skills improve, you will notice that you apply different strategies to fit the different purposes for reading. For example, if you are reading for entertainment, you might read quickly, but if you read to gather information or follow directions, you might read more slowly, take notes, construct a graphic organizer, or reread sections of text.

Draw on Personal Background

Drawing on personal background may also be called activating prior knowledge. Before you start reading a text, ask yourself questions like these:

- What have I heard or read about this topic?
- Do I have any personal experience relating to this topic?

Using a K-W-L Chart A K-W-L chart is a good device for organizing information you gather before, during, and after reading. In the first column, list what you already **know,** then list what you **want** to know in the middle column. Use the third column when you review and assess what you **learned.** You can also add more columns to record places where you found information and places where you can look for more information.

K (What I already know)	W (What I want to know)	L (What I have learned)

Adjust Your Reading Speed Your reading speed is a key factor in how well you understand what you are reading. You will need to adjust your speed depending on your reading purpose.

Scanning means running your eyes quickly over the material to look for words or phrases. Scan when you need a specific piece of information.

Skimming means reading a passage quickly to find its main idea or to get an overview. Skim a text when you preview to determine what the material is about.

Reading for detail involves careful reading while paying attention to text structure and monitoring your understanding. Read for detail when you are learning concepts, following complicated directions, or preparing to analyze a text.

► Techniques to Understand and Remember What You Read

Preview

Before beginning a selection, it is helpful to **preview** what you are about to read.

> **Previewing Strategies**
>
> ◆ Read the title, headings, and subheadings of the selection.
> ◆ Look at the illustrations and notice how the text is organized.
> ◆ Skim the selection: Take a glance at the whole thing.
> ◆ Decide what the main idea might be.
> ◆ Predict what a selection will be about.

Predict

Have you ever read a mystery, decided who committed the crime, and then changed your mind as more clues were revealed? You were adjusting your predictions. Did you smile when you found out that you guessed who committed the crime? You were verifying your predictions.

As you read, take educated guesses about story events and outcomes; that is, **make predictions** before and during reading. This will help you focus your attention on the text and it will improve your understanding.

Determine the Main Idea

When you look for the **main idea**, you are looking for the most important statement in a text. Depending on what kind of text you are reading, the main idea can be located at the very beginning (news stories in newspaper or a magazine) or at the end (scientific research document). Ask yourself the following questions:

• What is each sentence about?
• Is there one sentence that is more important than all the others?
• What idea do details support or point out?

Taking Notes

Cornell Note-Taking System There are many methods for note taking. The **Cornell Note-Taking System** is a well-known method that can help you organize what you read. To the right is a note-taking activity based on the Cornell Note-Taking System.

Graphic Organizers Using a graphic organizer to retell content in a visual representation will help you remember and retain content. You might make a **chart** or **diagram,** organizing what you have read. Here are some examples of graphic organizers:

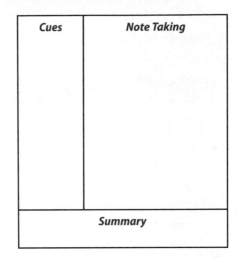

Venn diagrams When mapping out a compare-and-contrast text structure, you can use a Venn diagram. The outer portions of the circles will show how two characters, ideas, or items contrast, or are different, and the overlapping part will compare two things, or show how they are similar.

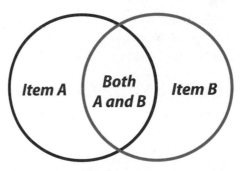

Flow charts To help you track the sequence of events, or cause and effect, use a flow chart. Arrange ideas or events in their logical, sequential order. Then, draw arrows between your ideas to indicate how one idea or event flows into another.

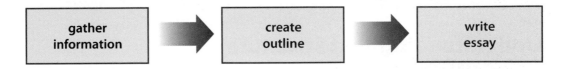

Visualize

Try to form a mental picture of scenes, characters, and events as you read. Use the details and descriptions the author gives you. If you can **visualize** what you read, it will be more interesting and you will remember it better.

Question

Ask yourself questions about the text while you read. Ask yourself about the importance of the sentences, how they relate to one another, if you understand what you just read, and what you think is going to come next.

Clarify

If you feel you do not understand meaning (through questioning), try these techniques:

> **What to Do When You Do Not Understand**
>
> ◆ Reread confusing parts of the text.
> ◆ Diagram (chart) relationships between chunks of text, ideas, and sentences.
> ◆ Look up unfamiliar words.
> ◆ Talk out the text to yourself.
> ◆ Read the passage once more.

Review

Take time to stop and review what you have read. Use your note-taking tools (graphic organizers or Cornell notes charts). Also, review and consider your K-W-L chart.

Monitor Your Comprehension

Continue to check your understanding by using the following two strategies:

Summarize Pause and tell yourself the main ideas of the text and the key supporting details. Try to answer the following questions: Who? What? When? Where? Why? How?

Paraphrase Pause, close the book, and try to retell what you have just read in your own words. It might help to pretend you are explaining the text to someone who has not read it and does not know the material.

▶ Understanding Text Structure

Good writers do not just put together sentences and paragraphs, they organize their writing with a specific purpose in mind. That organization is called text structure. When you understand and follow the structure of a text, it is easier to remember the information you are reading. There are many ways text may be structured. Watch for **signal words**. They will help you follow the text's organization (also, remember to use these techniques when you write).

Compare and Contrast

This structure shows similarities and differences between people, things, and ideas. This is often used to demonstrate that things that seem alike are really different, or vice versa.

Signal words: similarly, more, less, on the one hand / on the other hand, in contrast, but, however

Cause and Effect

Writers use the cause-and-effect structure to explore the reasons for something happening and to examine the results or consequences of events.

Signal words: so, because, as a result, therefore, for the following reasons

Problem and Solution

When they organize text around the question "how?" writers state a problem and suggest solutions.

Signal words: how, help, problem, obstruction, overcome, difficulty, need, attempt, have to, must

Sequence

Sequencing tells you in which order to consider thoughts or facts. Examples of sequencing are:

Chronological order refers to the order in which events take place.

Signal words: first, next, then, finally

Spatial order describes the organization of things in space (to describe a room, for example).

Signal words: above, below, behind, next to

Order of importance lists things or thoughts from the most important to the least important (or the other way around).

Signal words: principal, central, main, important, fundamental

▶ Reading for Meaning

It is important to think about what you are reading to get the most information out of a text, to understand the consequences of what the text says, to remember the content, and to form your own opinion about what the content means.

Interpret

Interpreting is asking yourself, "What is the writer really saying?" and then using what you already know to answer that question.

Infer

Writers do not always state exactly everything they want you to understand. By providing clues and details, they sometimes imply certain information. An **inference** involves using your reason and experience to develop the idea on your own, based on what an author implies or suggests. What is most important when drawing inferences is to be sure that you have accurately based your guesses on supporting details from the text. If you cannot point to a place in the selection to help back up your inference, you may need to rethink your guess.

Draw Conclusions

A conclusion is a general statement you can make and explain with reasoning, or with supporting details from a text. If you read a story describing a sport where five players bounce a ball and throw it through a high hoop, you may conclude that the sport is basketball.

Analyze

To understand persuasive nonfiction (a text that discusses facts and opinions to arrive at a conclusion), you need to analyze statements and examples to see if they support the main idea. To understand an informational text (a text, such as a textbook, that gives you information, not opinions), you need to keep track of how the ideas are organized to find the main points.

Hint: Use your graphic organizers and notes charts.

Distinguish Facts from Opinions

This is one of the most important reading skills you can learn. A fact is a statement that can be proven. An opinion is what the writer believes. A writer may support opinions with facts, but an opinion cannot be proven. For example:

Fact: California produces fruit and other agricultural products.

Opinion: California produces the best fruit and other agricultural products.

Evaluate

Would you take seriously an article on nuclear fission if you knew it was written by a comedic actor? If you need to rely on accurate information, you need to find out who wrote what you are reading and why. Where did the writer get information? Is the information one-sided? Can you verify the information?

▶ Reading for Research

You will need to **read actively** in order to research a topic. You might also need to generate an interesting, relevant, and researchable **question** on your own and locate appropriate print and nonprint information from a wide variety of sources. Then you will need to **categorize** that information, evaluate it, and **organize** it in a new way in order to produce a research project for a specific audience. Finally, **draw conclusions** about your original research question. These conclusions may lead you to other areas for further inquiry.

Locate Appropriate Print and Nonprint Information

In your research, try to use a variety of sources. Because different sources present information in different ways, your research project will be more interesting and balanced when you read a variety of sources.

Literature and Textbooks These texts include any book used as a basis for instruction or a source of information.

Book Indices A book index, or a bibliography, is an alphabetical listing of books. Some book indices list books on specific subjects; others are more general. Other indices list a variety of topics or resources.

Periodicals Magazines and journals are issued at regular intervals, such as weekly or monthly. One way to locate information in magazines is to use the *Readers' Guide to Periodical Literature.* This guide is available in print form in most libraries.

Technical Manuals A manual is a guide or handbook intended to give instruction on how to perform a task or operate something. A vehicle owner's manual might give information on how to operate and service a car.

Reference Books Reference books include encyclopedias and almanacs, and are used to locate specific pieces of information.

Electronic Encyclopedias, Databases, and the Internet There are many ways to locate extensive information using your computer. Infotrac, for instance, acts as an online reader's guide. CD encyclopedias can provide easy access to all subjects.

Organize and Convert Information

As you gather information from different sources, taking careful notes, you will need to think about how to **synthesize** the information, that is, convert it into a unified whole, as well as how to change it into a form your audience will easily understand and that will meet your assignment guidelines.

1. First, ask yourself what you want your audience to know.
2. Then, think about a pattern of organization, a structure that will best show your main ideas. You might ask yourself the following questions:
   - When comparing items or ideas, what graphic aids can I use?
   - When showing the reasons something happened and the effects of certain actions, what text structure would be best?
   - How can I briefly and clearly show important information to my audience?
   - Would an illustration or even a cartoon help to make a certain point?

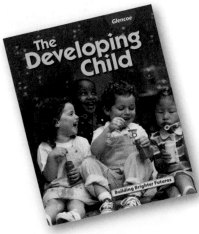

How to Use Technology

Introduction

Technology affects your life in almost every way, both at home and at work. Computers can do wonderful things. They are a path to the libraries of the world. They enhance and enrich your life. You can find the answers to many of your questions on the Internet, often as quickly as the click of your mouse. However, they can also be misused. Knowing some simple guidelines will help you use technology in a safe and secure way.

Practice Safe Surfing!

The Internet can also be a dangerous place. Although there are many Web sites you can freely and safely visit, many others are ones you want to avoid. Before you sign on to any site or visit a chat room, there are several things to consider:

- ◇ **Know to whom you are giving the information.** Check that the URL in your browser matches the domain you intended to visit and that you have not been redirected to another site.

- ◇ **Never give personal information of any sort** to someone you meet on a Web site or in a chat room, including your name, gender, age, or contact information.

- ◇ **Think about why you are giving the information.** For example, if a parent orders something online to be delivered, he or she will need to give an address. But you should never give out your social security number, your birth date, or your mother's maiden name without adult consent.

- ◇ **Check with a parent or other trusted adult** if you are still unsure whether it is safe to give the information.

Tips for Using the Internet for Research

The Internet is probably the single most important tool for research since the public library. There is so much information to access on the Internet that it can be difficult to know where to begin.

A good place to start is with a search engine, such as Google. Google is an automated piece of software that "crawls" the Web looking for information. By typing your topic into the search bar, the search engine looks for sites that contain the words you type. You may get many more sites than you are looking for. Here are some ways to get better results:

To get the best results when conducting a search online, be sure to spell all your search words correctly.

✧ **Place quotes around your topic,** for example, "sports medicine." This will allow you to find the sites where that exact phrase appears.

✧ **Use NEAR.** Typing "sports NEAR medicine" will return sites that contain both words and have the two words close to each other.

✧ **Exclude unwanted results.** Simply use a minus sign to indicate the words you do not want, for example, "sports medicine" –baseball.

✧ **Watch out for advertisements.** If you are using Google, know that the links on the right-hand side of the page, or sometimes at the top in color, are paid links. They may or may not be worth exploring.

✧ **Check for relevance.** Google displays a few lines of text from each page and shows your search phrase in bold. Check to see if it is appropriate for your work.

✧ **Look for news.** After you have entered your search phrase and have looked at the results, click on a *News* link on the page. This will show you recent stories about your topic.

✧ **Try again!** If you have made an extensive search and not found what you want, start a new search with a different set of words.

✧ **Check other sources.** Combine your Internet search with traditional research methods, such as books and magazines.

How to Use Technology

How to Evaluate Web Sites

Even though there is a ton of information available online, much of this information can be deceptive and misleading and often incorrect. The books in your library and classroom have been evaluated by scholars and experts. There is no such oversight on the Web. Learning to evaluate Web sites will make you a more savvy surfer and enable you to gather the information you need quickly and easily. When you are trying to decide whether a Web site provides trustworthy information, consider the following:

◇ **First, ask, "Who is the author?"** Once you have the name of the author, do a quick Web search to see what else the author has written. Search online for books he or she has written. This information will help you consider whether the person is credible.

◇ **Look at the group offering the information.** Be wary if they are trying to sell a product or service. Look for impartial organizations to provide unbiased information.

◇ **Look for Web sites that provide sources for each of their facts,** just as you do when you write a term paper. Also, look for clues that the information was written by someone knowledgeable. Spelling and grammatical errors are warning signs that the information may not be accurate.

◇ **Check for the date the article was written and when it was last updated.** The more recent the article, the more likely it will be accurate.

◇ **Finally, when using information from a Web site, treat it as you would treat print information.** Anyone can post information on a Web site. Never use information that you cannot verify with another source.

Plagiarism

Using your computer in an ethical manner is simple if you follow certain guidelines. Plagiarism is the act of taking someone else's ideas and passing them off as your own. It does not matter if it is just one or two phrases or an entire paper. Be on guard against falling into the trap of cutting and pasting. This makes plagiarism all too easy.

It is acceptable to quote sources in your work, but you must make sure to identify those sources and give them proper credit. Also, some Web sites do not allow you to quote from them. Be sure to check each site or resource you are quoting to make sure you are allowed to use the material. Remember to cite your sources properly.

Copyright

A copyright protects someone who creates an original work. This can be a single sentence, a book, a play, a piece of music. If you create it, you are the owner. Copyright protection is provided by the Copyright Act of 1976, a federal statute.

If you want to use a portion of a copyrighted work in your own work, you need to obtain permission from the copyright holder. That might be a publisher of a book, an author, or an organization or an estate. Most publishers are willing to grant permission to individuals for educational purposes. If you want to reproduce information you found on the Web, contact the Webmaster or author of the article to request permission.

Once a work's copyright has expired, it is considered to be in the public domain and anyone can reprint it as he or she pleases. Remember the following tips:

✧ **What is copyrighted?** All forms of original expression published in the United States since 1923.

✧ **Can I copy from the Internet?** Copying information from the Internet is a serious breach of copyright. Check the site's *Terms of Use* to see what you can and cannot do.

✧ **Can I edit copyrighted work?** You cannot change copyrighted material, that is, make "derivative works" based on existing material, without permission of the copyright holder.

Student Organizations

What Is a Student Organization?

A student organization is a group or association of students that is formed around activities, such as:

- Family and Consumer Sciences
- Student government
- Community service
- Social clubs
- Honor societies
- Multicultural alliances

- Technology education
- Artists and performers
- Politics
- Sports teams
- Professional career development

A student organization is usually required to follow a set of rules and regulations that apply equally to all student organizations at a particular school.

Why Should You Get Involved?

Being an active part of a student organization opens a variety of experiences to you. Many student clubs are part of a national network of students and professionals, which provides the chance to connect to a wider variety of students and opportunities.

What's in It for You?

Participation in student organizations can contribute to a more enriching learning experience. Here are some ways you can benefit:

- Gain leadership qualities and skills that make you more marketable to employers and universities.
- Demonstrate the ability to appreciate someone else's point of view.
- Interact with professionals to learn about their different industries.
- Explore your creative interests, share ideas, and collaborate with others.
- Take risks, build confidence, and grow creatively.
- Learn valuable skills while speaking or performing in front of an audience.
- Make a difference in your life and the lives of those around you.
- Learn the importance of civic responsibility and involvement.
- Build relationships with instructors, advisors, students, and other members of the community who share similar backgrounds/world views.

Find and Join a Student Organization!

Take a close look at the organizations offered at your school or within your community. Are there any organizations that interest you? Talk to your teachers, guidance counselors, or a parent or guardian. Usually posters or flyers for a variety of clubs and groups can be found on your school's Message Board or Web site. Try to locate more information about the organizations that meet your needs. Then think about how these organizations can help you gain valuable skills you can use at school, at work, and in your community.

What Is FCCLA?

Family, Career and Community Leaders of America is a nonprofit national career and technical student organization for young men and women in Family and consumer Sciences education in public and private school through grade 12. Everyone is part of a family, and FCCLA is the only national Career and Technical Student Organization with the family as its central focus. Since 1945, FCCLA members have been making a difference in their families, careers, and communities by addressing important personal, work, and societal issues through family and consumer sciences education.

Today over 220,000 members in nearly 7,000 chapters are active in a network of associations in 50 states as well as in the District of Columbia, the Virgin Islands, and Puerto Rico. Chapter projects focus on a variety of youth concerns, including teen pregnancy, parenting, family relationships, substance abuse, peer pressure, environment, nutrition and fitness, teen violence, and career exploration. Involvement in FCCLA offers members the opportunity to expand their leadership potential and develop skills for life—planning, goal setting, problem solving, decision making, and interpersonal communication—necessary in the home and workplace.

STAR Events Program

STAR Events (Students Taking Action with Recognition) are competitive events in which members are recognized for proficiency and achievement in chapter and individual projects, leadership skills, and occupational preparation. FCCLA provides opportunities for you to participate at local, state, and national levels.

What Is SkillsUSA?

SkillsUSA is a national organization serving teachers and high school and college students, who are preparing for careers in technical, skilled, and service occupations. More than 300,000 students and instructors join SkillsUSA annually.

One of the most visible programs of SkillsUSA is the annual SkillsUSA Championships. This competition showcases some of the best career and technical students in the nation. It allows students to compete in First Aid/CPR scenarios that will test their abilities to save a child's life. These contests begin locally and continue through state and national levels.

Unit 1

Children and Parenting

↑ Explore the Photo
Families that spend time together often build strong relationships. *Why would spending time together help to build strong relationships?*

Chapter 1 Learn about Children

Chapter 2 Responsibilities of Parenting

Chapter 3 Building Strong Families

Unit | Thematic Project Preview

Learn Parenting Skills

By completing this unit, you will learn that using positive parenting skills can help strengthen family relationships. In your unit thematic project, you can show how these skills help to build strong families.

 My Journal

Parenting 101 Write a journal entry about one of the topics below. This will help you prepare for the unit project at the end of the unit.
- Identify what kind of parent you think you would be someday.
- Determine what you would need to know about children before becoming a parent.
- List resources you could use to learn more about parenting.

1 Learn About Children

Chapter Objectives

After completing this chapter, you will be able to:

- **Explain** the best way to learn about children.
- **Identify** three areas of childhood that researchers have studied.
- **Summarize** how children learn and develop important skills.
- **List** the stages of development after childhood.
- **Determine** why observation is important in the study of child development.
- **Compare and contrast** different methods of observation and interpretation.

Writing Activity ✏ Freewriting

Caring Children of all ages need to be cared for. However, as they get older they need less care. Use freewriting to generate ways to show caring to a one-year-old child you are babysitting.

Writing Tips To jumpstart your writing, it can be helpful to write out ideas freely. This is called freewriting. Use these tips to start freewriting:

1. Write everything that comes to mind, in any order.
2. Do not worry about having an introduction or conclusion. You can go back and revise later.
3. Focus on ideas. Correct your grammar and spelling after you are done writing.

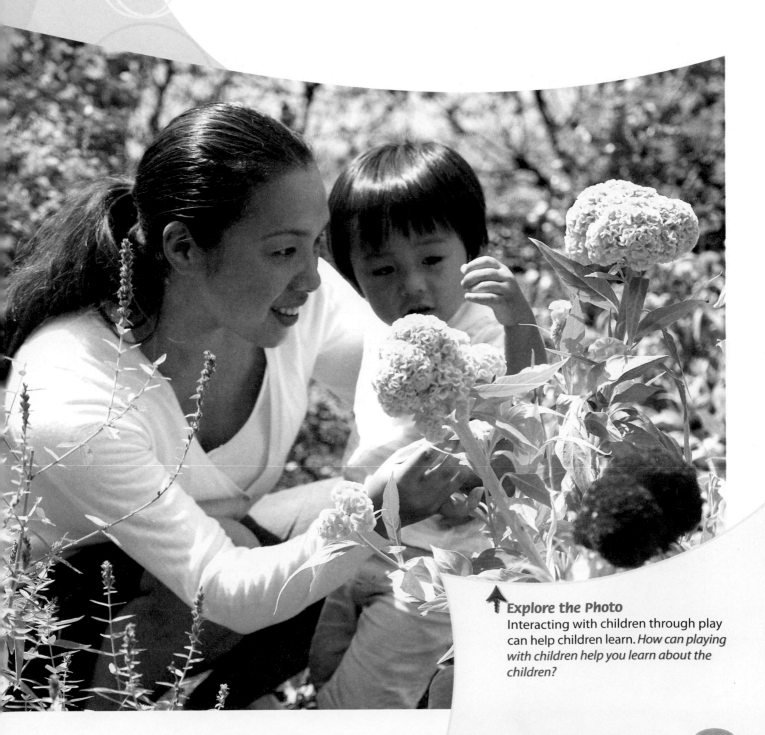

Explore the Photo
Interacting with children through play can help children learn. *How can playing with children help you learn about the children?*

Make a Difference in Children's Lives

Reading Guide

Before You Read

Preview Read the Key Concepts listed below. For each Key Concept, write a short paragraph that explains what you think you will learn in this section.

Read to Learn
Key Concepts
- **Explain** the best way to learn about children.
- **Identify** three areas of childhood that researchers have studied.

Main Idea
Caregivers use their skills and knowledge to interact with children. Caregivers can make a positive difference in a child's life. Childhood is viewed differently today than in past years.

Content Vocabulary
◇ typical behavior
◇ caregiver

Academic Vocabulary
You will find these words in your reading and on your tests. Use the glossary to look up their definitions if necessary.
■ impact
■ moral

 Graphic Organizer Go to this book's Online Learning Center at **glencoe.com** to print out this graphic organizer.

Graphic Organizer
As you read, compare childhood in the past with childhood in the present. Use a chart like the one shown to list the differences.

Childhood Past and Present		
	Past	**Present**
Health		
Education		
Love		
Work		
Play		
Dress		

Academic Standards . . . .

 English Language Arts
NCTE 4 Use written language to communicate effectively.

 Social Studies
NCSS V F Individuals, Groups, and Institutions Evaluate the role of institutions in furthering both continuity and change.

NCTE *National Council of Teachers of English*
NCTM *National Council of Teachers of Mathematics*

NSES *National Science Education Standards*
NCSS *National Council for the Social Studies*

Benefits of Studying Children

Why do babies like to chew on books? Why do toddlers throw their toys again after you have just picked them up? What should you do if a three-year-old lies? Children's behavior can be both fascinating and frustrating, especially when you do not understand it. As you study child development, you will find answers to questions such as these. You will also learn that taking care of children is one of the most important responsibilities you can have.

Understanding Children and Yourself

Have you ever really thought about the process by which children grow up and become independent adults? You might never have realized that you have an **impact**, or significant effect, on children's lives. People and events help shape who children become. When you live with children, you influence them every day.

If your contact with children is less frequent, what you say and how you act still matter. Even if you do not interact with children regularly, younger children still watch you and pay attention to how you behave. This is true whether the children are relatives, friends of your family, or even strangers that you pass in a store. Do you think that you are a good role model? Studying child development will help you learn how you can make a positive difference in a child's life.

Learning more about how children grow and develop will help you understand children better. It will also improve your understanding of yourself.

Many experts have written about how children learn and how best to care for them. No two children are alike, however, and no expert can explain every aspect of a child's behavior. The best way to learn about children is through your active involvement with them.

By interacting with children and studying their behaviors, you will:

- **Learn why children feel, think, and act the way they do.** It is not always easy to understand children's behavior, especially before they learn to talk. However, there are some typical behaviors. A **typical behavior** is a way of acting or responding that is common at each stage of childhood. Understanding these behaviors can help you respond to children more appropriately. For example, Carrie was puzzled by the actions of her brother Brett and their neighbor Curtis, both two-year-olds.

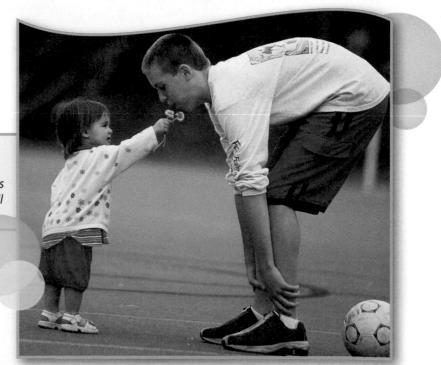

➤ Learn by Doing
Interacting with children is the best way to learn about them. *What can this teen learn about toddlers by playing ball with them?*

Learning Through PLAY

Playing with Babies

As babies grow and develop they learn new mental, physical, and social skills. As they learn more, their play changes. Very young babies learn physical skills by grasping toys such as rattles or stuffed animals. They interact and learn social skills when adults or older children talk to and play with them. Older babies learn social skills by playing games such as peek-a-boo. They might learn physical skills by clapping and moving in time to music. Their toys can be as simple as a bucket and some blocks. They can put the blocks into the bucket. Then they might turn the bucket upside down and dump out the blocks, and start over. Toys that make noise and change colors or have blinking lights can help babies learn to distinguish sounds and colors. For babies, play is their school. Through play, they continue to develop mentally, physically, and socially.

Think About It You are reading to your nine-month-old niece, Rihanna, who is very alert and playful. How is this helping her develop mental, physical, and social skills?

They never interacted when they played. Brett and Curtis usually sat near each other, but they played with different toys. In a child development class, Carrie learned that two-year-olds typically play *alongside* each other but not *with* each other. Carrie understood that her brother's style of play was typical for his age.

- **Discover caregivers' importance.** A person who takes care of a child is called a **caregiver**. Parents and others can be caregivers. As you learn more about how children develop, you will see why they are dependent upon others for many years. Caregivers provide more than food and clothes. They give the affection children need to grow emotionally. They help children learn, and teach children how to get along with others and how to know right from wrong.
- **Enjoy children more.** Learning about children can help you discover what a joy they can be. Spending time with them will give you chances to experience their honesty, humor, energy, and curiosity. Caring for children can be very rewarding.
- **Learn about career opportunities.** Throughout this book, you will be introduced to many jobs related to children. You may find one that interests you.

Apply What You Learn

You are in an excellent position to study child development. You are close enough to adulthood to think critically, but still young enough to remember what being a child feels like. As you learn about children, some of your views about childhood and child rearing may be reinforced, and you may rethink other views. Interacting and working with children and child care professionals can help you answer questions.

Gain New Skills

As you learn about children and ways to meet their needs, try to find opportunities to apply your knowledge. You might spend your summers working at a local park or pool, or looking after a younger sibling or a neighbor's child. Knowing how to bathe a baby, prepare a healthy meal for a toddler, or encourage a four-year-old to settle down for a nap can give you confidence. This confidence can help make the children you care for feel more secure with you.

Understand Yourself

As you gain a better understanding of children, you will also come to know yourself better. You may begin to see your own childhood differently. Think of your childhood.

Try to recall major events in your childhood. Think about how they revealed different parts of your personality, or how they influenced whom you have become.

If you want to work with children, many career paths, such as teacher, children's librarian, or pediatric nurse, are open to you. You may not intend to work with children as an occupation, but you or someone close to you may be a parent someday.

✓ **Reading Check** **Define** What is a typical behavior?

Views of Childhood

Childhood means different things to different people. The way you think about childhood can depend in part on what your own childhood was like. If your childhood was fairly easy and comfortable, you may think of it as a carefree time of security. If your parents struggled to provide for you, you may think of childhood as a time of hardship. For everyone, childhood is a period of rapid development, dependence on caregivers, and preparation for adult life.

Researchers have made a special study of childhood and its phases. They have looked at how children develop, what their needs are, and how those needs can best be met. One of their most important findings is that childhood has a profound influence on later life.

Childhood has not always been considered a separate, important stage of life. In fact, childhood as it is now known is a fairly recent viewpoint.

{ **Expert Advice...** }

"Children need people in order to become human . . . It is primarily through observing, playing, and working with others older and younger than himself that a child discovers both what he can do and who he can become."

—Urie Bronfenbrenner, psychologist and family advocate

Explore Careers
Summer jobs can be a great way to explore career options. *How can this teen's job help him prepare for a career?*

Compare Childhood Past and Present

Until the twentieth century, some people believed that there was nothing special or important about the early years of life. Some adults believed children were meant to be "seen and not heard." Little was known about the emotional and intellectual needs of children. Changing attitudes, social changes, and advances in technology and medicine have changed views about childhood.

Health

Before the twentieth century, diseases caused deaths in almost every family, particularly among children. Today, many deadly diseases can be controlled, and better nutrition has helped children to grow and thrive as never before. However, not all children eat well. Some do not have enough food. Others eat too many high-fat, high-sugar foods. Also, lack of regular exercise is increasingly common. The rate of childhood obesity and related problems has increased.

Education

Public education for all children did not become common in the United States until the early 1800s. Schools were small, and often children of different ages and abilities were in the same classroom. In today's schools, students are grouped according to age and sometimes learning levels. Technology has enhanced learning options. Schools work to meet the special needs of individual students.

Love

One thing that has not changed through the years is children's need for love. Most parents and other caregivers work hard to build a good life for their children and to raise them as **moral**, or ethical, people who are also responsible and independent.

↑ **Changing Times**
Toys children play with have changed dramatically over time. *Do you think children learn more by playing with today's toys? Explain your answer.*

Work

For settlers in America, a primary concern was survival. Children helped greatly with chores, gathering wood, sewing, and even plowing. Up until the twentieth century, children were expected to work at an early age. Then laws were enacted banning children from working in factories or other adult workplaces. Today, most young children are only expected to work at growing, learning, and playing. Teens may hold jobs, but laws specify the minimum working age and number of hours worked, and most dangerous jobs are banned. Most children are expected to help out at home by cleaning their rooms, feeding pets, helping with yard work, or helping care for siblings.

Play

Play has always been important to children. It is how they learn. How much children play and what they play with have changed. In the past, children had far fewer toys, and they were simple. Parents often showed their love for their children by making them toys out of materials at hand. A child might have had a doll made of cloth or an animal carved from wood. Toys encouraged children to use their imagination.

Sports like baseball and basketball were not developed until the 1800s. Video and computer games first became available in the 1970s. Today, the variety of toys seems endless. Many toys are electronic and do not involve as much use of the imagination. However, children still enjoy books and other traditional toys. Children today spend much of their time playing.

Dress

If you look at old pictures, you will quickly notice that children dressed more formally in the past. Infants and toddlers of both genders often wore long gowns. Older boys wore suits, while girls wore dresses. Today, casual clothes for boys and girls are often similar in style. It is not uncommon for infants to wear onesies or t-shirts. They are washable, comfortable, and loose enough to allow freedom of movement.

Section 1.1   After You Read

Review Key Concepts

1. **Describe** two ways learning about children can benefit you.
2. **List** six areas in which views about children have changed over the years.

Practice Academic Skills

English Language Arts

3. Use your personal experience and any observations you have made over the years to explain what is meant by the phrase, "Children are dependent upon others for many years." Write your explanation in a paragraph.

> **NCTE 4** Use written language to communicate effectively.

Social Studies

4. Children have better health today due to advances in medical technology. Many diseases that were responsible for childhood deaths in the past are treatable today. Conduct research and write a list of four ways medical advances affect our society today.

> **NCSS V F** Evaluate the role of institutions in furthering both continuity and change.

Check Your Answers Check your answers at this book's Online Learning Center at **glencoe.com**.

Reading Guide

Before You Read

Cause and Effect A cause is an action or event that makes something happen. An effect is the result of the cause. As you read, look for causes and effects to better understand how the material is related.

Read to Learn
Key Concepts
- **Summarize** how children learn and develop important skills.
- **List** the stages of development after childhood.

Main Idea

Childhood is an important time of physical, mental, and emotional development. A child's heredity and environment affect development. Development continues throughout the life cycle.

Content Vocabulary
◇ stimulation
◇ heredity
◇ environment
◇ self-esteem
◇ human life cycle
◇ developmental task

Academic Vocabulary

You will find these words in your reading and on your tests. Use the glossary to look up their definitions if necessary.
- theory
- sequence

Graphic Organizer

As you read, note three effects of low self-esteem on a developing child. Use a chart like the one shown to help organize your information.

 Graphic Organizer Go to this book's Online Learning Center at **glencoe.com** to print out this graphic organizer.

Academic Standards ·

 English Language Arts

NCTE 12 Use language to accomplish individual purposes.

 Social Studies

NCSS IV C Individual Development and Identity Describe the ways family and cultural influences contribute to the development of a sense of self.

NCTE *National Council of Teachers of English*
NCTM *National Council of Teachers of Mathematics*

NSES *National Science Education Standards*
NCSS *National Council for the Social Studies*

Importance of Childhood Development

Imagine spending your whole career researching child development. By the time you retired, do you think you could solve all its mysteries? Many researchers have devoted their careers to the study of children, yet there are still many unanswered questions.

What has been learned, however, has dramatically changed how parents raise children, how educators teach them, and how we think of development today. Today we know development is a lifelong process.

Childhood prepares us for adulthood. Research has shown that early childhood may be the most important life stage for brain development. A child's brain is not yet fully developed at birth. The brain is the least developed of the organs. A baby's brain is about one-fourth the size of an adult's. By age three, it has made trillions of connections among the brain cells.

Scientists have found that a baby's brain develops in direct response to stimulation. **Stimulation** is any activity that arouses a baby's sense of sight, sound, touch, taste, and smell. Such activities can improve a baby's curiosity, attention span, memory, and nervous system development. Babies who receive stimulation develop more quickly and have a more secure self-image.

By the time babies are three to four months old, they are beginning to connect what they see with what they smell, feel, and taste. By the time toddlers start walking, the brain is sending messages faster and more clearly. Repetition of actions, such as throwing a ball, reinforces pathways in the brain. This makes it easier to perform the same action the next time.

What Researchers Have Found

Child development theorists have provided valuable information about how children learn and develop skills. Some perform experiments involving children to test a **theory**, or belief. For example, children's perception of volume can be tested using the same amount of water in containers of various shapes. Other theories cannot be tested, such as Erik Erikson's belief that each stage of development includes a personal crisis.

Not everyone agrees on how parents, caregivers, and educators should apply theories and research findings. **Figure 1.1** on page 15 summarizes the study and research findings of some of the major child development theorists.

Although they do not always agree, scientific researchers have given us insight about how best to nurture and educate children. They have also laid the foundations upon which future researchers can build. There are five basic areas of child development: physical, emotional, social, intellectual, and moral.

Physical Development
Toddlers cannot learn to walk until their bodies are physically developed and ready. *What happens when a toddler is just learning to walk? Why does it happen?*

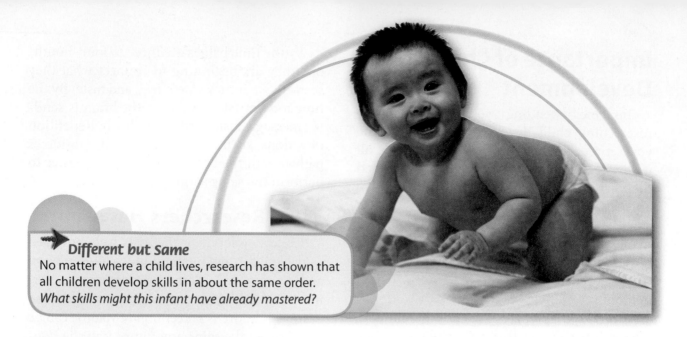

Different but Same
No matter where a child lives, research has shown that all children develop skills in about the same order. *What skills might this infant have already mastered?*

Characteristics of Development

Researchers have found that child development follows five general rules:

- **Development is similar for each individual.** Children go through the same stages in about the same order. All babies lift their heads before they lift their bodies.
- **Development builds upon earlier learning.** Development follows a **sequence**, or an order of steps. The skills learned at one stage build on those mastered earlier.

- **Development proceeds at an individual rate.** While all children pass through the same stages of development, each child goes through these stages at his or her own pace.
- **The different areas of development are interrelated.** Though research tends to focus on one area at a time, changes occur in many areas at the same time.
- **Development is continuous throughout life.** The rate of development varies. No matter what the pace is, development does not stop.

THE DEVELOPING BRAIN

Neural Connections

Babies learn alot in the first three years of life. Newborn babies' brains contain about 100 billion nerve cells, called neurons. Those neurons have about 50 trillion connections. These connections increase rapidly, and by the age of three, a child has twice as many connections as an adult. As a child matures, unused pathways are removed. This means that babies who live in an environment where they learn more will keep more connections.

■ **Science Inquiry** A stimulating environment is important for babies' brains to develop to their fullest potential. How would a stimulating environment lead to an increased number of neurological connections?

Influences on Development

If you traveled the world visiting families in various countries, you would see that babies are cared for in different ways in different cultures. However, all infants follow a predictable sequence of development at about the same ages. Babies must learn to lift their heads before they can sit or crawl, stand, and walk.

Children develop at different rates because each has a unique combination of factors influencing their development. These factors fall into one of two categories:

- **Heredity** is the biological transfer of certain characteristics from earlier generations. Blood type, eye color, and hair color are just a few of the characteristics determined by heredity.
- **Environment** is the people, places, and things that surround and influence a person, including family, home, school, and community.

Figure **1.1** **Child Development Theorists**

These are some of the researchers who have made a major contribution to the study of child development. *Which theorist said that each stage of development includes a psychological crisis? Why is this important?*

Theorist	Findings or Ideas	Significance
Sigmund Freud (1856–1939)	Believed that personality develops through a series of stages. Experiences in childhood profoundly affect adult life.	Childhood is much more important than previously thought, and its effects are longer lasting.
Jean Piaget (1896–1980)	The first to study children scientifically. Focused on how children learned. Believed that children go through four stages of learning.	Children must be given learning tasks appropriate to their level of development.
Lev Vygotsky (1896–1934)	Wrote that biological development and cultural experience influence children's ability to learn. Social contact is essential to intellectual development.	Children should be given the opportunity for frequent social interaction.
Erik Erikson (1902–1994)	Like Freud, said that personality develops in stages. Thought that each stage includes a unique psychological crisis. If that crisis is met in a positive way, the individual develops normally.	Parents and other caregivers must be aware of, and sensitive to, children's needs at each stage of development and support them through crises.
B. F. Skinner (1904–1990)	Argued that when a child's actions have positive results, they will be repeated. Negative results will make the actions stop.	Parents and other caregivers can affect a child's behavior through the use of negative and positive feedback.
Urie Bronfenbrenner (1917–2005)	Outlined layers of environment that affect a child's development, such as the child's own biology, family/community environment, and society.	Child's primary relationship with a caregiver needs to be stable, loving, and lasting.
Albert Bandura (b. 1925)	Said that children learn by imitating others. Disagreed with Skinner. Pointed out that although the environment shapes behavior, behavior also affects environment.	Caregivers must provide good examples for children to follow.

A Healthy Environment

Anne is a pediatric nurse. She has two nine-year-old patients, Ian and Seth, who have asthma. Aside from their age and diagnosis, their situations are different. "Seth has been to the hospital only once for an asthma attack," Anne says. "His mom also has asthma, so they have learned together how to manage their symptoms. They keep emergency medication on hand and clean their house often to reduce dust. Ian, on the other hand, spends a lot of time in the hospital for asthma attacks." Anne continues, "Two conditions in his home can make his asthma worse: his family has a cat and one of his parents smokes." Ian's parents asked how to help reduce his number of attacks.

✐ *Write About It* How might Ian's parents change his environment to reduce the number of his asthma attacks? Write a brief article for the Health section of your local newspaper to offer ideas for Ian's parents.

Heredity is often referred to as *nature*. For example, if someone says, "Dylan is musically talented—it's in his nature," they mean that he was born with this gift. *Nurture* is used to refer to influences and conditions in a child's environment. Dylan may play the piano well because he practices each day. For years, scientists and philosophers have debated whether nature or nurture has more influence. Most agree, however, that they work together.

Children inherit certain physical characteristics from their parents and ancestors. For example, Alejandra has brown hair and brown eyes, as do her parents. Children learn attitudes and beliefs from their environment. Samira's parents take helping family and friends very seriously, and so does she.

Children are also greatly influenced by the world around them. What they read, the music they listen to, the movies and television shows they watch, the type of community in which they grow up, and many other influences play a part in who they become. If you spend time around children, you can count yourself as one of these influences.

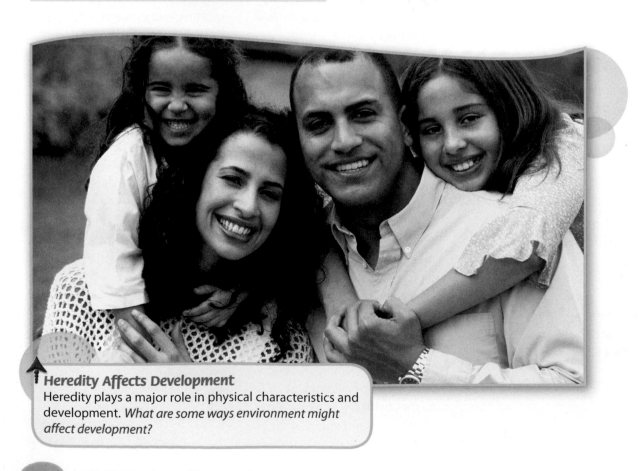

Heredity Affects Development
Heredity plays a major role in physical characteristics and development. *What are some ways environment might affect development?*

Of course, children do not always copy the attitudes and actions of others, and no two children are exactly alike. They react to outside influences in their own ways. That is one reason that brothers and sisters who grow up in the same home may experience life differently. This is also why they may become very different people.

No two children have exactly the same environment. Even children who grow up in the same home have different environments. Their choice of friends, food, and activities will differ, and so will they. They might belong to different clubs. They will be exposed to different classmates. All of these things make up their environment.

During infancy and early childhood, environment plays a particularly important role in development. That is why working with young children is such an important responsibility and such a challenging opportunity.

The Role of Self-Esteem in Development

Self-esteem, or self-worth, is the value people place on themselves. Self-esteem plays a role in people's ability to face and overcome the challenges of each developmental stage, including those of young childhood.

People with low self-esteem often feel that they are failing or constantly disappointing others. Researchers have found a link between low self-esteem and poor school performance, truancy, and criminal behavior.

A sense of self-worth is critical to children's development. Children who feel good about themselves are more likely to show enthusiasm for learning, form friendships, and make healthy choices. Having a sense of self-worth can help children deal with life's frustrations and disappointments, as well as its successes.

✓ **Reading Check** **Identify** Explain what is meant by *nature versus nurture*.

Parenting Skills

Help Children Develop Self-Esteem

Parents and other caregivers play a major role in developing a child's sense of self-esteem. Here are a few ways to have a positive effect.

- **Give praise.** Praise children for their accomplishments or real effort.
- **Do not be overly critical.** When children do not do things quite right, try to find the good in what they have done and discuss how they can do better the next time.
- **Set realistic goals.** Help children set goals that they can reach. Reaching realistic goals makes children feel good about their accomplishments.
- **Encourage new activities.** Help children learn to enjoy trying new things.
- **Model self-esteem.** Children learn by example. If the adults in their lives say negative things about themselves, children will imitate this negative behavior.
- **Be honest about mistakes.** Children need to see that adults have faults and make mistakes, too.

Take Charge Write a journal entry that describes a time when someone's criticism lowered your self-esteem. Explain how that person might have encouraged you instead.

Stages of Life After Childhood

Development does not end when childhood does. It continues from birth to death in the human life cycle. The **human life cycle** is a set of stages of human development that each present different challenges to be met or skills to be acquired. The challenge to be met or skill to be acquired in each stage is known as a **developmental task**. These tasks can be such things as creating an identity or starting a career. Individuals differ in how they approach the challenges. Mastering the tasks of one stage helps prepare a person for the next stage.

- **Adolescence** This is the stage of life between childhood and adulthood. Teens work on three developmental tasks: creating an identity, becoming independent, and pursuing education and careers.
- **Young Adulthood** This stage refers to people in their twenties, when many young adults finish their education and begin working. Many marry in this period.
- **The Thirties** This stage presents the challenges of establishing roots, reevaluating life choices made earlier, and finding stability in career and relationships.
- **Middle Age** This stage lasts from about ages 40–55. Parents adjust as their children become more independent. Adults in this stage may make life changes, such as starting a new career.
- **Late Adulthood** At some point during this stage (ages 55–75), many adults retire. They may become more politically or socially active, travel, take classes, or enjoy hobbies they did not have time for before. Some take on a part-time job. Others enjoy having more time with their grandchildren. Health issues may arise.
- **Very Late Adulthood** It is in this stage (beyond age 75) when health problems become more common. However, many older adults are still active, and they contribute their knowledge and experience to society. Those in fragile health often need more assistance or care.

Section 1.2 After You Read

Review Key Concepts

1. **Explain** why early childhood is considered the most important period for brain development.
2. **Identify** common characteristics of late adulthood.

Practice Academic Skills

 English Language Arts

3. Imagine that you will participate in a panel discussion on *Nature versus Nurture*. Create notes to use that explain how heredity and the environment can work together to shape a child.

> **NCTE 12** Use language to accomplish individual purposes.

 Social Studies

4. Having a sense of self-worth helps children deal with life's successes and challenges. Research someone who has overcome obstacles in his or her life. Write a paragraph explaining how you think having a sense of self-worth helped them to succeed in life.

> **NCSS IV C** Describe the ways family and cultural influences contribute to the development of a sense of self.

 Check Your Answers Check your answers at this book's Online Learning Center at **glencoe.com**.

Reading Guide

Before You Read

Vocabulary Read the Content and Academic Vocabulary. Choose a term that you are not familiar with and when you see it in the text, write down the definition.

Read to Learn
Key Concepts
- **Determine** why observation is important in the study of child development.
- **Compare and contrast** different methods of observation and interpretation.

Main Idea
An important component in learning and understanding child development is observation. Observation allows caregivers to better understand individual children and their particular needs.

Content Vocabulary
◇ subjective
◇ objective
◇ running record
◇ anecdotal record
◇ frequency count
◇ baseline
◇ developmental checklist
◇ interpretation
◇ confidentiality

Academic Vocabulary
You will find these words in your reading and on your tests. Use the glossary to look up their definitions if necessary.
- assumption
- judgment

Graphic Organizer
As you read, note the four methods of recording observations described in the text. Use a chart like the one shown to help organize your information.

Types of Observation Records

 Graphic Organizer Go to this book's Online Learning Center at **glencoe.com** to print out this graphic organizer.

Academic Standards . . . .

 English Language Arts

NCTE 4 Use written language to communicate effectively.

 Science

NSES A Develop abilities necessary to do scientific inquiry, understandings about scientific inquiry.

NCTE *National Council of Teachers of English*
NCTM *National Council of Teachers of Mathematics*

NSES *National Science Education Standards*
NCSS *National Council for the Social Studies*

Learning by Observation
Observation can help you learn traits and personalities of individual children. *What have you learned by observing children?*

Why Observe Children?

While you can learn a great deal from reading about children, observing them is even more helpful. Observing offers you the chance to see children as individuals. You see them meeting the challenges of development in their own ways and in their own time. Child development comes to life when you observe children in action. Learning how to observe children is an important skill for teachers, parents, and other caregivers.

Observing young children and interpreting their behavior are skills that take time to learn. You will see how one stage leads to the next, for example, as an infant learns to sit up, then pull up, then stand alone, and finally walk. Caregivers who are familiar with the various stages of development can help and encourage children as they progress.

Observing a child will let you see his or her unique personality. If you get to know a child, you will be able to adapt activities to that child's needs. Parents and caregivers who are careful observers often can identify children who may have disabilities or require extra care.

Children developing slowly can be evaluated and treated. Researchers have found that children whose special needs are spotted and treated early do better over the long term.

Finally, observing children provides caregivers with useful feedback. Watch how children respond to your attempts at guiding their behavior, and you will see how successful your methods are. If you stick to what works, you will be more effective at earning children's cooperation and trust.

✓ **Reading Check** **Recall** Why is it useful to get to know a child?

How to Observe Young Children

Knowing how to record what you observe and analyze it later will give you insight into children's development. Observing means more than just watching. It means following certain steps so that your observations will be useful. You must have a written record of your observation to refer to for analysis.

Objective Versus Subjective Observations

When observing, you must learn to separate fact from opinion. Compare the two observations of the same event in **Figure 1.2.**

Observation A is subjective. **Subjective** means to rely on personal opinions and feelings, rather than facts, to judge an event. From reading the observation, it is hard to tell what really happened between Ethan and Cody. The observer in this example recorded an opinion about how Ethan felt.

Observation B is objective. **Objective** means something is factual, and leaves aside personal feelings and prejudices. The observer describes only what was actually seen and heard. You know exactly what actions Ethan and Cody performed. Analyzing the observation later will help determine why those actions occurred.

Subjective observations are based on the false assumption that the observer knows what is going on in the child's mind. An **assumption** is a fact that is taken for granted. Subjective observations can be misleading. Ethan might not have been acting selfishly. He might have had an earlier agreement with Cody about taking turns. He might be angry because Cody is not holding up his end of the deal.

Subjective observations do not record facts, so they are hard for others to use. A teacher who knew that Ethan was generally shy at school would probably prefer to hear the objective facts presented in Observation B. The teacher might interpret Ethan's behavior as a sign of growing self-assertion. Ethan might not be behaving appropriately, but the teacher might be pleased that he is sticking up for himself. The teacher might also realize that Cody needs more practice at sharing.

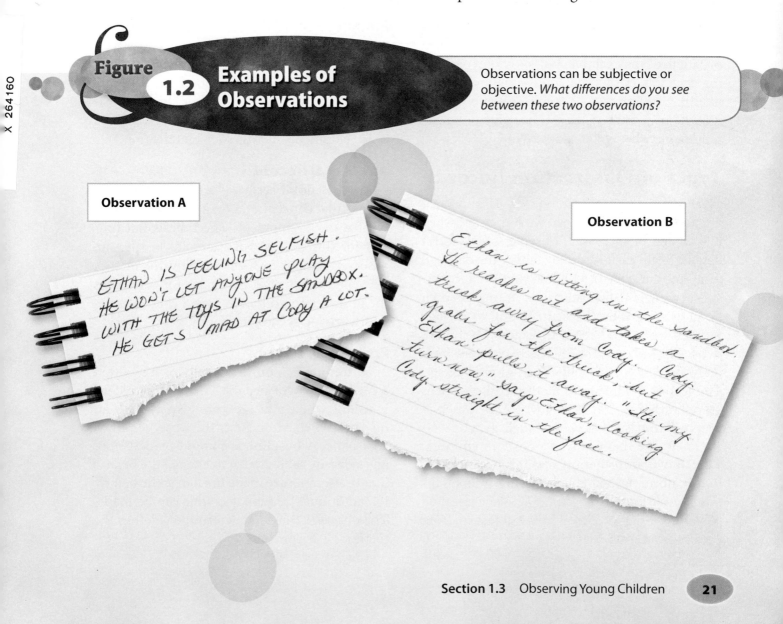

Figure 1.2 Examples of Observations

Observations can be subjective or objective. *What differences do you see between these two observations?*

Observation A

ETHAN IS FEELING SELFISH. HE WON'T LET ANYONE PLAY WITH THE TOYS IN THE SANDBOX. HE GETS MAD AT CODY A LOT.

Observation B

Ethan is sitting in the sandbox. He reaches out and takes a truck away from Cody. Cody grabs for the truck, but Ethan pulls it away. "It's my turn now," says Ethan, looking Cody straight in the face.

X 264160

Observe to Learn
Observing young children is an important way to learn about child development. *Why do you need to have a specific focus or purpose for an observation?*

Writing objective observations takes practice. An observer can note that a child smiled or laughed, for example, but should avoid saying that this means the child is happy. That is making a **judgment**, or opinion. Remember to record only what you see and hear. Do not make judgments when you are observing.

Types of Observation Records

When making observations, it is important for observers to write down what they see when it happens. If they wait, observers may forget details. Begin each record by noting the date and time, the number of children and adults present, and their names and ages. Young children develop so quickly that it is helpful to include months when you record their ages. A child of two years and one month is quite different from one who is two years and eleven months of age. The record should also note the setting, such as school or home, and exactly where the observation occurred, such as on the jungle gym.

There are many ways to observe children. The above information should be included in any observation. The following four methods are particularly useful. Choose a method based on what you are hoping to learn from the observation.

Running Record

A **running record** is a record of everything observed for a set period, such as 15 minutes. This method is useful for observers who are just getting to know the child or children. It is also good when concentrating on a certain area of development, such as social interaction.

Anecdotal Record

An **anecdotal record** is a report of a child's actions that concentrates on a specific behavior or area of development. The time is not limited for this record. For example, suppose an observer wanted to focus on adjustment to a new child care center. Every day for two weeks the observer could record how a child behaves upon arriving at the center.

Frequency Count

A **frequency count** is a tally of how often a certain behavior occurs. This kind of record is useful when you are trying to change an unwanted behavior. First, the observer finds a baseline. A **baseline** is a count made before any steps are taken to try to change the behavior. As attempts are made to change the behavior, additional frequency counts can be made. The observer can then determine whether the methods are working.

Developmental Checklist

A list of skills children should master, or behaviors they should exhibit at a certain age, is called a **developmental checklist**. Observers can use this checklist and simply check off the skills or behaviors they see.

How to Act While Observing

There are two different ways you can observe young children: formally and informally. A formal observation might be something you set up with a child care center or a family. An informal observation is one where you do not make yourself so obvious. This could be sitting at a mall or airport watching children. When you make informal observations, you will have to estimate the ages of the children you observe. Avoid making quick judgments about children, since you are only getting glimpses of their abilities and behavior.

Whether you observe children formally or informally, you do not want to be noticed. When you observe children, it is generally important to try to blend into the environment as much as possible. Avoid calling attention to yourself. If your presence affects the children's behavior, it may not be possible to gather objective information. Sit or stand slightly outside the area where the children are, and be ready to take notes. Make sure you clearly understand your observation assignment before you begin. Also make sure you have noted the basic information. When you are observing children, things happen very quickly. You need to be prepared. **Figure 1.3** offers more tips on how to take notes that will be useful for later analysis.

Figure 1.3 How to Take Notes During an Observation

Preparing ahead of time will help ensure a successful observation. *How might you prepare your paper to help you complete all the aspects of your observation?*

Action	Explanation
Know your purpose.	Before you do your observation, define the purpose of your observation. Ask yourself what you are supposed to observe.
Identify the when, where, who, and what.	Take note of the physical features of the setting. Who is there? What activities are going on? Make a record of the time and place.
Be descriptive.	You can use words and phrases to capture the moment. Think of it as giving a picture of what you see.
Make comparisons.	Look for similarities and differences. If you are watching groups of children, evaluate what each group is doing. If you are focusing your observation on one child, how do his or her skills compare to those of another child of the same age?
Uncover the data.	Record as much factual information as you can, focusing on the evidence at hand.
Review and clarify.	At the end, read through your comments, make clarifications or corrections, and add any additional notes.

An Observer's Role

Children often do not have the judgment or skills to realize that they are in danger. While observing, if you see a child in a dangerous situation, you must intervene and get help from a teacher or caregiver. For example, imagine you are observing children at a child care center and you notice a young toddler put a small puzzle piece in his mouth. You should get help from a child care worker immediately. Getting help quickly often prevents harm from coming to children.

Be Prepared Think of a dangerous situation in which you would intervene immediately. Decide what you would do in the situation. Develop a step-by-step procedure that you would follow in the situation and create a poster with the steps. Hang the poster in the classroom.

Always be respectful of others. If you are doing a formal observation, arrive on time. Be sure to follow any sign-in procedures or other rules a center might have.

Children are naturally curious, and they will want to find out who you are and what you are doing. Answer questions honestly but briefly. You can also just smile and say you are working. Avoid asking questions, which will encourage conversation. If the children need to be persuaded to return to their activities, you might say, "I am writing a story about how children play. If you go back to playing, I can write about you in my story."

There are some situations when you may need to interact with a child. For example, if you are updating a developmental checklist you might need to know how well a child can catch and throw a ball. You could pull the child aside for a few minutes and test for these skills. The Safe Child, Healthy Child feature describes other reasons you might need to step in.

Time to Understand
It takes time to develop good observation skills and to be able to interpret observations accurately. *Why should you discuss questions about what you observe with your teacher rather than your friends?*

How To Interpret Observations

Before you use your observations, you will need to finalize your paperwork. In many cases, you will want to transfer your notes to another sheet, or use your notes to write a longer observation record. Some observations are kept in a child's file for future reference, so make sure that your final report appears neat and professional. You might want to type your report using word-processing software. This will allow you to save an electronic file for reference and print a copy for the child's file.

Simply having a half-hour's running record of a child's behavior is of little use unless you analyze it. The analysis an observer forms and expresses about what was observed is called an **interpretation**. In recording the information, it was your job to remain objective. Now it is time to form and express ideas about what you saw. Your study of child development will help you do so.

Anyone who observes children and interprets information about them must maintain confidentiality. **Confidentiality** (ˌkän-fə-ˌden(t)-shē-ˈa-lə-tē) is the protection of another person's privacy by limiting access to personal information. You may share your information only with the child's parents or your child development teacher. It is not ethical to discuss children outside of class.

Remember that most observations are short in length. For this reason, your interpretation may not be accurate. You are just developing your observation skills, so your interpretation may not match that of a professional. These are further reasons that you must avoid discussing the child's behavior with your friends. Comments such as "Lauren is spoiled" or "Caleb is a slow learner" might lead to gossip that could hurt the child or the family. If you have questions or concerns about a child you observed, discuss them only with your child development teacher.

Section 1.3   After You Read

Review Key Concepts

1. **List** two reasons why observing children is helpful in your study of child development.

2. **Identify** four basic facts an observation record should include.

Practice Academic Skills

 English Language Arts

3. Imagine that you have just completed your observation of a kindergarten-age boy. Write a paragraph to discuss how you would go about interpreting his behavior. List the steps you would take after recording your information.

NCTE 4 Use written language to communicate effectively.

 Science

4. With a partner, observe one child for at least ten minutes. One of you will write a running record of all the behaviors observed. The other will write an anecdotal record, focusing on one aspect of behavior, such as attitude toward learning. How are your records similar or different? .

 Check Your Answers Check your answers at this book's Online Learning Center at **glencoe.com**.

NSES A Develop abilities necessary to do scientific inquiry, understandings about scientific inquiry.

Parent Educator

Sometimes parents want to do more for their children outside of the home and classroom. Parent educators are trained in child development. They use their training to help educate parents about parenting skills.

What Does a Parent Educator Do?

Parent educators provide assistance, instruction, and materials in a variety of areas. These can include academic areas as well as nutrition, parenting styles, and behavioral management. Parent educators can demonstrate techniques to enhance parent-child growth. One primary responsibility of these educators is to teach parents about the resources available to them. They provide referral information for books, Web sites, and workshops.

Where Does a Parent Educator Work?

Depending on the area in which they specialize, parent educators have the flexibility of working in schools, community centers, and hospitals. Some parent educators visit the homes of the people they work with.

Preparation and Skills

Education and Training
Most parent educators have bachelor's degrees with an emphasis in early childhood education or psychology. Some hold master's degrees in social work or developmental psychology.

Aptitudes, Abilities, and Skills
Parent educators must be proficient in communication and language skills. They should possess a knowledge of early childhood behavior, characteristics, and development. Effective parenting skills, mentoring abilities, and record-keeping abilities are also needed.

Academic Skills
Parent educators use English language arts, such as speaking and listening, when they talk to parents or groups of parents. They also use mathematics, science, and social studies skills in the research and skills they teach to parents.

Explore Careers

Research a career related to parent educator, such as teacher or family counselor. Write a paragraph describing the career. Explain why you would or would not pursue that career.

 Careers Online For more information on careers, visit the Occupational Outlook Handbook Web site through the link on this book's Online Learning Center at **glencoe.com**.

Chapter Summary

By studying children, you can learn why they act the way they do, discover why caregivers are an important influence, and enjoy children more. As more has been learned about children through research, attitudes and practices have changed. Experiences in the first years of life promote rapid brain development. Heredity and environment both impact development. Self-esteem influences a person's ability to face life's challenges.

You can learn things by observing children that you cannot learn from a book. There are several types of observation methods. All observations should be conducted carefully and kept confidential.

Vocabulary Review

1. Use each of these content and academic vocabulary words in a sentence.

Content Vocabulary
- ◇ typical behavior (p. 7)
- ◇ caregiver (p. 8)
- ◇ stimulation (p. 13)
- ◇ heredity (p. 14)
- ◇ environment (p. 14)
- ◇ self-esteem (p. 17)
- ◇ human life cycle (p. 18)
- ◇ developmental task (p. 18)
- ◇ subjective (p. 21)

- ◇ objective (p. 21)
- ◇ running record (p. 22)
- ◇ anecdotal record (p. 22)
- ◇ frequency count (p. 22)
- ◇ baseline (p. 22)
- ◇ developmental checklist (p. 23)
- ◇ interpretation (p. 25)
- ◇ confidentiality (p. 25)

Academic Vocabulary
- ■ impact (p. 7)
- ■ moral (p. 10)
- ■ theory (p. 13)
- ■ sequence (p. 14)
- ■ assumption (p. 21)
- ■ judgment (p. 22)

Review Key Concepts

2. Explain the best way to learn about children.

3. Identify three areas of childhood that researchers have studied.

4. Summarize how children learn and develop important skills.

5. List the stages of development after childhood.

6. Determine why observation is important in the study of child development.

7. Compare and contrast different methods of observation and interpretation.

Critical Thinking

8. Examine How might studying the different aspects of child development better help you understand yourself?

9. Conclude What are two reasons adults might have less responsibility as they settle into middle age?

10. Infer Why might the conclusions of scientific studies, such as those in child development, later be viewed as invalid?

Family & Community Connection

11. Shadow a Teacher Work with your teacher to set up a time when you can shadow, or observe, a preschool or kindergarten teacher. Notice how the teacher interacts with the children. Take notes on the techniques used to stimulate learning. Prepare an oral presentation to share your observations with your class.

Health Skills

12. Research Childhood Vaccinations One of the main reasons for the decline in childhood deaths from disease is the development of vaccines. Select and research two vaccines. Find out at what ages they are given to children. Research what diseases they will protect against. How do the vaccines work? Do the vaccines have any side effects? Record your findings in a chart.

 Observation Skills

13 Observe Child Interaction Obtain permission to observe elementary school–age children in a class setting. Choose an age in which you have a particular interest. Be sure the class has both boys and girls in it.

Procedure Pay close attention to the children's interactions with one another. Do they all get along well? Is there one who does not seem to fit in?

Analysis Take notes during your observation. After the observation, rewrite your notes into a short report. Be sure to note any behaviors that show an inability to interact positively with others.

> **NSES 1** Develop an understanding of science unifying concepts and processes; evidence, models, and explanations.

Real-World Skills

Problem-Solving Skills

14. Making Conclusions A three-year-old child consistently tries to get in the front of the line for the playground slide. Answer the following questions in a short report: What conclusions can you make about the child's behavior? What are some ways that might help this child learn to take turns?

Technology Skills

15. Research a Theorist Conduct research about one of the child development theorists mentioned in this chapter. How does this theory help caregivers, parents, and teachers understand children? Use presentation software to create a presentation about your selected theorist and include your answers to the questions. Share your presentation with the class.

Financial Literacy Skills

16. Compare Video Games Imagine that your brother is celebrating his 10th birthday. You want to buy him an educational computer game that teaches map skills. Do research to find the best game at the best price. Record the name of each game researched, the cost of each game, and its strengths and weaknesses. Which game would you buy? Why?

 Additional Activities For additional activities, go to this book's Online Learning Center at **glencoe.com**.

Academic Skills

English Language Arts

17. Campaign for Change Imagine that you are campaigning to promote longer recess times in elementary schools. Write a letter to the editor of a local newspaper stating why you feel children this age need more play time. Use the information you have learned about child development to support your arguments.

> **NCTE 12** Use language to accomplish individual purposes.

Mathematics

18. Respiratory Diseases Young children spend most of their time at home, where they are exposed to a wide range of hazards. These exposures affect 8.5 million children below the age of 15 every year. 2.5 million of those children have respiratory diseases. What percentage of children exposed to environmental hazards contracted respiratory diseases?

Math Concept **Percentages** A percent is a ratio that compares a number to 100.

Starting Hint Divide the number of children with respiratory diseases by the total number of affected children. Multiply by 100 to convert the answer to a percent.

 For math help, go to the Math Appendix at the back of the book.

> **NCTM Number and Operations** Understand numbers, ways of representing numbers, relationships among numbers, and number systems.

Science

19. Graph Communicable Diseases Public health services track communicable diseases that may affect public health. They keep statistics that help them determine when they might have a health disaster and how to avoid it. They also offer prevention services.

Procedure Contact your local public health agency to obtain statistics related to communicable childhood diseases in your area during the past ten years.

Analysis Create a bar graph to show the incidences of childhood diseases in your area for the past ten years.

> **NSES F** Develop understanding of personal and community health.

Standardized Test Practice

MULTIPLE CHOICE

Read the passage, then answer the question.

Whether you observe children formally or informally, you do not want to be noticed. When you observe children, it is important to try to blend into the environment as much as possible. If your presence affects the children's behavior, it may not be possible to get objective information. Stay slightly outside the area where the children are.

20. In this passage, the phrase *blend into the environment* means:

  a. wear camouflage clothing.
  b. ignore the children if they talk to you.
  c. stay slightly outside the area where the children are.
  d. participate in the children's activities.

> **Test-Taking Tip** In a multiple-choice test, read the question first, then read all the answer choices. Eliminate answers that you know are incorrect.

Chapter Objectives

After completing this chapter, you will be able to:

- **Explain** who can benefit from knowing about child development and parenting.
- **Describe** the five areas of responsibilities for parents.
- **Identify** pressures involved in sexual development.
- **Summarize** the benefits of abstinence.
- **Describe** the possible consequences of sexual activity.
- **Compare and contrast** the options available to a teen parent.
- **Explain** what it means to be sexually responsible.

Writing Activity — Prewriting

Responsible Parenting Until you become a parent, it is impossible to understand all of the responsibilities of parenting. Imagine that you need to write a one-page essay about the responsibilities of parenting. Before you can write the essay, you should do a prewriting activity. This will help your essay be more organized. Talk to some parents about their experiences as new parents. Include their responses in your writing.

Writing Tips Use these tips to effectively prewrite:
1. Freewrite or collect ideas from other sources.
2. List ideas and see how they relate to each other.
3. Ask questions to explore and clarify ideas.

Section 2.1 Parenting and Families

Section 2.2 Teen Parenthood

Explore the Photo
No matter your age, you will always be your parents' child. *At what age do you think parents should stop being responsible for their children?*

Parenting and Families

Reading Guide

Before You Read

Predict Look at the photos in this section and read their captions. Write one or two sentences predicting what the section will be about.

Read to Learn
Key Concepts

- **Explain** who can benefit from knowing about child development and parenting.
- **Describe** the five areas of responsibilities for parents.

Main Idea

Parenting is a learning process with many demands and rewards. There are many decisions that must be made before and during parenthood.

Content Vocabulary

◇ parenting
◇ emotional maturity

Academic Vocabulary

You will find these words in your reading and on your tests. Use the glossary to look up their definitions if necessary.

- pride
- prospective

Graphic Organizer

As you read, list five elements necessary to prepare for parenting. Use a chart like the one shown to organize your information.

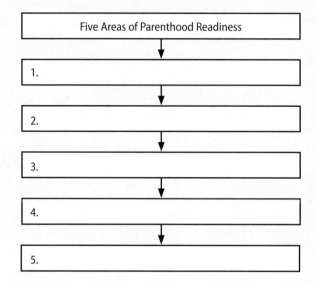

Five Areas of Parenthood Readiness
1.
2.
3.
4.
5.

 Graphic Organizer Go to this book's Online Learning Center at **glencoe.com** to print out this graphic organizer.

Academic Standards . . . .

 English Language Arts

NCTE 12 Use language to accomplish individual purposes.

 Social Studies

NCSS I A Culture Analyze and explain the ways groups, societies, and cultures address human needs and concerns.

NCSS VII F Production, Distribution, and Consumption Compare how values and beliefs influence economic decisions in different societies.

NCTE *National Council of Teachers of English*
NCTM *National Council of Teachers of Mathematics*

NSES *National Science Education Standards*
NCSS *National Council for the Social Studies*

Preparation for Parenthood

Being a parent is a job unlike any other. Parents work hard but are not paid. They are on call 24 hours a day, seven days a week. Fortunately, being a parent can bring unique rewards. Parents cherish those times when the family seems especially close or has fun together. They watch with **pride**, or pleasure, as their children become adults, ready to start independent lives of their own. For most parents, the joys outweigh the challenges.

Parenting is complicated. **Parenting** is the process of caring for children and helping them grow and develop. It impacts individuals, families, and societies. Parenting requires knowing and understanding a child's needs and then meeting those needs. It also requires good judgment.

- Parents need to know when to help and when to let children try a task on their own. Sometimes this means the children will fail. Children should learn how to bounce back after setbacks and try again.

- Parents must decide when to encourage children to try different activities. It is important to allow children the freedom to explore their own likes and dislikes. Parents need to avoid pushing children into activities they are not yet ready for. However, parents need to encourage children to engage in enjoyable activities.

- The skills needed by parents will change as the children get older. Parents must adapt their parenting skills to each stage of their children's development.

Being a parent is one of the most important roles a person has in life. It is also a role for which few people are educated and trained. People rarely learn about children and the skills needed for parenting before having children.

It is not just parents who need parenting skills. Anyone who lives or works with children can benefit from knowing about child development and parenting. This includes adult caregivers, older siblings, or other family members. By learning about parenting skills, people who interact with children can have a positive influence on them.

Normal Behavior
Knowing how children develop helps caregivers have reasonable expectations about what a child can do. *How can this help prevent some parenting frustrations?*

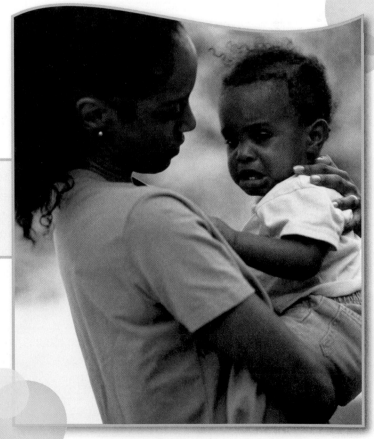

Having Reasonable Expectations

"Act your age." "How old are you, anyway?" "Would you grow up?" Do any of these sound familiar? Many parents have made remarks like these to their children. What adults often do not realize is that children usually do act their age. It is adults who do not always know what to expect from children at different ages. That is why understanding child development is so important.

Having reasonable expectations for children is the first step in effective parenting. For example, Kristin grew increasingly frustrated when two-year-old Adam said no to everything. Then her mother told her that children usually go through a negative stage at that age. Relieved that Adam would outgrow the behavior, Kristin was better able to cope with it.

Just knowing what children are like at different ages is not enough. It is important for parents and caregivers to remember that each child is an individual. Some children learn to walk earlier than others. Some need extra encouragement to make friends. Some children immediately respond when given directions. Others may need gentle reminders and more time to complete tasks. It is important to accept and respect the differences among children.

Parenthood Readiness

People considering parenthood should take a close look at what parenting involves. This includes looking at their own emotional maturity as well as health considerations, financial concerns, and how skilled they are at managing personal resources. Making a careful decision to have a child benefits both you and your child. People should learn about the myths and realities of parenting. Children deserve to be born to parents who are ready for parenthood.

Parenting Skills

Make a Positive Difference

You are probably aware that younger siblings pick up cues on how they should act by watching your behavior. Make sure you are sending appropriate, positive cues!

- **Treat others with kindness and consideration.** Make time in your day for younger siblings. Ask about school, friends, and activities they enjoy.
- **Some neighborhood children can benefit from having a teen friend.** You might be able to help a struggling reader by listening to him or her practice reading. You might work on a craft project with a group of neighborhood children.
- **Volunteer and paid jobs also provide opportunities to work with children.** Volunteer jobs might include tutoring or helping with a sports program. Possible paid jobs include babysitter, swim or dance teacher, and camp counselor. Whatever the job, the interaction with children enriches your own life as much as it does the children's lives.

Take Charge Write a paragraph that describes a time when you were a positive influence for a child. How might working with children now prepare you for parenthood later?

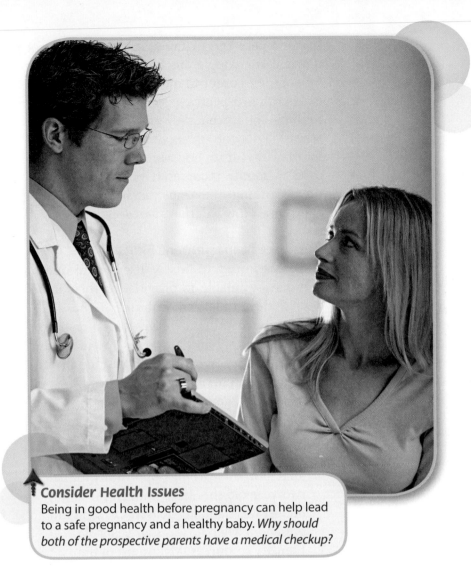

Consider Health Issues
Being in good health before pregnancy can help lead to a safe pregnancy and a healthy baby. *Why should both of the prospective parents have a medical checkup?*

Emotional Maturity

To handle the changes and demands that parenthood brings, a person needs emotional maturity. **Emotional maturity** means being responsible enough to consistently put someone else's needs before your own needs. People with emotional maturity are secure enough to devote their attention to a child without expecting anything in return. They can control their temper when an infant cries for hours on end or a child breaks a favorite possession. They are able to handle being constantly on call.

Prospective, or likely, parents should take an inventory of their own emotional maturity. Are they truly equipped to handle the challenges of parenthood? If there are doubts, it is best to put aside the desire for a child until they are convinced they have the maturity it takes to raise one.

Some prospective parents hope that having a child will help them solve some personal problems, such as low self-esteem or marriage difficulties. It will not. These are some of the reasons for wanting children that do not show emotional maturity or a real readiness for parenthood.

Health Considerations

Before pregnancy, it is best for both prospective parents to have a medical checkup. Some medical problems can affect the health of a baby or the parent's ability to care for a child. The age of the prospective mother is another consideration. If she is under 17 or over 35, pregnancy is riskier for both her and the baby.

Pregnant teens, for example, are less likely than older expectant mothers to get proper nutrition, gain adequate weight, and seek good prenatal care. These issues can be harmful to the teen's health as well as her baby's. Women over 35 are at a greater risk for developing diabetes and a potentially dangerous type of high blood pressure during pregnancy. There are also higher rates of birth defects among children born to older mothers.

Financial Concerns

Raising a child is expensive. It requires the financial resources to pay for clothes, health care, food, equipment, and other expenses. Before deciding on parenthood, couples should consider the costs of having a child during the first year and in the years ahead. It is not unusual for couples to have to change their way of life in order to meet these expenses.

If both prospective parents work, they need to think about what they will do after the baby arrives. Will one parent stop working to care for the baby? If so, how will they cope with the drop in family income? If both parents continue working, they must arrange for reliable child care. How will they pay for it?

Resource Management Skills

Parents need to wisely use the resources they have available to provide for their families. Money is just one resource. Time, skills, and energy are others. Because most resources are limited, applying a process for managing them can help parents do their best for all family members. There are five key steps to good resource management:

1. **Set goals.** Decide what is important and then turn those things into personal goals. For example, Sara considered preschool an important learning opportunity for her two-year-old son, Eli. Although the family budget was tight, her goal was to send him to preschool when he was four years old.

2. **Identify resources.** Make a list of the resources needed to achieve the goal. Sara checked into the cost of a local preschool program. She had some savings that could pay for part of the tuition. She would need to work part time to earn the rest.

3. **Make a plan.** Decide how to use the identified resources to achieve the desired goal. Sara realized she needed more money to afford Eli's preschool. Because that was two years away, she figured out how much she would need to save each month to have the tuition when Eli turned four. To achieve her goal, she also started looking for a job she could do at home.

4. **Put the plan into action.** Start working toward the goals using the steps outlined in the plan. Sara started watching her neighbor's kindergartener after school. Instead of spending the money, she put it into her savings account. She was actively working toward her goal of saving enough money.

5. Re-evaluate from time to time. Step back and take stock of progress. Are more or different resources needed? Was the goal achieved? What are some new goals to work toward? That August after Eli's fourth birthday, Sara was pleased to be able to take him to preschool. And, she had already decided on a new savings goal. She would save for a family vacation.

Parenting Skills

Can parenting be learned? Absolutely! There are many different ways to gain these skills. Classes in child development and parenting are good sources for information and support. Hospitals, schools, community groups, and private instructors offer courses or workshops on parenting skills. Some courses are targeted to age-related issues of children. Others may focus on certain behavioral or health challenges.

Still other courses may focus on helping a parent cope with difficult personal issues that can affect family life, such as financial stress or relationship problems.

There are other ways to build parenting skills too:

- Read reliable books, magazine articles, and online information about parenting.
- Gain experience working with or caring for children, informally or as a job.
- Ask the advice of family and friends who have parenting experience.
- Observe parents and children whenever and wherever possible.

Take advantage of as many learning opportunities as possible. Because each child is different, techniques that work with some do not work with every child. By learning different strategies, you are more likely to find one to match a particular child and situation.

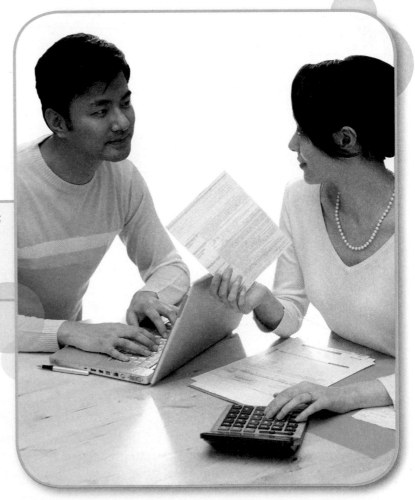

Manage Financial Resources Parents must learn to handle money wisely. *What are some expenses that must be considered when planning to meet a child's needs?*

Stages of Parenthood

In her book, *Between Generations: The Six Stages of Parenthood*, psychologist Ellen Galinsky describes how parents typically develop through their interactions with their children. Her findings were based on interviews with parents. **Figure 2.1** summarizes Galinsky's six stages.

The stages of parenthood that Galinsky identified are important because they describe how parents develop and change as their children do. When parents are aware of these stages, they can be more prepared for parenthood. By being prepared, they are more likely to be effective parents and lead happier, more satisfied lives.

✓ **Reading Check** **Explain** Why is it important for adults to understand child development?

Parenting Responsibilities and Rewards

When a new child joins the family, parents feel great joy. This is true whether the child joins by birth, remarriage, or adoption. Some parents also feel that a great burden has been placed on their shoulders. The decision to become a parent is a serious one. Being a parent radically changes a person's life and creates new long-term responsibilities.

When Dominique and Ross adopted baby Tanya from Russia, they were thrilled. The waiting was finally over. Everything felt right. Dominique's parents stayed with them for a week to help with the baby's care. Life with Tanya seemed relatively easy. However, after the baby's grandparents left, the challenges and responsibility of raising a child began to feel overwhelming.

Figure 2.1 Galinsky's Stages of Parenthood

The role of the parents changes as the child grows and matures. *During which stage does Galinsky feel parents rethink their role as parents?*

Stage	Time Period	Parents' Tasks
Image-Making	Pregnancy	❖ Begin to imagine themselves as parents
Nurturing	Birth to Age 2	❖ Become emotionally attached to the child ❖ May question relative worth of other priorities
Authority	Age 2 to Ages 4–5	❖ Determine rules ❖ Clarify role as authority figure
Interpretive	Ages 4–5 to Age 13	❖ Rethink their role as parents ❖ Decide what knowledge, skills, and values the child needs
Interdependent	Adolescence	❖ Establish boundaries ❖ Find disciplinary methods appropriate for teens
Departure	Child Leaves Home	❖ Evaluate their parenting

Giving New Parents a Break

New parents need all the help they can get from family, community, and society. In Finland, one parent (mother or father) has the right to ten months' fully paid leave from work after the birth of a child. Or couples can split the time. Even a prime minister took two weeks off from work after the birth of his child. The idea behind maternal, paternal, and parental leave is to protect the health of both the mother and child. It also allows parents the chance to take care of their child during the first few months of its life.

⭐ **Build Connections** *Parents in the United States do not get as much parental leave as those in Finland. What effect do you think this may have on the health of the mother and child?*

NCSS I A Culture Analyze and explain the ways groups, societies, and cultures address human needs and concerns.

Tanya hardly slept at night, so Dominique and Ross did not get much sleep either. Ross went to work each day feeling exhausted. Meanwhile, Dominique was left with the baby. She felt alone and uncertain. They both wondered how so many people managed to raise families. It was clearly not as easy as it seemed.

New Responsibilities

Many new parents say that having children changes everything. Becoming a parent does present many challenges. However, as the newness of parenthood passes, many parents adjust to the changes and find that their lives are enriched by the presence of a child.

Once people become parents, they can no longer think of only their own needs. They have much less time for themselves. They must always consider their child's needs first. Children need physical care, financial support, love, and guidance.

First-time parents can feel overwhelmed by so many new responsibilities. Family and friends can help in many ways. They can offer to watch the baby while the parent goes shopping, just listen, or help solve a problem.

Communities have many resources too, including religious organizations, government agencies, and support groups.

Lifestyle Changes

New parents have to adjust to major changes in their daily lives. Caring for a child takes a huge amount of time and energy. This is especially true for a newborn. A newborn needs to be fed every few hours, day and night. Babies also must be diapered, played with, comforted, and supervised for safety.

With children of any age, parents have limits placed on their personal freedom. They have less time to spend with friends. Instead of unwinding after work, they must spend time with their children, feed them, bathe them, and put them to bed. While it can be disappointing, sometimes plans have to be changed. Dennis and Shawna had looked forward to his brother's party for weeks, but had to cancel at the last minute. Their toddler was sick, and they did not feel right leaving him with a babysitter.

Parents are better able to adjust to these changes if they prepare for them. Taking classes and caring for a friend's child can help give an idea of what it is really like to live with a child.

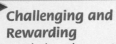

Challenging and Rewarding

Raising a baby takes patience and dedication. It also brings rewards. *What kinds of rewards do you think parenting might bring?*

There is no substitute for the experience of parenting. Making an effort, though, to learn about child development and parenthood can make the demands of the job less surprising and unsettling.

Emotional Adjustments

Parenthood requires many emotional adjustments. Going through so many changes is stressful in itself. On top of that, many parents feel conflicting, and sometimes difficult, emotions, such as:

- Fear of not being a good parent.
- Frustration at the loss of personal freedom and the addition of new responsibilities.
- Worry over money matters.
- Jealousy of the baby and the attention he or she gets from the other parent, friends, and relatives.
- Depression due to exhaustion and the physical changes of pregnancy and birth.

Parents can feel confused and troubled by these negative emotions. In time, most parents get over these rough spots. They learn that these emotions are common among new parents. They learn how to handle them. If these feelings persist, however, it is important to talk to a doctor. The doctor can help determine what assistance is needed. A new mother might need medication, or she might need counseling or just sleep and exercise.

Relationship Changes

When people become parents, they are likely to notice changes in how they interact with each other and with other family members. This is especially true for first-time parents.

The birth of a baby is an exciting time. Sometimes, though, parents may feel overwhelmed by concerns, negative emotions, and lack of sleep. They may argue with one another. Having patience and trying to be understanding can reduce the danger of frustration turning into anger. One key to getting past such trouble spots is for the couple to communicate effectively.

A new baby changes the relationship between the new parents and their own parents. Most grandparents feel love and joy of their own and want to spend time with their grandchild. Some may offer to help with child care or household chores. Some freely share advice based on their own parenting experience. Sometimes, however, offers of help or advice cause friction. New parents may resent advice that they feel is criticism. At the same time, the grandparents may feel hurt if their suggestions or offers of help are rejected.

On the other hand, new parents often find that having a baby brings them closer to their own parents. Understanding the sacrifices and work involved in parenting, they can now appreciate their own parents more.

Employment Adjustments

Having children can have an impact on careers. Some parents stop working or cut back on their hours to care for their children. People who work overtime and weekends, or travel for their jobs, may be less willing to do so once they become parents. Some parents will decide to change their careers. They might look for a career path that requires less travel or that is simply less stressful.

Some employers have policies to help working parents. They may offer flexible hours, part-time work, or work-at-home options. Others have child care facilities at or near the workplace. Couples planning to become parents should find out what benefits or programs their employers offer to help parents.

Legal Responsibilities

Parents, both mothers and fathers, are legally responsible to provide food, shelter, clothing, medical care, an education, and legal help for their children. Physically, fathers can walk away from parenthood more easily than mothers, but the law holds them equally responsible. A father is legally bound to support his child until the child turns 18. This is regardless of the father's age or whether he is married to the child's mother. It does not matter if he ever sees his child. Fathers as young as 14 have been sued for child support.

Rewards of Parenthood

While parenthood is a lot of work and responsibility, it brings many joys as well. There is nothing quite like a baby's first smile or hearing a toddler say, "I love you, Daddy." Parents feel happiness, pride, and love that they have never felt before.

By helping children discover the world, parents often see it with new eyes themselves. Having children can also enrich an already strong marriage. Finally, raising children can give parents a great sense of accomplishment.

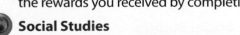

Section 2.1 After You Read

Review Key Concepts

1. **Identify** three ways to build parenting skills.
2. **Describe** the types of conflicting emotions new parents often experience.

Practice Academic Skills

 English Language Arts

3. Think of a time when you experienced something for the first time. Create a list of the steps you had to take to accomplish the task. Write a paragraph describing some of the challenges you faced and some of the rewards you received by completing the task.

> **NCTE 12** Use language to accomplish individual purposes.

Social Studies

4. What sorts of changes in buying habits do you think parents should make to be able to provide for their family? Research how parents in a different culture would prepare for a new child. Write a one-page essay that compares the culture you researched with the changes you predicted for parents in your culture.

> **NCSS VII F** Compare how values and beliefs influence economic decisions in different societies.

 Check Your Answers Check your answers at this book's Online Learning Center at **glencoe.com**.

Reading Guide

Before You Read

Be Organized A messy environment can be distracting. To lessen distractions, organize an area where you can read comfortably.

Read to Learn
Key Concepts

- **Identify** pressures involved in sexual development.
- **Summarize** the benefits of abstinence.
- **Describe** the possible consequences of sexual activity.
- **Compare and contrast** the options available to a teen parent.
- **Explain** what it means to be sexually responsible.

Main Idea

Choosing abstinence from sexual activity allows you to take responsibility for your well-being.

Content Vocabulary

◇ sexuality
◇ hormone
◇ abstinence
◇ sexually transmitted infection (STI)
◇ paternity
◇ confidential adoption
◇ open adoption
◇ fidelity

Academic Vocabulary

You will find these words in your reading and on your tests. Use the glossary to look up their definitions if necessary.

- intimacy
- essential

Graphic Organizer

As you read, list the consequences associated with teen pregnancy. Use a chart like the one shown to help organize your information.

Teen Pregnancy

 Graphic Organizer Go to this book's Online Learning Center at **glencoe.com** to print out this graphic organizer.

Academic Standards . . . .

 English Language Arts

NCTE 5 Use different writing process elements to communicate effectively.

 Social Studies

NCSS IV F Individual Development and Identity Analyze the role of perceptions, attitudes, values, and beliefs in the development of personal identity.

NCTE *National Council of Teachers of English*
NCTM *National Council of Teachers of Mathematics*

NSES *National Science Education Standards*
NCSS *National Council for the Social Studies*

Sexual Development

The teen years bring on many physical changes. These changes are the start of adult sexual development. Sexual traits develop. Teens become physically able to reproduce. Interest in the opposite gender increases. Sexual interest is common. The decisions you make about sexual behavior will have a great impact on your life. Choosing to make responsible decisions about sexual behavior is part of becoming mature.

Sexuality

Sexuality and sexual activity are not the same thing. **Sexuality** is your beliefs and values about sexual behavior. It involves more than physical maturity or the ability to be sexually active. Sexuality includes how people feel about themselves and their sense of responsibility for and understanding of other people and their feelings. Thus, sexuality has physical, intellectual, emotional, and social aspects. Individuals show their sexuality in their attitudes and the way they walk, talk, move, and dress. It affects your behavior and your relationships.

Adolescence is a time when boys and girls begin to develop a sense of their own sexuality. A **hormone** is a chemical in the body that controls the changes that occur as teens become sexually mature. These changes have an emotional and physical impact. They can cause mood swings and emotional ups and downs.

Sexual Pressures

Social development also shifts into high gear during puberty. Children will have attractions to new friends. Relationships with family members often change as teens become more independent. They want to spend more time with friends. They sometimes question parental authority.

In the midst of these changes, messages about sexual activity seem to be everywhere. Music, television, radio, movies, and advertising often send the messages that sexual activity is a necessary part of sexuality. Peer pressure, the influence of friends and other teens, may come with the mind-set of "Everyone's doing it. Why aren't you?"

With all these pressures, it is easy to lose sight of what is important. Dating can be fun without becoming sexually active. Teens can date as couples or in groups. Dating helps teens discover which qualities and characteristics they find desirable in another person. Teens can learn more about building relationships through dating.

Sexual activity is not the same as intimacy. **Intimacy** is a closeness between two people. You can develop intimacy and express affection by holding hands or hugging. Sharing thoughts, feelings, and dreams also helps build intimacy. A lasting and loving relationship is not based on sexual activity. Sexual activity does not make you an adult. It cannot save a poor relationship either.

Attraction
During the teen years, interest in the opposite gender increases. *How might a responsible person deal with these feelings?*

Group Dates
Dating does not have to include sexual activity. It can be just getting to know someone. *What can people learn about one another by going on dates?*

Physical and emotional changes often create a desire to act on sexual feelings. Even teens who reject the outside pressures to become sexually active have to be strong about resisting their own sexual feelings. Sexual feelings are natural, and they can be powerful. The best defense is to plan ahead and avoid situations where you may be tempted to engage in sexual activity.

Decisions related to sexuality are too important to be made casually. They deserve careful consideration, because they can have serious lifelong consequences. It can be helpful to discuss decisions about sexuality with other people. While teens often turn to friends for advice, most teens can benefit from talking to a responsible adult. Trusted adults can be valuable resources. A trusted adult might be a parent, an older family member, a religious leader, a school counselor, or a doctor.

Family Values

One role of families is to pass on the family's and society's values. These are the principles they consider important and the rules they use to guide their lives. Values are based on ideas about what is right, good and desirable. They include trust, self-respect, respect for others, commitment, and loyalty.

Family can help answer questions about sexuality based on values. For example, "How should I treat people of the opposite sex?" "How can I balance old friendships and new relationships with someone of the other sex?" Values help shape each person's response to these questions.

By drawing on their values, teens can choose to build a sense of their own sexuality without becoming sexually active.

✓ Reading Check **Describe** What are some values commonly passed on by families?

Abstinence

Choosing abstinence from sexual activity allows you to take responsibility for your well-being. **Abstinence** is a deliberate decision to avoid high-risk behaviors, including sexual activity and the use of tobacco, alcohol, and other drugs. You show your values and beliefs when you choose abstinence. Abstinence is not always easy. Use these tips to stay firm in your decision.

- **Talk about your feelings before you get in an intimate situation.** Make sure your partner understands your point of view.
- **Say no to any situation that does not feel right.** Refusing to participate in something you believe is wrong is your responsibility to yourself. Choose dating locations and activities that avoid the pressure for sexual activity. This might include a group date or a party with adults present.
- **Show affection in nonsexual ways.** There are nonsexual ways of showing love that can be satisfying, such as holding hands, hugging, or kissing. Talking and sharing dreams and interests can also create a sense of intimacy and closeness. Small sacrifices can express caring more than sexual behavior does.

"It can't happen to me." Countless teens have thought that. They were wrong. The threat of sexually transmitted infections is very real, as is the threat of pregnancy. Abstaining from sexual activity is the only guaranteed way of avoiding these problems.

This is a decision that each individual needs to take time to think about thoroughly before encountering a sexual situation. It is much more difficult to reach the decision to abstain in a moment of passion. Once a person has decided to abstain, it is important to stick to the decision. It can help to remember why the decision was made in the first place.

✓ **Reading Check** **Identify** What are three things teens can do to help themselves remain abstinent?

Consequences of Sexual Activity

Saying yes to sexual pressures as a teen has serious consequences. Those who engage in sexual activity too soon may have major problems. Some of these are emotional, such as trust issues, difficulty committing in future relationships, and a loss of self-respect. Problems can also include physical consequences, such as sexually transmitted infections or pregnancy.

Sexually Transmitted Infections

A **sexually transmitted infection (STI)** is a disease that is spread from one person to another by sexual contact. These are sometimes called sexually transmitted diseases (STDs). It is estimated that one in five people in the United States has an STI, and 25 percent of new cases of STIs are infected teens. All STIs are preventable. The only way to completely prevent STIs is through abstinence.

Some STIs can be treated. Others last a person's entire life. **Figure 2.2** on page 46 describes some common STIs. Some of the symptoms for an STI may also indicate other diseases or conditions. Anyone who has symptoms should see a doctor for diagnosis and treatment.

HIV/AIDS

One STI with deadly results is acquired immune deficiency syndrome (AIDS). AIDS is caused by the human immunodeficiency virus (HIV). HIV can stay in a person's blood for many years before it develops into AIDS. AIDS does not directly kill its victims, but it allows other diseases to invade the body. One or more of these diseases usually causes the person's death. There is no known cure for AIDS at this time, although research is continuing.

Abstinence Takes Courage
The decision to abstain can be a difficult one. *What are the benefits that make abstinence worth the effort?*

Figure 2.2 **Sexually Transmitted Infections**

Anyone who experiences any of these symptoms should be tested so that his or her exact condition can be determined and treatment begun. *Which STIs have no cure?*

STI	Symptoms	Effects	Treatment
Chlamydia (klə-ˈmi-dē-ə)	Pain when urinating. Women may feel abdominal pain, nausea, and low fever. Some people show no symptoms.	Can cause *sterility*, the inability to have children.	Can be cured with antibiotics.
Genital herpes	Open sores on sex organs, which go away in a few weeks. Painful urination, fever.	Can cause brain damage or death if passed to a baby during childbirth.	There is no cure. Symptoms can be treated.
Genital warts	Small growths on the sex organs, which cause discomfort and itching.	If left alone, they may become cancerous.	There is no cure, but a doctor can remove them. A vaccine is available to prevent the disease.
Hepatitis B (ˌhe-pə-ˈtī-təs)	Causes flu-like symptoms.	Can lead to liver disease or cancer.	There is no cure. A vaccine is available to prevent the disease.
Gonorrhea (ˌgä-nə-ˈrē-ə)	Burning, itching, and the discharge of liquids from infected areas.	Can cause sterility in females. A baby born to an infected mother can suffer eye damage.	Can be treated with antibiotics.
Syphilis (ˈsi-f(ə-)ləs)	In early stages, sores on the sex organs, fever, rash, and hair loss.	Can cause insanity and death.	Can be cured with antibiotics.
HIV/AIDS	No visible symptoms in first stage of infection. Later stages include fever, headache, sore throat, rashes, diarrhea, swollen glands, body aches, diminished appetite, and weight loss.	AIDS lessens immunity to other illnesses, which can cause death.	There is no cure. Some medicines can delay the development of AIDS.

Pregnancy

Another possible consequence of sexual activity is pregnancy. Pregnancy causes many problems. These problems affect both the teen mother and father. When Tracy became pregnant, she and Parker married. Parker took a job, planning to finish high school after a year. Before that could happen, their car broke down and he needed to work overtime to pay for the repairs. Soon after, Tracy became pregnant again. By the time their second child was a year old, Parker had been out of high school almost three years. He did not feel like going back, even though he knew he could earn more with a diploma or a GED.

Teen pregnancy creates four basic types of problems. These include health risks, education challenges, financial issues, and emotional and social stress. These problems also affect the teens' families and society.

Health Risks

Pregnancy presents special health risks for both a teen mother and her baby. A teen is not yet physically or emotionally mature and may not be ready for the extra demands of pregnancy. Teens are also at greater risk than adult women for experiencing serious medical complications from a pregnancy. One such complication is significant iron deficiency, which can deprive the baby and mother of oxygen. A teen is also at greater risk for a dangerous condition called *toxemia*, which can lead to the premature delivery of the baby.

A female teen has high nutritional needs. If she becomes pregnant and there is no extra emphasis on nutrition, her body may not be able to provide the nutrients that she and her growing baby both need. In addition, a critical period of development occurs before most mothers are even aware they are pregnant. Babies of teen mothers are more likely to be born early and have low birth weights. These conditions are linked to other problems, including learning difficulties.

Education Challenges

It is important for pregnant teens to complete their schooling, at least through high school. Unfortunately, many drop out of school. Nearly half of the teen mothers who leave school never finish their education. This is true even for those who plan to return. Without a high school diploma, it is hard to find a job, especially one with a salary to support a small family. This puts a greater strain on society to help support the family.

RESPOND TO SPECIAL NEEDS

Low Birth Weight Babies

Low birth weight babies are born weighing less than five pounds, eight ounces. These babies are at risk for serious health problems and death. Low birth weight babies may have disabilities such as vision and hearing loss, learning difficulties, mental retardation, and cerebral palsy. These babies need specialized care both as babies and as they grow older.

There are many factors that can cause babies to be born with a low birth weight. These include illness in the mother or fetus, premature birth, the baby is a twin or other multiple, the mother smoked while pregnant, the mother used alcohol or illegal drugs while pregnant, and the age of the mother. Women under the age of 17 and over the age of 35 have an increased risk of delivering a low birth weight baby.

Critical Thinking Research steps a woman can take to reduce her risk of delivering a low birth weight baby. Create a poster that includes a list of the steps you find.

Pregnant and parenting teens can work with school counselors and social service agencies to find solutions to such problems. These resources can help find ways to provide care for the babies while their parents take classes. Graduating should be a high-priority goal for young mothers and fathers.

Financial Issues

Most teen parents experience financial problems. Teen mothers need good medical care. That care costs money, as does childbirth. Teen parents who keep their child must provide food, clothing, housing, and health care. This continues for at least 18 years.

Even when teen parents do not marry, both are legally responsible for providing for their child. If the father chooses not to stay involved with the child, it is especially important to establish paternity. **Paternity** is the legal identification of a man as the biological father of a child. Paternity will legally ensure the father's responsibilities toward the child. A medical test can prove paternity.

For many teen couples, the burden of child care expenses becomes overwhelming. In order to meet financial needs, a young couple's goals and plans for the future must be changed. This tension can lead to arguments. The stress from financial issues can affect other family members and even the baby. Sometimes society must help care for the child through government and welfare programs.

Emotional and Social Stress

Adjusting to new relationships can cause great stress. Changes to old relationships can also cause stress. Teen parents may miss their old friends, but find they no longer have much in common with them. Teens who enjoyed sports or other after-school activities may have to give them up or cut back. Teen parents quickly realize that their lives have changed in profound ways.

✓ **Reading Check** **Recall** What is the only way to completely prevent sexually transmitted infections?

Teen Parenting Options

Teens can and do get pregnant. Many, though, have trouble believing and acknowledging the symptoms when it happens. A girl who fears she might be pregnant may try to ignore the possibility. However, for her health and the baby's health, it is **essential**, or necessary, that she confirm the pregnancy and get good care as soon as possible.

A teen who suspects she is pregnant should discuss her concerns with someone close. This could be her boyfriend, a parent or other family member, a trusted friend, or a teacher or counselor. She should also see a doctor as soon as possible to confirm the pregnancy.

Once her pregnancy has been confirmed, a teen can begin to make plans. Her partner

Parenting and Education
The birth of a child prompts many teens to drop out of school. *Why is it so important to stay in school?*

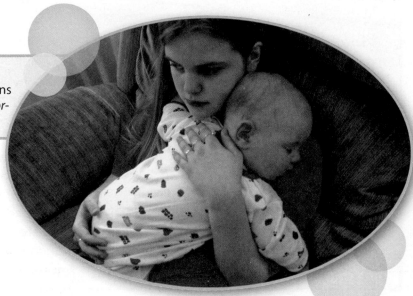

should be involved, too. After all, the father has rights and responsibilities. The pregnancy will have a long-lasting effect on the lives of both parents. In order to make responsible plans, both teens will have to carefully consider the options and their consequences. Family can be a good resource for support and guidance at this time.

When faced with pregnancy, teens have several options. Each one must be considered seriously. There are several factors that must be considered for each option.

Marriage

Marriage has many benefits for both the teen parents and their child. At any age, however, marriage is not easy. It takes a special commitment, responsibility, and work.

Married teens face a special set of problems. As the initial excitement of marriage wears off, the strains of responsibility and the new social situation set in. Teens who marry because of a pregnancy face an additional problem. They have to adjust to parenthood at the same time they are adjusting to being married.

Married teens who are able to meet these challenges can find themselves with a strong and rewarding relationship. Having two people share the child care lessens the work of each. With hard work and commitment, married teens can build a caring home for a child.

Single Parenthood

Having a tiny baby to cuddle and love can seem very appealing. Indeed, it can be rewarding to care for someone who is so small, helpless, and dependent. However, caring for a newborn is a huge responsibility, and becoming a parent is a lifelong commitment.

All these responsibilities can be draining for an adult. They can be even harder for a teen. Not surprisingly, many teen parents suffer from burnout or depression. They need to find support.

Teens considering single parenthood need to be realistic and ask a lot of questions. How much emotional and financial help can one teen parent expect from the other? From his or her own parents and other family members? A

teen considering single parenthood must guard against romanticizing the situation. For example, a teen who is not interested in marriage during the pregnancy is unlikely to change his or her mind after the birth. Parents, counselors, and other adults can help teens develop realistic expectations for their own situations as single parents.

Adoption

Adoption is another option for pregnant teens. In adoption, the birth mother and father legally give up their rights and responsibilities for raising the child to another family.

The decision to place a baby for adoption is not easy. Teens considering adoption need to think it through carefully, because it is a permanent decision. Many teens choose adoption because they feel they are giving their child an opportunity for more care, guidance, and love than they are able to provide at this stage of their lives. Placing a baby for adoption for these reasons is an act of love. However, even when the decision is made with careful thought and consideration, it is an emotional decision.

There are two different types of adoption. A **confidential adoption** is an adoption in which the birth parents do not know the names of the adoptive parents. There is no exchange of information after the adoption. The access to information about the birth parents is limited by law in a confidential adoption.

An **open adoption** is an adoption in which the birth parents and adoptive parents know something about each other. There are different levels of open adoption based on how much information is shared with both sets of parents. The parents may or may not meet each other.

✓ **Reading Check** **Define** What is adoption?

Take Responsibility

What does it mean to be sexually responsible? It means knowing the facts about sexuality. It means thinking about the outcome of your decisions and actions. It means knowing your values and living by them.

Most people want sexual activity to be special. They want their strong feelings of desire to go along with a strong bond to one beloved person. Many people are willing to wait. They want a sexual relationship based on fidelity. **Fidelity** is faithfulness to an obligation, duty, or trust. Saving sexual activity for the committed framework of marriage provides a way to show your responsibility. It also shows respect for yourself and others.

Remember that you and your partner or date both deserve to be treated with consideration and respect. You should be able to communicate your thoughts and feelings honestly with one another. Talk with a trusted adult, such as a parent or guardian, to help you manage your feelings and make informed choices.

Parenthood is a challenging and rewarding time of life, but it can be especially challenging for teens. When people wait to have children until they are physically, emotionally, and financially prepared, it helps assure a bright future for both the children and the parents.

Section 2.2 — After You Read

Review Key Concepts

1. **Explain** the difference between sexuality and sexual activity.
2. **Define** abstinence.
3. **Analyze** two risks a teen pregnancy has on the baby.
4. **Distinguish** between confidential and open adoption.
5. **Explain** why people should wait to have children until they are physically, emotionally, and financially prepared.

Practice Academic Skills

 English Language Arts

6. Imagine that you write an advice column for a local newspaper. A seventeen-year-old unmarried teen has written to you saying that she thinks she is pregnant. How would you respond? Write an advice column to the teen.

 Social Studies

7. A decision to abstain from sexual activity is strongly influenced by personal values. Write a paragraph in which you explain how values influence a person's decision to abstain.

 Check Your Answers Check your answers at this book's Online Learning Center at **glencoe.com**.

NCTE 5 Use different writing process elements to communicate effectively.

NCSS IV F Analyze the role of perceptions, attitudes, values, and beliefs in the development of personal identity.

Chapter Summary

Parenting is a learning process, and offers many challenges and rewards. Before deciding to become parents, it is important to seriously consider one's readiness for parenthood. People who are ready for parenthood have considered their own emotional maturity, health issues, financial concerns, resource management skills, and parenting skills.

Decisions related to sexuality cannot be made casually. Abstinence is the only guaranteed way to prevent pregnancy and sexually transmitted infections. There are several options for teens who are pregnant.

Vocabulary Review

1. Create a multiple-choice test question for each content and academic vocabulary term.

Content Vocabulary
◇ parenting (p. 33)
◇ emotional maturity (p. 35)
◇ sexuality (p. 43)
◇ hormone (p. 43)
◇ abstinence (p. 44)
◇ sexually transmitted infection (STI) (p. 45)

◇ paternity (p. 48)
◇ confidential adoption (p. 49)
◇ open adoption (p. 49)
◇ fidelity (p. 50)

Academic Vocabulary
■ pride (p. 33)
■ prospective (p. 35)
■ intimacy (p. 43)
■ essential (p. 48)

Review Key Concepts

2. Explain who can benefit from knowing about child development and parenting.
3. Describe the five areas of responsibilities for parents.
4. Identify pressures involved in sexual development.
5. Summarize the benefits of abstinence.
6. Describe the possible consequences of sexual activity.
7. Compare and contrast the options available to a teen parent.
8. Explain what it means to be sexually responsible.

Critical Thinking

9. Summarize How can people who care for one another show intimacy without sexual activity?
10. Apply What should a teen do if she suspects she is pregnant?

Family & Community Connection

11. Conduct a Survey Create a brief survey in which you ask people why they chose to become a parent. Distribute the survey to at least 10 family members or friends who are parents. Be sure the surveys are anonymous. Make a list of the responses and compile your results in a bar graph. Compare your results graph with your classmates' results.

Health Skills

12. Research Healthy Babies Use the online or print resources to find out more about the health concerns related to teen pregnancy. What can teens do to make sure that they will stay healthy? What can they do to ensure they will deliver a healthy baby? Use what you learn in your research to create a brochure. The brochure should include a list of steps teens can take to remain healthy during pregnancy.

Observation Skills

13. Observe Newborn Caregivers Caregivers of newborns spend much of their time caring for the baby. Work with your teacher to arrange to observe caregivers of newborn babies at your local hospital.

Procedure Choose one baby to observe and take notes on the care provided such as feeding, changing, cleaning, and comforting. Also note the length of your observation.

Analysis Use your notes to write a half-page report in which you list the care provided to the newborn, the number of times the baby was cared for, and the length of your observation. Determine the average number of times per hour the baby was cared for.

> **NCSS I A Culture** Analyze and explain the ways groups, societies, and cultures address human needs and concerns.

Real-World Skills

Interpersonal and Collaborative Skills

14. Work in Teams Work in groups determined by your teacher to develop questions for a self-assessment test for potential parents. Include at least 25 questions and a scoring system. Use information from Section 2.1 of this chapter to help you write the questions.

Technology Skills

15. Create a Document Use word-processing software to write a scene for a play in which a young couple discusses whether to start a family. You can end the scene with either decision, but be sure both characters show good communication skills as they talk about the issue.

Financial Literacy

16. Calculate Diaper Costs Research diapers that would fit a nine-pound baby and record the price of a box and the quantity in the box. If a baby uses seven of these diapers a day, how much would it cost per day to diaper the baby? How much per week? Per year?

 Additional Activities For additional activities, go to this book's Online Learning Center at **glencoe.com**.

Academic Skills

 English Language Arts

17. Think About Your Future Parenting requires a lot of time and effort. Think about what kind of parent you want to be. What will be more important to you: spending time with your family or making lots of money? With this in mind, how might you approach a career path? Why? Write a one-page essay of your thoughts.

> **NCTE 4** Use written language to communicate effectively.

 Mathematics

18. Savings Account for a Newborn Micah wants to open a savings account for his newborn son. Eastern Bank offers simple interest of 1.5 percent per year. If Micah has $100 to open a savings account, how much money would be in the savings account after 16 years?

Math Concept **Multiply Percentages** A percent is a ratio that compares a number to 100. To multiply by a percent, first convert the percent to a decimal.

Starting Hint Rewrite the percent (1.5%) as a fraction with a denominator of 100. Convert the fraction to a decimal. Multiply this decimal by the number ($100), and then multiply it by 16. Add your result to the original amount ($100).

 For math help, go to the Math Appendix at the back of the book.

> **NCTM Number and Operations** Understand numbers, ways of representing numbers, relationships among numbers, and number systems.

 Science

19. Investigate a Research Claim Research reveals that some pregnant teens do not receive adequate care throughout pregnancy. One reason for this is that medical care can be expensive, and teens have no way to pay for that care.

Procedure Conduct your own research with print or online resources to learn how this research finding can be useful to parents and other caregivers.

Analysis Use the information from your research to write a one-page report.

> **NSES C** Develop understanding of the interdependence of organisms; matter, energy, and organization in living systems; and behavior of organisms.

Standardized Test Practice

TRUE/FALSE

Read the passage, then answer the question.

Many teen mothers are unable to continue attending high school once they have a baby to care for. Statistics show that the dropout rate is higher for teen mothers than for other female teens. Identify programs that help teen mothers stay in school while they raise their child.

20. According to the passage, teen mothers never finish high school.
  a. True
  b. False

> **Test-Taking Tip** Statements that contain extreme words, such as all, none, never, or always, or that have unsupported opinions, are often false.

Chapter Objectives

After completing this chapter, you will be able to:

- **Summarize** the qualities that contribute to building a strong family.
- **Describe** the different family structures.
- **Discuss** the trends affecting families.
- **List** the basic categories of children's needs.
- **Identify** the three parenting styles.
- **Summarize** effective ways to guide children's behavior.

Writing Activity — Journal Entry

Working Together When families work together to complete household tasks or take care of younger family members, it helps build a strong family. Write a journal entry about a time when you worked together with one or more of your family members.

Writing Tips A journal is a record of experiences, ideas, and reflections. To write an effective journal entry, follow these tips:

1. Date your entry.
2. Let one idea lead to another.
3. Write about experiences, reactions, and observations.

Section **3.1** **Family Characteristics**

Section **3.2** **Parenting Skills**

Explore the Photo
Families can enjoy many types of activities together. *What activities does your family enjoy doing together?*

Reading Guide

Before You Read

Preview Write a list of what you want to know about qualities that contribute to a strong family, family structures, and trends that affect families.

Read to Learn

Key Concepts

- **Summarize** the qualities that contribute to building a strong family.
- **Describe** the different family structures.
- **Discuss** the trends affecting families.

Main Idea

There are many different family structures. Family members must work together to overcome challenges and to build a strong foundation for the family.

Content Vocabulary

◇ nuclear family
◇ single-parent family
◇ custodial parent
◇ blended family

◇ extended family
◇ legal guardian
◇ foster child
◇ intergenerational

 Graphic Organizer Go to this book's Online Learning Center at **glencoe.com** to print out this graphic organizer.

Academic Vocabulary

You will find these words in your reading and on your tests. Use the glossary to look up their definitions if necessary.

- ■ vital
- ■ venture

Graphic Organizer

As you read, list the three types of family traditions described in the text. Use a chart like the one shown to record your answers.

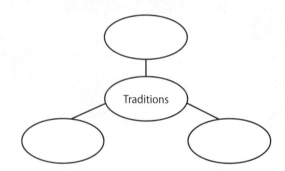

Traditions

Academic Standards . . . .

 English Language Arts

NCTE 4 Use written language to communicate effectively.

 Science

NSES F Develop understanding of science and technology in local, national, and global challenges.

 Social Studies

NCSS I A Culture Analyze and explain the ways groups, societies, and cultures address human needs and concerns.

NCTE *National Council of Teachers of English*
NCTM *National Council of Teachers of Mathematics*

NSES *National Science Education Standards*
NCSS *National Council for the Social Studies*

Qualities of Strong Families

Within every culture, there are families. A family can be different from group to group. In some cultures, family includes only parents and children. In others, aunts, uncles, grandmothers, and grandfathers are important parts of the family. Families are the foundation on which every human culture is built.

Families are not just a group of individuals who happen to be related. They are a group where all members can feel accepted and safe. In families, adults and children can learn and grow together. Families provide children with a sense of belonging, emotional support, nurturing, protection, and security. As families spend more time together, they form stronger bonds and traditions. Families also give children their first lessons in values and acceptable social behavior. These are lessons they will carry with them throughout their lives.

Developing family relationships is not an easy task. This is especially true when families are spread out. However, just living together under one roof does not guarantee smooth relationships. When individuals need to work together as a group, there are going to be differences of opinion, problems, and conflict. Each family member can help make a family stronger. Strong families can act as a buffer against many of life's problems.

Strong families have a variety of characteristics. Family members work together to provide for the needs of the family and prepare the children to live in our society. They spend time together, share responsibilities, and work together to resolve differences. They listen to each other with an open mind and allow each person to express opinions and share feelings. Families share goals and values and also show appreciation for each other. These are **vital**, or necessary, lessons for life.

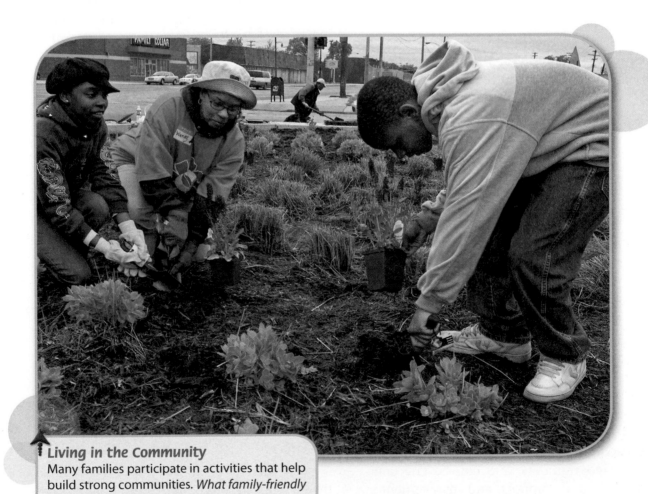

▲ Living in the Community
Many families participate in activities that help build strong communities. *What family-friendly activities are available in your community?*

Learning Through PLAY

Families Playing Together

One of the many rewards of parenthood is being able to play again! Play is more than just a time for fun. It is also a great learning experience for children. Play teaches children about trust, honesty, cooperation, taking turns, following rules, counting, colors, and having fun. With so much to learn, children need lots of opportunities for play. Parents should set aside time for play and have a variety of toys and games available. Some ideas for engaging in family play include singing nursery rhymes together; using puppets, dolls, or action figures for pretend play; or doing puzzles and playing games together. Activities should be appropriate for the child's age. What a parent and child play is not important. What matters is that families spend time together playing, learning, and enjoying each other.

Think About It Your family is traveling by car to visit relatives in a different city. Your 10-year-old brother is bored and beginning to annoy you. What activities can you suggest your family do to help entertain your brother?

Functions of the Family

Each day after band practice, Marisa picks up her little brother from the after-care program at his school. When they arrive home, they share a snack. Then they read, do homework, or watch television together. While this may sound routine, Marisa's actions show the importance of family. Family members help meet each other's basic needs.

Meet Basic Needs

Everyone needs food, clothing, and shelter. Families need to make sure that these basic needs, as well as health and safety needs, are met. Family members care for one another when they are sick and teach children basic rules about safety.

Strong families meet emotional and social needs, too. Family members have the chance to love and be loved, to care and be cared for, to help others and receive help. Living in a family teaches sharing and teamwork.

Strong families meet their members' intellectual needs as well. The family is a child's first teacher. The family teaches concepts such as language, numbers, and colors. The family's expectations, support, and involvement in learning can affect success in school.

Prepare Children to Live in Society

Author Robert Fulghum wrote a book called *All I Really Need to Know I Learned in Kindergarten*. His point was that children learn the basic rules of life in kindergarten, such as "share everything," "play fair," and "don't hit people." Fulghum could have said the same thing about family. By learning how to live with others in the family, children are prepared to live with others in society.

Adults teach children what is important to people in their society. They pass on these values in three ways:

- **Through Example** When adults treat children and each other with respect, they show children how to behave.
- **Through Communication** Parents who explain to toddlers why hitting is wrong, or talk to teens about respecting others' individuality, are passing on values through communication.
- **Through Religious Training** In houses of worship, of any faith, children learn the principles of what is right and what is wrong as taught by people of that faith.

Each society has its own way of life revealed through its art and music, its cooking and clothing styles, and its views of work and play.

Families introduce children to their society's way of life. Society can include neighborhoods, cities, states, countries, or nations.

Adults teach children about the traditions of their society, such as holidays. Adults also explain and demonstrate acceptable behavior. What kind of language is appropriate? How should children speak to adults? These and similar questions are first answered in families.

Provide Support

Family members support each other. However, with all the demands and stresses put on families, parents need to have a support system. This will help them get through rough spots and sometimes just everyday life. Talking to a friend, relative, or coworker can help. These same people may be willing to watch the children so a parent can have a short break.

When stress causes health or relationship problems, it is helpful to consult a professional such as a family doctor, counselor, social worker, or religious advisor. Seeking additional sources of support can help a parent get through the more difficult times.

Some families may feel as though they do not have a support system, but there are people and services ready to help. Besides communicating with friends, neighbors, coworkers, and relatives, a parent can talk to caregivers, teachers, religious leaders, or counselors. A local hospital or place of worship may provide lists of support groups. Local family service agencies are also available for support. By using these sources, parents can help strengthen family relationships and relieve some of their stress.

Form Traditions

Spending time together is the foundation to building a strong family. This includes doing special activities, such as a family vacation, as well as following everyday routines, such as eating dinner together. These activities and the ways that families do things are what become family traditions. A *tradition* is a custom that is followed over time. It can be simple or elaborate. Families that form many traditions form strong ties with each other. Friends will come and go through a lifetime, but your family is always there.

Seeking Help
It is important for parents to find help when they need it. Sometimes just having someone to listen to you or give another point of view helps a parent get through a difficult time. *When might a parent seek help?*

➡ **Forming Traditions**
Celebrations often turn into family traditions. *What traditions take place in your family?*

Traditions provide a sense of continuity, understanding, and appreciation that brings a family together. They are also opportunities for families to have fun times and establish good memories that will carry them through tough times. Traditions provide a family with time together to communicate, heal from a loss, adapt to new events, affirm family values, celebrate, and connect to the past.

Traditions will vary from family to family and from generation to generation. However, there are three types of traditions that families form:

- **Celebration Traditions** These are activities or events formed around special occasions, such as holidays and birthdays.

- **Family Traditions** These include events and special activities created to fit a family's lifestyle, such as vacations or family meetings.

- **Patterned Family Interactions** These are actions that are centered on daily routines in life, such as dinner time and bedtime.

Traditions are the threads of life that create a sense of togetherness and appreciation in families. It is the little things done together that not only create strong family ties, but also memories to last a lifetime. Quinn enjoyed his families' weekly game nights so much as a child that he plans to build the same tradition with his family someday.

Share Values

Values are the beliefs held by an individual, family, community, or society. They include feelings about the importance of acceptable behavior in terms of honesty, respect, responsibility, friendliness, kindness, and tolerance. The values that parents pass on to their children are largely shaped by the values that were passed on to them as children, their own life experiences, and their religious beliefs. Society also helps shape a family's values. Society relies on values, such as honesty, to keep order and to function well.

{ **Expert Advice...** }

"The family is the corner stone of our society. More than any other force it shapes the attitude, the hopes, the ambitions, and the values of the child."

—Lyndon Baines Johnson, former U.S. president

In a strong family, everyone is committed to one another. Family members respect one another and see that each person is different. The family is built on a foundation of shared values. For example, when parents and other caregivers teach children the value of honesty, they foster that trait in their children. When a problem or conflict arises, their children have learned to be honest and that the family will not judge or criticize them. Their children then communicate more openly, and, as a family, they work together to solve the problem.

With a strong foundation of shared values, children feel more at ease. People who learn trust in the family tend to see theworld as a safe place. They experience more success when they **venture**, or proceed, away from the family to meet new people, take on challenges, and become valuable members of society.

Handle Family Conflict

There is no way around it: Families argue. Sometimes they bicker over seemingly minor issues such as what show to watch or whose turn it is to take out the trash. Other times the conflicts are more serious. Many families have conflicts about money or curfews, for example.

Whether the issue is big or small, families need to know how to resolve their differences. Parents and children need to try to understand each other's viewpoints and feelings. Strong families figure out ways to approach and solve their problems together.

When families resolve their conflicts successfully, the whole family is stronger. Here are some tips for handling conflicts effectively:

- **Keep cool.** When people are angry, they say and do things they do not really mean. It is always a good idea to calm down before trying to resolve a conflict. This lets you use reason and empathy to solve the issue. Physical conflict, such as hitting, should never be a part of teen or adult relationships. If a discussion gets heated, it is wise to call a time out.
- **Be an active listener.** Even in the middle of a conflict it is important to listen carefully to each other's concerns without immediately judging them. Repeat back what you heard to help avoid confusion about feelings and attitudes. Often people are so concerned about what they will say next that they fail to really listen. Active listening encourages problem solving and better communication.

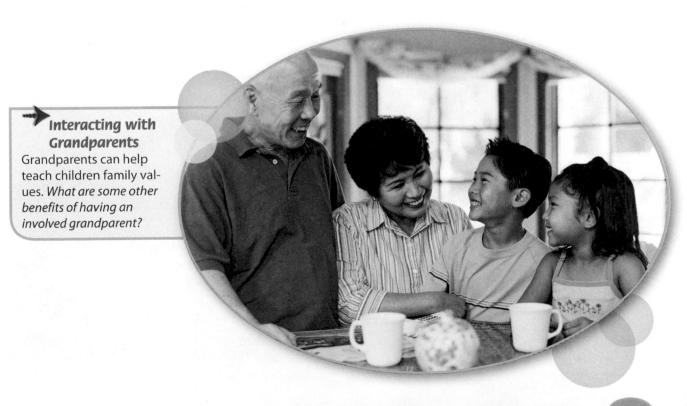

Interacting with Grandparents
Grandparents can help teach children family values. *What are some other benefits of having an involved grandparent?*

- **Use positive body language.** People who make eye contact and sit up straight send the message that they are truly listening and do care about the other person. When appropriate, a pat on the back or a hug can do wonders to help break the tension and make the other person feel loved and more at ease.

How would you rate your family's conflict resolution skills? Which technique could you use to improve your own?

✓ **Reading Check** **Shaping Values** What three things shape the values that parents pass on to their children?

Family Structure

While each family has individual characteristics, most can be categorized as nuclear, single-parent, or blended families.

Nuclear Families

A **nuclear family** is a family that includes a mother and father and at least one child. In a nuclear family there are two parents to help raise the children. The families may differ depending on how many children there are, whether the parents work outside the home, and other characteristics.

Single-Parent Families

A **single-parent family** is one that includes either a mother or a father and at least one child. The absent parent might have died or left after a divorce, or the parents may never have married. While single parenting presents special challenges, it can still be effective.

Raising a child alone is a demanding job. A single parent typically has little free time, since there is no one with whom to share the work or to help solve problems related to parenthood. Single-parent families usually have less income than two-parent families. The added cost of child care can increase the challenges for a working single parent.

Many single parents receive help from friends or relatives. They may provide child care while the parent works. They may help simply by giving the parent someone to talk to about frustrations, problems, or challenges, as well as rewards and successes. In the case of a divorce, many children make scheduled visits to the parent who does not live with them. These visits give the custodial parent a needed break from the challenges of single parenthood. A **custodial parent** is the parent with whom the child resides. It also preserves the relationship between the other parent and child.

➤ **A Real Family**
Adoption pairs children who need parents with those who want to build a family. *What rights do adopted children have?*

Blended Families
Trying to blend two unique families into one strong family can create some challenges. *When parents remarry, what can they do to make the transition easier for their children?*

Blended Families

A **blended family** is formed when a single parent marries another person, who may or may not have children. To a child, the parent's new spouse becomes a stepparent. To the couple, each child of the new spouse is a stepchild. If both spouses have children when they marry, these children become stepbrothers or stepsisters to each other.

Becoming a strong family unit can be a challenge for a blended family. Parents and children need time to adjust to one another. Everyone has to learn about and adapt to each other's habits, likes, and dislikes. Even topics such as how to celebrate holidays can cause conflict. Patience, tolerance for different opinions and habits, and a sense of humor can help families overcome the challenges they face.

Extended Families

An **extended family** is a family that includes a parent or parents, at least one child, and other relatives who live with them. For example, a grandparent may live with a nuclear family or an aunt may live with a single-parent family. Sometimes extended family is used to refer to family members who do not live with the family but still play important roles in the child's life.

What Would You Do?

Finding a Family

Bree is a typical nine-year-old girl. She lives with Mr. and Mrs. Mason, her foster parents. When Bree was seven, her biological mother and father were not able to care for her, so they gave her up for adoption. For two years, Bree moved from family to family. Going from home to home was hard for her. Sometimes she had to change schools. Each time meant she had to make new friends and leave her old friends. Bree has lived with the Masons for a year now. They would like to formally adopt her. Bree is happy and likes the Masons. She is not sure she wants to become part of their family, though. The Masons have other adopted children who are not always kind to Bree.

✐ **Write About It** Bree has sent a letter to the local newspaper's advice column asking for help with her problem. Based on your knowledge of families, write a column in response to Bree's letter. Be sure to address Bree's concern that the other children in the family are not always kind to her, and give suggestions for how she might handle it.

Joining a Family

A child can join a family in many ways. In the majority of cases, a child is born into a family. This is a *biological child*. In other cases, a child joins a family through a legal process. A **legal guardian** is a person who is designated by a legal process to assume responsibility for raising a child.

Adoption is a legal process in which children enter a family they were not born into. The adopted child has the same rights as any biological children those parents have.

Some children join a family as foster children. A **foster child** is a child that comes from a troubled family or difficult circumstances and is placed in the temporary care of another person or family. Foster parents care for foster children, giving them a home while their parents solve their problems, or sometimes until a permanent adoptive home can be found. Adults apply to the state government to become licensed foster parents. They receive payment to help with the expense of caring for the child.

✓ **Reading Check** **Family Structure**
Which type of family is formed when two people with children marry?

Trends Affecting Families

All families are affected by trends in the society around them. These trends may support families or put additional pressure on them. Some current trends include mobility, an aging population, changes in the economy, workplace changes, and the impact of technology. Which of these trends do you think has had an effect on your family?

Figure 3.1 The Family Life Cycle

The six stages of family development provide a pattern that most families follow. Families will spend different amounts of time in the same stage. *Do you think moving from one stage to the next is an easy process?*

Stage 1

Couple Stage
Couples grow closer as they share activities. They work together to establish a home and marriage relationship.

Stage 3

Developing Stage
As children grow, parents work to meet children's changing needs. The focus of the family is the socialization and developing independence of children.

Stage 2

Expanding Stage The arrival of a child signals the beginning of parenthood. The couple prepares for and adjusts to parenthood.

Mobility

Today many adults move from the community where they were raised. As a result, many families lack close, supportive connections with extended family. Grandparents, aunts, uncles, and cousins may be spread out across the globe. In this situation, families must rely on themselves, neighbors, and close friends for support and assistance.

When extended family members are far away, it takes time and effort to remain close. Many families value a strong family connection and find it worth the extra effort. Such connections help build traditions and reinforce the importance of family history.

This increased mobility also places added stress on children when a family moves to a new home or neighborhood. Children must make new friends and find ways to stay in touch with old friends.

Aging Population

There are a larger number of older people today than in the past. People are living longer than they used to. Advances in medicine and nutrition have contributed to the longer average lifespan. As a result, more people find themselves caring not only for children, but also helping and caring for aging parents. This can create stress as well as opportunities for intergenerational interaction. **Intergenerational** means occuring between older and younger age groups.

A related trend is that more grandparents are helping to raise their grandchildren because their children are not able to parent on their own. Some grandparents live with the core family, while others just help with babysitting. Having a grandparent involved in raising a child means that the child will learn values and traditions from the grandparent. It also helps teach the child the importance of a strong family.

Stage 4

Launching Stage Children gradually leave home to support themselves. Parents help their children adapt to life on their own. Events such as graduation signal the child's independence.

Stage 6

Retirement Stage The couple stops full-time work and adjusts to having more free time. Life may be slower paced but couples still enjoy each other's company.

Stage 5

Middle Stage A couple renews their relationship and prepares for retirement. They may have time and money for special interests. If they had children who have left home, this is called the "empty nest" stage.

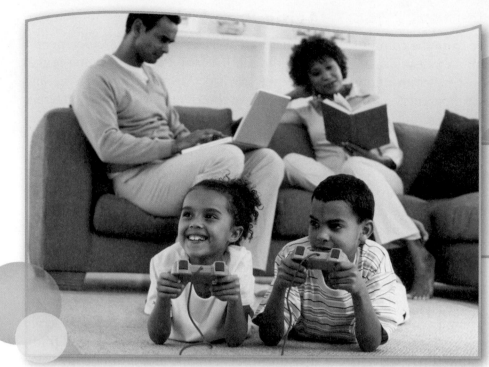

Establish Limits Families must set limits to manage the technology that they use. *What effect can video games have on a family?*

Science in Action

Technology and the Family

In today's society, we have many technological inventions available for work, home, and entertainment. This includes newer inventions such as cell phones, MP3 players, and video games. Technology also includes older technology such as television and computers. How might these inventions affect a family?

Procedure

Create a survey that lists five technological inventions and asks how much time people feel they spend using these inventions. Ask if they think using these technologies takes away from or adds to their family time. Distribute the survey to at least ten people of various ages.

Analysis

Find the average amount of time each invention is used. Then find the overall average. Chart your findings in a bar graph. Write a summary of your research that explains the results and describes people's opinions about whether these technologies are taking away from family time.

> **NSES F** Develop understanding of science and technology in local, national, and global challenges.

Economic Changes

Many families struggle to make ends meet. This is particularly true in times of economic downturn. Finances are often the primary reason why both parents in a nuclear family are employed. This trend has had a significant impact on families.

Many families are smaller than they used to be, and some couples are having their first child later in life. The rise in two-income families has also added to the demand for child care, including before- and after-school care for school-age children. Some families count on extra income or child care services from teens or extended family members. Some nuclear families become extended families to help share finances.

Workplace Changes

The working world is changing rapidly. Many companies employ fewer workers. The types of available jobs are shifting. For example, the number of manufacturing jobs in this country has declined, while jobs in health and technology have expanded. Such changes affect families. After a layoff, a parent may be unemployed for a time. New jobs available may pay less or may not have health insurance as a benefit.

In a changing work environment, there is a continuing need to learn new skills. Many workers invest time and money in additional education. When Marianna's mother needed to learn more advanced computer skills, she decided to take a night course. Marianna was happy for her mother, but she also missed having her at home.

Another trend is the growing number of people who work outside of the home. This has both benefits and drawbacks for families. It may increase the family's income and fill a need for socialization. It also means that child care arrangements may be needed for small children and the family will have less time to spend together. Some families may be able to rely on extended family to help with child care.

Technology

Advances in technology continue to make family life both easier and more complicated. Technology can increase efficiency at home and at work. For example, the Internet allows people to find information in minutes, rather than searching books and archives.

There is a growing need to be sure children use technology safely and within reasonable limits. Critics claim that these new devices isolate people from one another. Linda felt that way when she took her niece on a shopping trip. Thirteen-year-old Ashley passed the time in the car by text-messaging her friends and playing games. Linda had hoped they would spend the day talking to each other.

Even older technology like televisions and video games need to be used within reasonable limits. Parents should monitor children to ensure that enough time is spent on other activities for physical development and social skills.

Strong families find ways to use technology to strengthen their bonds. They make choices based on their values. They manage their resources so that technology is a tool to bring the family together.

Section 3.1 After You Read

Review Key Concepts

1. **List** two functions of families.
2. **Analyze** the similarities and differences among the four family structures described.
3. **Identify** three trends that affect families.

Practice Academic Skills

English Language Arts

4. Determine which family structure fits your family—nuclear, single-parent, blended, or extended. Now choose one of the other family structures. Write a one-page story about how your life would be different if you lived in the other family structure.

> **NCTE 4** Use written language to communicate effectively.

Social Studies

5. Choose a country other than the United States and study their family structures. Write a one-page report in which you answer these questions: What are the family structures? How are they similar to and different from the family structures in the United States?

> **NCSS I A** Analyze and explain the ways groups, societies, and cultures address human needs and concerns.

 Check Your Answers Check your answers at this book's Online Learning Center at **glencoe.com**.

Section 3.2 Parenting Skills

Reading Guide

Before You Read

Preview Choose a Key Concept that is new to you and write it down. When you find the concept in the text, write one or two sentences to explain it.

Read to Learn
Key Concepts
- **List** the basic categories of children's needs.
- **Identify** the three parenting styles.
- **Summarize** effective ways to guide children's behavior.

Main Idea
Parents use a variety of parenting styles to raise children and deal with the responsibilities of being a parent.

Content Vocabulary
◇ deprivation
◇ parenting style
◇ guidance
◇ self-discipline
◇ conscience
◇ positive reinforcement
◇ negative reinforcement
◇ time-out

 Graphic Organizer Go to this book's Online Learning Center at **glencoe.com** to print out this graphic organizer.

Academic Vocabulary
You will find these words in your reading and on your tests. Use the glossary to look up their definitions if necessary.
- dispute
- consistent

Graphic Organizer
As you read, list the four types of negative reinforcement discussed in the text and write a brief description of each one. Use a chart like the one shown to record your answers.

Negative Reinforcement	Description

Academic Standards . . . .

 English Language Arts

NCTE 12 Use language to accomplish individual purposes.

 Science

NSES A Develop abilities necessary to do scientific inquiry, understandings about scientific inquiry.

NCTE *National Council of Teachers of English*
NCTM *National Council of Teachers of Mathematics*

NSES *National Science Education Standards*
NCSS *National Council for the Social Studies*

Children's Needs

Having a child makes a person a parent. It does not make a person an effective parent though. Parenting skills do not always come naturally or easily. Parenting is a learning process that occurs each day. Parents must work to develop the skills required to meet their children's needs, guide their children's behavior, and help their children develop positive relationships. It takes time to figure out what works for each parent, child, and family. Sometimes effective parenting means learning from mistakes and trying to do better each day.

Maria wakes up to Ryan's cries at 4:30 in the morning. She changes his diaper and feeds him. Although she is ready to go back to sleep, Ryan is wide awake and wants to play. She puts him in his bouncy seat on the floor and talks to him about his colorful toys. After an hour, Ryan seems sleepy, so Maria rocks him a bit and returns him to his crib. Just as she is ready to go back to bed, Maria hears, "Mommy?" Two-year-old Karenna is awake and ready for a fresh diaper. Unfortunately, Maria will not be going back to sleep. She goes to the kitchen instead to make breakfast and start the day.

Parents often must put their own needs aside to take care of their children. The list of parenting tasks can seem to be endless. In addition, all children are different, with unique characteristics and needs. Ask a group of parents what it takes to raise happy, healthy, well-adjusted children, and you will hear many different answers.

Children's needs can be grouped into three categories:

- **Physical Needs** These include food, clothing, and shelter.
- **Emotional and Social Needs** Meeting these needs means making sure that children feel safe, loved, and cared for. This allows the children to learn how to make friends and work with other people.
- **Intellectual Needs** All children need stimulation and the opportunity to learn about the world and become educated. By fulfilling this need, parents and caregivers help prepare children for life as independent adults.

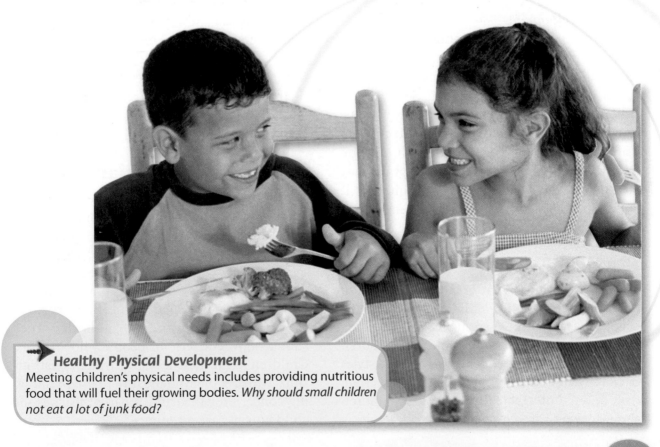

Healthy Physical Development
Meeting children's physical needs includes providing nutritious food that will fuel their growing bodies. *Why should small children not eat a lot of junk food?*

Developing Social Skills
Children need plenty of opportunities to play.
How does play help children develop social skills?

Unfortunately, some parents cannot or do not meet all of their children's physical, emotional, social, or intellectual needs. These children tend to lag behind other children in their overall development.

They suffer from deprivation. **Deprivation** is a lack of the critical needs and encouraging environment that are essential for physical, emotional, and intellectual well-being. Some people believe that deprivation and poverty are the same things. This is not true. Deprived children can come from families that are rich or poor, or anywhere in between. Money is not the only factor. Children can be deprived of time, nutrients, stimulation, or love. What matters most is whether a child's basic needs are being met.

Physical Needs

The most important and obvious task of parenthood is meeting children's basic physical needs. Parents are responsible for providing nourishing meals for their children. Children do not need the latest or most expensive styles of clothes, but their clothes do need to be clean, dry, and comfortable. In addition, children should have a safe, clean place to call home.

Parents are also responsible for the health and safety of their children. Parents schedule regular checkups and provide care when children are sick or hurt. Ensuring children's safety includes using a car seat and seat belt while in a vehicle. It also means making sure toys are safe and appropriate for the child's age, and eliminating hazards in the home so that children can safely explore their environment. Parents should always make an effort to know where their children are, whom they are with, and what they are doing.

Emotional and Social Needs

A major goal of parents is to raise children who will become happy, independent adults who can support themselves. They may even go on to raise their own children. To become independent, children need to learn how to function in the world and get along with others. For example, children need to learn to show respect for figures of authority. They should show concern for people who are hurt. Children learn these lessons through relationships with people who nurture them. By showing concern for the child, a parent teaches the child how to care for others.

Nurture Children

Nurturing children means giving them plenty of love, support, concern, and opportunities for enrichment. These factors help meet children's emotional and social needs and help prepare them for their adult lives. Parents aid children's emotional and social development by helping them explore the world on their own, while still keeping them safe. For a preschooler, this might mean letting her play in the sandbox without worrying about whether her clothes will get dirty. With reassurance and freedom to explore, a child develops a healthy emotional well-being.

Parents can show children love and support in many different ways such as a hug, a kiss, or a smile. Unfortunately, some parents find it hard to show affection for their child. They may be embarrassed or feel that affection will make their child too "soft." When parents fail to recognize a child's accomplishments, the child may feel insecure or worthless. He may have a difficult time forming healthy relationships later because he did not learn how to give and receive love.

Communicating with a child shows love and support. Giving time and attention also shows that you care about a child. Actively listening shows children that they are important.

Show Restraint

Some parents become overprotective, overattentive, or both. They give a child too much attention, too many toys, and too many treats. They may try to shield the child from all unpleasant experiences. This can harm children, too. Children learn from trial and error. They need to make mistakes so they can learn from them. They must also learn to cope with the ups and downs of life.

Intellectual Needs

Children begin learning at birth. Parents are a child's first teacher. Researchers have found that with stimulation, the brain undergoes tremendous growth during a child's first years. In the past, it was thought that a baby could not learn much in the first few months of life. Researchers now know that infancy can be a time of constant learning if a baby is given opportunities to learn.

Learning Through the Senses

Early on, children's lessons come through touching, tasting, hearing, and looking at the objects around them. Parents can nurture this early learning by playing with their children. The child's environment should be filled with interesting sounds, smells, sights, and textures.

RESPOND TO SPECIAL NEEDS — Autism

Autism is a brain development disorder that affects the way people relate to others. People with severe autism have an impaired ability to interact and communicate with others. Signs of autism usually appear before a child turns three. Autistic children tend to avoid eye contact and cuddling. They often have restricted interests and repetitive behaviors. They do not like changes in routine and they may be very sensitive to lights and sounds. They may not respond to their own names, and they may start talking late. Early diagnosis is important. A child with autism needs a special treatment program.

Therapy and special education help children with autism lead fuller lives. Special diets may also help. Parents can help by showing love and understanding, setting up routines, and praising successes.

Critical Thinking Research the causes of autism. Describe the major theories and explain why some theories are controversial. Summarize your findings in a one-page essay. Cite your sources.

When parents stimulate young children in these ways, they help encourage brain development and a lifetime love of learning.

As children grow older, their intellectual needs expand. They want to play games and explore more of their environment. Parents and caregivers meet these intellectual needs by continuing to provide opportunities for play and learning. These opportunities can be as simple as playing ball in the park or visiting the zoo.

Learning Through Reading

Children can also help choose books to borrow from the library. Learning to read and enjoying books are keys to intellectual development. Sharing books together can begin at birth. Infants simply enjoy the sound of the reader's voice. As they grow a bit older, they enjoy the pictures and story. They soon learn that the words on the page have meaning. Sharing books with children helps foster a love of books and a joy for reading. It also helps them learn about the world around them.

Learning Through Exploring

It is a myth that children need a lot of expensive toys. Everyday objects and experiences with nurturing adults can provide great opportunities for learning. The best way to get children ready and excited about learning is to allow them to explore in a safe environment. When intellectual needs are met at an early age, children are better prepared for school.

✓ **Reading Check** **Define** What is deprivation?

Parenting Styles

A **parenting style** is how parents and other caregivers care for and discipline children. Effective parents use a style they feel comfortable with. This style matches their personality and values. For this reason, no *one* parenting style is considered right. No *one* style works best with all children. Parents also often change their parenting style as children grow and change.

There are three main styles of parenting:

- **Authoritarian** An authoritarian parent believes children should obey their parents without question. The parent tells a child what to do, and the child's responsibility is to do it. When rules are broken, the authoritarian parent typically responds quickly and firmly.

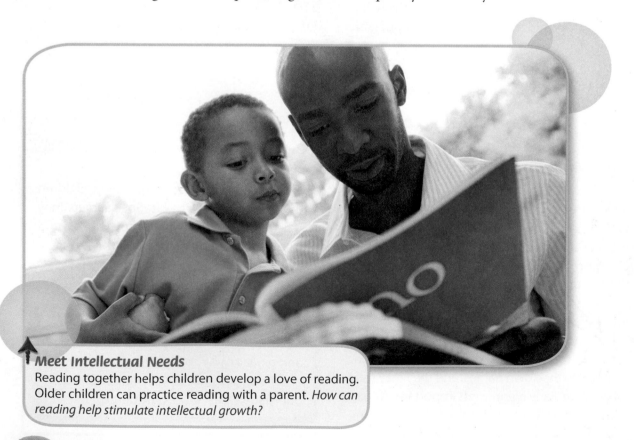

↑ Meet Intellectual Needs
Reading together helps children develop a love of reading. Older children can practice reading with a parent. *How can reading help stimulate intellectual growth?*

- **Assertive-Democratic** In this style, children have more input into the rules and limits of the home. Learning to take responsibility is important, so children are given a certain amount of independence and freedom of choice within the rules. When rules are broken, the assertive-democratic parent believes children learn best from accepting the results of their actions or by problem solving together to find an acceptable punishment.
- **Permissive** In the permissive style, parents give children a wide range of freedom. Children of permissive parents may set their own rules. They are encouraged to think for themselves and not follow trends. Permissive parents typically ignore rule breaking.

Few parents follow just one style at all times. A parent may use a more authoritarian style on issues such as health or safety. The same parent may be more assertive-democratic about clothing or hairstyles. Parents may feel that before children become teens, they need firm rules, but that as teens they should be allowed the freedom to make more of their own choices.

✓ **Reading Check** **Determine** Which parenting style allows the child to provide input into the rules?

Guide Children's Behavior

Amy was frustrated because Grace, age four, never put her toys away. She tried reminding Grace, scolding her, and even banning television until the toys were picked up. Nothing seemed to work. Amy did not know what to do.

Acceptable behavior does not come naturally to children. This is true whether it is putting toys away, getting along with a sibling, or saying please and thank you. Children need to be taught what is acceptable, what is *not* acceptable, and what is expected of them. As children grow, their minds develop and they test their limits. Doing so helps them to learn about the world and their place in it.

Guiding children's behavior can be both the hardest and the most rewarding task of parenting. For years, Ella felt as though she was always reminding her children to get along with each

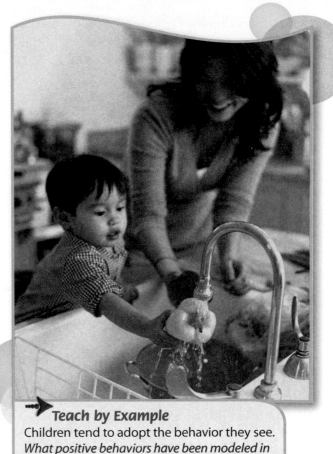

▶ Teach by Example
Children tend to adopt the behavior they see. *What positive behaviors have been modeled in your family?*

other and showing them effective ways to settle a **dispute**, or quarrel. Nothing worked. Finally, one day her message seemed to click, and the two managed to settle a disagreement on their own before it became a shouting match. The children became increasingly more effective at avoiding disputes and finding better ways to resolve their differences. Ella's guidance and patience had paid off. All three of them were able to benefit from it.

Understand Guidance

Guidance means using firmness and understanding to help children learn how to behave. Children learn self-discipline with effective guidance. **Self-discipline** is the ability to control one's own behavior. They also learn how to get along with others and how to handle their feelings in acceptable ways. Guidance promotes security and positive self-esteem. It also helps children learn the difference between what is right and wrong. Very young children understand right from wrong only in terms of being praised or scolded. Gradually, they develop a conscience. A **conscience** is an inner sense of what is right. As children mature, they use their conscience to decide how to act in new situations.

Parents can successfully guide their children in three basic ways. They can be positive role models. They can set limits and redirect their children's behavior. Finally, they can use positive reinforcement to let children know when their behavior is on the right track.

Be a Role Model

Children are great imitators. They learn best by being shown what to do, rather than just being told what to do. Parents and other people in a child's life serve as role models. Children constantly watch those around them and then imitate the behaviors they see. The old saying is true: Actions speak louder than words. That is why parents need to demonstrate at all times the behaviors they would like to see in their own children. For instance, parents who want their child to talk politely to others need to speak politely themselves.

The desire to imitate applies to all behaviors, not just the acceptable ones. Five-year-old Mark sees his older brothers yell at each other when they disagree. It is no surprise then that Mark yells at his friends when he is upset with them. Parents and other family members should model respect, honesty, and kindness.

Give Effective Direction

Parents and other caregivers often need to tell children what to do. Sometimes children do not seem to listen, but often the real problem is lack of understanding. These tips can help children understand and follow directions:

- **Be sure you have the child's attention.** Make eye contact. You may have to stoop down or sit beside a young child to do so.
- **Be polite.** A child will respond better if you speak politely in a normal voice.
- **Use positive statements.** Say, "Please walk," rather than, "Don't run."
- **Use specific words that the child can understand.** Say, "Keep the paint on the paper," not, "Don't be sloppy."
- **Begin with an action verb.** Beginning this way helps keep directions simple. Say, "Pick up your socks" or "Get ready for bed."
- **Give a limited number of directions at a time.** Very young children can only remember one step. You can increase the number as the child's memory improves. Remember, though, that fewer directions are easier to understand, remember, and follow.

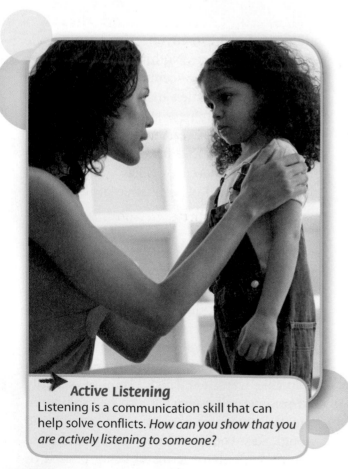

Active Listening
Listening is a communication skill that can help solve conflicts. *How can you show that you are actively listening to someone?*

Give Directions
Parents must be sure the child is attentive before giving directions. *How can you tell this child is attentive to the parent?*

- **Be clear.** Think in terms of the child's point of view as you decide what to say.
- **Give praise and love.** All people need to hear good things about themselves. This is especially true of young children. Praise encourages cooperation.

Set Limits

Setting limits is another way to guide children toward appropriate, safe behavior. Limits include physical restrictions, such as preventing a child from crossing the street alone. A rule of behavior can also be a limit. For example, hitting other people or using certain words is not allowed.

Children need limits to grow into responsible adults. Having limits helps them to understand expectations and acceptable behavior, and to develop self-control. Children of any age will test limits, but parents should be consistent in enforcing them. A limit will not mean anything if the child is allowed to break it from time to time.

When setting limits, parents and other caregivers often follow this general guideline: Limits should keep children from hurting themselves, other people, or property. Children will respect and follow guidelines if they are reasonable.

The following questions can help parents determine limits:

- **Does the limit allow the child to learn, explore, and grow?** Too much restriction hinders development.
- **Is the limit fair and appropriate for the child's age?** A toddler might be restricted to a fenced-in yard. A school-age child might be allowed to visit a friend living down the street.
- **Does the limit benefit the child, or is it just for the adult's convenience?** Restrictions should be for the child's good, not because they fit a routine.

Children must be told what is expected of them in ways they can understand. Limits should be stated simply and briefly and in a calm, direct tone of voice. For example, "We don't throw toys," stated calmly is a simple limit that is easily understood. If a young child throws a toy, he or she should be reminded of the rule and then redirected to an acceptable behavior. "We don't throw toys. You can go outside to throw a ball."

Redirection is important because it helps the child to do something else *and* it suggests another, acceptable behavior. However, the redirection must be appropriate for the child's age. Infants, for example, may need to be physically moved to another, acceptable activity.

Appropriate Behavior
Preschoolers are capable of learning appropriate behavior. *How can caregivers encourage that behavior?*

Limits must also be clear. Telling three-year-old Madeline that she can have a little snack is not a clear limit. She might not know what makes a snack little. A better limit suggests a specific snack Madeline can have, such as half an apple.

Limits often have to be repeated each time the situation arises. Children, especially young ones, do not always remember limits from one day to the next. They also may not realize that limits stated one day still apply another day.

With very young children, it is not necessary to explain the reasons for expected behaviors. For a one-year-old, the instruction "Be gentle with the kitty," combined with modeling of gentle handling, is enough. Around age three, however, children begin to understand simple reasoning. Then they can understand limits that include the reason for them: "Don't pull the kitty's tail. It hurts the kitty when you pull his tail. If you want to play with him, you need to be gentle."

Once established and explained, limits should be firmly and consistently enforced. Children can become confused if throwing blocks is ignored one day and punished the next. Parents who are not consistent with limits also teach their children that they do not mean what they say. Children take rules more seriously if they are enforced at all times.

Provide Positive Reinforcement

"You didn't clean your room *again*." "How many times do I have to tell you to pick up your toys?" All too often, parents remind children of all the things they do wrong without noting what they do right. Constant scolding does not change children's behavior. It makes them feel as though they cannot do anything right. After a while, they may decide to stop trying.

Children, like all people, are more likely to change their behavior when they are praised for the things they do right. Giving children attention when their actions are appropriate is an example of positive reinforcement. **Positive reinforcement** is a response that encourages a particular behavior. When children learn that an action wins attention and approval from adults, they are likely to repeat that action.

Positive reinforcement can be used to help change a problem behavior and to strengthen good behavior. Use these guidelines to encourage appropriate behavior:

- **Be specific.** Clearly comment on the behavior being acknowledged: "That was such a nice letter you wrote to Grandpa."
- **Comment on the behavior as soon as possible.** Recognize the behavior right away to help the child link the action and the praise.

- **Recognize small steps.** Encourage steps in the right direction. Do not wait for perfect behavior. If a child usually leaves toys all over the floor, acknowledge the effort of putting even some of the toys away. This will encourage him to do it again next time, and he will likely do a little more.
- **Help children take pride in their actions.** Saying "That was hard work to get dressed by yourself, but you did it!" helps a young child feel competent.
- **Tailor the encouragement to the needs of the child.** Praise behaviors that are hard for that child. The child who usually forgets to wash his hands should be rewarded with approval for remembering to do so.
- **Use positive reinforcement wisely.** If children are praised for everything they do, it no longer motivates them. The praise must be genuine and deserved.

✓ **Reading Check** **Recall** How can positive reinforcement be used?

Deal with Inappropriate Behavior

No matter how hard adults try to encourage appropriate behavior, all children misbehave from time to time. Then adults must deal with the situation appropriately and effectively.

The child's age should shape an adult's response to inappropriate behavior. A one-year-old who bites another child can be told "We don't bite." However, the child cannot be expected to understand the meaning of his or her action. A four-year-old should understand why biting is unacceptable.

Here are some questions to consider when deciding how to respond to misbehavior:
- Is the expected behavior appropriate, given the child's age and development?
- Does the child understand that the behavior was wrong?
- Did the child do the behavior knowingly and deliberately, or was it beyond the child's control?

Reinforce Positive Behavior
Children should be praised for positive behavior. *Do you think it is possible for a parent to praise a child too much?*

Unintentional Misbehavior

With children of any age, misbehavior is sometimes unintentional. A young child may drop a glass of milk that is too heavy or accidentally break something. Such unintentional actions should not be punished.

Misbehavior is also unintentional if the child had no way of knowing it was wrong. For example, Ana picked a flower in the park and brought it to her father. People should not pick flowers in parks, but Ana had never been told that. Rather than scolding her, Ana's father simply explained that she should not have done it. He told her that flowers in the park are there for everyone's enjoyment. He asked her to draw a picture of a flower instead.

Effective Punishment

By guiding children's behavior, parents and other caregivers are more likely to teach a child acceptable behavior. Still, when children test the limits and misbehave, punishment can be effective if used thoughtfully and with good judgment.

Punishment can help remind children that correct behavior is important and teach them that there are consequences for poor choices. When using punishment, parents should clearly show that they disapprove of the behavior but that they still love the child. They can do this by avoiding blame and criticism.

The first time a child breaks a rule, parents may choose to give a warning rather than a punishment. Even a child with good self-control makes an occasional mistake. A warning reminds the child of the rule and why it is important. It also gives the child a chance to regain self-control.

After a rule has been broken another time, punishment is appropriate. However, the punishment given should be in proportion to and related to the misbehavior. Forgetting to put dirty clothes in the hamper one day does not call for severe punishment. In this case, a simple reminder would be sufficient. Repeated failure to stop throwing sand in the sandbox calls for more action, such as leaving the park or not visiting the park for a few days.

Effective Punishment
Even when being punished, children should still understand that they are loved. *What types of misbehavior should not be punished?*

Negative Reinforcement

Negative reinforcement is a response aimed at strengthening desired behavior by removing an unpleasant trigger. Several different methods can be used. These include natural consequences, logical consequences, loss of privileges, and time-out.

When deciding which method of negative reinforcement to use, parents and other caregivers often find that what works for one child may not be effective for another. The same method may not work every time for the same child, or for the same child at different ages.

Parents need to think about which method of negative reinforcement is most appropriate for the child's personality and their own values. For the method to be effective, parents must also be consistent in their use of it. Ideally, punishment should be linked to a child's age and emotional, social, and intellectual development.

Natural Consequences With natural consequences, children suffer from the actual result of their action. For example, suppose Kwan loses his new jacket. Using natural consequences, his parents do not replace it and he has to wear his old one.

When a natural consequence occurs, parents should not lecture. For children, it is often difficult enough to have to live with the consequences. Nor should parents attempt to remedy a situation for their children. This defeats the purpose of the consequence. Children who are rescued from their choices will expect to be saved whenever they make poor choices.

Logical Consequences Parents may choose to address a child's misbehavior with consequences that have a connection to the misbehavior. Parents often choose logical consequences when natural consequences are inappropriate. For example, when Katy colored on the table with crayons, the natural consequence of a messy table bothered her mother more than it bothered Katy. Instead, her mother told Katy that she was taking the crayons away for the day. This was a logical consequence.

Parents who use logical consequences need to be prepared to follow through. They should think about the logical consequence before giving it and ask themselves "Am I ready to do

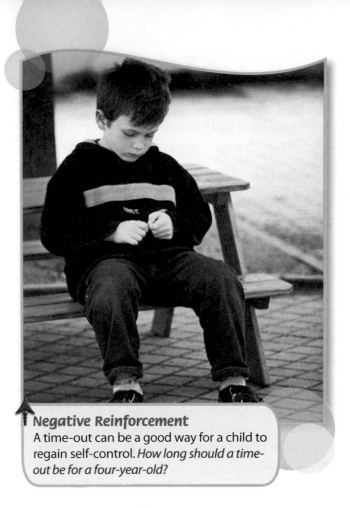

Negative Reinforcement
A time-out can be a good way for a child to regain self-control. *How long should a time-out be for a four-year-old?*

this?" After all, lack of follow-through shows children that they do not need to take their parents or their limits seriously.

Loss of Privileges Sometimes using natural or logical consequences is not appropriate. If a child runs into the street, the natural consequence of being hit by a car is far too dangerous. A parent might take away a privilege instead. This type of punishment is most effective for children ages five and older. It also works best if the privilege taken away is related to the misbehavior. That way, the child is likely to associate the two. In our example, the child might lose the privilege of playing outside to remind him not to run into the street.

Time-out Another way to respond to misbehavior is with a time-out. A **time-out** is a short period of time in which a child sits away from other people and the center of activity. The purpose of a time-out is to give children a chance to calm down and regain self-control. Time-outs can be especially effective when emotions are running high and the child simply needs a

Spanking as Discipline

Few parenting issues are as controversial as spanking. Some parents believe that spanking is an effective way to punish children and teach them how to behave. Other parents feel that certain misbehaviors call for spanking, such as when children push the limits of safety. Most child development experts believe there are more effective ways to get children to behave appropriately. They argue that there are problems with spanking. For example, spanking can physically harm children. Parents who spank serve as models for hitting and other aggressive behaviors. Spanking does not teach lessons about behavior. Children younger than two are unable to make the connection between their behavior and a spanking. Parents must set firm limits and follow through with warnings, redirection, and if necessary, punishment. This helps children make a connection between their actions and the consequences.

Be Prepared Choose a country outside of North America. Research the methods used there to guide children's behavior. Be sure to include both positive and negative reinforcement methods. Share your findings with the class in an oral report.

break. One minute of time-out for each year of a child's age is generally a good length of time.

Five-year-old Teresa, for example, took pretzels away from her playmates. She continued to do this, even after her teacher gave her a warning and redirected her to other activities. The third time it happened, her teacher immediately intervened. She explained again why the behavior was inappropriate, and instructed Teresa to sit in the "thinking chair" for five minutes. After five minutes, Teresa had calmed down, and her teacher invited her to do a puzzle.

Poor Disciplinary Measures

Well-meaning parents and caregivers sometimes use disciplinary methods that are less effective than others and sometimes even harmful. Those who follow the positive discipline techniques already described in this chapter will likely find that they do not need to use the following measures.

- **Bribing** Bribing children so they stop misbehaving can backfire. Instead of learning self-control, children learn to expect rewards for ending inappropriate behavior. Children may even misbehave on purpose, knowing that by stopping they will earn a treat or privilege. Bribing is not the same as rewarding desirable behavior though. Positive reinforcement for acceptable behavior is a more effective way to guide children's behavior.

- **Making Children Promise to Behave** In the process of learning to control their behavior, children will naturally make mistakes. If they made a promise to be good, children may feel forced to lie about misbehavior rather than disappointing someone they love. Children need to know that a parent's love is unconditional.

- **Shouting or Yelling** When children misbehave, parents and caregivers should talk to them in a calm, reasonable voice. A loud, harsh voice can frighten young children. Older children may learn to tune out, or ignore, yelling. Also, adults who yell are not modeling acceptable behavior. If the adult yells, the child might yell back.

- **Shaming or Belittling** Parents and caregivers should not ridicule children's mistakes or make comments such as "If you chew with your mouth open, no one will want to sit with you at the lunch table!" This can make a child feel worthless.

- **Threatening to Withhold Love** Caregivers should never stop loving a child. They should also not threaten to do so. Children take statements very seriously and literally. Statements such as "Treat your brother better or I won't love you anymore" create the fear of being rejected or abandoned. Children should always know that they are loved, even when they misbehave. Children need to understand that the parent is unhappy with the misbehavior, not with the child.

- **Exaggerating Consequences** Parents and caregivers sometimes threaten wildly impractical consequences. When a child refuses to leave a toy aisle in a department store, a tired parent might say "If you don't come now, I'm going to leave you at the store." Such statements frighten children. They also cause a parent to lose credibility. When children see that a parent will not follow through on such exaggerated claims, they may begin to wonder if anything a parent says will actually be done. The child loses trust and respect for the parent.

Consistency in Guidance

Being **consistent**, or continually the same, is the key to guiding children's behavior. Consistency is a matter of clearly making rules and applying them in the same way whenever the situation occurs. Consistency helps children know what is expected of them. It also lets them know what responses to expect from parents.

Children lose trust and confidence in caregivers who constantly change rules or fail to enforce rules in a consistent way. If parents permit a behavior one day and punish children for the same behavior the next, children will feel confused and insecure. They will pay little attention to the next limit that is set.

Consistency is an especially important issue when more than one person cares for a child. All caregivers need to agree on rules and ways to enforce them. For example, Steve's parents are divorced. When he asked to change his bedtime from eight to nine, his mother first talked to his father to get agreement. If caregivers do not agree, children can use the inconsistency to their advantage, playing one adult against the other.

Section 3.2 — After You Read

Review Key Concepts

1. **Identify** four factors that are part of nurturing.
2. **Explain** why it is important to set limits.
3. **List** two ways to deal with inappropriate behavior.

Practice Academic Skills

 English Language Arts

4. Think back to your own childhood and the parenting styles used in your home. Which style or styles were used? Do you think they were effective? Why or why not? Would you follow the same parenting style with your children? Write a journal entry explaining your answers.

> **NCTE 12** Use language to accomplish individual purposes.

 Science

5. On a sheet of paper, list the methods used to guide children's behavior. Get permission to observe supervised children on a playground. Note the methods used by caregivers by putting a checkmark beside the method each time it is used. Create a pie chart to present the information you gather.

> **NSES A** Develop abilities necessary to do scientific inquiry, understandings about scientific inquiry.

 Check Your Answers Check your answers at this book's Online Learning Center at **glencoe.com**.

Family court judges decide who should get custody of children when parents divorce, how much money one spouse should pay to the other, how often parents are allowed to visit their children, and where abused children should live.

What Does a Family Court Judge Do?

Judges make sure everyone in the courtroom is treated fairly. They decide what evidence may be presented, settle disputes between sides, and interpret laws. Judges are responsible for ensuring rules and procedures are followed.

Family court judges determine guilt or innocence for crimes committed by youth. They often try to arrange for help and treatment, instead of prison time. They try to keep families together whenever possible. Family court judges also decide who can provide foster care or adopt children.

Where Do Family Court Judges Work?

Judges most often work in courtrooms and private offices. They must also spend time in law libraries to research past decisions about cases.

Preparation and Skills

Education and Training

A family court judge needs a bachelor's degree and law degree. Judges are usually required to have several years of experience, as well as knowledge of family and child problems.

Aptitudes, Abilities, and Skills

Family court judges need listening skills, intelligence, fairness, ability to deal with stress, and an interest in the problems of children and families. They must be able to listen to both sides of a case and make fair, unbiased decisions.

Academic Skills

Strong English language arts skills are necessary for family court judges to complete research and to communicate clearly and effectively with each person involved in the court. Social studies skills are useful in understanding people's culture and motivation behind actions.

Explore Careers

Research other careers in the area of family law. Choose one career and write a paragraph describing it. Tell whether or not you think you would be a good candidate for this job.

 Careers Online For more information on careers, visit the Occupational Outlook Handbook Web site through the link on this book's Online Learning Center at **glencoe.com**.

Chapter Summary

Families today serve many functions. Families need to meet children's basic needs and prepare children to live in society. There are three basic family structures. Each structure has unique challenges. Most families follow a series of stages called the family life cycle. Families are affected by trends in society and sometimes need support. Parents use many skills to raise children. Children have physical, emotional, social, and intellectual needs that should be met by a family. Parents must find the parenting style that works best for them and their children. Parents must also learn positive ways to guide children's behavior and deal with misbehavior.

Vocabulary Review

1. Use at least seven of these content and academic vocabulary terms in an essay about your family.

Content Vocabulary
- nuclear family (p. 62)
- single-parent family (p. 62)
- custodial parent (p. 62)
- blended family (p. 63)
- extended family (p. 63)
- legal guardian (p. 64)
- foster child (p. 64)
- intergenerational (p. 65)
- deprivation (p. 70)
- parenting style (p. 72)
- guidance (p. 73)
- self-discipline (p. 73)
- conscience (p. 74)
- positive reinforcement (p. 76)
- negative reinforcement (p. 79)
- time-out (p. 79)

Academic Vocabulary
- vital (p. 57)
- venture (p. 61)
- dispute (p. 73)
- consistent (p. 81)

Review Key Concepts

2. **Summarize** the qualities that contribute to building a strong family.
3. **Describe** the different family structures.
4. **Discuss** the trends affecting families.
5. **List** the basic categories of children's needs.
6. **Identify** the three parenting styles.
7. **Summarize** effective ways to guide children's behavior.

Critical Thinking

8. **Analyze** This chapter notes that traditions help to strengthen a family. Do you think this is so? Why or why not?
9. **Compare and contrast** How are guidance and punishment similar? How do they differ?
10. **Apply** Nathan lost a library book. His father says Nathan can no longer borrow books from the library. Do you think this is an appropriate punishment? Why or why not?

Family & Community Connection

11. Interview Blended-Family Members Talk with one or both parents and one or more children in a blended family. Note how many children are in the family. What were the children's ages when the parents married? Create a list of questions to ask each member. You might ask, "How did you deal with the blending process?" "How do you think the family is doing now?" Conduct the interviews. Then, record your answers in a table.

Health Skills

12. Research Emotional Balance The emotional balance in blended families can be fragile. Parents must build effective relationships with each other and with stepchildren. The stepchildren must also build relationships among themselves. Research to identify strategies that can help parents create harmony in blended families. Write an advice column for a newspaper sharing these strategies.

Observation Skills

13. Observe a Parent-Child Interaction Ask family members or friends who have young children if you can observe them interacting with their children. Or go to a public place and observe caregivers interacting with young children.

Procedure Watch the interaction between the adult and the child. Take notes during your observation. Write down answers to questions such as: How would you describe the parenting style you observe? Was the parenting style effective? How did the child respond to the parent?

Analysis Use your notes to write a report of your observation. Include an analysis of the type of parenting style used and whether you think it was effective.

NCSS IV D Individual Development and Identity Apply concepts, methods, and theories about the study of human growth and development, such as behavior, perception, and personality.

Real-World Skills

Problem-Solving Skills	**14. Compromise** Imagine that you see a child in a restaurant who refuses to eat at dinner. One parent has an authoritarian parenting style, and the other has a permissive parenting style. Write a dialogue between the two parents that shows how they might compromise to find a solution.
Technology Skills	**15. Cultural Presentation** A family adopts an older child from a culture very different from their own. How might the parents help the child maintain his or her culture's traditions? Create an oral report using presentation software or other media to present your answer to the class.
Financial Literacy Skills	**16. Comparison Shop** Your family has decided that everyone must cut back on spending to help stick to a family budget. You have volunteered to help cut grocery bills by comparison shopping. List the steps you can take to reduce grocery costs.

 Additional Activities For additional activities, go to this book's Online Learning Center at **glencoe.com**.

Academic Skills

English Language Arts

17. Apply Your Knowledge Think of a book you have read about a family with children. Consider the interaction between the parents and children. Which parenting style was used? Were the parents' actions effective in teaching and training their children? Explain your answers in a one-page analysis of the book.

> **NCTE 2** Read literature to build an understanding of the human experience.

Mathematics

18. The Importance of Family Suppose that out of 20,000 American teenagers, 65 percent said they have dinner with their family each night. What is the total number of those teens that do not eat dinner with their family?

Math Concept **Ratios** A ratio is a comparison of two numbers using division.

Starting Hint Subtract 65 percent from 100 percent. Then divide that number by 100 and multiply it by the total number of teenagers (20,000).

 For math help, go to the Math Appendix at the back of the book.

> **NCTM Number and Operations** Understand numbers, ways of representing numbers, relationships among numbers, and number systems.

Science

19. Environmental Awareness Making decisions that show respect for the environment is important. There are many ways you and your family can work together to make a positive impact on your local environment. One easy way to help the environment is through recycling.

Procedure Research recycling facilities near you. Find out what items can be recycled. Discuss with your family how you might develop a plan to recycle.

Analysis Create a poster of your family's recycling plan to place on a wall at home.

> **NSES F** Develop understanding of personal and community health; natural resources; environmental quality in local, national, and global challenges.

Standardized Test Practice

ESSAY

Read and consider the statement about child development. Then read the writing prompt and write your essay.

> Many child development experts believe that the best way to teach children how to behave is by providing positive reinforcement for appropriate behaviors.

20. Write a one-page essay in which you identify positive reinforcement techniques. Explain how families can use the techniques effectively. Be sure to proofread your paper and correct any spelling and grammar errors.

> **Test-Taking Tip** Read, re-read, and think about an essay question before you begin writing. Then write a short outline with your main points. Make sure your outline addresses all the questions in the essay writing prompt.

Unit Thematic Project

Learn Parenting Skills

In this unit, you have learned the importance of being ready to parent. You have also learned that parenting is a full-time job for about 18 years. In this project, you will find a parenting role model. You will create a handbook of things to know before becoming a parent.

 My Journal

If you completed the journal entry from page 3, refer to it to see if your thoughts have changed after reading the unit.

Project Assignment

In this project, you will:
- Choose a person you know who you believe can teach you good parenting skills.
- Identify four good parenting qualities this person possesses.
- Arrange to meet the parent. Ask prepared questions. Be sure to take a pen and paper to record the answers.
- Use what you learned from the parent to create a parenting handbook.

Child Development Skills Behind the Project

- Evaluate qualities of a good parent.
- Describe ways to put parenting skills into practice.
- Identify positive parenting qualities in action.

Academic Skills

 English Language Arts

> **NCTE 4** Use written language to communicate effectively.
>
> **NCTE 12** Use language to accomplish individual purposes.

Step 1 Choose a Parent Role Model

The parent you choose as a role model can be anyone in your community. A possible parent to talk to might include:
- Friend
- Teacher
- Religious leader
- Neighbor
- Counselor
- Child care worker
- Relative

Step 2 Create a List of Questions About Parenting

What qualities do you think make a good parent? You might think a good parent treats his or her children with respect, explains what is right or wrong, does not yell or scream, and provides emotional support. Use complete sentences to write a list of four or five questions that can help you learn about parenting with your parenting role model.

Writing Skills
★ Organize your thoughts.
★ Use complete sentences.
★ Use correct spelling and grammar.
★ Consider your audience.

Step 3 Connect to Your Community

Arrange to speak with the parent role model you chose in Step 1. Use the questions you wrote in Step 2 to interview the parent. Questions should focus on the positive parenting qualities you identified in this person. How does the parent use this quality in his or her day-to-day parenting duties? Accurately record the answers to your questions.

Interpersonal Skills

★ Be polite. Do not interrupt the parent while he or she is talking.

★ Use standard English to communicate.

★ Listen attentively.

★ Ask additional questions to better understand the parent's answers.

Step 4 Create and Present Your Parenting Handbook

Use the Unit Thematic Project Checklist on the right to plan and create your handbook and make your presentation.

Handbook Skills

★ Use language appropriate for your audience.

★ Enhance your handbook with illustrations and graphics.

★ Correct all spelling and grammar errors.

Step 5 Evaluate Your Child Development Skills and Academic Skills

Your project will be evaluated based on:

● Content and organization of your information.

● Mechanics—presentation and neatness.

● Speaking and listening skills.

Evaluation Rubric Go to this book's Online Learning Center at **glencoe.com** for a rubric you can use to evaluate your final project.

Unit Thematic Project Checklist

Handbook	✓ Make a handbook that illustrates with words and pictures the parenting skills you learned from your model parent. ✓ In your handbook, list one skill on each page and include an explanation or example of how the skill might be used. ✓ Use illustrations throughout the handbook to support your content and to enhance it visually.
Presentation	✓ Create a presentation to share your handbook with your class and discuss what you learned. ✓ Invite the students in your class to ask you any questions they may have. Answer three questions. ✓ When students ask you questions, demonstrate in your answers that you respect their perspectives. ✓ Turn in your handbook and the questions and answers from your interview to your teacher.
Academic Skills	✓ Be creative in writing and illustrating the content of the handbook. ✓ Create an outline to organize your presentation. ✓ Arrange your presentation so the audience can view your handbook as you discuss it. ✓ Speak clearly and use proper language (not slang).

Unit 2

Pregnancy and Childbirth

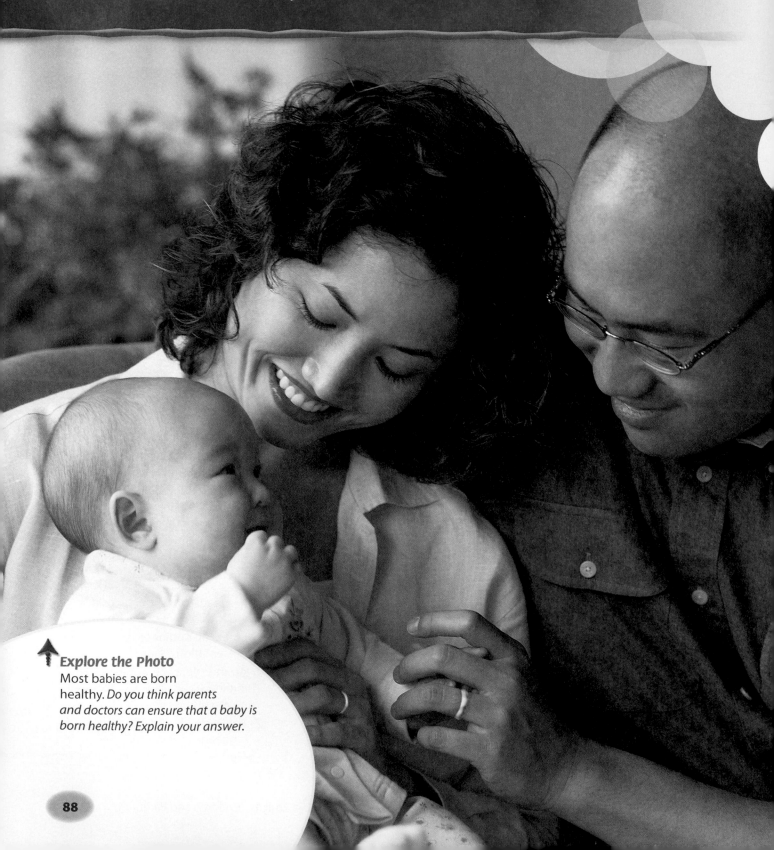

Explore the Photo
Most babies are born healthy. *Do you think parents and doctors can ensure that a baby is born healthy? Explain your answer.*

Chapter 4   Prenatal Development

Chapter 5   Preparing for Birth

Chapter 6   The Baby's Arrival

Unit   Thematic Project Preview

Promote Good Health During Pregnancy

By completing this unit, you will learn that there are steps a mother can take to help ensure the safety and health of herself and her baby during pregnancy and childbirth. In your unit thematic project, you can examine the importance of the mother's diet during pregnancy.

 My Journal

Keeping Fit and Healthy Write a journal entry about one of the topics below. This will help you prepare for the unit project at the end of the unit.

- Why is it important to eat healthfully during all stages of life?
- Why is exercise important to help keep a body fit?
- Where can you learn how to develop an exercise routine that is right for you?

4 Prenatal Development

Chapter Objectives

After completing this chapter, you will be able to:

- **List** the methods of family planning.
- **Outline** what occurs during each of the three stages of prenatal development.
- **Contrast** miscarriage and stillbirth.
- **Identify** how ten major birth defects can be diagnosed.
- **Summarize** the hazards that alcohol and other drugs pose to prenatal development.
- **Assess** why environmental hazards must be avoided during pregnancy.
- **Describe** how a fetus can be affected by certain illnesses the mother may contract.

Writing Activity / Outline

Examining Text Structure Good authors write text that is well structured. They clearly state their main points. Then they add details to these main points as needed. Use the following Writing Tips to create an outline of Section 4.1: The Developing Baby.

Writing Tips Outlining can help you identify an author's main points and understand how these points have been expanded. Use these tips when you are outlining text:

1. Determine the major points or topics.
2. Divide each major point into two or more subpoints.
3. Continue subdividing until you have covered the important details.

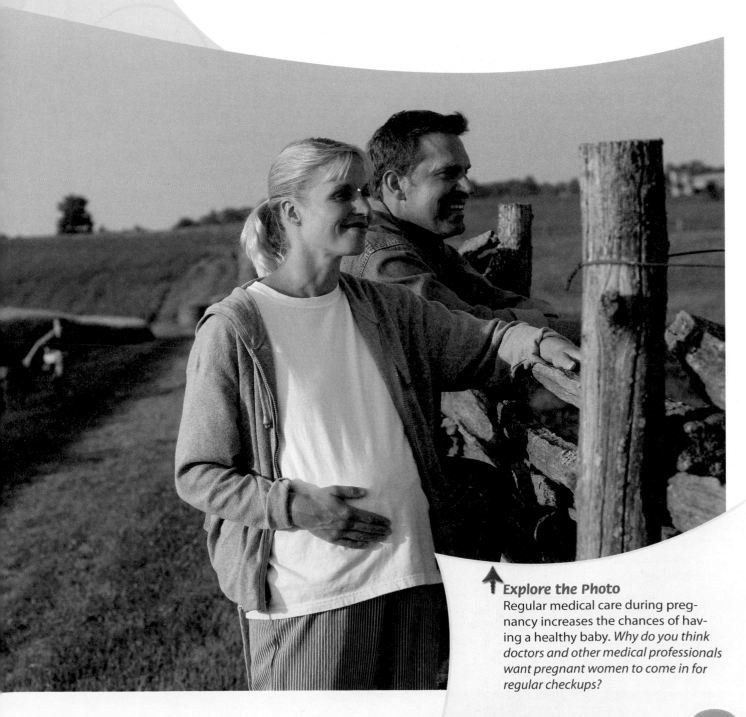

Explore the Photo
Regular medical care during pregnancy increases the chances of having a healthy baby. *Why do you think doctors and other medical professionals want pregnant women to come in for regular checkups?*

Reading Guide

Before You Read

Compare and Contrast When a chapter discusses more than one way of performing the same task, try to compare and contrast the different methods.

Read to Learn
Key Concepts
- **List** the methods of family planning.
- **Outline** what occurs during each of the three stages of prenatal development.

Main Idea
A man's sperm fertilizes a woman's egg to begin developing an infant. Many contraception methods are available.

Content Vocabulary
◇ ovum
◇ uterus
◇ fallopian tube
◇ sperm
◇ conception
◇ chromosome
◇ gene
◇ genome
◇ DNA
◇ infertility
◇ surrogate
◇ prenatal development
◇ zygote
◇ embryo
◇ amniotic fluid
◇ placenta
◇ umbilical cord
◇ fetus

Academic Vocabulary
You will find these words in your reading and on your tests. Use the glossary to look up their definitions if necessary.
■ controversial
■ spontaneous

Graphic Organizer
As you read this section, note each of the three stages of prenatal development. Use a chart like the one shown to help organize your information.

Three Stages of Prenatal Development

 Graphic Organizer Go to this book's Online Learning Center at **glencoe.com** to print out this graphic organizer.

Academic Standards

 English Language Arts

NCTE 7 Conduct research and gather, evaluate, and synthesize data to communicate discoveries.

 Science

NSES C Develop an understanding of the cell; molecular basis of heredity; and biological evolution.

 Social Studies

NCSS I A Culture Analyze and explain the ways groups, societies, and cultures address human needs and concerns.

NCSS II B Time, Continuity, and Change Apply key concepts such as time and change to analyze and show connections among patterns of historical change and continuity.

NCTE *National Council of Teachers of English*
NCTM *National Council of Teachers of Mathematics*

NSES *National Science Education Standards*
NCSS *National Council for the Social Studies*

Family Planning

Many families carefully consider whether to have children and when to have them. However, anytime a couple has sexual intercourse, a pregnancy can occur. The only sure way to prevent pregnancy is abstinence, or avoiding sexual activity.

There are other methods of contraception, which can help prevent pregnancy. It is important to understand that most methods of contraception do not prevent sexually transmitted infections (STIs). Abstinence, however, prevents both STIs and pregnancy.

Most family planning methods have possible side effects. These problems develop among some, but not all, users. **Figure 4.1** on page 94 compares different methods of family planning. It also indicates if there are side effects. Families should check with their doctors for complete listings of side effects.

Effectiveness is given as a percentage. A method that is 100 percent effective, such as abstinence, works all the time. If a method is 80 percent effective, there is a one in five chance that a pregnancy could occur when that method is used.

Conception

About once every 28 days, an ovum ('ō-vəm) is released by one of a woman's two ovaries. An **ovum** is an egg cell. This release is part of a woman's menstrual cycle and is called *ovulation*. At the same time, a woman's body releases specific hormones. These hormones prepare the uterus in the event that the ovum is fertilized. The **uterus** is the organ in a woman's body in which a baby develops during pregnancy. It is a pear-shaped muscle able to expand during pregnancy.

During ovulation, the inner lining of the uterus grows and thickens. If the ovum is not fertilized, the lining breaks down and passes out of the body. This is the bleeding that women experience as a menstrual period.

When an ovum is released from the ovary, it moves through a fallopian tube into the uterus. The **fallopian tube** is a tube that connects the ovary to the uterus. The journey from the ovary to the uterus takes about two or three days.

When the ovum reaches the uterus, it usually breaks up and leaves the body with the menstrual flow. The male cell is known as a **sperm**. When a sperm reaches the fallopian tube, it may penetrate and fertilize the ovum.

Pregnancy
For many couples, looking forward to a new baby is an exciting time. *What kinds of things do you think a couple might talk about during the pregnancy?*

Figure 4.1 Methods of Family Planning

There are many different methods of birth control. Some are more effective than others. *Which of the methods listed here can have the lowest rate of effectiveness?*

Method	Characteristics	Effectiveness
Abstinence	Only method that is 100% effective.	100%
Hormonal implants	Capsules placed under skin of upper arm. Possible side effects include hair loss or growth, acne, headaches, and moodiness.	99% effective, for up to 5 years
Hormonal patch	Thin patch worn on skin for 3 weeks each month. Possible side effects such as weight gain or moodiness.	99%
Hormonal injections	Hormones given by physician monthly or once every 3 months. May cause irregular bleeding.	up to 99%
Intrauterine device (IUD) and Uterine implant	Device placed inside the uterus to prevent sperm from fertilizing the egg. May cause discomfort and side effects first 3 months of use.	up to 99%
Vaginal implant	Ring worn internally for 3 weeks each month. Side effects can include vaginal bleeding.	95–99%
Birth control pills	Daily pill that contains hormones. Possible side effects such as weight gain or moodiness.	95–98%
Condom	Available for females, but more frequently used by males. Helps reduce spread of STDs.	86% to 97%
Diaphragm	Covers the cervix to prevent sperm from entering the uterus. Used with spermicide. Increases risk of urinary infections.	80–94%
Cervical cap	Small latex thimble that must remain in place eight hours. Increases risk of infection.	60–91%
Natural family planning	Known as the rhythm method. Determines when a female can get pregnant based on her menstrual cycle.	53–80%
Spermicide	Foams, creams, and gels. May cause allergic reactions. Should be used with condom, diaphragm, and cervical cap.	72%

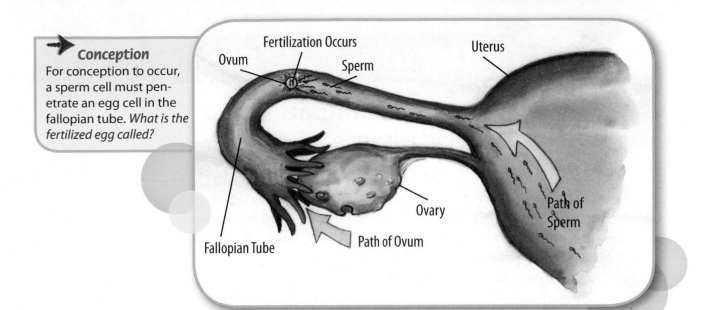

→ Conception
For conception to occur, a sperm cell must penetrate an egg cell in the fallopian tube. *What is the fertilized egg called?*

**Diagram labels:** Ovum · Fertilization Occurs · Sperm · Uterus · Ovary · Path of Sperm · Fallopian Tube · Path of Ovum

The process of the sperm fertilizing the ovum is called **conception**. An ovum usually lives 12 to 24 hours, while a sperm is capable of fertilizing an ovum for about 48 to 72 hours. During a woman's menstrual cycle, there are approximately three to four days during which intercourse could lead to conception.

Pregnancy, which lasts about nine months, begins at that time. During this time, a single cell grows and develops into a human being capable of life outside the mother's body.

An *ectopic pregnancy* is one in which the baby starts to grow somewhere other than the uterus, such as the fallopian tube. Ectopic pregnancies are dangerous for the mother. They do not end in a live birth.

The Role of Genetics

Why do I have this hair color? Why do I have blue eyes like my mom instead of brown eyes like my dad? Figuring out why people have certain traits can be confusing.

Have you ever compared your relative's looks to your own? Maybe you looked a lot like your father when you were both seven years old. People inherit many physical traits from their parents. These traits may include skin color, hair texture and color, eye color, the size and shape of ears, and more.

Some children are more likely to have certain talents, such as musical or athletic ability, because their parents have those talents. Some medical conditions are also inherited. How does this happen? Scientists are constantly learning more and more about how heredity, the passing on of characteristics, works.

At the moment of conception, every human baby receives 46 chromosomes. A **chromosome** is a tiny threadlike structure in the nucleus of every cell. These chromosomes come in 23 pairs. The father's sperm and mother's ovum each contribute one chromosome to each pair. Each chromosome has hundreds to thousands of genes. A **gene** is a unit that determines a human's inherited characteristics. The complete blueprint for the creation of a person is called a **genome**. The complex molecules that make up genes are called **DNA** (deoxyribonucleic acid).

{ Expert Advice... }

"The development of a baby is quite an intricate journey. From the moment that the egg and sperm meet, a baby is beginning the developmental process. This early part of development lays the foundation for a healthy pregnancy and the birth of a healthy baby."

— The American Pregnancy Association

Isolated Communities and Genetic Diseases

Isolated communities, especially those on islands, often have few people. This means that residents might marry individuals to whom they are at least distantly related. The South Atlantic island of Tristan da Cunha, or simply Tristan to residents, is one such community. All 300 residents of Tristan are cousins. Genetic disease is widespread, and over half of Tristan's residents have asthma.

Close relatives are likely to have similar genetic combinations, which means that their children are more likely to have genetic diseases. These diseases are less likely to appear in places with large numbers of people where parents typically are not related to one another.

⭐ **Build Connections** *Do you think that the residents of Tristan da Cunha should make their genetic information available for scientific research? Explain your answer.*

NCSS I A Culture Analyze and explain the ways groups, societies, and cultures address human needs and concerns.

A human's 46 chromosomes form that person's unique DNA. No two people, except identical twins, have identical DNA.

Dominant and Recessive Genes For each inherited characteristic, a person receives two copies of a gene. One copy comes from the mother and one from the father. When both genes are the same, the child automatically has that characteristic. In many cases, a person receives two different genes. What factors determine the characteristic that person will express? The characteristic is controlled by the dominant gene. A *dominant gene* is a stronger gene. The *recessive gene* is a weaker gene. The recessive gene will not be expressed. The terms *dominant* and *recessive* only refer to the relationship of genes to each other. It does not mean that one characteristic is actually weaker than another.

Some people may not look much like their mother or father. They may look a lot like one of their grandparents, though. Some traits may skip a generation when recessive genes are inherited. For example, red hair often skips a generation because the gene for red hair is recessive. A recessive gene is only expressed when it is received from both parents.

Most traits are influenced by multiple genes. Height, weight, personality, and intelligence are examples of these traits. They are determined by a specific combination of genes that are brought together at conception. See the Science in Action feature on page 97 for more information.

Making a Unique Person Heredity explains why people in the same family often look alike. You may have a friend who looks a lot like his or her sibling. Heredity also explains why two family members can look quite different.

Each sperm and egg cell contains a different combination of genes. When these genes combine, they make a unique individual. That is why one child in a family can have light brown hair and another can have black or blonde hair. If each child in a family inherited the same genes from both parents, all of the children in the family would look exactly the same.

The gender of the child is determined at conception. The sex chromosomes come in two types, X and Y. Each ovum in the woman's ovaries carries an X chromosome. Each sperm cell in the man's body carries either an X or a Y chromosome. If the sperm that fertilizes the egg carries an X chromosome, the child receives an X chromosome from each parent. A child with the XX combination is a girl. If the sperm carries a Y chromosome, the child receives an X chromosome from the mother and a Y chromosome from the father. A child with the XY combination is a boy.

Multiple Births

The number of children a woman will give birth to at one time is determined at conception or soon after. When a woman gives birth to more than one child at a time, it is called a *multiple birth*. The most common instance of multiple births is twins.

There are two types of twins: identical and fraternal. When a sperm fertilizes a woman's ovum, the cell begins to divide right away. As the cells continue to divide, the mass of cells may split in half, creating two separate cell masses. Each cell mass continues to divide and grow into a separate embryo. The result is identical twins. Because only one ovum and sperm were involved in conception, identical twins have very similar physical characteristics and are always the same gender.

Fraternal twins form when two eggs are released from the ovaries at the same time and are fertilized by two different sperm. Because of the different eggs and sperm, fraternal twins may not look alike. They just happen to be in the mother's uterus at the same time. It is common for fraternal twins to be opposite genders.

In a general population, three in 100 births, or about 3 percent, are twins. Identical twins are much less common than fraternal twins. Out of 1,000 births, about 23 will be fraternal twins and about four will be identical twins.

The birth of three or more babies is much more rare than the birth of twins. However, a rise in the use of treatments to help women become pregnant has increased the frequency of multiple births. One potential drawback to some of these treatments is that they can cause more than one egg to be released at a time, making multiple births more likely. The more children a pregnant woman carries, the more difficult it is for all of them to survive.

Infertility

Not all couples who want to become parents are able to have a child. These couples are considered infertile. **Infertility** is the inability to conceive a child. There are many causes of infertility in both men and women. About 40 percent of cases are due to female infertility, and about 40 percent are due to male infertility. The other 20 percent have unknown causes or are linked to both partners.

Science in Action

Understanding Genetic Traits

All people have physical traits that are controlled by the genes they inherit. For each trait, one gene comes from the father, and one comes from the mother. Whether a physical trait is related to a dominate or recessive gene determines the chances of a child inheriting it.

Procedure

Suppose that two parents each have a dominant gene for brown hair and a recessive gene for red hair. Fill in the following table with the child's four possible gene combinations.

	Mother	
Father	BROWN	red
BROWN		
red		

Possible gene combinations of child

Analysis

1. What are the chances (in percent) of this child having red hair?
2. What are the chances of brown hair?
3. What are the chances of blonde hair?

NSES C Develop an understanding of the cell; molecular basis of heredity; and biological evolution.

Multiple Births
Twins may be identical or fraternal. *What is the difference between the two types of twins?*

People with infertility problems may feel isolated or abnormal. There are support groups available to help couples in this situation. Also, advances in medicine have helped couples overcome infertility. The treatments used depend on the cause. For example, a doctor can prescribe medication when a woman's ovaries do not release an ovum each month. Some fertility medications, however, can cause uncomfortable or potentially serious side effects, and require the careful supervision of a doctor. As time passes, research is improving the safety and effectiveness of a variety of infertility treatments.

Options for Infertile Couples

After attempts to treat infertility, some couples still cannot conceive a child. There are several other options they may discuss with each other and with their doctors:

- **Adoption** By adopting a child, a couple legally takes on all responsibilities and rights for raising, loving, and caring for a child in need of a permanent home.
- **Artificial Insemination** In this process, a doctor injects sperm into a woman's uterus. This procedure is timed to take place when a woman's ovary releases an ovum. Often, the sperm is from the woman's husband.

If the spouse has a genetic disorder that prevents his sperm from being used, sperm from a male donor can be used.

- **In Vitro Fertilization** This process is used to treat many causes of infertility, such as when a woman has damaged fallopian tubes. With the help of a microscope, the doctor combines a mature ovum from the woman with sperm from her husband. If the ovum becomes fertilized, the doctor places it in the woman's uterus. Pregnancy occurs if the fertilized egg attaches itself to the uterus.
- **Ovum Transfer** This procedure is similar to in vitro fertilization, except an ovum has been donated by another woman. The ovum is fertilized in a laboratory and placed in the mother's uterus. This procedure is an option for women who lack working ovaries, have poor ovum quality, or who have inherited disorders.
- **Surrogate Mother** A **surrogate** ('sər-ə-ˌgāt) is a substitute. A surrogate mother is a woman who becomes pregnant to have a baby for another woman. This option requires legal arrangements be made for everyone involved, including the child. Each state has laws regarding surrogate motherhood.

Questions Raised

Medical specialists can help some infertile couples. Infertility treatments are often very expensive. Medical insurance plans may exclude or limit coverage for these treatments.

As technology and knowledge continue to advance, other options for the treatment of infertility may be discovered. However, personal beliefs may limit a couple's options. Not everyone believes that these alternatives are acceptable. The use of surrogate mothers or sperm and ovum donors is considered **controversial**, or causing opposing views. These practices raise many moral questions. New procedures in the future will raise questions as well.

✓ Reading Check **Recall** What is the most common type of multiple birth?

Three Stages of Pregnancy

The baby's development during a pregnancy is called **prenatal development**. It is often grouped into three stages, called the germinal stage, embryonic stage, and fetal stage. Different developmental milestones are reached during each of the three stages. **Figure 4.2** on pages 102–103 shows month-by-month development of each stage.

The Germinal Stage

The germinal stage is the first stage in a baby's development. It includes the formation of the zygote. The **zygote** ('zī-ˌgōt) is the fertilized egg. This stage lasts only about two weeks, but includes the key steps in establishing a pregnancy.

Cell Division

The zygote begins to grow by cell division while it is still in the Fallopian tube. The single cell splits into two cells. Then the two cells rapidly multiply to four, then to eight, and so on. Within a few days, the zygote has grown to about 500 living cells. After about four days of growth and slow movement, the zygote reaches the opening to the uterus.

Implantation

The lining of the uterus has now thickened enough to provide a place for the zygote to attach itself and continue to grow. The zygote implants in the lining of the uterus and is covered by that lining. Despite the rapid growth of the zygote during the two weeks after fertilization, it is only the size of the head of a pin. Although it is barely big enough to see without a microscope, it is ready to grow into a fully developed human being.

Infertility
Consulting a doctor is the first step for couples who suspect a problem with infertility. *Why would a couple want to consult a doctor if they were having problems conceiving?*

➡ **Embryo Attaches to Uterus**
The embryo must become implanted in the lining of the uterus in order to grow. *What stage does this occur in?*

Fallopian Tube

Embryo

Ovary

Uterus

The Embryonic Stage

The second stage of pregnancy is the embryonic stage. The **embryo** is what the developing baby is called from about the third week of pregnancy through the eighth week. The embryo grows rapidly during this time. It is also during this stage that many important and amazing changes occur. It is during the first eight weeks that the face, eyes, ears, limbs, and bones begin to form.

Organs and Body Systems

The cells begin to separate and develop into the major systems of the human body. These systems include the heart, lungs, bones, and muscles. However, these internal organs and their systems are not yet ready to function. They will continue to develop throughout the pregnancy.

About 27 days after conception, the neural tube has closed. The neural tube is a tube in the back of the developing baby that will become the brain and spinal cord.

At this point, the brain begins to take control of the various body systems. By about the sixth week after conception, the connections between the brain and the spine allow the first movements of the embryo. The developing brain is sensitive to damage from any drugs or alcohol the mother might take. This is especially true at this crucial stage. It is vital that a pregnant woman avoid these substances throughout her pregnancy.

Amniotic Sac

A sac filled with liquid forms around the embryo. The liquid that surrounds and protects the developing baby in the uterus is called **amniotic fluid** (ˌam-nē-'ä-tik). The amniotic sac is formed from special layers of cells in the uterus. It cushions the embryo from any bumps or falls that the mother might have. At this point in development, the embryo is still very small (about 1 inch, or 2.5 cm, long). It can float freely in the amniotic fluid.

Placenta and Umbilical Cord

Also at this stage, the placenta (plə-'sen-tə) develops. The **placenta** is a tissue that connects the developing baby to the uterus. It is formed from special layers of cells in the uterus. The placenta is rich in blood vessels that allow food and oxygen to flow to the baby.

The placenta's job is to absorb oxygen and nourishment from the mother's blood to be sent to the baby through the umbilical cord. The **umbilical cord** is a long tube that connects the baby to the placenta. The umbilical cord also takes carbon dioxide and other waste products away from the baby. These waste products go to the placenta, which releases them into the mother's bloodstream.

The umbilical cord is usually stiff and firm, like a garden hose filled with water. It is generally not flexible enough to loop around the fetus, although this may occur in rare cases. The placenta and umbilical cord provide all of a baby's needs until birth.

The Fetal Stage

The fetal stage is the third and final stage of development. It is also the longest stage. It begins around the eighth or ninth week of pregnancy and lasts until birth. During this stage, the developing baby is called a **fetus** ('fē-təs). The vocal cords develop, and the digestive system and kidneys begin to function. **Spontaneous**, or unplanned, movements are possible by the end of the third month.

Making Movements

Sometime during the fourth or fifth month, the kicks and other movements of the fetus touch the wall of the uterus. These movements are faint and infrequent at first. These are usually the first fetal movements that the mother can feel. She may feel the movement as a kind of fluttering, like a butterfly. Gradually, these sensations become stronger and more frequent, letting the mother know that she really is carrying a live child within her.

A pregnant woman's doctor usually asks her when she first felt these movements. This information helps the doctor estimate the baby's age and make sure the baby is developing normally. This information can also be used to help project an accurate due date.

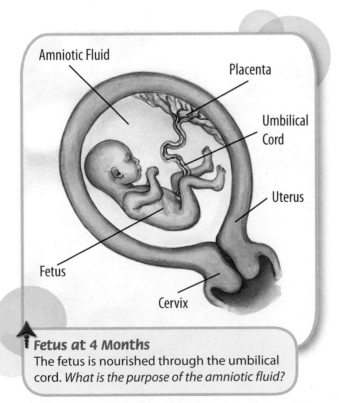

↑ Fetus at 4 Months
The fetus is nourished through the umbilical cord. *What is the purpose of the amniotic fluid?*

Labels on diagram: Amniotic Fluid, Placenta, Umbilical Cord, Uterus, Cervix, Fetus

Sometimes a fetus will roll or stretch just to get more comfortable. A fetus will also move in response to loud noises or familiar voices. Many parents talk, read, or sing to the developing fetus to encourage movement. This also helps the fetus become familiar with the parents' voices. The baby can recognize these voices after birth.

Completing Development

During the last few months of pregnancy, development continues, preparing the fetus to live independently. By the seventh month, the baby is capable of living outside the uterus, but only with a lot of medical help.

The body's major organs become ready to function without any help from the mother's body. The fetus also gains weight quickly. Fat deposits are formed under the skin. These will help the baby hold body heat after delivery. The fetus goes from thin and wrinkled to the smoother, rounder appearance of a baby. The fetus also stores nutrients and builds immunity to diseases and infections.

By the eighth month of pregnancy, the fetus sleeps about 90 percent of the day. Brain scans have shown rapid eye movement (REM) in some fetuses during this time. That means that fetuses can dream while they sleep!

Staying Active

The fetus can do a surprising number of things. It uses all five senses. It can suck its thumb, cough, sneeze, yawn, kick, and hiccup. A fetus can even cry. Even though the uterus is crowded, the fetus is still very active and can change positions. Sometimes, around the eighth month, babies will lodge their feet between their mother's ribs. This can be painful for the mother. She can often dislodge the foot with gentle exercises or stretches. Once the baby has moved down, in the ninth month, he usually cannot reach this high anymore.

During the eighth month of pregnancy, the baby should settle into the proper position for delivery. This means the head is angled down to lead the way out of the uterus. The baby will continue to kick and stretch though. By the ninth month, these kicks can be quite powerful, and sometimes painful for the mother.

Figure 4.2 Fetal Development Month by Month

The fetus develops in the uterus for approximately nine months. *When does hair begin to appear?*

Month 1
❖ Size: At two weeks, the size of a pin head.
❖ Egg attaches to lining of uterus.
❖ Critical stage for brain and spinal cord development.
❖ Internal organs and circulatory system begin to form.
❖ The heart begins to beat.

Month 2
❖ Size: About ¼ inch (6 mm) long as month begins.
❖ Face, eyes, ears, and limbs take shape.
❖ Bones begin to form.

Month 3
❖ Size: About 1 inch (25 mm) long as month begins.
❖ Nostrils, mouth, lips, and eyelids form.
❖ Buds for all 20 baby teeth appear.
❖ Fingers and toes almost complete.
❖ All organs present but still immature.

Month 4
❖ Size: About 3 inches (7.6 cm) long, weighs 1 ounce (28 g) as month begins.
❖ Can suck its thumb, swallow, hiccup, and move around.
❖ Facial features become clearer.

Month 5
❖ Size: About 6½–7 inches (16–18 cm) long, weighs about 4–5 ounces (113–142 g) as month begins.
❖ Hair, eyelashes, and eyebrows appear.
❖ Teeth continue to develop.
❖ Organs are maturing.
❖ Becomes more active.

Month 6
✤ Size: About 8–10 inches (21–25 cm) long, weighs about 8–12 ounces (227–340 g) as month begins.
✤ Fat deposits under skin, but fetus appears wrinkled.
✤ Breathing movements begin.

Month 7
✤ Size: About 10–12 inches (25–31 cm) long, weighs about 1½–2 pounds (680–907 g) as month begins.
✤ Has periods of activity followed by periods of rest and quiet.

Month 8
✤ Size: About 14–16 inches (36–41 cm) long, weighs about 2½–3 pounds (1.0–1.4 kg) as month begins.
✤ Rapid weight gain continues.
✤ May react to loud noises with a reflex jerking action.
✤ Moves into a head-down position.

Month 9
✤ Size: About 17–18 inches (43–46 cm) long, weighs about 5–6 pounds (2.3–2.7 kg) as month begins.
✤ Weight gain continues.
✤ Skin becomes smooth as fat deposits continue.
✤ Movements decrease as the fetus has less room to move around.
✤ Acquires disease-fighting antibodies from the mother's blood.
✤ Descends into pelvis, ready for birth.

Growing Bigger

As the fetus grows, so does the amount of surrounding amniotic fluid. The uterus also expands, causing the woman's stomach to grow. When the fetus grows large during the last few months of pregnancy, it no longer has room to stretch out. It curls up in what is called the fetal position. This means the baby is curled into a ball. The head is bowed forward and the arms and legs are drawn in.

Ready for Birth

The common length of pregnancy is about 40 weeks, or 280 days, from the first day of the last menstrual cycle. By the ninth month, the fetus is fully developed and can usually survive outside the mother's body with little medical assistance. Some babies are born either a few weeks early or a few weeks late. This is usually not a problem. Advances in technology allow many babies to survive that are born early.

Fetus at 9 Months
As the end of pregnancy nears the fetus is folded in the fetal position. *Given its current position in the uterus, how will this baby be positioned when it is born?*

Section 4.1 After You Read

Review Key Concepts

1. **Describe** two options for an infertile couple that wants children.
2. **Explain** how the developing baby receives oxygen and nutrition during the second and third stages of prenatal development?

Practice Academic Skills

 English Language Arts

3. Ask students to interview a mother with two or more children. They should ask questions such as: How were the pregnancies different? Did you have any worries about each baby's health? Have students create a chart comparing the mother's experiences.

> **NCTE 7** Conduct research and gather, evaluate, and synthesize data to communicate discoveries.

 Social Studies

4. Attitudes about pregnancy and pregnant women have changed over the years. Pregnant women were treated differently in the past. Conduct research to find out how pregnancy was viewed in the United States in the 1950s. Include print or online resources, and consider talking to older family members about their memories. Write a paragraph comparing these attitudes to today's attitudes.

> **NCSS II B** Apply key concepts such as time and change to analyze and show connections among patterns of historical change and continuity.

 Check Your Answers Check your answers at this book's Online Learning Center at **glencoe.com**.

Section 4.2 Problems in Prenatal Development

Reading Guide

Before You Read

Adjust Your Reading Speed Learning to adjust your reading speed can help you remember information. Reading more slowly can help you to understand more complex concepts.

Read to Learn
Key Concepts
- **Contrast** miscarriage and stillbirth.
- **Identify** how ten major birth defects can be diagnosed.

Main Idea
Not all pregnancies end in the birth of a healthy infant. Some end early with the unborn baby's death. Some babies are born with health problems.

Content Vocabulary
◇ miscarriage
◇ stillbirth
◇ ultrasound
◇ amniocentesis

Academic Vocabulary
You will find these words in your reading and on your tests. Use the glossary to look up their definitions if necessary.
■ predisposition
■ serious

Graphic Organizer
As you read, look for types of prenatal tests that can be used to check for birth defects. Use a chart like the one shown to help organize your information.

Prenatal Tests

 Graphic Organizer Go to this book's Online Learning Center at **glencoe.com** to print out this graphic organizer.

Academic Standards ·

 English Language Arts

NCTE 8 Use information resources to gather information and create and communicate knowledge.

Science

NSES A Develop abilities necessary to do scientific inquiry, understanding about scientific inquiry.

NCTE *National Council of Teachers of English*
NCTM *National Council of Teachers of Mathematics*

NSES *National Science Education Standards*
NCSS *National Council for the Social Studies*

Losing a Baby

Will the baby be healthy? This is a major concern for all expectant parents. Most babies develop normally and are born healthy. However, sometimes the baby does not develop normally. Sometimes the developing baby dies. When the developing baby dies prior to the twentieth week of pregnancy, the event is called a **miscarriage**. If the baby dies after the twentieth week, it is called a **stillbirth**.

Unfortunately, miscarriages are fairly common. About 15 percent of recognized pregnancies end in miscarriage. Medical professionals do not completely understand the causes.

Stillbirth occurs in about 2 percent of pregnancies. The most common causes are problems with the placenta, abnormal chromosomes, poor growth, and infections.

Dealing with Grief

The loss of a child by miscarriage or stillbirth can be very unexpected and painful for the parents. Most couples look forward to a baby's birth. They feel a great sense of attachment long before the birth. When they lose their baby, they may go through stages of grief similar to those experienced by the loss of a child that was already born. Sometimes these parents feel alone, and may blame themselves for the death. In most cases, however, these deaths are completely beyond the parents' control. Couples may need support to work through their grief. Most couples who suffer a miscarriage or stillbirth are able to have healthy children later.

✓ **Reading Check** **Recall** What percentage of pregnancies end in miscarriage?

Birth Defects

Some babies survive pregnancy, but are born with serious problems that threaten their health or even their lives. A serious problem that threatens a baby's health, and is present at birth, is called a birth defect. There are hundreds of types of birth defects, each with its own set of symptoms. Some are so mild that no one would ever know the child has a birth defect. Others can result in lifelong disabilities or even death.

Approximately 120,000 babies are born each year in the United States with a birth defect. Scientists and medical professionals are working hard to understand the causes of birth defects. They hope that knowing the causes will help to decrease the number of babies born with birth defects, and improve the lives of children with birth defects.

↑ Losing a Baby
Sadly, some pregnancies end in a miscarriage or stillbirth. *Do you think experiencing a miscarriage would be different from a stillbirth? Why?*

For some couples, thinking of having a baby brings up concerns about genetic birth defects. This typically happens when the diseases seem to occur in the family of one or both of the parents. The couple should share their concerns with their family doctor or obstetrician. If there is a family history of one specific disease or symptoms of a genetic disorder, individuals may wish to be tested.

There are different types of genetic testing. Prior to pregnancy, testing can determine whether a person carries the traits for cystic fibrosis, Tay-Sachs disease, or sickle cell. If needed, the doctor can refer the couple to a genetic counselor. The counselor can discuss with the couple the likelihood of their passing on the condition, and the various options.

Critical Thinking Research the ethical, legal, and social issues regarding genetic testing. Then write a report in which you analyze how these issues can affect a couple's decision concerning whether to have children.

Types and Causes of Birth Defects

Some birth defects cause an abnormality in the structure of the body. For example, an affected baby might have a misshapen foot, or an extra or missing finger. Other birth defects cause one or more systems of the body not to function properly. Blindness, deafness, and mental retardation are examples.

Not all birth defects are obvious at birth. Sometimes the abnormality is not discovered until months or years later. **Figure 4.3** on pages 108–109 describes types of birth defects as well as their causes, how to detect them, and treatment for them.

Scientists do not fully understand the causes of most birth defects. However, research continues to be done to find out why the defects occur. Scientists hope this understanding will lead to cures for the defects. So far, they have determined that there are four main causes for birth defects:

- Factors in the environment
- Hereditary factors
- Errors in chromosomes
- A combination of environmental and hereditary factors.

Research is continuing in each area.

Environmental Causes

In the first few weeks after conception, a baby develops all the bodily systems needed for survival and a healthy, normal life. During this time, the baby depends on the mother's body for nourishment and oxygen.

This early development of the embryo is critical. Many choices the mother makes can affect the lifelong health of her baby. Some of these choices can occur before she even knows she is pregnant.

There may be environmental factors that the mother is unaware of that can affect the development of the baby. Here is a list of some of the environmental causes of birth defects. Which of these factors do you think the mother can control?

- The nutritional balance of the mother's diet.
- Any diseases or infections the mother has during pregnancy.
- Harmful substances the mother consumes, such as alcohol, over-the-counter medications, tobacco, and illegal drugs.
- Some medicines that benefit the mother but hurt the baby.
- Air pollution.
- Exposure to X-rays and high levels of radiation, or to certain chemicals such as solvents and pesticides, especially early in pregnancy.

Figure 4.3 Birth Defects

A birth defect can be a serious threat to a baby's health. *Which of these birth defects can be detected before the baby is born?*

Birth Defect	Causes	Detections	Treatments
Cerebral Palsy *A general term for a variety of problems of the motor system. Symptoms can include lack of coordination, stiffness, difficulty with speech, and paralysis.*	Causes vary but include damage to the brain before, during, or shortly after birth.	Motor skills are typically slow to develop during the first year of life.	Damage caused to the brain is irreversible. Physical therapy, speech therapy, surgery, and medication can often lessen the effects.
Cleft Lip and Cleft Palate *A gap in the upper lip or palate (the roof of the mouth) that causes problems with eating, swallowing, speech, and appearance.*	May be caused by hereditary, environmental factors, or both.	Conditions are apparent at birth. Often detectable by ultrasound before birth.	Surgery corrects the gap and helps eliminate problems associated with it.
Cystic Fibrosis (CF) *Affects respiratory and digestive systems. Many with CF die before adulthood, although treatment now allows sufferers to live longer.*	Caused by inheriting defective recessive genes from both parents. Most commonly affects Caucasians.	Blood tests can identify carriers of the gene. Sweat tests can diagnose an affected child.	No known cure. Special diets, lung exercises, therapies, and medication can treat symptoms.
Down Syndrome *A group of problems that may include mental retardation; heart, blood, and digestive system difficulties; and poor muscle tone.*	The presence of an extra chromosome 21.	Can be detected in a fetus by amniocentesis or chorionic villi sampling, or after birth with a blood test.	No known cure. Treatment includes therapy, special educational assistance, and in some cases corrective surgery.
Muscular Dystrophy *There are many different types; all involve a progressive weakness and shrinking of the muscles. Most common form begins between the ages of two and six.*	Most types are hereditary. Most common form is transmitted by female carriers of the gene but affects only males.	Recognizable once symptoms appear. Genetic counseling can identify carriers.	No known cure. Physical therapy can minimize the disabilities.

Birth Defect	Causes	Detections	Treatments
PKU (phenylketonuria) *Condition in which the body is unable to process and use a specific protein present in nearly all foods. Brain damage and mental retardation can result.*	Defective recessive genes inherited from both parents.	Newborns are tested for PKU, as required by law in all states.	No known cure. If diagnosed early, a special diet can reduce or prevent brain damage.
Sickle Cell Anemia *Malformed red blood cells interfere with the supply of oxygen to all parts of the body. Symptoms include tiredness, lack of appetite, and pain. Can lead to early death.*	Defective recessive genes inherited from both parents. Most common in African Americans.	Genetic counseling can identify parents who carry the gene. Amniocentesis or chorionic villi sampling can identify it in a fetus. Blood tests can detect it after birth.	No known cure. Medication can help treat the symptoms.
Spina Bifida and Hydrocephalus *In spina bifida, an incompletely formed spinal cord may lead to stiff joints, partial paralysis, and problems with the kidneys and urinary tract. Seventy of every 100 children with spina bifida also have hydrocephalus, in which an excess of fluid surrounds the brain.*	Seems to be a combination of hereditary and environmental factors. Taking a folic acid supplement during pregnancy may reduce incidence.	Spina bifida is apparent at birth. Hydrocephalus is indicated by overly rapid growth of the head. Tests of the mother's blood, amniocentesis, and ultrasound can reveal suspected cases in a fetus.	Corrective surgery, physical therapy, and special schooling can minimize disabilities caused by spina bifida. Hydrocephalus can be helped by surgically implanting a shunt that relieves fluid build-up.
Tay-Sachs Disease *Caused by the lack of a specific chemical in the baby's blood. The body cannot process and use certain fats. This leads to severe brain damage and death, usually by age four.*	Defective recessive genes inherited from both parents. Most common in families of eastern European Jewish descent.	Amniocentesis or chorionic villi sampling can identify it in a fetus. Blood tests can identify carriers and can test for the condition after birth.	No known cure. Treatment involves trying to make the child comfortable.

Hereditary Causes

Every person has approximately 20,000 to 25,000 genes that determine traits, such as eye color and height. These genes also direct the growth and development of all body systems. Half of the genes come from the mother and half from the father. It is normal for children to get five or six imperfect recessive genes passed on to them.

In most cases, a single copy of a faulty recessive gene will have no effect on the baby's development. However, sometimes both parents will pass on the same faulty recessive gene. This causes the baby to have a birth defect. When this happens, it is called *recessive inheritance*. Two conditions caused by recessive inheritance are Tay-Sachs disease and cystic fibrosis.

Sometimes a child will inherit a defective gene that is dominant. It is only necessary for this gene to be passed on by one parent for the child to have the resulting birth defect. This is called *dominant inheritance*. Huntington's disease, a birth defect that does not appear until middle age, is caused by dominant inheritance.

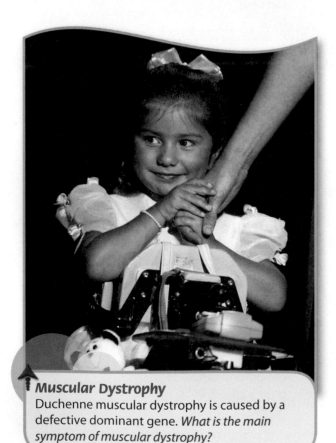

Muscular Dystrophy
Duchenne muscular dystrophy is caused by a defective dominant gene. *What is the main symptom of muscular dystrophy?*

Some inherited conditions only affect one gender. Hemophilia is a condition that prevents the blood from clotting. Like color blindness and Duchenne muscular dystrophy, hemophilia usually only affects males.

Errors in Chromosomes

Several types of birth defects are caused by problems in the number or structure of chromosomes. An error may occur when an egg or sperm cell is developing. This can cause a baby to have too many or too few chromosomes, or to have broken or rearranged chromosomes. These are not hereditary defects because neither parent has the abnormal chromosome.

The most common birth defect of this type is Down syndrome. A child with Down syndrome may have some degree of mental retardation, plus physical problems. One in 800 babies has this condition. Under normal conditions, each sperm and egg cell carries 23 chromosomes. Sometimes an error occurs when an egg or sperm cell is forming, causing an extra copy of chromosome 21. Instead of having two copies of chromosome 21, the child has three. Because each chromosome carries hundreds of genes, the defect can interfere with development in many ways. This includes an increased risk of heart defects and leukemia, poor muscle tone, vision and hearing problems, delayed physical growth and motor development, and distinctive physical characteristics. The risk for having a child with Down syndrome is higher for mothers over the age of 35.

Interaction of Heredity and Environment

Some birth defects are caused by a combination of heredity and the environment. For example, a child may inherit a tendency that may later lead to a heart defect. If a factor such as a drug or virus affects the baby during pregnancy, the baby will have the heart defect. If the baby did not inherit the gene for the heart defect *or* did not get exposed to the drug or virus, the heart would be normal. Because both the inherited factor and the environmental factor were present, the baby's heart had a defect.

Birth defects such as cleft lip, cleft palate, and spina bifida may be caused by a combination of hereditary and environmental fac-

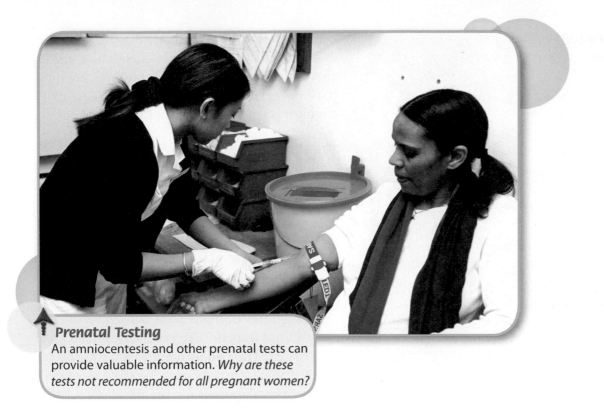

Prenatal Testing
An amniocentesis and other prenatal tests can provide valuable information. *Why are these tests not recommended for all pregnant women?*

tors. See Figure 4.3 on pages 108–109 for more information on these birth defects. Both cleft lip and cleft palate may be caused by a number of inherited genes joined with exposure during pregnancy to certain medications, infections, illnesses, or tobacco or alcohol. A genetic **predisposition**, or tendency, for spina bifida, combined with the use of certain medications during pregnancy, will increase the chance of a child having the defect.

Prevention and Diagnosis of Birth Defects

It can be challenging for a child born with a **serious**, or severe, birth defect to lead a normal, productive life. Other family members are affected by the emotional and financial strain the defect causes. However, advances in treatment and support groups are helping children and their families cope. Not all causes of birth defects can be anticipated or controlled. There are several things that couples can do, though, to lessen the chances of having a child with birth defects.

Couples who are planning to become parents should get a checkup to evaluate their overall health before trying to conceive. They can discuss lifestyle changes that may improve their chances for a healthy baby. For example, women should stop using tobacco and alcohol prior to pregnancy. Both of these can lead to health problems and birth defects.

Because many women do not know they are pregnant in the early weeks, it is safer to quit smoking and drinking before there is a possibility of pregnancy. Men are also advised to avoid or drink less alcohol, since it has been linked to low sperm count.

Once a woman is pregnant, she should visit her doctor for prenatal care. This care helps ensure a successful pregnancy. The doctor can monitor the mother's health and the baby's growth and development throughout the pregnancy. The mother should continue to avoid substances such as alcohol, drugs, and tobacco. She can talk to her doctor or pharmacist about the effects of any over-the-counter and prescription medications on her baby. A pregnant woman should not take any medication without her doctor's approval.

Genetic Counseling

Some people seek genetic counseling to assess their risk of having a child with a birth defect that is caused by a defect in the genes.

Down Syndrome
The fluid obtained from amniocentesis can be used to check chromosomes. *In these chromosomes, Down syndrome is shown by what unusual circumstance?*

There may be a history of birth defects in the family. Some couples may already have a child with a birth defect and want to learn more about the risks for future children. Genetic counselors can explain the options and risks.

Family doctors can perform genetic counseling, but most patients are referred to a genetic counselor. This specialist usually begins by evaluating the family history of both members of the couple. This includes information such as the medical histories, diseases, and causes of death of all known family members.

Along with the family history, a genetic counselor will usually request a physical exam for both parents. If specific birth defects are of concern, some other members of the family may receive physical exams as well. Special lab tests may also be performed. Small samples of blood and body tissue may be analyzed. For example, a blood sample can be tested to determine whether the parents are carriers for the gene that causes cystic fibrosis.

Once all of the testing is complete, the genetic counselor can usually tell the couple what their risks are for having a child with certain genetic birth defects. It is the couple's decision whether or not to have children. If they do, they will be aware of extra testing that may be needed during pregnancy to closely monitor the development of the baby.

Prenatal Tests

More than 100 kinds of birth defects can now be detected before a baby is born. There are many tests that are standard for prenatal care in this country. These help a doctor decide whether or not a baby might have a birth defect. These tests can help determine what treatments, if any, are needed for the child before or after birth.

Sometimes prenatal tests are simple blood tests. Other tests involve procedures that carry more risks. The couple must weigh the potential value of the information to be gained against possible risks for the developing baby or the mother. Here are examples of some common prenatal tests.

Alpha-fetoprotein (AFP) This blood test is performed on the expectant mother between weeks 15 and 20 of a pregnancy. AFP is a protein produced in the liver of the fetus that is evident in the mother's blood. Abnormal AFP levels can indicate a possible birth defect. Further testing can be done to determine if a birth defect does exist, and what it might be.

Ultrasound Ultrasound is a test that uses sound waves to make a video image of an unborn baby. This image is called a *sonogram*. It can help the doctor monitor the development of the baby, pinpoint the baby's age, and detect certain birth defects. Problems with the baby's skeletal, circulatory, or nervous system may be detected during an ultrasound. The sonogram also helps confirm the due date and the presence of more than one fetus.

Many women will have an ultrasound during their pregnancy, usually near the 20th week. Many doctors now do 3D ultrasounds, which give more detailed images and information about the baby's development. Research has shown that an ultrasound poses no threat to the unborn child or the mother. However, it should be performed only when there is a valid medical reason for doing so.

Amniocentesis The process of withdrawing a sample of the amniotic fluid surrounding the unborn baby is called **amniocentesis** (ˌam-nē-ō-(ˌ)sen-ˈtē-səs). The doctor uses the view from an ultrasound to guide a needle through the mother's abdomen into the amniotic sac. Some cells from the fetus are in the amniotic fluid. These cells are then taken to a lab and tested for evidence of birth defects and other health problems.

Amniocentesis is most often used as a test for Down syndrome when the expectant mother is age 35 or older. The test may also be given if uncertain results have been obtained from an ultrasound or AFP blood test. Amniocentesis involves some risk to the fetus and is performed only when there is a strong medical reason to do so. It can be done between the 15th and 20th week of pregnancy.

Chorionic Villi Sampling A prenatal test that uses a sample of the tissue from the membrane that encases the fetus to check for specific birth defects is called chorionic villi sampling (ˌkȯr-ē-ˈä-nik ˈvi-ˌlī). Samples of the tissue are cut or suctioned off and analyzed.

Chorionic villi sampling tests for the same disorders as amniocentesis. This test does not detect neural tube defects though. It is used less often because its risks are greater. One advantage is that it can be done much earlier in the pregnancy than amniocentesis. Chorionic villi sampling is usually done between the 10th and 12th week of pregnancy.

New Prenatal Diagnosis Several methods of prenatal diagnosis are now in experimental stages. These may someday provide more accurate information earlier in a pregnancy. For example, it is possible to view the fetus directly through a special instrument called a *laparoscope*. Doctors can get samples of fetal blood and tissue, and even do surgery on an unborn child. Currently, these procedures carry a risk. New technology may make these procedures safe for widespread use in the future.

Section 4.2 — After You Read

Review Key Concepts

1. **Summarize** the causes of stillbirth.
2. **List** the four categories of birth defects.

Practice Academic Skills

 English Language Arts

3. Studies show that taking prenatal vitamins with folic acid can help prevent birth defects. Research the amounts of folic acid recommended and how it can help prevent defects. Use the information from your research to create a handout promoting the use of prenatal vitamins. Use art or photos to make your handout visually appealing.

> **NCTE 8** Use information resources to gather information and create and communicate knowledge.

 Science

4. Choose one of the birth defects listed in Figure 4.3. Use print or online resources to learn about the current research being done on the causes or treatments of this birth defect. Write a brief report explaining what you learned.

> **NSES A** Develop abilities necessary to do scientific inquiry, understanding about scientific inquiry.

 Check Your Answers Check your answers at this book's Online Learning Center at **glencoe.com**.

Reading Guide

Before You Read

Categorize Before reading, skim this section to determine whether the dangers to baby can be placed into categories. As you read, categorize each type of danger to help you see the big picture.

Read to Learn
Key Concepts
- **Summarize** the hazards that alcohol and other drugs pose to prenatal development.
- **Assess** why environmental hazards must be avoided during pregnancy.
- **Describe** how a fetus can be affected by certain illnesses the mother may contract.

Main Idea
A fetus needs to be protected from many dangers. These include the mother drinking alcohol or taking other drugs, environmental hazards, diseases, and infections.

Content Vocabulary
◇ fetal alcohol syndrome (FAS)
◇ fetal alcohol effects
◇ SIDS
◇ toxoplasmosis

 Graphic Organizer Go to this book's Online Learning Center at **glencoe.com** to print out this graphic organizer.

Academic Vocabulary
You will find these words in your reading and on your tests. Use the glossary to look up their definitions if necessary.
■ deformity
■ congenital

Graphic Organizer
As you read, list examples of each of the three types of dangers that can affect a baby. Use a chart like the one shown to help organize your information. Add additional boxes as needed.

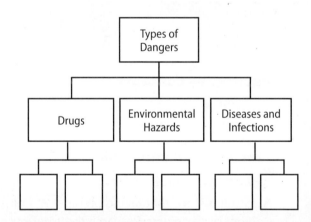

Academic Standards •

 English Language Arts
NCTE 5 Use different writing process elements to communicate effectively.

 Science
NSES F Develop understanding of personal and community health; and environmental quality.

NCTE *National Council of Teachers of English*
NCTM *National Council of Teachers of Mathematics*

NSES *National Science Education Standards*
NCSS *National Council for the Social Studies*

Effects of Alcohol and Other Drugs on Pregnancy

The mother-to-be has a big responsibility throughout her pregnancy. She must do everything possible to increase the chances of having a healthy baby. She needs to consider the effects of her actions on her unborn child. She must take care of herself physically and emotionally, and avoid potential dangers.

An essential part of good prenatal care is avoiding hazards such as alcohol and other drugs, smoking, X-rays, hazardous chemicals and other substances, and infections. Researchers and doctors believe that drugs consumed during pregnancy are among the major causes of birth defects linked to environmental factors. These drugs include:

- Alcohol, in any form.
- Prescription and over-the-counter medicines.
- Caffeine. This is found in foods such as chocolate, and beverages. The safety of caffeine during pregnancy is controversial. However, until researchers know more about its effects, it is wise to avoid caffeine.

- Nicotine and other toxic chemicals found in cigarettes.
- Illegal drugs such as heroin, LSD, ecstasy, marijuana, and cocaine.
- Inhalants. These are fumes that are inhaled into the lungs.

Alcohol

Sometimes people forget that alcohol is a drug. It is an especially dangerous one for unborn children. When a pregnant woman drinks alcohol, she puts her baby at great risk. Anything the mother consumes or inhales is passed directly to her child through the placenta. This is true for alcohol too. Even a small amount of alcohol can harm the developing systems of the baby.

Doctors do not know how much alcohol it takes to endanger a developing baby. There is no known safe amount of alcohol that a pregnant woman can drink. For this reason, most doctors recommend that women consume no alcohol when they are trying to become pregnant or during the pregnancy. Abstaining from alcohol will prevent any negative effects on the baby related to alcohol.

Drugs and Fetal Harm
Birth defects caused by drinking, smoking, and other drugs are preventable. *How do you think a mother feels if she finds out her behavior caused her child's birth defect?*

How Does Alcohol Affect a Fetus?

The dangers of alcohol to an unborn fetus may seem like common sense. Many people are unaware just how dangerous this common drug can be though.

Consuming alcohol during pregnancy can also cause serious health problems for the baby. The alcohol passes directly to the baby through the placenta. It may cause problems in development, especially that of the brain. Even small amounts of alcohol can harm the baby. Greater amounts have been linked to fetal alcohol syndrome (FAS), which causes life-long physical and mental disabilities. Expectant mothers can avoid these risks by completely avoiding alcohol during pregnancy.

Be Prepared Imagine that your aunt is pregnant and thinks it is fine to drink occasionally. Conduct research to learn more about how even occasional drinking can affect a fetus. Create a one-page report explaining why any amount of alcohol is unsafe.

Fetal alcohol syndrome (FAS) is an incurable condition found in some children of mothers who consumed alcohol during pregnancy. FAS includes a wide range of physical and mental disabilities that last a lifetime.

One in five babies born with FAS does not live to see his or her first birthday. Those who do survive can suffer many problems. These can include delayed physical growth; heart, liver, or kidney defects; hyperactivity; and facial deformity. A **deformity** is a defect in a structure.

Some babies with FAS are mentally retarded. Others have difficulties with learning, attention, memory, or problem solving. Alcohol can interfere with tissue growth and development. Brain tissue is easily injured by alcohol. Other common problems include poor coordination and difficulty controlling behavior.

Some children may suffer from fetal alcohol effects. Like FAS, **fetal alcohol effects** are abnormalities caused by the mother consuming alcohol during pregnancy. These children suffer from many of the same problems as those with FAS, but to a lesser degree.

The extent of damage to the child is often directly related to the amount of alcohol the mother consumed during pregnancy. It may also be affected by the stage of pregnancy when she drank. For example, women who binge drink in the early stages of pregnancy may have an increased risk of having a baby with FAS. Binge drinking means to drink a lot in a short amount of time. The combination of alcohol with other drugs also affects the degree of damage to the child.

Prescription Drugs and Over-the-Counter Drugs

An expectant mother should check with her doctor every time she considers using any type of medication, vitamin, or herbal supplement. There is no such thing as a completely safe drug for a developing fetus.

An extreme example of an unsafe medication is thalidomide. This drug was prescribed to women in the 1950s to relieve morning sickness. Before its devastating effects were discovered, more than 5,000 babies were born with severe birth defects, such as missing or deformed arms and legs. Had doctors known the effects of this drug, they never would have prescribed it.

More recently, a prescription medicine for acne proved harmful to unborn children. When taken during pregnancy, the drug can cause serious birth defects. Therefore, it is not prescribed for pregnant women or those who may become pregnant.

The first three months of pregnancy are the most critical because the baby's body systems, including the brain, are being formed. The chemicals found in some medications can cause severe harm, including mental retardation. This includes drugs sold without prescriptions, or over-the-counter (OTC) medications. Even something as seemingly harmless as an antacid can harm a fetus.

In the fourth through ninth months of pregnancy, harmful substances may cause slow growth, infections, or bleeding at birth. Drugs taken shortly before delivery will still be in the baby's bloodstream after birth.

Sometimes the expectant mother needs medication for a specific medical condition. For example, some women may need to take medications for epilepsy, diabetes, or high blood pressure. A pregnant woman can take these, as long as her doctor prescribes them and she takes them correctly. Medications that are not absolutely necessary should be avoided.

Caffeine

Caffeine is in the beverages many people drink each day, such as coffee, tea, cocoa, and most soft drinks. It is also present in some foods and many over-the-counter medications. Because it is consumed so frequently, caffeine is often not considered a drug, but it is.

Caffeine passes easily from a mother to her fetus through the placenta. The fetus may have higher blood levels of caffeine than the mother because of its immature metabolism. Caffeine can increase fetal heart rate and movement.

Small amounts of caffeine, such as two cups of coffee or soft drinks per day, do not appear to pose great pregnancy risks. However, larger quantities have been associated with a variety of prenatal problems. That is why most doctors advise women to avoid caffeine during pregnancy.

When women consume large amounts of caffeine during pregnancy, there is an increased risk of miscarriage, premature birth, and low birth weight. There is also a higher risk of infant death. Birth weight is a critical factor to a baby's survival. Low birth weight is a weight of less than 5 pounds, 8 ounces (2.5 kg) at birth. Babies with low birth weight may have serious health problems as newborns and are at greater risk of long-term problems.

Caffeine can draw fluid and calcium out of the body. It may also interfere with the absorption of iron. These are all vital to the health of the mother and the developing fetus. In addition, drinks with caffeine, such as coffee and tea, can make you feel full. This will spoil your appetite for nutritious foods. Soft drinks may have other chemicals and large amounts of sugar, in addition to the caffeine. The caffeine and sugar can also worsen mood swings and prevent the mother from getting needed rest.

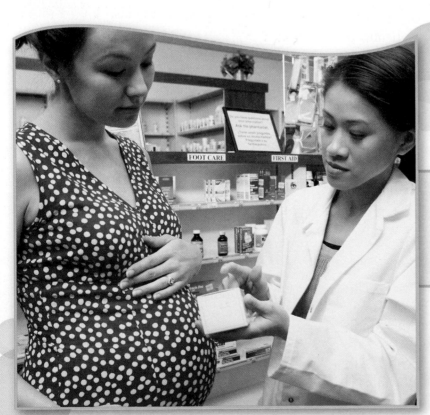

OTC Drugs and Pregnancy Even common medicines that are sold in pharmacies and supermarkets may be unsafe for an unborn baby. *How can a pregnant woman be sure that a medicine is safe?*

What Would You Do?

Stopping Smoking

Lori and her husband want to have a baby, so Lori has been exercising and watching what she eats. Unfortunately, Lori has been a smoker for several years. She knows that she needs to stop smoking before she becomes pregnant. Lori says, "I have tried almost everything to quit: the nicotine patch, other over-the-counter treatments, classes. Nothing worked. I've got to make it work this time. I want to do everything possible to improve my baby's chances for a healthy life. But it's hard when I've failed so many times in the past."

Write About It Imagine you are a friend of Lori's. Write a script in which you talk with Lori about specific problems for both her and her baby associated with smoking. Also offer tips that might help her quit. If possible, base your tips on what you have done to break a bad habit.

Tobacco

Many studies have shown that the nicotine found in tobacco is harmful to the health of any person. It is especially harmful to a baby's development before birth. Smoking has been shown to cause low birth weights. The more a mother smokes, the smaller her baby is likely to be at birth. Heavy smoking is believed to cause premature birth as well. Finally, smoking during pregnancy is linked to respiratory infections and allergies among children after they are born. Nicotine from secondhand smoke has similar effects.

Illegal Drugs

Illegal drugs should never be used. This is especially true for women who are pregnant.In addition to the effects on the mother's health, the use of illegal drugs can have devastating effects for an unborn baby. This includes cocaine, marijuana, and other illegal substances.

A mother who is addicted to a drug usually passes the addiction on to her baby. All drugs in the mother's bloodstream pass through the placenta to the baby. As a result, addicted newborns may suffer the consequences throughout their lives.

Right after birth, infants with an inherited drug addiction must go through a painful period of withdrawal. This is because the body is no longer receiving the drug upon which it depends. Babies that survive withdrawal have an uncertain future. Many experts believe that the long-term effects of prenatal addiction can be severe. Many of these children have learning and behavioral difficulties.

Cocaine has been proven to increase the risk of miscarriage when used during the early stages of pregnancy. It may also cause stillbirth or premature birth. Cocaine may cause the unborn child to have a stroke. This can result in brain damage, a heart attack, serious birth defects, or even death. Fetuses exposed to cocaine tend to have a low birth weight, smaller heads than other newborns, and a risk of seizures and sudden infant death syndrome. **SIDS**, or sudden infant death syndrome, is the sudden, unexpected death of a baby under one year of age with no clear cause. Marijuana and methamphetamine use are also linked to low birth weight and premature delivery.

Babies exposed to cocaine may also have tremors, exaggerated startle response, sleep and feeding difficulties, irritability, and developmental delay. All of these problems may persist into the school years. Use of marijuana and methamphetamines during pregnancy can cause breathing difficulties, poor attention span, drowsiness, or heart defects in children.

Researchers are still learning about the effects of the drug ecstasy on unborn children. The results are not good. Recent studies have shown that babies of women who take ecstasy are more likely to be born with heart disease or a physical abnormality. This drug is not safe to take any time, but it is especially unsafe during pregnancy.

✓ **Reading Check** **List** What kinds of drugs, other than alcohol, can harm a developing baby?

Environmental Hazards

Environmental hazards are all around us. However, they may not be obvious. For these reasons, it is vital that pregnant women be aware of them. Two possible hazards to unborn babies are X-rays and chemicals such as pesticides and mercury.

X-rays

X-rays present a potential danger to the unborn baby. Radiation from X-rays, or from other sources, can cause birth defects. There has been a great deal of debate about the safety of X-rays during pregnancy. If an X-ray is necessary due to an accident, illness, or dental work, the mother should inform the medical staff that she is pregnant. Special precautions can be taken to make sure the fetus is not exposed to much radiation. Patients should always wear abdominal shields during an X-ray to reduce the amount of radiation they are exposed to.

Dental X-rays are generally considered safe, because they are focused very far from the uterus. Many dentists still delay routine X-rays for a patient until after she has given birth.

Hazardous Substances and Chemicals

A pregnant woman must be careful about hazardous substances in her home and work environment. Some of these substances include:

- Paint. Low-odor latex paint in a well-ventilated area may not pose a problem. A woman should check with her doctor before any exposure.
- Pesticides used to exterminate bugs.
- Lead, in water and paint.
- Carbon monoxide.
- Mercury, found in some fish such as swordfish and shark.
- Solvents, paint thinners, and formaldehyde (used in some workplaces).

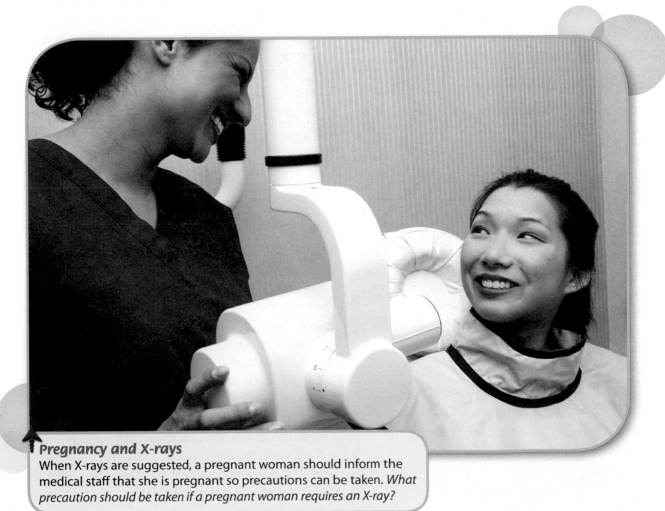

Pregnancy and X-rays
When X-rays are suggested, a pregnant woman should inform the medical staff that she is pregnant so precautions can be taken. *What precaution should be taken if a pregnant woman requires an X-ray?*

If a pregnant woman must live or work around some of these substances, she should consult her doctor immediately. She should also take extra precautions to minimize her exposure to any of these substances.

✓ Reading Check **Explain** Why should a woman tell a dentist when she is pregnant?

Diseases and Infections

Occasionally, an expectant mother might get an infection during the course of her pregnancy. Some infections pose more of a risk to a fetus than others. The timing of an infection also may have an effect on the level of risk to a fetus. Some infections can be treated without any harm to the unborn baby, if they are found early and treated properly.

Rubella

If a pregnant woman contracts rubella, also known as German measles, it can have terrible consequences for her unborn baby. The infection can cause severe birth defects, especially in the first three months of pregnancy. These can include blindness, deafness, heart disease, and mental retardation.

{ **Expert Advice...** }

"Each system of the body is most vulnerable to harmful outside influences at the time that it is forming. Since so many body systems are forming in the first weeks and months of pregnancy, this is the time when the risks are greatest of birth defects caused by exposures to certain medications, drugs, radiation, infections, or nutritional problems."

— Robert Needlman, pediatrician,
The Dr. Spock Company

A vaccine for rubella is available, and millions of children have been vaccinated. The vaccine may be dangerous, however, for women who are pregnant or who become pregnant shortly after receiving it. A woman who is unsure whether she has been vaccinated can check her health records or ask her doctor to test her. Every woman should be sure she is immune to rubella before she considers becoming pregnant.

Toxoplasmosis

Toxoplasmosis (ˌtäk-sə-ˌplaz-ˈmō-səs) is an infection caused by a parasite. This parasite is found all over the world, so the infection is quite common. It is estimated that 60 million people in the United States carry the parasite. Most people have immune systems that are strong enough to keep them from feeling any ill effects. However, developing babies are at risk if their mothers get the disease. Toxoplasmosis can cause blindness, hearing loss, and learning disabilities in babies. Some cases are so severe that a baby dies shortly after birth or has long-term mental disabilities. Toxoplasmosis can also cause miscarriage or stillbirth.

An expectant mother can take several precautions to avoid exposing her baby to toxoplasmosis. She should never clean a cat's litter box, because cats carry the parasite that causes the infection. She should not eat undercooked meat and should wash her hands immediately and thoroughly after touching raw meat.

Chicken Pox

Varicella is a viral infection that generally occurs in childhood. It is more commonly known as chicken pox. Some women who have not had chicken pox will get the infection during pregnancy. Depending upon when the infection occurs, there can be serious consequences to the fetus. If an expectant mother gets chicken pox during the first half of her pregnancy, her baby has a slight risk of getting a condition called congenital varicella syndrome. **Congenital** means present at birth. This condition can cause scarring of the skin, limb defects, eye problems, and other serious abnormalities. In a very small number of cases, it can cause miscarriage.

Ounce of Prevention
Washing hands immediately after handling raw meat can help avoid toxoplasmosis. *What other precautions can a pregnant woman take to prevent infections?*

Women who have not had chicken pox should get the vaccine before getting pregnant. They should also avoid contact with people who have chicken pox.

Sexually Transmitted Infections

As with rubella, sexually transmitted infections (STIs) can do great harm to unborn babies. In some instances, STIs may be passed to the child during the birth process. As you read in Chapter 2, some STIs include syphilis, gonorrhea, hepatitis B, genital herpes, acquired immune deficiency syndrome (AIDS), and chlamydia.

Many of these diseases can be passed on from the pregnant woman to the unborn child. This occurs in the same way that the child receives nutrients from the mother. Some of these diseases can result in serious illnesses, physical disabilities, or even death.

People can get a sexually transmitted infection without realizing it. They may never have any symptoms to indicate a problem. For this reason, special measures are usually taken to protect babies from the effects of STIs. Most

doctors routinely test pregnant women for syphilis and group B streptococcus. Many states require these tests by law. Doctors also usually treat the eyes of newborns with a solution that will kill any gonorrhea germs that could cause blindness.

Medical treatment can cure syphilis and gonorrhea and can relieve the symptoms of herpes in adults. No drug can cure the damage to a newborn that comes from a delay in diagnosis and treatment. Any pregnant woman who thinks she might have been exposed to an STI should discuss this possibility with her doctor as soon as possible.

Syphilis

The effects of syphilis on an unborn baby can usually be treated if the infection is discovered before the sixteenth week of pregnancy. If left untreated, syphilis can cause a skin rash or lesions, bone or facial deformities, deafness, or brain damage. Many babies infected with syphilis will develop anemia, jaundice, or pneumonia in the first few months of life. About two in five pregnancies with untreated syphilis end in miscarriage, a stillbirth, or a baby who dies soon after birth.

AIDS

When an expectant mother has AIDS, there can be serious consequences for her unborn baby. There is a 35 to 65 percent risk that the virus will be passed on to the baby. AIDS attacks the brain, and infected babies often have seizures and retarded mental development.

Most states now require an AIDS test early in a pregnancy. If a doctor knows that a pregnant woman has AIDS or the virus that causes it, special steps can be taken to reduce the baby's exposure to the disease. For example, the mother can take medication to reduce the chance of the baby being infected with the virus. Also, most babies exposed to the AIDS virus and other STIs are delivered by cesarean section, a surgical procedure. This avoids exposure to the disease that may exist in the birth canal. AIDS testing also helps doctors to prepare for a newborn infected with the HIV virus that causes AIDS.

Genital Herpes

Managing genital herpes during pregnancy is important to the health of the developing fetus. When the mother develops her first genital herpes infection during pregnancy, the risk to the infant is greater. Herpes simplex can cause the infant to be born with a brain infection or mental retardation. Some newborns will die from a herpes simplex infection.

In most cases, the infection is transmitted to the newborn during the birth process. For this reason, if a doctor knows that the mother is infected, he will often schedule a cesarean birth. You will learn more about this surgical procedure to deliver the baby in Chapter 6. In addition, there are medications that are safe to treat genital herpes during pregnancy. As with any sexually transmitted infection, couples should honestly discuss with their doctor the possibility of either parent having a herpes infection.

Section 4.3 After You Read

Review Key Concepts

1. **Explain** what causes FAS. How can it be avoided?
2. **Identify** three common chemicals a woman should avoid during pregnancy.
3. **Describe** why a woman should be vaccinated against rubella and chicken pox before becoming pregnant.

Practice Academic Skills

 English Language Arts

4. Suppose you are having coffee with a friend when she tells you that she is pregnant. Write a skit in which you urge your friend to avoid caffeine during the pregnancy, explaining the possible effects on her developing baby.

 Science

5. Health care professionals are concerned about pregnant women eating certain types of fish. Because of environmental pollution, these fish can contain high levels of mercury. Conduct research and create a chart showing the quantities of different types of fish a pregnant woman can safely eat.

NCTE 5 Use different writing process elements to communicate effectively.

NSES F Develop understanding of personal and community health; and environmental quality.

 Check Your Answers Check your answers at this book's Online Learning Center at **glencoe.com**.

Chapter Summary

Any time sexual intercourse takes place, a pregnancy may occur. There are many family planning methods available. Chromosomes from each parent determine the baby's inherited traits. There are three stages in prenatal development. Couples who cannot conceive may seek infertility treatment or adopt a child. Some pregnancies end in miscarriage or stillbirth. Birth defects have a variety of causes. There are tests to help diagnose potential problems. Everything a pregnant woman eats, drinks, and breathes affects her developing baby.

Vocabulary Review

1. Use each of these content and academic vocabulary words in a sentence.

Content Vocabulary

◇ ovum (p. 93)
◇ uterus (p. 93)
◇ fallopian tube (p. 93)
◇ sperm (p. 93)
◇ conception (p. 95)
◇ chromosome (p. 95)
◇ gene (p. 95)
◇ genome (p. 95)
◇ DNA (p. 95)
◇ infertility (p. 97)
◇ surrogate (p. 98)

◇ prenatal development (p. 99)
◇ zygote (p. 99)
◇ embryo (p. 100)
◇ amniotic fluid (p. 100)
◇ placenta (p. 100)
◇ umbilical cord (p. 100)
◇ fetus (p. 101)
◇ miscarriage (p. 106)
◇ stillbirth (p. 106)
◇ ultrasound (p. 112)
◇ amniocentesis (p. 113)

◇ fetal alcohol syndrome (FAS) (p. 116)
◇ fetal alcohol effects (p. 116)
◇ SIDS (p. 118)
◇ toxoplasmosis (p. 120)

Academic Vocabulary

■ controversial (p. 99)
■ spontaneous (p. 101)
■ predisposition (p. 111)
■ serious (p. 111)
■ deformity (p. 116)
■ congenital (p. 120)

Review Key Concepts

2. List the methods of family planning.

3. Outline what occurs during each of the three stages of prenatal development.

4. Contrast miscarriage and stillbirth.

5. Identify how ten major birth defects can be diagnosed.

6. Summarize the hazards that alcohol and other drugs pose to prenatal development.

7. Assess why environmental hazards must be avoided during pregnancy.

8. Describe how a fetus can be affected by certain illnesses the mother may contract.

Critical Thinking

9. Analyze Why do babies born at full term have a better chance for survival than babies born a few months early?

10. Predict What could be the consequences if someone denies that she is pregnant and does not seek any medical care?

Family & Community Connection

11. Local Organizations There are many organizations that offer support to families with children with birth defects. The March of Dimes and Special Olympics are just two examples. Choose and research one of this type of organization in your community. Find out what the organization's purpose is and what services it provides. Prepare an oral report on what you learn, and, if possible, present it to the class or another group.

Health Skills

12. Investigate Ultrasound Research the latest advances in ultrasound technology. How can these advances help with the diagnosis of birth defects? What specific birth defects can they identify? What else can these new technologies reveal about a developing fetus?

Observation Skills

13. Observe Pregnant Women Most pregnant women enjoy active lives, despite difficulties such as fatigue. What kinds of changes do you think the average pregnant woman makes in her daily routine? Make a list of your ideas.

Procedure Observe pregnant women around you. Write down any accommodations they appear to have made, such as sitting more than usual or wearing different clothes.

Draw Conclusions Write a summary describing ways in which pregnant women appear to have changed their lives. Compare your observations to the list of ideas you wrote before you made your observations.

> **NCTE 7** Conduct research and gather, evaluate, and synthesize data to communicate discoveries.

Real-World Skills

Problem-Solving Skills

14. Make Decisions Follow your teacher's instructions to form groups. Discuss with your group what you might do if a genetic counselor told you any future children might have Tay-Sachs disease. Would you plan to have children? Why or why not? Share your group's response with the class.

Technology Skills

15. Research Fetal Development Conduct research to learn more about fetal development during the last three months of pregnancy. Then use presentation software to prepare a presentation for middle-school students explaining development during this time. Use illustrations and language that is appropriate for this age group.

Financial Literacy

16. Family Planning A couple is planning on having their first baby three years from now. They want to save $10,000 before they have the baby to help with the expenses of the first year. How much money do they need to save each month to have the $10,000 saved in three years?

 Additional Activities For additional activities, go to this book's Online Learning Center at **glencoe.com**.

Academic Skills

 English Language Arts

17. Write a Persuasive Letter Imagine you are a pregnant woman who is exposed to solvents, such as paint thinners, at the factory where you work. Write a persuasive letter to your boss explaining why these solvents present a risk to the baby. Also propose a solution. Conduct research to gather information to strengthen your argument.

NCTE 12 Use language to accomplish individual purposes.

 Mathematics

18. Prenatal Development Alcohol consumed during pregnancy increases the risk of alcohol related birth defects. A report from the U.S. Surgeon General states that up to two out of every thousand births show signs of fetal alcohol syndrome. Suppose there are 4.1 million children born in a year. How many of those might have fetal alcohol syndrome?

Math Concept **Variables and Expressions** Translate verbal phrases into algebraic expressions by defining a variable.

Starting Hint Write your expression as

$$\frac{x}{4.1 \text{ million}} = \frac{2}{1,000}$$

Math For math help, go to the Math Appendix at the back of the book.

NCTM Algebra Represent and analyze mathematical situations and structures using algebraic symbols.

 Science

19. Pregnancy and Painkillers Over-the-counter medications such as acetaminophen and ibuprofen are widely used by the public. Pregnant women may be tempted to use these due to the added aches and pains caused by pregnancy. However, scientists and health care professionals are concerned about any effects these painkillers may have on a developing baby.

Procedure Choose one type of over-the-counter painkiller. Research to find what is known about its effects on fetuses.

Analysis Imagine you are an obstetrician and a pregnant patient has asked you about your chosen painkiller's safety. What would you say? Write a dialogue showing how you would respond to the patient. Be sure to include reasons why she should or should not use that particular painkiller.

NSES A Develop abilities necessary to do scientific inquiry, understand about scientific inquiry.

Standardized Test Practice

ESSAY QUESTIONS
Answering essay questions can be challenging, especially if time is limited. Before writing a response to an essay question, spend a few moments thinking about the main points you want to make. Think about the structure of your response and how much detail you want to include. Apply these skills to answer this essay question.

20. Describe the major changes that occur in a developing baby during the embryonic stage.

Test-Taking Tip When answering essay questions, begin by creating a brief outline. Keep the outline in mind as you write your response.

Chapter

5 Preparing for Birth

Chapter Objectives

After completing this chapter, you will be able to:

- **Identify** the early signs of pregnancy.
- **Explain** the importance of proper nutrition during pregnancy.
- **List** six categories of basic baby supplies.
- **Describe** why parents need to develop a budget.
- **Identify** ways expectant parents can prepare for the birth of a child.
- **Compare and contrast** the options for the delivery of a baby.

Writing Activity 🖋 Topic Sentence

A Healthy Pregnancy Developing a topic sentence is like building a house's frame. If the frame is poorly built, the entire building will collapse. Write a paragraph that includes a topic sentence about how a woman can remain healthy during her pregnancy.

Writing Tips A topic sentence provides an overview of a paragraph. Here are some tips for writing a good topic sentence:

1. **State** the main idea of the paragraph.
2. **Place** the ideas in the order in which they will be covered in the paragraph.
3. **Avoid** making the topic sentence overly detailed.

▲ **Explore the Photo**
A pregnancy affects all members of the family, not just the mother. *How do you think each person in this photo is affected by this pregnancy?*

Section 5.1 A Healthy Pregnancy

Reading Guide

Before You Read

Create a KWL Chart Create a chart with three columns labeled "What I Know," "What I Want to Know," and "What I Learned." Skim the section and fill in the first two columns. Then fill in the last column after you read.

Read to Learn

Key Concepts

- **Identify** the early signs of pregnancy.
- **Explain** the importance of proper nutrition during pregnancy.

Main Idea

It is important that pregnant women have regular doctor checkups and practice good nutrition. They also should follow appropriate exercise routines and avoid excess stress.

Content Vocabulary

◇ obstetrician
◇ anemia
◇ Rh factor
◇ gestational diabetes
◇ preeclampsia
◇ osteoporosis
◇ lactose intolerance
◇ lactase

Academic Vocabulary

You will find these words in your reading and on your tests. Use the glossary to look up their definitions if necessary.

■ robust
■ alleviate

Graphic Organizer

As you read, note the food groups pregnant women should eat. List two foods in each group. Use a chart like the one shown to organize your information.

Food Group	Example 1	Example 2
Grains		
Fruit		
Vegetables		
Milk		
Meat and Beans		
Oils		

 Graphic Organizer Go to this book's Online Learning Center at **glencoe.com** to print out this graphic organizer.

Academic Standards

 English Language Arts

NCTE 8 Use information resources to gather information and create and communicate knowledge.

 Science

NSES F Develop understanding of personal and community health.

 Social Studies

NCSS I A Culture Analyze and explain the ways groups, societies, and cultures address human needs and concerns.

NCTE *National Council of Teachers of English*
NCTM *National Council of Teachers of Mathematics*

NSES *National Science Education Standards*
NCSS *National Council for the Social Studies*

Health During Pregnancy

A pregnant woman's responsibilities grow along with her baby. What happens to a baby during prenatal development can affect both the baby's and parents' lives. Mothers-to-be need to eat a well-balanced diet, exercise moderately, get plenty of sleep, and manage stress. This is important for both the mother's and the baby's health.

Early Signs of Pregnancy

How do women discover that they are pregnant? Within a few weeks of conception, women usually experience one or more of the following signs of pregnancy:

- A missed menstrual period (often the first indicator)
- A full feeling or mild ache in the lower abdomen
- Tiredness or faintness
- A frequent, urgent need to urinate
- Swollen breasts, causing discomfort or tenderness
- Nausea or vomiting, particularly in the morning

These symptoms are common, but they do not always mean that a woman is pregnant. If a woman believes she is pregnant, she should take a pregnancy test as soon as possible. Doctors can conduct tests to confirm pregnancy. There are also a variety of home pregnancy tests available. They are easy to use and fairly accurate. Early detection of pregnancy is crucial to the health of the expectant mother and her baby.

Medical Care

Once pregnancy is determined, it is important for a woman to schedule a doctor's visit. Most pregnant women choose an obstetrician for medical care during pregnancy. An **obstetrician** (ˌäb-stə-'tri-shən) is a doctor who specializes in pregnancy and childbirth.

Obstetricians will schedule regular checkups during pregnancy. These checkups will become more frequent as the pregnancy progresses. The doctor also assists during childbirth and examines the newborn. It is important that expectant mothers find a doctor they like, feel comfortable with, and trust.

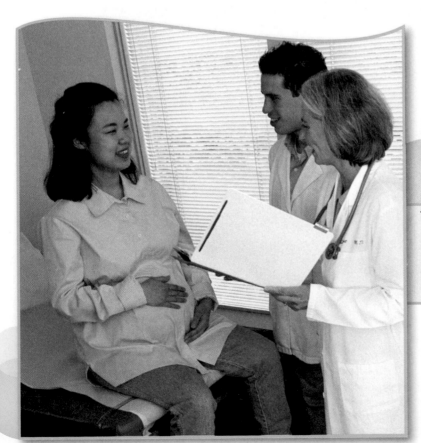

Meeting with Obstetricians
A pregnant woman often meets all the doctors in a medical office or clinic. *How can meeting the other doctors help a woman prepare for childbirth?*

Many obstetricians work as part of a team with other doctors, taking turns caring for patients at night and on weekends. Although pregnant women usually have a primary doctor, they typically meet all the doctors who work in the office. This is so they know and feel comfortable with all the doctors.

The primary doctor performs most of the woman's checkups. However, if he is not on duty when the woman is ready to deliver, another doctor on the team will deliver the baby. Since no one knows when labor will begin, it could happen on the primary doctor's day off. He also could be ill or on vacation.

Some women believe they will save money by seeing a doctor only when the baby is ready to be born. This is not the case. Most obstetricians set a fee for all the services they provide throughout the pregnancy, from the first exam to the follow-up visits after the baby is born. Nothing is more important to the health of the baby than for the mother to get regular medical care and advice from the beginning to the end of the pregnancy.

The First Exam

When pregnancy is confirmed, the woman receives a thorough examination that includes:

- A check of her blood pressure, pulse, respiration, and weight.
- A discussion of her medical history, including existing medical conditions, such as high blood pressure, that may require special treatment or observation during pregnancy.
- A measurement of her pelvis to determine whether it is wide enough to allow a baby of normal size to pass through.
- An analysis of her urine for signs of infection or diabetes, a condition characterized by excessive amounts of urine. Diabetes develops when the body is not able to produce enough insulin to keep blood sugar (glucose) within an acceptable range. This condition affects the body's ability to burn energy.
- Blood tests to rule out anemia. **Anemia** is a condition that results from not having enough red blood cells. Symptoms include fatigue, shortness of breath, rapid heartbeat, and feeling cold and weak.

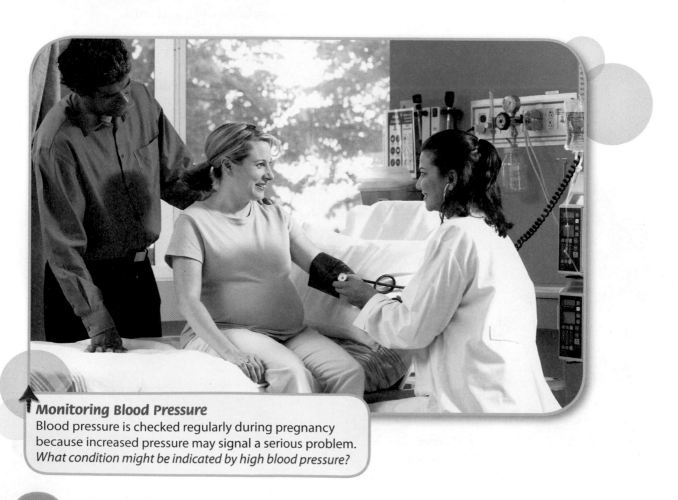

Monitoring Blood Pressure
Blood pressure is checked regularly during pregnancy because increased pressure may signal a serious problem. *What condition might be indicated by high blood pressure?*

Korean Taegyo

In Korea, many pregnant women learn a set of practices that have been transmitted to women by word of mouth and through literature for centuries. The word for these practices is taegyo ('tīg-yō). This means fetal education. Koreans believe that fetal education is more important than the first ten years of a child's schooling. Pregnant women are taught to read inspiring books; eat colorful, attractive foods; sit or stand up straight; and listen to beautiful music. They should not deceive anyone or think about anything unpleasant. Koreans believe that the fetus is extremely sensitive to what the mother feels.

Build Connections *Korean women believe that what happens to an unborn baby can affect his or her entire life. Do you think this is true? If yes, in what ways do you think this is true?*

NCSS I A Culture Analyze and explain the ways groups, societies, and cultures address human needs and concerns.

The blood test also shows whether or not the mother's blood contains a certain protein. This protein is referred to as the **Rh factor**. Knowing about the presence (Rh positive) or absence (Rh negative) of this protein is very important. The Rh factor is determined genetically. If the mother's blood does not have the protein and the fetus's blood does, the mother's blood builds up antibodies that attack the protein in the fetus's blood. This does not affect a first pregnancy, but it can endanger any future pregnancies. Once identified, the mother can receive an injection that will prevent the antibodies from forming, thus protecting any Rh positive fetus.

- A check of the woman's immunity to rubella, also called German measles. If a pregnant woman has not been vaccinated against this disease and has never had it, she must be especially careful to avoid anyone who has it. If she contracts rubella during pregnancy, the fetus could be harmed.

One question every pregnant woman has is "When will my baby be born?" The approximate birth date is easy to calculate. Nine months and one week after the first day of her final period before pregnancy is her baby's due date.

Of course, doctors know that even in a typical pregnancy a variation of up to two weeks before or after that date can be expected.

Periodic Checkups

Expectant mothers have checkups, or prenatal visits, once a month until about the sixth or seventh month of pregnancy. After that, women see the doctor twice a month. In the final month, checkups occur once a week. During these visits, the doctor monitors the baby's development and the mother's health. Regular checkups allow immediate response should a problem arise.

Between the 24th and 28th weeks of the pregnancy, most women take a glucose tolerance test to check for signs of gestational diabetes. **Gestational diabetes** is a form of diabetes that occurs only during pregnancy. If left untreated, gestational diabetes can cause the baby to be heavier than is normal or healthy.

Some women who do not normally have diabetes develop the condition when they are pregnant. This type of diabetes usually goes away after the baby is born. Gestational diabetes can usually be controlled by a special diet but may require medication.

Aches and Pains
Many pregnant women experience difficulties such as tiredness and back pain. *Why should pregnant women not take over-the-counter remedies for common problems such as headaches?*

Another serious condition that can occur during the second half of pregnancy is preeclampsia. **Preeclampsia** (ˌprē-i-ˈklam(p)-sē-ə) is a condition characterized by high blood pressure and the presence of protein in the mother's urine. It can prevent the baby from getting enough blood, which provides oxygen and food. Treatment for preeclampsia depends on how far along in the pregnancy a woman is. Treatment might include bed rest or medication. The doctor can recommend the best treatment option.

Most doctors welcome the father or another person who will be attending the birth to accompany the pregnant woman at prenatal visits. This gives the support person a chance to meet the doctor and follow the baby's growth. Also, sometimes it is helpful to have someone else to ask questions and remember important information.

Discomforts of Pregnancy

Most women experience few problems during pregnancy. In fact, some women say that pregnancy is a time of **robust**, or thriving, health. Many women experience an increase in energy and well-being. Other women feel some discomfort. This usually does not indicate serious problems. However, if a woman experi-

ences one or more of the following symptoms, she should discuss it with her doctor.

- **Nausea or Vomiting** While this is commonly called morning sickness, it can occur at any time of the day. Morning sickness is the most common complaint of pregnant women. It rarely lasts beyond the fourth month of pregnancy. If it is severe or prolonged, however, women should alert their doctors.

- **Sleepiness** Due to hormonal changes, sleepiness is quite common early in pregnancy. Many women feel more energetic in the middle months of pregnancy. For most women, fatigue returns in the final months, since the baby weighs more and takes up more room.

- **Heartburn** This is a burning feeling in the upper abdomen. It has nothing to do with the heart. Women with heartburn should ask their doctors about safe forms of relief.

- **Shortness of Breath** Pressure on the lungs from the baby can cause shortness of breath. This is particularly common late in pregnancy.

- **Varicose Veins** When there is pressure on the blood vessels in the legs, varicose veins can appear. These are swollen veins, or blood vessels, that are close to the skin's surface. Getting plenty of exercise, resting with the legs elevated, and using support stockings can help relieve the swelling.

- **Muscle Cramps in the Legs** Gentle stretches, rest, and a diet rich in calcium may **alleviate**, or ease, the pain caused by leg cramps.
- **Lower Back Pain** Wearing low-heeled shoes and learning to lift properly, or avoiding lifting altogether, can minimize back problems. Exercises that strengthen the back can also help.

Possible Serious Complications

A few women experience more serious problems during pregnancy. Any of the following symptoms should be reported to a doctor immediately:

- Vaginal bleeding
- Unusual weight gain or loss
- Excessive thirst
- Diminished need to urinate or pain during urination
- Severe abdominal pain
- Persistent headaches
- Severe vomiting
- Fever
- Increased vaginal mucus
- Swelling of the face, hands, or ankles
- Blurred vision or dizziness
- Prolonged backache

Physical Changes

The common length of pregnancy is about 40 weeks, or 280 days, from the first day of the last menstrual cycle. See **Figure 5.1** on page 134 for a description of physical changes a woman can expect each month of her pregnancy.

Toward the end of the 40 weeks, the baby's weight seems to shift downward, and most mothers feel more comfortable in their upper abdomen. This shift is called lightening. Sometimes there is a visible change in the shape of the mother's abdomen, giving signs that the baby has dropped into the birth canal. The birth canal is the channel through which the baby passes during birth.

In most births, the fetus is usually upside down at this point, with the head nestled in the mother's pelvis. This is the easiest and safest position for birth. Once the head is out of the mother's body, the rest of the body usually delivers easily.

In some cases, the fetus does not turn to the head-down position in the last few weeks. Instead, the fetus is in a seat-down position in the mother's pelvis. This is called a breech presentation. In many of these instances, a doctor uses a surgical procedure called a cesarean section to deliver the baby. A complete discussion of cesarean birth appears in Chapter 6.

In the last few weeks of pregnancy, the skin of the mother's abdomen appears stretched to capacity. This is when stretch marks will generally appear. The muscles of the uterus and abdomen can be stretched to many times their original size during pregnancy. At the end of pregnancy, the muscles of the uterus contract to push out the baby during delivery. The mother's abdominal and uterine muscles generally return to near-normal sizes approximately six weeks after delivery.

What Would You Do?

Keep On Moving

"I guess you'll have to stop working out with me now that you're pregnant," Gwen said to her friend Holly. "I don't know, actually," Holly told Gwen. "I'll ask Dr. Wallace."

From the doctor, Holly learned that a woman *can* and *should* exercise while pregnant. Some aspects of her usual exercise regimen might need to be adjusted to her changing body. Dr. Wallace said, "If you exercised before becoming pregnant, it's okay to continue, with modifications. After the first trimester, do not do any exercises that require you to be on your back and do not do any abdominal work."

Write About It Imagine that you are Holly. Write a paragraph describing the exercise routine you are going to follow while pregnant. Also list any activities you would plan to avoid.

Figure 5.1

Pregnancy Development Month by Month

Specific changes occur during each month of pregnancy. *During which months is a mother most likely to experience morning sickness?*

Month	Pregnancy Development
Month 1	✤ Missed menstrual period. ✤ Other signs of pregnancy may not yet be noticeable.
Month 2	✤ Breasts begin to swell. ✤ Pressure on bladder from enlarging uterus results in need to urinate more frequently. ✤ Possible nausea (morning sickness) and fatigue.
Month 3	✤ Breasts become firmer and fuller, may ache. ✤ Nausea, fatigue, and frequent urination may continue. ✤ Abdomen becomes slightly larger. The uterus is about the size of an orange. ✤ Weight gain may total 2–4 pounds (0.9–1.8 kg).
Month 4	✤ Abdomen continues to grow slowly. ✤ Most discomforts of early pregnancy are usually gone. ✤ Appetite increases.
Month 5	✤ Enlarged abdomen becomes apparent. ✤ Slight fetal movements felt. ✤ Increased size may begin to affect posture.
Month 6	✤ Fetal movements sensed as strong kicks, thumps, and bumps. Some may be visible. ✤ Weight gain by the beginning of this month may total 10–12 pounds (4.5–5.4 kg).
Month 7	✤ Increased size may affect posture.
Month 8	✤ Discomfort may result from increased size. Backache, leg cramps, shortness of breath, and fatigue are common. ✤ Fetal kicks may disturb the mother's rest. ✤ At the beginning of this month, weight gain totals about 18–20 pounds (8.2–9.1 kg).
Month 9	✤ Lightening is felt as the fetus drops into the pelvis. Breathing becomes easier. ✤ Other discomforts may continue. ✤ A total weight gain of 25–35 pounds (11.3–15.9 kg) is typical. ✤ False labor pains may be experienced.

Weight Gain During Pregnancy

Women typically gain between 24 and 30 pounds during a healthy pregnancy. This weight is from the baby itself and from changes to the mother's body. **Figure 5.2** shows how that weight is usually distributed.

Recommended weight gain is about a pound a month during the first three months. In the fourth through ninth months, weight gain should be about three to four pounds per month.

Gaining too little weight can increase the risk of fetal death or premature birth. Gaining too much weight can put added stress on the mother's body and increase the risk of complications. Women who begin a pregnancy underweight or overweight will require special monitoring.

Maternity Clothes

By around the fourth or fifth month, a pregnant woman needs looser clothing to allow for freedom of movement and circulation as the baby grows. Maternity pants often have a stretch panel in the front. Shirts also are made looser to allow room for the growing baby. When choosing clothing, an expectant mother should consider how garments will fit during her ninth month.

Daily Routines

Pregnant women can take care of themselves in many ways. While pregnant women can usually follow some of the same daily routines they had before pregnancy, they should also do the following:

- **Eat a healthful diet.** Eat a variety of nutritious meals and snacks to get the nutrients that both mother and baby need.
- **Get plenty of rest.** Taking frequent breaks during the day may provide more energy.
- **Exercise.** Moderate exercise is important to everyone, including pregnant women.

Figure 5.2 Weight Gain During Pregnancy

Weight gain during pregnancy is due to many factors besides the actual weight of the baby. *Next to the baby itself, what causes the greatest weight gain during pregnancy?*

Factor	Pounds
Weight of average baby at birth	7–8
Placenta	1–2
Amniotic fluid	1½–2
Increased size of uterus and supporting muscles	2
Increase in breast tissue	1
Increase in blood volume	1½–3
Increase in fat stores	5
Increase in body fluids	5–7
Total	**24–30**

Doctors may recommend walking, yoga, or swimming. Look for exercise classes that are designed for pregnant women.

- **Practice good hygiene.** Keeping the skin clean helps the body maintain a healthy temperature and eliminate waste. A warm bath or shower before bedtime also may help pregnant women relax.

Pregnant women do not need to radically change their activities during pregnancy. Moderation is advised, but most activities can continue as before. Most women are able to continue working throughout their pregnancy.

Emotional Health During Pregnancy

Pregnancy and birth are major events in a couple's life. They are also times of emotional adjustments. It is vital to talk to each other. Spending time alone together can help. Family and friends can also be sources of information and support.

Pregnancy causes hormonal changes that may lead to mood swings. Most women feel upset and worried at some time during pregnancy. This is why effective stress-reduction techniques are important.

Depression

Emotional and physical stress can lead to deep and lasting feelings of sadness. This is known as depression. Expectant mothers who feel overwhelmed need to seek help. There are a number of ways to find support. A woman's doctor may recommend a professional counselor or local support group. Often, women who are going through, or have been through, similar experiences can help the expectant mother. Some books also can help expectant mothers understand their concerns and improve their outlook.

Stress

If you have experienced stress, you know how it affects you. You may feel moody, anxious, annoyed, or scared. Perhaps you lose your appetite, have nightmares, or feel sweaty and shaky. Pregnancy can be a stressful time.

It is important that pregnant women find ways to ease the stress for themselves and their babies. There are many ways to cope with stress while pregnant.

- **Avoid sugary foods and caffeine.** These can make pregnant women nervous or jumpy.

Dealing with Stress
There are many ways to handle the emotional stress that may occur during pregnancy. *What could happen if a woman does not find ways to relieve stress?*

- **Exercise.** Gentle exercises, such as stretching, and moderate physical activity, such as walking, can help pregnant women feel lighter and more energetic.
- **Take a time-out.** Taking time to relax and enjoy a favorite activity or hobby can help relieve stress.
- **Practice relaxation techniques.** Pregnant women can learn breathing or visualization exercises through books or classes.
- **Talk about concerns.** Mothers-to-be can benefit from talking to supportive friends or family members, especially those who have children of their own. They can also talk to their doctors or seek a counselor.
- **Take a class for expectant parents.** The more pregnant women know about the birth process, the greater their sense of control. Feeling prepared can help reduce stress.

✓ **Reading Check** **Explain** Why is it best for pregnant women to avoid sugary foods and caffeine?

Nutrition During Pregnancy

Good nutrition is the single most important requirement during pregnancy. The baby's growth and development, including crucial brain development, depend on nutrients from the mother. By eating a nutritious, balanced diet, a pregnant woman promotes her baby's development and maintains her own health.

Five Food Groups Plus Oils

Expecting mothers need a variety of nutrients to keep themselves and their developing babies healthy. The U.S. Department of Agriculture has developed nutritional guidelines for pregnant women. These guidelines are known as MyPyramid for Moms. The guidelines divide foods into five food groups, plus the oils category. (See **Figure 5.3**.)

Grains

Eating grains is essential to any well-balanced diet. They contain carbohydrates, which provide

THE DEVELOPING BRAIN

Nutrition and Fetal Brain Development

Some pregnant women do not follow a sensible and balanced diet. Others, wrongly concerned about gaining weight, severely restrict their food intake. Either way, the developing fetus is put in serious danger. One possible outcome of failing to supply adequate nutrition to the fetus is that brain development could be stunted and the baby could be mentally retarded. Alcohol consumption, cigarette smoking, and drug abuse during pregnancy can have similar results.

■ **Science Inquiry** Dieting during pregnancy can cause problems with fetal brain development. Why do you think a pregnant woman might diet even though she knows this?

our body with energy. Grains fortified with folic acid can help prevent defects to the baby's nervous system. The nutrients in grain also reduce the risk of heart disease and keep the digestive system working properly. The grains group includes any food made from wheat, rice, cornmeal, barley, or other grains. Examples include bread, pasta, oatmeal, and tortillas.

Grains are divided into whole grains and refined grains. Whole grains, such as whole-wheat flour and oatmeal, contain the entire grain kernel. Refined grains have been milled, causing parts of the grain to be removed. This gives them a finer texture and slows down the rate at which they spoil. However, refining also removes fiber, iron, and some vitamins. Examples of refined grain products include white bread and white rice. Most refined grains are enriched. This means that some vitamins and iron have been added back into them. However, they are still missing the fiber and some of the vitamins of whole grains.

Because whole grains are generally more nutritious than refined grains, it is recommended that at least half of the grains eaten be whole grains. Look to see that grains such as wheat, rice, oats, or corn are referred to as "whole" in the list of ingredients.

Vegetables

Eating vegetables keeps the mother's heart healthy. Vegetables also can reduce her chances of getting diabetes, high blood presure, and some kinds of cancer.

Vegetables are rich in potassium and dietary fiber. Many are rich in folic acids and vitamins A, C, and E. Most are low in fat and calories, and therefore can help to control the mother's weight. Different colored vegetables typically provide different nutrients. They are divided into the following categories:

- Dark green vegetables, such as broccoli and spinach
- Orange vegetables, such as carrots and pumpkin
- Dry beans and peas
- Starchy vegetables, such as potatoes and corn
- Other vegetables, such as celery and onions

Fruits

Any fruit or 100 percent fruit juice is part of this group. Some common fruits include apples, bananas, tomatoes, avocados, strawberries, and oranges. Fruit juices are high in calories and do not contain fiber. Eat a variety of fruits rather than just fruit juice for most of your fruit choices. Fruits can be fresh, frozen, canned, or dried.

Fruits have many of the same benefits as vegetables. Fruits also help maintain a healthy heart and blood vessels. Fruits can help control body weight. Many fruits are good sources of potassium, dietary fiber, vitamins A and C, and folic acid.

Milk Products

Foods in the milk group include all varieties of milk, cheese, ice cream, and yogurt.

Figure 5.3 MyPyramid for Moms

MyPyramid for Moms divides foods into five basic groups, plus oils. *Which group contains nuts and seeds?*

MyPyramid.gov

Vegetable Group Vary your veggies. In general, more colorful vegetables, such as broccoli, carrots, and kidney beans, have more vitamins and minerals than lighter colored ones.

Grains Group Make half your grains whole. Eat at least three ounces of whole-grains every day. One ounce is about one slice of bread, one cup of breakfast cereal, or ½ cup of cooked rice or pasta.

Fruit Group Focus on fruits. In general, two cups of fruit should be eaten each day. For example, have one small banana, one large orange, and ¼ cup of dried apricots or peaches.

Nutrients in milk products include calcium, potassium, vitamin D, and protein. Calcium is vital for building healthy bones and teeth. It is important that pregnant women get adequate calcium to prevent osteoporosis. **Osteoporosis** is a condition in which bones become fragile and break easily.

Choosing milk products that are low-fat or fat-free is important. High-fat milk products contain saturated fats and cholesterol that can lead to a greater risk of heart disease. If you cannot consume milk, choose lactose-free milk products and calcium-fortified foods and beverages.

Meat and Beans

Meat, poultry, fish, dried beans, nuts, and eggs belong to this group. Choose meat and poultry cuts that are low-fat. They provide protein, which is vital to the baby's growth and development of bones and teeth. Protein also helps keep the mother's body healthy. Expectant mothers need more protein than they did before they were pregnant.

Oils

Oils are fats that are liquid at room temperature. They can come from either plants or fish. Common oils include olive oil, corn oil, and canola oil. Many foods are naturally high in oils, including nuts, olives, and some fish.

Solid fats, such as butter, contain more saturated or trans fats than oils. These kinds of fats can increase your risk for heart disease. Oils have more monounsaturated and polyunsaturated fats, which are healthier. Oils are healthier than solid fats, but they are still high in calories, so their intake should be limited.

Milk Group Eat calcium-rich foods. Get three cups of low-fat or fat-free milk, or an equivalent amount of low-fat yogurt or low-fat cheese, every day. Note that 1½ ounces of cheese equals 1 cup of milk.

Oils Choose healthy oils. Read the Nutrition Facts label on foods. Look for polyunsaturated and monounsaturated oils such as olive oil or canola oil.

Meat & Beans Group Go lean with protein. Choose lean meats and poultry. Bake it, broil it, or grill it. And vary your protein choices with more fish, beans, nuts, and seeds.

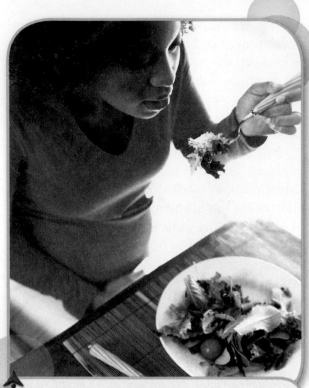

Nutrition and Pregnancy
Eating nutritiously is one of the best gifts a pregnant mother can give her unborn baby. *What can happen if a mother does not eat a balanced diet?*

Vitamins and Minerals

A variety of vitamins and minerals are vital to both the fetus and the mother. Whenever possible, it is best to get these from a healthy diet, rather than by taking supplements. Pregnant women should take vitamins, minerals, or other supplements only with their doctor's approval.

{ **Expert Advice...** }

"Pregnancy is such a demanding time nutritionally on a woman's body. If she can make even one positive change, it can make all the difference in her health, as well as in the health of her developing child."

— Maggie McHugh, registered dietitian and certified nutritionist

Vitamins

Vitamins help to maintain a healthy pregnancy. Research has determined some birth defects, such as spina bifida, are linked to vitamin deficiency. Women usually need more vitamins during pregnancy. Here are some of the most important ones.

- Vitamin A ensures proper eye development and helps keep skin healthy.
- The B vitamins assist in general fetal development.
- Vitamin C helps build healthy teeth and gums. It also helps form the connective tissue of skin, bone, and organs.
- Vitamin D aids in the creation of bones and teeth.
- Folic acid is necessary for normal spinal development in the fetus. Lack of folic acid can lead to spina bifida. Pregnant women need twice the normal amount. Even women who are considering becoming pregnant should increase their intake of folic acid.

Minerals

Pregnant women need iron, a mineral that helps prevent anemia and assists in developing the baby's own blood supply. Extra iron is stored in the baby's liver and is used in the months right after birth. During this time, a baby who lives on breast milk lacks iron in the diet. The mother can get iron from dried beans, raisins, dates, meat, and leafy green vegetables.

Calcium and phosphorous are also important minerals during pregnancy. These nutrients work together to produce strong bones and teeth and ensure regular elimination of waste from the body. Milk and other dairy products are good sources of calcium and phosphorous.

Food Quantities

All pregnant women should eat a wide variety of healthy foods. However, the exact quantities needed vary depending on the mother's age, weight, and activity level, as well as the stage of pregnancy.

When you visit the MyPyramid for Moms Web site, you can create a specific plan based on these factors. **Figure 5.4** shows a sample nutrition plan made using this Web site. The nutrition plan will show you how much food you need from each food group, during each stage of pregnancy.

Within each food group, pregnant women should choose foods that are rich in the vitamins and minerals needed. For example, carrots, winter squash, and spinach are good choices from the vegetable group for pregnant women.

Nutrition and Pregnant Teens

Teens' bodies have special nutritional needs because they are still developing. Pregnancy places additional strain on the body. Many teens fill up on high-calorie, low-nutrient foods. Pregnant teens must be especially careful to eat nutritious meals and snacks. It is essential for a teen's own body and for her growing baby to get all the needed nutrients for proper growth and development.

It is especially important for pregnant teens to get enough calcium and iron. Calcium is essential for growing bones. Iron helps the blood carry oxygen to all parts of the body. During pregnancy, a woman has more blood in her body, so iron is even more important to her health. As with any pregnant woman, pregnant teens should discuss their nutritional needs with their doctor.

Special Diets

Some people are sensitive to certain foods, such as dairy. Some people choose to avoid certain foods for personal reasons, such as vegetarians. A pregnant woman needs to discuss these considerations with her doctor to ensure that her fetus gets the needed nutrients for healthy growth and developoment.

Sensitivities to Milk

Milk and other dairy products are a rich source of calcium, protein, and other key nutrients. Expectant mothers who cannot tolerate milk products need special eating strategies. One alternative is to eat larger amounts of other calcium-rich foods, such as broccoli,

Figure 5.4 **MyPyramid for Moms Sample Nutrition Plan**

This nutrition plan is for a 30-year-old woman who weighs 140 pounds. *Amounts in which groups increase over the course of the pregnancy?*

	1st Trimester	2nd Trimester	3rd Trimester
	Jan - Mar	Apr - Jun	Jul - Oct
▶ Grains	7 ounces	9 ounces	9 ounces
▶ Vegetables	3 cups	3½ cups	3½ cups
▶ Fruits	2 cups	2 cups	2 cups
▶ Milk	3 cups	3 cups	3 cups
▶ Meat & Beans	6 ounces	6½ ounces	6½ ounces

For more tips and information, visit **MyPyramid.gov**.

tofu, and leafy green vegtables. Protein can come from meat, fish, dried beans, and nuts.

Some people are lactose intolerant. Lactose is a type of sugar found in milk. A person is **lactose intolerant** if milk products cause symptoms such as abdominal pain and gas. Many people who have problems digesting lactose can still eat dairy foods, if they are served in small quantities or eaten with other foods. Fortified soy milk can also provide nutrients for people who are lactose intolerant.

Lactase is an enzyme that helps digest lactose. Eating foods with lactase, such as yogurt, helps some people digest milk. Taking lactase in liquid or tablet form can also relieve symptoms. Before taking a lactase supplement, pregnant women should consult their doctors.

Vegetarians

Vegetarians do not eat meat, which is high in protein. Some vegetarians, called *vegans*, do not eat any animal products at all, including eggs and milk. Vegetarians eat food from plant sources, such as vegetables, fruits, grains, beans, nuts, and seeds. People may choose this diet for religious or cultural reasons, because of their concern for animals, or health reasons. By eating enough tofu and other soybean products, dried beans, nuts, and nut butters such as peanut butter, pregnant vegetarians can still get the protein they need. As with any pregnant woman, pregnant vegetarians should discuss their diet with their doctor. This will help ensure they get the needed nutrients for a healthy baby and a healthy mother.

Section 5.1   After You Read

Review Key Concepts

1. **Explain** why it is important for a pregnant woman to receive prenatal care from the beginning through the end of her pregnancy.

2. **List** three vitamins and explain each one's purpose.

Practice Academic Skills

 English Language Skills

3. Visit the MyPyramid for Moms Web site and explore the tools for an expectant mother. Use what you have learned to make a poster explaining MyPyramid for Moms. Use simple language and art to emphasize the importance of good nutrition, both for the mother and the developing baby.

 Science

4. Pregnant women often feel more tired than normal and require extra sleep. However, women often find it difficult to sleep due to the discomforts of pregnancy. Conduct research to find out what pregnant women can do to help them sleep better without medication. Include talking to women with children, or women who are pregnant as part of your research.

 Check Your Answers Check your answers at this book's Online Learning Center at **glencoe.com**.

NCTE 8 Use information resources to gather information and create and communicate knowledge.

NSES F Develop understanding of personal and community health.

Section 5.2 Preparing for the Baby's Arrival

Reading Guide

Before You Read

Self-Checking As you read, stop when you come to a new heading. Ask yourself questions about what you have just read. If you cannot remember the answers, go back and find them. This is called self-checking.

Read to Learn
Key Concepts
- **List** six categories of basic baby supplies.
- **Describe** why parents need to develop a budget.

Main Idea
New babies require items such as clothing, equipment, and a place to sleep. Parents also should create a budget and prepare any siblings for the new baby.

Content Vocabulary
◇ formula
◇ pediatrician
◇ fixed expense
◇ flexible expense
◇ maternity leave
◇ paternity leave

 Graphic Organizer Go to this book's Online Learning Center at **glencoe.com** to print out this graphic organizer.

Academic Vocabulary
You will find these words in your reading and on your tests. Use the glossary to look up their definitions if necessary.
- slat
- reimbursement

Graphic Organizer
As you read this section, note three advantages of breast-feeding and three advantages of bottle-feeding. Use a T-chart like the one shown to organize your information.

Feeding Decisions	
Breast-Feeding	**Bottle-Feeding**

Academic Standards . . . .

 English

NCTE 7 Conduct research and gather, evaluate, and synthesize data to communicate discoveries.

 Mathematics

NCTM Number and Operations Understand numbers, ways of representing numbers, relationships among numbers, and number systems.

 Science

NSES B Develop an understanding of the structure and properties of matter, chemical reactions.

NCTE *National Council of Teachers of English*
NCTM *National Council of Teachers of Mathematics*

NSES *National Science Education Standards*
NCSS *National Council for the Social Studies*

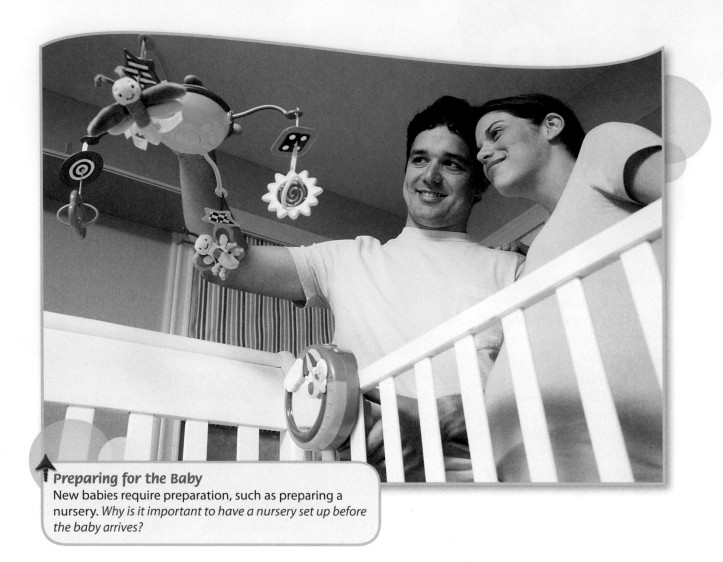

Preparing for the Baby
New babies require preparation, such as preparing a nursery. *Why is it important to have a nursery set up before the baby arrives?*

Preparing for Parenthood

Pregnancy is a time of anticipation and preparation. It is also a time for expectant parents to think about what their baby's physical, emotional, and intellectual needs will be and how they are going to meet them. Many expectant parents worry that they may not be up to the demands of raising a child. This is especially true for first-time parents. Parents should discuss their hopes, fears, worries, and other aspects of parenting with each other before the baby's arrival.

How will they handle guidance and discipline? How will parenting tasks be shared? How will they manage the new expenses? Of course, no one can plan for every situation. Parents' ideas often change as they gain parenting experience. Agreeing on certain ground rules, however, can help reduce confusion and conflict in relationships later on.

Parents-to-be must also prepare for their changing responsibilities. They may already be spouses, employees, students, volunteers, sisters or brothers, or daughters or sons. Now they will become parents as well. Some of the existing roles will change due to the time and energy that parenthood demands.

Everyone can benefit from good time-management skills. These skills are especially important for parents. Developing a basic daily schedule helps keep things on track. Routines also help infants and young children know what to expect and when to expect it. This helps them feel secure. Using time wisely can help staying on a schedule easier. For example, combining errands or taking advantage of nap times can help parents feel less overwhelmed.

Other Children in the Family

It is not always easy for children to accept a new baby in their lives. Older siblings may not be excited about the new addition to the family. Who can blame them? All of a sudden their world is turned upside down. They have to share their parents' attention, their toys, and their space. It is a big adjustment. Of course, many children are happy to have a sibling. They look forward to helping care for the new baby. They also enjoy showing their sibling how things work.

How children react to a new sister or brother depends on how well prepared they were before the baby's arrival, how they react to change, and their age. Parents should be prepared for a wide range of attitudes, from jealousy and confusion to excitement and love. A two-year-old does not really understand what is happening. Adjusting takes time. Talking about concerns and acceptance of a child's feelings can help foster a positive relationship between siblings.

Clothes, Equipment, and Space

The list of basic supplies for a baby can be overwhelming for many new parents. Babies need clothes, bedding, bath supplies, and travel equipment such as a stroller. Parents who choose bottle-feeding need bottles, plastic nipples, and lids. **Figure 5.5** describes basic baby supplies. Parents can get specific suggestions from doctors, family, friends, and magazines and books that test products.

Baby's Room

Newborns may sleep as many as 18 to 22 hours a day. During the first six months, most babies sleep 15 to 18 hours a day. Some parents feel that babies sleep better in their parents' room. This arrangement makes late-night feedings easier. Others think that babies need a quiet space of their own in which to sleep. Of course, many babies share a sibling's room. Comfortable conditions are more important than a large amount of space. If the baby does not have a separate room, curtains or other room dividers can be used to create a quieter, more private space.

Parenting Skills

Accepting the New Family Member

Many parents are concerned about how an older child will react to having a new baby brother or sister. Here are some tips parents can use to reassure an older sibling:

- Try not to change the older child's routine any more than necessary.
- If your local hospital offers sibling classes, consider enrolling your child.
- If possible, have the child come to the hospital to see the new baby.
- When relatives and friends visit, make sure the older child feels included.
- Encourage the older child to help with the baby's care. For example, he can bring you a diaper or entertain the baby while you are changing her clothes.
- Set aside time each day to spend with the older child without the baby being around.

Take Charge Imagine that a friend recently had a second child. Your friend is worried that visitors will pay attention to the new baby, but ignore the older child. Write an advice column on how your friend might handle this situation.

Figure 5.5 Basic Baby Supplies

It is important to have baby supplies ready when the infant first arrives home. *Why do you think sun hats or bonnets are important?*

Needed Baby Items	
Diapering Needs	❖ A changing table, or some surface to use for changing the baby ❖ If using disposable diapers, about 70 (a week's supply) ❖ If using cloth diapers: 3–4 dozen diapers and diaper pins ❖ Covered diaper pail ❖ Washcloths or disposable wipes, and diaper rash ointment
Clothing	❖ 6–8 undershirts; 4–6 one-piece footed sleepers or gowns ❖ 6 cotton receiving blankets; 1 warm outer wrapping blanket ❖ 1–2 sun hats or bonnets ❖ 1 sweater, 1 coat or warm wrap, and warm hat (if weather is cold)
Feeding Equipment	❖ Breast-feeding: Breast pump and pads; plastic bottles or bags for storing breast milk ❖ Bottle-feeding: 6–8 small bottles; nipples and bottle caps; bottle and nipple brush ❖ Bibs ❖ High chair
Bedding/Bedroom	❖ Crib and waterproof mattress (if the baby will sleep alone); bumper pad ❖ Waterproof mattress cover ❖ 4 fitted crib sheets ❖ 2–3 lightweight blankets and a heavier crib blanket ❖ Storage space, such as chest of drawers
Bathing and Other Supplies	❖ Baby bathtub ❖ Rubbing alcohol and cotton swabs (for umbilical cord) ❖ Mild, pure soap; baby shampoo ❖ Several washcloths and 2 soft cotton bath towels ❖ Cotton balls, baby oil, and baby lotion ❖ Blunt-tipped nail scissors ❖ Baby comb and brush set ❖ Thermometer
Travel Equipment	❖ Car seat that meets the government safety standards ❖ Tote bag for carrying supplies ❖ Stroller, carriage, or infant carrier (optional)

The Crib Babies spend countless hours alone in a crib. That means crib safety should be a high priority. Here are the characteristics of a safe crib:

- **Slats** Slats should be no more than 2⅜ inches apart. A **slat** is the flat, narrow strip of wood on the sides of a crib. If they are farther apart than this, a baby's head could become trapped between them.
- **Paint** If the crib is painted, the paint should not contain lead and should be smooth, with no flaking.
- **Structure** Corner posts should all be the same height. If some corner posts are taller than the sides of the crib, the baby's clothing or bedding could catch on the posts.
- **Sides** When lowered, crib sides should be about 9 inches above the mattress to keep the baby from falling out. When they are raised, they should be at least 26 inches above the mattress.
- **Latch** The latch to raise and lower the sides should lock securely. Never use a crib with a broken latch.
- **Mattress** The mattress should be firm and fit the crib exactly. There should be no space between the crib and the mattress. Infants can get trapped in this space.
- **Safe Bedding** Soft bedding should *not* be placed in a crib. While soft bedding such as pillows and quilts may look cute and comfortable, babies can suffocate on it. Even stuffed toys should be removed when a baby is in the crib. Basic bumper pads around the crib, just above the mattress, can be used to protect the baby from the crib's sides though.
- **End Panels** If the end panels have decorative cutouts, they should be very small, so the baby's head, arms, and legs cannot become caught in them.
- **Age** If the crib was pre-owned, it should be carefully checked to be sure it meets these current safety standards.

Parents may choose to put a baby monitor near the crib. The device picks up sounds from the room and sends them to a speaker in another part of the home. Baby monitors let parents know if the baby needs attention.

SAFE CHILD HEALTHY CHILD

Car Seat Safety

Children should be restrained using the appropriate car seats for their size and weight. There are three classes of car seats.

- Infant-only seats fit babies up to 22 pounds. The infant faces to the rear. The seat should be placed in the back seat.
- Convertible seats fit children from birth to about 40 pounds. They are used facing to the rear for the first year, then can be turned around when the baby is at least one year old and weighs at least 20 pounds.
- Children between four and seven years old should use booster seats locked securely in place with adult seat belts.

Be Prepared Most parents are careful to properly place their babies in car seats. However, many parents do not place children in the four to seven age group in booster seats. Conduct research to determine the percentage of injuries that could be prevented if all four- to seven-year-olds were placed in booster seats.

The Diaper-Changing Area Parents need to set aside a space where the baby can be changed and dressed. They can buy a changing table or use almost any sturdy, flat surface. Whatever surface is used, it should be covered with a cloth or towel that can be washed regularly.

Many changing tables or pads have rails around the sides to help prevent falls. They also come with a restraint strap to help secure the baby. Even young babies can wiggle, roll, or move quickly. That is why a baby should never be left unattended on any elevated surface such as a changing table or a bed, even if restraint straps are used. Even babies who cannot yet roll can still wiggle out of them if not properly supervised. Falls can occur within seconds.

Figure

5.6

Breast-Feeding vs. Bottle-Feeding

Both breast-feeding and bottle-feeding have advantages. *What factor do you think is most important in determining if a mother will breast-feed her baby? Why?*

	Advantages	Disadvantages
Breast-feeding	❧ Best source of nutrition for baby. ❧ Gives the baby some immunity against diseases. ❧ Creates a bond through physical closeness with the mother. ❧ May boost brain development. ❧ Reduces baby's risk of allergies. ❧ Causes fewer digestive upsets. ❧ Speeds the return of the mother's uterus to normal size. ❧ Reduces the mother's risk of later having breast or ovarian cancer. ❧ Reduces the risk that the mother will feel depressed. ❧ Is available at all times. ❧ Is free, though a nursing mother needs additional food.	❧ Baby has to be fed more often. ❧ In rare cases, may be medical reasons that suggest breast-feeding is not desirable or possible. ❧ May be painful for some mothers. ❧ May be difficult because of work schedule.
Bottle-feeding	❧ Allows mother to have a more flexible schedule. ❧ Eliminates concern about mother's diet or medications she takes. ❧ Ensures that baby gets essential nutrients. ❧ Babies need feeding less often. ❧ Available in shelf-stable forms for easier storage and portability.	❧ Can be expensive. ❧ Does not give the baby any natural immunities to disease. ❧ Involves a greater chance of baby developing allergies. ❧ Creates risk that baby may not be given close physical contact during feeding.

Decisions About Feeding

All parents must decide whether to breast- or bottle-feed their baby. There are several factors for parents to consider when making that choice. **Figure 5.6** lists many advantages and disadvantages of breast-feeding and bottle-feeding.

Breast milk has many benefits. Health care professionals recommend it whenever possible, even for a short time. There are breast pumps available that allow many mothers to successfully store breast milk. Other caregivers can then feed the baby when the mother is not available. This is an option for mothers who must return to work but want to continue breast-feeding their child.

Using bottles enables the baby's father or other caregivers to enjoy time alone with the baby. Babies who are bottle-fed drink formula. **Formula** is a mixture of milk or milk substitutes, water, and essential nutrients. It comes in either a powdered form, which is mixed with water, or in liquid form.

Whether a baby is bottle-fed or breast-fed, the nurturing and touch that comes with being held and fed is as important as the food itself.

Choosing a Pediatrician

Before the baby is born, parents should choose a doctor to care for the child. Many parents choose pediatricians. A **pediatrician** is a doctor who specializes in treating children. This doctor may be the child's primary doctor for years.

Some families choose a family doctor or family practice medical group so the whole family can go to one place for medical care. A family doctor may treat people of all ages. The medical group may include a pediatrician to care for children.

Parents can ask their own doctors for recommendations for pediatricians. Parents can also ask friends who have children for suggested doctors. Once they have a few names,

Mothers and Work
If a new mother plans to provide breast milk for her baby, she needs to discuss these plans with her employer ahead of time. *What other work arrangements should be considered?*

parents should interview each doctor to see if they like the doctor and agree with his or her ideas about caring for children. Most pediatricians welcome this opportunity to talk with prospective patients.

When choosing a doctor, some considerations are practical. Where is the doctor's office? What are the office hours? What are the fees for checkups, tests, and vaccinations? Which insurance plans are accepted? Other considerations are emotional. Do you feel comfortable with the doctor and staff?

✓ Reading Check **Compare** How is a pediatrician different from a family doctor?

Making a Budget

Prenatal care is an important expense that can be quite costly. Add these costs to the extra expenses involved with having a baby, and the

amount of money needed to support a baby climbs higher than many new parents expect. Planning can help parents meet these expenses. Creating a budget is one way to plan.

A budget is simply a spending plan that people use to help estimate their present and future income and expenses. A budget allows people to set goals for saving and to develop a spending plan that meets their needs. Budgets are helpful for everyone, but especially for expectant and new parents.

The first step in making a budget is to identify income, such as money from jobs. The next step is to list where that income currently goes. A **fixed expense** is a payment that generally cannot be changed. This can include bills such as a car payment, housing payment and expenses, and taxes. A **flexible expense** is an expense that can be changed, such as food costs, household items, clothes, and entertainment. For example, you could go out to eat less often to reduce food costs if necessary.

Estimating Health Care Expenses

Health care costs for pregnancy and childbirth can be high. This includes doctors' fees and the cost of staying in the hospital or birthing center. Hospitals charge different fees based on the care provided. Most health insurance plans will cover these expenses, but only if the woman has insurance coverage at the time she becomes pregnant. If a pregnant woman does not have insurance, some hospitals have free or lower-cost clinics to help people who cannot pay the full fees. Some hospitals will make arrangements for payment plans. There are also government programs that offer financial assistance for health care costs.

Many employers offer health insurance to their employees, and these plans often cover their spouses and children, too. Workers should find out what part of the expenses insurance will cover and what they must pay on their own.

If employers do not provide insurance, people can purchase their own health insurance. It is always a good idea to shop around for a health care plan before buying into one. Insurance companies charge different amounts, and

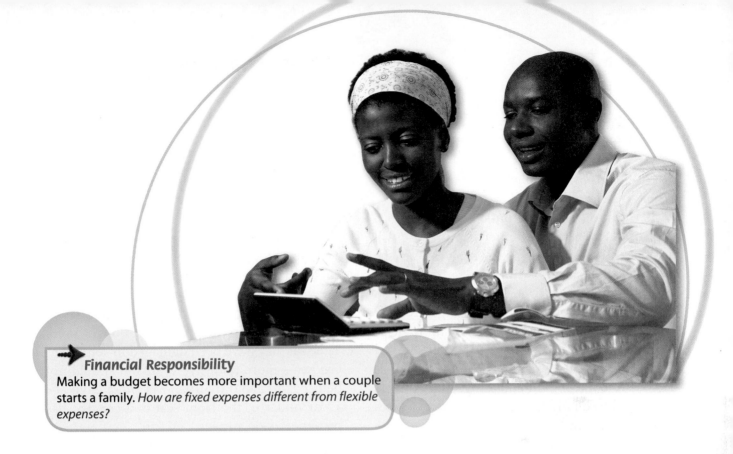

Financial Responsibility
Making a budget becomes more important when a couple starts a family. *How are fixed expenses different from flexible expenses?*

people can save money by making comparisons. As part of this process, it is important to carefully check the cost of the insurance and know exactly what services it will cover. Some insurance plans pay doctors and hospitals directly. Other plans require the insured persons to pay the bills themselves and then submit a claim for **reimbursement**, or repayment.

Consider Child Care Options

Once expectant parents have developed their budget, they need to review their options for child care. Parents must consider many factors when deciding how to care for their child. These factors include each other's goals, skills, and time available. Will one parent be able to cut back on working hours or stay at home full-time to care for the child? What other child care options are available, and what are their costs?

Many new parents who work take maternity or paternity leave. **Maternity leave** is time taken off work by a mother after the birth of a baby. **Paternity leave** is when the father takes time off work after a baby's birth. Under a federal law called the Family Medical Leave Act, employers with more than 50 workers must offer 12 weeks of unpaid family or medical

leave to new mothers and fathers. Many workers do not take the entire 12 weeks of leave for financial reasons. Many employers also offer some time off with full or partial pay. Many parents choose to take maternity or paternity leave to help bond with their new child.

Couples sometimes decide that one parent will care for the child and not work outside the home. In the past, this was usually the mother. Today, many fathers are full-time caregivers.

Regardless of who takes primary responsibility for daily caregiving, both parents should share the work of caring for their children. In many families, both parents decide to return to work. In others, there is just one parent to support the family. These single parents need to consider child care options.

Estimate Other Expenses

In addition to health care expenses, there are other costs that expectant parents must think about. Some of these include:
- Maternity clothes
- The supplies listed in Figure 5.5 on page 146
- Formula, if a baby is bottle-fed, which can cost between $1,200 and $2,200 per year
- Substitute child care, if needed

Make a Plan

Once parents have made a list of all the expected expenses, they can compare the expenses to their income and savings. If the couple's monthly income is less than their projected monthly expenses, it may be necessary to cut back on flexible expenses or to explore other sources of income.

If the mother works outside of the home, she should consider whether her income will be disrupted when the baby arrives and she is off work. Parents who have saved money will have an easier time. Even those with no prior savings should include saving a regular amount in their budget. This cushion helps families deal with unexpected expenses and future needs. Parents should use their plan as a guide to control their spending. Adjustments may need to be made periodically as expenses or income changes.

Reduce Expenses

There are several ways to reduce costs. Shopping for baby clothes at store sales, garage sales, or secondhand stores can save money. Using coupons can help decrease the family's food budget. Borrowing baby equipment and clothes is another way to save money. However, all used or borrowed items should be carefully cleaned. You should also make sure the items meet any current safety standards.

One of the most important duties of a parent is to make sure children are as safe as possible when traveling in a car. Restraining a child properly is the best way to prevent injuries in a crash. Car seats should not be bought used. The seat may have been damaged in some way. Car seats more than five years old should not be used. To avoid injury, never put a child age 12 or under in the front seat of a car that has passenger-side airbags.

Section 5.2 After You Read

Review Key Concepts

1. **Identify** some important safety considerations when choosing a crib.
2. **Describe** factors parents must consider when deciding on child care for a new baby.

Practice Academic Skills

English

3. Disposable diapers have become increasingly popular over the last 40 years. Conduct research to compare the advantages of using cloth or disposable diapers. Pay particular attention to cost and environmental issues. Create a chart comparing the two. Then write a paragraph stating which you believe is the better choice and why.

Science

4. Research has shown that breast-fed babies have fewer allergies than bottle-fed babies. Conduct research using print and online resources to determine why scientists believe this is true. Write a summary explaining what you have learned.

NCTE 7 Conduct research and gather, evaluate, and synthesize data to communicate discoveries.

NSES B Develop an understanding of the structure and properties of matter, chemical reactions.

 Check Your Answers Check your answers at this book's Online Learning Center at **glencoe.com**.

Reading Guide

Before You Read

Re-reading If you do not understand a difficult topic, stop immediately and re-read the section. Continuing on in the text will only make you feel discouraged.

Read to Learn

Key Concepts
- **Identify** ways expectant parents can prepare for the birth of a child.
- **Compare and contrast** the options for the delivery of a baby.

Main Idea

Taking childbirth classes can help prepare parents for the birth. Parents must decide who will deliver the baby and where the birth will take place.

Content Vocabulary

◇ prepared childbirth
◇ labor
◇ delivery
◇ midwife
◇ alternative birth center

 Graphic Organizer Go to this book's Online Learning Center at **glencoe.com** to print out this graphic organizer.

Academic Vocabulary

You will find these words in your reading and on your tests. Use the glossary to look up their definitions if necessary.

■ complication
■ compressed

Graphic Organizer

As you read, compare and contrast the places women might give birth. Use a Venn diagram like the one shown to organize your information.

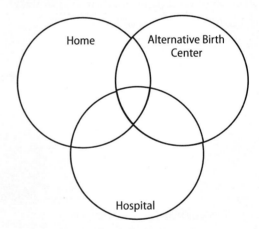

Academic Standards . . . .

 English Language Arts

NCTE 2 Read literature to build an understanding of the human experience.

Social Studies

NCSS I A Culture Analyze and explain the ways groups, societies, and cultures address human needs and concerns.

NCTE *National Council of Teachers of English*
NCTM *National Council of Teachers of Mathematics*

NSES *National Science Education Standards*
NCSS *National Council for the Social Studies*

Prepared Childbirth

Prepared childbirth means reducing pain and fear during the birth process through education and the use of breathing and conditioning exercises. Many expectant parents attend childbirth education classes to help them prepare for labor. **Labor** is the process in which the baby gradually moves out of the uterus and into the vagina to be born. This leads to delivery. **Delivery** is the birth of the baby. The father or another designated person can offer support to the mother during labor and delivery.

Childbirth education classes may be offered by hospitals, health care providers, or private teachers. In addition to learning breathing techniques, participants learn so much more, including the following:

- How the baby grows and develops throughout pregnancy
- Tests that may be performed during the pregnancy, such as amniocentesis
- Warning signs that may indicate a serious problem during pregnancy
- What to expect during labor and delivery, including the stages of labor
- The role of the support person
- Breathing and conditioning exercises to make pregnancy, labor, and delivery more comfortable and less painful
- What to expect after the baby is born

Classes offered by hospitals may also include a tour of the facility. Parents-to-be are shown where to go when they arrive and where they will be during labor and delivery, and after delivery. Classes might also review specific rules of the hospital regarding visitors, support persons, and electronics. For example, some hospitals will not allow cameras in the delivery room. Most hospitals have specified areas where cell phones can be used.

Childbirth education classes will also help parents make a plan for the labor and delivery. This is called a birth plan. This tells the medical staff what the couple would like to have happen during the childbirth process, including the possible use of pain medication.

✓ **Reading Check** **List** What are three things parents might learn about in a childbirth education class?

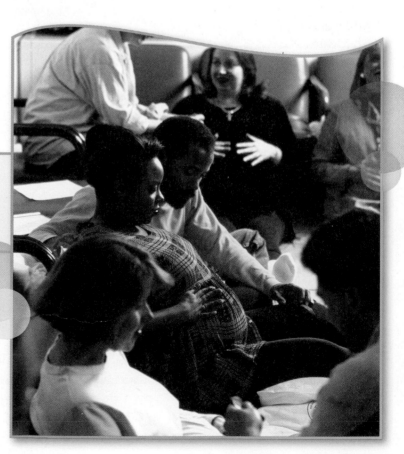

▸▸▸▸ Preparing for Childbirth
Many hospitals and health care providers offer childbirth education classes. *How can taking a class help reduce expectant parents' fears?*

Delivery Options

Years ago, most babies were born at home, often with the aid of a midwife. Mothers did not have the option of going to a hospital or the availability of today's lifesaving technology. Today, there are many options for where a baby will be born and the type of health care professional who will attend the birth.

Health Care Professionals

A health care professional attends most births, regardless of where the birth occurs. There are several types of professionals that can assist with the labor and delivery. The following health care professionals are qualified to deliver babies:

- **Obstetricians** Because these doctors specialize in the care of mothers and babies both before and right after birth, they are qualified to handle any emergencies or problems that might occur.
- **Family Doctors** Some family doctors provide prenatal care and deliver babies. If problems arise, however, they may call in an obstetrician.
- **Licensed Midwives** A **midwife** is a health care professional trained to assist women in childbirth. There are two types of midwives: certified nurse-midwives (CNMs) and certified midwives. CNMs are registered nurses. Both types of midwives have advanced training in normal pregnancy and birth. All midwives must pass a certification exam before they can practice. Midwives will usually call in an obstetrician if a **complication**, or problem, occurs.

The health care professional chosen will generally be involved in the care of the mother and baby throughout the pregnancy. This helps the doctor or midwife be better prepared for possible complications. It is important that the parents feel comfortable with their health care professional.

Many mothers also choose to have a *doula* present during their labor and delivery. A doula is a woman experienced in childbirth who provides advice and support to a mother during labor and delivery, and after childbirth.

Doulas often have suggestions for how to cope with labor pains. They can help keep the mother calm and focused during the delivery. Most hospitals will allow both the father and a doula in the delivery room to support the mother.

Places to Give Birth

Not all babies are born in a hospital. Parents have a choice of where the birth will occur. Expectant parents should explore the hospitals or birth centers in their area before deciding where to deliver their baby.

Their options may be limited by their health insurance or by which hospital their doctor uses. Many hospitals offer tours and will gladly discuss concerns and special needs. Parents should discuss their options with their doctor before making a final decision.

➤ **Delivery Options**
There are many factors to be considered when deciding where to give birth. *Why is it helpful to visit different facilities before making your decision?*

Home

It is only in the last 100 years that most babies have been born in hospitals. Some women still choose a home birth. If a couple is considering a home birth, they should consult their doctor. Together, a decision can be made that will take into account all risk factors.

Unfortunately, it is not possible to know what problems might arise. For example, the umbilical cord might become **compressed**, or flattened. This can threaten the baby's oxygen supply and force the need for a special or early delivery. No one can predict these types of problems. Parents should have a plan for dealing with the unexpected.

Many couples who choose home births have a midwife present to assist with the delivery. A couple should interview many midwives and find one that they are comfortable with prior to the birth. Remember, a midwife can assist with labor and delivery, but does not have the training of a doctor should problems arise. A doula, or a non-medical assistant, may also be used at a home birth, but does not have the training of a midwife.

Hospital

Depending on health insurance and other issues, new mothers and their babies may spend two to three days in a hospital after a routine delivery, or up to a week in the hospital if there are complications. The government requires insurance companies to cover at least two days in the hospital after delivery for women who have routine, vaginal births.

Hospitals have a full staff of medical professionals to help parents through labor and delivery. They also have staff to assist with the care of both mother and child after the delivery. In addition to doctors and nurses, many hospitals have staff to teach parents how to care for their new baby, including how to change a diaper and feed the child.

The trained personnel, sanitary conditions, and presence of high-tech medical equipment make many parents more comfortable with a hospital birth. Should a complication arise during or after delivery, a hospital has the staff and resources necessary to respond right away. Hospitals also may offer several types of services to meet the needs of expectant parents.

{ **Expert Advice...** }

"Pregnancy and the birth of a child are ranked as one of the most memorable experiences for women, so being well informed of all your options can help ensure a gratifying experience for you and your family."

— American Pregnancy Association

Parents should ask if the hospital offers any of the following:

- Classes that prepare parents for delivery and infant care.
- Programs for siblings and fathers.
- Private rooms that provide soft lighting, music, and comfortable furniture. Mothers and their families can stay in these rooms for labor, delivery, and recovery, unless a complication occurs. Additional medical equipment is kept out of sight but is ready for immediate use.
- The option for mother and baby to room together during their time in the hospital.

Alternative Birth Center

Some couples choose an alternative birth center for their delivery. These centers may or may not be part of a hospital. An **alternative birth center** is a facility that provides a more homelike environment for labor and delivery. Food and drink is generally offered during labor.

Most hospitals allow the mother to eat only ice chips after admittance, as anything else might interfere with anesthesia. Birth centers emphasize prepared, natural childbirth and so do not offer pain medication during labor.

Alternative birth centers also might offer beds large enough for both the mother and father to rest. Music and friends are generally allowed. Many birth centers have birthing tubs for women who choose a water birth. A water birth means the mother is in water during the birth. This would be discussed and agreed upon prior to the birth, as part of the birth plan.

Midwives generally handle births in these centers. Most accept only mothers with a low risk of complications. A nearby hospital or obstetrician is on call to handle any problems that may develop. These centers typically charge less than hospitals do. Time spent at the facility is usually shorter. Parents and their baby typically leave the center within 24 hours if there are no complications.

Section 5.3   **After You Read**

Review Key Concepts

1. **Explain** what is meant by the term *prepared childbirth*.
2. **Describe** three types of health care professionals who can assist with the birth of babies.

Practice Academic Skills

 English Language Skills

3. Locate a novel that contains a description of childbirth. If necessary, ask your teacher, parent, or another appropriate adult for ideas. Read the portion of the novel describing childbirth and write a summary. Was it presented as a pleasant or unpleasant experience?

> **NCTE 2** Read literature to build an understanding of the human experience.

 Social Studies

4. There are a number of different types of childbirth classes available. Two popular ones are the Lamaze method and the Bradley method. Research these two methods and write a report briefly describing each one. In your report, discuss whether you think the methods might appeal to different kinds of parents and why.

> **NCSS I A** Analyze and explain the ways groups, societies, and cultures address human needs and concerns.

 Check Your Answers Check your answers at this book's Online Learning Center at **glencoe.com**.

Toy designers create everything from simple rattles to complex, computer-controlled educational games. They begin with a basic concept. They then go through rigid development guidelines to come up with a final product.

What Does a Toy Designer Do?

Designing toys is challenging work. Toys must be attractive, interesting enough to capture a child's attention, safe, and easy to keep clean. New toys must look original, must function properly, and are often expected to be educational. The toy designer might get ideas from watching children play with existing toys. They might design a new toy based on a make-believe toy that a child thought up.

Where Do Toy Designers Work?

Most toy designers work for toy manufacturers. There is a lot of competition for jobs, so successful candidates must have skills that make them stand out from the crowd. Some designers start their own companies to create the toys they want to sell.

Preparation and Skills

Education and Training

Recommended courses of study include child psychology, graphic design, children's literature, and fine arts. Most toy designers apply for internships with toy companies.

Aptitudes, Abilities, and Skills

Toy designers need the ability to take an idea and turn it into a product. It is also helpful to know how to use computer design programs or how video games work. Knowledge of children's likes and dislikes, and a sense of fun are also needed to be successful as a toy designer.

Academic Skills

Design and basic engineering skills are used to determine how a new toy will work and how it will be built. Knowledge of child development allows a designer to create toys that children will want to use.

Explore Careers

Some toy designers work independently to develop ideas that they then submit to toy manufacturers. These people are called *entrepreneurs*. Use the Internet to learn more about being an independent toy designer. Write a report presenting what you learn.

 Careers Online For more information on careers, visit the Occupational Outlook Handbook Web site through the link on this book's Online Learning Center at **glencoe.com**.

Chapter Summary

A woman should see a doctor when she thinks she is pregnant. She should receive regular prenatal care during her pregnancy. Eating a well-balanced diet with foods from each of the five food groups is essential to the health of the developing baby and the mother. Moderate exercise and stress management also are important. Parents-to-be should prepare for the birth of the child. They should create a budget and decide how they will balance their lives after the baby is born. Prepared childbirth helps expectant parents get ready for labor and delivery. They must choose a health care professional to attend the birth and decide where the birth will occur.

Vocabulary Review

1. Use these content and academic vocabulary terms to create a crossword puzzle on graph paper. Use the definitions as clues.

Content Vocabulary

◇ obstetrician (p. 129)
◇ anemia (p. 130)
◇ Rh factor (p. 131)
◇ gestational diabetes (p. 131)
◇ preeclampsia (p. 132)
◇ osteoporosis (p. 139)
◇ lactose intolerance (p. 142)
◇ lactase (p. 142)

◇ formula (p. 149)
◇ pediatrician (p. 149)
◇ fixed expense (p. 150)
◇ flexible expense (p. 150)
◇ maternity leave (p. 151)
◇ paternity leave (p. 151)
◇ prepared childbirth (p. 154)
◇ labor (p. 154)
◇ delivery (p. 154)

◇ midwife (p. 155)
◇ alternative birth center (p. 156)

Academic Vocabulary

■ robust (p. 132)
■ alleviate (p. 133)
■ slat (p. 147)
■ reimbursement (p. 151)
■ complication (p. 155)
■ compressed (p. 156)

Review Key Concepts

2. Identify the early signs of pregnancy.
3. Explain the importance of proper nutrition during pregnancy.
4. List six categories of basic baby supplies.
5. Describe why parents need to develop a budget.
6. Identify ways expectant parents can prepare for the birth of a child.
7. Compare and contrast the options for the delivery of a baby.

Critical Thinking

8. Drawing Conclusions Why do you think some women might suffer more from emotional stress during pregnancy than at other times in their lives?
9. Apply If you knew a pregnant couple who had a very limited budget, what suggestions might you offer for preparing for the baby?
10. Infer Why might someone choose a midwife instead of a doctor to deliver her baby?

Family & Community Connection

11. Interview a Mom Talk to your mother or another relative or friend about her childbirth experience. Ask the following questions: Where did you give birth? What health care professionals assisted you? Who else was with you during your labor and delivery? Create a chart to compare and contrast the information from your interview with the information you learned in the text.

Health Skills

12. Midwife Requirements Requirements for becoming a licensed midwife vary from state to state. For example, some states require midwives to be registered nurses, and others do not. Use print or online resources, or contact the state medical board, to research your state's requirements. Create an oral report to share what you learn with your class.

Observation Skills

13. Shopping for Baby Supplies Many factors go into making purchases for a new baby. Go to a store that sells baby equipment. Choose one item, such as a crib, stroller, or car seat. Watch at least four different people shopping for the chosen item.

Procedure As you watch the shoppers, keep track of their main concerns. For example, do they seem more concerned with the product's features or its appearance?

Analysis Create a chart in which you summarize the features of the product that seemed most important to each shopper. List the factors they took into consideration when making purchasing decisions.

NCTE 7 Conduct research and gather, evaluate, and synthesize data to communicate discoveries.

Real-World Skills

Interpersonal and Collaborative Skills

14. Write a Radio Announcement Follow your teacher's instructions to form into groups. Work with your group to create the script for a one-minute public service announcement for the radio. The script should emphasize the importance of car safety seats and discuss the kinds of seats appropriate for different aged children.

Technology Skills

15. Create a Spreadsheet Use a spreadsheet software program to track the monthly budget for a family expecting a baby. Divide the budget into fixed expenses and flexible expenses. The spreadsheet should calculate a fixed expense total, a flexible expense total, and a total of all expenses.

Financial Literacy

16. Thrifty Shopping Choose three items new babies need, such as strollers, cribs, and sleepers. Use the Internet to find average prices for each item. Then check classified ads and secondhand stores to determine their secondhand cost. Create a table showing the difference in prices.

 Additional Activities For additional activities, go to this book's Online Learning Center at **glencoe.com**.

Academic Skills

 English Language Arts

17. Letter to Your Child Imagine you are the father or mother of a new baby. Write a letter to your child to read when he or she is older describing what you did to keep the baby safe and healthy during pregnancy. For example, if you were a new mother, how did you adjust your eating habits? Why did you do this? If you were a new father, how did you support the mother? Did you talk to the baby in the womb?

> **NCTE 4** Use written language to communicate effectively.

 Mathematics

18. Child Care Costs Many new parents must include the cost of child care in their monthly budgets. According to the National Association of Child Care Resources, day care costs for young babies can be as low as $366 per month and as high as $1,221 per month. What is the range of child care costs?

Math Concept **Range** Range is a statistical measure used with a set of numbers. Calculate range by subtracting the lowest value in the set from the highest value.

Starting Hint Subtract the minimum ($366) from the maximum ($1,221) costs for monthly day care.

 For math help, go to the Math Appendix at the back of the book.

> **NCTM Data Analysis and Probability** Select and use appropriate statistical methods to analyze data.

 Science

19. Rate Anesthesia Use Whether or not to have pain-relieving medication during a birth is an important decision each pregnant woman must make. Many women have local anesthesia. Others choose to have a natural childbirth, without pain-relieving medication.

Procedure Speak to several mothers. Ask them if they used local anesthesia. Try to find some women who did use anesthesia and some who did not. Ask each woman to rate her discomfort on a scale of 1 to 10, with 1 being completely comfortable and at ease and 10 being in unbearable pain.

Analysis Find the average rating for each group. Write a summary discussing which group appeared to have the least discomfort during childbirth.

> **NSES A** Develop abilities necessary to do scientific inquiry, understandings about scientific inquiry.

Standardized Test Practice

TRUE/FALSE QUESTIONS
Carefully read the statement and determine if it is true or false.

20. While following established nutritional guidelines is important for the health of a developing fetus, it matters little to the health of the mother.
   a. True
   b. False

> **Test-Taking Tip** If you have time at the end of a true/false test, check your answers. Did you read the statement carefully? Was there any part of the statement that was false? If so, the entire statement is false.

6 The Baby's Arrival

Chapter Objectives

After completing this chapter, you will be able to:

- **Describe** the progression of labor.
- **Explain** what happens during a cesarean birth.
- **List** the factors that can contribute to a premature birth.
- **Describe** a newborn's appearance immediately after birth.
- **Identify** the exams and procedures given to a newborn in the first few days.
- **Review** what occurs during the hospital stay after delivery.
- **Summarize** the physical and emotional needs of a new mother.

Writing Activity — *Write Using Details*

Describe Emotions Having a new baby in the home is an emotional time for every family member. Imagine that you are five years old and your parents have just brought home your new baby brother. Write two paragraphs using details to describe your emotions.

Writing Tips Before you write, create an outline to organize the details you will include in your paragraphs.

1. Create a head for the main idea for each paragraph.
2. List specific details under each head.
3. Follow the outline to write your paragraphs.

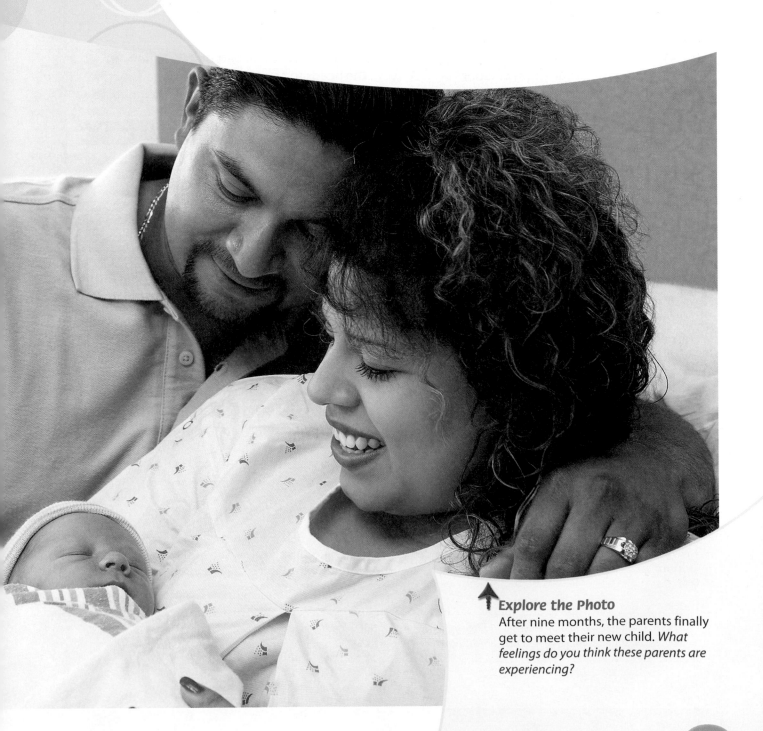

Explore the Photo
After nine months, the parents finally get to meet their new child. *What feelings do you think these parents are experiencing?*

Reading Guide

Before You Read

Predict Look at the photos in this section and read their captions. Write one or two sentences predicting what you think the section will be about.

Read to Learn

Key Concepts

- **Describe** the progression of labor.
- **Explain** what happens during a cesarean birth.
- **List** the factors that can contribute to a premature birth.

Main Idea

Pregnant women go through different stages of labor before delivering a baby. Some women have a cesarean or premature birth.

Content Vocabulary

◇ cervix
◇ contraction
◇ fetal monitoring
◇ dilate
◇ cord blood
◇ stem cells
◇ cesarean birth
◇ incubator

Academic Vocabulary

You will find these words in your reading and on your tests. Use the glossary to look up their definitions if necessary.

■ induce
■ anesthesia

Graphic Organizer

As you read the first part of this section, use the heads to create an outline. Use a structure like the one shown to help build your outline.

The Progression of Labor
1. _____
a. _____
b. _____
c. _____
d. _____
2. _____
a. _____
b. _____
c. _____
d. _____

 Graphic Organizer Go to this book's Online Learning Center at **glencoe.com** to print out this graphic organizer.

Academic Standards . . . .

 English Language Arts

NCTE 12 Use language to accomplish individual purposes.

 Social Studies

NCSS I A Culture Analyze and explain the ways groups, societies, and cultures address human needs and concerns.

NCTE *National Council of Teachers of English*
NCTM *National Council of Teachers of Mathematics*

NSES *National Science Education Standards*
NCSS *National Council for the Social Studies*

The Progression of Labor

Nine months is a long time to wait to hold a new baby. Many expectant mothers have felt like their due date would never come. Finally, though, it does. A nervous, excited woman goes into labor, and her baby arrives.

Giving birth is a powerful physical and emotional experience. It leaves most new mothers feeling both exhausted and exhilarated. Giving birth, or labor, occurs in two basic parts: the beginning of labor and the stages of labor.

The Beginning of Labor

During the last few weeks of pregnancy, time often seems to slow down for the expectant mother. Many women become anxious for the baby to be born. During this time, they feel what is called lightening. This occurs when the baby settles deep in the pelvis near the time of birth. Because the baby has moved down, the pressure on the woman's upper abdomen is reduced, or lightened. With a first pregnancy, lightening may occur days or weeks before labor. A woman who has already had a baby may experience this change just before labor begins.

Early Signs of Labor

There are many signs that the baby is on its way. A new mother may experience one or more of these signs. A woman in her first pregnancy may have more trouble recognizing some of the early signs.

One is commonly called the "show" or "bloody show." This refers to the few drops of blood or a pinkish vaginal stain that occurs when the mucus that plugs the uterus during pregnancy dissolves. This plug seals the cervix ('sər-viks) and prevents bacteria from moving into the uterus. This may occur as early as a few days prior to birth. The **cervix** is the lower part of the uterus.

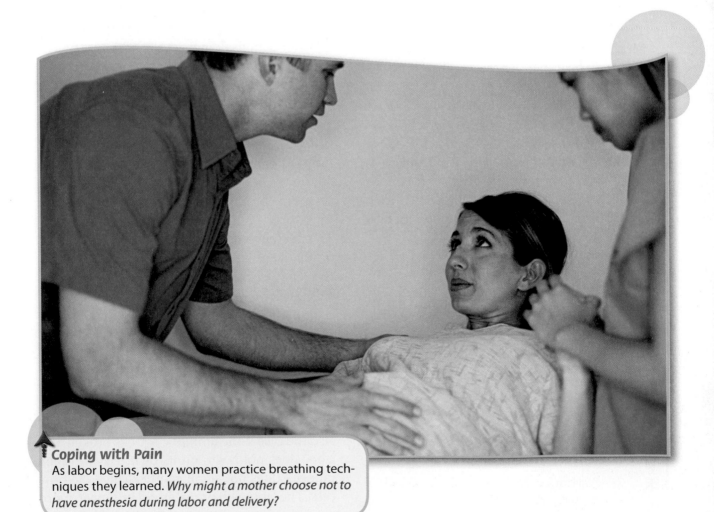

Coping with Pain
As labor begins, many women practice breathing techniques they learned. *Why might a mother choose not to have anesthesia during labor and delivery?*

Some women realize that they are in labor when they feel a trickle or gush of warm fluid from the vagina. This indicates that the membrane, or amniotic sac, holding the fluid around the baby has broken. Often, the membrane does not rupture until much later in labor. This is what is meant when a woman says that her water has broken.

If the mother experiences this, she should note the time, the amount of fluid, and the color and odor of the fluid. She should call her doctor or midwife and report this information. Once the membrane has broken, delivery should be within 24 to 48 hours to protect the baby from infection.

A **contraction** is the tightening and releasing of the muscles of the uterus. This is also a sign of labor. When the uterus contracts, it shortens and closes, pushing the fetus against the cervix. Then the uterus relaxes before the next contraction. This is why contractions may last a few minutes. Earlier in labor, the period between them is longer. This time gets shorter as labor advances.

Mothers often report that contractions are painful but bearable. There is time between them to rest and recover. After the baby is born and the placenta is also pushed out, contractions end and there is no lingering pain.

As labor and contractions begin, the baby's heart can be monitored. **Fetal monitoring** is the watching of an unborn baby's heart rate for indications of stress. This is usually done during labor and birth. There are different types of fetal monitoring. One of the most common methods is with an ultrasound device. This method provides a beat-to-beat picture of the baby's heart in relationship to the mother's contractions.

Premature Labor

A full-term pregnancy usually lasts 40 weeks. Giving birth a week or two earlier or later is still considered normal though. Premature, or preterm, labor occurs when the fetus has been developing in the womb for 37 weeks or less. Warning signs of premature labor include having contractions every ten minutes or less; feeling a constant, dull backache; or leaking fluid or blood. Sometimes, doctors can give medication to stop premature labor.

False Labor

Some women feel what is called false labor hours or even days before their real labor starts. They begin to feel strong contractions and believe that labor may have begun. Doctors look for three signs that indicate false labor:

- Contractions are not regular or rhythmic.
- Contractions do not get stronger over time.
- Contractions end with light exercise, such as walking or stretching.

When contractions follow a regular pattern and grow in intensity, a woman is having real labor. The woman and her labor coach should time the contractions by noting how long they last and how often they occur.

It can be difficult to determine the right time to go to the hospital or birthing center. The doctor or nurses at the obstetrician's office or medical center can provide guidance.

Inducing Labor

If necessary, the doctor can **induce**, or start, labor by artificial means. This can be done by using medication or puncturing the amniotic sac. Labor is often induced for medical reasons or in emergencies. If the baby has been slow to develop or is still in the womb after 42 weeks, the doctor may decide to induce labor. This is also the case if the amniotic sac has broken and labor does not begin on its own. Having labor induced does not significantly change the process. The labor will probably *not* be longer, more painful, or more difficult than natural labor.

{ Expert Advice... }

"Some mothers start their labor with a bang—suddenly, undoubtedly, powerfully—and progress fast. Others ease into labor slowly, sometimes unconvincingly, and progress gradually, yet efficiently."

— William and Martha Sears, pediatric medical specialists

Stages of Labor

Once labor begins, it moves through three basic stages:

- **Stage 1** Contractions open the cervix.
- **Stage 2** The baby is born.
- **Stage 3** The placenta is expelled.

See **Figure 6.1** on pages 168–169 for more details about each stage. During these three stages, the baby makes its way out of the mother's womb and into the world. The amount of time it takes to give birth depends on the mother and baby. It often takes longer if the baby is the woman's first. For a first birth, the first stage may last from six to 18 hours. It may be two to five hours for a later child.

It is often hard to tell exactly when real labor starts. This makes it hard to determine a typical length for the first stage of labor. The second stage is usually one to two hours for a first child. However, it is often only 15 to 30 minutes for a later child. The third stage is the shortest. It can take anywhere from 10 to 30 minutes.

The First Stage

The first stage of labor officially begins when contractions are coming at regular intervals. The contractions in the uterine muscle pull up on the cervix, slowly softening and thinning it and allowing it to open. Contractions increase in strength, length, and frequency. When this stage begins, contractions usually last for about 30 seconds and occur up to 20 minutes apart. When they last about 60 seconds and occur two to five minutes apart, then the woman is in "active labor". Some hospitals prefer not to admit the mother until she is in active labor.

To cope with the demands of labor, the woman becomes more focused and needs support from her partner. This is when the woman will use the coping techniques that she may have learned, such as breathing exercises or walking. It is during this stage that the mother would receive pain medication if she wanted it. Some medications may affect how long this stage of labor will last.

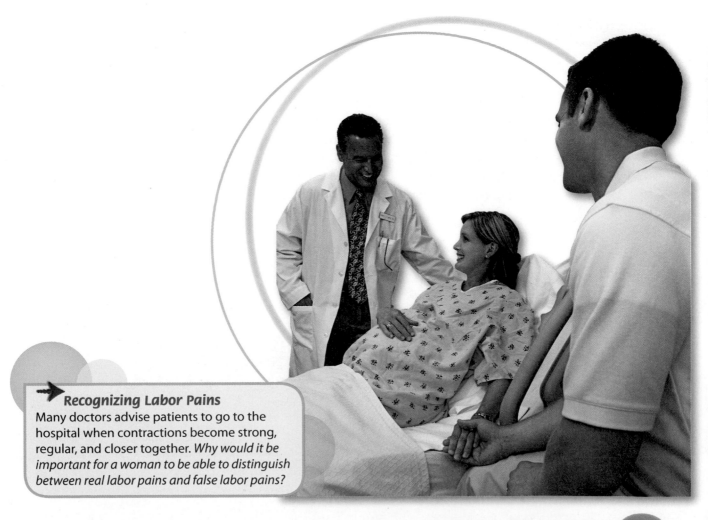

Recognizing Labor Pains
Many doctors advise patients to go to the hospital when contractions become strong, regular, and closer together. *Why would it be important for a woman to be able to distinguish between real labor pains and false labor pains?*

Figure
6.1 The Stages of Labor

Women who go through natural child-birth will go through each of these stages of labor. *How can knowing these steps in advance help a mother during labor?*

Cervix (closed)

Birth canal

Before Labor Begins
The cervix is its normal size and shape.

Cervix (beginning to open)

Birth canal

First Stage of Labor Contractions make the cervix dilate, or widen. The cervix also becomes thinner, changing from its usual thickness of about ¾ inch (19 mm) to become as thin as a sheet of paper. This thinning is called *effacement.*

Cervix (fully dilated)

Birth canal

Transition Transition completes the work of the first stage. The cervix becomes fully dilated to a size of 4 inches (10 cm) and the baby's head slips out of the uterus into the birth canal.

Second Stage of Labor: Crowning
When the top of the head appears at the opening of the birth canal, it is called *crowning*.

Second Stage of Labor: Head Emerges The baby's head emerges first. The head has changed its shape to ease passage through the birth canal. It will later return to normal. After the head, the shoulders follow. Then the rest of the baby slips out easily.

Third Stage of Labor The woman gives birth to the placenta, no longer needed by the baby.

What's in a Name?

What is the best way to choose a name for a baby? Children are often named after relatives, living or deceased. In China, parents' hopes for a healthy, prosperous life for their children are reflected in the names they choose. Girls' names typically include words relating to elements of beauty or composure, such as *ting* (graceful) or *hua* (flower). Boys' names are designed to honor ancestors or indicate strength, such as *shaozu* (bring honor to our ancestors) and *gang* (steel). Some Chinese names are combinations of elements, such as *po yee*, meaning treasured child.

Build Connections *How can names link children to past generations?*

NCSS I A Culture Analyze and explain the ways groups, societies, and cultures address human needs and concerns.

As the cervix dilates, the baby moves into the lower pelvis. **Dilate** means to widen or open. Most babies enter the world headfirst. However, some enter the pelvis with their feet or buttocks first. These positions are known as breech presentation. Babies in these positions may have a difficult time moving through the pelvis. The doctor will decide whether a normal delivery is possible.

The first stage ends with a period called transition. A transition is a change. In labor, the change refers to the cervix. Transition is when the cervix becomes fully dilated to a diameter of about 10 centimeters (4 inches). Strong contractions that last up to 90 seconds and are two to three minutes apart occur in this period. This is the more difficult part of labor. A woman needs encouragement and reassurance from her support partner at this time.

The Second Stage

Contractions during the second stage are more productive, pushing the baby through the pelvis and out of the vagina, or birth canal. During this stage, it is safe for a woman to push. When she pushes, she uses her muscles to expel the baby. Earlier pushing might have resulted in tearing of delicate tissues, or other types of injuries.

How can a baby fit through such a narrow space? Ligaments, or connective tissue, join the bones of the mother's pelvis. During labor, a hormone called relaxin allows this tissue to stretch like rubber bands. This stretching moves apart the pelvic bones. Relaxin also makes it possible for the walls of the vagina to stretch so that the baby can safely pass through.

A baby's body is designed for this journey. A soft skull lets the baby's head become longer and narrower than usual. The skull consists of five separate bones that move together and allow for the baby's head to fit through the pelvis and vagina.

Sometimes the opening in the mother's body is too small to accommodate the baby's passage. In this case, the doctor may widen it with a surgical cut called an episiotomy.

As the baby's head emerges, the doctor or midwife provides gentle support and help guide the baby out. The head is followed by one shoulder, and then the other. The rest of the baby follows quickly.

Sometimes doctors use surgical tongs called forceps to grasp the baby's body and guide its movement. A vacuum extractor that applies suction to the baby's head once it appears may be used if the baby needs to be moved through the birth canal quickly.

The Third Stage

After birth, the mother may be able to rest briefly, and then may feel a few contractions and a desire to push. These contractions usually are not painful. They help the placenta, the organ that develops in the mother and helps supply oxygen to the fetus, separate from the uterine wall.

Once the mother pushes the placenta out of her body, the birth process is complete. The new mother may begin bonding with her child. If needed, the doctor or midwife will stitch up the episiotomy or tears that may have occurred during the birth. The final stage of labor is brief but important.

Scientists have discovered that cord blood contains stem cells. **Cord blood** is the blood left behind in the umbilical cord and placenta following birth. **Stem cells** are cells capable of producing all types of blood cells. The stem cells can be used to treat many serious blood-related illnesses in the baby or other family members. Parents can arrange to have the cord blood stored in case there is a future medical need. It may also be donated for use by others.

How to Cope with Labor

Most first-time mothers worry about how much pain is involved in the birth process. The answer is it varies. Some women find it very painful and tiring, while others do not. There are many ways to cope with the pain, including medication.

Mothers and fathers can participate in childbirth classes. These classes teach breathing and relaxation techniques, as well as focusing exercises that may help distract a woman from pain. These classes are often referred to as Lamaze classes. However, Lamaze is just one approach to childbirth education. Some classes teach a form of self-hypnosis that can significantly reduce pain.

When choosing a childbirth class, parents should consider:

- Who is teaching the class? If it is offered by the hospital, it is probably a nurse. Does the teacher's philosophy agree with yours?
- How big is the class? Smaller is better.
- What is the format of the class? Does the class offer time for practicing techniques?

There are several types of **anesthesia**, or drugs that cause a loss of feeling, used for pain relief during childbirth. Some are injected into veins or muscles, where they act on the entire body. These do not slow labor but may make women and their babies sleepy. Others, called epidural blocks, are injected into the lower back, where they numb the lower half of the body. Epidural blocks still allow women to feel some pressure as the baby's head descends. Sometimes, if the pain is worse than expected, or there are other problems, more medication may be needed.

✓ **Reading Check** **Summarize** What happens during the third stage of labor?

Learning to Cope
Many couples take childbirth classes together. *Why is it important for the father to attend childbirth classes?*

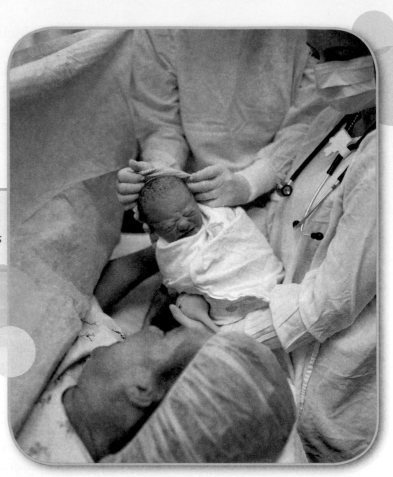

Cesarean Birth

A cesarean birth may be necessary when complications arise during labor. *How does a cesarean birth differ from natural birth?*

Cesarean Birth

Not all births progress through the stages of labor. If complications arise during pregnancy or labor, a cesarean birth (si-ˈzer-ē-ən), also known as a cesarean section or c-section, may become necessary. A **cesarean birth** is the delivery of a baby through a surgical incision in the mother's abdomen.

Cesarean delivery might be performed for several reasons. It could be due to lack of normal progress during labor or discovering that the baby is in distress or turned in the wrong direction. Cesarean deliveries are often planned for multiple births. If a cesarean birth is anticipated during pregnancy, special childbirth classes can help parents prepare.

Pain medication is used for cesarean births. With certain types of medication, such as an epidural, women can remain awake during the surgery. In other situations, general anesthesia that puts the mother to sleep is used. With the doctor's permission, the father or other support partner may be present.

Because a cesarean birth is surgery, it carries some risks. However, when necessary, it can relieve stress on the baby and speed up delivery. It also allows the doctor to better control the birth process.

The mother may be able to hold the baby in the delivery room after a cesarean delivery. This will depend on hospital rules as well as the mother's condition. If the mother cannot hold the baby, the father may be able to. In some hospitals, it is standard procedure to take the baby to an intensive care nursery after a cesarean. This is not necessarily cause for alarm.

After a cesarean delivery, mothers are taken to a recovery area where they stay for a few hours. They are encouraged to stand or walk with help as soon as possible to speed the healing process. Women who have had cesarean births may need up to six weeks to fully recover.

✔ **Reading Check** **List** What are three reasons a mother might have a cesarean delivery?

Premature Birth

Between 5 and 6 percent of all babies are born prematurely. Premature babies are those born before reaching 37 weeks of development and weighing less than five pounds, eight ounces (2.5 kg). The earlier babies are born, the less developed their organs are and the lower their birth weight.

Why are babies born prematurely? No one knows for sure. However, mothers who have had other premature births, are carrying more than one baby, or have other medical problems are more likely to have premature babies. Teen mothers also are more likely to give birth prematurely. Women can reduce their risks by eating well and getting proper prenatal care.

Premature babies, or preemies, require special care. They are not really ready to live outside their mother's body. Their systems for controlling body temperature, breathing, and feeding are not yet mature. These systems are controlled by the brain. A premature baby's brain is not yet ready to control these systems. Doctors are sometimes able to delay an infant's birth. Even a few extra days in the womb can help promote the baby's development.

To help control the undeveloped body systems, a premature baby is usually placed in an incubator. An **incubator** is a special enclosed crib where the oxygen supply, temperature, and humidity can be closely controlled. Some preemies are able to suck and can be breast-fed or fed using a bottle. This allows the mother to begin bonding with her child while still in the hospital.

Some preemies will have long-term health problems, learning problems, or even brain damage. However, advances in medical technology allow many to survive and grow to be healthy. Many premature infants will reach developmental milestones in the first year a little later than the average child. By the time they are toddlers, though, it is often impossible to know if a child was born prematurely.

Section 6.1   After You Read

Review Key Concepts

1. **Identify** two early signs of labor.
2. **List** three reasons for cesarean birth.
3. **Explain** why premature babies require special care.

Practice Academic Skills

 English Language Arts

4. Think about when you have seen babies being born on television or at the movies. Write a half-page essay in which you compare and contrast what you have seen in the media with what you read in this section.

> **NCTE 12** Use language to accomplish individual purposes.

 Social Studies

5. Childbirth in the United States is generally done with the guidance and assistance of a medical professional. This is not always the case in other countries. Select a country other than the United States and learn about its childbirth process. Prepare an oral report to share your findings with the class.

> **NCSS I A** Analyze and explain the ways groups, societies, and cultures address human needs and concerns.

 Check Your Answers Check your answers at this book's Online Learning Center at **glencoe.com**.

Reading Guide

Before You Read

Explain Read the Key Concepts and Content Vocabulary. Write one or two sentences to explain what you think the section will be about.

Read to Learn

Key Concepts
- **Describe** a newborn's appearance immediately after birth.
- **Identify** the exams and procedures given to a newborn in the first few days.

Main Idea

A newborn baby is examined immediately after birth. A newborn also receives numerous tests shortly after birth.

Content Vocabulary

◇ fontanel
◇ lanugo
◇ vernix
◇ Apgar scale

Academic Vocabulary

You will find these words in your reading and on your tests. Use the glossary to look up their definitions if necessary.

■ fuse
■ secure

Graphic Organizer

As you read, find the five factors that are checked during a baby's first exam. Use a fishbone diagram like the one shown to organize your information.

Apgar scale

 Graphic Organizer Go to this book's Online Learning Center at **glencoe.com** to print out this graphic organizer.

Academic Standards . . . .

 English Language Arts

NCTE 5 Use different writing process elements to communicate effectively.

 Social Studies

NCSS VIII C Science, Technology, and Society Analyze how science influences the core values, beliefs, and attitudes of society, and how core values of society shape scientific change.

NCTE *National Council of Teachers of English*
NCTM *National Council of Teachers of Mathematics*

NSES *National Science Education Standards*
NCSS *National Council for the Social Studies*

The Baby Arrives

At birth, a newborn goes through many physical changes that are necessary for the baby's survival outside of the mother's body. Before birth, parents often wonder, "What will my baby look like?"

When parents imagine the answers to this question, they usually imagine a sturdy, smiling baby of about six months. Newborns look nothing like that. It will take some time before they are picture perfect.

A newborn baby has a tiny measure of independence. No longer reliant on the mother for oxygen, the baby will take a first breath. During the pregnancy, the baby's lungs are collapsed. Oxygen is delivered through the mother's blood, and the lungs are not used.

During delivery, the lungs fill with the amniotic fluid that was in the baby's trachea. This is the tube that delivers air from the mouth to the lungs. Most of the fluid is squeezed out during the trip through the birth canal.

Whatever remains in the mouth is suctioned out immediately after birth. Newborns usually breathe naturally. If the baby needs help, medical personnel may gently rub or pat the baby's back to encourage breathing.

For the first few months, newborns breathe through their noses. Their breathing may be irregular. They may even pause briefly in their breathing while they sleep. This is perfectly normal. Newborns may sneeze often in order to clear mucus from their noses. A newborn's breathing becomes regular a month or two after birth.

Once the lungs have begun to take in oxygen, the baby's circulatory system changes. Blood now circulates to and from the lungs, rather than bypassing them as before.

The heart changes, too. The heart must pump harder to get more blood to the lungs. Two small openings in the heart begin to close. A new type of hemoglobin develops. Hemoglobin is a part of the red blood cell that delivers oxygen to the body.

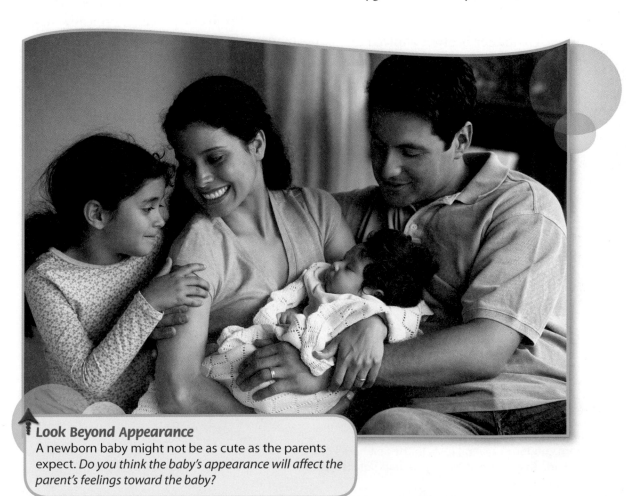

↑ Look Beyond Appearance
A newborn baby might not be as cute as the parents expect. *Do you think the baby's appearance will affect the parent's feelings toward the baby?*

Brain Size and Growth

At birth, a baby's head is about one-fourth of the baby's total height, which averages about 20 inches (50 centimeters). That is twice the size, compared to the rest of the body, of an adult's head. An infant's head is big because the brain is big. After birth, the head and brain grow much less than the rest of the baby's body.

■ **Science Inquiry** Having a bigger head and brain does not necessarily mean a smarter baby. Why does size not determine intelligence?

The umbilical cord once provided the baby with nourishment and oxygen. This cord is no longer needed. Within a few minutes of birth, the cord stops pulsing with the mother's heartbeat and begins to shrink. The cord is clamped and cut off, leaving a small stump at the baby's navel. The father is often allowed to cut the cord. The stump will fall off in the first few weeks. The navel should be kept clean and dry until the cord stump falls off.

The Newborn's Appearance

Most people think of bright eyes and plump arms and legs when they picture babies. Newborns tend to look a little different though. Their limbs may be skinny, and their features sometimes appear flattened.

The newborn's head is wobbly and looks too large for the body. The baby's skull may appear pointed or lopsided due to the passage through the birth canal. A baby's skull bones are not fully fused. The skull will have soft spots, or fontanels. A **fontanel** is an open space found on the baby's head where the bones are not yet joined. One of these soft spots is just above the baby's forehead. The other is toward the back of the skull. Fontanels allow the bones to move together during birth. As the baby develops during the first year and a half of life, the bones grow together and **fuse**, or combine. The fused bones cover the fontanels. In the meantime, a thick layer of skin covers them and protects the brain.

The face of the newborn may be swollen or puffy after the birth process. Typically, newborns have fat cheeks; short, flat noses; and receding chins. The small features make it easier for the baby to nurse at the mother's breasts. At birth, babies' eyes are nearly adult-size.

Evaluating the Newborn
Newborns undergo several tests in the first hours of their lives outside the womb. *Why do you think babies are tested so soon after birth?*

Colleen's parents had heard the saying, "A baby whose sweat tastes salty will have a miserable life." What they did not know is that very salty sweat is one of the signs of a genetic disease called cystic fibrosis. While it affects all racial groups, the disease is most common in Caucasians, and affects both boys and girls equally. Doctors tested Colleen, a newborn, by taking a few drops of her sweat and measuring the chloride (a body salt) in it. The test was painless, and the results came back the same day. Colleen tested positive for the disease. This did not mean she would have a miserable life. Some people with the disease have breathing problems and trouble digesting food. However, Others show no signs of the disease except very salty sweat. Currently, there is no cure for cystic fibrosis, but there are many promising treatments in use.

Critical Thinking Research treatments currently in use for cystic fibrosis. Explain how one treatment works and whether it is for all people with cystic fibrosis. Record your findings in a one-page report. Be sure to cite your sources.

Babies of African, Asian, and Hispanic descent often have brown eyes at birth, and they remain this color. Caucasian babies' eyes are usually a dark grayish-blue at birth, but the color may change. The color becomes permanent at three to six months.

Babies' circulatory systems must make adjustments to the changing temperatures of the outside world. Tiny fingers and toes may be slightly cooler than the rest of the body for the first 24 hours. Keeping babies wrapped in blankets makes them feel more **secure**, or safe. A knitted cap keeps their heads warm. Hospitals may put babies under warming lamps immediately after birth.

Some babies, especially preemies, have lanugo (lə-'nü-(,)gō). **Lanugo** is fine, downy hair growing on newborns' foreheads, backs, and shoulders. This hair soon disappears.

While in the uterus, the baby is floating in amniotic fluid, and is covered with vernix. **Vernix** is a thick, white, pasty substance made up of the fetus's old skin cells and the secretions of skin glands. It acts as a protection against constant exposure to the amniotic fluid. Any remaining vernix is washed off during the baby's first bath.

Many babies have tiny, white bumps called milia, or baby acne, on their nose and cheeks. They are plugged oil ducts caused by stimulation from the mother's hormones, which remain in the baby's system for a short time after delivery. The milia disappear in a week or so.

✓ **Reading Check** **Recall** What is the first measure of independence a newborn baby has?

Examining the Newborn

When babies are born, their condition is usually evaluated using the Apgar scale. The **Apgar scale** is a system of rating the physical condition of a newborn baby. The baby is also given other tests soon after birth.

First Exam

Using the Apgar scale, five factors are checked when the baby is one minute old. The same factors are checked again five minutes after birth. These factors are heart rate, breathing, muscle tone, response to stimulation, and skin color. Crying is a desired response to stimulation and shows good breathing. Many newborns have a blue tint to their skin tone.

The Apgar scale rates each of the five areas from zero to two. A normal total score is in the six-to-ten range. Ten is a perfect score. A lower score indicates that the baby may need some medical assistance.

Nurses also examine the baby for any condition that might require special care. They weigh, measure, and dry the baby. They apply antibiotic to the baby's eyes to prevent infection. The baby often receives an injection of vitamin K to prevent a rare bleeding disorder.

Shortly after birth, certain records are created. The baby's foot is printed in ink for the public record. Plastic bands are fastened to the mother's wrist, to the baby's wrist or ankle, and to the wrist of someone of the mother's choosing. The bands have matching numbers and are checked each time the baby leaves the mother's room. The baby may be moved to the hospital nursery. In most hospitals, only hospital staff members with the appropriate identification are permitted into the hospital nursery.

Later Tests

Newborns are given several other tests and medical procedures during their first few days of life. Most newborns receive at least one and often two hearing screenings. Blood is taken from the umbilical cord immediately after birth to check the baby's blood type and to screen for certain diseases.

While the baby is still in the hospital, blood will be taken from the heel to test for certain diseases and disorders. Which tests are done currently varies from state to state. Some hospitals will also give the first hepatitis B vaccine before the baby is discharged.

Babies that are born at home should still receive the same tests as those born in a hospital. Parents should plan ahead and discuss the birth with their doctor. If a midwife is present, she may be able to perform some of the initial tests. Parents should schedule visits with a pediatrician for routine shots and tests.

Section 6.2   After You Read

Review Key Concepts

1. **Explain** why the face of a newborn might be swollen after birth.
2. **List** the five characteristics that are rated on the Apgar scale.

Practice Academic Skills

 English Language Arts

3. Imagine that you have learned that your older cousin is about to give birth for the first time. She is excited and a little nervous. She knows what to expect during the birth process, but is not sure what happens to the baby immediately after birth. Write a letter to your cousin explaining what happens to the newborn immediately after birth.

> **NCTE 5** Use different writing process elements to communicate effectively.

 Social Studies

4. Stem cells can be used in the treatment and cure of many human diseases and disorders. There is a lot of debate over the ethical use of stem cells for research. Conduct research to find out why stem cell research is controversial. Write a brief essay on your findings.

> **NCSS VIII C** Analyze how science influences the core values, beliefs, and attitudes of society, and how core values of society shape scientific change.

 Check Your Answers Check your answers at this book's Online Learning Center at **glencoe.com**.

Reading Guide

Before You Read

Discover Choose a Content or Academic Vocabulary term that is new to you. When you find it in the text, write down the definition.

Read to Learn
Key Concepts
- **Review** what occurs during the hospital stay after delivery.
- **Summarize** the physical and emotional needs of a new mother.

Main Idea
After the baby is born, the parents begin to bond with the baby while still at the hospital. Both mother and baby receive postnatal care.

Content Vocabulary
◇ neonatal period
◇ jaundice
◇ bilirubin
◇ bonding
◇ colostrum
◇ lactation consultant
◇ rooming-in
◇ postnatal period
◇ postpartum depression

Academic Vocabulary
You will find these words in your reading and on your tests. Use the glossary to look up their definitions if necessary.
- major
- stable

Graphic Organizer
As you read, write a one-sentence summary of each physical need of the mother after the baby is born. Use a chart like the one shown to organize your information.

Postnatal Need	Summary
Rest	
Exercise	
Medical checkups	

 Graphic Organizer Go to this book's Online Learning Center at **glencoe.com** to print out this graphic organizer.

Academic Standards . . . .

 English Language Arts

NCTE 4 Use written language to communicate effectively.

 Science

NSES F Develop understanding of personal and community health.

NCTE *National Council of Teachers of English*
NCTM *National Council of Teachers of Mathematics*

NSES *National Science Education Standards*
NCSS *National Council for the Social Studies*

After the Birth

Once the baby has arrived, parents quickly begin forming emotional ties with their newborn. This enjoyable process plays an important role in the emotional and physical development of the baby. It also helps the parents. Mothers go through emotional changes, and it is important that they receive needed support.

The neonatal period involves **major**, or significant, adjustments for mother and baby. The **neonatal period** is the first month after the baby is born. Labor and delivery are tiring. Both mother and baby need time to rest and recover. In some facilities, a healthy mother and baby may go home as soon as 12 hours after birth. In hospitals, the average stay following birth is one to two days.

Jaundice ('jȯn-dəs) causes the baby's skin and eyes to look slightly yellow. This condition occurs in more than 50 percent of newborns because the liver cannot remove bilirubin (,bi-li-'rü-bən). **Bilirubin** is a substance produced by the breakdown of red blood cells. The baby's body may be producing too much of this substance, or the developing liver may not be able to remove it fast enough. If left untreated, jaundice can damage the nervous system.

In the hospital, doctors may prescribe phototherapy to help the liver do its job. Phototherapy is treatment using ultraviolet light. Sometimes the treatment is continued at home.

Bonding

In recent years, many researchers have given attention to the emotional needs of the newborn. Studies have emphasized bonding. **Bonding** is forming emotional ties between parents and child. Knowing how important bonding is, most hospitals now delay some of the routine procedures after birth, if there are no complications. Parents are allowed to hold the child and begin forming an attachment sooner. When complications do occur and the parents are not able to hold the baby right away, bonding can still occur later.

Immediately after birth, nurses may place the baby on the mother's stomach. This lets the baby feel the warmth of her mother's skin. The baby can also hear the mother's voice and heartbeat that became so familiar in the uterus. At this point, many fathers examine their newborn's tiny toes and fingers. Parents often begin touching and talking to the baby, looking into the baby's eyes and stroking the baby's cheeks. By instinct, the newborn focuses on the human face. This helps the newborn bond.

Bonding also helps brain development. During the first year, a baby's brain cells are making millions of connections. Parents' efforts to bond with their baby help build connections in the brain. Through simple interactions, such as holding or singing to the baby, parents help strengthen the baby's brain development.

Neonatal Care
A newborn with jaundice is placed under an ultraviolet light that is absorbed by the baby's skin to change the bilirubin into a form that can be eliminated from the baby's kidneys. *What is bilirubin?*

If the baby will be breast-fed, the mother may begin nursing right away. Newborns are born with a strong sucking reflex. They are usually alert right after delivery. Each breast-feeding session tells the mother's body to continue making milk. It also helps the mother's uterus contract after birth, stopping any bleeding.

Colostrum (kə-'läs-trəm) is a high-calorie, high-protein early breast milk. It satisfies the baby's appetite and provides protection from illnesses. When the baby becomes too sleepy to nurse, the father or another relative can hold the baby while the mother rests.

Help with Feeding

All babies lose weight during the first few days of life, but gain it back later. By the fourth day, breast-feeding mothers begin producing more milk. Some mothers have trouble with breast- or bottle-feeding. Parents can get help while they are still in the hospital.

Many hospitals offer lactation consultants. A **lactation consultant** is a professional breast-feeding specialist who shows mothers how to encourage adequate milk production and how to position babies properly so that they can nurse. Nurses can also help. During the first few days of life, some babies are too sleepy to eat. To wake them, mothers can try unwrapping their babies to expose them to the air in the room. A little stimulation, such as a light massage, can also help wake the baby for a feeding.

Rooming-in

Many hospitals offer the option of full or partial **rooming-in**. Full rooming-in means that the baby remains with the mother in her room during the entire hospital stay. Partial rooming-in means that the baby stays in the nursery part of the time, such as during the night. Mothers can ask that their babies be brought to their rooms for night feedings. Hospitals that offer rooming-in generally allow the father to visit whenever he wishes.

Parenting Skills

Bonding with a Baby

Babies crave touch. Close emotional ties help their brains and bodies develop. When parents include the baby in their usual activities, they give the baby varied experiences and strengthen their own relationship. Here are some ideas to promote bonding.

- **Use a baby carrier.** Being comfortably strapped to a parent's body keeps the baby close to the heart. The rhythm of a heartbeat comforts babies.
- **Sing or read to the baby.** It is not necessary to wait until the baby is old enough to understand what is being read. The sound of a familiar voice can be very comforting.
- **Allow dad time with the baby.** Fathers who spend time alone with their babies get to know them better. Giving a late-night bottle or going for walks can enhance the bonding experience.
- **Let the baby handle you.** Babies are interested in different textures, like beards and long hair. But be careful! Babies have a tight grasp and do not like to let go.

Take Charge Playing with babies is another way for parents and babies to bond. Can you think of some ways to play with a baby that would promote bonding?

Rooming-in programs have advantages for the entire family. Rooming-in babies tend to have only one main caregiver, usually a nurse, attending to their needs. These babies seem to cry less. As a result, a rooming-in mother gets more rest and does not worry about her baby in the nursery. Also, parents start learning how to take care of them right away.

Legal Documents

A birth certificate is the most important piece of personal identification anyone has. It is required for entrance into school. Getting one is simple. The parents fill out a form provided by the hospital or birthing center. Several weeks later, the parents receive one copy of the birth certificate. Another one is sent to a government office to be filed. Processes for filing a birth certificate for a home birth will vary by state.

The federal government recommends that a baby receive a social security number in the first year. Hospitals provide new parents with the necessary forms. Parents should fill out the forms to obtain a number for their child. They can then claim an exemption on their income taxes, obtain medical coverage for the child, and take part in government programs.

Caring for Premature Babies

Premature babies are born before 37 weeks of development. Many premature babies spend time in a hospital's neonatal intensive-care unit (NICU). The NICU has special equipment and highly trained nurses. Not all hospitals have these units. In many areas, babies are transferred to a larger hospital that has a NICU.

There are three levels of NICU care. Level I facilities provide routine care for preemies. This includes keeping them warm and nourished. Level II care is for preemies who need to be monitored closely. Some states have only one or two hospitals with Level III facilities. These provide care for very premature (less than 34 weeks) babies or full-term infants who have serious or life-threatening conditions. A baby born far from a Level III facility may be taken there by ambulance or helicopter, depending on the baby's condition.

Special Needs

Premature babies do not have enough body fat to maintain their temperature, even with blankets. NICUs have incubators and special warmers for preemies. These decrease the chance of infection and surround the baby with warm air.

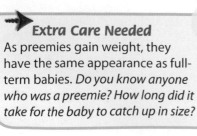

Extra Care Needed
As preemies gain weight, they have the same appearance as full-term babies. *Do you know anyone who was a preemie? How long did it take for the baby to catch up in size?*

Preemies also need special types of nourishment because they grow more quickly than full-term babies. Their digestive systems are immature. Most preemies are fed breast milk through feeding tubes. Breast milk helps protect against infection and disease. Many preemies receive extra vitamins and nutrients. Once they are in a **stable**, or unchanging, condition and show signs of sucking, the doctor determines whether they can breast-feed. Sometimes preemies need special pacifiers to help them learn how to suck properly. Preemies may be fed through a tube in the stomach until they learn to suck and swallow milk.

Babies in the NICU are frequently tested for infections. Their blood cell and blood sugar levels are also checked often. Nurses and doctors will change individual care plans to reflect each baby's needs.

Premature babies stay in the hospital until their organs develop enough to function without help. This may take from a few days to a month, or more. Breathing machines are often used to help babies whose lungs are immature.

Improved Care

The care for premature babies has improved greatly over the years. They still have an increased risk of medical and developmental problems though. How well a preemie thrives often depends on how close the baby was born to the due date. Premature babies can experience long-term difficulties such as cerebral palsy and developmental delays. The earlier the baby is born, the more risks the baby faces.

As premature babies grow, doctors decide when they can leave incubators and be placed in open cribs. Babies must be able to breathe without a machine, drink, maintain a steady body temperature, and maintain a weight of 5 pounds or more before they can leave the hospital. Other problems may require a longer hospital stay.

Premature babies need constant monitoring, which can interrupt parent-child bonding. Incubators and machines can be scary to parents. If a baby is extremely premature, the parents may touch the baby through special openings in the incubator. As the babies grow, parents can hold, sing, talk to, and bathe them.

As with full-term babies, contact helps them develop faster. Breast-feeding mothers also can provide milk for their babies.

✓ Reading Check **List** What four criteria must premature babies meet before they are allowed to go home?

Mother's Postnatal Care

The **postnatal period** is the time following the baby's birth. During this time, a new mother has special needs. She may be physically exhausted from birth, and she is now responsible for the well-being of a newborn. Nurses will explain how the new mother should care for herself as she meets the needs of her baby. Mothers who give birth by cesarean section have a longer recovery time since they have had major surgery.

Physical Needs

Recovery from pregnancy and childbirth takes time. The new mother's hormone levels change. Her sleep may be interrupted by the baby's feedings. Breast-feeding mothers experience additional changes related to producing milk. Women who have had a cesarean section require additional care. They are generally required to stay in the hospital longer and will be more fatigued. The physical needs of the new mother include rest, exercise, nutrition, and checkups.

{ **Expert Advice...** }

"Babies enter the world with only one power—the power to elicit the emotion of tenderness and a caring response to them from other humans, especially and specifically from their mothers."

— James Kimmel, author, *Whatever Happened to Mother?*

- **Rest** During the first few weeks, the new mother may be tired. She should try to sleep whenever the baby does. Relatives and friends can help by preparing meals, doing chores, or watching the baby for a few hours.
- **Exercise** With her doctor's approval, a new mother can usually begin exercising gently. Stretching and walking short distances can help her lose weight and feel more energetic.
- **Good Nutrition** As during pregnancy, eating right is important for new mothers. They should continue to follow the USDA's MyPyramid Plan. Breast-feeding mothers are providing nutrition for their own bodies and for their babies. They need about 300 calories per day more than before pregnancy. They also need plenty of fluids.
- **Medical Checkups** Four to six weeks after birth, a new mother should have a postnatal checkup. Her doctor makes sure her uterus is returning to normal and that there are no other problems.

Emotional Needs

In addition to physical changes, a new mother goes through emotional changes. Many women feel confused a few days after birth. Some have mood swings. The "baby blues" are very common. The mother may cry for no reason. She may feel irritable, lonely, anxious, or sad. Joining a support group for new mothers or talking with other mothers often helps.

A small percentage of new mothers experience these symptoms to a greater degree. The blues do not go away. Instead, they get worse. **Postpartum depression** is a condition in which new mothers may feel very sad, cry a lot, have little energy, feel overly anxious about the baby or have little interest in the baby, and, in extreme cases, think of harming the baby.

Treatment is available for postpartum depression. It is very important for women who have any of these symptoms to talk with their doctors about treatment. Talking to a therapist can help, as can medication.

Section 6.3   After You Read

Review Key Concepts

1. **Explain** how bonding is promoted between parents and their baby in the hospital.
2. **Describe** four areas of physical needs in a mother's postnatal care.

Practice Academic Skills

 English Language Arts

3. Imagine that your cousin, who is pregnant, has told you that she and her husband have toured the local NICU. She is confused about the purpose of a NICU. Write a letter to your cousin explaining the services NICUs provide.

NCTE 4 Use written language to communicate effectively.

 Science

4. In many countries, people do not understand the importance of postnatal care for the mother. Write a one-page report in which you summarize the reasons for postnatal care for the mother and what forms that care should take.

NSES F Develop understanding of personal and community health.

Check Your Answers Check your answers at this book's Online Learning Center at **glencoe.com**.

Chapter Summary

There are three main stages of labor. A cesarean birth may be necessary if the mother's or baby's health is in danger. A premature baby will require special medical care. Immediately after birth, a newborn's physical condition is evaluated through a variety of tests. Bonding after birth strengthens the emotional connection between parents and their child. A new mother needs postnatal care. New mothers need rest, exercise, good nutrition, and follow-up medical care. They may also have emotional needs.

Vocabulary Review

1. Arrange the vocabulary terms below into groups of related words. Explain why you put the words together.

Content Vocabulary
- cervix (p. 165)
- contraction (p. 166)
- fetal monitoring (p. 166)
- dilate (p. 170)
- cord blood (p. 171)
- stem cells (p. 171)
- cesarean birth (p. 172)
- incubator (p. 173)
- fontanel (p. 176)
- lanugo (p. 177)
- vernix (p. 177)
- Apgar scale (p. 177)
- neonatal period (p. 180)
- jaundice (p. 180)
- bilirubin (p. 180)
- bonding (p. 180)
- colostrum (p. 181)
- lactation consultant (p. 181)
- rooming-in (p. 181)
- postnatal period (p. 183)
- postpartum depression (p. 184)

Academic Vocabulary
- induce (p. 166)
- anesthesia (p. 171)
- fuse (p. 176)
- secure (p. 177)
- major (p. 180)
- stable (p. 183)

Review Key Concepts

2. Describe the progression of labor.
3. Explain what happens during a cesarean birth.
4. List the factors that can contribute to a premature birth.
5. Describe a newborn's appearance immediately after birth.
6. Identify the exams and procedures given to a newborn in the first few days.
7. Review what occurs during the hospital stay after delivery.
8. Summarize the physical and emotional needs of a new mother.

Critical Thinking

9. Draw Conclusions What are some reasons a woman might choose labor without pain medication?
10. Infer What feelings might a new mother have during the postnatal period? Why might she have these feelings?

Family & Community Connection

11. Interview a Mother Talk to a mother about her experience with the birth of her first child. Questions to ask might include: If you delivered naturally, were you prepared for the reality of labor? Did you use pain medication? What were your concerns after the baby was born? Use your notes to write a one-page report describing the mother's experience.

Health Skills

12. Research Congenital Heart Defects In 8 out of every 1,000 live births, the newborn has some kind of congenital heart defect. Conduct research to answer these questions: Which of these heart defects are mild? Which of them are severe? What are their possible causes and treatments? Use the answers from your research to create a flyer or brochure that raises awareness of these conditions.

Observation Skills

13. Observe a Hospital Nursery Work with your teacher to arrange to observe your local hospital's nursery. Note that you will probably not be allowed into the nursery. Your observation may be through the viewing window.

Procedure As you observe, take note of the number of babies in the nursery and the number of health care workers. Note how many times the babies are touched by the workers and how often the infants are checked or tested. Note how long you observed the nursery.

Analysis Write a report of your observation. Include the ratio of babies to health care workers. Note the frequency of touch, as well as frequency and nature of checking on the babies.

> **NCTE 7** Conduct research and gather, evaluate, and synthesize data to communicate discoveries.

Real-World Skills

Problem-Solving

14. Recommend Action Imagine that your cousin has delivered her first baby and is feeling a little anxious. She thinks something might be wrong because she should be happy, but she is not. Write a letter with tips to ensure her physical and emotional health are provided for.

Technology Skills

15. Create a Graph Use online resources to research information about infant mortality rates in different countries. Search for answers to these questions: Which nation has the highest infant mortality rate? Which has the lowest? Where does the United States rank? Use graph-making software to create a graph that illustrates your findings.

Financial Literacy

16. Calculate the Cost of Child-Rearing Talk to two or more people you know who have children. Ask them to estimate the costs for items such as food, clothing, education, and medical costs for each child for one year. Present your data in a table.

 Additional Activities For additional activities, go to this book's Online Learning Center at **glencoe.com**.

Academic Skills

English Language Arts

17. Use Your Knowledge A new mother is worried because her baby's face is not round and chubby like babies on television. She writes an e-mail to her sister expressing her concern. Use your knowledge of a newborn's appeareance to write a reassuring e-mail reply from the perspective of her sister.

> **NCTE 12** Use language to accomplish individual purposes.

Mathematics

18. The Baby's Arrival A magazine published a survey of 2,000 women. It showed that in the first four months of a baby's life, most mothers averaged 5 hours of sleep per night. If adults require 8 hours of sleep, how many hours of sleep are lost per mother over the four-month period? Assume that each of the four months has 30 days.

Math Concept **Multi-Step Problems** When solving problems with more than one step, think through the steps before you start.

Starting Hint Calculate how many hours are lost in one night. Then, determine how many days are in four months, and multiply that number by the number of hours lost per night.

 For math help, go to the Math Appendix at the back of the book.

> **NCTM Number and Operations** Understand numbers, ways of representing numbers, relationships among numbers, and number systems.

Science

19. Research Postpartum Depression Postpartum depression is a serious complication in 10 to 15 percent of all deliveries. For adolescents who give birth, the incidence is between 26 and 32 percent.

Procedure Conduct research to answer these questions: Why is the percentage higher in adolescents? What are some of the warning signs of postpartum depression? Identify treatment alternatives.

Analysis Take notes as you do your research. Write a speech based on your notes. Deliver the speech to your class. Include answers to all of the questions in your speech.

> **NSES F** Develop understanding of personal and community health.

 Standardized Test Practice

READING COMPREHENSION
Read the passage, then answer the question.

Mothers often report that contractions are painful but bearable. There is time between them to rest and recover. After the baby is born and the placenta is also pushed out, contractions end. There is no lingering pain.

20. In this passage, the word *bearable* means:
  a. able to be endured
  b. having characteristics of a bear
  c. extremely difficult
  d. not to be endured

> **Test-Taking Tip** Read the paragraph carefully to make sure you understand what it is about. Read the answer choices. Then read the paragraph again before choosing the answer.

Promote Good Health During Pregnancy

In this unit, you have learned that there are many things health care professionals and mothers-to-be can do to help ensure the delivery of a healthy baby. In this project, you will research nutrition for the different phases of pregnancy. You will use what you learned to develop menus for women in one of the stages related to pregnancy.

My Journal

If you completed the journal entry from page 89, refer to it to see if your thoughts have changed after reading the unit.

Project Assignment

In this project, you will:
- Choose a pregnancy-related time period, like pre-conception, pregnancy, or post-natal, you want to know more about.
- Conduct research on recommended nutrition for the time period you have chosen.

Child Development Skills Behind the Project

- Identify actions that can affect the health of an unborn baby.
- Determine the nutrition needs of an unborn baby.
- Identify professionals who can offer guidelines to enhance the health of the unborn baby.

Academic Skills

English Language Arts

> **NCTE 7** Conduct research and gather, evaluate, and synthesize data to communicate discoveries.
>
> **NCTE 12** Use language to accomplish individual purposes.

- Identify and interview a health care provider or nutrition specialist in the community who works with women in different stages of pregnancy.
- Arrange the interview and take notes.
- Use what you learned in the interviews to create menus.

Step 1 Choose Your Topic

The health of the mother before, during, and after pregnancy, is critical to the health of the baby. If the mother does not eat healthful foods or keep her body fit, the chances are greater that the baby will have one or more medical issues. Choose a time period to focus on.
- Before conception
- During pregnancy
- After giving birth

Step 2 Complete Your Research

Conduct research to determine what you need to know about a woman's nutritional needs during the time period you chose. Write a summary of your research.

Research Skills

★ Use reputable Web sites.
★ Use dictionaries and encyclopedias.
★ Cite the sources you use. Give credit to the author of the information.

Step 3 Connect to Your Community

Discuss your research findings from Step 2 with a health care provider or nutrition specialist in your community. During the discussion, share your research findings. Ask the health care provider or nutrition specialist for their comments or feedback on the material. Take notes of their responses. Ask for advice about nutrition for the stage you researched.

Discussion Skills

★ Know the material you will be discussing.

★ State your findings clearly.

★ Ask for feedback or comments.

★ Listen attentively.

Step 4 Create and Present Your Menu

Use the Unit Thematic Project Checklist on the right to plan and create your menu and make your presentation.

Presentation Skills

★ Present your ideas clearly.

★ Engage your audience.

★ Organize your presentation by developing an outline.

★ Speak concisely (briefly but completely).

Step 5 Evaluate Your Child Development Skills and Academic Skills

Your project will be evaluated based on:

- Content and organization of your information.
- Mechanics—presentation and neatness.
- Speaking and listening skills.

 Evaluation Rubric Go to this book's Online Learning Center at **glencoe.com** for a rubric you can use to evaluate your final project.

Unit Thematic Project Checklist

Menus	✔ Research the nutritional needs of a woman during the time of pregnancy you have selected and summarize your findings.
	✔ Discuss your findings with a health care provider or nutrition specialist in your community and take notes of your discussion.
	✔ Use presentation software or make a poster of menus based on your research and discussion.
	✔ In your menus, show how the nutritional needs suggested by your research and your discussion are met.
	✔ Make menus for breakfast, lunch, and dinner for two days.
Presentation	✔ Make a presentation to your class to share your menus and discuss what you learned.
	✔ Invite the students in your class to ask you any questions they may have. Answer three questions.
	✔ When students ask you questions, demonstrate in your answers that you respect their perspectives.
	✔ Turn in your research summary, the notes from your discussion, and your menus to your teacher.
Academic Skills	✔ Create visuals to enhance a presentation.
	✔ Organize a presentation.
	✔ Speak clearly and concisely.

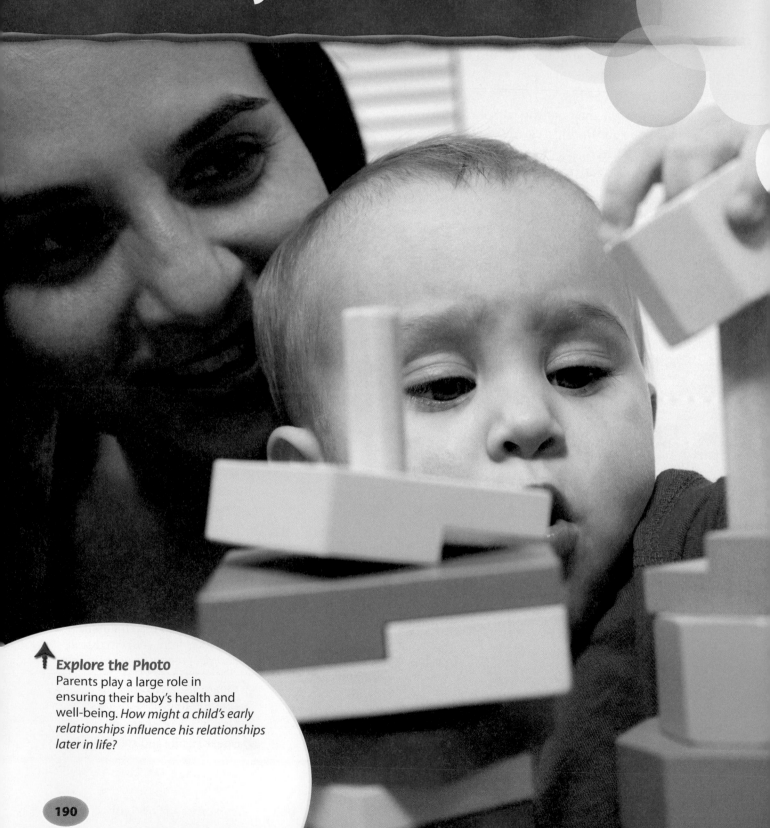

Unit 3

The Baby's First Year

Explore the Photo
Parents play a large role in ensuring their baby's health and well-being. *How might a child's early relationships influence his relationships later in life?*

Chapter 7 Physical Development of Infants

Chapter 8 Emotional and Social Development of Infants

Chapter 9 Intellectual Development of Infants

Unit | Thematic Project Preview

Raise a Healthy Baby

In this unit, you will learn how infants grow and develop during their first twelve months. You will also learn about the important role of parents and caregivers in a baby's physical and mental health. In your unit thematic project, you will explore how caregivers can support a baby's healthy growth and development.

My Journal

Healthy Development Write a journal entry about one of the topics below. This will help you prepare for the project at the end of this unit.

- How can a parent or caregiver help a baby grow up physically healthy?
- How can a parent or caregiver help a baby develop trusting relationships with adults and siblings?
- How can a parent or caregiver help a baby develop language skills?

Chapter

7 Physical Development of Infants

Chapter Objectives

After completing this chapter, you will be able to:

- **Identify** the four major influences on an infant's growth and development.
- **Summarize** how a baby typically grows in the first year.
- **Explain** how to safely hold a baby.
- **Identify** how to meet a baby's nutritional needs.
- **Describe** the best type of clothing suitable for a baby.
- **Describe** how to bathe a baby.
- **Explain** why checkups and immunizations are important for babies.

Writing Activity · Paragraph

Growing a Happy Baby During the first year of life, babies grow and develop in many ways. Caregivers have many responsibilities to make sure a baby's needs are met. For example, the caregiver must feed the baby and change the baby's diapers. These are just two of the many physical needs. Infants also have emotional needs that must be met. Write a paragraph in which you describe what you think makes a happy, healthy baby.

Writing Tips To write a good paragraph, follow these tips:
1. Make sure the paragraph focuses on one main idea.
2. Use transition words to link ideas. These include words such as then, however, and because.
3. Make sure all the sentences in each paragraph support the main idea.

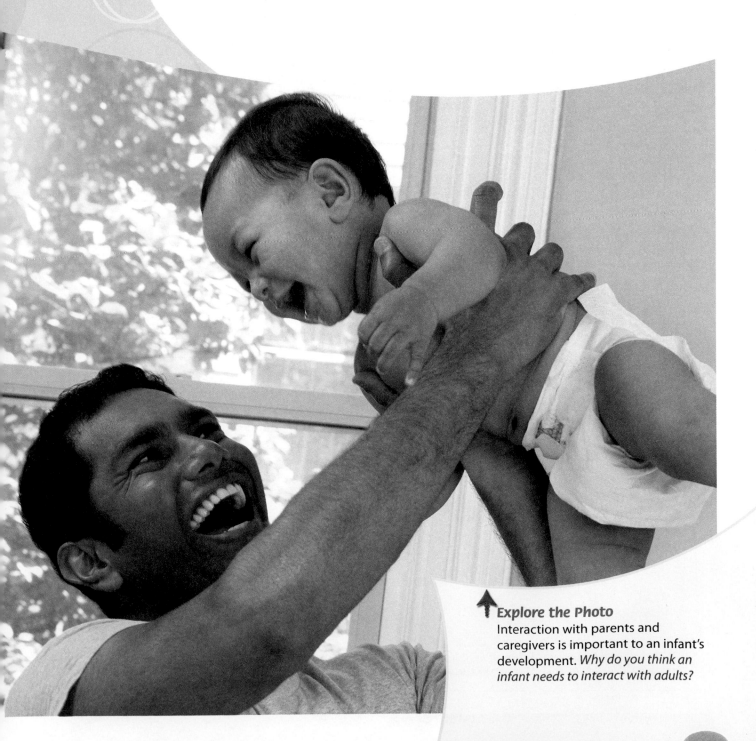

Explore the Photo
Interaction with parents and caregivers is important to an infant's development. *Why do you think an infant needs to interact with adults?*

Infant Growth and Development

Reading Guide

Before You Read

Contribute Share at least one piece of information you expect to learn with your classmates.

Read to Learn

Key Concepts

- **Identify** the four major influences on an infant's growth and development.
- **Summarize** how a baby typically grows in the first year.

Main Idea

There are four main influences on a baby's growth and development. An infant's growth and development follow many patterns.

Content Vocabulary

◇ developmental milestone
◇ depth perception
◇ reflex
◇ stimulating environment
◇ gross motor skill
◇ fine motor skill
◇ growth chart
◇ hand-eye coordination
◇ proportion

Academic Vocabulary

You will find these words in your reading and on your tests. Use the glossary to look up their definitions if necessary.

■ makeup   ■ accommodate

Graphic Organizer

As you read, list the six areas an infant develops in his first year of life. Use a diagram like the one shown to help organize your information. The first area has been filled in for you.

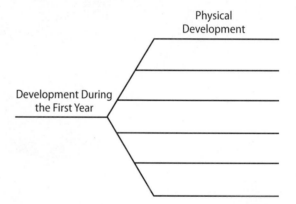

Physical Development

Development During the First Year

 Graphic Organizer Go to this book's Online Learning Center at **glencoe.com** to print out this graphic organizer.

Academic Standards ....

 English Language Arts

NCTE 4 Use written language to communicate effectively.

 Science

NSES C Develop understanding of molecular basis of heredity; biological evolution; matter, energy, and organization in living systems.

NSES A Develop abilities necessary to do scientific inquiry, understandings about scientific inquiry.

NCTE *National Council of Teachers of English*
NCTM *National Council of Teachers of Mathematics*

NSES *National Science Education Standards*
NCSS *National Council for the Social Studies*

Influences on Growth and Development

Babies experience a tremendous amount of physical growth and development in their first year of life. In just twelve months, babies who begin as helpless newborns learn to stand alone, feed themselves, and even walk. While babies typically follow the same development patterns, they do so at their own rate. Parents have the responsibility to help their baby grow and develop normally.

The terms growth and development are often used interchangeably, but they are not the same things. Growth refers to changes in size, such as weight and length. Development refers to increases and changes in physical, emotional, social, or intellectual skills.

Researchers have found that both heredity and environment play important roles in a baby's growth and development. Heredity is sometimes referred to as nature. It includes the physical **makeup**, or structure, that a baby inherits from his or her parents. Environment is a more complex concept. It includes influences such as nutrition, amount of stimulation, health, and relationships. Environment is also known as nurture. All these factors work together to influence a baby's physical growth and development. However, at various times one or more of these factors can play a larger role than the others in an infant's growth and development.

Development experts have studied the range of ages to determine the average ages at which children acquire certain skills. A key skill used to check a child's progress is called a **developmental milestone**. For example, Jeffrey may inherit a strong, healthy body from his parents. But if Jeffrey becomes sick for an extended period, he may miss out on opportunities for active play that would strengthen the large muscles of his legs. As a result, he may reach some developmental milestones, such as learning to walk or climb steps, later than a healthy baby. Another baby, Aisha, inherits a strong, healthy body and enjoys good health. She therefore has more opportunities for physical play than Jeffrey had and will more likely develop at a normal rate.

Heredity

As explained in Chapter 4, genes provide a blueprint for the development of the human body and how it functions throughout life. Children inherit a unique combination of genes

Hereditary Traits
Children inherit many physical characteristics from their parents. *What other factors influence a baby's growth and development?*

from their parents. This combination of genes determines traits such as eye and hair color, when the teeth first emerge, whether certain diseases are likely to develop, and much more. The genes also shape or influence larger traits, such as a person's intellectual potential or artistic abilities.

Having certain genes, though, does not mean a person will automatically exhibit those traits. Nature and nurture both play a role in determining how a child grows and develops. For example, a girl's genes may give her the potential to be musically gifted, but if she is never given the opportunity to sing or play an instrument, her talent may never emerge. Think of people you know who seem to have inherited physical characteristics or artistic abilities from their parents.

Nutrition

The body needs essential nutrients to grow and develop. Eating foods that contain these nutrients is vital to a child's lifelong health. Even newborns who spend most of their time sleeping are growing and developing. Proper nutrition fuels that development. Research has shown that nutrition affects many aspects of a baby's physical growth and development, including bone strength, brain development, and height.

When a baby does not get enough calories or necessary nutrients, he or she is at risk for illness, delayed growth, or even death. You will learn more about proper nutrition for an infant in Section 7.2 of this chapter.

Health

Staying healthy is closely linked to other factors that influence growth and development. A baby who is healthy is more likely to eat well and have the energy to be active. A healthy baby is more likely to have varied experiences that stimulate the brain and aid in muscle development. An infant with poor health is at risk of falling behind developmentally.

Parents and other caregivers must guard children's health. In addition to providing good nutrition, they must provide a safe environment. Children also need regular medical checkups and care.

Environment

An infant's experiences are an important part of development. Brain development, which impacts all areas of development, is linked to the quantity and variety of experiences a child has. Infancy is a critical period. Failure to achieve normal brain development at this stage can have lifelong effects.

Learning Through PLAY

Interactive Play

Babies may seem too young to play games, but even a six-month-old infant can enjoy simple interactive play. All that is usually needed is an adult, a baby, and some creativity. Peek-a-boo and hide-and-seek with toys are favorites. Babies also enjoy listening to music and clapping hands together. They like to hear an adult sing nursery rhymes or mimic animal sounds. Whatever the activity, it is important to remember that it is not the type of play that matters. It is the benefits that count. Playing with babies is not only fun, it helps promote physical development, brain development, and social interaction. The contact that occurs during play also helps nurture a baby's sense of security and well-being.

Think About It Imagine that you are helping care for your seven-month-old niece. She is not hungry or tired, but she is getting fussy. What could you do to help entertain her?

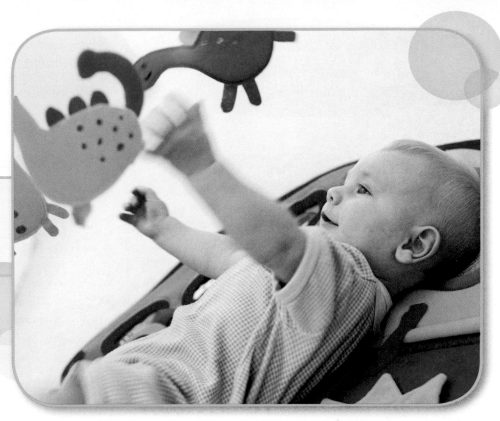

Stimulating Baby Interaction with toys helps stimulate development in a baby. *How can toys help a baby develop?*

A stimulating environment promotes brain development. A **stimulating environment** is an environment in which the baby has a wide variety of things to see, taste, smell, hear, and touch. A world with plenty of ways to use all the senses provides wonderful opportunities for an infant. While investigating their world, all that they experience is stored in the brain. As associations form, such as the high chair means food, more brain connections are made.

An environment lacking in stimulation can result in fewer or weaker connections in the brain and delayed or slow development in other areas. For example, infants are not born with language skills. During the first few months of life, connections form in the part of the brain responsible for language. This eventually allows the child to begin speaking. If the child is not exposed to language and not encouraged to speak during this time, there will be fewer connections in the brain. This can delay normal language development.

Other environmental factors can have a harmful impact on a child's development as well. For example, children who breathe secondhand smoke are more likely to suffer from poor health. It increases the risk of sudden infant death syndrome. Other possible health problems can include respiratory infections, ear infections, bronchitis, and asthma. These conditions can make it more difficult for a child to develop normally. They also increase the chances of lung cancer and heart disease later in life.

✓ **Reading Check** **Explain** What is the difference between nature and nurture?

THE DEVELOPING BRAIN

Language Development

Some people think, "How silly!" when they see adults talking to newborns. Is it a waste of time? How can a baby possibly understand? In fact, talking to and playing with infants are important for brain development and learning. These activities help babies to learn language and to develop social skills.

▪ **Science Inquiry** Babies need interaction with humans to develop their language and social skills. Would a baby develop language skills if adults did not talk to them?

Figure 7.1 — Average Lengths and Weights

A baby's length and weight increase rapidly during the first year. *Should a parent be concerned if their child's length or weight does not match the averages on this growth chart?*

Age	MALES Length/Inches	MALES Weight/Pounds	FEMALES Length/Inches	FEMALES Weight/Pounds
Birth	19¾	7½	19½	7½
3 months	24	13	23½	12¼
6 months	26½	17½	25½	15½
9 months	28	20½	27½	18¾
12 months	29	22½	29	21

Growth and Development During the First Year

Babies go through remarkable changes during their first year. They grow faster physically than during any other time of their life. They also grow emotionally, socially, and intellectually.

Growth During the First Year

From birth to age one, babies typically triple their birth weight. They usually increase their length by about 50 percent. One way doctors can judge whether a baby is growing at a healthy pace is by using growth charts. A **growth chart** shows the average weight and height of girls and boys at various ages. **Figure 7.1** focuses on average heights and weights for boys and girls from birth to age one. Boys and girls are shown separately because their growth rates and patterns differ.

Very few babies match the average measurements on growth charts. That is because children grow at their own rate. Instead of focusing on any one measurement, doctors watch for a steady pattern of growth. Sudden drops in a baby's weight could indicate health concerns. If parents are concerned about their baby's growth, they should talk to the doctor.

Weight

Weight gain is one of the best signs of good health. Most newborns lose about 10 percent of their birth weight in the first five days of life. After that, they begin to gain weight rapidly. In the first six months, a healthy baby gains about one to two pounds (0.45 to 0.9 kilograms) per month. In the following six months, the average monthly weight gain is about one pound (0.45 kilograms). A baby's birth weight usually doubles in the first few months and triples by the twelfth month. The average weight of a one-year-old is 20 to 22 pounds (9 to 10 kilograms). However, boys tend to weigh slightly more than girls during infancy.

Length

In the first year, physicians talk about the length of a baby rather than the height. This is because babies are measured while lying down.

Babies steadily grow in length during the first year, in part because bone growth is rapid at that time. For example, the average newborn measures 20 inches (51 cm) long. One year later, the average is about 30 inches (76 cm) long.

Again, not all babies grow at the same rate, and boys tend to be slightly longer than girls. Heredity has a stronger influence on height than weight. A baby with tall parents is more likely to be tall as an adult than a baby with short parents.

Body Shape

Newborns tend to hold themselves in a tightly curled position with their fists clenched, legs bent, and feet curved inward. The head may have an elongated shape from moving through the birth canal. Arms and legs are skinny, and the abdomen is large. The umbilical cord stump usually dries up and drops off within about three weeks after birth, revealing the navel. Babies will gradually stretch out their arms and legs and uncurl their fingers. Their legs and feet generally straighten out over the first six months.

Babies typically look chubby by three months of age, but they usually lose that look as they grow longer and become more active. After about eight months, when babies begin to practice standing, their typical posture includes a protruding belly and a slight lean forward.

Science in Action

Interpreting Infant Development

One way that doctors monitor infants' growth is by measuring their length. By recording this information each month, the doctor can ensure that the baby is continuing to grow and develop.

Procedure

Make a bar graph of the following data.

Infant Development	
End of Month	Length (inches)
3	24
4	25
5	25.5
6	26
7	27
8	27.5
9	28

Analysis

1. During which month does the greatest increase in length occur?
2. On average, how many inches does the baby grow per month?

NSES A Develop abilities necessary to do scientific inquiry, understandings about scientific inquiry.

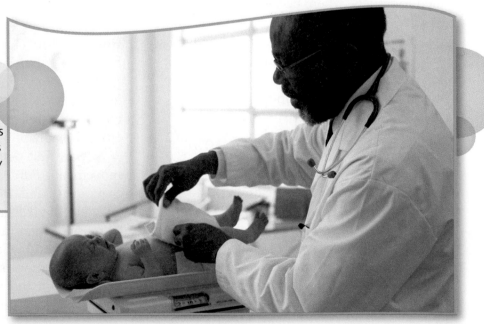

➡ Measuring Growth
During the first year, physicians talk about and track an infant's length rather than height. *Why do doctors track a baby's length instead of height?*

Dramatic Changes
The growth and development of a child during the first year of life is dramatic. *What changes are obvious from these two photos?*

Proportion

In child growth, **proportion** refers to the size relationship between different parts of the body. Compared to the rest of the body, a baby's head and abdomen are large. The legs and arms are short and small. A baby's head grows rapidly during the first year to **accommodate**, or make room for, the swiftly developing brain. More than half the total growth of the head occurs during this time. As you read in Chapter 6, the bones of a newborn's skull have gaps called fontanels, where bones of the skull have not yet joined together. During birth, these gaps allowed the head to change shape to pass through the birth canal. During infancy, they allow the head to grow as the brain develops. They later close up permanently.

Development During the First Year

A baby's growth and development are both quite rapid during the first year. Each month brings changes and new abilities. Growth and development are not nearly as obvious in older children. There are dramatic changes in appearance and abilities between a one-year-old and a two-year-old. The same is true of a two- and a three-year-old. In a group of teens you could probably tell older teens from younger ones, but it would be difficult to guess their exact age. A fifteen-year-old and a sixteen-year-old sister look and act much alike.

Patterns of Physical Development

An infant's physical development follows three basic patterns. Infants develop from head to foot, from near to far, and from simple to complex. Understanding these patterns can help you understand and follow the sequence of a typical baby's development.

Head to Foot This pattern of development begins long before birth. It starts during the prenatal stage, when a baby's head takes the lead in development. This pattern continues after birth and can be seen in the increasing control that babies gain over their body.

Babies first develop some control of head movement. For example, they will support their own head when being held. Then they will raise their head to see an object. Control of muscles then moves down the body to the arms and hands. Control of the baby's legs and feet occurs more slowly. It is not until about the age of one that a baby develops all the skills needed to walk.

Near to Far An infant's development also starts close to the body and moves outward. For example, babies will first simply wave their arms when they see an object they want. Later, they develop more precise hand and finger control and can point to an object they want. Later still, they can reach out and grasp for an object with their fingers.

Simple to Complex In the developmental pattern of simple to complex, babies first develop their large muscle groups. This includes those in the neck, arms, torso, and legs. The *torso* is the upper body. As babies strengthen and gain control over these muscles, they learn to do increasingly complex tasks. These tasks begin with controlling the head, rolling, reaching, and crawling. They continue through to walking. Even more complex movements that need small muscle development come later. Coloring, for example, requires good control of the fingers to grasp, hold, and direct a crayon.

Senses

As babies grow and develop during their first year, their senses are also developing. Babies' perception of the world increases through their vision, hearing, touch, smell and taste.

Vision A baby's eyesight improves rapidly during the first year. At first, vision is blurry. Within a week or so, a newborn is increasingly aware of the environment and can focus on objects that are seven to ten inches away. Babies' eyes can also follow an object moved slowly past their face. By one month, babies can focus on objects up to three feet away. By six months, their eyesight reaches the clarity and sharpness of the adult level.

At first, a baby sees the world in two-dimensions. This means it is like looking at a picture. Infants begin to demonstrate depth perception in their second month of life. **Depth perception** is the ability to perceive objects that are three-dimensional. This ability has a major impact on a child's interaction with the world. They can track people's movements. They also learn to reach for objects by judging how far away they are.

Patterns and colors are also important to a baby's world. Young babies seem to prefer patterns that show high contrast, such as alternating stripes, bull's-eyes, or simple faces. When shown the same object in different colors, they typically look at red or blue objects most often. Aside from an inability to focus in the early days, some babies appear to have

RESPOND TO SPECIAL NEEDS · Down Syndrome

Down syndrome is a genetic condition that affects the development of the body and brain. It is the most common cause of birth defects in humans. Children with Down syndrome have certain physical characteristics. The head may be smaller than normal and abnormally shaped. The inner corner of the eyes may be rounded instead of pointed. They also may have decreased muscle tone at birth, a flattened nose, a single crease in the palm of the hand, small ears, a small mouth, upward slanting eyes, or wide, short hands with short fingers. Physical development in children with Down syndrome is often slower than normal. Most children with

Down syndrome never reach their average adult height. Social and mental development may also be delayed. According to the National Institute of Child Health and Human Development, most people with Down syndrome have mild to moderate mental retardation.

Critical Thinking Children with Down syndrome often have one or more medical conditions. Research some of those conditions and write a one-page report of your findings.

Exploring the World
For much of the first year, children explore the world through the senses of sight, sound, and taste. After they learn to grasp objects, they begin to explore more of the world through touch. *What kinds of small objects can present hazards for babies?*

Getting Help

Three-month-old Landon was a happy baby. He smiled and gurgled when his parents held him and talked to him. He also ate well and had good sleeping habits. Landon's father commented that his son was so easygoing that even the dog's loud bark at the door did not seem to bother him. But his mother was puzzled that Landon was not starting to imitate sounds. When she stood a few feet behind him and clapped, Landon flinched and looked around, but when she gently rustled paper by his right ear, he did not seem to notice. Landon's mother was not sure what to do. Landon's father told her not to worry. He said that Landon was just a calm, quiet child. Landon's mother did not know whether Landon's behavior was normal though. She wanted to believe her husband but was afraid something was wrong.

✒ **Write About It** Suppose Landon's mother wrote a letter to the local paper asking advice. Write an advice column for Landon's mother with suggestions for what she should do.

eyes that are slightly crossed, or one eye that seems to wander outward. This condition typically improves by the fourth month as the eye muscles strengthen.

Hearing A baby's sense of hearing develops even before birth. Unborn babies often respond to sounds with changes in heart rate or activity level. A young pregnant woman who attended a loud concert found that out firsthand. For an hour after the concert, the baby continued to move to the beat of the music.

At birth, a full-term baby can already tell the general direction that a sound comes from. Newborns respond to the tone of a voice, rather than to the words. A soothing, loving voice calms them, and an angry or loud voice alarms them. By the age of seven months, babies recognize their parents and other caregivers by their voices. Some people believe that the baby will recognize these voices at birth if they heard them enough in the womb.

Language development begins with hearing spoken words first, and then imitating and understanding them. Premature babies and those who have had frequent ear infections tend to have more hearing problems. This can delay language development.

Touch Newborns lack both sufficient brain development and movement skills to explore their world through the sense of touch. However, they rely on the touch of others to teach them about their environment. Meeting a young baby's needs promptly and with a gentle touch builds trust.

Touch becomes a more important sense for learning as the first year progresses. At first, a baby may begin to notice different textures such as a soft blanket or a father's scratchy chin. As the ability to reach and grab objects develops, a baby uses touch for exploration.

Smell and Taste Since babies are surrounded by amniotic fluid until birth, their sense of smell does not have an opportunity to develop until after birth. A study has shown, however, that even newborns have some sense of smell. They respond differently to different scents. The sense of smell develops quickly. Within ten days, they can distinguish their mother from another person by smell.

The sense of taste also develops rapidly in children. Research studies have shown that two-week-old babies can taste the difference between water, sour liquids, sugar solutions, salt solutions, and milk. Even at this early age, babies show a preference for sweet tastes.

Throughout the first year, babies put anything and everything into their mouths. This is one of the main ways babies learn about their world. It is important to be sure that anything a baby grabs is clean, not sharp, and not so small that it could cause choking. Any object that can fit into a paper towel tube is likely too small for a baby to play with. Even food can be harmful for an infant.

Voice

The newborn's cry is shrill, but it softens as the baby's lungs mature. The change in the voice of the child also results from the physical growth of the throat muscles, tongue, lips, teeth, and vocal cords. The tongue and the inside of the mouth change in shape and proportion during the first months of life. This growth makes speech development possible. Babies prepare for speech by making word-related sounds. They begin babbling vowel sounds, such as *ooh* and *ah* as early as two months of age. By the age of one year, many babies can imitate some speech sounds and understand simple phrases. It is important to talk and sing to babies as much as possible. The more babies hear speech, the more opportunities they have to learn it.

Automatic Reflexes
A newborn shows an automatic reflex when grabbing a finger. *What are some other automatic reflexes?*

Figure 7.2

Physical Developmental Milestones—1st Year

During the first year babies reach many developmental milestones. *At which age does a baby typically begin to pull herself up?*

Age	Developmental Milestone
1 Month	❖ Lifts head and turns it from one side to the other when placed on stomach ❖ Focuses on objects from about 10 inches to up to 3 feet away ❖ Reacts to parent's voice
2 Months	❖ Makes sounds such as "ooh" and "aah" ❖ Watches objects moved about 6 inches away from face ❖ Responds to more sounds and different pitches of voice
3 Months	❖ Opens and closes hands ❖ Holds head steadily when held up ❖ Lifts head and chest when on stomach ❖ Swipes at objects ❖ Brings hands together
4 Months	❖ Supports upper body on hands when lying on stomach ❖ Shows preference for red and blue over yellow ❖ May begin to use vowels and consonants in babbling, such as "ah ga" ❖ Grasps rattle ❖ Puts hands in mouth ❖ Rolls from tummy to back
5 Months	❖ Rocks on stomach while kicking legs and making swimming motions with arms ❖ Reaches out and grabs toys ❖ Turns head in direction of sound ❖ Knows positive speech from unhappy speech
6 Months	❖ Passes a block from one hand to the other ❖ Puts objects to mouth with hand ❖ May begin creeping ❖ Recognizes basic sounds of native language

Age	Developmental Milestone
7 Months	❖ Rolls over both ways ❖ Sits up steadily ❖ Stands with assistance ❖ Knows parents and caregivers by their voices and by sight ❖ Can follow a path of moving objects with eyes ❖ Babbles with strings of vowels and consonants, such as "ba, ba, ba" ❖ Grabs for objects with raking motion
8 Months	❖ Pulls self up to standing ❖ Bangs blocks together ❖ Propels self by arms, knees, or squirming motion ❖ Looks at objects with sustained attention
9 Months	❖ Uses index finger to poke ❖ Puts objects in containers ❖ Leans forward to pick up toy ❖ Notices small objects ❖ May start associating sounds with objects
10 Months	❖ Crawls well ❖ Can put objects in containers ❖ Uses index finger to start pointing ❖ Imitates new word sounds more frequently
11 Months	❖ Walks while holding onto furniture or crib rails for support ❖ Uses gestures like shaking head for no ❖ Releases objects intentionally ❖ Grasps with thumb and forefinger
12 Months	❖ May walk a few steps alone ❖ Stands alone for short time ❖ Picks up small objects using thumb and forefinger ❖ Puts objects into and takes them out of containers ❖ Holds and drinks from cup

Reflexes

At birth, babies have little control over their muscles. Most movements are due to reflexes. A **reflex** is an instinctive, automatic response, such as grasping or sucking. Newborns begin life with many reflexes to help them survive in the first weeks of life. Most of these reflexes go away within a few months. Babies learn to control their muscles and develop motor skills.

The Sucking Reflex This reflex is stimulated when something is put in a baby's mouth. This reflex allows a newborn baby to feed from the mother's breast or a bottle.

The Rooting Reflex This happens when the baby's cheek is stroked. The baby turns toward the side of his or her face that was stroked.

Other Automatic Reflexes These include shutting the eyes under bright lights, grabbing a finger when it is placed in the hand, or stepping motions when the feet touch the floor. The Moro reflex causes a baby to throw the arms back with fists clenched when the arms are held and suddenly released.

Motor Skills

Much of a baby's physical development in the first year is in muscle movement, also called motor skills. These skills depend mainly on direct control and use of muscles. For example, the arms and legs must get stronger and become coordinated before a baby can crawl.

There are two basic types of motor skills. A **gross motor skill** is a skill that involves the large muscles of the body such as those of the legs and shoulders. These are sometimes called large motor skills. Gross motor skills have to do with the ability to make large movements, such as jumping and running.

A **fine motor skill** involves the smaller muscles of the body such as those in the fingers. These are also called small motor skills. Fine motor skills require small, precise movements, such as using scissors or writing.

During their first year, babies' gross motor skills develop more rapidly than fine motor skills. **Figure 7.2** on pages 204–205 shows some of the major gross motor and fine motor skill milestones during the first year.

Gross Motor Skills The large muscles of the body involved in gross motor skills are primarily in the legs, arms, torso, and neck. Newborns can turn their head, wave their arms, and kick their legs. However, these movements occur as the result of reflexes and not because the baby purposefully controls the muscles.

One of the first motor skills that infants acquire is control of the head. A newborn's head is large and heavy, and the neck muscles are weak. For example, by age one month, when Chen was placed on his stomach he could lift his head slightly. By three months, he was able to prop himself up with his arms and lift his

Safely Exploring
The increased development of gross motor skills during the first year gives a child great mobility. *What can a caregiver do to let a child explore without getting hurt?*

head and chest. In the next few months, Chen learned to roll over, and keep his head steady when he was held in a sitting position. By his first birthday, he could stand while holding on to something. This sequence of development is typical during a baby's first year.

By about nine months, many babies are crawling. They begin to explore their world. This is an exciting time for babies. They have more independence than ever before. This newfound mobility adds many new opportunities for learning.

Fine Motor Skills Fine motor skills involve the smaller muscles of the body, such as those of the fingers. By three months of age, babies' clenched fists have relaxed and they can open and close their hands. This is an important milestone in the development of fine motor skills. It means the child can grab objects by choice. By about five or six months, babies can reach for toys and pass a block from one hand to the other. By about seven months, babies can pick up objects by raking at them with the fingers and hand. Between nine and twelve months, babies fine-tune the ability to self-feed. They also learn to pick up objects with the thumb and forefinger.

Hand-Eye Coordination

The ability to move the hands and fingers precisely in relation to what is seen is called **hand-eye coordination**. This is an essential skill for many tasks in life. It is what allows people to eat, catch a ball, color pictures, and tie shoes.

Newborns have poor hand-eye coordination. It develops as vision and motor skills improve. Around the age of three or four months, babies begin to reach and grab for objects they see and bring them to their mouths. By the end of their first year, babies can pick up an object and put it in another place.

Section 7.1 — After You Read

Review Key Concepts

1. **Explain** how growth differs from development.
2. **Describe** the head to foot, near-to-far, and simple to complex patterns of development.

Practice Academic Skills

 English Language Arts

3. Imagine that you have a friend who is pregnant for the first time. How would you explain to her the importance of an infant's health and environment? Write a letter to your friend describing the effect they might have on the baby's growth and development.

NCTE 4 Use written language to communicate effectively.

 Science

4. Gina's baby weighed 7 pounds when she was born. The baby has been sick and is now a year old and weighs 15 pounds. Gina is concerned that the baby does not weigh enough. Should Gina be concerned? Write a paragraph explaining whether Gina should be concerned and what advice you would offer her.

 Check Your Answers Check your answers at this book's Online Learning Center at **glencoe.com**.

NSES C Develop understanding of molecular basis of heredity; biological evolution; matter, energy, and organization in living systems.

Section **7.2** **Caring for an Infant**

Reading Guide

Before You Read

Buddy Up for Success One advantage to sharing your notes with a buddy is that you can fill in gaps in each other's information. You can also compare notes before you start quizzing each other.

Read to Learn

Key Concepts

- **Explain** how to safely hold a baby.
- **Identify** how to meet a baby's nutritional needs.
- **Describe** the best type of clothing suitable for a baby.

Main Idea

Caregivers need to know the proper ways of handling, feeding, and dressing a baby. This knowledge will help keep a baby healthy.

Content Vocabulary

◇ shaken baby syndrome
◇ antibody
◇ weaning
◇ malnutrition

Academic Vocabulary

You will find these words in your reading and on your tests. Use the glossary to look up their definitions if necessary.

■ aggravate
■ curb

Graphic Organizer

As you read, look for things a frustrated caregiver might do when they are unable to get a baby to stop crying. Use a chart like the one shown to help organize your information.

How to Relieve Stress if a Baby Will Not Stop Crying
1.
2.
3.
4.

 Graphic Organizer Go to this book's Online Learning Center at **glencoe.com** to print out this graphic organizer.

Academic Standards . . . .

 English Language Arts

NCTE 8 Use information resources to gather information and create and communicate knowledge.

 Social Studies

NCSS I A Culture Analyze and explain the ways groups, societies, and cultures address human needs and concerns.

NCTE *National Council of Teachers of English*
NCTM *National Council of Teachers of Mathematics*

NSES *National Science Education Standards*
NCSS *National Council for the Social Studies*

Handling a Baby

A baby requires a huge amount of physical care. Each simple need, from a clean diaper to being comforted, requires someone's help. When caregivers pick up and hold a baby they can strengthen emotional bonds as well.

Holding the Baby

Babies need to be held for many reasons. They need to be changed, fed, bathed, dressed, cuddled, and hugged. Safety, physical care, and emotional bonding are all involved in picking up and holding a baby.

Newborns and very young babies require the most careful handling. A newborn's neck muscles are not strong enough to support the head. For that reason, anyone picking up and holding a newborn must support the baby's neck and head at all times. **Figure 7.3** on pages 210–211 shows how to safely pick up, hold, and put down a newborn.

By about four months of age, babies can hold up their head without support. Even then, handling babies gently and holding them close gives the babies a sense of security. Whenever picking up or putting down an infant, try to move smoothly and gently to avoid startling him. A crying baby can often be calmed by being picked up and held. Sometimes rocking the baby and gently patting the back can also be soothing.

Bedtime Routines

Sleep is essential for growth and development. It also appears to be necessary for the brain to work properly. In babies, children, and teens, sleep allows the release of chemicals in the body that contribute to growth. In addition, the body's cells are hard at work during sleep, building and repairing themselves.

Some infants sleep more than others. Generally, a baby who is active needs more sleep than an inactive baby. Babies also need more sleep on some days than on others. Additional stimulation can cause a baby to sleep more, even if the baby is not more active.

As harmless as sleeping may seem, there are safety precautions to follow when putting babies to sleep. You need to do more than just choose a safe bed. Pillows, fluffy blankets, puffy bumper pads, and stuffed toys need to be removed. They can cause suffocation.

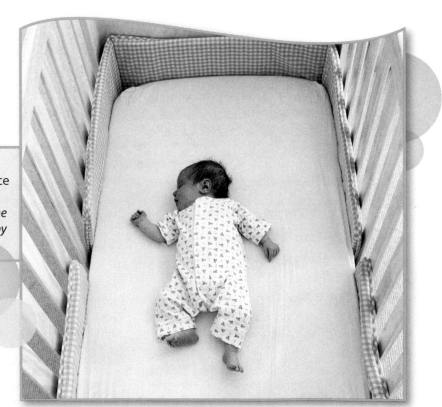

Bed Time Safety
While a crib may seem like a safe place for infants to sleep, there are safety hazards to be aware of. *What are some safety precautions when putting a baby to sleep in a crib?*

Babies should be placed face up when put to bed. This is to help prevent a death from sudden infant death syndrome. Read more about this in the Parenting Skills feature on page 212.

Putting a baby to sleep should be a relaxed and pleasant experience. A consistent bedtime routine is one of the best ways to help a baby calm down and go to sleep. Some common routines include a warm bath, reading a story, and rocking the baby gently. Parents need to find a routine that works for them. Put the baby in the crib, gently pat the baby goodnight, and leave the room. The baby may cry or whimper a bit but usually will fall asleep within a few minutes.

Lupe wants to begin a bedtime routine with her three-month-old son, Miguel. The first night, she gives Miguel a warm bath and puts a fresh diaper and some pajamas on him.

She then rocks Miguel gently as she sings him a lullaby. After a few minutes, Miguel seems drowsy. Lupe gently lays him in his crib and creeps out of his room.

Experts vary in their advice about what to do if a baby continues to cry. Some recommend leaving the baby alone to cry it out. Others say the baby should be held and comforted immediately.

Today, many experts say to go to the baby after a few minutes of crying, offer comfort without picking up the baby, and then leave the room. If the baby cries again, stay away a bit longer than before and repeat the sequence. This process reassures the baby that a parent will always be near. However, any baby who continues to cry for more than 15 minutes should be checked for a wet diaper, sickness, or other problems.

Figure 7.3 Handling a Newborn Safely

Newborns must be handled with extreme care. *Why is it important to support a newborn's neck and head when lifting and holding him?*

Lifting a Newborn Slide one hand under the baby's bottom and the other under the shoulders and head. Use your forearm to support the neck and head as you raise your hands together to lift the newborn.

Holding a Newborn in Your Arms Hold the baby upright, cradled in the curve of your arm. Your arm supports the baby's head and neck. You can easily maintain eye contact with the baby.

Sleep Patterns

The amount of time a baby spends sleeping decreases greatly during the first year. A newborn may sleep a total of 12 to 20 hours a day. By one year, however, a baby often has as few as two or three sleep periods, including naps. **Figure 7.4** on page 213 shows how much sleep babies typically need during the course of the first year.

Responding to Cries

It is important to respond to a baby's cries. Doctors say that a prompt response to a very young baby does not spoil the baby. As discussed earlier, the only time parents and other caregivers may be advised to let a baby cry is at bedtime, when they are trying to establish good sleep habits. At other times, the reason for crying may be as simple as a wet diaper or feeling cold or hungry. Pain or sickness may also cause crying. Some babies may simply be startled by loud noises. First, make sure a crying baby is comfortable, fed, and dry. Next, try rocking, talking, singing, or other comforting techniques to soothe the baby.

Shaken Baby Syndrome

No one should ever vigorously shake or jiggle a baby. These actions are extremely dangerous. Every year thousands of babies suffer serious problems due to shaken baby syndrome. **Shaken baby syndrome** is a condition that occurs when someone severely shakes a baby, usually in an effort to make her stop crying. Shaken baby syndrome can lead to brain damage, including mental retardation, cerebral palsy, or blindness. Sometimes the shaking breaks bones or injures the neck and spine. It can even cause death.

Holding a Newborn Against Your Chest Hold the baby against your chest, so that the baby faces or peeks over your shoulder. Use your hand to support the baby's neck and head.

Putting a Newborn Down Continue to support the neck, head, and body. Bend over and rest the child on a surface that can support the baby's body. Then remove your arms.

The baby cries and cries and nothing you do seems to help. You are scared, frustrated, and angry. You are afraid you will lose control and hurt the baby. You may think this could never happen to you, but it might. Even experienced adults sometimes come close to losing control. For new parents and child care providers, the odds are higher. What can you do in such a situation?

- Put the baby down in a safe place, go into another room, and take some deep breaths or look out the window to calm down.
- Ask a friend or relative to care for the baby for a few hours.
- Call someone and talk about the problem.
- Call a parenting hotline or take the baby to a crisis nursery if available in your area. Both can give immediate help and teach you how to handle stress in the future.

Gently rocking or playfully bouncing a baby on the knee is not dangerous. However, shaking or hitting a baby can be deadly. A baby cannot purposely **aggravate**, or anger, a parent. If you or someone you know is ever in this situation, ask for help.

✓ **Reading Check** **Explain** Why is it important to respond to a baby's cries?

Feeding an Infant

Mealtime provides babies with the nutrients they need to grow and develop. It also gives them much more though. It is an opportunity for babies to interact with others, learn more about their world, and practice skills. The cuddling, body contact, and encouragement that go along with feeding babies are almost as important as the food. Feeding an infant is a great opportunity for parents to bond with their child.

Parenting Skills

What Is Sudden Infant Death Syndrome?

Sudden infant death syndrome (SIDS) is the unexpected death of an infant with no obvious cause. The baby dies during sleep, with no crying and no evidence of struggle. The vast majority of children who die of SIDS are between two and four months old. However, SIDS can affect infants up to twelve months old. SIDS happens to about 2,500 infants each year in the United States.

The cause of SIDS is unknown, but researchers have identified some groups who are more at risk. Among those groups, the most likely victims are male babies who had a low birth weight. Premature babies, babies who live with a person who smokes, and babies who sleep on their stomachs also have a greater risk of SIDS.

To reduce the risk of SIDS:

- Put babies to sleep on their backs.
- Avoid smoking both during pregnancy and after the baby is born.
- Avoid exposing the baby to smoke from others.

Take Charge Research to find out more about the Back to Sleep campaign sponsored by the National Institute of Child Health and Human Development. Create a flyer to explain the 10 ways you can help prevent SIDS.

Figure 7.4 How Much Do Babies Sleep?

Babies up to a year old sleep more than half the time. *Why do babies need so much sleep?*

Age	Hours of Sleep	Description
Newborn	16	❧ Takes four or five naps a day, each about 3 to 4 hours. ❧ Between each nap is a period of wakefulness that may last a few hours.
3 months	14 to 15	❧ Total amount of sleep decreases but takes longer naps—about 4 to 5 hours long. ❧ Longer sleeping periods at night.
4 months	12 to 14	❧ Takes naps midmorning and late afternoon. ❧ Sleeps at night.
6 months	12 to 14	❧ Sleeps about six hours at night. ❧ Takes two long naps in the day.
1 year	12 hours	❧ Sleeps about 9 to 10 hours at night. ❧ May take one or two naps in the day.

Nutritional Needs

In the first year, a baby's basic source of nutrition is breast milk or formula. In fact, for the first six months of life, a healthy baby's nutritional needs can be met solely through breast milk or iron-fortified formula.

At about six months, solid foods can be introduced. Watery rice cereal is offered first, followed by other thin cereals and strained fruits and vegetables. These foods are key sources of the calories, or food energy, needed for growth. After about eight months of age, babies can get about half of their calories from solid food and half from breast milk or formula. The amount of solid food should continue to increase gradually. By the first birthday, most nutrition usually comes from solid foods.

Babies under age one should not be fed cow's milk because it is hard for them to digest. It lacks important nutrients that breast milk and formula provide. Fruit juice seems like a nutritious food for infants. However, fruit juice promotes tooth decay and may **curb**, or limit, a child's appetite for more nutritious foods. It is usually best to wait until the baby is six months old before introducing fruit juice. Then, it should be watered down for the baby. Parents should discuss their baby's eating plan with the baby's doctor.

Breast Milk

If a mother is capable, nutrition experts recommend breast-feeding. There are many advantages to breast milk:

- It contains all the nutrients a baby needs.
- It also contains antibodies. An **antibody** is a substance produced by the body to fight off germs. Antibodies boost a baby's defenses against infection. Colostrum, or the first breast milk, is especially rich in nutrients and antibodies.

- It is germ-free and easy to digest.
- Breast-fed babies get fewer ear infections, respiratory infections, and allergies than formula-fed babies. They are also less likely to develop asthma.

Breast milk lacks vitamin D, a nutrient important for bone growth. Fortunately, the skin makes this vitamin when it is exposed to sunlight. A young baby in a cold climate might need extra vitamin D in the winter. Parents should check with the baby's doctor.

The World Health Organization encourages mothers to breast-feed for at least one year. This gives babies the best possible nutrition and a good start in life. Refer back to Section 5.2 for more information on breast milk and baby formula.

Baby Formula

Many babies are fed formula for part or all of their infancy. Not every mother is physically able to breast-feed. Other parents choose to use formula.

Baby formula is specially made to meet babies' nutritional needs. Milk-based formula is used most often. The cow's milk used as an ingredient has been modified to eliminate digestive problems. Soy-based formula is also available. Formula comes in three forms: ready to use, a concentrated liquid that is mixed with water, and a powder that is mixed with water.

Feeding Schedules

A newborn's schedule of eating and sleeping is unpredictable. Pediatricians recommend that newborns be fed as much and as often as they want to eat. A newborn will generally stop eating when he or she is full.

Frequent feedings are necessary because a newborn's stomach can hold only a small amount. In the first few weeks of life, breast-fed babies may want to eat as many as eight to twelve times a day or more. Formula-fed babies may eat every three to four hours for the first few weeks.

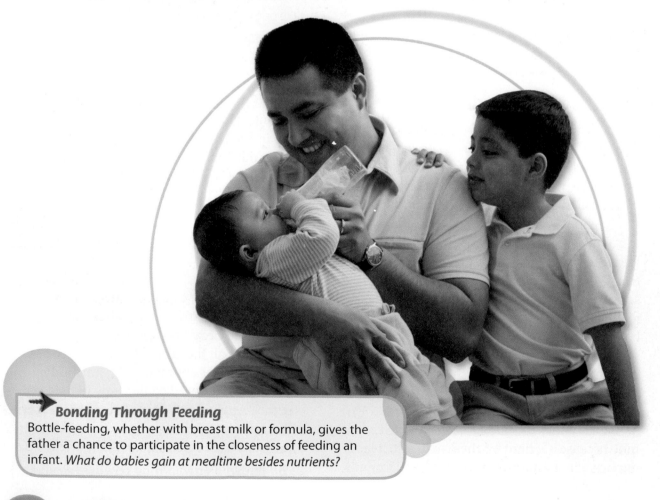

Bonding Through Feeding
Bottle-feeding, whether with breast milk or formula, gives the father a chance to participate in the closeness of feeding an infant. *What do babies gain at mealtime besides nutrients?*

By the second or third month, most babies are eating on a regular schedule. They may wake for a feeding every three or four hours. Eventually babies no longer need a late-night feeding. This is typically when they weigh about 12 pounds (5.4 kg). At this weight, their stomach is usually large enough to allow them to sleep through the night, about six hours.

Feeding Methods

Most babies under the age of six months eat only breast milk or formula. This means there are only two ways they can be fed: by breast or bottle. With either method, babies should be allowed to eat until they are satisfied. Healthy babies usually eat only the amount they need, so overeating is generally not an issue with young babies.

Breast-Feeding

Breast-feeding is very natural, but it does not always come naturally. It can take practice. Many hospitals have consultants on staff to offer assistance if needed. They can help new mothers learn how to find the best way to hold the baby and get the baby to eat. They can also give advice on the mother's nutritional needs and how to deal with problems.

Bottle-Feeding

There are certain guidelines for bottle-feeding. The first deals with preparing the formula. If using a powdered or concentrated formula, mix it with sterile (germ-free) bottled water or water that has been boiled.

Bottles should be washed in a dishwasher or with hot, sudsy water followed by a boiling water rinse. Bottles with disposable liners are a popular alternative. Bottles can be prepared up to 24 hours ahead and stored in the refrigerator.

Most infants prefer their bottles at room temperature or warm. To warm a bottle, place it in a pan of warm water. Heat the formula until it is lukewarm. Special bottle warmers are also now available. Always test the temperature by dripping a small amount of formula onto the inside of your wrist. If it is hot, allow it to cool down before feeding. Formula should never be warmed in a microwave oven. The microwave

SAFE CHILD HEALTHY CHILD

Food Poisoning

Watching children enjoy new foods for the first time can be a wonderful experience. But there are some important things, such as food poisoning, to keep in mind as new foods are introduced. Botulism is a deadly form of food poisoning. Food poisoning can make children very sick. Some of the milder symptoms may include diarrhea, vomiting, nausea, stomachache, headache, weakness, and fever. Food poisoning is caused by eating foods that have not been handled properly, or by bacteria in the foods.

Be Prepared Research to find other common types of food poisoning parents and caregivers should be aware of. Write a brief report about one type of food poisoning. Explain what it is, how it might affect a baby, and how to avoid it.

can leave pockets of hot liquid that will burn a baby's mouth.

For bottle-feeding, hold the baby close to you in a semi-upright position. The head needs support in the first few months. You should never prop up the baby and bottle and leave the baby to drink alone. It deprives the baby of important physical contact. In addition, babies should not be put to bed with a bottle. The milk can pool around the gums and cause decay in developing teeth. This practice also leads to an increased risk of ear infections.

If a baby does not finish the contents of the entire bottle, the remainder should be thrown away. Disease-causing bacteria can grow quickly in leftover formula and if eaten, could lead to illness.

Burping the Baby

Babies often swallow air as they drink whether they are bottle- or breast-fed. To feel comfortable, a baby must be burped from time to time to expel the air. Without burping, a baby may spit up, become irritable, or have gas. Burping is a technique that anyone who cares for a baby needs to know.

- Burp a baby at least twice during a feeding. Depending on how much the baby is drinking, try burping at least once during a feeding and once after a feeding.

- Find the most comfortable position to burp a baby. Many caregivers lay the baby across their knees. Others hold the baby across their chests with the baby's head above their shoulders. Some prefer to hold the baby in a sitting position for burping.

- Pat the baby on the back to cause the burp. A gentle tap works as well as a firmer one, so be very gentle.

- Protect your clothing. Put a towel or cloth under the baby's head to catch any liquid that comes up.

- Remember that it is perfectly normal for a baby not to burp each time. Each baby's liquid intake is different. Although a baby may not burp each time, it is important to try.

It is also common for most babies to spit up from time to time. This may occur after the baby has eaten more than his or her stomach can hold. Sometimes a baby will spit up while burping. It is a good idea to protect your clothes with a cloth while holding or burping a baby. Avoid placing the baby in a seated position after eating because this can put pressure on the stomach and cause the baby to spit up. If a baby vomits forcefully, or does not appear to be gaining weight, consult a doctor.

Introducing Solid Foods

Babies are typically given their first solid foods around the age of four to six months. There is no rush to start, however. Once babies have started to eat cereal, other new foods can be introduced. It is not unusual for a baby to have a bad reaction to a certain food. It may cause a skin rash, digestive trouble, or an allergic reaction. By introducing new foods at least four days apart, it is easier to figure out which food is the problem.

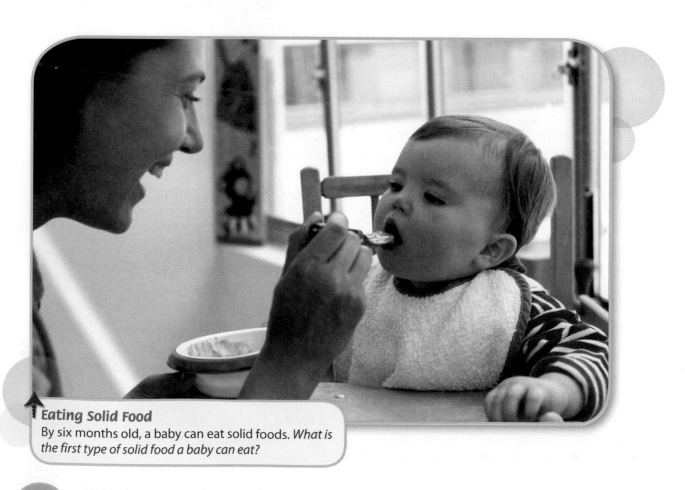

Eating Solid Food
By six months old, a baby can eat solid foods. *What is the first type of solid food a baby can eat?*

Weaning

Sometime around their first birthday, many babies are ready for weaning. **Weaning** is changing from drinking from the bottle or breast to a cup. Weaning is an important sign of a baby's increasing independence.

There is no absolute time at which a baby should be weaned. Many babies show signs that they are ready. They may show less interest in breast- or bottle-feeding. Typically this occurs between nine and twelve months of age. Other signs that a baby is ready to be weaned may include playing or looking around while feeding, pushing the breast or bottle away, or showing a preference for eating solids.

It is best to approach the weaning gradually. If a mother is breast-feeding, her body can adjust to decreasing demands on milk production. The slower transition also gives children time to get used to drinking formula or milk, depending on their age. Forced weaning may result in other feeding or behavior problems for the child.

Some pediatricians suggest going directly from breast-feeding to a cup if the child is old enough to drink from one. This avoids later transitions from bottles to cups. If an infant moves from breast-feeding to a bottle, the breast milk should slowly be replaced with formula or milk first.

Self-feeding

When babies can sit up steadily in a high chair, they can start to eat with their fingers and reach for a spoon. This is often at about eight or ten months. Being able to pick up food and self-feed is an important developmental milestone because it signals increased independence. Finger foods are small pieces of food that can easily be picked up with the fingers and eaten. They encourage self-feeding.

When a baby begins to self-feed, it is important to avoid foods that could get stuck in a baby's throat. Some of the foods to avoid include raw vegetables, hot dogs, nuts, peanut butter, whole grapes, candy, chips, pretzels, and popcorn. Any hard, round food can get stuck in a baby's throat. Foods that break up easily in the mouth are best. This might include dry toast, cereal pieces, small pieces of chicken, small pieces of cooked pasta, and chunks of banana.

A baby's first efforts at self-feeding with a spoon will probably be fun for the baby but not very productive. At first, mealtime may consist of the baby trying to self-feed finger foods while the caregiver spoons in extra food whenever possible. Babies may not become expert spoon users until eighteen months of age or later. It takes patience and a sense of humor. You should allow plenty of time for each meal and anticipate some messiness.

Nutritional Concerns

Just like adults, babies who are eating solid foods should eat nutritious, well-balanced meals that include grains, fruits or vegetables, and protein. They should be able to eat whenever they are hungry, rather than on a rigid schedule. Foods should be soft and easy to gum or chew and swallow. Salty snack foods should be limited because they are likely to be low in nutritional value. Certain other foods may contain substances that are not good for a baby. Babies have very specific nutritional needs. They include the following:

- Enough calories to provide for activity and rapid growth
- Foods that provide key nutrients, such as vitamins and minerals
- Adequate amounts of liquid

Some babies do not receive enough of the right types of food. Others may have a medical condition that prevents them from absorbing enough nutrients after they eat. Malnutrition in infancy can cause lasting physical problems.

{ **Expert Advice...** }

"When you comfort your baby, you are letting her know the world is a safe place and that someone cares about her feelings."

— Claire Lerner, LCSW; Amy Dombro, MS; and Karen Levine, coauthors, *The Magic of Everyday Moments: 0–4 months*

How to Dress a Baby

Dressing and undressing a baby quickly and smoothly takes some practice. It is easy to understand why babies do not really like the process. There is usually an abrupt change in temperature, as well as being pushed and pulled through clothes. Here are some hints for dressing babies in different types of clothing.

Pullover Garments

These clothes have a stretchable neck opening. If the neck opening is large, put the opening around the baby's face first, and then pull it over the back of the head. If the opening is small, gather the garment into a loop and slip it over the back of the baby's head. Stretch the garment forward, down, and away from the face and ears. Put the baby's fist into the armhole and pull the arm through with the other hand. Repeat with the other arm, and then straighten out the bottom of the garment.

When undressing the child, carefully stretch the garment away from the chin and face as it is lifted off.

Open-Front Shirt

Set the shirt out, with the front open. Lay the baby down on the shirt, face up. Gently pull the baby's arms through the sleeves. Fasten the front.

One-Piece Garment with Feet

Putting on this type of garment is easier when the zipper or the snaps go from neck to toes. Lay the baby on the open garment. Start with the bottom part of the garment. If the zipper or snaps go down only one leg, put the baby's leg on the side without the zipper or snaps first. Follow this by putting in the other leg. Then gently pull the sleeves over the baby's arms. Finish by zipping or snapping the garment closed.

Section 7.2 — After You Read

Review Key Concepts

1. **Describe** a possible routine to use when putting a baby to bed at night.
2. **Identify** signs that a baby has a food allergy.
3. **List** three factors you should consider when choosing a clothing gift for a newborn.

Practice Academic Skills

 English Language Arts

4. Many new parents do not recognize when a young baby is not getting the proper nutrition. Do research to learn the warning signs of malnutrition in a baby. Use the information you learn to create a poster titled Signs of Malnutrition in Babies.

> **NCTE 8** Use information resources to gather information and create and communicate knowledge.

 Social Studies

5. Research organizations in your community that help meet the nutritional needs and clothing needs of young children. Combine your findings with those of your classmates and create a directory to provide to parents of young children.

> **NCSS I A** Analyze and explain the ways groups, societies, and cultures address human needs and concerns.

 Check Your Answers Check your answers at this book's Online Learning Center at **glencoe.com**.

Reading Guide

Before You Read
Understanding Write down any questions you have while reading. Many of them will be answered as you continue. If they are not, you will have a list ready for your teacher when you finish.

Read to Learn
Key Concepts
- **Describe** how to bathe a baby.
- **Explain** why checkups and immunizations are important for babies.

Main Idea
Keeping a baby healthy involves bathing, diapering, and taking care of baby's teeth. A baby needs regular checkups and scheduled immunizations.

Content Vocabulary
◇ cradle cap
◇ diaper rash
◇ teething
◇ immunization
◇ vaccine

Academic Vocabulary
You will find these words in your reading and on your tests. Use the glossary to look up their definitions if necessary.
■ designate
■ emerge

 Graphic Organizer Go to this book's Online Learning Center at **glencoe.com** to print out this graphic organizer.

Graphic Organizer
As you read, note the steps for changing a baby's diaper. Use a chart like the one shown to record your information.

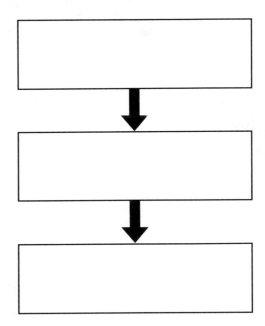

Academic Standards . . . .

 English Language Arts
NCTE 4 Use written language to communicate effectively.

 Social Studies
NCSS I A Culture Analyze and explain the ways groups, societies, and cultures address human needs and concerns.

NCTE *National Council of Teachers of English*
NCTM *National Council of Teachers of Mathematics*

NSES *National Science Education Standards*
NCSS *National Council for the Social Studies*

Keeping Baby Clean

The first year of a baby's life can be very demanding for the parents. Beyond the everyday care of a baby, parents have to maintain their baby's overall wellness. Positive caregiving techniques include everything from bathing the baby to keeping the baby safe.

Bathing a Baby

Regular baths help keep babies clean and healthy. There are two types of baby baths: a sponge bath and a tub bath. Newborns should have sponge baths until the navel heals. This is usually about two weeks after birth. After that, the baby can be given a tub bath. Many parents use a portable baby bathtub or a sink. It is best to wait until a baby can sit up on his own before using a full-size tub.

A sponge bath can be done any time a baby needs to be cleaned. Use a soft, clean sponge and warm water to gently clean the baby. Avoid the naval area. Your doctor may advise you to clean the naval using rubbing alcohol and a cotton swab. Immediately pat dry the baby and dress her to prevent chills.

Around age two to three months, babies should have baths two or three times a week. By age seven to eight months, when most babies can sit up steadily in the bath, they tend to really enjoy bath time. They love to splash and play in the water with floating toys and plastic cups. Through much of early childhood, the bathtub can be a favorite play place. Bath toys and a child's imagination merge for delightful play.

How to Bathe a Baby

Bath time can be a lot of fun for babies. Some like to kick and splash in the water or play with bath toys. Caregivers often talk, sing, or play games with a baby. It is important to handle a slippery baby carefully. Follow these guidelines for safely bathing a baby.

- **Prepare for the baby's bath.** Gather everything needed for the baby's bath ahead of time. Set up the baby bathtub, towels, washcloths, shampoo, and other supplies. Put about two inches of warm water in the baby's bathtub. Test the temperature of the water with your arm. When the bath is ready, undress the baby.
- **Put the baby in the tub.** Support a very young baby's head and neck with one hand and arm. Hold the baby's body with the other hand. Lower the baby into the tub feet first. Many baby bathtubs will support the baby in a reclined position until they can sit up on their own. However, you must stay with the baby at all times.

▶ Keeping Baby Healthy
Bathing is an important step in keeping a baby clean. *Why should you never leave a baby alone in a bathtub?*

- **Wash the baby's face.** Use clear water and a damp, soft washcloth to wash the baby's face. Then gently pat it dry.
- **Wash and rinse the baby's hair.** About twice a week, wash the baby's hair with baby shampoo. Wet the baby's hair. Add a bit of shampoo and rub gently. Rinse by pouring water toward the sides and back of the baby's head.
- **Wash the baby's body.** While supporting the baby's body, use your free hand to wash and rinse the baby.
- **Dry the baby's body.** To prevent chills, wrap the baby in a clean towel immediately. Pat the baby dry. Diaper and dress the baby right away.

Sometimes infants develop cradle cap. **Cradle cap** is a skin condition known for yellowish, crusty patches on the scalp. Most cases disappear after a few weeks or months. Parents can treat it by washing the baby's scalp daily with a mild shampoo. Other treatments, such as baby oil or excessive shampooing, can worsen the scales or dry the skin.

Bath time is also a good time to trim a baby's nails. If needed, use baby nail clippers or nail scissors to trim the nails. You might also want to use a baby file to help smooth the sharp edges. Baby nails are soft but sharp, and they can scratch the baby's face.

Diapering a Baby

Diapers are the most essential part of a baby's wardrobe. A very young baby may need diaper changes 12 to 15 times each day. A newborn wets several times an hour but in small amounts that do not require changing each time. An older baby probably needs fewer diaper changes each day. The older baby might let you know when a clean diaper is needed. Many babies are uncomfortable in a wet or dirty diaper. They will cry when they need a clean diaper.

A common problem that occurs is diaper rash. **Diaper rash** is a condition that includes patches of rough, red, irritated skin in the diaper area. Sometimes painful raw spots develop. Controlling bacteria in diapers helps prevent this condition.

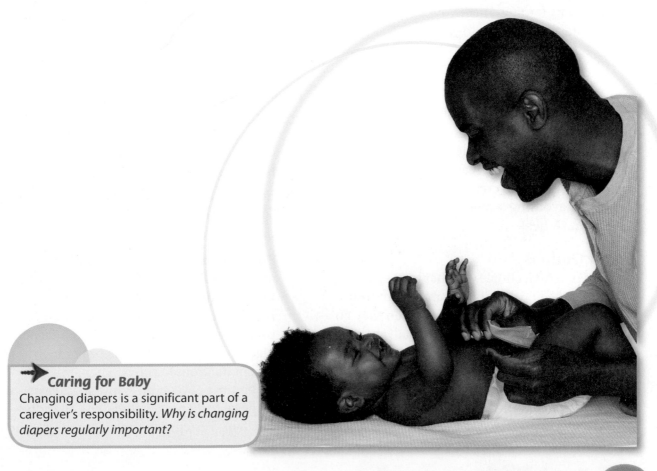

→ **Caring for Baby**
Changing diapers is a significant part of a caregiver's responsibility. *Why is changing diapers regularly important?*

Respiratory Syncytial Virus

Respiratory syncytial virus (RSV) affects nearly all babies by the age of two. In adults and children, RSV usually causes mild, cold-like symptoms. In premature babies, it can develop into a serious respiratory illness. High-risk children who are infected with RSV often need to be hospitalized. Parents and other caregivers should follow these steps to help a baby stay free of RSV.

- Always wash hands with warm water and soap before touching the baby.
- Keep the baby away from anyone with a runny nose, cold, or fever.
- Avoid taking the baby to crowded areas.
- Keep the baby away from smoke.

Be Prepared All babies are at risk for RSV. Many are infected with it. When diagnosed, there are a number of treatments depending on the severity and risk level of the baby. Do research to find common treatments for RSV. Share your information in an oral presentation to your class.

Mild cases of diaper rash can be treated by changing the diaper more frequently and being sure to thoroughly clean the baby at each changing. More severe cases need treatment such as a medicated cream. Exposing the area to air and avoiding waterproof pants can also help the rash heal.

Diaper Options

It is a personal choice whether to use disposable or cloth diapers. Some parents opt to use cloth at home but use disposable when they go out. Each has advantages and disadvantages. Parents will need to consider each option carefully before making the best decision for their child. Doctors and nurses can offer advice if needed when making these decisions. Here are a few things to consider in the decision.

- **Disposable Diapers** Many people feel that these are more convenient and more effective at keeping babies dry and comfortable than cloth diapers. Some babies develop a sensitivity to disposables, causing a rash. Infant care centers generally use disposable diapers for convenience and sanitation. Disposable diapers add significantly to environmental waste.
- **Cloth Diapers** These are the most economical choice if they are washed at home. However, they cost more than disposable diapers if they are provided and cleaned by a commercial diaper service. Cloth diapers are more environmentally friendly.

You should **designate**, or specify, a changing area. This makes it easy to keep diapers and other supplies close at hand. Any flat, clean surface may be used. A changing table is a good choice because it has sides to help keep the baby from rolling off. However, it is never safe to leave a child alone on a raised surface. Diapering supplies may include wet washcloths, disposable wipes, and dry cloths for cleanup.

For outings away from home, a diaper bag can hold diapers and supplies. It is also a good idea to include extra clothes and a plastic bag for diaper disposal.

How to Change a Diaper

Diaper changes are an opportunity for positive interaction by talking and laughing with the baby while changing the baby's diaper. There are three basic steps to changing a diaper:

1. **Remove the diaper and clean the baby.** Thoroughly clean the diaper area with a damp washcloth or disposable wipe.

2. **Put on a fresh diaper.** Hold the baby's ankles and lift the body to slide the diaper underneath the baby. With disposable diapers, be sure the adhesive tabs are on the back side of the diaper. With cloth diapers, place the folded side in the back for girls and in the front for boys. Then, bring the diaper up between the baby's legs. Fasten a disposable diaper together with the adhesive tabs. Fasten a cloth diaper with diaper

pins or diaper tape. When using pins, keep a finger between the pin and the baby's skin. Parents may choose to add plastic or cloth diaper covers over cloth diapers.

3. **Dispose of used supplies.** Throw out all used wipes and disposable diapers, preferably in a trash container with a lid. Disposable diapers clog plumbing, so never flush one down a toilet. Dirty cloth diapers should be rinsed in a clean, flushing toilet and soaked in a covered container that is filled with water, detergent, and bleach. Later, they should be washed in hot water with mild detergent.

✓ **Reading Check** **Explain** What is cradle cap?

Health Care

Parents and caregivers must be careful to help keep the baby healthy. Cleaning teeth is one part of baby's health care. Regular check-ups and immunizations and watching for illness are also important parts of maintaining a baby's health.

Teeth

The development of a baby's teeth begins about the sixth week of pregnancy. However, a baby's teeth do not begin to break through the gums until about six months of age or later. The first set of teeth a baby gets are called primary teeth, or baby teeth. The complete set of primary teeth generally comes in by the time a child is twenty months old. The timetable for when each tooth will appear varies somewhat from child to child. Children can start teething as early as four months. Some children do not get the last primary teeth until they are almost three years old.

Teething is the process of the teeth pushing their way through the gums. The gums around the new teeth swell and become tender, so it can be a painful experience. During teething, a baby may become cranky, fuss during meals, drool a lot, develop a low-grade fever, and want to chew on something hard. Teething can cause different reactions in different children.

Massaging the gums and allowing the baby to chew on a cold, hard, unbreakable object, such as a refrigerated teething ring, can bring relief to some. Babies will often put anything they can grab into their mouths at this time to chew for relief. Also note that what soothes one child may not work for another child.

Most physicians do not recommend using medications to soothe the pain. Teething medication does not always bring much relief because it washes out of the mouth in minutes. Also, numbing medications can make it difficult for the baby to eat. If a baby develops a higher fever or cannot be comforted, parents should check with a doctor. You should never give an infant any medication without first asking the baby's doctor. This is true even for over-the-counter medications that are labelled for infants.

Once the baby's first teeth **emerge**, or appear, it is a good idea to begin cleaning them regularly. The best way is to wipe them with a soft, damp cloth or gently brush them with a soft baby's toothbrush. Some dentists recommend cleaning the gums even before the first teeth emerge.

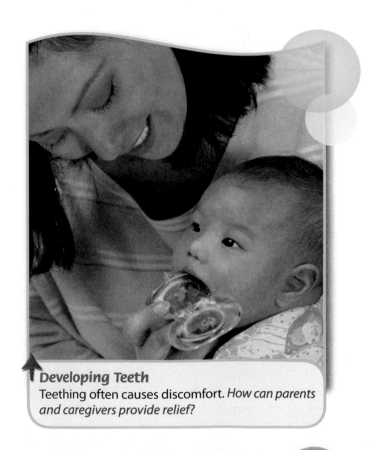

↑ **Developing Teeth**
Teething often causes discomfort. *How can parents and caregivers provide relief?*

It is important for babies to get fluoride after six months of age to build healthy teeth. However, most babies do not need fluoride toothpaste. Usually babies get enough fluoride from their drinking water or water used in formula. If their local drinking water does not contain fluoride, a doctor can determine if a baby needs fluoride supplements.

Infant Safety Concerns

Keeping children safe is one of a caregiver's greatest responsibilities. Caregivers can help prevent accidents before they happen by learning how to keep infants safe. The following are some safety guidelines for infants:

- **Choking** Keep floors clear of small objects such as buttons, coins, and safety pins. Do not feed infants solid food until the child's doctor says it is safe. Then be sure to follow the doctor's guidelines on what foods are safe to eat. Some foods are choking hazards for children until they are three years old.
- **Suffocation** Soft, flexible objects that can cover an infant's nose and mouth may cause suffocation. Keep all plastic bags away from infants. Do not put stuffed animals or loose blankets in a child's crib.
- **Water** Never leave a baby alone near or in water. This includes water in a bucket, bathtub, or wading pool. A baby can drown in as little as one to two inches of water.

{ **Expert Advice...** }

"Even healthy infants have days when they don't feel so good. Germs are all around us, and infections such as coughs and colds, stomach upsets and eye problems are not uncommon in young infants."

— Donald Schiff, MD, and Steven Shelov, MD, co-editors, *The American Academy of Pediatrics Guide to Your Child's Symptoms: The Official, Complete Home Reference, Birth Through Adolescence*

- **Falls** Do not leave a baby alone on *any* raised area, including an adult bed or a changing table.
- **Poisoning** Babies put everything into their mouths. Keep all medicines, household cleaners, paints, and other poisonous substances in locked storage areas.
- **Burns** Never leave children alone around hot liquids, ovens, or irons. Use safety covers on all electrical outlets. Keep the water heater set at no higher than 120°F (49°C).
- **Sun** Infants should wear sunglasses and hats with a brim when outdoors. Avoiding direct sun exposure and dressing babies in lightweight long pants and long-sleeved shirts are the best ways to protect them from sunburn. For infants older than six months of age, sunscreen should be used when adequate clothing and shade are not available.
- **Animals** Babies do not know how to act around animals, even pets. Never leave a child alone with any animal.
- **Clothing** It is very important that a baby's clothing be flame retardant. This is especially true for sleepwear. Check clothing labels for this information.

Regular Checkups

An infant's first checkup usually occurs within a day of birth. A doctor does a thorough check of the newborn, including all parts of the body, the baby's reflexes, the fontanels, the heart rate and breathing, the skin color, the umbilical stump, the nostrils and mouth, and the eyes. The health care staff will also record the first measurement of the baby's weight, length, and head circumference. These measurements will be tracked over the next year. A blood sample will be drawn to test for a range of disorders and diseases. A follow-up visit often occurs two or three days after a baby is born.

Additional checkups are often scheduled at 1 month, 2 months, 4 months, 6 months, 9 months, and 12 months. During these exams, the doctor will continue to track the baby's growth and development, thoroughly examine and measure the baby, and respond to parents' questions and concerns.

The Importance of Immunizations

Some checkups include immunizations. An **immunization** is a shot of a small amount of a dead or weakened disease-carrying germ given so that the body may build resistance to the disease. The most common way to immunize against a disease is with a vaccine. A **vaccine** is the disease-carrying germ that usually is injected in the body.

Immunizations are one of the most important ways caregivers can protect children against certain diseases. After being immunized, the body produces antibodies to fight off the germs for that disease. If the person is later exposed to the disease, he or she already has antibodies that fight it and will be less likely to get the disease or will only get a mild form of it. Only in very rare cases does a child have a bad reaction to a vaccine.

State regulations and schools typically require that children have certain immunizations before being admitted to a school. Many child care centers also require babies and toddlers to have immunizations before they are allowed in the center.

It is up to parents and other caregivers to keep a record of their child's immunizations and to make sure that they receive immunizations on time. To find out what types of vaccines infants need and when they need them, refer to the recommended schedule of immunizations in Chapter 20.

Watching for Illness

Babies cannot say when they do not feel well. Therefore, it is important to watch for signs of illness. Such signs may include irritability, lack of energy, constipation, nasal congestion, persistent coughing, diarrhea, rashes, vomiting, or fever. Parents and caregivers should never hesitate to call the doctor if a child shows any significant symptoms that are of concern.

Many illnesses do not require medication. In fact, many experts now feel that infants should be allowed to fight off some infections on their own so they can build stronger immune systems. The child's doctor can direct you on the best course of action for your child. For more information on illnesses, see Chapter 20.

Section 7.3 After You Read

Review Key Concepts

1. **Explain** how a sponge bath is different from a tub bath.
2. **Describe** what happens during a baby's regular checkup.

Practice Academic Skills

 English Language Arts

3. Imagine that you are caring for a six-month-old baby. You have put her down for a nap but she begins to cry. What techniques could you use to get the baby to stop crying? Write a list of suggestions.

> **NCTE 4** Use written language to communicate effectively.

 Social Studies

4. Methods for diapering a baby differ from country to country. Choose a country in a different part of the world and research the baby diapering methods used. Write step-by-step directions and demonstrate the method for the class.

> **NCSS I A** Analyze and explain the ways groups, societies, and cultures address human needs and concerns.

 Check Your Answers Check your answers at this book's Online Learning Center at **glencoe.com**.

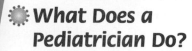

Careers With Children

Pediatrician

Pediatricians are doctors who specialize in treating children. Pediatricians work in offices, clinics, hospitals, and pharmaceutical companies. Some specialize in caring for children who have diseases such as cancer or diabetes.

What Does a Pediatrician Do?

Pediatricians keep track of children's growth and development. They also vaccinate children against disease. They diagnose and treat injured or sick children. In addition, they show parents how to care for sick children. Many children are afraid of doctors, so pediatricians must be patient and kind.

Where Do Pediatricians Work?

Most pediatricians see patients in their offices. Some pediatricians work in a group office or hospital. Others have a private practice. They also visit patients in the hospital. The hours can be long, and some pediatricians remain on duty when they are at home. This means they can be called into the office for emergencies.

Preparation and Skills

Education and Training
Pediatricians earn bachelor's and medical degrees. This is followed by three years of training in pediatric medicine. Pediatricians must pass a state exam to earn their medical license.

Aptitudes, Abilities, and Skills
Pediatricians must have strong communication skills and compassion to talk to both sick children and their families. They need keen observation abilities to analyze a child's illness, even though children often cannot explain what is wrong. Respect for patients' privacy is also a must.

Academic Skills
English language arts skills are used to talk to parents and medical associates. Pediatricians also need science and math skills to learn and understand anatomy and medical procedures.

Explore Careers

Work with your teacher to set up a time when you can talk with or observe a pediatrician or pediatric nurse. Prepare questions in advance and take notes as you talk. Share the information in an oral report to your class.

 Careers Online For more information on careers, visit the Occupational Outlook Handbook Web site through the link on this book's Online Learning Center at **glencoe.com**.

Chapter Summary

Heredity, nutrition, health, and environment all play a role in a baby's growth and development. Babies grow rapidly in the first year. Babies must be handled carefully and must never be shaken. Feeding babies breast milk or formula meets the nutrition needs for the first six months. Other foods should be introduced gradually. A baby's clothing should be comfortable and easy to put on and take off. Babies should be bathed regularly but never be left alone in the bathtub. Parents should follow a recommended schedule of checkups and immunizations.

Vocabulary Review

1. Create a fill-in-the-blank sentence for each vocabulary term. The sentence should contain enough information to help determine the missing term.

Content Vocabulary

◇ developmental milestone (p. 195)
◇ stimulating environment (p. 197)
◇ growth chart (p. 198)
◇ proportion (p. 200)
◇ depth perception (p. 201)
◇ reflex (p. 206)
◇ gross motor skill (p. 206)
◇ fine motor skill (p. 206)

◇ hand-eye coordination (p. 207)
◇ shaken baby syndrome (p. 211)
◇ antibody (p. 213)
◇ weaning (p. 217)
◇ malnutrition (p. 218)
◇ cradle cap (p. 223)
◇ diaper rash (p. 223)
◇ teething (p. 225)

◇ immunization (p. 227)
◇ vaccine (p. 227)

Academic Vocabulary

■ makeup (p. 195)
■ accommodate (p. 200)
■ aggravate (p. 212)
■ curb (p. 213)
■ designate (p. 224)
■ emerge (p. 225)

Review Key Concepts

2. Identify the four major influences on an infant's growth and development.
3. Summarize how a baby typically grows in the first year.
4. Explain how to safely hold a baby.
5. Identify how to meet a baby's nutritional needs.
6. Describe the best type of clothing suitable for a baby.
7. Describe how to bathe a baby.
8. Explain why checkups and immunizations are important for babies.

Critical Thinking

9. Compare and Contrast the role heredity and nutrition play in an infant's growth and development.
10. Examine why it is or is not acceptable for an eight-month-old to drink the same milk as the rest of the family.

Family & Community Connection

11. Interview Caregivers Work with your teacher to set up an interview with a parent or caregiver. Ask the caregiver about the techniques he or she uses to bathe and diaper an infant. Take good notes during the interview. Using your notes, write a report in which you compare and contrast the techniques described in the interview with the techniques described in this text. End your report with a brief summary of any differences noted. Why do you think the caregiver used a different technique?

Health Skills

12. Research State Rules Contact a local licensed childcare facility and ask for an answer to this question: What are the state rules for appropriate sanitation and hygiene for infants, toddlers, children, and staff at a licensed childcare facility? If necessary, conduct additional research to adequately answer the question. Write a brief essay to report your findings.

Observation Skills

13. Observe a Baby Work with your teacher to arrange to observe a baby in a home or childcare center. The baby should be under the age of 12 months. Children this age are developing more physical abilities and independence.

Procedure Be sure to note the age of the baby and if there are other children present. As you observe, note how interested the baby is in moving around independently. What signs of such interest do you see?

Analysis Complete an observation record to formally record the baby's actions. You can use an anecdotal record or a running record. Share your findings in an oral report to your class. Be sure not to reveal personal information such as the child's name in your report.

NCTE 7 Conduct research and gather, evaluate, and synthesize data to communicate discoveries.

Real-World Skills

Interpersonal and Collaborative Skills

14. Work in Teams Follow your teacher's instructions to form into groups. Work with your group to practice dressing and undressing baby-sized dolls. As team members take turns, offer comments about their techniques. Be sure your comments are constructive and not critical. Then, as a group, create a list of tips for dressing and undressing an infant.

Technology Skills

15. Create a Time Line Use graphics software to create a time line that shows the physical developmental milestones for a baby's first year. Refer to Figure 7.2 for information to include on your time line.

Financial Literacy

16. Determine Baby Food Costs Your friends have been paying $0.23 per ounce for baby food. They can make their own baby food with the same nutritional value for about $0.08 per ounce. How much will they save on 200 ounces of baby food by making their own?

 Additional Activities For additional activities, go to this book's Online Learning Center at **glencoe.com**.

Academic Skills

 English Language Arts

17. Use Your Knowledge Research has found that infants who are confined to carriers, strollers, and playpens for extended periods of time will roll over, crawl, and walk later than other children. Write a one-page essay to describe interactive activities that can help children develop gross motor skills.

> **NCTE 4** Use written language to communicate effectively.

 Mathematics

18. Rolling Distance An infant four to six months of age can roll over. The amount of distance an infant can cover in one turn is 1½ feet. If an infant is placed in the middle of a play yard that is 6 feet wide, how many rolls can the baby make before reaching the side?

Math Concept **Dividing with Fractions** To divide a whole number by a fraction, first convert the fraction to a decimal.

Starting Hint Since the baby is in the middle of the play yard, divide 6 by 2. to find out how many total feet are between the baby and the side. Then divide your answer by the amount of feet covered in each roll (1½).

 For math help, go to the Math Appendix at the back of the book.

> **NCTM Number and Operations** Understand numbers, ways of representing numbers, relationships among numbers, and number systems.

 Science

19. Motor Skills Development Research has found that an iron deficiency in infants leads to lower mental functioning and delays in motor skills development. In addition, infants need more iron as their growth accelerates during the second half of the first year.

Procedure Use print or online resources to identify good sources of iron for infants. Remember that the sources will probably change as an infant gets older and is able to eat more foods. Explain why this information is important for parents and other caregivers.

Analysis Create a brochure for parents and caregivers that states the reasons children need iron as well as good sources of iron for infants.

> **NSES F** Develop understanding of personal and community health.

Standardized Test Practice

OPEN-ENDED RESPONSE
Read the passage and follow the directions.

20. Cara is caring for her 15-month-old nephew, Jamie. Jamie is asleep and Cara is on the phone with her best friend. Jamie wakes up and begins to cry. He cries for several minutes while Cara continues to talk with her friend. Write a paragraph that describes what Cara should do.

> **Test-Taking Tip** Open-ended test questions are often looking for a specific response rather than an opinion. These may include definitions, comparisons, or examples.

Emotional and Social Development of Infants

Chapter Objectives

After completing this chapter, you will be able to:

- **List** six basic emotions that babies experience.
- **Explain** the role of attachment in a baby's emotional development.
- **Describe** how temperament affects a baby's social development.
- **Explain** how the emotional climate of the home can affect a baby's development.
- **Explain** how a baby learns social behavior.
- **Identify** how play and exploration help a baby develop socially.

Writing Activity / Freewriting

Building Relationships From the first moment she is born, a baby begins to develop relationships with her parents or caregivers. Use freewriting to describe your idea of a positive, healthy relationship.

Writing Tips To jumpstart your writing, it can be helpful to write out ideas freely. This is called freewriting. Use these tips to start freewriting:

1. Write everything that comes to mind, in any order.
2. Do not worry about having an introduction or conclusion. You can go back and revise later.
3. Focus on ideas. Correct your grammar and spelling after you are done writing.

Section 8.1 Understanding Emotional Development of Infants

Section 8.2 Understanding Social Development of Infants

Explore the Photo
This baby's healthy bond with his caregiver can help him form healthy relationships later in life. *Why do you think a baby's early experiences can affect his self-esteem later in life?*

Section 8.1 Understanding Emotional Development of Infants

Reading Guide

Before You Read

Preview Look at each photo in this section and read the photo captions. Write one or two sentences explaining what you think the section will be about.

Read to Learn
Key Concepts
- **List** six basic emotions that babies experience.
- **Explain** the role of attachment in a baby's emotional development.
- **Describe** how temperament affects a baby's social development.
- **Explain** how the emotional climate of the home can affect a baby's development.

Main Idea
Caregivers play a large role in babies' emotional development, helping them learn to express feelings and develop a personal identity.

Content Vocabulary
◇ emotional development
◇ emotion
◇ colic
◇ reflux
◇ attachment
◇ failure to thrive
◇ temperament

Academic Vocabulary
You will find these words in your reading and on your tests. Use the glossary to look up their definitions if necessary.
■ crucial
■ hinder

Graphic Organizer
As you read, list things a caregiver can do to promote a baby's healthy emotional development. Use a chart like the one shown to help organize your information.

Healthy Emotional Development
1.
2.
3.
4.

 Graphic Organizer Go to this book's Online Learning Center at **glencoe.com** to print out this graphic organizer.

Academic Standards . . . .

 English Language Arts

NCTE 4 Use written language to communicate effectively.

 Social Studies

NCSS I C Culture Apply an understanding of culture as an integrated whole that explains the functions and interactions of behavior patterns.

NCSS IV C Individual Development and Identity Describe influences that contribute to the development of a sense of self.

NCTE *National Council of Teachers of English*
NCTM *National Council of Teachers of Mathematics*

NSES *National Science Education Standards*
NCSS *National Council for the Social Studies*

Emotions and Emotional Development

Emotional and social development begin at birth and continue throughout life. They are as important as physical development to becoming a healthy and happy adult.

Emotional development is the process of learning to recognize and express feelings and to establish a personal identity. A personal identity is a sense of being a unique individual. A child who experiences healthy emotional development will be self-confident. He or she will be able to handle stress and will have empathy for others.

The most important influences on a child's emotional development are the bond between the caregiver and the child, the temperament of the child, and the atmosphere of the home.

Emotions in Infancy

We are all born with the ability to experience emotions. An **emotion** is a feeling response to the world around us. Even newborns can feel basic emotions such as contentment and distress. Emotions grow more complex with age. **Figure 8.1** on page 236 shows the development of some basic emotions during a child's first year.

Learning Emotions Through Interaction

Parents and caregivers play a large role in shaping a baby's emotions. Parents can encourage positive emotions. Parents can also help infants cope with negative emotions. Returning a baby's smile, for example, encourages his joyful expression. Rocking a frightened baby teaches her to become calm again after a scary experience.

Babies also learn from their caregivers how to react to situations. A baby whose caregiver is often joyful may learn to approach life with happiness and interest. A baby whose caregiver is often anxious may learn to approach life with fear.

Emotions and Crying

Infants do not have words, so they show many of their needs and emotions through crying. At around two months of age, babies start to vary their cries to express different feelings.

Healthy Emotional Development
Touch can help an infant develop healthy emotions. *Why is physical touch important to emotional development?*

Parents may eventually learn what each cry means. This adds to the baby's comfort and encourages the expression of emotions. It also strengthens the parent-child bond.

Some babies rarely cry and are easy to comfort when they do. Often these babies are labeled as "easy" or "good" babies. Other babies may cry loudly and often. It can be difficult to comfort them.

A baby who is crying needs attention and care. How should you comfort him? First, check for a physical problem. Is the baby hungry? Does he need a diaper change? Is he cold or hot? Did he burp at the last feeding? If none of these is the cause and the baby does not seem ill, he probably needs something else. Perhaps he needs company or cuddling. These are real needs, too. Sometimes, babies just need help to go to sleep.

Getting to know the baby helps you to discover which comforting measures work best. Here are a few time-tested techniques.

- **Cuddle** Cuddle up with the baby in a rocking chair or hold the baby close while walking around. The combination of being held and rocked is soothing.
- **Move the Baby** Move the baby to a new position. The baby may be too young to roll over on her own. Try placing her in an infant seat so she can see what is happening.
- **Sing** Talk softly or sing to the baby. The tone and rhythm of your voice may comfort him.
- **Offer a Toy** Offer a toy to interest the baby. She may be bored and want something to do.
- **Massage** Stroke or gently rub the baby's back. You can also try rubbing baby lotion on his back and legs.

Figure 8.1 Development of Basic Emotions

By nine months of age, babies experience and show many basic emotions. *How would you judge whether a baby was angry or sad?*

Parents and caregivers play a large role in shaping babies' emotions. Basic emotions lead to more complex emotions—such as pride, shame, and embarrassment—later in life.

Sadness Very young babies express discomfort or unhappiness by crying.

Interest Babies watch their mothers very closely. Often, this is the first sign of interest in babies.

Self-Comforting

Babies also find ways to comfort themselves. Many babies soothe themselves with a favorite blanket or stuffed toy. Babies may develop a special attachment to the object and use it for comfort when they are sleepy or anxious. Other babies comfort themselves by twisting their hair or by rocking themselves back and forth. Children usually give up these habits when they are ready.

Thumb Sucking

The most common self-comforting technique is sucking. A baby will suck on a thumb, a fist, or a pacifier. Sucking is a basic urge in infants. Many babies stop sucking their thumbs on their own at six or seven months of age, when their first teeth appear. Parents should only be concerned about thumb sucking if it starts to change the shape of a child's teeth or mouth. A pediatrician can check to see whether thumb sucking is causing physical problems.

Pacifiers

Many infants find comfort in sucking on a pacifier. A pacifier can help a baby calm down and fall asleep. Some people fear that pacifiers can cause physical or emotional harm. The American Academy of Pediatrics disagrees. The Academy recommends that, if using a pacifier, caregivers should use one that is the correct size and shape for their baby's age. The pacifier shield should be large enough to prevent the entire pacifier from fitting in the baby's mouth. Caregivers should sanitize a pacifier frequently. They should never tie a pacifier around a baby's neck or hand or use it as a replacement for food.

Joy Babies show joy by smiling, perhaps in response to an adult who is making funny faces at them.

Anger Babies show anger through crying. Signs of anger may appear as early as three to six months of age.

Disgust Babies begin to show their dislikes very clearly.

Fear Babies show fear by startling, turning away, and screaming, especially in response to strangers.

Uncontrollable Crying

It is normal for infants to cry between one and three hours a day. Some healthy babies cry more than this and can be difficult to comfort. Two common causes for excessive crying in infants are colic and reflux.

Colic

Some babies who cry for long periods may have colic. **Colic** is uncontrollable crying by an otherwise healthy baby. A colicky baby cries for three hours or more each day, for three or more days a week, for three weeks or more. Babies with colic usually cry at the same time each day. The crying is often worst between six o'clock in the evening and midnight. A colicky baby is difficult or impossible to comfort. The symptoms of colic are often the most intense when the baby is about six weeks old. These periods of crying usually end around three or four months of age.

Doctors are not sure why babies get colic. It may be caused by anxiety or allergies. It may be caused by gas in the stomach. Caregivers can try burping the baby more frequently or rubbing the baby's belly. Colic may be caused by sensitivity to certain foods, such as milk or wheat. The solution can sometimes be as simple as eliminating a problem food. Breast-feeding mothers can try avoiding strong foods such as cabbage, onions, and spicy foods.

Reflux

If an infant cries constantly, she might have a physical problem, such as reflux. **Reflux** is a condition in which partially digested food rises in the throat. Reflux can cause forceful vomiting and intense crying. Parents should talk to their pediatrician if they cannot figure out why their baby is constantly crying. The doctor can advise a course of action to help and can prescribe medication if needed.

✓ **Reading Check** **Summarize** How should you respond to a crying baby?

Parenting Skills

Helping a Baby Develop a Sense of Trust

Meeting a baby's physical and emotional needs helps a baby build a sense of trust. Try these strategies to help a baby develop trust.

❧ **Follow a predictable routine.** Routine care helps a baby learn to trust a parent or caregiver. Establish regular times for feeding, baths, and naps.

❧ **Get to know the baby.** Appreciate the baby's uniqueness. Learn about the baby's likes and dislikes. Learn the baby's signs for hunger, tiredness, and boredom.

❧ **Bond with the baby.** Spend time nurturing and holding the baby. Talk to the baby in a soft, positive tone. Smile and establish eye contact. Enjoy physical closeness.

❧ **Meet the baby's needs.** Strive to meet a baby's physical, social, and emotional needs. Provide loving care and affection.

Take Charge If you were a caregiver, how could you learn what a baby's different cries mean? Write a one-page journal entry sharing your thoughts.

Physical Contact
Babies need physical contact to grow and develop normally. *How can a caregiver help a child grow up to trust others?*

Attachment and Emotional Development

Attachments are **crucial**, or essential, to the healthy emotional development of an infant. An **attachment** is a baby's bond to his or her main caregiver. A healthy attachment helps a baby develop trust, self-esteem, and social and emotional skills.

Attachment begins to develop in the first few months of life. It is fully formed around age two. A child who has not formed a strong attachment by age two may have difficulty with relationships later in life.

A baby's attachment to a caregiver helps her build healthy, loving relationships later in life. Psychologist Erik Erikson suggested that people learn to trust or mistrust the world during their first year. Love and affection from parents and other caregivers fosters a sense of trust.

Building Attachment Through Touch

Physical contact helps build attachment. Infants have a basic need for physical contact. They need to be held and cuddled. Touch helps build trust and affection between a baby and a caregiver. Touch is a primary sense for infants. Touch is how babies experience and respond to their environment. Being held or massaged helps to soothe crying babies. This is a natural way for a caregiver to show love or affection to a child. The baby is learning that the parent or caregiver will be there when needed.

Building Attachment Through Consistent Care

Babies develop trusting relationships when caregivers meet their needs. The world is a strange place for newborns. Depending on a baby's early experiences, it may be a comfortable place or a confusing, difficult place. If the newborn's needs are met and he bonds with adults, he learns that the world is a comfortable place and he develops a sense of security.

THE DEVELOPING BRAIN

Touch Builds the Brain

Touching babies does more than comfort them. It helps their brains grow. Touch causes new pathways, or networks of neurons, to form in a baby's brain. Experiences of loving touch also cause a baby's brain to trust human contact. Lack of contact can also affect brain development. Abused and neglected children who do not receive love, touch, and opportunities for learning can have brains that are 20 to 30 percent smaller than average.

■■ **Science Inquiry** Physical touch is especially helpful for the mental and emotional development of deafblind babies. What might explain this?

Holding a Baby Close

Carrying babies close to the body is the norm in many cultures. In Somalia, women tie their babies to their backs with long scarves. In Nepal, mothers carry their babies in a garment that also holds money and tools. The Inuit people of the Canadian Arctic can snuggle their babies in the furry linings of their parkas. Baby slings are now growing more popular in North America and Europe. Carrying a baby close provides the baby with a sense of security and lets him feel, see, and smell the parent. It also lets the baby see the world from a different vantage point.

⭐ **Build Connections** *What are the advantages of sharing space? What are the disadvantages?*

NCSS I C Culture Apply an understanding of culture as an integrated whole that explains the functions and interactions of behavior patterns.

Caregivers need to try to be consistent in their care and responses toward an infant. If schedules change often, or if caregivers are patient and loving at times and impatient and harsh at other times, babies have difficulty building trust.

Building Attachment Through Communication

Communication between infants and caregivers is also important in building attachment. Infants respond to a caregiver's voice, facial expressions, and eye contact. Babies gaze into the eyes of those who care for them, track their movements, and cuddle. These are signs of growing attachment. As babies get older, they respond to their caregivers with sounds and hugs. Later, babies crawl or walk to their caregivers.

Failure to Thrive

Infants enjoy healthy emotional development when their emotional and physical needs are met. Lack of love and attention can cause failure to thrive. **Failure to thrive** is a condition in which babies do not grow and develop properly. They do not respond to people and objects.

Their cries weaken and their smiles fade. They become withdrawn. As adults, they may be unable to develop caring relationships with others, even with psychological help.

Failure to thrive can be caused by neglect, abuse, or another form of stress. Babies can fail to thrive if they are left alone most of the time or do not receive enough physical contact. Children who live in poverty are more likely to fail to thrive than other children.

✓ **Reading Check** **Identify** How can parents build an attachment with their child?

Understanding Temperament

Temperament is another key factor in a baby's emotional development. **Temperament** is a person's unique emotional makeup. Each person is born with a unique temperament. A baby's temperament helps determine how he reacts to his environment. Understanding a baby's temperament can help you give him exactly the type of care he needs. **Figure 8.2** on page 242 can help you identify a baby's temperament traits.

How can you tell a baby's temperament? Observe her in different situations. Is she relaxed or bursting with energy? Does she love or hate surprises? Is she cautious or the first to try something new? You can also note her eating and sleeping patterns, and her general mood.

By recognizing a baby's temperament, you can learn to work with the baby to ensure a happy and healthy emotional development. Parents and caregivers should always keep in mind that every baby is unique. There are many definitions of normal infant behavior. Parents need to accept and nurture their baby's individual style to develop the best relationship possible.

Resolving Temperament Conflicts

Parents should remember that temperament traits cannot be changed. Rather, parents should learn to adapt their reactions to a child's specific traits. A child should not be punished for a temperament trait. If a child is shy, try holding him when you introduce him to someone new. Give him time to warm up to the new person, instead of handing him to the new person right away.

Caregivers have their own temperaments, too. One of a caregiver's responsibilities is to adapt to the temperament of the child, even if they are different. Look for positive ways to adapt to these differences. Suppose that you have a low energy level, but your infant is constantly on the move. You should provide safe opportunities for energetic play. Enjoy a trip to the park or dancing to music. Avoid activities that require the child to sit a lot. Can you think of other strategies you might try?

✓ **Reading Check** **Analyze** Why is it important to understand a baby's temperament?

Unique Temperaments
Each baby is a unique individual with a different combination of temperament traits. *Why is it useful to know a baby's temperament?*

Figure 8.2 Nine Temperament Traits

A baby's temperament is a combination of different temperament traits. Each person has these traits in different amounts. *Do you recognize these traits in the babies you know?*

Trait	Description
Intensity *How strong are a child's emotional responses?*	Highly intense children have powerful responses. They may cry and scream loudly. Less intense children tend to be calmer and quieter.
Persistence *How determined is a child to complete a task?*	Very persistent children take on challenges. They do not like to stop in the middle of a project. Less persistent children can be persuaded to move on to new activities. They can accept no for an answer.
Sensitivity *How strongly does a child notice her own and others' feelings?*	Highly sensitive children have their feelings hurt easily. They may be bothered by sights, sounds, or smells. Less sensitive children are not as concerned with others' opinions of them. They may not perceive other people's emotions as easily.
Perceptiveness *How aware is a child of all that is around him?*	Highly perceptive children get distracted easily. They have a hard time following complex directions. Less perceptive children notice less of what is going on around them. This makes it easier to follow through on multistep tasks.
Adaptability *How easily does a child accept changes?*	Highly adaptable children are not bothered by surprises or changes of plans. Less adaptable children resist change.
Regularity *Does a child's behavior follow regular patterns?*	Highly regular children like to eat, sleep, and go to the bathroom at about the same time each day. Less regular children have a different schedule each day.
Activity *What is a child's energy level?*	High-energy children love to move. They often squirm and move around in their seats. They would often rather run than walk. Low-energy children move much less and may seem more relaxed.
Approach *How does a child face new situations and people?*	High-approach children dive right in. These children are open to new activities and willing to try new foods. Low-approach children are more shy and cautious.
Mood *Is a child typically cheerful or down?*	Children with a positive mood have a rosy outlook. They expect the best from people. Children with a negative mood may be more suspicious. They may easily feel angry or disappointed.

Emotional Climate of the Home

Babies are very sensitive to the feelings of people around them. Long before they know the meanings of words, they are influenced by adults' emotions, tone of voice, gestures, and facial expressions. Worried or angry caregivers are likely to be tense in handling their babies. Babies sense these feelings and can become irritable and anxious.

Every family has ups and downs, and a baby adapts to them. It is normal for caregivers to feel occasional frustration and anger toward a beloved child. However, a baby needs to feel that affection and caring are the basis of the family's interactions. Feelings of bitterness, mistrust, and anger can **hinder**, or delay, an infant's emotional development.

Handling unwanted feelings, such as anger, frustration, and sadness, is a challenge for every parent and caregiver. It can be an even greater challenge for single parents. Single parents have no other adult to share the work or the worries, and they may feel alone and overwhelmed.

It is important for all parents to find ways of releasing negative feelings away from their children. Dealing with challenging feelings can help parents find the patience to create a caring environment. Every parent needs someone who can give them emotional support.

Section 8.1   After You Read

Review Key Concepts

1. **List** the most important influences on a child's emotional development.
2. **Explain** ways to build attachment to support a baby's emotional development.
3. **Describe** ways to resolve temperament conflicts.
4. **Explain** why it is important for parents to *not* express negative feelings around their children.

Practice Academic Skills

English Language Arts

5. Describe your temperament using the nine temperament traits described in the section. Now imagine that you are caring for a child whose temperament is very different from yours. Write a letter to a friend describing how this could be challenging and what strategies you might use to handle the challenge.

> **NCTE 4** Use written language to communicate effectively.

Social Studies

6. Temperament, family, culture, and institutions such as schools and churches are important influences on your identity. You are also influenced by your *peers*, or people your same age. Write a report describing the people, places, and things that you think have influenced your identity since you were a baby, and why.

> **NCSS IV C** Describe influences that contribute to the development of a sense of self.

Check Your Answers Check your answers at this book's Online Learning Center at **glencoe.com**.

Reading Guide

Before You Read

Preview Look at the headings and key terms in the section. Write one or two sentences explaining what the section will be about.

Read to Learn

Key Concepts

- **Explain** how a baby learns social behavior.
- **Identify** how play and exploration help a baby develop socially.

Main Idea

Caregivers play a large role in a baby's social development. They help the infant learn to form relationships and feel comfortable in his or her world.

Content Vocabulary

◇ social development
◇ cause and effect
◇ model
◇ stranger anxiety
◇ play environment

Academic Vocabulary

You will find these words in your reading and on your tests. Use the glossary to look up their definitions if necessary.

■ lead
■ motivate

Graphic Organizer

As you read, describe actions a caregiver can take to assist in a baby's healthy social development. Use a chart like the one shown to help organize your information. Add more circles as necessary.

Healthy Social Development

 Graphic Organizer Go to this book's Online Learning Center at **glencoe.com** to print out this graphic organizer.

Academic Standards

 English Language Arts

NCTE 4 Use written language to communicate effectively.

 Social Studies

NCSS IV C Individual Development and Identity Describe the ways family, and other group and cultural influences contribute to the development of a sense of self.

NCTE *National Council of Teachers of English*
NCTM *National Council of Teachers of Mathematics*

NSES *National Science Education Standards*
NCSS *National Council for the Social Studies*

Social Development and Learning

Social development is the process of learning how to interact and express oneself with others. A child who experiences healthy social development will be able to communicate well with others, connect with others, and show tolerance for others.

Social development is closely related to emotional development. Children who have good feelings about themselves relate well with others. Children who relate well to others feel good about themselves.

Figure 8.3 on page 246 shows common steps in an infant's social development. Children grow and develop at their own pace. They may reach these milestones at different times or in a different order.

Learning Through Cause and Effect

Babies learn by observing cause and effect. **Cause and effect** is a relationship between events in which one event, the effect, is caused by another event. For example, infants learn that they can get their needs met by crying. They learn that letting go of a toy will cause it to fall.

Babies learn that certain behaviors earn a positive response from adults. When babies coo and smile, for example, they are rewarded with laughter, hugs, and praise. Love is important to babies, so they repeat these behaviors. Babies also learn that other behaviors bring frowning or other unwanted behaviors from adults. They are less likely to repeat these behaviors.

Learning Through Imitation

Babies learn through imitation too. As children grow, they watch the behavior of important adults in their lives and then imitate those actions. Parents and caregivers should model desirable behaviors, such as kindness and patience. To **model** a behavior means to teach it through example.

Sending Clear Messages

Babies develop better social behaviors if they get many more positive responses than negative responses. Always try to give a baby clear messages. Smiling while expressing love or approval sends a clear message. Smiling while expressing disapproval sends an unclear message. Babies become confused if the same behavior leads to a positive response one time and a negative response another time. Provide consistent responses to help a baby understand what behaviors are desirable.

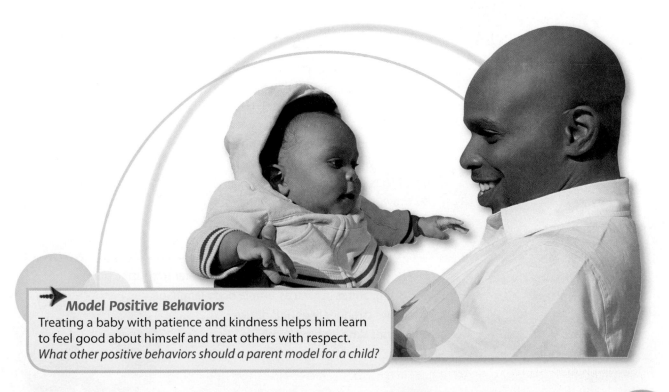

Model Positive Behaviors
Treating a baby with patience and kindness helps him learn to feel good about himself and treat others with respect.
What other positive behaviors should a parent model for a child?

Age		Developmental Milestone
1 Month		✤ Coos and babbles ✤ May cry a lot, but quiets down when he sees the caregiver's face, hears the caregiver's voice, or is lifted or touched
2–3 Months		✤ Maintains brief eye contact while being fed ✤ Makes different crying sounds for different needs ✤ Begins to smile and show excitement ✤ Eyes can follow moving objects ✤ Wants companionship ✤ May like being tickled ✤ Can tell a smile from a frown
4–6 Months		✤ Turns to sound of familiar voices ✤ Laughs, squeals, babbles ✤ Can tell the difference between family members ✤ Reaches out to play ✤ May cry when left alone
7–8 Months		✤ Tries to imitate sounds made by adults ✤ Plays alone and plays longer with other people and toys ✤ Enjoys other children ✤ Begins to experience stranger anxiety and clings to familiar caregivers
9–10 Months		✤ Responds to "no" and own name ✤ Says simple words, such as "no," "bye-bye," "dada," and "mama" ✤ Objects if a toy is taken away ✤ Crawls around to look for parents ✤ Enjoys playing peek-a-boo and sound games
11–12 Months		✤ Uses the words "Dada" and "Mama" to refer to specific people ✤ Uses gestures as well as simple body language ✤ Shows stronger likes and dislikes ✤ Spends time looking in mirrors

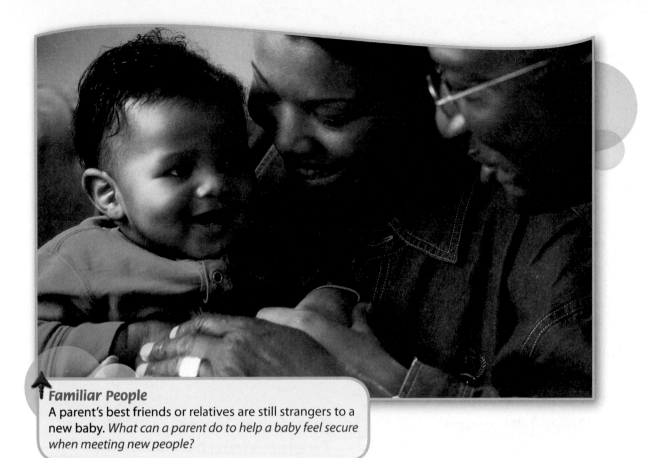

Familiar People
A parent's best friends or relatives are still strangers to a new baby. *What can a parent do to help a baby feel secure when meeting new people?*

Stranger Anxiety

Beginning at around eight months of age, many babies show signs of stranger anxiety. **Stranger anxiety** is a fear of unfamiliar people, usually expressed by crying. A baby who used to sit cheerfully on a stranger's lap suddenly screams and bursts into tears when an unfamiliar person approaches. Some babies bury their heads in a parent's shoulder.

Stranger anxiety is a normal part of social development. Most babies simply need time and understanding. A caregiver can help a baby through this fear by providing consistent responses. Act welcoming toward new people. Encourage friends and relatives to quietly let the baby get used to them. Never force a baby to be held by an unfamiliar person. Instead, hold the baby yourself and sit next to the person to introduce them. While still holding the baby in your lap, encourage him to play with the new person. Give the baby time to become comfortable. When the baby seems ready, hand him to the new person. Stay nearby to provide comfort and reassurance.

A baby might feel this same anxiety with a parent if he or she looks different. For example, if a father puts on a hat and then greets the baby, the baby might not recognize him. This is normal. When the baby hears the father's voice, and smells his scent, he will recognize him again.

✓ **Reading Check** **Explain** How can toys help a baby learn cause and effect?

{ Expert Advice... }

"For infants and toddlers, learning and living are the same thing. If they feel secure, treasured, loved, their own energy and curiosity will bring them new understanding and new skills."

— Amy Laura Dombro and Leah Wallach, early childhood authors, *The Ordinary Is Extraordinary.*

Learning Through PLAY

Social Development Through Play

The job of a baby is to play. Babies learn about the world around them through play. Play strengthens all areas of growth and development. Play helps children learn to interact with adults and other children. Caregivers and babies strengthen their attachment through play. Play also helps babies develop motor skills and learn about the world.

Play from Birth to Six Months

Try these strategies with babies who are in their first six months of life:

- Play games with toys or objects that the baby can grasp.
- Place colorful toys where the baby can learn to recognize and reach them. Name the colors of the toy as the baby chooses one to play with.
- Make noise with a rattle or other toy.
- Gently shake, stretch, and exercise the baby's arms and legs while smiling and talking to the baby.
- Follow the baby's **lead**, or example. Laugh and smile after the baby laughs and smiles.

Play from Six to Twelve Months

Babies from six to twelve months of age can play somewhat more complicated games and handle more toys. Try these play strategies with older babies:

- Play peek-a-boo with the baby. Hold a blanket up to hide your face and then pull it away. As the baby gets older, let her pull the blanket away to find you.
- Set toys just out of reach so that the baby has to crawl to them. Encourage the baby to crawl to the object and praise his success.
- Read to the baby from simple books that have big pictures. It is never too soon to start introducing a child to books.
- Play silly songs and dance with the baby. Help the baby clap or bounce in rhythm with the music.
- Give babies plastic buckets or other containers that they can fill up with water, sand, or toys and dump out. Talk the baby through the activity, describing what can be done.

After each play activity, reward the baby for success by showing positive responses. Babies love to see their parents clapping hands, smiling, laughing. The parent should also tell the baby what a great job he or she did.

Create a Safe Play Environment for Infants

Parents and other caregivers need to provide a safe play environment for babies to explore. A **play environment** is a comfortable space free of dangers and with toys that are safe and interesting. Many caregivers use safety gates to keep infants away from dangerous areas like stairs.

Infants love toys that are colorful and that move around and make noise. Hanging mobiles, rattles, and stuffed animals are wonderful toys for infants. Babies from six to twelve months of age enjoy more complicated toys, such as those they can push or pull.

Choose Safe Toys

It is important to choose toys that are safe and appropriate for the age of the baby. Toys should be big enough so that babies cannot put them all the way in their mouths. Choose toys that do not have small parts. Babies can swallow and choke on small parts, or stick them in their nose or ears. Toys should also be sturdy.

SAFE CHILD HEALTHY CHILD

Exploring Through Taste

Babies' mouths are more sensitive than their hands, so it is no wonder that babies use their mouths to explore tastes, textures, and shapes. *Mouthing* is normal, but it can be dangerous. A baby can choke on small objects or be poisoned by chemicals. Make sure that all toys are too large to fit all the way into a baby's mouth. Keep soaps, medicines, and chemicals out of reach. You can satisfy a baby's need to explore by choosing toys and foods with interesting shapes and textures.

Be Prepared Use the library or the Internet to conduct research on child safety. Make a safety checklist of 20 common choking hazards for babies, including toys and toy parts, household objects, and foods. Share your checklist with the class.

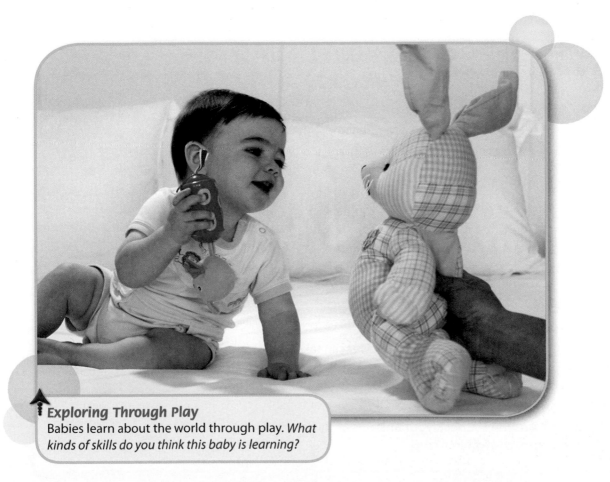

Exploring Through Play
Babies learn about the world through play. *What kinds of skills do you think this baby is learning?*

Use a safety checklist to make sure the rooms where a baby plays do not have any hidden dangers. See Chapter 10 for tips on how to child-proof a room. It is also important to keep toys clean. Wash new toys with soap and water. Wash them again each time the baby plays with them.

Social Development Through Exploration

Babies have a need to explore. They explore with all their senses: touch, vision, hearing, smell, and taste. Babies often put toys, stuffed animals, and other objects into their mouths. Sometimes babies repeatedly throw or drop things just to see what happens.

When babies start rolling, and later crawling and walking, they can explore more of their environment. Many babies will try to pull themselves up to reach objects on furniture. They will often try to take away keys or telephones from their parents. To a baby, these items look like new toys. As infants get older, they will want to explore and learn about everything in their environment.

Play and Exploration

Play and exploration are related. Babies use play to explore their world. They look at and play with toys to explore colors and textures. Blocks, for example, let babies explore how things stack up and balance. Caregivers can help babies explore by giving them safe and interesting objects to explore. Even basic household items such as plastic spoons or cups and empty boxes that can be filled are interesting to infants. A kitchen pot and wooden spoon make an instant drum set for an infant.

Encouragement and positive responses from adults **motivate**, or provide a reason for, babies to explore and learn. Everything in the world is new to a baby. By participating in explorations with the baby, caregivers can deepen their attachment to their children. For example, a parent could take the baby to a park or garden. The parent can participate in the exploration by showing the baby the different colors and shapes of flowers and trees. The parent can help the baby feel the textures of the leaves and bark.

Section 8.2 After You Read

Review Key Concepts

1. **Describe** how a parent can give a baby clear messages about behavior.
2. **Explain** how parents can help babies to explore and learn.

Practice Academic Skills

English Language Arts

3. Imagine that you write an advice column on parenting. A young parent asks for advice on how to handle her nine-month-old son, who cries and acts terrified around friends and neighbors. Write an answer to explain why the baby is behaving this way and give some tips on how to help him feel more comfortable.

> **NCTE 4** Use written language to communicate effectively.

Social Studies

4. Brainstorm actions that a parent or caregiver can take to help a baby's healthy social development. Group your ideas into major topics, such as "play" and "modeling positive behaviors." Create a table of information, devoting three activities to each of your major topics.

> **NCSS IV C** Describe the ways family, and other group and cultural influences contribute to the development of a sense of self.

Check Your Answers Check your answers at this book's Online Learning Center at **glencoe.com**.

Chapter Summary

Emotional development is the process of learning to recognize and express feelings and to establish a personal identity. Caregivers can help shape babies' emotional development by providing consistent, responsive, and loving care. Babies' unique temperaments and the emotional climate of the home also influence their emotional development. Social development is the process of learning how to interact and express oneself with others. Babies learn social behavior by watching and interacting with others. One normal sign of social development is stranger anxiety. Babies learn about the world by playing and exploring.

Vocabulary Review

1. Use each of these content and academic vocabulary words in a sentence.

Content Vocabulary

◇ emotional development (p. 235)
◇ emotion (p. 235)
◇ colic (p. 238)
◇ reflux (p. 238)
◇ attachment (p. 239)
◇ failure to thrive (p. 240)
◇ temperament (p. 240)
◇ social development (p. 245)
◇ cause and effect (p. 245)
◇ model (p. 245)
◇ stranger anxiety (p. 247)
◇ play environment (p. 249)

Academic Vocabulary

■ crucial (p. 239)
■ hinder (p. 243)
■ lead (p. 248)
■ motivate (p. 250)

Review Key Concepts

2. List six basic emotions that babies experience.
3. Explain the role of attachment in a baby's emotional development.
4. Describe how temperament affects a baby's social development.
5. Explain how the emotional climate of the home can affect a baby's development.
6. Explain how a baby learns social behavior.
7. Identify how play and exploration help a baby develop socially.

Critical Thinking

8. Analyze A baby builds attachment through touch, consistent care, and communication. Do you think a baby could still bond with a parent if one of these elements were missing? Explain your opinion.
9. Synthesize Stranger anxiety and attachment to a caregiver develop at around the same time. How might these two developments be related?
10. Predict What combination of temperament traits might help a baby cope with a stressful family environment? What combination of traits might make a baby less able to cope with a stressful environment? Why?

Chapter 8 Review and Applications

 Family & Community Connection

11. Interview a Single Parent Interview a single parent about how he or she copes with negative emotions, such as stress, frustration, anger, and fear. What strategies does he or she have for resolving negative emotions? Who does he or she rely on for emotional support? How does he or she try to create a positive emotional climate in the home? Take notes during your interview, and share what you learned with the class.

Health Skills

12. Research Infant Massage Go online to research massage techniques for babies. What is infant massage? What are the benefits? How is it performed? Are there any times when massage should not be used on babies? Write a summary of what you learned and state whether you would be interested in trying infant massage.

Observation Skills

13. Observe Babies at Play Work with your teacher to arrange to observe a baby in a home or at a child care center. Note that an infant six months or older will probably be much more active than a baby five months or younger.

Procedure Pay attention to how the baby explores objects in the environment as well as how the baby interacts with the caregivers during playtime.

Analysis Write a report to describe your observations. Include an analysis of the physical, social, and emotional skills you think the baby was learning through play.

NSES 1 Develop an understanding of science unifying concepts and processes: evidence, models, and explanations.

Real-World Skills

Problem-Solving Skills

14. Generate Solutions What would you do to care for a crying baby? Explain in a report how you would identify the cause of the crying and what strategies you would use to comfort the baby. Also explain what you would do if you were unable to comfort the baby.

Technology Skills

15. Create a Table Research three developmental disabilities that may affect a baby's social and emotional development. Use word-processing software to create a table that defines each disability and explains how it is diagnosed and treated.

Financial Literacy Skills

16. Shop for a Safe Play Environment Imagine that you have $150 to create a safe play environment for your three-month-old baby. You will need two baby gates, a play mat, and age-appropriate toys. Conduct research to comparison shop for the best quality and prices. How many toys can you buy and stay within your budget? Create a list of the products you would buy, identifying the source or place of purchase and the prices.

 Additional Activities For additional activities, go to this book's Online Learning Center at **glencoe.com**.

Academic Skills

English Language Arts

17. Reflect on Your Skills Parents need many emotional and social skills, such as self-control, empathy, patience, responsibility, caring, and kindness. List and describe the skills that a parent should have in order to care for a baby's emotional and social needs. Which of these skills do you have? Which could you develop further? Summarize your thoughts in a one-page essay.

> **NCTE 4** Use written language to communicate effectively.

Mathematics

18. Calculate Food Costs According to the United States Department of Agriculture, the average married couple will spend about $200,000 to raise a child to the age of 17. If food is about 18% of this total, how much does the average couple spend on food for a child through age 17?

Math Concept **Multiply Decimals by Whole Numbers** A percent is a ratio that compares a number to 100.

Starting Hint Rewrite the percent (18%) as a fraction with a denominator of 100. Convert the fraction to a decimal. Multiply this decimal by the total amount ($200,000).

Math For math help, go to the Math Appendix at the back of the book.

> **NCTM Number and Operations** Understand numbers, ways of representing numbers, relationships among numbers, and number systems.

Science

19. Design an Experiment The scientific method is a way to answer questions. You must collect information, form a hypothesis, study the results, and draw conclusions that other scientists can test. One hypothesis might read: Two-month-old babies can identify the emotions they see on their mothers' faces.

Procedure Describe an experiment that would test this hypothesis.

Analysis Write a speech to explain how your experiment would prove whether this hypothesis is correct or incorrect.

> **NSES A** Develop abilities necessary to do scientific inquiry, understandings about scientific inquiry.

Standardized Test Practice

READING COMPREHENSION

Read the passage, then answer the question.

A baby is playing at home when a stranger walks by the window and waves. Confused, the baby looks at his mother, who seems delighted. She waves back at the passerby and smiles. The baby is reassured and returns to playing. This baby has just demonstrated social referencing, the process of assessing other people's facial expressions to help decide how to react to a new situation.

20. According to the passage, social referencing:
   a. only occurs in babies.
   b. involves facial expressions.
   c. is a self-comforting technique.
   d. usually happens when strangers are present.

> **Test-Taking Tip** Read the passage carefully, noting key statements as you go. Answer the questions based only on what you just read in the passage, not based on your previous knowledge.

Chapter Objectives

After completing this chapter, you will be able to:

- **Describe** how a baby's experiences increase brain function.
- **Explain** how the brain becomes organized.
- **List** four abilities that show intellectual growth in infants.
- **Identify** specific abilities that babies learn during Piaget's first period of learning.
- **Name** five ways caregivers can encourage learning.
- **Discuss** how to choose toys appropriate for babies of different ages.

Writing Activity Personal Letter

Understanding Babies Having a baby can be an exciting adventure for adult couples. You may know someone who has a new baby. Write a personal letter to a real or imaginary friend who has a new baby. Ask your friend questions that will give you a better understanding of the baby's growth and development.

Writing Tips Use the following tips to write your personal letter effectively:

1. Express your thoughts and feelings.
2. Ask clear questions that are not too personal.
3. Check your grammar and spelling.

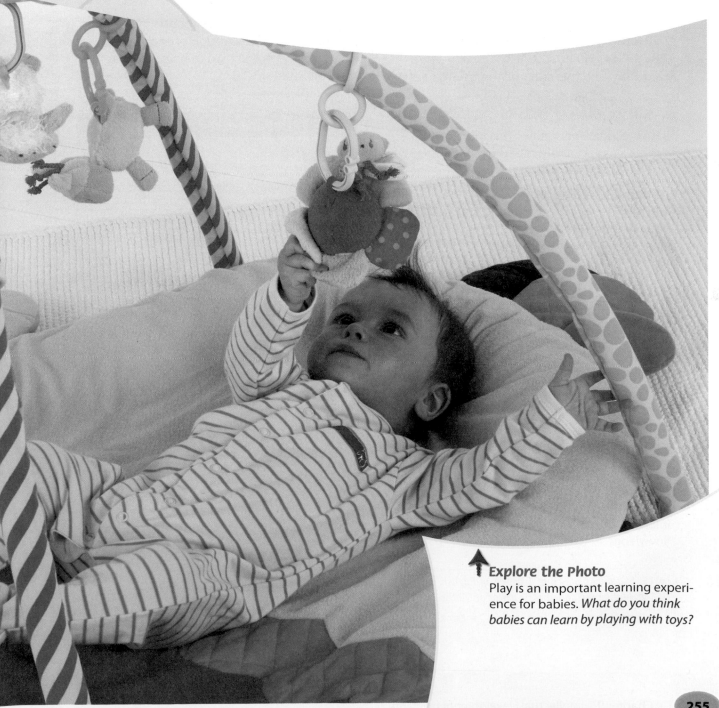

▲ **Explore the Photo**
Play is an important learning experience for babies. *What do you think babies can learn by playing with toys?*

Section 9.1 Early Brain Development

Reading Guide

Before You Read

Examine As you read the section, write down any questions you have about the material. Then write the answers as you find them.

Read to Learn

Key Concepts

- **Describe** how a baby's experiences increase brain function.
- **Explain** how the brain becomes organized.

Main Idea

The information in babies' brains develops as they acquire new skills. This information evolves at a very rapid rate during the first few years of life.

Content Vocabulary

◇ neuron
◇ neural pathway
◇ cortex
◇ axon

◇ myelin
◇ dendrite
◇ synapse
◇ neurotransmitter

Academic Vocabulary

You will find these words in your reading and on your tests. Use the glossary to look up their definitions if necessary.

■ function
■ receptor

Graphic Organizer

As you read, list six different parts of the brain and give a brief description of each. Use a chart like the one shown to help organize your information.

Parts of the Brain
1.
2.
3.
4.
5.
6.

 Graphic Organizer Go to this book's Online Learning Center at **glencoe.com** to print out this graphic organizer.

Academic Standards ·

 English Language Arts

NCTE 8 Use information resources to gather information and create and communicate knowledge.

 Science

NSES F Develop understanding of personal and community health.

NCTE *National Council of Teachers of English*
NCTM *National Council of Teachers of Mathematics*

NSES *National Science Education Standards*
NCSS *National Council for the Social Studies*

The Structure of the Brain

Sabrina and Joe had watched six-month-old Abby's every twitch, gulp, burp, gurgle, and coo with rapt attention. They often worried whether Abby was developing as she should. The doctor said she was healthy, but they wanted her to be smart too. Their families and friends offered lots of advice, but some was conflicting. Sometimes they tried to guess what Abby was thinking, or if she was thinking. When they took a parenting class they were amazed to find out how much was already going on in a six-month-old's brain.

One of the most important areas of recent scientific research has been about the development of infant brain function. What scientists have learned has great significance for caregivers. It has long been known that in the first year, babies' intellectual and motor skills grow and change at an amazing rate. Development happens faster in the first year than at any other time of life. This growth is what allows babies to learn to sit, crawl, walk, and talk. Yet recent research has shown that the infant brain's capacities are even greater than scientists suspected.

Research shows that the environment has a major impact on brain development. By providing new activities, parents and other caregivers can stimulate, or awaken, a baby's senses of sight, sound, touch, taste, and smell. Doing so helps the infant's brain develop new abilities. In fact, it now appears that much of a baby's increased brain function is due to the quantity and quality of experiences the baby has.

At birth, the brain has billions of neurons. A **neuron** is a nerve cell. In response to experiences, babies' brains immediately begin to develop links between these neurons. The link between neurons is called a **neural pathway**. These pathways "wire" the brain so that it can control different body functions and thinking processes. Neural pathways are created quickly. For example, babies just four days old have demonstrated that they are able to make fine distinctions in hearing. This means they are able to distinguish between their parents' voices and other people's voices. This ability is the result of links in the brain that the baby has formed in the few days after birth. Such links form continuously during a child's early years. They reach their maximum number at around age ten.

Providing Brain Stimulation
One of the first skills a baby gains is the ability to visually track moving objects. *What experiences can help a baby learn this skill?*

How the brain develops in a baby's first year of life has profound effects on the baby's whole life. Before birth, the fetus's world is warm and dark. This changes radically at birth. The newborn child is showered with input to the senses. Eyes closed for so long are exposed to bright lights. There are new sounds and smells. The baby feels a sudden drop in temperature from the familiar 98.6 degrees Fahrenheit. It is no wonder that so many babies cry when they enter the world! However, it is this variety of sensory input that the brain uses to build neural pathways. Babies' brains will make use of every bit of noise and new sensations.

Newborns learn about the world through their senses. The senses include what they see, hear, smell, taste, and touch. A baby's mobile moves when it is touched, and brightly colored objects dance before the baby's eyes. It might play soothing lullabies to calm the baby. The voices of caregivers sound familiar. The smells of parents and caregivers are familiar too. A fist or a finger tastes different from milk. A blanket feels soft and warm.

In general, most of the responses of a newborn are reflexes. As you learned in Chapter 7, a reflex is an instinctive, automatic response. For example, the newborn will instinctively grasp a finger placed in its palm. An overheated baby will kick until a blanket falls off or is removed. These are not planned actions that come from learned responses. They are only reflexes.

By the time the baby is six months old, he or she is aware that blankets and socks can be kicked or pulled off. By the time a child is a year old, he or she has the ability to stack toys, stand up, and maybe even walk. All these skills result from the brain's growing ability to direct the body's actions.

Figure 9.1 Parts of the Brain

The brain is the master organ that controls the functions of the body. *Which part of the brain sends information throughout the body?*

Cerebrum Receives information from the senses and directs motor activities. Controls such functions as speech, memory, and problem solving. Most of these activities occur in the outer layer, called the *cortex*, or *cerebral cortex*.

Thalamus Relays sensory information from other parts of the brain to the cerebral cortex.

Cerebellum Controls muscular coordination, balance, and posture.

Pituitary Gland Secretes hormones that control growth, metabolism, and sexual development.

Spinal Cord Transmits information from the body to the brain and from the brain to the body. It controls simple reflexes that do not involve the brain.

Brain Stem Controls involuntary activities such as breathing, heart rate, and blood pressure.

Parts of the Brain

The brain is divided into different sections. Each section controls a specific **function**, or job, of the body. The major sections are shown in **Figure 9.1**, along with a description of the functions they control.

One of the most important parts of the brain is the cortex (ˈkȯr-ˌteks). The **cortex** is part of the brain's cerebrum and its growth permits more complex learning. At one year, a baby's cortex is far more developed than it was at birth.

As babies experience more input from the world around them, their brains respond by forming more connections in the brain. It is in this way that the quality of caregiving affects brain growth. As caregivers hold, play with, and talk to an infant, the baby actually uses these experiences to build the brain's capacity.

How the Brain Works

The brain contains billions of nerve cells called neurons. Neurons are tiny messenger cells that transmit information in the brain and nervous system through an electrical-chemical process.

Neurons are connected by axons (ˈak-ˌsäns) and dendrites. An **axon** is the connection between neurons that transmits instructions from the cell body to another neuron. Each axon is coated with myelin (ˈmī-ə-lən). **Myelin** is a fatty, insulating substance, which helps transmit information from one nerve cell to another. A **dendrite** is a branchlike feature at the end of each axon that receives the electrical messages from other neurons. This process actually begins when the baby is developing in the mother's uterus. After birth, it happens more quickly.

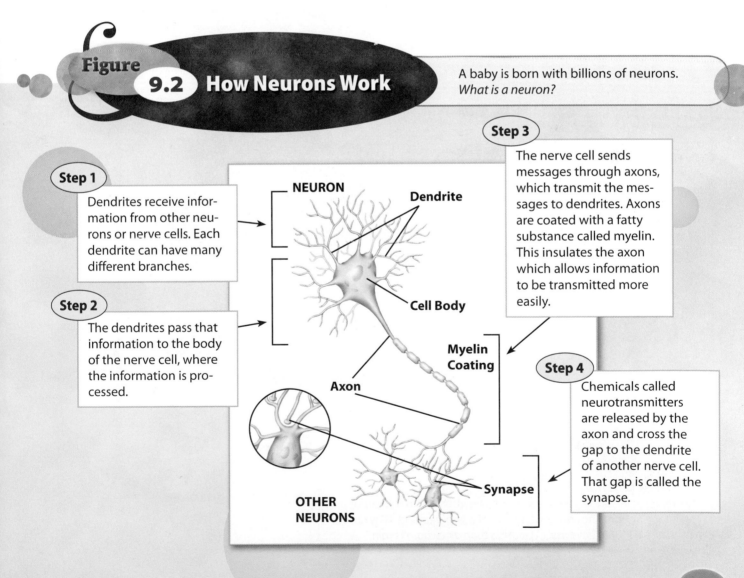

Figure 9.2 How Neurons Work

A baby is born with billions of neurons. *What is a neuron?*

Step 1
Dendrites receive information from other neurons or nerve cells. Each dendrite can have many different branches.

Step 2
The dendrites pass that information to the body of the nerve cell, where the information is processed.

Step 3
The nerve cell sends messages through axons, which transmit the messages to dendrites. Axons are coated with a fatty substance called myelin. This insulates the axon which allows information to be transmitted more easily.

Step 4
Chemicals called neurotransmitters are released by the axon and cross the gap to the dendrite of another nerve cell. That gap is called the synapse.

NEURON
Dendrite
Cell Body
Myelin Coating
Axon
Synapse
OTHER NEURONS

As **Figure 9.2** shows, dendrites reach out toward the axons of other neurons. The dendrites and axons do not touch, but they come close. A **synapse** (ˈsi-ˌnaps) is the tiny gap between the dendrites where messages are transmitted from one neuron to another.

A **neurotransmitter** (ˌnu̇r-ō-tran(t)s-ˈmi-tər) is a chemical released by the axon. The neurotransmitter acts as a messenger between the neurons. This chemical looks for a dendrite to attach to, but they can only attach to those dendrites with the right kind of **receptor**, or receiver. The more times the same axon and dendrite connect, the stronger the connection grows. As a result, they can send and receive messages more quickly.

✓ **Reading Check** **Analyze** Why is it important to provide infants with repeated sensory input?

Developing the Brain

More dendrites indicate increased learning. The more dendrites that neurons grow and the more links that develop between neurons, the more neural pathways are created in the brain. More pathways give the brain more power. It can do more tasks and control more actions. Think of a road system around a city. The more roads there are, the more places a driver can go, and the quicker he can get there.

The increased number of connections gives the brain more flexibility. Again, this is like a road system. The more roads there are, the more choices a driver has. If one road is shut down, there are alternate routes.

This increase in connections is the direct result of sensory input. The more the baby interacts with the world, the more complex the brain's "wiring" becomes.

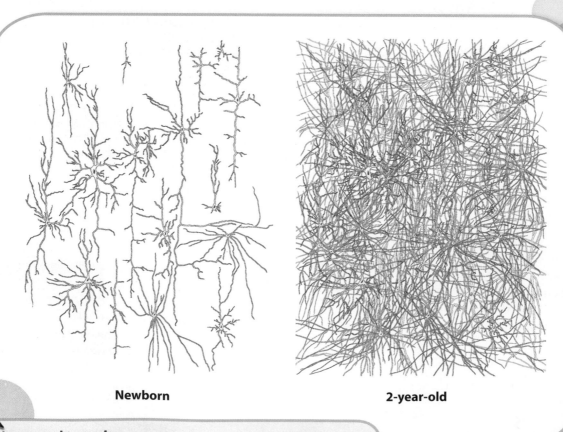

Newborn   **2-year-old**

Increased Learning
The image at left shows the neurons of a newborn, with few dendrites. The image at right shows the dendrites of a two-year-old. *Why does a two-year-old's brain have more dendrites than a newborn's brain?*

How the Brain Becomes Organized

Each child's brain becomes organized in a unique way. This is because the organization is based on the particular experiences unique to that child. As connections between dendrites and axons grow stronger, a group of neurons becomes linked together. They become systems of nerve cells that control a certain action or thinking task.

For instance, one group of neurons can work together to control drinking from a cup. Each time a ten-month-old drinks from a cup, this network of synaptic connections fires together, in a particular sequence. At first, the connections take time to move the muscles. Eventually, after many repetitions, the neurons work together so well that it becomes easy for the child to drink from a cup. The child's skills increase as a result of the greater number of neural pathways. The child learns.

These connections affect not only actions but all areas of behavior. Systems of neurons work together to influence how babies see and hear, as well as how they think and remember. This process is how all learning takes place. The system is so flexible that humans continue to learn new behaviors and form new ideas all their lives.

Note that the connections between neurons are not permanent. They can be broken when the behavior or idea is not repeated, and the synaptic pathways fade away if they are not used. This is called pruning. People lose synapses in this way all through their lives. They forget what they have learned.

At the same time that some connections are being lost, however, new ones are being added. This building of new connections is called branching. The new connections become part of the brain as new skills are learned or new experiences are stored as memories.

Indeed, children form so many synaptic connections that they must lose some surplus connections in the process of refining a new skill and becoming proficient at it. This branching and pruning helps the brain focus only on useful connections, and thus acquire more skills.

Is the Brain Organized Only Once?

The answer is no. There are many circumstances that prove this is not the case. Some children who suffered damage to the brain area that controls language have still learned to speak. Neurons in a specific area of the brain die during a stroke. Older people who suffer strokes can relearn skills by learning to use other areas of the brain.

The brain can be reorganized. In practical terms, that means a child does not have to be exposed to every possible activity in the first year, or even few years, of life. The brain will continue to develop through responses to life's experiences. It is important to give young children a stimulating environment. By doing so, parents and other caregivers help children's responsive brains develop many pathways and connections. See **Figure 9.3** on page 262 for tips on stimulating brain development.

What Would You Do?

Learning Through Music

Donna has always loved music, so it was only natural that she share it with her baby, Michael. Donna sings to Michael every night when she puts him to bed. She was pleased to learn that listening to music may have a positive effect on certain thinking skills. Musical stimulation helps strengthen pathways in the brain, increasing the ability to learn. Some researchers believe that musical training creates new pathways in the brain. Now Donna tries to include music in Michael's day in a number of ways. She wants to enroll Michael in a Music for Tots program at the park district. Donna's husband believes Michael is too young to be in a class. He believes babies should learn and grow naturally. He has asked Donna not to take Michael to the music class.

Write About It Write a letter from Donna to her husband in which she explains why it is good for Michael to attend music class. What does he learn there? How can it help him? How might it improve his learning in the future? Read your letter to the class.

Figure 9.3

Stimulate Infant Brain Development

There are many ways to help foster intellectual development in children. *How could you interact with a one-year-old to stimulate her intellectual development?*

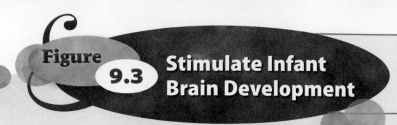

Keep it simple and natural. Everyday experiences, such as changing a diaper or giving a bath, build the pathways between neurons when combined with cuddling, talking, or singing to the baby. Experts urge parents to give children an environment rich with positive interaction and talking.

Match experiences to the child's mental abilities. Babies need physical experiences. That is how they learn. It is important to provide experiences at their level of understanding. For example, a safe interactive toy can help infants learn. However, flashcards are too advanced for a three-month-old.

Practice makes perfect. The more repetition, the stronger the connections between neurons become. Establish routines with the baby so the baby learns what to expect. Include reading a bedtime story, even when the baby cannot read. An infant will learn that sitting down with you and a book is important.

Actively involve the baby. Provide experiences in which the child takes part. Children of all ages learn best by doing.

Provide variety, but avoid overload. Some parents try to expose their baby to as many different experiences as possible to enhance brain development. Babies do benefit from a variety of experiences, but too many can overwhelm them.

Avoid pushing the child. Children learn better if they are interested in what they are doing. Look for clues as to whether the child shows interest in the activity. If not, do not pursue it.

Speeding the Brain's Work

Myelin, the fatty substance that coats axons, makes it easier for axons to transmit signals. It speeds the neuron's work. When a baby is born, only those nerves that control basic instincts, such as nursing, have this myelin coating.

Other axons get a coating of myelin as the child grows. This process continues until about age twenty. The myelin coating is added in different areas of the brain at different times. Axons in the area of the brain that controls motor skills, vision, and hearing receive the coating the earliest. As a result, those are the areas in which babies first show development. Myelin formation occurs in cycles that coincide with a child's mastery of increasingly complex learning.

The rate at which axons receive this fatty coating may explain why some children have difficulty learning certain tasks. If the nerves

Environment and the Brain

The number of connections in an infant's developing brain can be increased by a stimulating environment. Playing simple games like peek-a-boo stimulates a child to learn. This is proven when the child imitates the actions. The number of connections can also be decreased by a lack of stimulation. If no one talks to an infant, the connections for language will not form properly. The change can be as much as 25 percent in either direction. Babies love visual stimulation, and they have a preference for high-contrast images, such as black and white.

■ **Science Inquiry** Stimulating all of a baby's senses can dramatically increase the number of connections in a baby's brain. Why is it important to stimulate all of a baby's senses?

Stimulating the Brain
Touching and talking to a baby will stimulate dendrite growth in the baby's brain. *How do attention and experiences contribute to brain development?*

controlling a certain activity are not yet covered with myelin, it is difficult for a child to learn that activity. The presence of myelin makes learning much easier by speeding up the signal.

Myelin is so crucial to the speed at which nerves function that if this coating is lost, it affects the way the brain and body function. Multiple sclerosis is a disease in which the absence of myelin plays a role. Scientists are working hard to find new treatments for this and other diseases.

How Caregivers Can Help

Parents and caregivers can support the brain's work by giving the child a stimulating environment. The child needs opportunities to see, hear, smell, and touch new things. The child might learn the terms *red* and *flower* by looking at a picture. However, the child is more likely to learn the terms quicker if he can see and smell a real flower, and touch its petals.

Another important way to help the brain develop is with repetition. By doing the same task over and over, synaptic connections are strengthened. This improves memory. Caregivers are likely to tire of Itsy Bitsy Spider after singing it once or twice. The child may want to hear it over and over again for several minutes. This repetition is how the child learns.

{ Expert Advice... }

"Children need lots of practice doing things over and over again to succeed at a new skill. Think of the pride a baby feels when she can finally grasp the rattle and put it into her mouth by herself."

— Claire Lerner LCSW, and Lynette Ciervo, authors, *Getting Ready for School Begins at Birth: How to help your child learn in the early years*

Section 9.1   After You Read

Review Key Concepts

1. **Explain** how dendrites and axons function together in the brain.
2. **Describe** how repeated experiences help organize the brain.

Practice Academic Skills

 English Language Arts

3. Choose a country other than the United States and research the child-rearing practices. What kinds of practices do they typically use to stimulate intellectual growth and understanding in infants? Write your answer in a one-page report. Use illustrations if possible.

NCTE 8 Use information resources to gather information and create and communicate knowledge.

 Science

4. Conduct research on multiple sclerosis. In your report, be sure to provide answers to the following questions: What is multiple sclerosis (MS)? What are the typical symptoms of MS? What causes the symptoms?

NSES F Develop understanding of personal and community health.

 Check Your Answers Check your answers at this book's Online Learning Center at **glencoe.com**.

Reading Guide

Before You Read

Use Color As you read this section, try using different colored pens to take notes. For example, use blue to write main ideas and green to write vocabulary terms. This can help you learn new material and study for tests.

Read to Learn

Key Concepts

- **List** four abilities that show intellectual growth in infants.
- **Identify** specific abilities that babies learn during Piaget's first period of learning.

Main Idea

During the first year of a baby's life, growth occurs in many areas. These areas include size, intelligence, motor skills, social skills, and personality.

Content Vocabulary

◇ perception
◇ attention span
◇ concept
◇ sensorimotor period
◇ object permanence
◇ imaginative play
◇ symbolic thinking

Academic Vocabulary

You will find these words in your reading and on your tests. Use the glossary to look up their definitions if necessary.

■ elicit
■ determined

Graphic Organizer

As you read, compare the intellectual and sensorimotor development of 1–4 months old babies. Use a chart like the one shown to list the characteristics.

Developmental Milestones Ages 1–4 Months	
Intellectual	**Sensorimotor**

 Graphic Organizer Go to this book's Online Learning Center at **glencoe.com** to print out this graphic organizer.

Academic Standards ·

 English Language Arts

NCTE 5 Use different writing process elements to communicate effectively.

 Social Studies

NCSS I A Culture Analyze and explain the ways groups, societies, and cultures address human needs and concerns.

NCTE *National Council of Teachers of English*
NCTM *National Council of Teachers of Mathematics*

NSES *National Science Education Standards*
NCSS *National Council for the Social Studies*

Early Learning Abilities

During the first year of life, children undergo a greater change than they ever will again. In just 12 months, a helpless newborn becomes a whirlwind of energy and activity. Babies go from not being able to move, to crawling or walking. A newborn communicates only by crying. However, as social skills begin to appear, a one-year-old can use gestures or even a few words. By age one, a baby has likes and dislikes, an imagination, and a unique personality.

Babies have many abilities at birth. A newborn can hear, see, taste, smell, and feel. These abilities are the building blocks of learning. The brain is fed by what is experienced through the senses. A babies' perception improves as experiences are repeated. **Perception** is the ability to learn from sensory information. The brain's neurons begin to become organized, increasing the baby's learning and skills. A newborn cannot purposely grasp and lift objects, but a three-month-old can. In time, babies' hand-eye coordination improves further. They develop many skills. **Figure 9.4** on page 267 summarizes the intellectual developmental milestones for a baby's first 12 months.

Signs of Intellectual Growth

In just the first year of life, babies develop four abilities that show their growing intellectual abilities. They learn to remember experiences, make associations, understand cause and effect, and pay attention.

Remembering Experiences

In the first few months, babies develop the ability to remember. The information from the senses can be interpreted in light of past experiences. A two- or three-month-old baby may stop crying when someone enters the room because the baby anticipates being picked up.

Making Associations

When the baby ceases to cry, it also indicates association. The baby associates a parent or other caregiver with receiving comfort.

Understanding Cause and Effect

Babies also develop an understanding of cause and effect, the idea that one action results in another action or condition. Sucking causes milk to flow. If the baby stops sucking, the milk stops. In short, every time the infant does something, something else happens.

Increased Attention Span
During the first year, a baby's attention span becomes much longer. *At what age do babies begin to study objects carefully?*

Figure 9.4 **Intellectual Developmental Milestones—1st Year**

Motor skills are essential to intellectual development. *How might you encourage an 11-month-old baby who identifies objects in books?*

Months	Developmental Milestone
1–2 Months	❖ Gains information through senses ❖ Makes eye contact ❖ Prefers faces to objects ❖ Can distinguish between familiar and unfamiliar voices
3–4 Months	❖ Can distinguish between familiar and unfamiliar faces ❖ Makes vowel-consonant combinations such as "ah-goo" ❖ Can tell a smile from a frown
5–6 Months	❖ Is alert for longer periods of time, up to two hours ❖ Studies objects carefully ❖ Recognizes own name ❖ Distinguishes between friendly and angry voices ❖ Recognizes basic sounds of native language
7–8 Months	❖ Imitates the actions of others ❖ Begins to understand cause and effect ❖ Remembers things that have happened ❖ Sorts objects by size ❖ Solves simple problems ❖ Forms sounds such as *da, ga, ma, ba* ❖ Recognizes some words ❖ Babbling imitates speech inflections
9–10 Months	❖ Looks for dropped objects ❖ Responds to some words and phrases, such as "no" and "all gone" ❖ Takes objects out of containers and puts them back in ❖ May say a few words
11–12 Months	❖ Can point to and identify objects in books ❖ Fits blocks or boxes inside one another ❖ Says "Mama" and "Dada" for parents ❖ Understands simple words and phrases like "Come to Mommy" ❖ Speaks some words regularly

As babies' motor skills develop, cause-and-effect learning changes. By seven or eight months, babies can throw things deliberately. They can pull the cord on a toy and make the toy move. At this age, babies have a better understanding of their own power to make things happen.

Paying Attention

As babies grow, their attention span grows too. **Attention span** is the length of time a person can concentrate on a task without getting bored. If the same object is presented over and over again, the baby's response to the object will eventually become less enthusiastic. The baby's diminishing response is a way of saying, "That's old stuff. I've seen it before."

Generally, infants with above-average intelligence have a short attention span. They tend to lose interest sooner than babies of average or below-average intelligence. However, beyond infancy, children with above-average intelligence typically have a longer attention span than others their age.

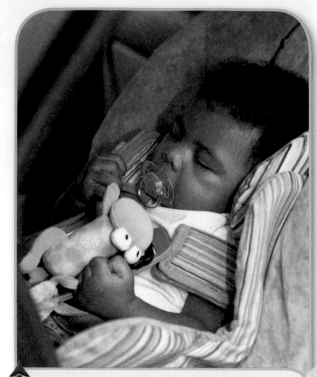

Safe and Stimulating Play
There are many ways to provide an infant with sensory stimulation. *What are some safe toys a baby could play with while riding in a car?*

THE DEVELOPING BRAIN

Human Contact Needed

When babies are bored, they will often announce their boredom by letting out a loud wail. Parents can come to the rescue by giving the infant a toy to play with. They might also talk to or play with the baby. Some parents and other caregivers use the television as a substitute. However, television cannot take the place of live interaction. Researchers have found that language not connected to the events around an infant is nothing but noise to the child. Studies show that no new pathways are being created when a child is watching television. Human contact, though, stimulates all of a child's senses.

■ **Science Inquiry** Human interaction is generally the best interaction for a baby. When might it be appropriate to use the television to entertain a baby?

Stimulating the Senses

A child's senses can be easily stimulated each and every day. For example, a baby's senses of touch and taste are routinely stimulated as he or she is changed and fed.

Very young infants prefer looking at people, rather than things. They can focus on and follow objects. They can also see shapes and forms. Hanging a mobile in an infant's crib will help stimulate a baby's sense of sight. Mobiles should be hung about 12 inches from the baby's eyes. Infants will respond to brightly colored objects, perhaps soft stuffed dolls with smiling faces and large eyes. Change the baby's position from time to time to vary the view.

Infants are very sensitive to sound. They recognize the voices of family and friends and can be calmed by a loving voice, even from another room. They are increasingly aware of their own voices and will babble back to an adult, mimicking the adult's tone of voice. Talking,

Learning Through PLAY

Sensory Play

During the sensorimotor period of development, children learn through their senses and their environment. In the first few months, babies learn about their own bodies. They learn how to move hands and feet at will, and hold bottles and small toys. At about eight months to one year, children learn to crawl and then to walk. This greatly expands the world they can explore. Everything in their path becomes an opportunity for learning. Besides seeing, touching, smelling, and listening, babies put almost everything into their mouths. Feedback from this sensory exploration teaches infants about their world.

By providing everyday objects and toys that will stimulate the child's senses, parents and other caregivers can enhance learning. As the baby grows, new objects and toys that stimulate all of the senses can be introduced.

Think About It Imagine you are baby-sitting your nine-month-old nephew. He spends his time crawling around, picking up things, and putting them in his mouth. You spend your time removing things from his mouth. What can you do so that you are not constantly removing things from his mouth?

reading, singing, and humming are wonderful ways to vary and stimulate an infant's hearing. These early stimulations from talking and singing will also help build the foundation for language development.

Touch is one of the most important ways to communicate love to an infant. The infant's sense of security and trust are built through cuddling, rocking, and patting. This also helps the infant gain a sense of his or her own body. This sense is crucial to the development of motor skills. A slowly swaying rocking chair or baby swing is a deeply comforting sensation for a baby, and helps him or her develop an awareness of space. In some areas, infant massage classes are available for learning more formal techniques to stimulate a baby's sense of touch.

Concept Development

As they continue to learn, young children between ages one and three begin to organize the information they receive from their senses. They start to form concepts. A **concept** is a general category of objects and information. Concepts range from categories for objects, such as fruit, to qualities, such as color or shape. Concepts also include abstract ideas, such as time.

Children learn words and concepts by using three principles:

- Children start by thinking that labels are for whole objects, not parts. Suppose Dwayne's father points to an animal and says "dog." How does Dwayne know that the label "dog" applies to the whole animal and not to its nose or its tail?
- Children believe that labels apply to the group to which the individual objects belong, not to the particular object. Any four-legged creature may **elicit**, or bring forth, "doggy!" from Dwayne.
- Young children tend to believe that an object can only have one label. That may be why it takes time for young children to learn to use pronouns. They have to learn to recognize that "mommy" and "she" can mean the same person.

As a child matures, concepts become more accurate. Babies begin with two broad concepts of "the baby" and "not the baby." Later, children make very broad distinctions between people and things.

✓ **Reading Check** **Explain** Why is the sense of touch so important to infants?

Periods of Learning

Jean Piaget, a psychologist, had a great influence on what is known about how children learn. In an effort to understand how children's intellectual skills developed, Piaget observed infants and children. He then recorded his observations about the growth of their ability to reason, or the increases in the level of their intellectual understanding. He found that intellectual development followed a pattern. His theory identified four major learning stages, or periods, that take place from birth to adulthood.

According to Piaget, these four periods appear in the same order in all children. They are the sensorimotor period, the preoperational period, the concrete operations period, and the formal operations period. Although the ages at which the periods emerge may vary from child to child, researchers have established average ages at which they appear. These periods are described in **Figure 9.5.**

Piaget **determined**, or reasoned, that children must learn to master one thinking skill before they can move on to another. Children cannot be forced to understand a concept or master a skill any faster than the speed at which their abilities mature. He also noted that children who do not get the opportunity to apply new skills during each stage might never reach their full potential. For this reason, it is important for children to have constant learning opportunities.

The Sensorimotor Period

The **sensorimotor period** is Piaget's first stage of learning and lasts from birth to about age two. During this period, babies learn mainly through their senses and their own actions. This period happens during the time when the neurons in the infant's brain establish pathways that enable learning.

The exact role played by the brain in infant learning was not known when Piaget first developed his theories. Later scientific discoveries about neural pathways confirmed Piaget's observations. Sensory stimulation in the first year of life is vital for fostering a child's intellectual development. The more stimulation a child receives, the more dendrites the child's brain creates.

Figure 9.5 Piaget's Four Periods of Learning

Most people go through these periods during the ages indicated. *What might cause a child to go through the periods at a later age than indicated?*

Period	Characteristics
Sensorimotor *Birth–2 years*	Children learn through their senses and own actions.
Preoperational *2–7 years*	Children think in terms of their own activities and what they perceive at the moment.
Concrete Operations *7–11 years*	Children can think logically but still learn best through experience.
Formal Operations *11–adult*	People are capable of abstract thinking.

Figure 9.6

Piaget's Sensorimotor Period: Birth to Age Two

Babies move from stage to stage as their sensorimotor skills develop. *How does a baby feeding itself a cracker demonstrate Stage 2?*

Stage	Approximate Ages	Characteristics
Stage 1	Birth to 1 month	❖ Practices inborn reflexes ❖ Does not understand self as separate person
Stage 2	1 to 4 months	❖ Combines two or more reflexes ❖ Develops hand-mouth coordination
Stage 3	4 to 8 months	❖ Acts intentionally to produce results ❖ Improves hand-eye coordination
Stage 4	8 to 12 months	❖ Begins to solve problems ❖ Finds partially hidden objects ❖ Imitates others
Stage 5	12 to 18 months	❖ Finds hidden objects ❖ Explores and experiments ❖ Understands that objects exist independently
Stage 6	18 to 24 months	❖ Solves problems by thinking through sequences ❖ Can think using symbols ❖ Begins imaginative thinking

Piaget noted that during the sensorimotor period, babies come to understand an important concept. This concept is called object permanence. **Object permanence** is the concept that objects will continue to exist, even when they are out of sight. This usually occurs at about ten months of age. For example, at four months, when Megan drops her rubber ring toy and it rolls behind her, she simply looks for something else to play with. But at eleven months, Megan actively looks for her ball when it rolls out of sight. She has learned the concept of object permanence. This is why babies enjoy playing peek-a-boo. They learn that Mommy is still there, even if they cannot see her face.

Six Stages

As seen in Figure 9.6, the sensorimotor period can be broken down into six shorter stages. At each stage, a baby has specific intellectual abilities. This can help you better understand how learning occurs.

Note that the child's abilities at each stage after Stage 1 build on the stage before. For example, the inborn grasping reflex in Stage 1 establishes a pattern that permits learning to grasp and hold a desired object. At Stage 2, an infant has learned how to grasp a desired object, such as a piece of food or a teething ring, and bring it to the mouth. Acquiring these abilities lets an infant move on to learn a more complex set of skills at each stage.

At the end of Stage 6, children have used their experiences of the physical world to construct a consistent view of the world they live in. At this point, children can hold an image in their minds of a period beyond the immediate moment. This is especially true if they have been read to regularly. Words such as soon or later now have meaning because the child is able to think of a time in the future.

Imaginative play also becomes possible at Stage 6. **Imaginative play** is pretending. The child can imagine things that might happen but have not happened yet. Children will start pretending by mimicking the actions of those around them. For example, after watching a parent cook a meal, they might pretend to cook. After visiting the doctor, they might go home and want to "listen" to mom's heartbeat or look in dad's throat.

This is also the time when symbolic thinking begins, and the foundations for reading are established. **Symbolic thinking** is the use of words and numbers to stand for ideas. Children can begin to learn pre-reading skills when they are read to on a daily basis. They might begin to understand that print stands for words. Many children will want to read and re-read the same book. They often will memorize the story before they know how to read. This allows them to match the words they know with the words and letters they see on the page. Books with rhyming and alliteration make it easier for the child to remember the story.

Remember that reading is not just for intellectual development though. Reading to a child is also a great way to bond with the child. It also teaches the child that reading is fun.

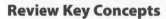

Section 9.2   After You Read

Review Key Concepts

1. **Define** *perception* and give an example of how a baby's perception changes during the first year of life.

2. **Identify** what babies use to learn during Piaget's first period of development.

Practice Academic Skills

 English Language Arts

3. When your friend babysits his six-month-old niece, he usually puts her in the crib so he can do homework. Write a convincing letter to your friend explaining how the loving touch of a caregiver helps a baby develop certain senses that are important to the development of motor skills.

> **NCTE 5** Use different writing process elements to communicate effectively.

 Social Studies

4. Though cosleeping is a recent trend in America, it has a long tradition in many other countries. *Cosleeping* is when a baby sleeps with one or both parents, rather than in a crib, for up to two years of his or her life. Conduct research on a culture that promotes cosleeping. Write a paragraph to answer the following questions: Why is it considered the most acceptable method of infant care in that society? What benefits does that society feel cosleeping has for a baby?

> **NCSS I A** Analyze and explain the ways groups, societies, and cultures address human needs and concerns.

 Check Your Answers Check your answers at this book's Online Learning Center at **glencoe.com**.

Reading Guide

Before You Read

Discuss Read the heads in the section and write a paragraph in which you discuss the meaning of the heads.

Read to Learn

Key Concepts

- **Name** five ways caregivers can encourage learning.
- **Discuss** how to choose toys appropriate for babies of different ages.

Main Idea

Caregivers need to recognize the importance of play and the development of communication skills. Toys should be selected for children based on the child's age and abilities.

Content Vocabulary

◇ age appropriate
◇ childproof
◇ manipulate

 Graphic Organizer Go to this book's Online Learning Center at **glencoe.com** to print out this graphic organizer.

Academic Vocabulary

You will find these words in your reading and on your tests. Use the glossary to look up their definitions if necessary.

- responsiveness
- hazard

Graphic Organizer

As you read, list toys appropriate for different ages. Use a spider web chart like the one shown to help organize your information.

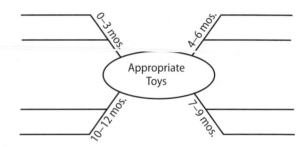

Appropriate Toys

0–3 mos.
4–6 mos.
10–12 mos.
7–9 mos.

Academic Standards ·

 English Language Arts

NCTE 12 Use language to accomplish individual purposes.

 Mathematics

NCTM Geometry Analyze characteristics and properties of two- and three-dimensional geometric shapes and develop mathematical arguments about geometric relationships.

 Social Studies

NCSS I C Culture Apply an understanding of culture as an integrated whole that explains the functions and interactions of traditions, beliefs and values, and behavior patterns.

NCTE *National Council of Teachers of English*
NCTM *National Council of Teachers of Mathematics*

NSES *National Science Education Standards*
NCSS *National Council for the Social Studies*

Encouraging Learning

Intellectual development in an infant is closely linked with the **responsiveness**, or reactions, of others in the baby's environment. This means babies learn more and learn faster when caregivers comfort them, smile at them, talk to them, and play with them. A baby treated in this way is likely to develop more skills more quickly than a child who receives less interactive care. Babies' most important teachers are the people who care for them every day.

Even the youngest babies learn about the world from the care they receive. When Tyler's stomach feels uncomfortable, he cries. Then his mother picks him up and nurses him, and he feels better. Everyday events like discomfort, crying, cuddling, and being fed are connected. The child learns to recognize this pattern. If the baby's cries are not answered, the baby sees no relationship between his or her needs and the caregiver's actions. There is no pattern to help the baby form new pathways in the child's brain. No new pathways means no new abilities or associations.

In addition to giving a child basic care, there are things that parents and other caregivers can do to help build and influence their child's learning, or intellectual development. Encouraging learning does not require money or special toys. Rather, it depends on the attention, knowledge, and time that parents and other caregivers can give to the child.

Here are some ways that parents and other caregivers can encourage learning:

- **Learn about child development.** Caregivers should understand how an average child develops. This can help caregivers provide toys and learning experiences that are age appropriate. **Age appropriate** means something is suitable for the age and individual needs of a child. Understanding age-appropriate behavior also helps caregivers have realistic expectations for what their child should be able to do.

Making Connections
When a person responds to a baby's needs, the baby learns to make connections between the events. *What might a baby learn from being held?*

- **Give the child time and attention.** Caregivers know to give a child attention when he or she cries. However, no baby needs attention every waking moment. A caregiver can help a baby thrive and learn just by talking to and playing simple games with the baby.
- **Provide positive feedback.** When the baby demonstrates a new skill or tries out a new activity, showing pleasure and responding with praise will encourage the baby to keep trying new things. You can show your pleasure to a child with a hug, by clapping your hands, or sometimes just by smiling or laughing.
- **Express love.** Caregivers who use their personal style to show their love for the baby are helping the baby grow in self-confidence. They are also encouraging the baby to try more and to learn more.
- **Read.** A child is never too young for books. Caregivers should make reading part of a daily routine.
- **Talk, talk, talk.** Talking has many benefits. When caregivers talk to infants, they help them learn about their environment and learn language. Current research shows that the more caregivers talk to a baby, the faster the child's brain develops. Talking builds feelings of security, too.

Developing Communication

One of an infant's major tasks is to learn to communicate with others. This skill depends on development in all areas: physical, emotional, social, and intellectual. There are wide differences in the rate of development from baby to baby. However, healthy babies should show steady improvement in communication skills.

Communicating Without Words

Babies communicate long before they can talk. Most children do not have the ability to speak with words until they are about 11-months-old. By the end of the first year, though, they can effectively make most of their needs and wants known without words.

At first, crying is simply an automatic way to communicate discomfort. However, babies quickly learn that crying produces a response.

SAFE CHILD HEALTHY CHILD

Safe Learning

To encourage learning, allow babies as much freedom of movement at home as possible. In the first few months, the baby should be moved from one room to another to be with the family. A baby who spends time with the family as they go about their daily routine learns more than a baby who is left alone in a crib. Older babies who can crawl or walk should not be restricted to playpens for long periods of time. It is better to childproof the home and monitor the child's activities. To **childproof** means to take steps to protect the child from possible dangers.

Be Prepared Research ways to childproof a home for a toddler. Choose three of the safety measures you learn and create a poster to illustrate them. With your teacher's permission, mount your poster in the classroom.

Someone will come and try to make them feel better. Within a month or so, the crying takes on a pattern. A cry is followed by a pause to listen for reactions. If no response arrives, the baby resumes crying. The baby soon develops different cries for different problems. A cry indicating hunger may be interrupted by wails of frustration as the baby learns to manipulate a bottle. A cry of pain may include groans and whimpers.

Babies also send messages with movements and gestures. An eleven-month-old who pushes away a bowl of a favorite food has had enough to eat. The baby who clings with both arms to a parent's leg is showing a sure sign of anxiety. The use of gestures continues into adulthood, but they are used more to reinforce words than as a substitute for words.

Finally, a baby communicates by making special sounds. Some sounds, such as giggles and cooing, carry obvious messages.

Sign Language In the United States and Canada, some parents are using sign language to communicate with babies between six and twelve months old. Experts say that babies as young as six months have the memory to recognize and remember signs their parents make, and to respond. Parents teach their babies to use simple hand signals for words such as "no," "eat," "more," "milk," and "dog."

Scientific studies have shown that signing enhances babies' language development by allowing them to learn language before they develop the ability to speak. The physical skills needed for speech include coordinating the movements of the tongue, jaw, and lips. These skills do not develop until babies are between eleven and eighteen months of age.

The motor skills needed to produce hand signals develop much sooner. Signing also helps children learn social skills by allowing them to express themselves. It is a relief to some children to have a way to communicate with their parents.

There are many resources available to help you learn basic signs to teach to your baby. These include books, Web sites, and classes. It is important to be consistent when you teach a baby sign language. The child should see the same signs for the same thing in different settings, and if possible from different people. This will reinforce the connection between the sign and the meaning.

Chase's mom has started using the sign for drink each time she offers Chase a cup. If Chase only sees this sign at home and from his mom, he may associate it with his mom. When his grandpa uses the same sign in a restaurant, Chase begins to understand that the sign goes with the action. Next time Chase is thirsty, he may try to make the sign himself.

It is best to choose three or four signs to teach your baby. Try to use them consistently for several days or weeks. Once your child has mastered them, then you can add a few more to expand his vocabulary.

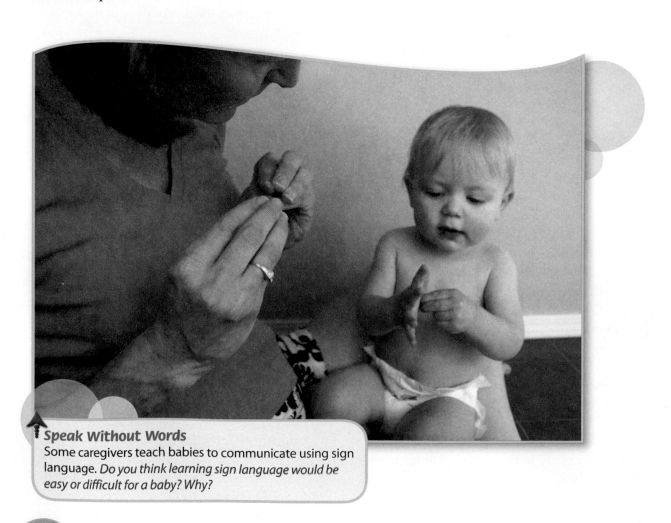

Speak Without Words
Some caregivers teach babies to communicate using sign language. *Do you think learning sign language would be easy or difficult for a baby? Why?*

Math in Action

Geometric Shapes

Researchers recommend adding abstract props to a baby's play area. One such prop is a set of wooden geometric shapes called tangrams. These shapes can be triangles, squares, rectangles, or trapezoids. They fit together to create larger geometric shapes. What geometric shape do two equal-size trapezoids create when their longer bases are placed side by side?

Math Concept **Geometric two-dimensional shapes** A trapezoid is a shape with four sides where two of the sides are parallel.

Starting Hint Draw two trapezoids that are the same size. Cut them out and place the two long bases together.

> **NCTM Geometry** Analyze characteristics and properties of two- and three-dimensional geometric shapes and develop mathematical arguments about geometric relationships.

 Math For math help, go to the Math Appendix at the back of the book.

Learning to Speak

Before learning to talk, a baby must learn to associate meanings with words. This is a gradual process. It depends on caregivers talking to the baby, even when the baby does not appear to respond. For example, when taking the baby for a walk, caregivers can talk about what they see.

When talking to a baby, use simple words, but avoid baby talk. Children are experts at repeating what they hear. If they learn baby talk first, regular speech is more difficult. Caregivers should speak clearly using simple words. In this way, the child will become accustomed to hearing real words. For example, parents should say "Does Susie want a bottle?" instead of "Susie want baba?"

Although babies will not understand much of what caregivers say, they are beginning to establish an important habit. Listening to other people's talk is essential for an infant's language development. This is especially true if the talk

is directed to the baby. This interaction also helps build speech centers in the child's brain. Parents and caregivers can increase the amount of speech a baby hears by talking to the baby about everything they do. For instance, they can describe each step of the process as they change a baby's diaper.

Developmental Milestones A newborn is physically unable to speak. Over the first year, physical changes take place that allow the baby to make the sounds necessary for speech. Babies get ready for real speech by babbling, or repeating syllables and sounds. You may have heard babies endlessly repeating consonant and vowel sounds such as "babababababa" or "gogogogo." Babbling is a baby's preparation for saying recognizable words. To encourage babbling, respond to and imitate the baby's sounds. This encourages the baby to continue practicing.

A child's first real words are usually understandable between the ages of eight and fifteen months. Because the infant typically has been babbling and coming close to real word sounds for some time, it is not always easy to know exactly when a specific word is spoken on purpose. First words are usually common, simple words that have special meaning for the baby, such as "mama," "dada," or "bye-bye." Most children do not have a large vocabulary and cannot combine words into sentences until after their first birthday.

There are predictable stages that children go through as they develop speech. **Figure 9.7** on page 278 outlines some typical speech milestones. Of course, children vary in their development of speech, so these milestones serve only as a guide to normal development. They help doctors and caregivers determine when and if a child may need extra help to develop his or her speech. If parents are concerned about their child's development, they should speak to their pediatrician.

A baby's first words are one of the most exciting milestones parents and other caregivers experience with their child. A parent will love to hear "mama" or "dada" instead of a cry from their child. When a child learns to talk, it opens the door to a whole new world of communication and learning.

Figure 9.7

Speech Developmental Milestones—Birth–Age 5

Language development must be encouraged at each age level. *How might you encourage an eight-month-old baby to talk?*

Months	Developmental Milestone
Birth–3 Months	✤ Watches your face when you speak ✤ Babbles ✤ Cries to express hunger, anger, pain, or discomfort
4–6 Months	✤ Babbling sounds more like speech with different sounds such as *p*, *b*, and *m* ✤ Voices excitement and displeasure ✤ Gurgles
7 Months–1 Year	✤ Babbling has long and short groups of sounds ✤ Uses speech to get attention ✤ Imitates different speech sounds ✤ Says one or two words
1–2 Years	✤ Adds more words to vocabulary each month ✤ Makes animal sounds such as "moo" ✤ Begins using pronouns such as "mine" ✤ Asks one- to two-word questions, such as "Go bye-bye?" ✤ Puts two words together, such as "more milk"
2–3 Years	✤ Has a word for almost everything ✤ Uses two- to three-word sentences to talk about and ask for things ✤ Begins to use plurals such as "shoes" or "socks"
3–4 Years	✤ Talks about activities ✤ Uses four- or more words sentences
4–5 Years	✤ Voice is clear ✤ Uses sentences with a lot of details ✤ Tells stories ✤ Says most sounds correctly

Reading Teaches Speech Children need to hear speech and learn that sounds have meanings before they can develop language skills of their own. Parents and caregivers can help with this by reading to children.

- The vivid pictures in children's books help infants connect the sounds they are hearing to concrete objects. Rhymes help children remember words.
- Repetition is vital to children's learning. Reading favorite books over and over produces a familiar pattern of sounds. Children recognize these familiar patterns and attempt to repeat them, even if they do not know what the words mean.
- If children read with caregivers, they will start to associate books with attention and care. They will be much better prepared to learn to read when the time comes. They also will likely be more motivated to do so.
- Reading to young children helps to increase their vocabularies and promotes their ability to read aloud.

✓ **Reading Check** **Summarize** How does a baby learn from the care he or she receives?

The Importance of Play

For children, play is work as well as pleasure. Research has clearly shown that playtime is essential to intellectual development. Toys are the tools for learning.

Play is also a physical necessity through which development takes place. When a baby shakes a rattle, stacks blocks, throws a ball, or chews on a teething toy, it is not just for amusement. These are serious, absorbing tasks that let infants strengthen their muscles, refine their motor skills, and learn about the world.

Babies learn from listening too. The familiar voices of the primary caregivers are the first sounds a baby learns to recognize. Rattles and squeak toys introduce different sounds. Babies enjoy music from a wind-up toy, a CD, or a person singing. They can also enjoy different rhythms. With exciting music, they can dance in the arms of a caring adult. With soothing music, they can cuddle and be rocked.

Different Toys for Different Ages

Babies mature and change rapidly during the first year. They will need different toys to play with as they develop. A toy that delights a three-month-old may bore a ten-month-old. Also, a fun toy for a twelve-month-old might be dangerous for a two-month-old.

Birth to Three Months

A baby at this age needs little more than things to look at and listen to. Bright colors, moving objects, and interesting sounds stimulate development of the senses. A mobile hung safely above the crib is interesting for the baby to listen to and watch, and allows him or her to practice following objects with the eyes. Brightly colored wallpaper and pictures can also provide interest.

Four to Six Months

The sense of touch is important at this age. Babies need things to touch, handle, bang, shake, suck, and chew. Make sure that toys are small enough to handle easily but too large to swallow. All items and pieces should be at least 1½ inches across. A good rule of thumb is that it should be too large to fit into a standard paper towel tube.

Teething rings, cups, rattles, and plastic toys are good choices. Stuffed toys are fun to touch. Toys that squeak or make noise give results that the baby can learn to produce. Providing

---

{ **Expert Advice...** }

"Other scholars have shown that the most powerful factor influencing reading skills is auditory processing skill—the very skill that is honed as infants listen to parents speak to them in sophisticated, adult language."

— Clayton M. Christensen, author, *Disrupting Class: How Disruptive Innovation Will Change the Way the World Learns* objects with different textures helps the child learn by touch. Babies this age like simple picture books, and love being read to. Choose sturdy, washable books with big, colorful pictures of familiar objects.

Seven to Nine Months

Babies still need things to handle, throw, pound, bang, and shake. Anything that makes a noise fascinates infants at this age. Look for books that have different textures to feel, or places to press on the page that produce noises. Children of this age enjoy blocks, balls, large plastic beads that pop apart, and toys that can be pushed or kicked. Safe household items are just as interesting as purchased toys. Pots and pans with lids, and plastic containers to stack make great playthings. Be sure to thoroughly wash any used containers before giving them to a child. Make sure there are no sharp edges that could harm the child.

Ten to Twelve Months

By the end of their first year, babies need things to crawl after. Those who are already walking enjoy toys they can push or pull. Children this age especially enjoy toys that they can manipulate. **Manipulate** means to work with the hands. Baskets, boxes, and other containers are fun. Babies like to put things into them and then dump them out again. Picture books are good for looking at alone or for brief story times during the day or before bed. Vinyl books are now available that can even go in the tub. Floating toys are also great choices.

Choosing Toys

When choosing playthings for a young child, look for toys that encourage participation and use. Younger children need simpler toys. As a baby's abilities increase, toys can be more complex.

▲ **Alternative Toys**
Even simple household objects can make fun toys for babies. *What other household objects would be appropriate as toys for babies?*

Usefulness

Toys, especially those labeled educational, can be expensive. Sometimes they have limited usefulness. Parents can provide a baby with as much fun and learning by making common household items available. Items such as plastic measuring spoons and cups, a clean plastic bucket, plastic bowls, a metal pan or mixing bowl and a large wooden spoon, or a large cardboard box with a window cut in it all make great toys because young children can use them in many different ways. With any toy, however, supervision is important for safe play.

When buying toys, caregivers should look for ones that will remain interesting and appropriate for a number of years. A set of blocks is a good example. At the age of six months, Reynaldo grasped and inspected his blocks. By his first birthday, he could stack several blocks into a tower. At the age of three, he used the blocks to make roads for his cars. Now, at age six, Reynaldo creates elaborate houses and castles, using every available block.

Safety

Safety should also be a concern when considering toys for babies. A very tempting and common choking **hazard**, or danger, for babies is an older child's toys. Babies may see an older sibling playing with toys that look very inviting. It only takes a few seconds for a baby to pick up one of those toys and put it in his or her mouth. Make sure that babies are kept away from these toys while the older child is playing with them. Also, be sure to clean up all small pieces right away after playing, and store them out of a baby's reach. Babies are also interested in anything their caregivers use, such as keys, pens, and forks. Caregivers need to keep these out of babies' reach.

Section 9.3 After You Read

Review Key Concepts

1. **Discuss** whether or not babies communicate before they learn to talk. Explain your answer.
2. **Explain** why caregivers should choose toys that are age appropriate.

Practice Academic Skills

English Language Arts

3. Imagine that you write an advice column for your local newspaper. A young couple has written to you because they are worried about their six-month-old daughter. They are concerned because she cannot say any words. Write a column with your advice.

NCTE 12 Use language to accomplish individual purposes.

Social Studies

4. Many cultures use toys as part of celebrations and traditions. For example, in Mexico a piñata is a part of a birthday celebration. Kites are a traditional toy used in Japanese New Year celebrations. Choose a foreign culture and research the traditional toys that are still popular today. Write a one-page essay describing the toys and how they are used. Note any similarities the toys have to American toys that you may have played with. Include pictures, if possible.

NCSS I C Apply an understanding of culture as an integrated whole that explains the functions and interactions of traditions, beliefs and values, and behavior patterns.

Check Your Answers Check your answers at this book's Online Learning Center at **glencoe.com**.

Careers With Children — Storyteller

Before societies had written records, they had storytellers. Storytellers described battles and adventures and told tales of monsters and kings. Today's storytellers educate and entertain as they practice this ancient art. Many traditions are preserved with storytelling.

☀ What Does a Storyteller Do?

Storytellers captivate their audiences with words. Storytellers use their voices the way musicians use instruments. They write and memorize many stories and tell each one with enthusiasm and creativity. Many storytellers add songs and music to their stories, too. Some storytellers focus on certain traditions, such as African folk tales.

☀ Where Do Storytellers Work?

Storytellers perform in many different places, such as schools, libraries, museums, festivals, children's parties, senior centers, prisons, and hospitals. Some storytellers might perform on the radio or on television. Some sell recordings of their performances.

Preparation and Skills

Education and Training

Many storytellers study literature, folklore, music, and drama. Public speaking is also good preparation for storytelling. Look for a Storytellers Guild, or association, in your area to find a mentor or receive tips on developing this career. Some of these groups can help you find jobs to get started.

Aptitudes, Abilities, and Skills

Successful storytellers have imagination, self-motivation, a good memory, acting talent, and communication skills. Storytellers work hard, so they should be motivated and dedicated to their craft.

Academic Skills Required

English Language Arts are used by storytellers in reading and researching stories and ideas, and in writing stories to tell.

Explore Careers

Research other careers that involve performing with children or engaging them through play. Choose one career and write a paragraph describing it. Tell if the career interests you, and why.

 Careers Online For more information on careers, visit the Occupational Outlook Handbook Web site through the link on this book's Online Learning Center at **glencoe.com**.

Chapter Summary

An infant's brain undergoes major changes in response to stimulation. The transmission of information between nerve cells in the brain creates neural pathways that organize the brain. Piaget said that all children go through four periods of learning. During the sensorimotor period (birth–two years), children learn through their senses and own actions. A child learns and practices new skills through play. Appropriate toys can help babies learn. Children communicate before they can talk. Reading to a child promotes vocabulary.

Vocabulary Review

1. Create a multiple-choice test question for each content and academic vocabulary term.

Content Vocabulary
- ◇ neuron (p. 257)
- ◇ neural pathway (p. 257)
- ◇ cortex (p. 259)
- ◇ axon (p. 259)
- ◇ myelin (p. 259)
- ◇ dendrite (p. 259)
- ◇ synapse (p. 260)
- ◇ neurotransmitter (p. 260)
- ◇ perception (p. 266)
- ◇ attention span (p. 268)
- ◇ concept (p. 269)
- ◇ sensorimotor period (p. 271)
- ◇ object permanence (p. 271)
- ◇ imaginative play (p. 272)
- ◇ symbolic thinking (p. 272)
- ◇ age appropriate (p. 274)
- ◇ childproof (p. 275)
- ◇ manipulate (p. 280)

Academic Vocabulary
- ■ function (p. 259)
- ■ receptor (p. 260)
- ■ elicit (p. 270)
- ■ determined (p. 270)
- ■ responsiveness (p. 274)
- ■ hazard (p. 281)

Review Key Concepts

2. Describe how a baby's experiences increase brain function.
3. Explain how the brain becomes organized.
4. List four abilities that show intellectual growth in infants.
5. Identify specific abilities that babies learn during Piaget's first period of learning.
6. Name five ways caregivers can encourage learning.
7. Discuss how to choose toys appropriate for babies of different ages.

Critical Thinking

8. Analyze Why is it important to read and talk to a baby even if the baby does not understand?
9. Extend Piaget determined that children must learn to master one thinking skill before they can move on to another. Why is this so?
10. Compare How do the speech capabilities of two- to three-year-olds and four- to five-year-olds differ?

Family & Community Connection

11. Interview a Child Care Provider Interview a person who provides child care for one or more one-year-old infants. This could be in a home or in a child care center. Ask the provider to describe what he or she does to help stimulate the babies. How does he or she encourage the baby to learn? Compile a list of the answers. Does your list match with the information you have learned in this chapter?

Health Skills

12. Childproofing a Home Childproofing a home allows babies more freedom to explore their environment. There are many different ways to childproof a home, such as covering electrical outlets, moving small or fragile items out of a baby's reach, or installing cabinet locks. What steps could you take to temporarily childproof a room in your home for a visiting baby?

Observation Skills

13. Observe Babies Playing Work with your teacher to arrange to observe babies from ages six months to one year at play.

Procedure Find out the ages of the babies you observe. Write a list of the toys each baby plays with.

Analysis Compare and contrast the toys used by babies of different ages. How did the toys used by younger babies differ from the toys used by older babies? Were the toys used by older babies more complex than those used by younger babies? If so, in what way? Were any of the same toys used by children of varying ages? If so, were they used in different ways? Create a poster to present your findings.

> **NCTE 7** Conduct research and gather, evaluate, and synthesize data to communicate discoveries.

Real-World Skills

Problem-Solving

14. Make Decisions Imagine you are going to babysit a seven-month-old baby for a couple of hours. How will you keep the baby entertained? What activities or toys will you use? Make a list of how you plan to spend the two hours.

Technology Skills

15. Create a Chart Choose a researcher who studied intellectual development, such as B. F. Skinner or Albert Bandura, and compare their findings with those of Jean Piaget. How are they similar? How are they different? Use word processing software to create a chart showing your research results.

Financial Literacy

16. Birthday Shopping Imagine you have $25 to spend on a birthday gift for your neighbor who is turning one. How would you spend the money? Visit a local store and find age-appropriate toys and activities you could purchase. Create a list of your findings.

 Additional Activities For additional activities, go to this book's Online Learning Center at **glencoe.com**.

Academic Skills

English Language Arts

17. Research Literature Conduct research to find literature that describes how caregivers can help and encourage infants who are learning new skills. Use the information you find to write a scene that shows a caregiver providing an infant with encouragement while the baby is trying to master a new skill in intellectual development.

> **NCTE 2** Read literature to build an understanding of the human experience.

Mathematics

18. Semantic Development Research shows that the average child knows 200 words by age two and 10,000 words by age six. What is the rate of average words per year between the ages of two and six?

Math Concept **Determining Rates** A rate is a ratio of two measurements having different kinds of units. The rate for this problem is words per year.

Starting Hint Subtract the the number of words the child already knows at age two (200) from the number of words at age six (10,000). Divide your answer by the number of years spanned (4).

 For math help, go to the Math Appendix at the back of the book.

> **NCTM Algebra** Understand patterns, relations, and functions.

Science

19. Create a Flow Chart The nerves in the human body send and receive messages from the brain thousands of times a day. Conduct research using print or online resources to discover how this communication takes place.

Procedure List the steps involved when the nerves send and receive information from the brain.

Analysis Create a flow chart showing how nerves send information to the brain and send instructions from it.

> **NSES C** Develop understanding of the cell; interdependence of organisms; matter, energy, and organization in living systems; and behavior of organisms.

Standardized Test Practice

SHORT ANSWER

Read the passage, then answer the question.
    Some people believe that one way for a child's brain to grow intellectually is to expose the child to classical music during infancy. Other people do not agree with this.

20. Do you agree or disagree that classical music can help a child grow intellectually? Why? Use your knowledge of how a baby's brain develops to support your answer.

> **Test-Taking Tip** Put as much information into your answer as possible. Use easy-to-read, short sentences that define key words. Also give an example that explains your answer.

Unit Thematic Project

Raise a Healthy Baby

In this unit, you have learned that a child's first year is a time of great change. Parents and caregivers play a very important role in helping the child grow and develop. In this project, you will research a specific area of infant growth and development and explore what parents and caregivers can do to support a baby in this area.

My Journal

If you completed the journal entry from page 191, refer to it to see if your thoughts have changed after reading the unit.

Project Assignment

In this project, you will:

- Choose a feature of infant growth and development that interests you.
- Conduct research about the topic you have chosen.
- Interview a parent or child care professional about your topic.
- Prepare a presentation to share what you have learned with your class.

Child Development Skills Behind the Project

- Evaluate parenting roles and responsibilities.
- Identify a child's physical, emotional, and intellectual needs.
- Describe the growth and development of infants.

Academic Skills

English Language Arts Standards

> **NCTE 4** Use written language to communicate effectively.
>
> **NCTE 7** Conduct research and gather, evaluate, and synthesize data to communicate discoveries.

Step 1 Choose and Research Your Topic

The topics below are examples of areas in which infants grow and develop over their first year. Choose one of these topics, or select another topic approved by your teacher. Research its importance to healthy growth and development.

- Language skills
- Motor skills
- Development of emotions
- Vision
- Eating and sleeping
- Attachment to caregivers
- Relating to strangers
- Relating to other children

Write a summary of your research to:

- **Describe** milestones of infant growth or development in the chosen area.
- **Explain** how parents or caregivers can foster an infant's health in this area.
- **Identify** possible problems or disorders that can occur and how caregivers can identify and respond to them.

Step 2 Plan Your Interview

Use the results of your research to write a list of interview questions about your chosen topic to ask a parent or child care professional in your community.

Writing Skills

★ Use complete sentences.
★ Use correct spelling and grammar.
★ Organize your interview questions in the order you want to ask them.

Step 3 Connect with Your Community

Identify a child care professional or parent of a young child in your community who works with infants and toddlers. Conduct your interview using the questions you prepared in Step 2. Take notes during the interview and write a summary of the interview.

Interviewing Skills

★ Record interview responses and take notes.
★ Listen attentively.
★ Use correct spelling and grammar when you transcribe your notes.

Step 4 Share What You Have Learned

Use the Unit Thematic Project Checklist to plan and give an oral report to share what you have learned with your classmates.

Speaking Skills

★ Speak clearly and concisely.
★ Be sensitive to the needs of your audience.
★ Use standard English to communicate.

Step 5 Evaluate Your Child Development Skills and Academic Skills

Your project will be evaluated based on:

- Content and organization of your information.
- Proper use of standard English.
- Mechanics—presentation and neatness.
- Speaking and listening skills.

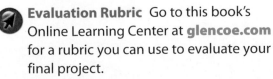 **Evaluation Rubric** Go to this book's Online Learning Center at **glencoe.com** for a rubric you can use to evaluate your final project.

Unit Thematic Project Checklist

Plan	✓ Select and research your topic and summarize your findings.
	✓ Plan and write your interview questions.
	✓ Interview a parent or child care professional and write a summary of what you learned.
Present	✓ Make a presentation to the class to discuss the results of your research and your interview.
	✓ Invite students to ask any questions. Answer these questions.
	✓ When students ask you questions, demonstrate in your answers that you respect their perspectives.
	✓ Turn in the summary of your research, your interview questions, and the summary of the interview to your teacher.
Academic Skills	✓ Communicate effectively.
	✓ Be sensitive to the needs of different audiences.
	✓ Adapt and modify language to suit different purposes.

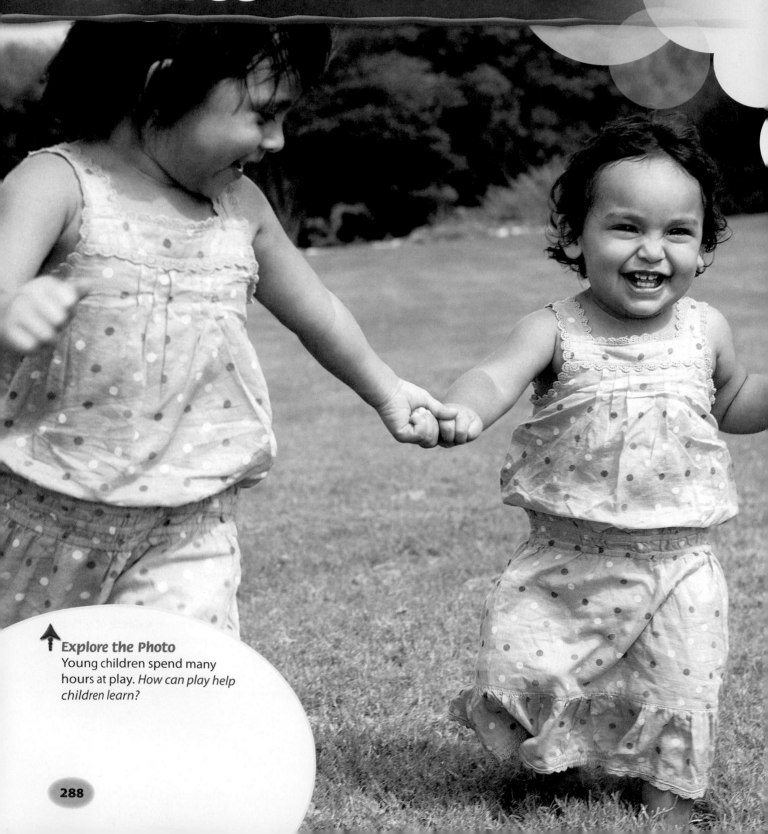

Unit 4

The Child from One to Three

Explore the Photo
Young children spend many hours at play. *How can play help children learn?*

288

Chapter 10 Physical Development from One to Three

Chapter 11 Emotional and Social Development from One to Three

Chapter 12 Intellectual Development from One to Three

Unit Thematic Project Preview

Help Children Learn

By completing this unit, you will learn that children ages one to three learn and develop physically, emotionally, socially, and intellectually. In your unit thematic project, you can create an activity to help children learn in one of these areas.

My Journal

Learning and Growing Write a journal entry about one of the topics below. This will help you prepare for the unit project at the end of the unit.

- Identify social activities in which one- to three-year-olds participate.
- Describe activities that will intellectually stimulate a one- to three-year-old.
- Tell about physical activities that are appropriate for one- to three-year-olds.

10 Physical Development from One to Three

Chapter Objectives

After completing this chapter, you will be able to:

- **Identify** five changes in a child's physical growth from ages one to three.
- **Explain** how developmental milestones are used.
- **Describe** how a parent should respond to typical changes in a child's sleeping patterns.
- **Explain** why it is important to establish good eating habits early in life.
- **Identify** why young children are particularly at risk for accidents.
- **List** four factors to consider when choosing clothing for young children.

Writing Activity Dialogue

Understanding Development Sometimes young children do not understand the limitations of toddlers. Write a dialog between a caregiver and a five-year-old who wants to play ball with a two-year-old. The caregiver should explain how the five-year-old can play with the two-year-old. Also be sure to answer any questions the five-year-old might ask.

Writing Tips To write an effective dialogue, you should
1. Let the people speak for themselves.
2. Use dialogue for a purpose.
3. Use language that sounds real and appropriate to the people talking.
4. Use quotation marks appropriately.

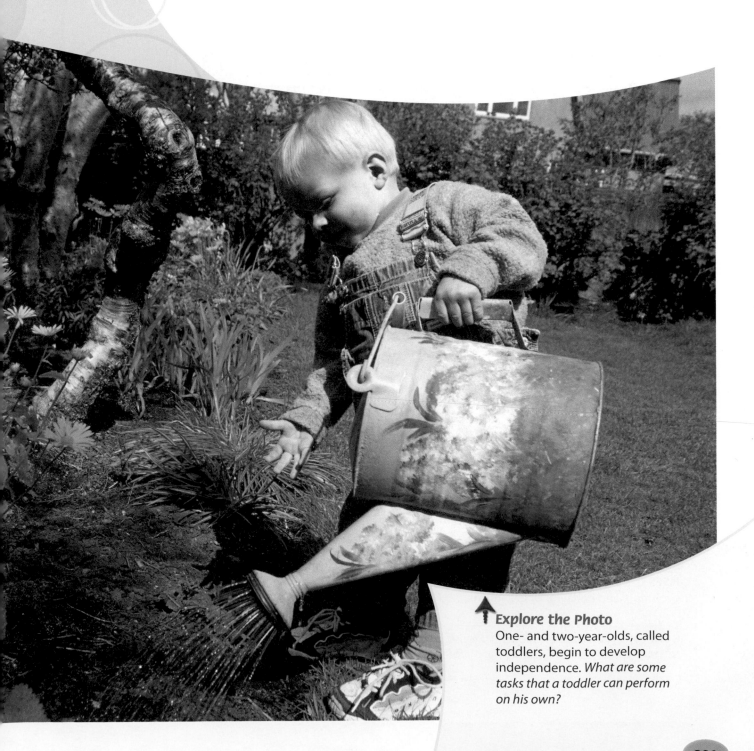

Explore the Photo
One- and two-year-olds, called toddlers, begin to develop independence. *What are some tasks that a toddler can perform on his own?*

Section 10.1

Growth and Development from One to Three

Reading Guide

Before You Read

Predict Look at the photos in this section and read their captions. Write one or two sentences predicting what the section will be about.

Read to Learn

Key Concepts

- **Identify** five changes in a child's physical growth from ages one to three.
- **Explain** how developmental milestones are used.

Main Idea

Children ages one-year-old to three-years-old grow, change, and develop in many ways. Motor skills improve noticeably.

Content Vocabulary

◇ toddler
◇ preschooler
◇ sensory integration
◇ developmentally appropriate
◇ dexterity

Academic Vocabulary

You will find these words in your reading and on your tests. Use the glossary to look up their definitions if necessary.

■ variation
■ proportion

Graphic Organizer

As you read, write down the gross motor skills for children one- to three-years-old. Use a time line like the one shown to illustrate your information.

| 12 months | 18 months | 24 months | 30 months | 36 months |

 Graphic Organizer Go to this book's Online Learning Center at **glencoe.com** to print out this graphic organizer.

Academic Standards ·

 English Language Arts

NCTE 4 Use written language to communicate effectively.

 Science

NSES C Develop understanding of the biological evolution; and behavior of organisms.

 Social Studies

NCSS I C Culture Apply an understanding of culture as an integrated whole that explains the functions and interactions of the arts, traditions, and behavior patterns.

NCTE *National Council of Teachers of English*
NCTM *National Council of Teachers of Mathematics*

NSES *National Science Education Standards*
NCSS *National Council for the Social Studies*

Growth from One to Three

The growth and development of a child from infancy to the preschool years is dramatic. A one-year-old still moves with some uncertainty, needs help dressing, and eats messily. A three-year-old can run and jump, get dressed alone, and eat fairly neatly with a fork and spoon.

A number of different influences impact the way children develop. Heredity plays a major role in child development. Physical traits such as body size, eye color, and even risk of disease can be passed on through genes. However, genes are not the only factor for growth and physical development. They act as a basic road map for physical development while other factors fill in the gaps. These other factors include nutrition, health, and life experiences.

Watching a child's growth during the toddler years can be amazing and informative. At this stage, changes in a child's physical growth are evidenced mainly by height, weight, body proportion, posture, and teeth. Motor development and ability progress as a child's physical development progresses.

Toddlers to Preschoolers

After the fast pace of the first year of life, physical growth slows somewhat. Children's skills improve dramatically between their first and fourth birthdays though. At about the age of one, most children begin to walk a few unsteady steps. The term **toddler** refers to one- and two-year-olds. By age three, children are typically far from toddling. Three-year-olds not only walk steadily but they also hop, skip, and run. Most of their other physical skills have advanced as well. A **preschooler** is a child from age three to about age five, when most children start going to school.

To build their physical skills, young children need plenty of space and room to move around. They need time each day for active play so they can exercise their muscles and use their stored-up energy. Although their attention span is longer than that of infants, they still want to change games and activities often. Each day brings new learning. Young children should have safe opportunities to explore, ask questions, use their imagination, and practice their growing motor skills.

Parental Influence
A child could have the same color eyes or hair as a parent. These physical traits are passed on by genes. *What other factors influence a toddler's growth and development?*

Figure 10.1

Average Heights and Weights: Ages 1–3

Growth charts help monitor a child's growth. *Should parents be overly concerned if their child does not fit within these ranges? Why or why not?*

AGE	BOYS		GIRLS	
	Height / Inches	Weight / Pounds	Height / Inches	Weight / Pounds
One year	29 to 30½	21 to 24½	28¼ to 29¾	19½ to 22½
Two years	33½ to 35¼	26 to 30	32¾ to 34¾	24½ to 28½
Three years	36¾ to 38¾	29¼ to 34	36¼ to 38½	28¼ to 33¼

Height and Weight

Children from ages one to three gain less than half the average monthly weight they did during the first year of life. Growth in height also slows by about half. **Figure 10.1** shows the average heights and weights for boys and girls from ages one to three.

Heredity and environment influence the rate at which children grow in height and weight. These influences are more noticeable among children ages one to three than among infants. After their first birthdays, children begin to show greater **variation**, or difference, in size. Some are much larger than average, while others are smaller. These size differences often continue through life. A tall two-year-old often grows to be a tall adult.

Proportion and Posture

Because of changes in physical **proportion**, or size, a child's posture generally improves between the ages one to three. Until age two, the circumference, or measurement around, of a child's head, abdomen, and chest are about the same. Between ages two and three, however, the chest becomes larger around than the head and abdomen. During this time, the arms, legs, and torso get longer. These changes in proportion help improve the child's balance and motor skills.

By the age of two, a child's posture is straighter but the child still does not stand completely erect. The typical toddler still has a protruding abdomen. The head is still bent forward somewhat. The toddler's knees and elbows are also slightly bent. By their third birthday, children stand straighter because their spines are stronger.

Teeth

A child's teeth emerge at different rates, but there are averages. One-year-olds typically have about eight teeth. During the second year of life, eight more teeth usually come in. For most children, the last four back teeth emerge early in the third year, giving them a complete set of 20 primary, or baby, teeth. These teeth will eventually fall out and be replaced by adult, or permanent, teeth.

There are several factors that influence the health of a child's teeth. These include diet, heredity, and dental care. Healthy teeth are important for eating and for preventing infection and pain.

Diet

Diet greatly influences the quality of a child's teeth. Teeth are formed before birth. This means the mother's diet during pregnancy affects the quality of her baby's teeth. The child's diet during the first two years is also important because adult teeth are forming under the primary teeth. Dairy products, which are rich in calcium and phosphorus, are especially important to good dental health. The vitamin D in milk also helps in the development of strong and healthy teeth and bones. Children should drink water that contains fluoride. Most tap water contains fluoride but most bottled waters do not. You can check with your dentist to be sure that a child is getting enough fluoride.

A poor diet can cause tooth decay. To promote good dental health, sweets should be limited in a child's diet. Gum-like candy, raisins, and fruit snacks that stick to the teeth are a particular problem. In addition to regular brushing, children should brush their teeth after eating sugary cereals. If left between the teeth, they can promote dental decay. Do not put a child to bed with a bottle unless it contains only water. When sweet liquids, such as juice or milk, are left in the mouth too long, they can cause tooth decay. In babies, it can lead to a condition called baby bottle decay, which destroys young children's teeth.

Heredity

Heredity appears to play a role in tooth quality. Dentists have identified a protective mechanism that discourages decay. Some children inherit this trait from their parents.

Dentist

Most doctors recommend taking children to a dentist at about the age of 18 months. This will help them become comfortable with dental visits from an early age and begin preventive care long before the permanent teeth come in.

Some family dentists will see toddlers. Others may refer you to a pediatric dentist. Toddlers can be challenging for a dentist due to their energy and temperaments. Pediatric dentists, just like pediatric doctors, are specially trained to deal with young children. They

Dental Development
During the second year of life, eight teeth usually come in, giving the two-year-old a set of sixteen teeth. *How many total primary teeth will there be?*

often have books and toys in the waiting room to entertain the children. Once in the exam room, many dentists will ask the child to sit on a parents lap for the exam. This gives them an added sense of security.

✓ **Reading Check** **Explain** How does diet influence the quality of a child's teeth?

{ **Expert Advice...** }

"The toddler stage is very important in a child's life. It is the time between infancy and childhood when a child learns and grows in many ways. Everything that happens to the toddler is meaningful. With each stage or skill the child masters, a new stage begins. This growth is unique to each child."

— Cathy Malley, child development educator, University of Connecticut

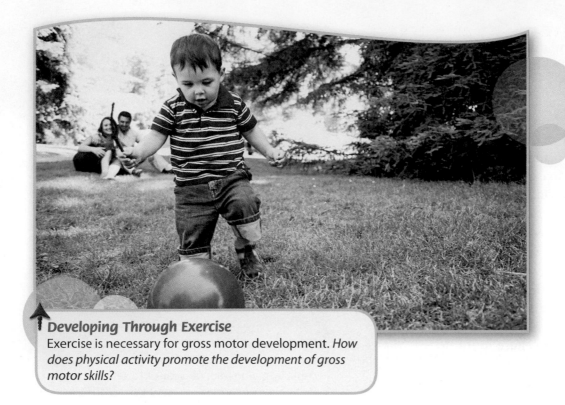

Developing Through Exercise
Exercise is necessary for gross motor development. *How does physical activity promote the development of gross motor skills?*

Development from One to Three

The three general patterns of physical development (from head to foot, from near to far, and from simple to complex) are evident in this age span. When you compare the skills of children at age one with those at the end of their third year, you can see big changes. Hand skills, for instance, show a pattern of development from simple to complex. At thirteen months, a child can bang blocks together or may manage to build a short stack of blocks. By age four, the same child can manipulate the blocks skillfully to create much more complex structures, such as towers, houses, and roads.

THE DEVELOPING BRAIN

Learning Abilities and Facts

Scientists have discovered that the learning of abilities, such as riding a bike, and the learning of facts, such as names and dates, are handled by different parts of the brain. Once a skill is learned, it forms a very durable memory. You never forget how to ride a bike. The same is not true of fact memories. Facts that are not used often slowly fade away until they are forgotten.

■ **Science Inquiry** Skills often become so automatic that you do not have to think about how to do them. What skills do you perform with little or no thought?

Sensory Integration

As children grow, their senses develop. This gives them greater awareness of their environment. **Sensory integration** is the process by which the brain combines information taken in through the senses to make a whole. This process is how a child knows how wide to open the mouth to eat a bite of orange. It also tells the child the orange dripped when he feels the juice on his chin. Some children are unable to normally process all the information their senses take in. These children are said to have sensory dysfunction. They may react more strongly to some types of stimulation, such as noises or lights, and less strongly to other types. When this happens, a child may have learning and behavioral problems.

Developmental Milestones

It is not always predictable when children from ages one to three will acquire various physical skills. Although they were born just two weeks apart, Blake and his cousin Damon have not mastered physical skills at the same pace. That is not surprising since some children learn skills earlier or later than average. These variations can be caused by differences in a child's physical size, health and diet, interests, temperament, and opportunities for physical play.

Child development experts have studied the range of ages at which children acquire certain important skills and have determined average ages. These developmental milestones for physical development of one-, two-, and three-year-olds are shown in **Figure10.2** on page 298 These are used to compare the average abilities of children of different ages. They also help caregivers plan developmentally appropriate activities. **Developmentally appropriate** describes toys, activities, and tasks that are suitable for a child at a specific age. For example, an 18-month-old can stack two blocks. That means activities that involve large building blocks would be developmentally appropriate for 18-month-olds.

Motor Skills

During this period, both gross and fine motor skills improve dramatically. Keep in mind that not all children develop physical skills at the same rate.

Gross Motor Skills

Physical exercise promotes the development of gross motor skills. Gross motor skills involve the use and control of the large muscles of the back, legs, shoulders, and arms. As children exercise, they slowly build the confidence, strength, and coordination that helps them run, jump, and kick a ball.

Walking is a significant gross motor milestone for children. It gives them a feeling of pride and much more mobility for exploration. Most children begin to walk at about one year of age. At first, children walk by holding on to furniture for stability. This is called cruising.

When they first let go of the furniture, they are wobbly and uncertain. Their toes are pointed outward, their feet are spread apart, and their arms are held out for balance. After a few shaky steps, they collapse into a sitting position. This is normal. With practice, children improve in steadiness, balance, and body control.

Learning Through PLAY

Changes in Play

How children play changes as they grow and develop. By the time they are one, children begin to discover what objects are used for. A one-year-old understands that a telephone is used for speaking to another person. However, by the time they are three, the role of imagination has begun to play a part in children's play. A telephone may no longer be a phone but could be used as a remote for turning on a pretend television. A two-year-old will play with small plates and silverware. However, by the age of three, the same child might use her imagination to pretend that a piece of paper is a plate and a crayon is a spoon. During this time period, children go from just being curious about objects to using their imagination with objects.

Think About It Your neighbor's three-year-old son is sitting in a box "driving" to the store. Your neighbor is concerned because her son has a toy car to play in. How can you assure your neighbor that her son is normal?

Figure
10.2

Physical Developmental Milestones—Ages 1–3

Children typically meet one mile-stone before moving on to the next. *At what age will a toddler likely be able to push herself on a wheeled toy?*

Age	Fine Motor Skills	Gross Motor Skills
12–18 Months	❖ Turns several pages of a book at a time ❖ Picks up small objects with thumb and forefinger ❖ Moves objects from hand to hand	❖ May walk alone or while holding a caregiver's hand ❖ Sits down without help ❖ Slides down stairs backwards, one step at a time
18–24 Months	❖ Stacks from two to four blocks ❖ Grasps crayons with a fist and scribbles	❖ Walks well ❖ Jumps in place ❖ Climbs up or down one stair ❖ Pulls toys with wheels
2–2½ Years	❖ Stacks six blocks ❖ Turns one page of a book at a time ❖ Picks up objects from the floor without losing balance	❖ Walks with more coordination and confidence ❖ Jumps off the bottom step ❖ Pushes self on wheeled toys
2½–3 Years	❖ Stacks eight blocks ❖ Screws lids on and off containers ❖ Draws circles and horizontal and vertical lines	❖ Alternates feet going up stairs but not going down ❖ Runs but may not be able to stop smoothly ❖ Throws a ball overhead but inaccurately
3–4 Years	❖ Stacks nine or ten blocks ❖ Cuts with scissors ❖ Draws recognizable pictures	❖ Jumps up and down in place with both feet ❖ Catches a ball with arms straight ❖ Rides a tricycle

Climbing skills follow a similar sequence if the child has stairs to climb. Climbing is not limited to stairs, however. Nothing is safe from the climbing toddler. Furniture, counters, shelves, and even people are conquered like mountains! This motion, of course, makes safety an important concern for caregivers. You will learn more about how to help make areas safer for children's exploration in Section 10.2.

Fine Motor Skills

One of the major developmental milestones that children reach at about age one is the ability to pick up small objects between their thumb and forefinger. This fine motor skill allows them to better grasp and lift small objects. This also increases the need to watch what they put in their mouth!

Between their first and second birthdays, children use fine motor skills as they learn to feed themselves and to drink from a cup. At first, young children often spill because they have poor hand-eye coordination. With practice, their success and neatness improve.

Toys offer children the chance to practice fine motor skills. One-year-olds usually enjoy playing with blocks, large beads, and stacking games. They might stack two or three blocks, only to knock them down and start over. They also like play phones, toys that roll, and musical toys.

Two-year-olds typically display greater dexterity. **Dexterity** is the skillful use of the hands and fingers. Two-year-olds can turn the pages of a book one at a time. They can turn on a faucet. They enjoy using crayons and typically color with such happy abandon that they leave marks running off the paper and on the table or floor. Another favorite activity of children in this age group is stacking blocks. They build small towers of blocks that usually topple after five or six blocks.

Three-year-olds show more success than younger children at tasks that require fine motor skills. They usually delight in taking things apart and putting them back together. Children this age have enough dexterity to draw circles, lines, and crosses.

Before the age of two, it is difficult to determine whether a child will be left-handed or right-handed. They generally use both hands equally as they continue to develop motor skills and build muscles and coordination. In fact, if a one-year-old seems to prefer one hand most of the time, it might indicate a physical problem with the other hand or arm. Parents should check with their physician if they feel there might be a problem.

Around age two or three, some children make their preference clear by favoring one hand over the other. This means they will consistently use the same hand to hold crayons, spoons, or toys. Other children, however, may continue switching between hands well into their preschool years. Physicians say that such switching back and forth is not a problem as long as it does not inhibit a child's ability to complete developmentally appropriate tasks.

Hand-Eye Coordination

Hand-eye coordination continues to improve among children in this age group, giving them the ability to zero in on small objects and pick them up for examination. Shortly after their first birthday, children start picking up very small objects between their thumb and forefinger. At first, this is difficult. With practice, however, their skill improves. By about eighteen months of age, children have mastered it.

This milestone in hand-eye coordination and fine motor skills gives children greater ability in using objects, poking fingers in holes, opening boxes, and playing with balls. It also aids them in building structures, sorting beads, and coloring with crayons. By their second birthday, children's coordination and strength has increased so much that they can turn doorknobs and pick up small objects on the ground without losing their balance.

Section 10.1　After You Read

Review Key Concepts

1. **Explain** the difference in growth between the ages of one and three and growth during the first year of life.
2. **Identify** what developmentally appropriate means.

Practice Academic Skills

 English Language Arts

3. Imagine that a parent said, "I can give my child whatever she wants to eat while she's little. Her baby teeth are going to fall out anyway." Write a short essay in which you explain what is wrong with this reasoning, as it pertains to teeth.

> **NCTE 4** Use written language to communicate effectively.

 Science

4. Three-year-old Tammy's mom has given her sorting beads, writing utensils, and dolls with removable clothing because she believes girls develop fine motor skills more quickly than boys. Write Tammy's mom a letter explaining why her viewpoint might be dangerous. Include suggestions on more age-appropriate toys.

> **NSES C** Develop understanding of the biological evolution; and behavior of organisms.

 Check Your Answers Check your answers at this book's Online Learning Center at **glencoe.com**.

Reading Guide

Before You Read

Discover Choose a Content or Academic Vocabulary term that is new to you. When you find it in the text, write down the definition.

Read to Learn

Key Concepts

- **Describe** how a parent should respond to typical changes in a child's sleeping patterns.
- **Explain** why it is important to establish good eating habits early in life.
- **Identify** why young children are particularly at risk for accidents.
- **List** four factors to consider when choosing clothing for young children.

Main Idea

One- to three-year-olds experience many changes in sleep patterns, nutritional needs, eating, hygiene, dressing, health, illness, and safety.

Content Vocabulary

◇ night terrors
◇ hygiene
◇ sphincter muscles
◇ synthetic fibers
◇ flame-resistant

Academic Vocabulary

You will find these words in your reading and on your tests. Use the glossary to look up their definitions if necessary.

■ incident
■ pollutant

Graphic Organizer

As you read, list five things a caregiver can focus on to make meals appealing to a young child. Use a chart like the one shown to help organize your information.

Promoting Nutritious Foods
1.
2.
3.
4.
5.

 Graphic Organizer Go to this book's Online Learning Center at **glencoe.com** to print out this graphic organizer.

Academic Standards ·

 English Language Arts

NCTE 4 Use written language to communicate effectively.

 Mathematics

NCTM Measurement Understand measurable attributes of objects and the units, systems, and processes of measurement.

 Social Studies

NCSS I A Culture Analyze and explain the ways groups, societies, and cultures address human needs and concerns.

NCTE *National Council of Teachers of English*
NCTM *National Council of Teachers of Mathematics*

NSES *National Science Education Standards*
NCSS *National Council for the Social Studies*

Sleeping

Changes in sleeping needs and patterns are common for children ages one to three. Sleeping habits often change around a child's second birthday. Children usually require less sleep than before, and they may not fall asleep as easily. It is important for parents to make sure their children still get enough rest.

Sleep Patterns

Most one-year-olds continue the pattern of sleeping eight or more hours at night. They typically take naps of several hours during the day. As they get older, daytime naps become shorter. The length of time they sleep at night slowly increases. By the age of two, most children no longer take a morning nap. Afternoon naps may continue for several years. In total, two-and three-year-olds sleep about 10 to 14 hours a day.

Fears or anxiety about separation from parents can make falling asleep difficult for toddlers and preschoolers. Some may call parents back into their room again and again, asking for a drink of water, another story, or one more trip to the bathroom. What they usually want, however, is just comfort and reassurance.

Children feel more comfortable when their lives are predictable. A nightly routine such as brushing teeth, reading stories, singing, and choosing a soft toy to take to bed can help prepare children for sleep. When the routine is broken because of a late bedtime or a lost toy, it is more difficult for a child to fall asleep. It is common for children to use self-comforting techniques at bedtime, such as thumb sucking or cuddling a favorite blanket.

Sleep Disturbances

Sometimes the quantity or quality of a child's sleep is upset. When this happens, the child may be tired and irritable the next day.

It is not unusual for toddlers to wake up briefly when sleeping. Some fall back to sleep. Others may begin to cry or try to get a caregiver's attention. The best response depends on the problem. For example, a trip to the bathroom may be needed.

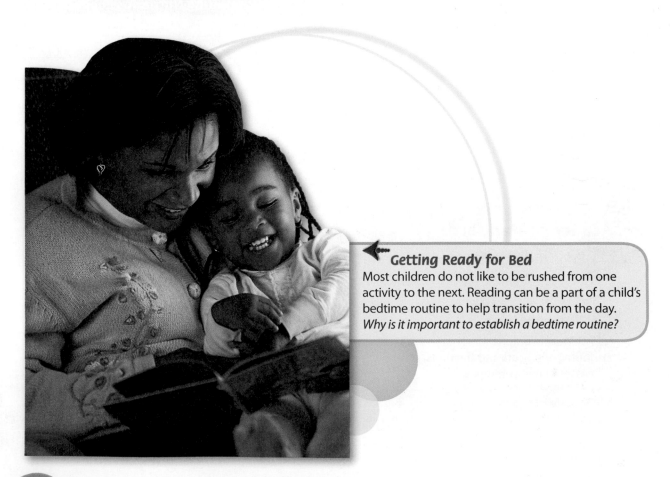

Getting Ready for Bed
Most children do not like to be rushed from one activity to the next. Reading can be a part of a child's bedtime routine to help transition from the day. *Why is it important to establish a bedtime routine?*

Fear of the dark is common at ages two and three and may prevent a child from falling asleep. A nightlight or calmly discussing fears may help. Never tease a child about fears.

Nightmares and night terrors sometimes disturb children's sleep. **Night terrors** are a type of sleep disturbance that occurs during the first few hours of sleep, when children are sleeping deeply. Children who are not fully awake may sit up with their eyes open and scream. Such children are often very upset but unable to explain what is wrong. By morning, the child usually does not remember anything about the **incident**, or action. In general, night terrors are not a cause for alarm. Children who experience them need reassurance.

Nightmares are frightening dreams that often seem real. Some children have difficulty separating dreams from reality. Experts recommend responding right away with words of comfort to a child who has had a nightmare.

Nightmares may occur because of stress or major changes in a child's life, such as starting preschool. Sometimes reassurance and reduction of pressure can help relieve a child's anxiety. Avoiding exposure to frightening images on television may also help.

✓ Reading Check **Recall** What seems to be the best way for caregivers to deal with a child's fear of the dark, night terrors, and nightmares?

Nutritional Needs and Eating

The habits and attitudes toward food that children learn at this stage will influence their eating habits throughout life. That is why it is vital to establish good eating habits early in life. Teaching good habits means helping children learn to enjoy nutritious foods and to eat correct portions of food.

Meals sometimes become a battle of wills between parents and young children. Experts suggest offering children a variety of healthy foods at mealtime and letting them choose what to eat. Like adults, children develop likes and dislikes. Children accept and try new

What Would You Do?

Getting a New Bed

Jamie, age two and one-half, kept climbing out of his crib, even when he was tired. His parents were concerned that he could hurt himself. They decided that it was time to get Jamie a toddler bed.

On an afternoon visit to his grandmother's, Jamie took a nap in a bed for the first time. His grandmother let him choose a blanket to use and bring his favorite stuffed animal. She read a story to him, and Jamie fell asleep.

Back at home, Jamie's parents asked him about his visit to Grandma's house. He proudly talked about sleeping in the big bed. Jamie's mother said she wanted to get him a big bed too. Jamie looked a little uncertain. His mother said she would need his help picking out sheets and a blanket to go with the bed. Then Jamie looked excited.

✏ **Write About It** Jamie's new bed had a rail on one side so he would not fall out. Besides getting a special toddler bed with a rail, how might you keep a child from getting hurt by falling out of bed? Create a list of your suggestions.

foods more easily if they are not pressured to try them. Adults can encourage children to try new foods and develop good habits by modeling those behaviors. Young children often mimic their parents. So if mom or dad likes a food, the child is more likely to try it.

Children this age like consistency at mealtimes. They may insist that a sandwich be cut just the right way. They may become upset if they do not get lunch on a certain plate or a drink in a favorite cup.

Self-Feeding

Children at this stage will want to feed themselves. This is a natural part of their growing independence. Self-feeding depends on a child's fine motor skills, and it also helps refine them.

One-Year-Olds

Children at this age eat a variety of foods. Finger foods, such as slices of banana, are popular. They should avoid hard foods like raw carrots that can cause choking. Using a spoon to eat usually begins before the age of one. There is still a lot of spilling though.

When children first start drinking from a cup, a training cup is a good choice. These are also called sippy cups. These cups' handles, lid, and spout or straw reduce spills.

Two-Year-Olds

Children in this age group can usually feed themselves and learn to use a fork, but they often take a long time to eat. They are still improving their fine motor skills, as well as getting nutrition. Most children drink from a cup fairly well by age two. At this age, a child should eat with the rest of the family.

Three-Year-Olds

By age three, most children are quite skillful using a spoon and fork. Three-year-olds have a full set of primary teeth, so chewing foods is not a problem. Three-year-olds generally eat meals with the family. They also eat the same food as the rest of the family. Meats and other tough foods should be cut into small pieces for them.

Nutritional Needs

Since they are growing less rapidly than in their first year of life, children ages one to three do not eat as much. Because their stomachs are still small, most need food every three or four hours. However, the amount that children eat may vary greatly from day to day, depending on appetite and level of activity. Nutritious snacks, such as fresh fruit, can help keep them full between meals.

Figure 10.3 Serving Sizes for Children Two and Three

Parents and caregivers need to know appropriate serving sizes for toddlers. *Why is it important to know the correct serving size for small children?*

Toddlers need smaller serving sizes of food but they still need to eat a variety of food from all five food groups.

Milk Group
Milk, yogurt—½ cup
Frozen yogurt,
 pudding—¼ to ½ cup
Cheese—½ to 1 oz.

Grain Group
Whole-grain bread—¼ to ½ slice
Ready-to-eat cereal—¼ to ⅓ cup
Spaghetti, rice, macaroni—¼ to ⅓ cup
Crackers—2 to 3
Hamburger bun—¼ to ½

Nutritious Foods

Children should be provided with a variety of beneficial foods to establish good health. Offer nutritious foods at both mealtimes and snack times. Avoid foods high in sugar, salt, and fat. Sticky foods such as raisins may cause tooth decay. Read the nutrition labels and ingredient lists on frozen, canned, and dried foods for help in making nutritious choices.

MyPyramid is a food guidance system from the U.S. Department of Agriculture (USDA). It was developed as a guide for healthful eating and active living for people ages two and older. Learn more about MyPyramid in Chapter 16.

Because their stomachs are smaller, young children need smaller servings, or portions, when they eat. **Figure 10.3** gives examples of a child-size serving for two- and three-year-olds in each food group. Children four and older need larger servings.

Teaching Children Good Nutrition

Parents and other caregivers are role models for children when it comes to food choices and eating habits. Sharing nutritious meals with children, trying new foods together, and letting children help in the kitchen all promote good eating habits. Parents should keep nutritious snacks, such as fruit, on hand. They should also let their child see them making good choices.

In addition to modeling good behavior, parents and other caregivers can encourage children to eat only when hungry and to eat slowly. Caregivers should not use food as a reward for good behavior. Likewise, they should not withhold food as a punishment. Children can also be encouraged to drink water when thirsty rather than milk or sugary drinks. If parents have nutritional concerns, they should consult their physician.

Meat and Beans Group
Egg—1
Chicken, hamburger,
 fish—1 to 2 oz.
Baked beans—¼ cup
Peanut butter— 1 to 2 Tbsp.

Vegetable Group
Carrots—¼ to ½
Corn, green beans,
 peas—¼ cup

Fruit Group
Apple, banana—¼ to ½
Fruit juice—⅓ cup
Grapes, strawberries,
 peaches—¼ cup

Math in Action

Overweight Children

What is the highest percent overweight reported in the graph below of a child 1–3 years of age?

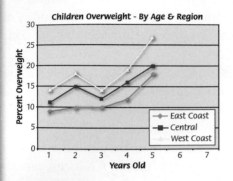

Children Overweight - By Age & Region

(Vertical axis: Percent Overweight, 0 to 30; Horizontal axis: Years Old, 1 to 7)

Legend:
- East Coast
- Central
- West Coast

Math Concept **Reading Graphs** A line graph represents data using different colored lines to show each value.

Starting Hint First, find the age range 1–3 on the horizontal axis. Look above to find the highest point.

 For math help, go to the Math Appendix at the back of the book.

NCTM Algebra Use mathematical models to represent and understand quantitative relationships.

Meal Appeal

One way to promote interest in nutritious foods is to try to make meals appealing for children. Think about the following elements as you plan their meals.

- **Color** Think about how dull a meal of fish, applesauce, milk, and vanilla pudding looks. Varying foods can add more color. Fresh fruits and vegetables are brightly colored and nutritious.
- **Texture** Foods with different textures add variety to a meal. Try adding crackers, cheese, or cut-up, juicy grapes to a child's plate to provide different textures.
- **Shape** Foods with a variety of shapes also add appeal. Your goal does not have to be to make a child's plate look like a circus, but you might cut sandwiches into rectangles or triangles or use large cookie cutters. Consider adding cucumber slices, zucchini sticks, or orange wedges to a plate. Help children identify the shapes.
- **Temperature** Try serving both hot and cold foods at a meal. Always check the temperature of any hot foods before serving them. If a food has been cooked or warmed in the microwave, stir it thoroughly to even out the temperature. Hot spots from foods warmed in a microwave can burn a child's mouth.

Gaining Independence It may be messy at first, but a child shows growing independence by using a spoon or drinking from a cup. *What beverages are appropriate for a child this age?*

- **Ease of Eating** Certain foods are easier than others for young children to eat. Ground beef, for example, is easier to chew and swallow than a pork chop. Many children like spaghetti, but they can handle it more easily when the strands are cut into short pieces.

✓ **Reading Check** **Explain** Why is it important for parents and caregivers to share nutritious meals with children and try new foods together?

Physical Health and Wellness

Keeping a child healthy and safe is a top priority for parents and other caregivers. Doing so requires knowing both how to prevent problems and how to deal with them when they occur. Children ages one to three are especially at risk for accidents. They are old enough to be mobile, but they are too young to understand the many hazards. They are also still unsteady as they are building their motor skills. Children at this age are also ready to begin learning personal hygiene.

Checkups

Most children have a checkup at 12 months. The physician checks the child's growth and development. The doctor may ask about the child's language ability, interest in learning and practicing new skills, and behavior. Additional checkups are often scheduled at 15, 18, and 24 months. These checkups will include growth measurements, immunizations, and routine examinations of the eyes, ears, teeth, genitals, and other body parts.

Immunizations

Immunizations protect children from a specific disease, usually by giving a child a vaccine. When a child is given a vaccine, a small amount of disease-carrying germs is introduced to the body on purpose so that the body can build resistance to that disease. Vaccines boost the immune system so that if a child is exposed to a certain disease, he or she can

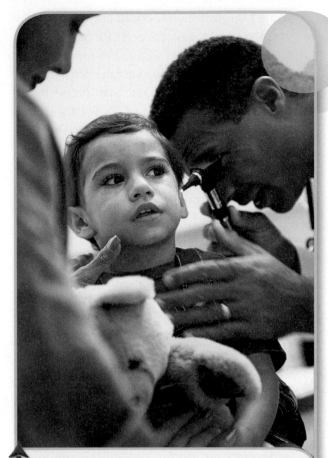

Staying Healthy
Regular checkups are important for the lifelong health of a child. *At what ages should children have checkups?*

more easily fight infection. Children at this age are more likely to get diseases since they spread easily in child care centers and preschools. For a complete list of childhood immunizations, see Chapter 20.

Many parents feel that keeping children at home when they are young helps prevent illness. Being in a child care center does tend to expose children to more germs. However, some studies have shown that children exposed to more germs through child care centers and older siblings had lower rates of asthma. This is probably because getting sick early in life stimulated their immune responses. No parent wants to see their child get sick. However, for common illnesses like a cold or the chicken pox, it is often better for a child to have them early in life. This allows their body to fight the illness and build resistance against future outbreaks, similar to an immunization.

Some people are concerned about the safety of vaccines, but severe complications from vaccines are *very* rare. State law requires that children receive certain vaccinations before entering school, and physicians recommend that children receive most of their immunizations by age two. Children are also required to have certain vaccinations to attend child care centers. To find out what types of vaccines children need and when they need them, refer to the recommended schedule of immunizations in Chapter 20.

Illnesses

It is not uncommon for children between the ages of one and three to get sick. Some common illnesses are respiratory and ear infections. These illnesses are often mild and usually require no medical intervention, although chronic ear infections do require attention. Other illnesses, such as the flu, can cause more severe problems. They are preventable with vaccinations.

Environmental Influences on Health

Pollutants can be found both in the home and outside it. A **pollutant** is something that makes the environment dirty. One of the chief indoor pollutants is environmental tobacco smoke (ETS), also known as second-hand smoke. This smoke comes from burning cigarettes. Researchers have shown that environmental tobacco smoke puts children at increased risk for respiratory infections, middle ear infections, and problems with asthma. Adults can avoid these increased risks for health problems by keeping children away from smokers and smoky areas.

Lead is another harmful substance that is found both inside and outside older homes, especially in paint. Caregivers must prevent children from putting bits of dried paint in their mouths. Children under the age of six are vulnerable to high levels of lead because their brain and central nervous system are still forming. Exposure to lead affects children in many ways, from delayed growth and hearing loss to irritability and hyperactivity.

Safety

Children ages one to three are interested in exploring their environment. They open drawers and cabinets, turn knobs, and put objects in their mouth. As they try to learn about their world, their curiosity can often put them in danger's path. Rather than trying to curb a child's curious nature, it is better to childproof the home and make it as safe as possible for the child.

➤ Protective Measures
Young children are usually not aware of dangerous situations. *How can parents and caregivers make an environment safe for young children?*

Childproof the Home

Young children love to explore the world around them. The average home contains a variety of conditions that can be hazardous. To ensure a child's safety while they explore, caregivers must childproof their homes.

To prevent falls, check to see that the floors and stairs are clear of clutter. Make sure floors are dry. Use safety gates on stairways until children learn to go up and down stairs safely. Remove furniture that might tip.

Check that open windows have screens with secure locks. Install window safety latches. Use window blinds with safety features. Keep blind cords away from children.

To prevent burns, teach children not to touch a range. Consider buying a stove guard. Use back burners when possible. Turn pot handles toward the range's center. Check the temperature of water from the faucet. Lower the water heater setting if it exceeds 120 degrees Fahrenheit (49 degrees Celsius). Place safety caps on unused electrical outlets. Keep toasters, irons, and other small appliances unplugged.

Store cleaning supplies, paints, insecticides, and medicines in locked containers. Keep knives, razors, scissors, and matches away from children. Inspect toys and other play equipment regularly for broken parts or sharp edges. It is usually best to throw away broken toys for young children rather than trying to fix them. Glueing toys together makes them easier to break again and exposes the child to harmful chemicals.

Environmental Concerns

There are hazards in a baby's environment, both inside and outside the home. The following tips are ways a caregiver can help provide a safer environment for children:

- **Choking Hazards** To help prevent choking, make sure that children stay seated while eating. Parents and other caregivers should encourage children to take small bites of food during meals, to chew all food thoroughly, and to swallow before taking another bite.
- **Toys** Take time to select toys that are age appropriate. Small toys or toys with small, removable parts are choking hazards.

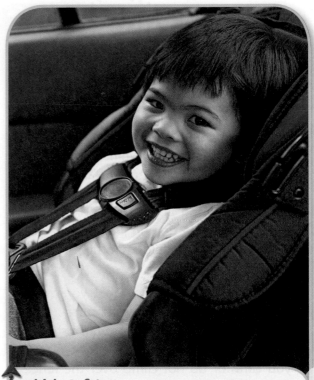

↑ Vehicle Safety
Children should always be safely buckled up in car seats when on the road. *What could happen to a child not secured in a car seat during an accident?*

- **Poisons in the Home** Avoid using strong household cleaning products. Keep all poisonous substances and medications locked up. Learn what to do in case a child ingests a poisonous substance. Keep the phone numbers of the poison control center and your local hospital handy. See the chart in Chapter 20 for a list of common household poisons.
- **Fire and Burns** Keep children away from candles, fireplaces, matches, and lighters. Teach children the stop, drop, and roll technique for extinguishing fire on their clothes or in their hair. If a burn looks more serious than a slight reddening of the skin, consult a doctor immediately.
- **Motor Vehicles** Children must ride in a car seat that is secured with seatbelts in the back seat of a vehicle. Children over 12 months of age and weighing 20 pounds or more may ride in a car seat that is facing forward. Always be sure children are wearing seatbelts while the vehicle is in motion.

Flushing toilets frighten some children. It may be better to flush the toilet after the child has left the bathroom.

Bowel training usually comes before bladder training, although some children learn at the same time. Most children are ready when they show awareness that a bowel movement is about to happen. When caregivers see this awareness in the child's facial expressions or gestures, they should suggest that the child sit on the toilet seat or potty chair. They should be encouraging. If caregivers are too demanding, toilet learning will become more difficult.

Many young children are encouraged in toileting when they are given cloth or disposable training pants in place of diapers. Training pants are heavy, absorbent underpants. Wearing training pants, instead of diapers, makes it possible for a young child to use a toilet or potty chair on their own. Most children also see wearing underpants instead of diapers as a sign of maturity.

✓ Reading Check **Review** How can you tell when a child is ready for toilet teaching?

Clothing

Parents and caregivers need to be aware of the types of clothing that are appropriate for young children. Appropriate clothing is important so that a child can learn to dress and undress himself. It is also important for comfort, durability, and economy.

Self-Dressing

Young children are eager to learn how to dress and undress themselves. Being able to put on her own clothes makes a child feel independent. It is important to encourage self-dressing whenever a child begins to show interest. Dressing involves a number of gross and fine motor skills that must be learned one step at a time. These skills require frequent practice. Caregivers need to be patient and encouraging. Be sure to allow plenty of time to get dressed so the child does not feel rushed.

Undressing is easier than dressing. Most children will start undressing themselves around thirteen or fourteen months of age. They generally will first pull off shoes, socks, or pants. They will then work up to removing loose t-shirts. Parents can make the process easier by buying clothes without buttons or fasteners.

Parenting Skills

Helping a Child Learn to Brush

Tooth decay occurs faster in children than in adults. It is important to clean a child's teeth in the first few years of life. Young children do not have the ability to brush teeth effectively, but they need to learn. The key to getting a child to brush is to make it fun.

Use only a pea-sized amount of mild-flavored toothpaste on the toothbrush. Brush gently and for at least one minute. Make sure the child spits out the toothpaste when finished instead of swallowing it. Swallowing toothpaste can lead to a condition called fluorosis, in which spots appear on the teeth. Helping a child learn to brush well and regularly can preserve a smile for a lifetime.

Take Charge How could you help make brushing fun for a child? Create a poster with at least three ideas for making brushing fun.

Learning to Self-Dress
Young children enjoy trying to dress themselves. *What should parents and caregivers look for when buying clothing for young children?*

About the same time, they might start helping to dress themselves by holding out an arm for the sleeve of a shirt. Next, they may learn to push an arm through a sleeve. By two years of age, the child can pull up pants, but putting on shirts is still difficult. Children may put their clothes on inside out or backwards. By age three, children can dress themselves but need help with fasteners like buttons and shoelaces. They may still put shoes on the wrong feet.

With self-dressing, a child learns independence and responsibility. This helps boost self-esteem. Caregivers can encourage self-dressing by choosing clothes that are easy to put on and take off. Shirts with loose necks and pants with elastic waists are easiest for young children to handle.

Choosing Clothes

When you shop for clothing, choose clothes that allow for growth. Look for deep hems or cuffs that can be let down. Check that the straps on overalls or jumpers are long enough to allow the buttons to be moved.

Consider buying pants that are a size larger but will fit when you roll up the pant legs. A child with a long torso will get more wear out of pants and a shirt than overalls or onesies.

Whenever possible, let children help choose their own clothes. They usually love bright colors and tend to choose their clothes more by color than for any other reason. Children also enjoy clothes printed with pictures of animals, toys, or familiar story characters. When choosing clothes for young children, there are several factors to consider.

Comfort

Look for clothes that allow a child to move freely. Knits that stretch as a child moves are good choices. Soft and sturdy fabrics are comfortable. Stiff or scratchy fabrics can bother children's skin. Size is an important factor in comfort. Clothes that are too small restrict movement, and clothes that are too large can get in the way. Look for clothes that are large enough to allow the child to move comfortably. All clothes labeled with the same size may not fit the same way.

Fabric

Cotton is a comfortable natural fiber often used in children's clothing. It absorbs moisture, wears well, and washes well. It may shrink though. **Synthetic fibers** are fabrics made from chemicals, rather than natural sources. Clothes made from synthetic fibers such as polyester and acrylic are durable, wrinkle resistant, and quick-drying.

Unlike cotton, most synthetic fibers do not absorb moisture well and hold heat and perspiration against the body. This characteristic makes them a good choice for clothes that will be worn in cool weather.

Often natural and synthetic fibers are blended to take advantage of the benefits of each. By law, all clothing must have a label that identifies the fibers used. Clothing labels also state how to care for each garment.

Federal law requires that the fabric used in children's sleepwear be flame-resistant. **Flame-resistant** means that the fabric can still catch on fire, but will not burn as quickly as other fabrics.

Durability

Children's clothes must withstand hard wear and repeated washings. Their *durability*, or ability to last, is influenced by the quality of the fabric and the construction of the clothing. When you check the construction of clothes, look for close, even stitching with strong thread. The stitching should be reinforced at points of strain.

All fasteners and trims should be firmly attached. Some pants have the knees reinforced with extra fabric which also helps improve durability.

Section 10.2   After You Read

Review Key Concepts

1. **Compare** the sleep needs of one-year-olds and three-year-olds.
2. **Describe** the most important consideration in preparing meals and snacks for young children.
3. **List** three ways children can develop good hygiene skills.
4. **Explain** why it is best to let a child help with dressing at an early age.

Practice Academic Skills

 English Language Arts

5. Oftentimes, children do not want to take a bath or brush their teeth. Imagine that you are a caregiver for young children. How can you encourage good hygiene with the children you care for? Write your ideas in a short essay.

> **NCTE 4** Use written language to communicate effectively.

 Social Studies

6. Many cultures take a different approach to toilet training. In some countries, toilet training begins when a child is only one month old. Research to find more information on toilet training in another culture. Create a chart to compare the practices in your chosen culture with the methods discussed in this chapter.

> **NCSS I A** Analyze and explain the ways groups, societies, and cultures address human needs and concerns.

 Check Your Answers Check your answers at this book's Online Learning Center at **glencoe.com**.

Chapter Summary

Heredity and environment play key roles in child development, affecting body size, eye color, and disease risk. A poor diet can cause tooth decay. As children grow, their senses develop, giving them greater awareness of their environment. Gross and fine motor skills improve as children get older. Some toddlers experience sleep disturbances. Children should be given nutritious foods and encouraged to feed themselves. Homes should be childproofed to help keep children safe. Toilet training should not be attempted before a child is ready. Parents should provide comfortable clothes and teach good hygiene.

Vocabulary Review

1. Label each of these content and academic vocabulary terms as a noun, verb, or adjective.

Content Vocabulary
- ◇ toddler (p. 293)
- ◇ preschooler (p. 293)
- ◇ sensory integration (p. 296)
- ◇ developmentally appropriate (p. 297)
- ◇ dexterity (p. 299)
- ◇ night terrors (p. 303)
- ◇ hygiene (p. 310)
- ◇ sphincter muscles (p. 311)
- ◇ synthetic fibers (p. 314)
- ◇ flame-resistant (p. 314)

Academic Vocabulary
- ■ variation (p. 294)
- ■ proportion (p. 294)
- ■ incident (p. 303)
- ■ pollutant (p. 308)

Review Key Concepts

2. Identify five changes in a child's physical growth from ages one to three.

3. Explain how developmental milestones are used.

4. Describe how a parent should respond to typical changes in a child's sleeping patterns.

5. Explain why it is important to establish good eating habits early in life.

6. Identify why young children are particularly at risk for accidents.

7. List four factors to consider when choosing clothing for young children.

Critical Thinking

8. Compare Toddlers' fine motor skills develop rapidly. How does self-feeding differ for a one-year-old and a three-year-old?

9. Differentiate Many young children experience night terrors and nightmares. What is the difference between night terrors and nightmares?

10. Examine Young children must be physically and emotinally ready for toilet training. How do physical and emotional factors play a role in toileting readiness?

Family & Community Connection

11. Interview a Preschool Teacher With your teacher's help, contact a local preschool teacher and set up a time for an interview. Prior to the interview, write questions to ask. Questions should focus on age-appropriate activities for preschoolers. For example, "What are some age-appropriate activities?" "How do you find or create these activities?" "Do any of the activities differ for the older preschoolers and the younger ones?" After the interview, write up your findings in a question-and-answer format.

Health Skills

12. Research Dental Hygiene Conduct online research to find dos and don'ts for parents and caregivers to use in promoting good dental health for children. Create and illustrate two posters with your findings. One poster should contain dos, the second poster should contain don'ts.

Observation Skills

13. Observe Preschoolers Work with your teacher to arrange to observe a group of children in a child care setting. The children should range in age from one to three years. You may need the help of the child care staff to identify children of different ages.

Procedure As you observe a one-year-old, a two-year-old, and a three-year-old, look for evidence of the fine and gross motor skill level of each child. This would be a good opportunity to use a developomental checklist.

Analysis Create a chart in which you record the fine and gross motor skills observed for the one-year-old, two-year-old, and three-year-old children.

NCSS IV D Individual Development and Identity Apply concepts, methods, and theories about the study of human growth and development, such as learning, motivation, and behavior.

Real-World Skills

Problem-Solving

14. Provide Solutions How might you make a bathroom safe for a two-year-old child? Look around a bathroom in your home and make a list of potential hazards for a two-year-old. Then generate a list of possible solutions to the hazards.

Technology Skills

15. Create a Table Research the average fine and gross motor skills developed in children ages four and five. Use word-processing software to create a table that shows the age and the fine and gross motor skills typical for that age.

Financial Literacy

16. Calculate Clothing Costs Conduct research to find out what clothes a two-year-old needs. Use a catalog or go to a store to estimate their cost. Write a report summarizing your findings. End your report with tips on how parents could save money on toddler clothes.

 Additional Activities For additional activities, go to this book's Online Learning Center at glencoe.com.

Academic Skills

 ### English Language Arts

17. Analyze the Text A child's fine motor skills typically improve as the child gets older. The chapter notes that self-feeding both depends on and helps improve children's fine motor skills. Write a half-page report to explain why this is true.

> **NCTE 12** Use language to accomplish individual purposes.

 ### Mathematics

18. Building Blocks Children ages 1 to 3 like to stack blocks. In the series shown below, how many blocks would a child need to build the fourth tower?

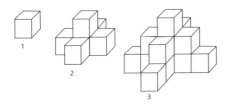

Math Concept **Multi-Step Problem** When solving problems with more than one step, think through each step before you start.

Starting Hint Remember the tower in the middle that you cannot see! Count how many blocks are in the first and second towers. Then subtract these amounts to find the amount of increase. Repeat this for the second and third in the series. Apply the pattern of increasing amounts to the third tower to predict the fourth.

 For math help, go to the Math Appendix at the back of the book.

> **NCTM Algebra** Use mathematical models to represent and understand quantitative relationships.

 ### Science

19. Test a Hypothesis A hypothesis is an assumption that is made to test the validity of a theory or idea. Use the data in Figure 10.2 on page 298 to choose a gross motor skill listed for a specific age group.

Procedure Use the chosen motor skill and age to form a hypothesis. For example: All two-year-olds can push themselves on wheeled toys. Describe an experiment you would conduct to test your hypothesis.

Analysis Create a step-by-step presentation that describes the experiment and explains how the experiment would test your hypothesis.

> **NSES A** Develop abilities necessary to do scientific inquiry, understandings about scientific inquiry.

 ## Standardized Test Practice

TIMED WRITING
Read the prompt and respond in a one-page essay.

20. Three-year-old Trina loves to build towers out of blocks. Her eighteen-month-old brother, James, loves to knock them down. Trina has begun to push James when she sees him approaching her play area. What are some specific ways that Trina and James's caregiver can address the problem?

> **Test-Taking Tip** Use the essay prompt as a basis for your thesis statement to help you focus your essay and ensure that you address the prompt in the time given. For example, you might say, "The children's caregiver can address the problem by . . ."

Chapter 11

Emotional and Social Development from One to Three

Chapter Objectives

After completing this chapter, you will be able to:

- **Identify** the factors that contribute to a child's emotional development.
- **Describe** six specific emotions children ages eighteen months to three years show.
- **List** the four signs of a healthy relationship between parents and a child.
- **Identify** four ways to help children get adequate sleep.
- **Compare and contrast** parallel play and cooperative play.
- **List** six ways to help children develop social skills.
- **Explain** the purpose of guidance.

Writing Activity 🖊 *Poem*

Temper Tantrum Imagine that a toddler is having a temper tantrum. She is frustrated that she cannot have her way. Write a poem about the tantrum. Make your poem funny or serious, but be sure it expresses emotion.

Writing Tips Remember that not all poems rhyme. Here are some tips to help you get started:

1. Use language that creates interesting images.
2. Use emotion-packed words.
3. Your poem should have a tempo or rhythm. Try setting your poem to music!

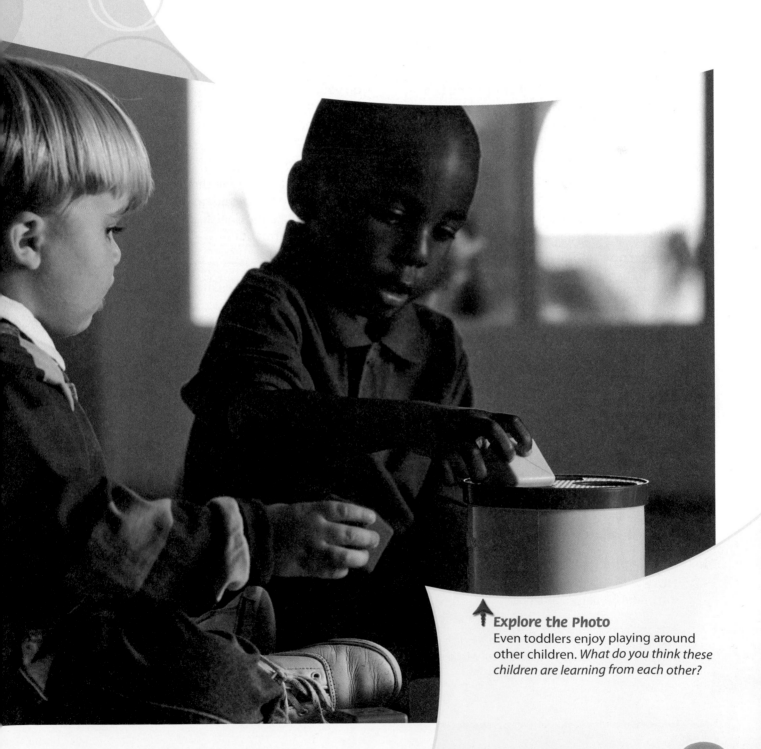

Section 11.1 Emotional Development from One to Three

Section 11.2 Social Development from One to Three

Explore the Photo
Even toddlers enjoy playing around other children. *What do you think these children are learning from each other?*

Emotional Development from One to Three

Reading Guide

Before You Read

Get Your Rest The better rested you are when you study, the more likely you will be to remember the information later. Studying in the same state of mind as when you take a test helps ensure your best performance.

Read to Learn
Key Concepts
- **Identify** the factors that contribute to a child's emotional development.
- **Describe** six specific emotions children ages eighteen months to three years show.
- **List** the four signs of a healthy relationship between parents and a child.
- **Identify** four ways to help children get adequate sleep.

Main Idea
Children go through a series of emotional stages. Each child develops differently based on his or her experiences and temperament. Adequate sleep is vital to good emotional development.

Content Vocabulary
◇ self-centered
◇ negativism
◇ temper tantrum
◇ phobia
◇ separation anxiety
◇ sibling rivalry
◇ empathy
◇ self-concept
◇ sleep-deprived
◇ REM sleep
◇ NREM sleep

Academic Vocabulary
You will find these words in your reading and on your tests. Use the glossary to look up their definitions if necessary.
■ perceptive
■ adequate

Graphic Organizer
As you read, look for the three types of positive guidance to use with a negative child. Use a chart like the one shown to help organize your information.

 Graphic Organizer Go to this book's Online Learning Center at **glencoe.com** to print out this graphic organizer.

Academic Standards · · · · · · · · · · · · · · · · ·

 English Language Arts

NCTE 2 Read literature to build an understanding of the human experience.

 Science

NSES A Develop abilities necessary to do scientific inquiry, understanding about scientific inquiry.

NCTE *National Council of Teachers of English*
NCTM *National Council of Teachers of Mathematics*

NSES *National Science Education Standards*
NCSS *National Council for the Social Studies*

Emotional Patterns

Emotional development tends to go in cycles throughout childhood. The cycles are especially pronounced in children ages one to three years old. They develop new emotions, such as jealousy, that they had not felt before. They have periods of frustration and rebellion, but they also have periods of happiness, calmness, and stability. Negative periods tend to alternate with positive periods, and they are generally related to the age of the child.

Of course, each child is an individual. Claire may go through a negative period at eighteen months, while Jamal may not experience this until age two. Matthew may not seem to go through it at all. Generally, though, children can be expected to go through certain distinct emotional phases at certain ages, as shown in **Figure 11.1** on pages 322–323.

Emotional development depends primarily on two factors: the child's experiences and the child's temperament. Understanding these factors can help in dealing with such issues as negativism, tantrums, or sibling rivalry. It also helps you guide a child to desirable behavior.

Individual Differences

There are general patterns to how children develop emotionally. However, each child is unique and will develop in a special way. Individual differences can be very noticeable between the first and fourth birthdays. The differences are partly due to the different experiences that each child has. An only child, for example, will have different experiences from a child who is one of five children. The experiences of twins or triplets will be different from the experiences of other children.

Individual differences in emotional development also result from the child's temperament. Temperament is the way the child naturally responds to other people and events. An intense child may become more frustrated than an adaptable child. A more **perceptive**, or observant, child may show more empathy than one who is less perceptive.

It is important to keep in mind these differences in temperament when teaching children how to control their emotions. Connor, for example, is very perceptive. He is aware of his environment. He can also be easily distracted.

Family Members
Each member of a family is an individual. *What are some ways that the emotional needs of a parent are different from those of a two-year-old?*

When Connor begins a temper tantrum, his mother tries to turn his attention to something new. She might point out a squirrel playing outside the window. Such a technique may not work on Nala, who adapts to change slowly. She dislikes surprises—even pleasant ones. Her parents have to give her plenty of warning and time to adjust before any change in her routine. This could include visitors arriving or even a new food for dinner.

Eighteen Months

By the age of eighteen months, children have become self-centered. The term **self-centered** refers to thinking about one's own needs and wants and not those of others. This is not surprising. During infancy caregivers promptly meet the child's needs and desires. This is appropriate for infants. By eighteen months, though, caregivers begin to teach the child that some desires will not be met right away. Some requests will never be met. This is a difficult lesson for the eighteen-month-old to begin learning.

Spoken instructions are not always successful with children of this age. The young toddler is likely to do the opposite of what is asked. At this age, the child's favorite response to everything is "no." Saying "no" allows the child to feel some control over his or her world.

It is important to realize that negativism is normal for a young toddler. **Negativism** means doing the opposite of what others want. It has a number of causes:

- **The Desire for Independence** Saying "no" is a child's way of saying, "Let me decide for myself." The child may even say "no" to things that he or she would really like to do. Children just want the chance to make the decision.

Figure 11.1 An Emotional Roller Coaster

Most young children go through predictable stages in their emotional development. *How do children typically change between eighteen months and two years of age?*

Two Years The two-year-old is affectionate and may often be in the caregiver's way.

Eighteen Months The eighteen-month-old is defiant, trying to establish some control over her life.

- **Frustration** Toddlers want to do more than their bodies are able to do. They do not have the language skills yet to express all their feelings. The frustration that results is often expressed in a simple and emphatic "No!"
- **The Realization of Being a Separate Person** This idea is both exciting and frightening. The child welcomes the power and independence of being a separate person. At times, though, he or she still wants a tight bond with a primary caregiver.

Negativism can produce a battle of wills between child and parent. There are strategies to help prevent conflicts. One is to eliminate as many restrictions as possible. For example, put fragile objects away instead of asking an eighteen-month-old not to touch them. As the child gets older, they can be put back in place.

Positive guidance can also help deal with a child who is negative. Use these tips:

- **Give Choices** Instead of saying "Pick up your books and toys," ask, "Which will you pick up first—the books or the toys?" Having choices allows the child to have control. Limit choices to two options, however. Toddlers cannot think about three or four things at a time.
- **Redirect the Child** If possible, distract the child from the issue that is causing the negative response. You may be able to go back to the issue later, when the child is calmer. For example, Julia was having trouble stacking her blocks. So her mother suggested instead that they read a book.
- **Encourage Talking** You can help children learn to use words to communicate how they feel. Being able to talk will help both you and the child understand and deal with those feelings. Asking "What's wrong, Susie?" or "Don't you like that?" encourages children to share what they are feeling.

Three Years The three-year-old is generally a happy child who is eager to help.

Two and One-Half Years At two and one-half, the child may feel overwhelmed. Frustration then becomes anger.

Three and One-Half Years At three and one-half years, a child is often bothered by fears.

Around eighteen months, a child may start to have temper tantrums. A **temper tantrum** is when children release anger or frustration by screaming, crying, kicking, pounding, and sometimes holding their breath. These tantrums may occur until age three or four. Even seemingly minor frustrations can cause temper tantrums. Try to help the child find calmer ways of expressing these feelings. For ways to calm a toddler who is having a temper tantrum, see the Parenting Skills feature on page 343.

Two Years

Emotionally, two-year-olds are less at odds with the world than eighteen-month-olds. The speech and motor skills of a two-year-old have improved. This eases some frustration. Christy can now say she wants milk instead of juice. A two-year-old also understands more and is able to wait longer for various needs to be met.

At age two, a child expresses love and affection freely and seeks approval and praise. Though the child still has some emotional outbursts, they are fewer and less intense. Two-year-olds are easier to reason with. They usually get along better with parents and other children. They tend to be more outgoing and friendly, and less self-centered.

Two and One-Half Years

Just as parents and caregivers begin to adjust to a smoother, less intense toddler, the child enters another difficult stage. This period may seem even more difficult for caregivers than the eighteen-month-old stage. At two and one-half, toddlers are not as easily distracted as they were at eighteen months.

Children this age are learning so much that they often feel overwhelmed. Their desires and their ability to understand tasks exceed their physical ability to perform. For example, they may want their blocks stacked up in a certain way. However, they might accidentally knock the blocks over before they finish the structure. They may know what they want to say but cannot always say it clearly. These situations produce frustrations that may boil over.

At two and one-half, children struggle with immaturity and a powerful need for independence. Their drive for independence causes children to resist pressures to conform. They are sensitive about being bossed, shown, helped, or directed during this stage. They can be stubborn, demanding, and domineering. However, their moods change rapidly, and within a short time they can become lovable and completely charming.

Children at this age have a need for consistency. They want the same routines, carried out the same way, every day. Following a routine is their way of coping with a confusing world. A routine helps children build confidence and a feeling of security.

At two and one-half, children feel both independent and dependent. Sometimes they seek help. Other times, they want to do things by themselves. They require love and patience, especially when their behavior is neither lovable nor patient. They need flexible limits rather than hard-and-fast rules.

Three Years

Three-year-olds generally have a happier nature than two-year-olds. They are more cooperative and are learning to be considerate. They are more physically capable and, therefore, less frustrated than two-year-olds.

Three-year-olds become more willing to take directions from others. They will modify their behavior to win the praise and affection they crave. In general, three-year-olds have fewer temper tantrums than younger children.

{ **Expert Advice...** }

"Emotional well-being and social competence provide a strong foundation for emerging cognitive abilities, and together they are the bricks and mortar that comprise the foundation of human development."

— *The Science of Early Childhood Development,* National Scientific Council on the Developing Child

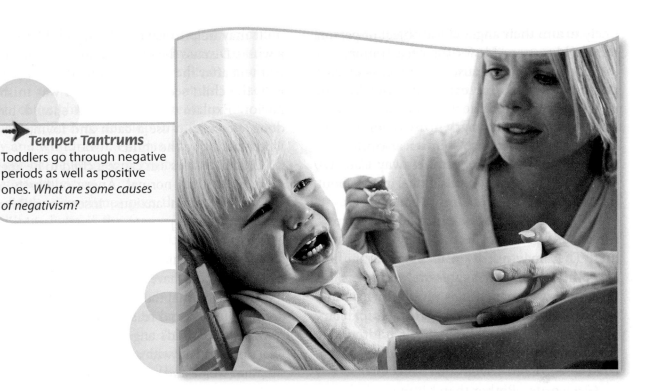

Temper Tantrums
Toddlers go through negative periods as well as positive ones. *What are some causes of negativism?*

At three, children like to talk and are much better at it. They talk to their toys, their playmates, themselves, and even to their imaginary friends. They often want to tell their parents all about their day. They also respond when others talk to them, and they can be reasoned with and controlled by words.

Three and One-Half Years

The self-confident three-year-old suddenly becomes very insecure at age three and one-half. Parents may feel that the child is going backward rather than forward emotionally.

Fears are common at this age. The child may be afraid of the dark, imaginary monsters, strangers, or loud noises. Emotional tension and insecurity often show up in physical ways too. Some children may start habits, such as thumb sucking or nail biting, to provide self-soothing. Others stumble or stutter.

At three and one-half, children try to ensure their own security by controlling their environment. They may issue insistent demands, such as "I want to sit on the floor to eat lunch!" or "Talk to me!"

> ✓ **Reading Check** **Identify** What are three ways a parent can help a child who is being negative?

Specific Emotions

Even young babies have specific emotions. How children express emotions changes as they get older. Children express their emotions openly until the age of two or three. They begin to learn socially acceptable ways of displaying feelings after the age of three. For example, eighteen-month-old Marta shows anger by kicking and screaming. Jonathan, at age three and one-half, expresses anger through words. The specific emotions children between the ages of eighteen months and three years generally show include anger, fear, jealousy, love, affection, and empathy.

Anger

Anger is often the child's way of reacting to frustration. How children show that anger changes over the years. By the time children are three years old, they are less violent and explosive. They are less likely to hit or kick. Physical attacks give way to name-calling, pouting, or scolding.

The target of a child's anger changes in these years as well. An eighteen-month-old who has a tantrum usually does not direct the anger toward a specific person or thing. Beginning around ages two to three, children are more

> **Toddlers and Jealousy**
> A new baby sometimes causes jealousy in a toddler. *What are some ways parents can help prevent sibling rivalry?*

Many children who feel separation anxiety have trouble going to sleep at night. A bedtime routine and a reminder that a parent is nearby can help lessen these fears. Here are some other ways to help toddlers deal with their fears:

- Offer support and understanding. Never make children feel ashamed of their fears.
- Encourage children to talk about their fears. Be sure to listen intently. Often talking about fears can diminish their impact.
- Sometimes, it is best to accept the fear and avoid trying to force the child to confront it. Often, it will go away on its own. Lily became suddenly afraid of lizards when she was two. By the time Lily was three, though, she enjoyed looking for the lizards. She was not afraid anymore.
- Read books together about a child who experiences fear. Talking about the book may help relieve the child's fears.
- Make unfamiliar situations more secure. Discuss new experiences and events in advance to help the child know what to expect. If possible, go with the child to new places.
- Teach the child how to control frightening situations. Getting in a swimming pool terrified Jacob, so his aunt showed him how to sit on the side and dangle his feet in the water.

Jealousy

Jealousy is an emotion that usually crops up some time during a child's second year. A twelve-month-old does not show any jealousy. By the age of eighteen months, though, jealousy becomes very pronounced. It reaches its peak when a child is about three. Then it becomes less intense as outside relationships begin to loosen a child's ties to home and parents. Sometimes parents become the target of a child's jealousy. For example, a toddler may resent any show of affection between parents because the child cannot yet understand that parents have enough love for everyone.

Sibling rivalry is the competition between brothers or sisters for parents' affection and attention. It is a common cause of jealousy. Children sometimes become jealous when a new baby is born. For example, a toddler finds that the attention he once received is now focused on a new baby. Some young children react to a new baby by trying to get more attention. They may show off or act in inappropriate ways. Sometimes they revert, or go back, to baby-like behaviors, such as wetting the bed or using baby talk. Some may behave aggressively towards the younger sibling.

Parents should understand that fear of losing the parent's love caused the negative behavior. The child needs more affection and reassurance, not punishment. Because of sibling rivalry, many experts say it is never safe to leave a baby alone with a toddler.

Sibling rivalry does not occur only when there is a newborn. One day Glen came home from work to find himself overwhelmed by hugs from both his four-year-old, Becky, and his three-year-old, Curt. The children soon began pushing and shoving, trying to block the other child from getting near their father.

There are steps a parent can take to help cut down on sibling rivalry:

- Make sure that each child feels love and appreciation.
- Set aside one-on-one time with each child.
- Avoid making comments that compare one child to another.
- Let the children take turns in choosing activities, such as a game the family plays together or a movie to watch.
- Make it clear that you will not accept one child tattling to get another one in trouble.

- Talk to children about their jealousy, how hard it can be to have siblings, and how lucky they are to have each other.

Love and Affection

The relationships that children have with others between the ages of one and three form the basis of their capacity for love and affection in later life. Young children must learn to love.

Babies first love those who satisfy their physical needs. Gradually, as children grow older, their affection expands to include siblings, pets, and people outside the home.

Loving relationships between parents or other caregivers and children need to be strong but not smothering. A child who depends entirely on caregivers for love has difficulty forming other relationships.

Empathy

For years, people believed that infants and toddlers were so self-centered they could not feel anything toward someone who was unhappy. Research shows that view to be false.

Showing Affection
Young children gradually learn to show love and affection for others. *Have you seen a young child try to comfort someone who seemed unhappy?*

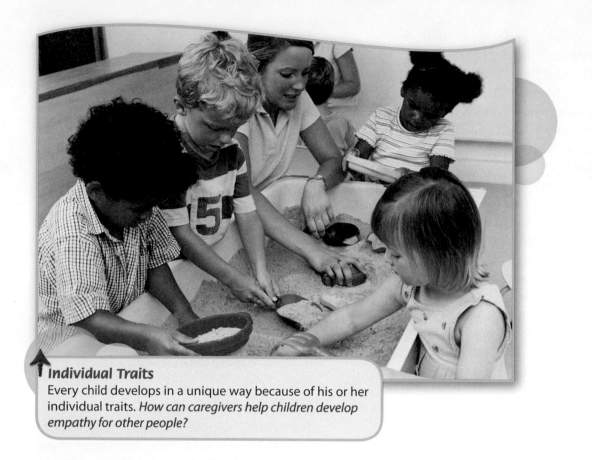

Individual Traits
Every child develops in a unique way because of his or her individual traits. *How can caregivers help children develop empathy for other people?*

It is true that a toddler is mainly self-focused. However, the self is not their only focus. Children this age are becoming more aware of people around them. They may be exposed to more children through child care or play groups.

Between twelve and eighteen months of age, children begin to understand that their actions can hurt others. This is the first step toward developing empathy. **Empathy** is the ability to understand how another person feels. Children as young as one year old may pat and talk to another child who is unhappy. By age two, a child can show empathy. For example, when two-year-old Antonio saw that Avery was upset, he offered Avery his favorite stuffed animal as a way to cheer him up.

Caregivers can help teach children to show empathy. If a child in your care does something to hurt someone's feelings, such as grabbing a toy, have the child give back the toy and apologize. Then ask the child to take an active step toward making the wronged child feel better, such as sharing another toy.

✓ **Reading Check**) **Describe** What types of children are more likely to feel angry ?

Emotional Adjustment

How can parents tell whether a child's emotional development is on the right track? Between their first and fourth birthdays, the most important clue is the relationship of children with their parents or other primary caregivers. The early pattern established between the familiar adults and the child will shape the child's relationships later in life as a friend, coworker, and spouse.

These are signs that a child has a healthy relationship with his or her parents:
- Seeks approval and praise
- Turns to parents and caregivers for comfort and help
- Tells caregivers about significant events so they can share in the joy and sorrow
- Accepts limits and discipline without too much resistance

Another indicator of emotional adjustment is a child's relationship with siblings. Some quarreling with brothers and sisters is bound to occur. However, the child who is continuously and bitterly at odds with brothers and sisters, in spite of parents' efforts to ease the friction, may need counseling. If emotional problems are dealt with early, it can make a difference for a lifetime.

Promote Positive Self-Concept

As they grow, children become more aware of their individual differences. The individual traits that make them special become part of their self-concept. **Self-concept** is how people see themselves. Self-concepts can be positive or negative. Children who see themselves as good and capable have a positive self-concept. Children who see themselves as bad or unable to do tasks have a negative self-concept.

Self-concept is different from self-esteem. Self-concept is what you think you are like as a person. Self-esteem is how highly you value yourself.

Children form their self-concept in response to the actions, attitudes, and comments of others. The years from one to three are crucial in a child's development of self-concept. Parents or primary caregivers usually spend the most time with the young child during this time. Therefore, they have the strongest influence on the child's self-concept.

Young children believe what others say about them. The opinions of others influence how children behave. Often, when children hear adults say that they are good, they try to act the part. If they constantly hear that they are bad or stupid, they will believe it and live up to that image.

Even young toddlers who cannot yet understand words are tuned in to the body language and tone of voice of adults. Adults' words and actions continue to have a strong influence on children until they are old enough to judge their own actions. By that time, however, their self-concept can be firmly established.

Another factor in building a positive self-concept is mastery of skills. For this reason, it is important to give infants and toddlers the chance to explore their world. Through exploration, children have the opportunity to master skills. Being able to learn skills such as finding toys and stacking blocks gives a sense of confidence. Self-confidence helps lead to a positive self-concept.

Discourage Negative Behavior

Some parents worry that correcting misbehavior will damage their child's self-concept. However, a positive self-concept is based on actual achievement. By teaching and praising young children for appropriate behaviors, self-esteem is enhanced. Here are some effective ways to discourage negative behaviors.

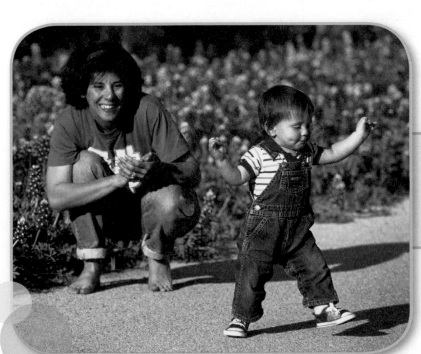

Giving Praise
It is important that young children have a good relationship with parents and other caregivers. *Why is it important that young children receive love from parents and caregivers?*

- **Explore feelings.** Read stories to a child or watch children's videos together. Then discuss ways that the characters handled their feelings or problems. This shows the child that others have the same feelings. It also helps the child cope with the feelings.

- **Acknowledge feelings.** When a playmate takes a toddler's toy, grabbing or hitting may be a natural reaction. Caregivers should explain why this response is not acceptable and give an alternative. They might say, "Everyone gets angry at times, but it's not okay to hurt people. Ask your friend for the toy back or choose another one."

- **Give choices.** Offer simple choices to empower children. Choosing what shirt to wear or what book to read makes a child feel important. Making a choice also gives them a sense of control.

✓ **Reading Check** **Summarize** What are three ways that a parent can discourage negative behavior?

Sleep and Emotional Behavior

A scream woke Joshua's parents in the middle of the night. It was not the first time that their three-year-old son had awakened terrified from a bad dream. Every time that Joshua woke up screaming, his parents rushed into his room and comforted him. Sometimes he was so scared that a parent had to stay with him so that he could go back to sleep.

Most sleep problems in children are normal. In fact, they are one of the most common problems that children experience. Parents can help ease sleep problems by understanding what causes them. Fears are a frequent cause of sleep problems. A bedtime routine and a reminder that a parent is nearby can help lessen these fears. Separation anxiety can also cause nightmares that wake the child. Asking the child to describe the nightmare can help calm him or her. Also, by hearing about a dream, the parent may gain insight into the cause of the nightmare.

Some children find it hard to fall back asleep after waking in the night. Children may associate a certain routine, such as being rocked or hearing a lullaby, with sleeping. Parents may need to repeat bedtime routines in the middle of the night to restore sleep.

Sleep problems also can be caused by something as simple as pajamas that are too tight. Or there could be a more serious cause such as an ear infection or other illness. Parents concerned about the cause of a child's sleep problem should talk to their pediatrician.

The Importance of Adequate Sleep

Adequate, or sufficient, sleep is as essential to good physical and emotional health as adequate nutrition. Without enough sleep, children can become sleep deprived. **Sleep deprived** means lacking adequate sleep. Being sleep deprived can affect a child's temperament and ability to do even simple tasks during the day. Children may be less alert, inattentive, and even hyperactive. To develop and function properly, one- to three-year-olds need twelve to fourteen hours of sleep each night.

Sleep Cycles

Children, like adults, go through cycles of sleep each night. **REM sleep** is a sleep cycle characterized by rapid eye movement. This is a light sleep during which dreams occur. **NREM sleep** is a cycle of sleep in which rapid eye movement does not occur. NREM sleep is a deep sleep. Children are more likely to wake up during the REM sleep cycle.

Newborns have short sleep cycles and can go through an entire cycle of REM and NREM in about an hour. By about four months of age, babies can sleep six to eight hours at a time. This increases to ten to twelve hours by six months of age.

Prevent Sleep Deprivation

What are signs of sleep deprivation? Children who do not get enough sleep must be awakened each morning and tend to be tired all day. They have trouble thinking and are at risk of hurting themselves while playing. They can also be fussy and hard to get along with. Sleep deprivation is more apparent when a child has to get up on a regular schedule. Here are some ways to help ensure that children get adequate sleep:

- **Determine a child's best bedtime.** People need different amounts of sleep. When does a child usually begin to get tired? Use that as a guide. Children who stay up past this normal bedtime may get a second wind and have trouble falling asleep.
- **Limit toys in the bed.** Toys might signal playtime rather than sleep time. A favorite stuffed animal is okay.
- **Establish a bedtime routine.** Every night, follow the same pattern such as a bath, brushing teeth, and a bedtime story.
- **Keep bedtime pleasant.** Talk and cuddle with the child. You might also try giving a soothing backrub.

Section 11.1 After You Read

Review Key Concepts

1. **Describe** the changes in emotions that occur in children between ages three and three and one-half years.
2. **Explain** the difference between self-concept and self-esteem.
3. **Identify** what separation anxiety is and at what age it typically becomes the strongest.
4. **Summarize** what parents can do to minimize sibling rivalry.

Practice Academic Skills

 English Language Skills

5. Locate a book for young children that deals with emotional issues such as a fear of the dark or a new baby in the family. Write a paragraph evaluating the book. Do you think it would help a young child?

 Science

6. Conduct research to learn more about sleep cycles and the differences between REM and NREM sleep. Write a report describing what you have learned. You may wish to include charts in your report.

 Check Your Answers Check your answers at this book's Online Learning Center at **glencoe.com**.

> **NCTE 2** Read literature to build an understanding of the human experience.

> **NSES A** Develop abilities necessary to do scientific inquiry, understanding about scientific inquiry.

Reading Guide

Before You Read

Prefixes Prefixes can help you determine a word's meaning. The prefix *co-* provides a clue to the meaning of *cooperation*. As you read, look for words with prefixes and check their meanings in a dictionary.

Read to Learn
Key Concepts
- **Compare and contrast** parallel play and cooperative play.
- **List** six ways to help children develop social skills.
- **Explain** the purpose of guidance.

Main Idea
Children learn to get along with others through a process called *socialization*. They begin to make friends and deal with conflict. With adult guidance, they gradually achieve self-discipline.

Content Vocabulary
◇ socialization
◇ parallel play
◇ cooperative play
◇ self-discipline
◇ autonomy
◇ time-out

 Graphic Organizer Go to this book's Online Learning Center at **glencoe.com** to print out this graphic organizer.

Academic Vocabulary
You will find these words in your reading and on your tests. Use the glossary to look up their definitions if necessary.
- gauge
- distraction

Graphic Organizer
As you read, look for ways to guide behavior. Note a brief description of each approach. Use a chart like the one shown to help organize your information. Add additional circles as needed.

Set Limits

Guidance

Promote Sharing

Academic Standards

 English Language Arts

NCTE 4 Use written language to communicate effectively.

 Social Studies

NCSS I A Culture Analyze and explain the ways groups, societies, and cultures address human needs and concerns.

NCTE *National Council of Teachers of English*
NCTM *National Council of Teachers of Mathematics*

NSES *National Science Education Standards*
NCSS *National Council for the Social Studies*

General Social Patterns

Young children gradually learn how to get along with other people. They first learn how to get along with members of their own families, and then with people in other groups. The process of learning to get along with others is called **socialization**. These social skills will stay with them throughout their lives. Through socialization, children can be expected to learn various social skills by certain ages, as seen in **Figure 11.2** on page 337. Of course, as with other areas of development, individual differences may influence when, and in what order, social skills are learned. If parents are concerned about a child's development, they should talk to their pediatrician.

Eighteen Months

Children usually begin developing some independence from the family unit by eighteen months of age. For most children, the closest relationships continue to be those with their families. However, toddlers need to learn about the outside world. This may mean trips to the playground or other opportunities to be with children and adults who are not part of the family, such as at child care centers.

Children at this age do not really interact with one another much, even when they are playing in the same area. Instead, children engage in parallel play. **Parallel play** is when children play near, but not actually with, other children. Each child plays independently. Two or more children may reach for the same toy, but the children are not really interacting with one another.

At eighteen months, toddlers often seem to treat other people more as objects than as human beings. At this stage, the toddler is intent on satisfying strong desires without regard for the person who interferes. There may be conflicts over toys that result in screaming, hitting, biting, or hair pulling. Suppose Billy really wants a certain truck, but Keith is playing with it. Billy might hit Keith to try and get the truck.

Children of this age can understand that their actions have consequences for others. However, this understanding is limited to actions that have direct, immediate, and physical results. For

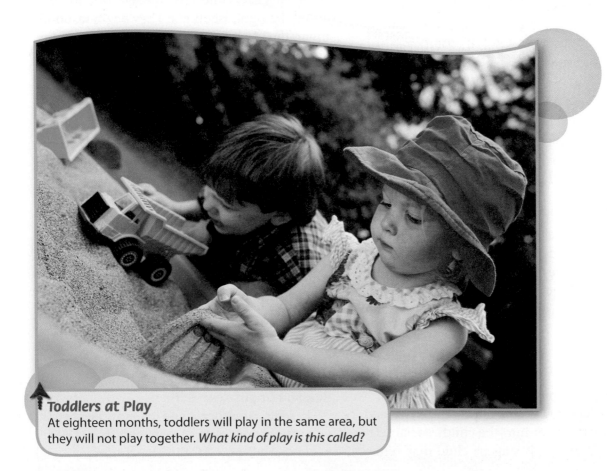

Toddlers at Play
At eighteen months, toddlers will play in the same area, but they will not play together. *What kind of play is this called?*

Cooperative Play
By the age of three, children engage in cooperative play. *What type of strategies do children use to resolve conflicts when playing together?*

example, eighteen-month-old Jill hits Rachel. Rachel cries. Jill can see the immediate result her action caused.

Two Years

By age two, children have begun to develop an impressive list of social skills. Two-year-olds are especially good at understanding and interacting with their main caregivers. Children can read their caregiver's moods and **gauge**, or judge, what kind of behavior the caregiver is likely to accept. As their speech abilities develop, toddlers are increasingly able to communicate with others.

Two-year-olds have fun playing with someone else, though they usually continue to engage in parallel play. At two, they start to understand the idea of sharing or taking turns. Children this age like to please other people. Occasionally, they are willing to put the wishes of someone else (usually an adult) above their own wishes.

Two and One-Half Years

The negativism that characterizes the emotional development of the child at age two and one-half carries over into the child's social relationships. During this stage, a child may refuse to do anything at all for one person, while happily doing almost anything another person asks. This can be especially frustrating if the child refuses to listen to a parent or caregiver.

At this age, children are beginning to learn about the rights of others. They begin responding to the idea of fairness, although at first they are more concerned with what is fair to them. Social play is still parallel and works best with only two children. There are frequent, but brief, squabbles during play. Children generally forget them quickly though.

Three Years

People become important to children of this age. A three-year-old will share, help, or do things another person's way just to please someone.

Three-year-olds begin to engage in cooperative play. **Cooperative play** is a type of play in which children play and interact with one another. They build sand castles together, push toy tractors down the same roads, and park their toy cars side by side in the same area. They also can work together in small groups to build with blocks, act out events for doll families, and fit puzzles together.

Parents or other main caregivers are still very important to three-year-olds, but they are no longer all-powerful in the children's social lives. Most toddlers of this age seek friends on their own. They also may prefer some children over others as friends.

Three and One-Half Years

By age three and one-half, children's play becomes more complex and includes more conversation. Disagreements with playmates occur less often. Because children this age enjoy the company of others, they realize they must share toys and accept some things they do not like in order to get along with friends.

At three and one-half, children can use several different strategies to resolve conflicts. Esteban tried to take a block that was behind Ramon, who was also playing with blocks. When Ramon said, "That's my block," Esteban replied, "Oh, okay," and put it down. Kelly and Rosa were playing with cars. When Kelly reached for Rosa's yellow car, Rosa objected and then said "You can have it if you give me that red one of yours."

Children this age show an increasing ability to evaluate friendships. For example, a child may say, "I don't like to have Kevin come here. He doesn't play nice." Children who are closer friends begin to exclude others. A child may become jealous and not want to "share" a friend with other children.

At this age, children also take more notice of what others are like. They become more likely to compare themselves to other children. The comparison is not always to their own advantage. One day, Allison asked her mother, "Why does Libby always win when we race?" Her mother agreed that Libby was faster but also pointed out things that Allison did well. In this way, she acknowledged that Allison was not as skilled as Libby in one area but had other skills of her own.

✓ **Reading Check** **Compare** Describe the social development of a child who just turned two. How does it differ from that of a child six months older?

Figure 11.2 **Social Developmental Milestones—Ages 1–3**

Children begin engaging in cooperative play and sharing when they are about three years old. *How do you think a child's social development reflects the child's emotional development?*

Age	Developmental Milestones
1 Year	❖ Plays alone but often near others ❖ Dislikes sharing toys ❖ Desires approval ❖ Fears some strangers
2 Years	❖ Engages in parallel play ❖ Plays simple games with others ❖ Bosses other children ❖ Says "please" if prompted
3 Years	❖ Engages in some cooperative play ❖ Takes turns ❖ Likes to help ❖ Shows affection

"Your preschool child is positively asking you to tell him what does and does not earn approval, so he is ready to learn any social refinement of being human which you will teach him . . . He knows now that he wants your love and he has learned how to ask for it."

— Penelope Leach, child development specialist and author, *Your Baby and Child*

Making Friends

The ability to make friends is important to normal social development. A child who is comfortable and friendly with others and who has at least one friend is usually developing normally. However, if a child is unable or unwilling to make friends, it is important to discover the cause and take steps to help. For example, a shy child sometimes needs coaching on what to say or how to act so that he or she can join others in play.

Even very young children need contact with other people. This is how they learn the give-and-take of socializing. Children who begin to play with others at the age of one or two are less likely to be afraid in these early social situations. They learn to cope with the occasional punches and toy snatching of other one- and two-year-olds.

When young children spend almost all of their time with adults, they may have difficulty interacting with others their own age. Adults are more polite and considerate than children. Children need to learn to enjoy the rough-and-tumble friendship of other children. If this learning is delayed until school age, the adjustment is more difficult. A five- or six-year-old's feelings are more easily hurt.

All children sometimes have disagreements and arguments. Whether or not a caregiver should step in depends on the situation.

If two children are relatively evenly matched and there is no physical or emotional harm being done, the caregiver can simply observe the situation. Children need to learn how to solve social problems on their own. If it looks as though someone might get hurt, the caregiver needs to help the children solve the problem. It is best for the children if the caregiver does not impose a solution but instead guides the children to find one for themselves.

Social Skills

Knowing how to get along with others is key to success and happiness. This ability depends upon social skills. Here are some ways to help children develop social skills:

- **Establish a basic set of rules to guide social behavior.** The rules will probably center on teaching respect for self, for others, and for things. For example, "No throwing toys." "Don't hit people."
- **Model good social skills.** Children are great imitators. They learn best by being shown what to do rather than by just being told. For instance, parents who talk politely to others are more likely to get their children to do so.
- **Help children understand and respect others' feelings.** You might show a child pictures of people's faces with a variety of expressions. Ask the child to guess how the person in the picture might be feeling, such as sad or angry. Talking about what these feelings mean can help the child develop empathy. Also, talk to the child about how you are feeling.
- **Show respect for other people's belongings.** Tell a child, for example, not to touch grandma's flower vase, because it might get broken. This would make grandma very sad.
- **Show children how to use words rather than physically striking out.** Explain how using appropriate words when they are angry is better than hitting or shoving.
- **Help children learn specific social skills.** Demonstrate how to share a toy, wait for a turn, and be kind to one another.

Many children do things such as biting and kicking other children that catch their parents and caregivers off guard. Occasionally, these behaviors go beyond what is considered normal. Some children never develop empathy. They consistently ignore the feelings and rights of others.

When this behavior is extreme, the child may be diagnosed with antisocial personality disorder. This is a serious psychiatric condition. Because individuals typically start showing signs of antisocial personality disorder in childhood, here are some signs caregivers should watch for:

- Is cruel to animals
- Sets fires
- Fights with other children much more frequently than others of that age
- Shows no concern when others are sad or hurt

Children with these symptoms need to be evaluated by a mental health professional. If they are diagnosed with antisocial personality disorder, treatment should begin as early as possible. Both medication and psychotherapy may be used to aid the child's social and emotional development.

Critical Thinking Conduct research to find out what mental health professionals believe causes antisocial personality disorder. Create an oral presentation discussing what you learned. Conclude by explaining what you think can be done to reduce its occurrence.

Imaginary Friends

Many toddlers begin to have imaginary friends. Some keep the same imaginary friend for a long time. It can last from several months to a year. Others have several different imaginary friends. Some toddlers have imaginary animals as friends. Some even have dragons or other imaginary creatures as friends. All of these are normal.

Imaginary friends may appear in a toddler's imagination as early as age two. These friends are even more common when a child is between ages three and four. This is when children have rich imaginations and are interested in fantasy.

Some parents worry that their child invents imaginary friends because he or she is unable to make real friends. They are concerned that an imaginary friend is a sign of unhappiness or problems coping with life. In fact, an imaginary friend helps a child experiment with different feelings. Some children use an imaginary friend as a way of working through their negative feelings. For others, the friend mirrors everything the child does or experiences. The child may then talk to the family about how the imaginary friend felt about these experiences. In this way, children can examine their own thoughts and feelings.

Imaginary friends usually fade away. Crystal simply stopped talking about her imaginary friend when she started school. Paul had an imaginary friend when he was three, but the friend was gone by the time Paul turned four. There is no cause for concern unless the child continues to talk to an imaginary friend after about age six. If a parent is concerned, a pediatrician or counselor may be able to help.

✓ **Reading Check** **Infer** What may happen to the social development of children who spend most of their time with adults?

Guiding Behavior

Guiding children's behavior does not simply mean making children behave and punishing them when they do something wrong. Punishment is only a small part of guidance. Guidance means using firmness and understanding to help children learn self-discipline. **Self-discipline** is the ability of children to control their own behavior. Effective guidance helps children learn to get along with others and to handle their own feelings. It promotes security and a positive feeling about self.

Guidance also helps children with moral development. Very young children understand right from wrong only in terms of being praised or scolded. Gradually, children develop a conscience, or an inner sense of what is right. As children mature, they use their conscience to act morally when facing new situations.

Approaches by Age

Effective guidance depends upon a child's age as well as emotional and social development. There is no one best approach to guidance.

Caregivers need to consider the unique personality of each child, as well as each child's age, stage of development, and ability to understand. Different approaches may be more or less effective at various ages. Parents may also need to use different approaches with each sibling.

Being consistent is a major factor in guiding children's behavior. Make clear rules and apply them in the same way in all situations. Consistency helps children know what is expected of them and what responses they can expect from caregivers. Consistency is especially important when more than one person cares for a child. Parents and other caregivers need to agree on rules and ways to enforce them.

One Year to Fifteen Months

Distracting children and physically removing them from forbidden activities or places works best for this age. This is because they cannot yet understand adult reasoning. For example, Kareem tried to follow the lawn mower around the yard when his brother was cutting the grass. His older sister picked Kareem up and took him into the house, saying, "Let's see if we can find the book about the bear."

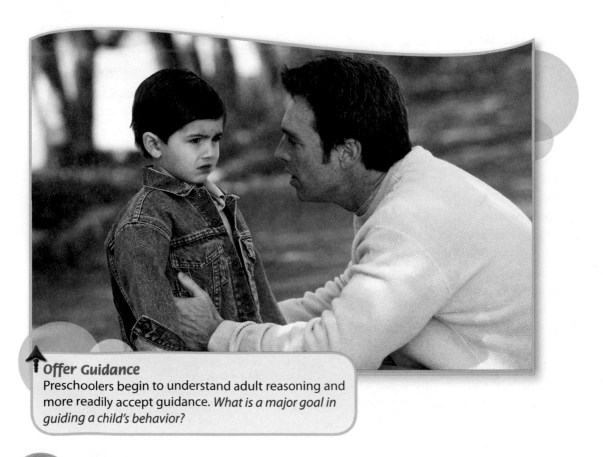

Offer Guidance
Preschoolers begin to understand adult reasoning and more readily accept guidance. *What is a major goal in guiding a child's behavior?*

What Would You Do?

Sharing

Madison and Morgan are sisters and love to play together. Madison is two and Morgan is three. Because they are so close in age, they share everything, from a bedroom to clothes to toys. Madison gets clothes and toys that her sister has outgrown, which is fine with her. She is delighted when she can finally call a toy her own. This can create a problem, however. Sometimes if Madison is playing with a toy that once belonged to Morgan, Morgan wants it back. She tries to snatch it away from her little sister. While both girls have difficulty sharing, Morgan is better able to understand the concept of taking turns. But for two-year-old Madison, if someone else is playing with her toy, she cries until it is returned to her. Morgan, however, has learned about sharing at preschool, where she must share things with eleven other children.

Write About It Imagine that you are these two girls' parent. Write a paragraph describing a situation where Morgan has grabbed a toy that used to belong to her. What might you say to Morgan to help her understand Madison's point of view?

Fifteen Months to Two Years

Children this age require spoken restrictions as well as a **distraction**, or diversion. Lee began playing with toy cars on the driveway. His father took him by the hand and said, "Let's take your cars into the backyard. You'll have more room there. The driveway isn't a safe place to play." His father removed him from the dangerous place, but also told him why. Lee may have to be reminded of the restriction a few times, but will eventually understand it.

Two to Three Years

By the age of two, children are usually able to understand spoken commands and simple explanations. Two-year-olds can begin to grasp the reasoning of adults. Caregivers who explain their reasons to children over age two get better results than those who only issue commands. When Kerri's mother saw that the two-and-one-half-year-old was still not dressed, she said, "Kerri, you need to get dressed now because Grandma will be here soon to go shopping with us. We can't go unless we are ready. Do you need any help?"

Three Years

Three-year-olds accept reasonable, loving guidance more readily than children of other ages. They like to please, and they may be quick to remind a parent that they are obedient. Marcus came inside on a rainy day and said, "I remembered to wear my boots today. See my clean shoes? I'm a good boy, right?"

Set Limits

Parents can help children learn self-regulation and self-discipline by setting and enforcing limits. Setting limits is another way of guiding children toward appropriate, safe behavior. When parents and caregivers set limits, it helps children begin to set limits for themselves.

Make sure you state limits clearly. Telling three-year-old Kyle that he can have a small snack does not set a clear limit. Kyle is not old enough to decide what makes a snack big or small. A better way to state the limit would be, "You can have either an apple or a banana." Speak in a calm, direct tone of voice to indicate that the limit is real and should be respected.

Setting limits includes four steps. Here is how a caregiver might set limits about where a toddler can draw pictures:

1. **Show an understanding of the child's desire.** "I know you think it's fun to draw on the wall."
2. **Set the limit and explain it.** "But you may not draw on the wall because it's hard to clean crayon marks off the wall."
3. **Acknowledge the child's feelings.** "I know you like drawing on the wall, but walls are not for drawing."
4. **Give alternatives.** If possible, give the child a chance to continue the same activity in an acceptable way. "If you want to draw, you may draw on this paper. Or you can play with your blocks. Which do you want to do?"

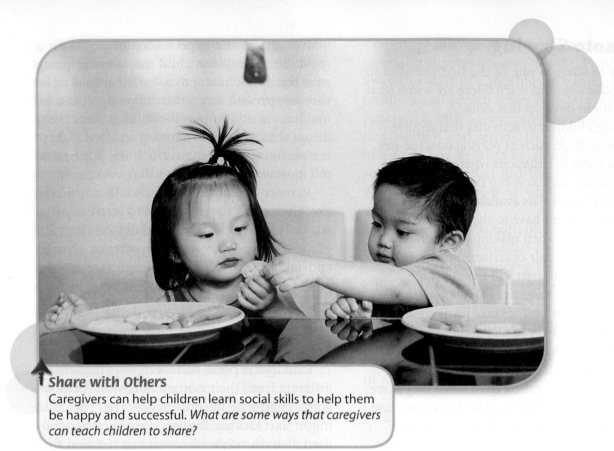

Share with Others
Caregivers can help children learn social skills to help them be happy and successful. *What are some ways that caregivers can teach children to share?*

Behavior is a form of communication. Inappropriate or aggressive behavior says that a child is upset or that some need is not being met. Young children can have a hard time using words to explain their feelings. Two-year-old Austin was jealous of his sister getting new toys for her birthday. Since Austin could not express his feelings with words, he started throwing toys. His parents realized why Austin was acting this way and calmly explained that he would have a birthday soon and get new toys too. On the other hand, sometimes children misbehave just because they enjoy the sensation. For example, Alex might repeatedly kick a table leg.

Caregivers need to look for and understand the problem behind aggressive or otherwise inappropriate behavior. Finding the cause of the behavioral problems can go a long way toward changing the behavior.

Biting

Marguerite was shocked when her two-year-old son ran up and bit her on the arm. He bit hard enough to leave a bruise.

It is not uncommon for young children to bite, and they bite for different reasons at different ages. Infants may bite because they fail to see any difference between chewing on a toy and chewing on a big brother or sister. One-year-olds may bite just to discover what happens when they do. Two- and three-year-olds may bite to get their way with other children or just to get attention. They may also bite when they are angry or frustrated.

Caregivers need to determine what is causing a child to bite. They can then take steps to guide the child toward more appropriate behavior. A teething baby, for example, can be given a teething ring or a soft cloth to bite on to relieve the discomfort of cutting teeth. A one-year-old needs to know biting is not okay and will not make his or her parents smile.

Wilson discovered his two-year-old daughter biting her brother in a fight over a toy wagon. He set her on his knee, looked directly into her eyes, and calmly but firmly told her, "Do not bite. Biting hurts your brother. It makes him cry."

Hitting, Kicking, and Shoving

Have you seen an adult react to a young child's aggressive behavior with anger? Unfortunately, this sends the message that anger and aggression are appropriate solutions to a problem.

Two- and three-year-olds have trouble controlling these impulses, or aggressive reactions to emotions and situations. At these ages, the part of the child's brain that controls impulses is not well developed. In addition, children are still very self-centered and concerned mainly with their own needs and desires. When something stops them from getting their needs met, they become angry or frustrated.

Hitting, kicking, and shoving are aggressive behaviors often seen in toddlers. Emma wanted a ball that Juan was playing with. Juan refused to let go, so Emma began hitting him.

Their preschool teacher intervened when Emma began to hit Juan. "I know that you want to play with the ball. I can see that it makes you angry when Juan will not give it up, but you must not hit people. Use words to tell Juan you are angry." The teacher then guided Emma toward some choices. "You can wait your turn to play with the ball, or you can color a picture. Which would you like to do?" At this age, it is still useful and sometimes necessary to offer a distraction. By suggesting Emma color a picture, the teacher gave Emma something besides the ball to focus on.

Many child development experts believe that time-outs are an effective way to help children understand that certain behaviors are not acceptable. A **time-out** is when a child is removed from the group, perhaps by being required to sit in a special chair for a short period of time. A time-out is another way of saying, "You cannot do that." A time-out can give a toddler time to calm down when they are upset.

Section 11.2 After You Read

Review Key Concepts

1. **Explain** why it is important to give young children opportunities to play with friends.
2. **Compare and contrast** shoes with laces and shoes with Velcro fasteners. Which ones would you choose for a three-year-old? Why?
3. **Identify** two ways that parents can communicate to their children that they respect them.

Practice Academic Skills

 English Language Skills

4. Write six negative statements that someone might say to a three-year-old child. Exchange papers with a partner. Turn each statement on the list into a more positive one that conveys the same message. Share your revised statements with the class.

> **NCTE 4** Use written language to communicate effectively.

Social Studies

5. The Montessori method of early childhood education was developed in the early 1900s by educator Maria Montessori. Conduct research to learn how the Montessori method encourages positive socialization among children. Create an oral presentation on what you learn.

> **NCSS I A** Analyze and explain the ways groups, societies, and cultures address human needs and concerns.

Check Your Answers Check your answers at this book's Online Learning Center at **glencoe.com**.

Careers With Children

Speech-Language Pathologist

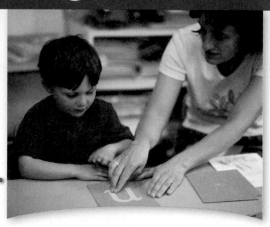

Speech-language pathologists help people overcome difficulties in communicating. For example, some children have problems making certain sounds. Others struggle with speech rhythm difficulties, such as stuttering. Speech-language pathologists can help these children communicate more effectively.

What Does a Speech-Language Pathologist Do?

Speech-language pathologists who work with children use special tests to find out each child's speech problem. Then they create a plan for working with that child. They teach sign language to children who cannot speak and help other children make sounds more clearly. They also advise parents on how to help their children practice speaking correctly.

Where Do Speech-Language Pathologists Work?

Many speech-language pathologists work in elementary schools. Others have jobs in hospitals, private clinics, or nursing homes.

Preparation and Skills

Education and Training
Speech-language pathologists must earn a master's degree and pass a national licensing exam. Then they must work a certain number of hours to become licensed. Specific requirements vary by state.

Aptitudes, Abilities, and Skills
Patience, optimism, excellent communication skills, and teaching ability are needed to excel in this career. Speech-language pathologists must also show a commitment to their client's care.

Academic Skills
A basic understanding of childhood development, an understanding of the physical aspects of speech, and knowledge of the appropriate therapies for different speech problems are required. Required courses cover anatomy and physiology, as well as psychological aspects of communication.

Explore Careers

Research the work speech-language pathologists do in schools. How do they find out which students need help? What kinds of therapy are provided? Write a summary of what you learn.

 Careers Online For more information on careers, visit the Occupational Outlook Handbook Web site through the link on this book's Online Learning Center at **glencoe.com**.

Chapter Summary

Children go through a series of emotional stages. Each child develops emotionally in his or her own way, based on temperament and past experiences. With help, children learn to show empathy for others and to handle emotions such as anger and jealousy. Adequate sleep is critical to many areas of a child's development. The socialization process involves gradually developing social skills and learning to get along with others. Behavior needs to be guided by caregivers. With the caregivers' guidance, children begin to develop a conscience.

Vocabulary Review

1. Arrange the vocabulary terms below into groups of related words. Explain why you put the words together.

Content Vocabulary

◇ self-centered (p. 322)
◇ negativism (p. 322)
◇ temper tantrum (p. 324)
◇ phobia (p. 327)
◇ separation anxiety (p. 327)
◇ sibling rivalry (p. 328)
◇ empathy (p. 330)
◇ self-concept (p. 331)

◇ sleep-deprived (p. 332)
◇ REM sleep (p. 333)
◇ NREM sleep (p. 333)
◇ socialization (p. 335)
◇ parallel play (p. 335)
◇ cooperative play (p. 336)
◇ self-discipline (p. 340)

◇ autonomy (p. 342)
◇ time-out (p. 345)

Academic Vocabulary

■ perceptive (p. 321)
■ adequate (p. 332)
■ gauge (p. 336)
■ distraction (p. 341)

Review Key Concepts

2. **Identify** the factors that contribute to a child's emotional development.
3. **Describe** six specific emotions children ages eighteen months to three years show.
4. **List** the four signs of a healthy relationship between parents and a child.
5. **Identify** four ways to help children get adequate sleep.
6. **Compare and contrast** parallel play and cooperative play.
7. **List** six ways to help children develop social skills.
8. **Explain** the purpose of guidance.

Critical Thinking

9. **Apply** What are two common behavioral problems? How would you deal with them in a three-year-old?
10. **Make Judgments** Eric is the father of two boys, ages three and four. To reduce fighting, he avoids situations in which the children must share. For example, if they are drawing, each child will have his own box of crayons. What do you think about Eric's plan for avoiding conflict?

Family & Community Connection

11. Cartoon Violence Interview the parent of a young child concerning violence in cartoons. Ask specific questions, such as "Do you think the make-believe violence in some cartoons increases children's aggressive behavior towards others?" "Do you restrict your child's viewing of such cartoons?" Write a summary of the parent's responses.

Health Skills

12. Child Care Center Nurse Imagine that a local child care center is looking for a nurse. Research the requirements to be a nurse at a child care center. What education is needed? What kinds of skills must the nurse have? How are these skills different from other nurses? Use what you learn to create a newspaper advertisement for the position.

Observation Skills

13. Analyzing Causes of Misbehavior Young children often misbehave, even to the extent of having temper tantrums. But these tantrums happen for a reason. Examining the situation from the child's point of view can be helpful in identifying the causes.

Procedure Go to a public place where you can observe parents and children. Watch for children having temper tantrums. Record what you observe during one of these tantrums.

Analysis Based on your record, write a paragraph describing what you think might have led to the tantrum. How do you think the child was feeling? Be specific.

> **NCSS IV F Individual Development and Identity**
> Analyze the role of perceptions, attitudes, values, and beliefs in the development of personal identity.

Real-World Skills

Problem-Solving

14. Antisocial Behavior A preschooler has begun to exhibit troubling behavior. She fights constantly with others and has no friends. She told a story about mistreating her puppy. What might you say to this child's parents?

Technology Skills

15. Emotional Development Suppose a parenting class teacher has asked you to create a presentation explaining the emotional stages of children ages one to three. Use software to create your presentation. Use illustrations where appropriate. Be sure your presentation looks good so it catches the attention of your audience.

Financial Literacy

16. Child Care Costs When choosing child care, parents must decide how to best meet their child's emotional and social needs. Most parents also must consider financial costs. Conduct research to learn about the cost of in-home child care as compared to child care centers. Create a chart comparing the costs.

 Additional Activities For additional activities, go to this book's Online Learning Center at **glencoe.com**.

Academic Skills

English Language Arts

17. Eight Stages Erik Erikson was a psycho-analyst who theorized that there are eight stages in a person's emotional and social development. The second stage involves children eighteen months to three years of age. Research the second stage of Erikson's theory and write a brief summary.

> **NCTE 3** Apply strategies to interpret texts.

Mathematics

18. Temper Tantrums Children ages one to three tend to have temper tantrums because they cannot put their needs into words. Translate the following verbal statement about tantrums into an algebraic expression: Cathy and Robert's baby has twice as many temper tantrums per day than Scott and Betsy's baby.

Math Concept **Algebraic Expressions** Algebraic expressions use variables as placeholders for changing value.

Starting Hint Assign a variable for Cathy and Robert's baby (x) and one for Scott and Betsy's baby (y).

 For math help, go to the Math Appendix at the back of the book.

> **NCTM Algebra** Represent and analyze mathematical situations and structures using algebraic symbols.

Science

19. Young Children and Play As you have learned in this chapter, parallel play is more common in young toddlers, while older children increasingly engage in cooperative play. Develop a hypothesis based on this fact. A sample hypothesis might be: two-and-one-half-year-olds engage in cooperative play more often than eighteen-month-olds.

Procedure Work with your teacher to arrange to observe a group of children at play. You will need to find out the ages of the children you are observing. Keep track of how children in different age groups play.

Analysis Calculate your results. Create a table that explains these results. State whether or not your hypothesis was true.

> **NSES A** Develop abilities necessary to do scientific inquiry, understandings about scientific inquiry.

Standardized Test Practice

SHORT ANSWER

Short answer questions are not the same as essay questions. These questions call for brief, to-the-point responses. Write a response to this short answer question:

20. At about eighteen months, many children begin to exhibit negativism. List three ways to deal with a toddler who is being negative.

> **Test-Taking Tip** Keep your language simple and direct in short answer questions. Avoid overly elaborate answers. Bulleted or numbered lists can help clarify your response.

Chapter Objectives

After completing this chapter, you will be able to:

- **Summarize** how heredity and the environment shape intelligence.
- **Describe** the four methods of learning used by young children.
- **List** the seven areas of intellectual activity.
- **List** 11 ways to help guide a child's learning.
- **Identify** four parts of language that children have an inborn ability to decipher.
- **Summarize** how to evaluate toys for young children.

Writing Activity — *Explanation*

Reading to a Child One of the most important things parents can do for their children is to read to them. Write a paragraph explaining why reading to children is essential.

Writing Tips People often write to explain, whether it is to defend a political view or to provide instructions on assembling a bike. When writing an explanation, keep these tips in mind:

1. Write clearly and avoid vague language.
2. Be specific in your explanation.
3. Keep your audience in mind.

Section **12.1** Brain Development from One to Three

Section **12.2** Encouraging Learning from One to Three

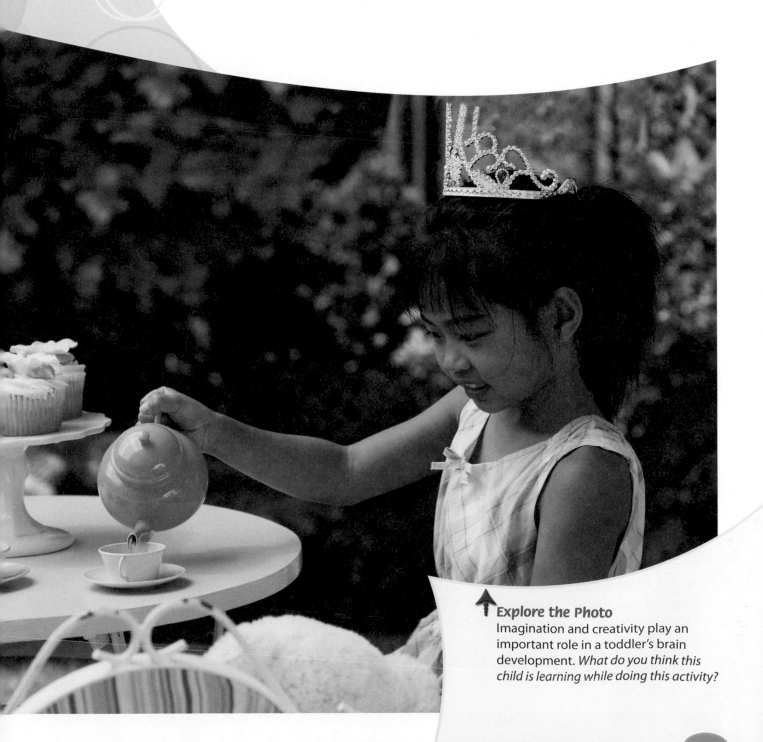

↑ Explore the Photo
Imagination and creativity play an important role in a toddler's brain development. *What do you think this child is learning while doing this activity?*

Brain Development from One to Three

Reading Guide

Before You Read

Restating Definitions Knowing the meanings of vocabulary words is vital to understanding what you are reading. Locate the content vocabulary words in this section. Read each word's definition. Then restate the definition using your own words.

Read to Learn

Key Concepts

- **Summarize** how heredity and the environment shape intelligence.
- **Describe** the four methods of learning used by young children.
- **List** the seven areas of intellectual activity.

Main Idea

Both heredity and environment play major roles in the development of a child's intelligence. Intellectual activity becomes increasingly complex.

Content Vocabulary

- ◇ neuroscience
- ◇ intelligence
- ◇ incidental learning
- ◇ trial-and-error learning
- ◇ imitation
- ◇ directed learning
- ◇ creativity

Graphic Organizer Go to this book's Online Learning Center at **glencoe.com** to print out this graphic organizer.

Academic Vocabulary

You will find these words in your reading and on your tests. Use the glossary to look up their definitions if necessary.

- ■ elicit
- ■ stifle

Graphic Organizer

As you read, look for two milestones of intellectual development for 1-, 2-, and 3-year-old children. Use a web diagram like the one shown to help organize your information. Add additional circles as needed.

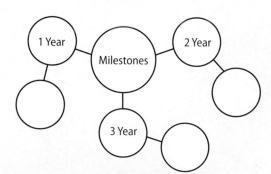

Academic Standards ·

 English Language Arts

NCTE 5 Use different writing process elements to communicate effectively.

 Mathematics

NCTM Data Analysis and Probability Select and use appropriate statistical methods to analyze data.

 Science

NSES 1 Develop an understanding of science unifying concepts and processes: systems, order, and organization; and evidence, models, and explanation.

NCTE *National Council of Teachers of English*
NCTM *National Council of Teachers of Mathematics*

NSES *National Science Education Standards*
NCSS *National Council for the Social Studies*

Brain Development

Lisa, age two and one-half, examined her doll with a toy stethoscope after returning from a visit to the pediatrician. This simple act of play revealed the growing power of her mind. A one-year-old is still much like a baby, just learning to make sense of the world. However, Lisa has learned so much by two and one-half that she can engage in imaginative play. She is using her imagination when she imitates the actions of her doctor or a character in her favorite book. In doing so, she develops her own ideas and extends her investigation of the world.

Most researchers agree that the brain plays a major part in directing behavior and determining intelligence. However, the exact functions of the brain were unknown until recent years. For a long time, people could do little but observe human behavior and guess about exactly how the brain controlled human actions and abilities.

Cells from the nervous system, called neurons, were observed to have fibers radiating from them, called axons and dendrites. As you learned in Chapter 9, these fibers were found to conduct information to and from other neurons in the brain. Later, scientists discovered that connections between axons and dendrites formed pathways in the brain that controlled particular actions or thinking tasks.

Since then, neuroscience has provided further important discoveries and insights about the functions of the human brain. **Neuroscience** is the modern study of the brain. These discoveries have greatly expanded the knowledge of how a child's brain develops. This knowledge has had an impact on recommendations for care of children.

People used to think that providing a child with food, clothing, and shelter in a loving, healthy, and safe environment was all a child needed for the development. Neuroscience has shown that a child's experiences can help determine the physical structure of the brain and the

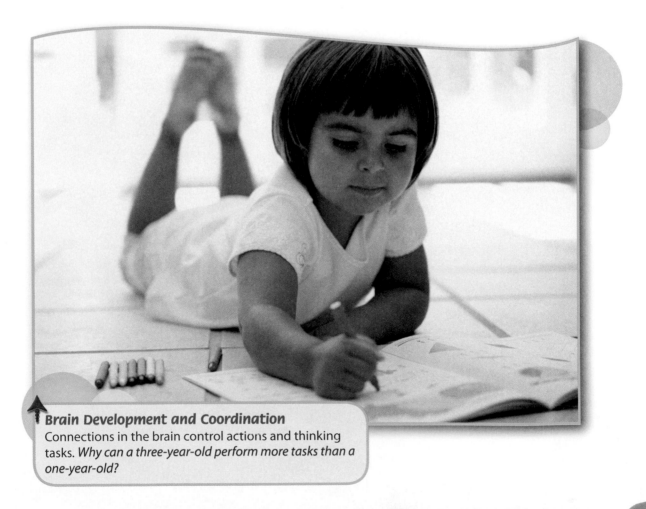

Brain Development and Coordination
Connections in the brain control actions and thinking tasks. *Why can a three-year-old perform more tasks than a one-year-old?*

extent to which a child reaches his or her potential. A parent can help ensure a child reaches his or her potential by offering a stimulating environment.

The Role of Intelligence

Intelligence is the ability to interpret and understand everyday situations and to use prior experiences when faced with new situations or problems. Intelligence is also the capacity to learn. Both heredity and environment shape intelligence. Everyone is born with certain limits of possible intellectual development. However, the extent to which a person's potential is actually developed is greatly influenced by that person's environment.

It is crucial for young children to have an environment that promotes learning and stimulates the senses. Such an environment includes interactions with caregivers and other children, a variety of appropriate toys, and plenty of encouragement. An enriched learning environment provides the best opportunity for learning. In fact, recent studies of brain development show that connections are made and the brain grows in complexity based partly on the opportunities for learning available to a child. A stimulating environment boosts learning. Children need bright colors and fun activities to learn.

Toddlers and preschoolers form attitudes about learning that can last a lifetime. If they are given many opportunities for learning, they are likely to develop a positive attitude toward learning.

Concept Development

Concepts are general categories of objects and information. Children learn concepts and the words for those concepts in stages. It takes time for misconceptions that result from a toddler's broad generalizations to be sorted out. Young children often over-apply labels. For example, toddlers may think that any round fruit is an orange. Young children gradually

Object Classification
By age three, many children can classify items by size, shape, or color. *What is an example of a misconception a toddler might have?*

learn to categorize objects by shape, color, and size. Balls are round, and so are cookies and plates. Grass and leaves are both green. Size distinctions come in two steps. The relationship between two items as big and little may be recognized as early as eighteen months. Not until age three, however, can children pick out the middle-sized ball from three possibilities.

Concepts concerning what is alive and what is not alive are not learned until later. A young child believes that anything that moves or works is alive. This includes clouds, toys, cartoon characters, and the washing machine!

Concepts of time improve during the second and third years. Two-year-olds may show more patience because they know what *soon* means and can wait a short time. They know the difference between before and after. However, a child may not understand today, tomorrow, and yesterday until kindergarten.

✓ **Reading Check** **Recall** What are concepts?

Methods of Learning

Children learn much from everyday experiences and play. There are four methods that children use for learning. These include incidental, trial-and-error, imitation, and directed learning.

Recall that Jean Piaget divided learning into four distinct periods, as shown in **Figure 12.1** on page 356. Between the ages of one and three years, toddlers progress from the sensorimotor period to the preoperational period. As you read about the four methods of learning, think about how they might fit into Piaget's periods of learning.

Incidental Learning

Incidental learning is unplanned learning. For example, five-month-old Evan pushes a button on a musical toy and discovers that this action causes music to play. After this happens a few times, Evan learns a cause-and-effect situation. Then he pushes the button on purpose to hear the music.

Science in Action

Video Games and Brain Development

Research studies have reported findings that playing video games may damage developing brains. These studies are primarily concerned with whether or not video games slow or prevent the maturing of specific brain regions.

Procedure

Conduct research to learn more about one of these studies. Also research whether any scientists think that these findings are incorrect.

Analysis

Study the results of your research. Draw a conclusion concerning whether you think that video games can damage developing brains. Write a report explaining your conclusion and how you reached it.

NSES 1 Develop an understanding of science unifying concepts and processes.

Trial-and-Error Learning

Trial-and-error learning is learning that takes place when a child tries several solutions to find one that works. At about twelve to eighteen months, this means experimenting. Trial-and-error learning may be more advanced for a three-year-old.

For example, three-year-old Krista wants to play with her younger brother's toy robot. First, Krista grabs the robot from her brother. He screams, and their mother makes her give it back. Next, Krista tells her brother to go play in the sandbox, but he does not want to. Finally, Krista offers to let her brother play with her stuffed horse if she can play with his toy. He agrees to the trade, and Krista gets what she wants. She has learned the best way to get what she wants from her brother by trying ways that did not work.

Imitation

Imitation is learning by watching and copying others. Older children are often annoyed when a younger sibling copies everything they do or say. The younger child uses the older as a model for behavior of all kinds. Both skills and attitudes can be learned by imitation. Toddlers also carefully watch and mimic the actions and attitudes of their parents and caregivers. Have you ever seen a toddler talking on a toy phone? He is imitating the action of the adults around him. The best way to teach children to eat their vegetables or say please and thank you is to do these things yourself!

Directed Learning

Learning that results from being taught, often by parents, other caregivers, teachers, or older siblings, is **directed learning**. Directed learning occurs in school or other places that offer formal instruction, as well as at home. Unlike incidental learning or trial-and-error learning, directed learning involves an older person purposely teaching a specific skill, fact,

or attitude to the child. Joel's kindergarten teacher helps him learn the letters of the alphabet by showing pictures of items that begin with each letter. At home, his sister demonstrates how to play Go Fish with playing cards. Joel learns how to play soccer from his coach. Directed learning begins in the early years and continues throughout life.

✓ **Reading Check** **Compare** How is directed learning different from imitation?

Intellectual Activity Areas

Intellectual activity can be broken down into seven areas. These are attention, memory, perception, reasoning, imagination, creativity, and curiosity. These areas develop throughout life, but their development from ages one to three is especially remarkable. As you read more about each area, try to think of ways that caregivers can encourage development in that area. Some basic intellectual milestones for these ages are described in **Figure 12.2** on page 359.

Figure 12.1 Piaget's Four Periods of Learning

Piaget's four periods of learning begin at birth and continue to adulthood. *At what age does a child begin thinking in terms of what they perceive at the moment?*

Period	Characteristics
Sensorimotor Birth-2 years	Children learn through their senses and own actions.
Preoperational 2–7 years	Children think in terms of their own activities and what they perceive at the moment.
Concrete Operations 7–11 years	Children can think logically but still learn best through experience.
Formal Operations 11-Adult	People are capable of abstract thinking.

Attention

At any given moment, the five senses are bombarded with information. Right now, for instance, you see the words on the page. You are aware of the size, shape, and color of the book and the amount of light in the room. You hear pages being turned, and perhaps you see other students jotting down notes. You feel the paper of the book. It is smooth and cool. If you were unable to screen out all of the extra information you take in, you would not be able to read.

In order to function, adults must be able to focus their attention on the task at hand. This means blocking out much of the sensory information they receive. Infants and young children are unable to do this. Their attention goes from one bit of sensory information to another as they try to make sense of it all. This is why toddlers are so easily distracted.

A caregiver may be struggling to dress a toddler. She may find that while she turned to get the shirt, the child wandered away to see what was going on outside the window. It is important for caregivers to understand how difficult it is for a child to pay attention to one thing at a time.

As children mature, they gradually build the ability to ignore most sensory information and to concentrate on one item of interest. Their learning becomes more focused on one topic or activity at a time. One- to three-year-olds tend to have very short attention spans. However, a three-year-old can focus on one activity for much longer than a one-year-old. The more children are able to block out distractions, the more they can learn. Caregivers may notice this as children spend more time interested in a story.

Memory

Without memory, there would be no learning. Experiences that are forgotten cannot affect later actions or thoughts.

Older children and adults have both short- and long-term memory. Short-term memory is brief and allows people to accomplish many everyday tasks without making the brain store

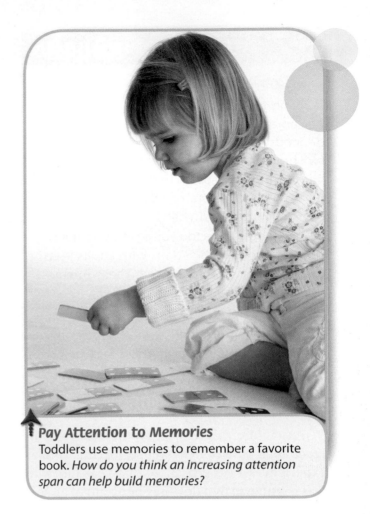

↑ Pay Attention to Memories
Toddlers use memories to remember a favorite book. *How do you think an increasing attention span can help build memories?*

unimportant information indefinitely. People use short-term memory when they look up a number in the phone book. They remember the number just long enough to place their call. They will look up the same number the next time they need to call it. Long-term memory is for more important data. First, this information must enter the short-term memory and be judged important enough to remember. Then it is stored in the long-term memory.

Babies begin to demonstrate memory early. They quickly learn to recognize the faces of their primary caregivers, for example. Much of babies' memory abilities have to do with faces and foods. Between six months and a year, babies develop recall memory. This is the ability to remember more information for longer periods of time. This is especially true for things that had a strong emotional impact. For example, by this time Kylee can remember that she did not like cats because one scratched her.

Long-Term Memory

Long-term memory is the ability to remember an event in one's life for a long time. It depends on connections between neurons in two brain areas called the frontal lobe and the hippocampus. Research has shown that these parts of the brain are not able to form long-term memories until a baby is 17 to 21 months old. Even if a baby is too young to remember a story or a song, interactions with adults keep the child alert and interested. These interactions also aid brain development.

■ **Science Inquiry** Children do not have long-term memory until at least 17 months. What must take place in the brain before long-term memory can occur?

As children develop, they become able to react to a situation by remembering similar experiences in the past. A one-year-old who was frightened by a dog may be afraid of all animals for a time. A three-year-old can remember the specific dog and compare it with others. A three-year-old also can recall a celebration and look forward to the next one.

Children develop more long-term memories at age three. This is when they can retain facts such as "the girl next door is named Keisha." They can remember observations such as "I love to go to the park." They can also recall their own personal history such as "I got a new puppy last year."

Perception

A newborn learns about the world through perceptions. Perception is the information received through the senses. This sensory information reinforces established connections in the brain. It also sparks new connections. Although a newborn's brain is developing these neural connections and pathways at a rapid rate, the infant is just starting to interpret the information. Gradually, the brain organizes itself to handle increasingly complex learning as a child grows. This allows sensory information to be used more effectively.

If you care for young children, you can play a key role in the development of perception. By talking about what you and the children are doing, you encourage children's perception. Use descriptive observations that children can understand and expand on. For example, when playing with blocks, you might say, "Look at the

Learning Through PLAY

Memory Games

As a toddler's intellectual abilities grow, so do the possibilities for play. A three-year-old is able to use his or her memory to play games. Do you remember playing card games where the object was to place cards face down, turn over one card, and then turn over another to find its match? Three-year-olds are able to successfully play such a memory game for two reasons. They are able to keep an idea in mind for longer periods of time than when they were younger. They also can complete a task without being easily distracted. Simple puzzles can be good for developing memory as well. Increasing a child's memory can help with later development of skills such as reading and writing.

Think About It Imagine you are babysitting a three-year-old. You bring along a memory game. The game involves matching 20 pairs of different animals. The child is having problems matching the cards. What might you do to make the game more appropriate for her age?

Figure 12.2 Intellectual Developmental Milestones—Ages 1–3

Toddlers reach certain milestones every year. *What change occurs in the ability to follow directions between ages 2 and 3?*

Age	Developmental Milestone
1 Year	❖ Begins to put two words together ❖ Names common objects and people ❖ Understands "no," but ignores it ❖ Finds hidden objects
2 Years	❖ Uses two- to three-word sentences ❖ Knows about 500 words ❖ Follows simple directions ❖ Identifies colors
3 Years	❖ Uses longer sentences ❖ Knows about 900 words ❖ Follows two-part directions ❖ Sorts by color and shape

blue block. Your shirt is blue, too. Let's build a tower using only blue blocks."

Two- and three-year-olds seem to ask questions constantly. "Why?" "What's that?" "How does it work?" Responding to these questions helps improve a child's perception. It can be hard for caregivers to answer these endless questions. However, when questions are ignored or dismissed a child loses opportunities for learning. If the response is often an absent-minded "Uh-huh" or "Don't bother me right now; I'm busy," the child may stop asking questions.

Reasoning

Reasoning is necessary to solve problems and make decisions. It is also important in recognizing relationships and forming concepts.

Babies show the signs of simple problem-solving skills at about four to six months of age. One-, two-, and three-year-olds gradually learn more sophisticated reasoning skills. At fourteen months, Jason solves problems by trying out all possible solutions. When playing with a shape sorter box, he tries to fit each piece into each hole until one works. By his third birthday, Jason's problem solving is less physical and more mental. He can think through possible solutions and eliminate those that will not work without actually acting out each one. He can see that the square shape will fit in the square hole, and not the round one.

Making decisions involves choosing from different alternatives. Children learn to make good decisions through practice. This is why it is important to give young children plenty of opportunities to make real decisions. At first, these decisions should be choosing between two options in which neither choice could cause any harm. For example, an eighteen-month-old can choose between two books to read at bedtime. A two-year-old child can choose between two different shirts.

Learning About Differences

Three-year-old Zack was curious about his surroundings, especially about other people. He was not at all shy, and his mother was happy that he so often smiled and greeted people. One day, Zack and his mother went grocery shopping. "What's wrong with her?" Zack asked loudly. "Why is she walking like that?" Zack's mother drew him into a nearby aisle, and after a quick review of the use of inside and outside voices, she assured him that there was nothing wrong with the person he had seen. She was using crutches to help her walk because her legs might not work the way that Zack's do. On their way home, she reminded Zack that all people are different. She told Zack that it might hurt people's feelings when he asks personal questions too loudly.

Write About It Suppose your child tells you that some children at the child care center are teasing a child who must wear a hearing aid. Write a scenario in which you describe how you would respond to this situation. In your scenario, state exactly what you would say to your child.

Parents of newly independent two-year-olds know that this approach has the added advantage of avoiding questions that may **elicit**, or bring about, a negative response. For example, a child could easily say no to the question, "Would you like to have fish for dinner?" A better question is, "Do you want beans or corn with your fish?" What kinds of decision-making opportunities might be appropriate to offer to a three-year-old?

Imagination

Imagination becomes very apparent at about two years of age. An active imagination improves learning because it allows the child to try new things. The child also can act out a variety of roles. Laundry baskets become airplanes, boxes are buildings, and closets are caves. The child becomes a ferocious lion or a busy airline pilot.

Children use their imagination to connect what they see and hear with themselves. For example, Yvonne may see an airplane. Then she imagines that she *is* an airplane, and zooms around the backyard with her arms outstretched. Imagination can also help children cope with anxiety and frightening new concepts. For instance, some children may pretend

Imagination
Children often use their imaginations to try out new ideas and roles. *Why should you not tell a toddler he is lying when he uses his imagination?*

to throw a scary monster out the bedroom window as a way of managing their fear. Using a toy doctor's kit and pretending to be a doctor can help calm fears about an upcoming medical procedure.

It is important to respect a child's imagination and respond carefully. When three-year-old Kim makes up a story, she is not lying. She is using her imagination. However, suppose Kim's mother says, "Don't be silly. You know that didn't really happen." Kim might be discouraged from using her imagination again. In fact, until about the age of five, children are not always sure where reality ends and imagination begins.

Creativity

An ability that is related to imagination is creativity. **Creativity** is a mental ability that involves using the imagination to produce original ideas. These ideas are often displayed through an object that others can see, such as a drawing or finger painting. The creative product is not always an object, though. It might be daydreams, dramatic play, or silly stories. Creativity is most readily developed in early childhood and is an asset throughout life. Creativity helps promote self-esteem and confidence.

Parenting Skills

Encourage Imagination and Creativity

While some children may naturally be more imaginative than others, all children need opportunities for creative play. Here are some ways to support a child's creativity:

- **Encourage exploration.** Promote activities that depend on exploration and imagination. Examples include drawing, dressing up in grown-up clothes, and telling stories.
- **Provide multipurpose toys.** Children need toys that can be used in more than one way. Wooden blocks can become cars, doll beds, or castle walls.
- **Allow for unstructured time.** Children need uninterrupted time to themselves. The less television they watch, the more their imaginations will grow.
- **Resist the inner critic.** Remember that the process of creating is more important than the product. There is more than one right way to paint or mold things from clay.
- **Reward the young creator.** Praise the child's efforts with both deeds and words. Display the child's pictures. Talk with others about what the child has made.

Take Charge Many caregivers worry about the mess resulting from creative play. Write a paragraph explaining what you might do to reduce the mess.

Readiness for Learning

Learning begins very early in life. However, children can learn a new skill only when they are physically and intellectually ready. For example, it would be a waste of time trying to teach a six-month-old to put on a coat. The baby has neither the physical nor intellectual maturity that the skill requires. Most two-year-olds lack the fine motor skills and conceptual development necessary to learn to write letters and words.

Sometimes adults push children to learn things they are not ready for. When children are not able to succeed, they may feel frustrated or feel they are a failure. These feelings may become stumbling blocks for learning. It is important to remember that children learn and grow at different rates. Therefore, worries such as "Brad is not talking as early as Mackenzie" should be minimized.

On the other hand, children should be taught skills they are ready to learn. For example, two-year-old Ben struggled with dressing himself. His mother helped by dressing him every day. She found out later that her helping was causing problems. When Ben was well past the age when he should be able to dress himself, he continued to ask for help. He had not developed enough confidence to complete the task on his own.

Most importantly, children need plenty of time for undirected play and safe exploration. As children explore their environment and everything in it, they will naturally make many discoveries.

Reading Readiness

A child's readiness to read depends in large part on the environment caregivers create. Enjoying books is vital for learning to read. The act of being read to should be a well-established, daily routine and a special time together. Even very brief sessions of reading to infants can be helpful in developing a joy of reading.

Interact with young children while reading to them. Let the children point at the pages and comment. Ask them to predict what will happen next. The more enthusiastic the reader is, the more enthusiastic children will become about story time.

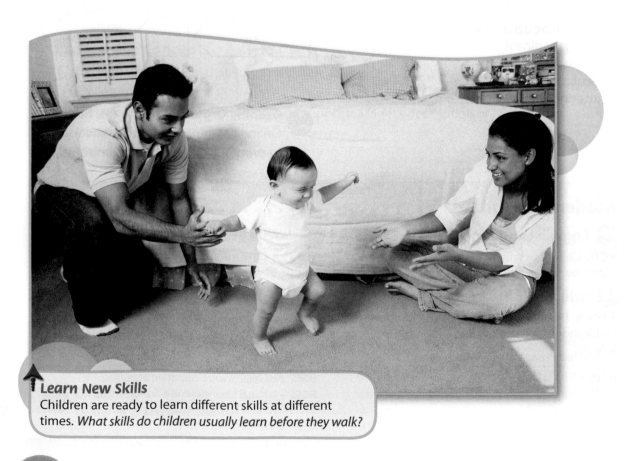

↑ Learn New Skills
Children are ready to learn different skills at different times. *What skills do children usually learn before they walk?*

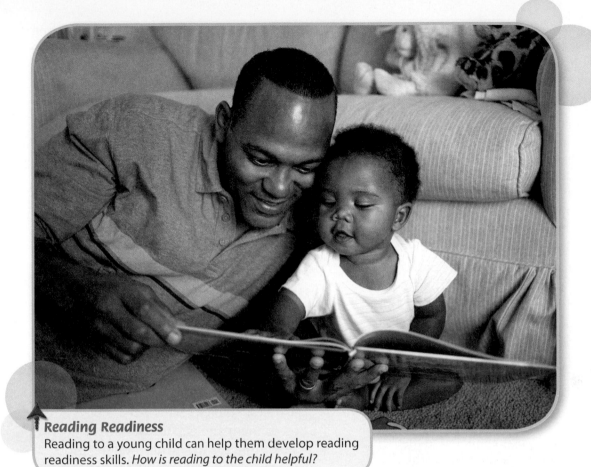

Reading Readiness
Reading to a young child can help them develop reading readiness skills. *How is reading to the child helpful?*

Reading readiness means learning the skills necessary for reading, including letter recognition and the understanding that letters of the alphabet combine to form words on a page. Before age three, reading readiness focuses on children's excitement about reading. The bedtime story accomplishes more than many parents realize.

- Children learn how to handle books and turn pages.
- They begin to associate written words that appear on the page with words being read aloud.
- Finishing a book creates a sense of accomplishment, especially when the child can choose what to read next.

The next stage of reading readiness involves letter recognition. This includes the understanding that letters of the alphabet combine to form words. Some children are ready to recognize letters at age three. During reading time, you can encourage the child to say the letters they see on the page. You might respond,

"You're right! That's a B. Your name begins with a B. B for Brianna!"

Children's readiness to read on their own may vary widely. Do not expect a strict timetable for gaining the preliminary skills needed for reading. It is more important that children learn to enjoy the process.

{ **Expert Advice...** }

"The kind of care a child receives plays a big role in how the brain chooses to wire itself. Parents who talk and read to their babies are helping them develop important language connections."

— Dr. Diane Bales, at-risk children, youth, and families coordinator, University of Georgia

Learning by Helping

Three-year-old Molly was excited when she woke up. Liz was taking care of her today! When Liz arrived that morning, Molly asked to have pancakes for breakfast. "I'll help you," said Molly confidently. While Liz got out the pancake mix, Molly watched. "How many cups of mix do we use, Molly?" asked Liz. "Two!" said Molly, "You put it in a bowl."

"That's right. Let's use the big blue bowl today." Molly got out the bowl and handed it to Liz. "Thank you," said Liz. "Now I'll measure the mix." Liz filled a measuring cup and let Molly level the cup with a spatula and put the mix in the blue bowl. Liz asked, "How many eggs?" "One!" "Right again!" Liz smiled at her helper. Liz measured the milk and Molly stirred it into the mix herself. Molly liked to count the pancakes in the pan as Liz cooked them. Molly also commented that the pancakes were the same color as the kitchen floor—brown!

🖊 **Write About It** Think of a task you perform frequently, such as making your bed or feeding a pet. Write a scenario in which you and a three-year-old perform the task together. Include what you would say and do to help the child learn during this activity.

Math Readiness

Math is a part of everyday life. People may count out a dozen apples, measure ingredients from a recipe, or count out coins. People use math so often and so unconsciously, they may miss experiences they could share with young children. **Math readiness** is the level of knowledge of basic math concepts, such as number recognition, needed for learning math. It also involves an interest in learning basic math concepts. As with reading, math can become a welcome and pleasant part of everyday experiences. Children can explore sizes, shapes, amounts, and proportions long before they ever enter a classroom.

To teach numbers, you can talk to children as they go about their daily routine. "Are there two bananas left this morning, or only one?" "How many plates are set out for dinner?" Counting and number recognition can be taught by making a game of finding numbers. How quickly can a child find a "3" on the signs in the grocery store?

Blocks and puzzles can teach shape recognition. They also help in learning the shape names. Sorting is a good mathematics skill. You can work with children to sort blocks and other items by shape, color, and size.

Guiding Learning

There are many ways to help guide children's learning. As you read the suggestions, try to remember a time when someone helped improve your learning in this way.

- **Give your time and attention.** Children learn best when a caring person pays attention to them and encourages them.
- **Allow time for thinking.** Solving problems and making decisions are new experiences for young children. They need time to consider choices and make decisions.
- **Give only as much help as the child needs.** If a toddler is struggling to put on a shirt, do not take over. Just help slip the shirt over the child's head before it gets caught. Children feel a sense of accomplishment when they do things on their own. Try to let children do the final step in any task they are struggling with.
- **Encourage children to draw their own conclusions.** "Let's find out" is better than an explanation. Seeing and doing helps reinforce learning and allows for discoveries that prompt further curiosity.
- **Demonstrate how to solve problems.** When a toddler's tower of blocks keeps falling down, demonstrate that stacking one block directly on top of another provides the balance. Then leave building the tower to the toddler.
- **Model problem solving.** Talk out loud as you solve everyday problems. This allows children to hear how you think your way to a solution.

- **Maintain a positive attitude.** Express confidence in the child's abilities. One way is to praise the child's efforts. "Thank you for helping me plant the daisies. You did a great job!" You can also point out improvements in a specific action, such as coloring.
- **Keep explanations simple and on the child's level.** Too much information can cause a young child to stop listening. When a child asks about why fish live in water, an appropriate explanation might be, "Fish breathe in water. People need air to breathe."
- **Allow children to explore and discover.** Exploration is often a messy business. It is important to give children opportunities to roll in the grass, splash in puddles, and squeeze mud through their fingers and toes. Safety is important, but constantly saying "Don't do this" and "Don't touch that" limits the sensory and motor experiences that promote learning.

- **Help children understand the world and how it works.** Take young children along, even on routine errands. On trips to the library, the supermarket, and the gas station, you could talk about what is happening and why it is happening. Helping out at home also boosts learning. While raking leaves together, for example, you might call attention to the different colors and the crackling sounds of the dried leaves.
- **Take frequent breaks.** Children need stimulation. They also need opportunities for unstructured play. **Unstructured** means lacking formal organization. Watch for clear signals that a child has had enough of an activity. Fussing, wiggling in a chair, or looking distracted suggest that it is time to move on.

✓ **Reading Check**) **Analyze** Why is it important that children be allowed to explore and discover on their own?

↑ **Exploration and Discovery**
Children learn by being able to explore on their own.
What might a child learn by playing in the mud?

Language Abilities

In the toddler and preschool years, language abilities grow at a very rapid pace. As with other areas of development, children's speech varies greatly. Brain development research has brought new insights into how children learn to use language. Children have an inborn ability to **decipher**, or interpret, sounds, words, sentences, and grammar from the language they hear. Most children develop language skills in the first three years of life.

Speech Development

Infants learn to recognize the speech of their parents and other caregivers early in life. Soon after, infants begin practicing the sounds of speech by babbling. Beginning at around twelve months of age, babbling gradually transforms into a child's first words.

Between their first and second birthdays, children work at learning new words. They like to learn the names of everything. They also enjoy listening to the sounds the words make. At this point, rhyming books that tell stories are ideal. At twelve months of age, a child may speak two to eight words, but by age two, that jumps to about 50 words. During this period, most children use one or two words rather than a whole sentence to express a thought. For example, Chloe points to a jar on the counter and says "cookie" to mean "I want a cookie."

Encourage language development by talking to young children about their lives. Speak clearly about children's everyday experiences. For example, take the time to describe whatever they are seeing or doing. "Look at the big bite you've taken out of that yellow banana. Does it taste sweet and yummy?"

At about age two, children usually start combining a few words to make short sentences, such as "Doggie bark" or "Jimmy fall down." Between ages one and two, a child typically calls himself or herself by name. At about two years of age, children begin to use pronouns, such as I, we, you, and they.

At about two and a half, children begin to learn some basic grammar rules. They learn by listening to other people talk, rather than by any formal teaching. For example, a child begins to add an *s* to words to make them plural. The child then applies this rule to all words. Foots and tooths make as much sense to them as hands and eyes.

Language skills continue to develop, but at varying rates. Most three-year-olds can:
- Say their name and age.
- Make all the vowel sounds and say the consonants P, B, M, W, H, D, T, and N.

Model Language
Children's language development is influenced by how adults around them speak. *Why is it important to use good grammar when speaking to a child?*

- Speak without repeating a word or syllable.
- Use sentences of at least four words.
- Usually be understood by others, even by strangers.
- Answer what and where questions.
- Understand what is meant by words such as *on*, *in*, and *under*.
- Follow a command with several parts.

Speech Difficulties

Parents become concerned when they believe their child is a late talker. Some make the mistake of pressuring the child. This pressure just makes the child aware of the problem, and possibly makes it worse.

A child who does not seem to understand what is said, does not speak at all, or speaks very little should have a thorough examination. Local public school districts often provide free screenings by a speech-language pathologist. A speech-language pathologist is a specialist who is trained to detect and help correct speech problems. Speech difficulties can often be treated beginning at age three or earlier. It is important to identify any physical problem that may be interfering with a child's language development as early as possible. Hearing problems, learning disabilities, and mood disorders may all hinder a child's speech development.

Children with speech difficulties need to be lovingly encouraged, but not pressured. Such an attitude can help the child cope with, and perhaps even overcome, the problem. Teasing or constant corrections only make the problem worse. Children need to know they are loved, regardless of any learning difficulties.

Articulation

The term **articulation** refers to the ability to use clear, distinct speech. It is normal for children to have trouble with articulation until at least age three or four. Some children skip syllables or leave off the endings of words. These problems usually correct themselves over time. A speech-language pathologist can determine whether a problem is likely to go away on its own or if speech therapy is needed.

Basic Toy Safety

Everyone involved in a child's life should make sure all toys are safe. Here are some safe toy guidelines:

- Any fabric should be labeled flame resistant or flame retardant.
- Paint must be lead-free.
- Crayons, paints, and other art materials should be labeled nontoxic.
- Toys should not be able to break into sharp pieces.

For younger children:

- Toys should not have long cords or strings that could wrap around a child's neck.
- Toys and rattles should not be able to get lodged in a child's mouth.
- Objects should be over 1.75 inches in diameter to avoid choking hazards.

Be Prepared Spend about a half hour examining the toys of a child under age four. If you need help finding a child, ask your parent or teacher for help. Check each toy for safety. Write a summary of what you find. Tell the child's parents if you find any toys you feel are unsafe.

Instead of constantly correcting a child's pronunciation of words, it is important for adults to set a good example with their own speech. Suppose a toddler says "ba" and reaches for a bottle. The caregiver can give the bottle to the child and say, "Here's your bottle."

Stuttering

Stuttering is a more serious speech difficulty for young children. **Stuttering** is when a person speaks with sporadic repetition or prolonged sounds. However, many adults mistake normal speech hesitations for stuttering. A child may repeat whole words or phrases: "Johnny . . . Johnny . . . Johnny. He . . . he . . . he hit Zoe!" This is not true stuttering. In this case, the child's speaking and thinking abilities are still immature. It is difficult to get the words out quickly and smoothly.

True stuttering can be identified by the rhythm, pitch, and speed of speech. It is rapid, forced, short, and sharp in sound. Usually, the child repeats only the beginning sound of a word: "I c—c—c—can't g—g—g—go outside." The child often also shows tension in some way, such as gasping, sputtering, or rapid blinking.

The cause or causes of stuttering are still not completely understood. Some children overcome the problem with speech therapy. However, most children who stutter outgrow it. Experts advise against finishing words for a child. Children who stutter need time to say the words on their own.

✓ **Reading Check** **Recall** What are three things that might interfere with a child's speech development?

Play Activities and Toys

Toys are an important part of play. They help children explore, imagine, and try out different roles. They encourage the development of motor skills and help children learn to share and cooperate with others, making further learning easier and more fun.

Stimulating Play Activities

Often a child's favorite toy is really a caregiver. A caregiver can respond instantly and individually to the child's efforts at play and imagination. A toy cannot respond in the same way. Some adults do not like to get on the floor and play with children. However, such interaction can expand the child's learning. At the same time, the parent or caregiver can learn more about the child's interests and talents.

Evaluating Toys

With thousands of toys to choose from, knowing what to buy is important. Parents should ask themselves these questions:

- **Is the toy safe?** This is the single most important consideration. Make sure there are no small parts that could be swallowed or sharp edges that could cut. Be aware that a toy that is safe for a three-year-old may not be safe for a one-year-old. Also make sure the toy is not flammable and indicates nontoxic when appropriate. The federal government's Consumer Products Safety Commission alerts the public about unsafe toys.

- **Is it well-made and durable?** There is nothing more discouraging for a child or an adult than having a toy break the first time it is played with. Can the toy withstand the rough treatment it will receive?
- **Will it be easy to care for?** A well-loved stuffed animal needs to be washable. Similarly, books with hard pages and wipe-clean covers are the most practical choice for toddlers.
- **Does it encourage the use of a child's imagination?** Some toys do everything for the child. With no need to pretend, the child's imagination develops more slowly. Look for simple toys that can be used in a variety of ways. A talking doll may say ten phrases, but a child can make an ordinary doll say anything!

- **Is it colorful?** Young children respond more readily to colorful objects. These toys also encourage children to learn the names of colors.
- **Will it be easy for the child to handle?** Think about the size of the toy and its level of difficulty. The excitement of receiving a motorized car is quickly lost if the child is too young to use it on her own.
- **Is it something the child will enjoy?** A toy that a child finds engaging is much better than a toy forced upon him by a well-intentioned parent or relative.

Age-Appropriate Toys

Toys should be appropriate for a child's age. Infant toys are usually not challenging enough for three-year-olds. An older child's toys are not able to hold the attention of most fourteen-month-olds. Children at different ages enjoy and learn from different kinds of toys. The following are some suggestions for age-appropriate toys.

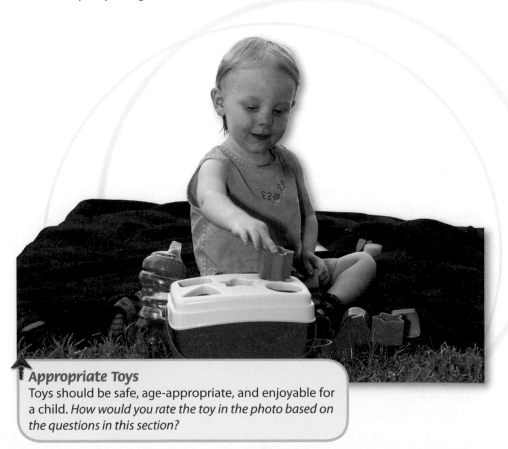

Appropriate Toys
Toys should be safe, age-appropriate, and enjoyable for a child. *How would you rate the toy in the photo based on the questions in this section?*

One to Two Years

At this age, a child practices motor control and learns through exploration. Some favorite toys are household items, such as metal pans, wooden spoons, and plastic storage bins. Pull toys, floating bath toys, toys that make music, and sorting toys are also popular.

Most toys that allow the child to use large muscles are also good choices. These toys may include swings, riding toys, balls, and cardboard boxes. One-year-olds also enjoy stuffed animals, sturdy books, simple puzzles, and toy cars. Avoid toys with parts that are small enough to fit into the cardboard tube from a roll of toilet paper.

Two to Three Years

Coordination and understanding improve greatly during this year. In addition, the child wants to do what adults are doing. The desire to imitate and role play provides ideas for many toys. Good choices are a child-size vacuum cleaner or lawn mower, telephone, plastic or wooden tools, play dishes, and empty food containers. Crayons, play dough, books, and large blocks are popular. A sandbox with a toy bucket and shovel can provide hours of enjoyment.

Three to Four Years

Preschoolers' improved motor skills and increased imagination bring interest in more complex toys. These often use fine motor skills. Dolls to dress, construction sets, and similar toys are popular. Three-year-olds love to mold play dough, color, cut with blunt scissors, and paint. Three-year-olds also spend longer periods with books than younger children. They enjoy listening to music. They like to do puzzles and use swings and slides. Many three-year-olds love to ride a tricycle.

Section 12.2   After You Read

Review Key Concepts

1. **Describe** one of the principles for guiding a child's learning and give an example of a caregiver putting it into practice.
2. **Identify** two kinds of speech difficulties that might indicate that speech therapy is needed.
3. **List** at least four toys that are appropriate and fun for toddlers between the ages of one and two.

Practice Academic Skills

 English Language Arts

4. Suppose you are applying for a summer job at a local preschool. You have heard that this preschool emphasizes reading readiness. Write a letter to the school's director explaining ways in which you would encourage reading readiness in young children.

> **NCTE 12** Use language to accomplish individual purposes.

 Science

5. Most researchers believe that genetic, neurological, and social factors all play a role in stuttering. Conduct research to learn more about how these factors are related to stuttering. Write a one-page report to share what you learn.

> **NSES A** Develop abilities necessary to do scientific inquiry, understandings about scientific inquiry.

 Check Your Answers Check your answers at this book's Online Learning Center at **glencoe.com**.

Chapter Summary

Intelligence is determined by both heredity and environment. Children learn concepts and the words for those concepts in stages. Learning methods include incidental, trial-and-error, imitation, and directed learning. There are seven areas of intellectual activity. Children's learning can be guided by adults. Caregivers should encourage reading and math readiness during play and everyday activities. Toys should be safe, appealing, and appropriate to a child's age. Speech difficulties include problems with articulation and stuttering.

Vocabulary Review

1. Write each of the vocabulary terms on an index card, and the definitions on separate cards. Work in pairs or small groups to match each term to its definition.

Content Vocabulary
- neuroscience (p. 353)
- intelligence (p. 354)
- incidental learning (p. 355)
- trial-and-error learning (p. 355)
- imitation (p. 356)
- directed learning (p. 356)
- creativity (p. 361)
- reading readiness (p. 365)
- math readiness (p. 366)
- articulation (p. 369)
- stuttering (p. 370)

Academic Vocabulary
- elicit (p. 360)
- stifle (p. 362)
- unstructured (p. 367)
- decipher (p. 368)

Review Key Concepts

2. **Summarize** how heredity and the environment shape intelligence.
3. **Describe** the four methods of learning used by young children.
4. **List** the seven areas of intellectual activity.
5. **List** 11 ways to help guide a child's learning.
6. **Identify** four parts of language that children have an inborn ability to decipher.
7. **Summarize** how to evaluate toys for young children.

Critical Thinking

8. **Evaluate** Recall a toy you enjoyed playing with as a child. Evaluate the benefits of that toy for young children.
9. **Apply** Suppose you are visiting a mother. Her toddler is feeding himself spaghetti. The mother gets upset at the mess. What might you say?
10. **Judge** Some people argue that in order to create an equal society, preschool must be free to all children. Do you agree? Explain your answer.

Help Children Learn

In this unit you have learned that one- to three-year-olds grow and develop physically, emotionally, socially, and intellectually. You have also learned that children often develop at different rates and in their own way. In this project, you will observe a group of one- to three-year-olds. You will use what you learned to create an activity that will help one- to three-year-olds learn a physical, emotional, social, or intellectual skill.

My Journal

If you completed the journal entry from page 289, refer to it to see if your thoughts have changed after reading the unit.

Project Assignment

In this project, you will:
- Choose an area of child development.
- Create an observation checklist.
- Arrange to observe one- to three-year-olds in a child care setting.
- Take notes during your observation.

Child Development Skills Behind the Project

- Evaluate the skill levels of one- to three-year-olds.
- Identify age-appropriate learning activities for one- to three-year-olds.
- Determine activities that would be enjoyed by one- to three-year-olds.

Academic Skills

 English Language Arts

> **NCTE 5** Use different writing process elements to communicate effectively.
>
> **NCTE 12** Use language to accomplish individual purposes.

- Ask a child care center worker to clarify any activities or procedures that you did not understand.
- Write an age-appropriate learning activity for one- to three-year olds in one of the four areas of child development.
- Present and demonstrate the learning activity to your class.

Step 1 Choose an Area of Child Development that Interests You

The topics below are four areas of development that can be observed in children. As you consider your area of interest, think about the types of activities that would help children develop skills in that area.
- Physical development
- Emotional development
- Social development
- Intellectual development

Step 2 Prepare for Your Observation

Make a checklist that will help you take notes during your observation. It may include such things as: name of the activity, number of children involved, materials needed, and behaviors observed.

Writing Skills

★ Organize the information on the checklist in a logical order. Keep like items together.

★ Leave enough space to fill in information about the observations.

★ Check your spelling.

Step 3 Connect to Your Community

Work with your teacher to arrange an observation at a child care center in your community. During your observation, note how the staff conduct activities with the children. Fill in your observation checklist.

Observation Skills

★ Sit or stand quietly outside of the activity area.

★ Do not engage the children in conversation.

★ Take careful notes.

★ After the activity, ask the child care workers for clarification if there is anything you do not understand.

Step 4 Write and Demonstrate Your Activity

Use the Unit Thematic Project Checklist on the right to plan, write, and demonstrate your activity.

Presentation Skills

★ Organize and distill information.

★ Write creatively.

★ Speak clearly and concisely.

Step 5 Evaluate Your Child Development Skills and Academic Skills

Your project will be evaluated based on:

• Content and organization of your information.

• Mechanics—presentation and neatness.

• Speaking and listening skills.

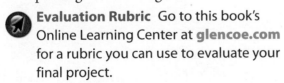 **Evaluation Rubric** Go to this book's Online Learning Center at **glencoe.com** for a rubric you can use to evaluate your final project.

Unit Thematic Project Checklist

Activity	✓ Develop an observation checklist to aid you in taking notes during your observation at a child care center. ✓ Write an original activity to promote physical, emotional, social, or intellectual growth for one- to three-year-olds. ✓ Label the parts of your activity: Goal (what you want the children to learn), Preparation (what must be done before the activity), Materials (all supplies needed for the activity), Step-by-Step Directions (how the activity is completed), Conclusion (how the activity will end such as asking the children questions or cleaning up).
Presentation	✓ Make a presentation to your class to demonstrate your new activity and discuss what you learned. Explain how the activity is promoting growth in your chosen area of development. ✓ Ask for class volunteers to participate in your demonstration. ✓ Invite the students to ask questions. Answer three questions. ✓ Demonstrate in your answers that you respect their perspectives. ✓ Turn in your observation checklist and the directions for completing your activity.
Academic Skills	✓ Communicate effectively. ✓ Organize your presentation so the audience can follow along easily. ✓ Thoughtfully express your ideas.

Unit 5

The Child from Four to Six

⬆ **Explore the Photo**
Four- to six-year-olds enjoy being active. *What kinds of activities might appeal to this age group?*

Chapter 13 Physical Development from Four to Six

Chapter 14 Emotional and Social Development from Four to Six

Chapter 15 Intellectual Development from Four to Six

Unit Thematic Project Preview

Teach New Skills

After completing this unit, you will learn that four- to six-year-olds are constantly learning new physical, emotional, social, and intellectual skills. In your unit thematic project you can identify activities that will help promote the development of these skills.

My Journal

Growth and Development Write a journal entry about one of the topics below. This will help you prepare for the unit project at the end of the unit.

- Identify how four- to six-year-olds differ physically from one- to three-year-olds.
- Describe intellectual activities a four- to six-year-old could do that a one- to three-year-old could not do.
- Discuss the difference in social skills between one- to three-year-olds and four- to six-year-olds.

Chapter

13 Physical Development from Four to Six

Chapter Objectives

After completing this chapter, you will be able to:

- **Summarize** how an average child's posture and body shape change from ages four to six.
- **Compare and contrast** average motor skills development for four-, five-, and six-year-olds.
- **Explain** why good nutrition is essential for children ages four to six.
- **Identify** three ways that four- to six-year-olds are able to care for themselves.
- **Describe** three steps that can help minimize toileting accidents.
- **List** three areas of outdoor safety to discuss with four- to six-year-old children.

Writing Activity *Question and Answer*

Caring for Four- to Six-Year-Olds There are many challenges associated with caring for four- to six-year-olds. Children this age are becoming more independent but still need a lot of care and guidance from their parents. Use your knowledge of children in this age range to write a question and answer. The question should focus on the concerns a caregiver might have. Answer the question in a detailed essay.

Writing Tips Use these tips to write an effective question and answer:
1. Develop a question that is challenging but realistic.
2. Plan an answer that connects to the key words of the question.
3. Organize your answer with an introduction, a body, and a conclusion.

Section 13.1 Growth and Development from Four to Six

Section 13.2 Caring for Children from Four to Six

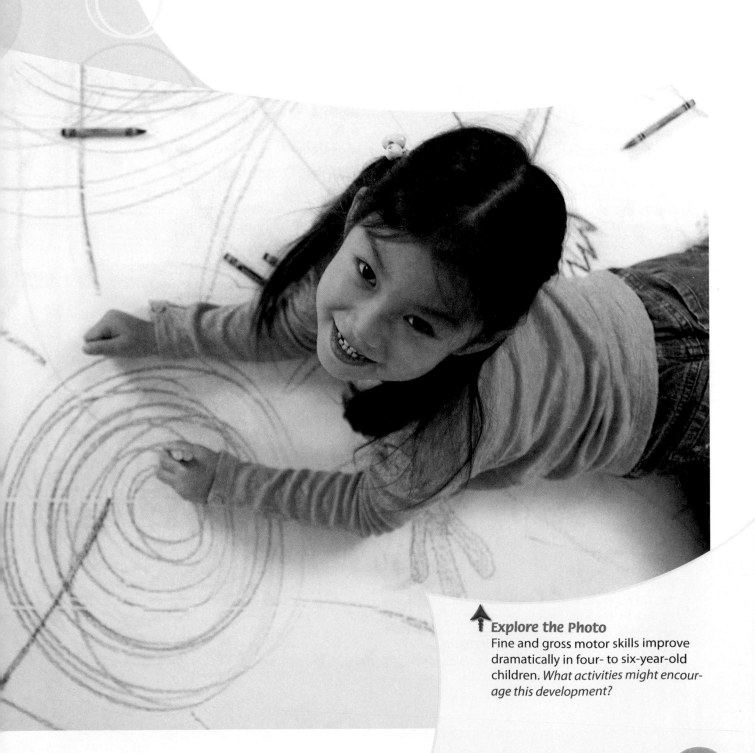

Explore the Photo
Fine and gross motor skills improve dramatically in four- to six-year-old children. *What activities might encourage this development?*

Growth and Development from Four to Six

Reading Guide

Before You Read

Stay Engaged One way to stay engaged when reading is to turn each of the headings into a question. Then read the section to find the answer.

Read to Learn
Key Concepts
- **Summarize** how an average child's posture and body shape change from ages four to six.
- **Compare and contrast** average motor skills development for four-, five-, and six-year-olds.

Main Idea
Four- to six-year-old children grow and develop in many areas. These include height, weight, posture, body shape, teeth, motor skills, and hand preference.

Content Vocabulary
◇ permanent teeth
◇ ambidextrous

 Graphic Organizer Go to this book's Online Learning Center at **glencoe.com** to print out this graphic organizer.

Academic Vocabulary
You will find these words in your reading and on your tests. Use the glossary to look up their definitions if necessary.
■ erect
■ dexterity

Graphic Organizer
As you read, list four facts about six-year-olds' teeth. Use a chart like the one shown to help organize your information.

Six-Year-Olds' Teeth
1.
2.
3.
4.

Academic Standards . . . .

 English Language Arts

NCTE 4 Use written language to communicate effectively.

Mathematics

NCTM Number and Operations Compute fluently and make reasonable estimates.

 Science

NSES C Develop understanding of matter, energy, and organization in living systems; and behavior of organisms.

NCTE *National Council of Teachers of English*
NCTM *National Council of Teachers of Mathematics*

NSES *National Science Education Standards*
NCSS *National Council for the Social Studies*

Growth from Four to Six

If you have ever been around four-, five-, or six-year-old children, you know how active they are at this time of life. Instead of sitting still, they wiggle. Rather than walk, they run. It is sometimes hard to get them to stay in one place long enough to put on their clothes or to eat. So what is the purpose behind all this activity? The answer is simple: Practice makes perfect. Children this age are constantly improving their physical skills.

Height and Weight

The rate of physical growth in children between the ages of four and six is only slightly slower than in children ages one to three. The average increase in height during these years is about 2½ to 3 inches (6.4 to 7.6 cm) per year. Most children gain about 4 to 5 pounds (1.8 to 2.3 kg) each year as well. These are just average gains among children, so larger or smaller gains are common, too. Boys tend to be slightly taller and heavier than girls during this period. See **Figure 13.1** on page 384 for the average heights and weights for boys and girls during each year of this age range.

Math in Action

Physical Education

An elementary school wants to improve its physical education program. An ideal physical education program in elementary school will offer three periods a week of approximately 45 minutes duration. If the school follows this recommendation, how many hours per month will each student spend in physical education?

Math Concept **Multi-Step Problem** When solving problems with more than one step, think through each of the steps before you start.

Starting Hint First, calculate how many minutes are spent in physical education class each week (3 periods × 45 minutes). Then multiply your answer by the number of weeks in a month (4). Convert your final answer to hours (60 min = 1 hour).

 For math help, go to the Math Appendix at the back of the book.

NCTM Number and Operations Compute fluently and make reasonable estimates.

▲ **Growing and Changing**
Four- to six-year-olds walk and run with their arms close to their bodies. *Why do four- to six-year-olds no longer hold their arms away from their bodies when they walk or run?*

Figure
13.1

Average Height and Weight: Ages 4–6

As children grow older, they experience significant differences in height and weight. *What is the average weight gain for a girl from age four to age six?*

Age	BOYS		GIRLS	
	Height / Inches	Weight / Pounds	Height / Inches	Weight / Pounds
Four years	40½	36	39½	35½
Five years	43	40½	42½	39¾
Six years	45½	46	45¼	44½

Posture and Body Shape

Children's posture changes noticeably between their fourth and seventh birthdays. Their bodies become straighter and slimmer, and the protruding tummy from babyhood flattens. Children this age hold their shoulders back and their upper bodies more **erect**, or straight. The chest, which had previously been rounded, broadens and flattens with improved abdominal strength. The legs also lengthen rapidly, growing straighter and firmer. Even the neck becomes longer.

Balance and coordination show improvement in these years as well. Four- to six-year-olds hold their arms nearer to their body when they walk or run.

Teeth

It is common for school pictures of a six-year-old to show a gaping hole in the child's smile. Children this age are losing their primary teeth. The larger permanent teeth generally begin to appear at about this time. **Permanent teeth** are teeth that will not be naturally replaced by another set. They replace the primary teeth that the child has lost. Children will eventually have a total of 32 teeth in the permanent set, to replace the 20 primary teeth.

The six-year-old molars are also called the first molars. These are the first permanent teeth to appear. These are new teeth, not replacements for primary teeth. There are four first molars. There are two upper ones and two lower ones. They are positioned behind the primary teeth. These molars act as an anchor. They keep all the teeth in front of them in place. The primary teeth are lost in the same order as they came in. This is generally the two lower front teeth first, then the two upper front teeth.

Thumb Sucking

Some four-, five-, and six-year-olds continue to suck their thumbs. This is a way to comfort themselves or handle stress. Adults may worry about this habit, but in most cases, it is best ignored. Trying to force a child to quit can cause more problems than the habit itself. Generally, children stop sucking their thumbs on their own.

If thumb sucking seems excessive, check with a dentist. After the child's fifth birthday, thumb sucking may cause changes in the shape of the roof of the mouth or in the way the teeth line up.

✓ **Reading Check** **Recall** Why are four-, five-, and six-year-old children so active?

Development from Four to Six

Children ages four to six change in many ways. They change in height and weight, and in posture and body shape. They also change in motor skills. Both gross and fine motor skills are improved. Children also usually develop a hand preference during this time period.

Motor Skills

Between the ages of four and six, most basic gross and fine motor skills improve significantly in children. Many motor skills, such as throwing a ball, must be taught. Children require guidance and practice. The timetable for the development of these skills varies. Just as in the earlier years, some children master one skill but are not as proficient at another.

For example, five-year-old Cheryl may have the skills to put together complex puzzles but not yet be able to jump rope. Her friend Gail may be comfortable with easier puzzles but may excel at jumping rope. Ishaan may be able to tie his shoes before he can write words. The chart in **Figure 13.2** on page 386 summarizes typical motor skills at each age.

Gross Motor Skills

Recall that gross motor skills are also called large motor skills. This is because they use the large muscle groups, such as those in the arms, legs, abdomen, and back. Four-, five-, and six-year-olds are very energetic. Their favorite activities are usually physical actions such as running, jumping, climbing, or turning somersaults. After age four, children are learning how to throw and catch both large and small balls. Five-year-olds show improved speed and coordination in all their activities. The movements of six-year-olds are even more smoothly coordinated. Six-year-olds enjoy balancing activities, such as walking on a curb or learning to ride a bicycle. Also, activities that involve rhythm appeal to them. This includes such activities as dancing to music and jumping rope to chanted songs.

Children need plenty of opportunities to develop their motor skills. Giving them time and space to run, jump, and climb on play structures helps them develop their large motor skills. As with any skill, motor skills take practice. If Michelle never plays with balls, then she will not develop the skills of throwing or catching a ball. Gabriel is not allowed to ride his bicycle because his mom is afraid

RESPOND TO SPECIAL NEEDS — Cerebral Palsy

The term *cerebral palsy* refers to a number of neurological disorders that appear in infancy or early childhood and permanently affect body movement and muscle coordination. These disorders do not worsen over time. The majority of children with cerebral palsy are born with it. However, it may not be detected until months or years later. The most common signs are a lack of muscle coordination when performing voluntary movements, stiff or tight muscles and exaggerated reflexes, and muscle tone that is either too stiff or too floppy.

Cerebral palsy cannot be cured. Treatment will often improve a child's capabilities, though. Treatment may include physical and occupational therapy; speech therapy; drugs to control seizures, relax muscle spasms, and alleviate pain; surgery; braces and other orthotic devices; wheelchairs and walkers; and communication aids such as computers with attached voice synthesizers.

Critical Thinking Research the causes of cerebral palsy. Summarize your findings in a one-page report and be ready to share your findings with the rest of the class.

Figure 13.2

Physical Developmental Milestones—Ages 4–6

A four-year-old can cut on a line with scissors. *What fine motor skills does a six-year-old have?*

Age	Fine Motor Skills	Gross Motor Skills
4 Years	❖ Dresses and undresses self ❖ Cuts on line with scissors ❖ Copies a circle and a cross	❖ Hops on one foot ❖ Throws ball overhand ❖ Alternates feet walking up and down stairs ❖ Walks backward easily
5 Years	❖ Draws a person with head, body, arms, and legs ❖ Prints some letters ❖ Buttons clothing ❖ Copies a triangle and a square ❖ Uses spoon and fork to eat, but still uses fingers for some foods	❖ Turns somersaults ❖ Skips with alternating feet ❖ Balances on each foot for short period
6 Years	❖ Cuts, pastes, and colors skillfully ❖ Writes entire words ❖ Ties shoelaces	❖ Can ride a two-wheel bicycle with training wheels ❖ Jumps rope ❖ Throws and catches a ball with more ease and accuracy (also requires fine motor skills and good hand-eye coordination)

he will fall and get hurt. However, he can only learn with practice. Gabriel's mother can help him develop the skills and still keep him safe by ensuring that he wears a bicycle helmet and safety pads.

Fine Motor Skills

Fine motor skills are also called small motor skills. This is because they involve coordination of small muscle groups such as those in the fingers, wrists, and ankles. Four- and five-year-olds show improved dexterity. **Dexterity** is ease and skill in physical activity. So improved dexterity means physical activity comes more easily. Children can use their hands and fingers skill-

fully. Most four-year-olds can learn to lace their shoes. However, most children cannot tie their shoelaces until they are five or six. While most four-year-olds can dress themselves, they may not be able to fasten buttons until they are five.

Five-year-olds' hand-eye coordination has improved to the point that they can pour liquids from a pitcher into a glass, as long as the pitcher is not too heavy or too full. They enjoy cutting, pasting, and using glue. They also can print some letters but might have trouble printing words. Six-year-olds show even greater fine motor skills and hand-eye coordination. Most children this age are able to draw detailed pictures, use scissors, and write their own names.

Hand-eye coordination also improves some skills children already had. For example, Mia enjoyed playing catch with her dad. When she was four, she usually had to chase the ball across the yard. By the time she was six, Mia could catch the ball most of the time.

Activities such as making cards, painting pictures, drawing, tracing outlines, cutting, and playing games help improve fine motor skills. Many child care centers will encourage children this age to do crafts, such as making animal masks from paper plates or making cards for Mother's Day. Children with well-developed fine motor skills may be more successful at learning to print.

Hand Preference

As mentioned in Chapter 10, some children express a preference for using one hand more than the other after the age of two. Others may continue to switch off during the preschool years. By about the second half of the fifth year, most children consistently use either their right or left hand for most activities, such as holding crayons or feeding themselves. Naturally, whichever hand they choose becomes the stronger, more skillful one. About 85 percent of all children prefer to use their right hand for most activities. Only a few people are ambidextrous. **Ambidextrous** means being able to use both hands with equal skill.

Research continues on how a preference for one hand develops. Some people believe that heredity is probably the source of right- or left-handedness. Others think it depends on which hand parents usually put objects in during the child's early years. Some research links hand preference to the areas of the brain controlling motor skills or language. Whatever the cause, professionals now agree that there is no reason to influence a child toward using one hand over the other.

Section 13.1   After You Read

Review Key Concepts

1. **Explain** the best way to generally deal with a five-year-old who sucks his or her thumb.
2. **List** three motor skills that an average six-year-old has mastered that most three-year-olds would not be able to do.

Practice Academic Skills

English Language Arts

3. Brainstorm activities that can help children this age refine their fine motor skills. Suggest activities that are not mentioned in the chapter. Be sure to include activities that use different tools and implements. Create a poster that shows at least three ideas.

Science

4. Research teeth in the human body. Find out when teeth typically come in and in what order. Do this for both the primary and permanent teeth. Do primary and permanent teeth come in the same order? What makes primary teeth fall out? Write a one-page report with your findings.

Check Your Answers Check your answers at this book's Online Learning Center at **glencoe.com**.

> **NCTE 5** Use different writing process elements to communicate effectively.

> **NSES C** Develop understanding of matter, energy, and organization in living systems; and behavior of organisms.

Reading Guide

Before You Read

Understanding Write down questions while reading. Many of them will be answered as you read. If they are not, share the list with your teacher.

Read to Learn
Key Concepts

- **Explain** why good nutrition is essential for children ages four to six.
- **Identify** three ways that four- to six-year-olds are able to care for themselves.
- **Describe** three steps that can help minimize toileting accidents.
- **List** three areas of outdoor safety to discuss with four- to six-year-old children.

Main Idea

Caregivers must provide for children's nutritional needs, teach them about good nutrition, and teach them self-care. School-age children need to be taught about outdoor safety.

Content Vocabulary

◇ group identification
◇ fluoride
◇ enamel

Academic Vocabulary

You will find these words in your reading and on your tests. Use the glossary to look up their definitions if necessary.

- persuade
- undermine

Graphic Organizer

As you read, look for six reasons children may have poor nutrition. Use a diagram like the one shown to help organize your information.

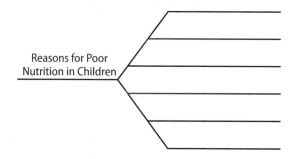

Reasons for Poor Nutrition in Children

 Graphic Organizer Go to this book's Online Learning Center at **glencoe.com** to print out this graphic organizer.

Academic Standards

 English Language Arts

NCTE 7 Conduct research and gather, evaluate, and synthesize data to communicate discoveries.

 Science

NSES F Develop understanding of personal and community health.

NCTE *National Council of Teachers of English*
NCTM *National Council of Teachers of Mathematics*

NSES *National Science Education Standards*
NCSS *National Council for the Social Studies*

Health and Wellness

A steady and varied supply of nutritious foods is the best fuel for children's physical and intellectual development. The recommendations in MyPyramid can help parents choose foods for good nutrition. The amount of food children need varies depending on their weight and level of physical activity.

For example, Stephanie spends hours kicking a soccer ball, running with her dog, and riding her bike. She needs more food energy than her cousin, who prefers coloring and building with blocks. Older or very active children need more food daily. Younger or less active children require less food each day. The USDA's MyPyramid Plan gives guidance. You will learn more about MyPyramid in Chapter 16.

Research has shown that four- to six-year-old children do better when they eat five or six small, nutritious meals and snacks a day instead of three large ones. Small meals and snacks are better suited to their small stomach size and provide a more constant level of energy. Snacks should be nutritious, appealing foods rather than convenience foods that are high in salt, sugar, or fat. Apple slices, grapes,

cheese, yogurt, and raisins are nutritious and popular with this age group.

Parents and other caregivers can encourage good eating habits by making food appealing and by modeling good food habits. Researchers have found that forcing a child to eat, making an issue of eating certain foods, or using foods as a reward may lead to poor eating habits and weight issues.

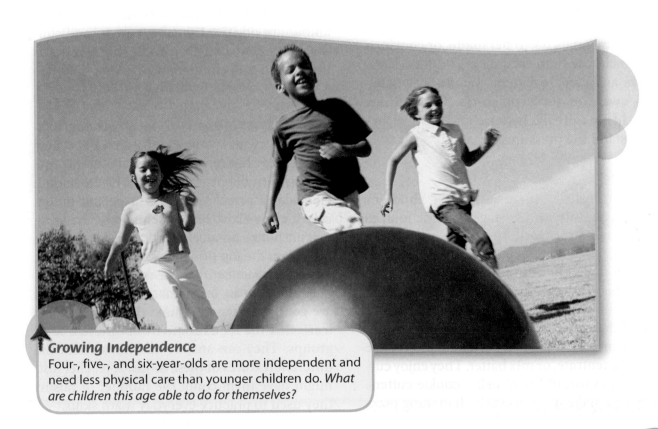

Growing Independence
Four-, five-, and six-year-olds are more independent and need less physical care than younger children do. *What are children this age able to do for themselves?*

➤ **Family Fun Time**
Doing physical activities as a family instills good lifetime habits in children. *What physical activities can families do together?*

Some adults set a poor example by frequently snacking on high-calorie foods. Some allow young children to choose their own food without guidance. It is the responsibility of parents and caregivers to provide children with healthful food and help them to learn to make appropriate choices.

Poor nutrition will **undermine**, or weaken, the health of children. Children who lack essential nutrition have less resistance to illness. They also may not grow adequately and may have learning difficulties.

Weight Problems

Children from four to six vary in their body type. They may look chunky or slim and still be healthy. When there are concerns about a child's weight, parents should consult the child's doctor. The doctor can accurately decide if the child is overweight or underweight.

If the doctor detects an issue with weight, there are many ways to help the child. Parents and caregivers might record the child's physical activity and what he or she eats for one week. Often, this record alone will help the doctor identify needed changes.

MyPyramid is always a good place to start in planning healthful meals and snacks. Other resources are available when the child has a more severe weight problem though. A dietitian or nutritionist can help parents and caregivers design a program to promote changes in diet or activity level.

When a child eats more calories than the body uses through physical activity, the body stores the extra calories as fat. If this happens consistently over time, the child is at risk for being overweight. The opposite is also true. A child who consistently eats fewer calories than his or her body needs may become underweight. Neither of these conditions typically occurs suddenly. Instead, both result from poor eating habits over time. If a child has a sudden weight gain or loss, a pediatrician should be consulted. This could indicate a medical problem.

The number of overweight children has been rising. Overweight children are at increased risk of being overweight or obese as adults. They also have a greater chance of developing life-threatening diseases, such as diabetes and heart disease. Good nutrition is the first step in preventing a child from becoming overweight.

Checkups and Immunizations

Most children will begin kindergarten at age five or six. Before they can attend school, they are typically required to receive a medical checkup and certain immunizations. Most schools require immunizations against hepatitis B, diphtheria, tetanus, pertussis (whooping cough), polio, measles, mumps, and rubella (German measles). More and more schools also require immunization against chicken pox. Parents should check with the school to find out the specific requirements.

✓ **Reading Check** **Explain** What happens when a child eats more calories than his body uses through physical exercise?

Self-Care Skills

As the physical strength and motor skills of four- to six-year-olds improve, they become increasingly able to care for themselves. They can wash and dress themselves, brush their own teeth, and begin to care for their clothes. Parents and caregivers should encourage this increasing independence. They should also remember, though, that the child is still learning and will need help to do things correctly.

Clothing

Despite their increased level of independence, four- to six-year-olds still need guidance in developing self-care skills. Choosing clothes, dressing, and caring for clothes are areas where children in this age group continue to learn and develop.

Dressing and Choosing Clothes

Four-, five-, and six-year-olds are usually able to dress themselves. Some may need help with certain fasteners such as shoelaces or buttons down the back.

Many children have difficulty figuring out which clothes match. Parents can help a child learn about matching colors and clothes. Help the child select coordinating outfits ahead of time and store them together.

Comfort, durability, and economy are still the main guidelines for choosing clothes. However, as children start school, two other factors become important in clothes selection.

First, children this age have definite likes and dislikes. Some become attached to a favorite garment, as they might have in the past to a specific toy. Second, group identification becomes important at this age. Children may have a desire to wear clothes like those of classmates.

Learning Through PLAY

Taking on Roles

Children of all ages frequently take on roles of other people when they play. Using dress-up clothes and other props, children love to pretend to be other people. Very young children choose roles in play that are close to their own experience. Children will frequently pretend to be a parent or teacher. However, as children learn more about the world, other characters become a part of their play. Some of these characters include firefighters, police officers, nurses, or doctors. Children may begin to pretend by suggesting a plan, such as "Let's drive to the store and get something to eat." Playing different roles is a way for children to express their creativity and to explore a world outside of their own.

Think About It Suppose you are baby-sitting three-year-old, Sam, and his six-year-old sister, Olivia. Olivia is trying to get Sam to play school with her, but Sam just takes the pencil and scribbles on the paper. Olivia is getting upset. What can you do?

Group identification is a feeling of belonging with others. Collin was excited to be starting first grade. When his mother took him shopping for clothes, he wanted only those with his favorite cartoon character on them.

Parents can help satisfy a child's desire to wear certain clothes by allowing him to select some of his own clothes. Children this age might enjoy shopping for their clothes. Collin's mom told him he could pick out two of his shirts by himself, but that she got to help choose the rest. Collin's mom was able to stay within their family's budget. And Collin was able to practice his independence by making his own choices.

Caring for Clothes

Once children begin to care about what they wear, they can learn basic clothing care. To start, they can put dirty items in the appropriate place. When it is laundry time, children can help sort their clothes. Then they can help fold and hang up clean clothes. Putting clothes away is easier if the child has storage within reach. Hooks at eye level, low rods, and handy shelves and drawers are helpful.

Good habits for taking care of clothes will not develop overnight. They will require consistent but gentle reminders. To many parents, it just seems easier to continue doing such tasks for their children. However, this is the stage of development when children need to increase their independence and sense of responsibility. Parents who continue to pick up and put away clothes for their children run the risk of having teens who expect the same service.

Washing and Bathing

Although bath time continues to be fun for some children, many this age are less interested in washing and bathing regularly than they were when they were younger. Some children just do not like to stop playing to bathe.

Praising children for taking a bath or shower is much more effective than nagging them to do so. Parents should set up and maintain hygiene routines. This helps children accept these tasks as expected behavior.

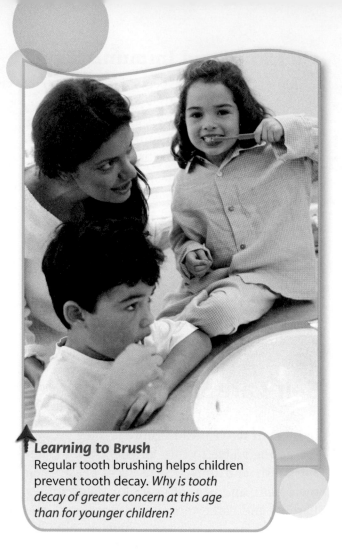

Learning to Brush
Regular tooth brushing helps children prevent tooth decay. *Why is tooth decay of greater concern at this age than for younger children?*

Caring for Teeth

Regular tooth brushing and flossing is another essential routine that parents can teach their children. Until a child handles a toothbrush well, at about the age of five, dentists recommend that parents help with brushing and flossing, especially at night.

Tooth decay is a special concern at this age because permanent teeth are coming in. Regular dental checkups and cleanings are important. Sometimes dentists apply a coating of fluoride to children's teeth. **Fluoride** is a substance that strengthens the enamel of teeth to help prevent decay. **Enamel** is the hard, outer coating of teeth. Fluoride is often added to drinking water and most toothpastes.

✓ **Reading Check** Summarize Why is group identification important for children in this age group?

Sleeping and Toileting

For most four- to six-year-olds, their need for sleep, especially naps, decreases while their independence in toileting increases. In spite of this, parents and caregivers must continue to monitor these two important areas of children's development.

Sleeping

By the age of four, many children no longer take an afternoon nap. Some continue taking a daily nap until they begin a full day of school, depending on their needs. Without an afternoon nap, nighttime sleep becomes even more important. Most children this age need ten to twelve hours of sleep each night.

In order to ensure this amount of sleep, parents and caregivers need to decide on an appropriate bedtime. If the child has to wake up early for school or child care, an early bedtime is best. This can often be hard on parents who work all day and do not have much time to spend with their children. However, it is important to keep in mind that a well-rested child will be healthier and happier than a tired and irritable one.

Children this age are generally more cooperative about going to bed. Some use delaying tactics, but many will ask to go to bed. After saying goodnight and perhaps looking at a book or listening to soft music for a few minutes, most go to sleep easily. Some children may need conversation, companionship, or the comfort of a stuffed toy or favorite blanket to sleep. Reading bedtime stories continues to be a way that parents can nurture children and encourage an interest in books and reading. Ongoing bedtime rituals remain comforting to many young children.

Toileting

By their fourth birthday, most children have few toileting accidents, either at night or during the day. When accidents do occur, it is often because the child is concentrating on an activity and forgets to go to the bathroom. Sometimes a child is in a new place and feels uncomfortable asking where the bathroom is.

Parenting Skills

What Is the Best Way to Handle Bedwetting?

It is not unusual for children who have learned to use the toilet to occasionally wet the bed at night. Either the child's bladder is not large enough to hold urine during the night, or the child is not awakened by the feeling of a full bladder. Sometimes the cause is an infection in the urinary tract. Here are some tips for dealing with bedwetting:

- Treat bedwetting accidents casually. Shaming or scolding a child does not help.
- Make sure the child understands that bedwetting is not his or her fault and that it will eventually stop.
- Reduce the amount of fluid the child drinks before bed.
- A small percentage of children continue to wet the bed as they get older, but almost all stop by the time they are teens. Children need continued support and reassurance that they will outgrow the problem.

Take Charge Imagine you are the parent of a six-year-old child who has episodes of wetting the bed. How would you respond if someone invited your child to sleep over?

Keep Children Safe from Strangers

Strangers are not always people who will harm children. Nonetheless, children should be taught to avoid contact with people they do not know unless the stranger is accompanied by an adult whom they do know. Help the child recite the names of the adults they know and can trust.

Children need to understand that it is not their job to help strangers. If a stranger asks for help, children should know to go tell an adult they can trust. Children should also be taught that if a stranger says, "Your mommy sent me to pick you up," they should not go with the person. They should tell a trusted adult right away.

Be Prepared Some children, because of age or disability, cannot be taught to follow the guidelines above. Research ways to keep these children safe from strangers that might want to harm them. Create a detailed list of your findings.

A child who has been dry at night may wet the bed again in response to stress or changes happening around him. If bedwetting recurs, put the child back in training pants at bedtime for a while. In some cases, a toileting accident is an indication that the child has an illness or infection. If problems with toileting persist, consult a physician.

In most cases, the following steps can help minimize accidents:

- Make sure the child uses the bathroom before leaving home.
- When arriving at a public place, point out where the bathroom is and remind the child to ask to use it.
- Keep an extra outfit available in the event of an accident. Handle the situation quietly, without calling unnecessary attention to it.

When they begin school, some children may suffer from constipation. Other children sometimes wet their pants. The stress children sometimes feel in their new school and with their routine can cause these problems. Most children adjust to the school routine within a few weeks. The adjustment period depends on the individual child though. For some children, the problem may recur at the beginning of school for several years. Children should not be punished when this occurs. Rather, they need to be reassured that they are still loved. Parents and teachers should work together to help relieve the stress the child is feeling. The child will probably overcome the toileting problems once he or she is more comfortable with the new routine.

✓ **Reading Check** **Explain** How many hours of sleep do four-year-olds need each day?

Outdoor Safety

Children ages four to six spend much of their time playing outside. For this reason, it is very important to teach children about outdoor safety. Here are some safety guidelines for outdoor play.

Bicycles

Bicycles can be fun for five- and six-year-olds, but can also pose dangers to the rider. A safety helmet should always be worn to protect the head from injury. Children should be taught the rules of the road when riding a bike. For more information on bicycle safety, see the Learning Through Play feature on page 560.

Traffic

Traffic is one of the most dangerous situations children can encounter when playing outside. Children must be taught to look both ways before crossing the street. Children should never play near parked cars.

Playgrounds

Public playgrounds are a great place for children this age to play outside. Children can socialize with other children. Playgrounds also offer a variety of equipment to help develop motor skills. There are safety precautions to take when using this equipment though.

Swings

Swings are the most common cause of injury from moving equipment on a playground. To reduce the risk of injuries on swings, children should always sit in the swing, not stand or kneel. Only one child at a time should sit in a swing. Children need to stay a safe distance away from other children who are swinging. Children should not be allowed to jump out of a moving swing.

Slides

Slides are safe if children are careful when using them. Children should always hold onto the handrails when climbing ladders to the top. They should also slide down feet-first and one at a time, not in groups. Be aware that slides may get too hot in the sun.

Climbing Equipment

Climbing equipment poses the greatest risk of any stationary, or non-moving, equipment on public playgrounds. Falling is the most common cause of injury for children of all ages.

Equipment must be properly anchored to the ground. Wood-framed structures should be inspected to ensure that they have been properly treated and have not splintered. There should be adequate cushioning material under playground equipment. This could include grass, mulch, or shredded tires.

Make sure there are not too many children on the equipment at once. Adult supervision is especially important for younger children, who might not have the arm strength necessary to play on climbing equipment. Make sure any equipment is age-appropriate for the child.

Section 13.2   After You Read

Review Key Concepts

1. **List** the factors that influence the amount of food a child needs.

2. **Describe** two things parents and caregivers can do to encourage children who do not like to bathe.

3. **Explain** three reasons why toileting accidents might occur.

4. **Recall** the most common cause of injury from moving equipment on a playground.

Practice Academic Skills

 English Language Arts

5. Review the MyPyramid Web site to determine which foods are nutritious. Talk to a child who is between the ages of four and six about foods. Does the child know which foods are nutritious and which are not? What nutritious foods does he or she like to eat? Summarize your interview in a report.

 Science

6. Use your knowledge of the personal hygiene needs of four- to six-year-olds to develop a checklist of hygiene routines. Put the checklist on a poster and illustrate. If possible, give the poster to a four- to six-year-old to use.

 Check Your Answers Check your answers at this book's Online Learning Center at **glencoe.com**.

> **NCTE 7** Conduct research and gather, evaluate, and synthesize data to communicate discoveries.

> **NSES F** Develop understanding of personal and community health.

Careers With Children

Children's Activity Director

Some cities, counties, states, and organizations such as churches have public facilities. These may include beaches, picnic grounds, gardens, or swimming pools. Children's activity directors plan and coordinate events for the different facilities. These events include concerts, sports, and educational programs for children.

What Does a Children's Activity Director Do?

Activity directors must begin planning events months in advance. They contact and make arrangements with performers. They decide how long the event should last, and whether food or seats need to be ordered. Children's activity directors make sure that events are appealing to children and safe for all involved.

Where Do Children's Activity Directors Work?

Children's activity directors for cities, counties, and states typically work in offices, but they often visit the parks and other facilities. Sometimes the activity directors are directly involved in the programs and work with the children.

Preparation and Skills

Education and Training
Many children's activity directors study management of nonprofit organizations. They usually have a background in recreation. Some learn a second language. An understanding of child development and age-appropriate activities is also helpful.

Aptitudes, Abilities, and Skills
Successful children's activity directors have energy, good organizational skills, resourcefulness, and an ability to make budgets. They also need imagination and a sense of fun to think of events and programs to sponsor.

Academic Skills
English language arts are used to communicate with others. Those who work in areas with large immigrant populations may need to know a second language.

Explore Careers

Work with your teacher to arrange to shadow a children's activity director. Ask the director if you may help teach a group of children a song or finger play. Write a one-page report of your experience and include whether you think you would enjoy this career.

Careers Online For more information on careers, visit the Occupational Outlook Handbook Web site through the link on this book's Online Learning Center at **glencoe.com**.

Chapter Summary

Children between the ages of four and six grow steadily, and their body shape changes. Permanent teeth begin replacing the primary teeth. From ages four to six, children refine their motor skills. The eating habits children learn will influence their adult eating habits and health. Physical inactivity is a major cause of overweight in children. Four- to six-year-olds can wash and dress themselves and can help care for their own clothes. They may still have toileting accidents.

Vocabulary Review

1. Create a fill-in-the-blank sentence for each of these vocabulary terms. The sentence should contain enough information to help determine the missing word.

Content Vocabulary
◇ permanent teeth (p. 384)
◇ ambidextrous (p. 387)
◇ group identification (p. 394)

◇ fluoride (p. 394)
◇ enamel (p. 394)

Academic Vocabulary
■ erect (p. 384)
■ dexterity (p. 386)
■ persuade (p. 390)
■ undermine (p. 392)

Review Key Concepts

2. Summarize how an average child's posture and body shape change from ages four to six.

3. Compare and contrast average motor skills development for four-, five-, and six-year-olds.

4. Explain why good nutrition is essential for children ages four to six.

5. Identify three ways that four- to six-year-olds are able to care for themselves.

6. Describe three steps that can help minimize toileting accidents.

7. List three areas of outdoor safety to discuss with four- to six-year-old children.

Critical Thinking

8. Develop Imagine that you are the parent of a five-year-old. Plan three nutritious meals or snacks that you feel would appeal to your child.

9. Demonstrate Show the steps you would use to teach a five-year-old how to tie shoelaces. Use words that a child can understand.

10. Apply Suppose you are an advice columnist. A parent writes in to say that her six-year-old is having bedwetting accidents. Write a response in which you provide advice. Use what you have learned about child development to offer tips for helping her child.

Family & Community Connection

11. Consult a Librarian Ask a librarian to recommend a book that would be suitable as a bedtime story for a four- to six-year-old. Read the book and write a one-page report that describes the book and tells what aspects you feel would make it appealing to children.

Health Skills

12. Research Childhood Disabilities In this chapter you learned that cerebral palsy is a disease that can cause physical disabilities or impairments in young children. This is only one of many causes though. Research a different disease or cause of physical disabilities in young children. Look for the cause of the disease, symptoms, and treatments. Write an essay that summarizes your findings.

Observation Skills

13. Observe Children's Television Watch children's television programs for at least one hour. Saturday morning or early evening are usually good times to do this.

Procedure As you watch the programs, pay attention to the commercials. Keep track of the commercials for food items. Note whether they are snack foods, breakfast foods, and so on.

Analysis Create a chart of your observations. The chart should indicate the type of food, such as snack or breakfast, the number of commercials for that type of food, and whether you think the food advertised is nutritious for young children.

NSES 1 Develop an understanding of science unifying concepts and processes: systems, order, and organization; evidence, models, and explanation.

Real-World Skills

Interpersonal and Collaborative Skills

14. PlanAction Follow your teacher's instructions to form groups. Brainstorm with your group to come up with hygiene practices to follow for infants, toddlers, and staff in a child care center. Create two posters to remind children and staff members of these practices.

Technology Skills

15. Make a Graph Use the information in Figure 13.1 on page 384 to create a bar or line graph comparing the average height and weight for boys and girls at ages four, five, and six. Use word processing or spreadsheet software to create your graph.

Financial Literacy

16. Comparison Shop Research the cost of fast-food meals and frozen dinners created especially for children. Compare these costs against the cost to prepare a home-made nutritious meal. Which is the better buy? Should cost determine which meal to purchase? Why or why not?

Additional Activities For additional activities, go to this book's Online Learning Center at **glencoe.com**.

Academic Skills

 English Language Arts

17. Determine Necessary Knowledge Caregivers of young children need to know the average rate of development to provide appropriate care and to assess whether there might be a developmental problem. List and describe the knowledge that caregivers should know about the rate of development of four- to six-year-olds. Summarize your ideas in a one-page essay.

> **NCTE 4** Use written language to communicate effectively.

 Mathematics

18. Party Preparation When a toddler wants something, she typically wants it immediately. To reduce the amount of conflict at an upcoming party for eight children, a mother plans ahead to make sure there are enough materials for everyone. Each child needs 6 blocks, 8 crayons, 10 pieces of paper, 1 balloon, 1 pair of safety scissors, and 2 foam balls. How many of each item is needed for the party of eight?

Math Concept **Multiples** Multiples are the products of a given number and various integers.

Starting Hint Multiply each integer (the number of each item needed) by the given number of children. For example, the number of blocks needed is six and $6 \times 8 = 48$.

 For math help, go to the Math Appendix at the back of the book.

> **NCTM Number and Operations** Compute fluently and make reasonable estimates.

 Science

19. Conduct a Survey Research has linked television viewing to an increased intake of calories, especially from snack foods. Children who eat while watching television tend to eat more snacks and many of the snacks are fatty foods.

Procedure Survey parents or caregivers of four- to six-year-olds. Ask them what snack foods their children eat while watching television or videos. How much do they eat?

Analysis Create a list of the snacks from your survey and report whether the snacks are high in fat. Do your findings agree with the research results? Write a paragraph to summarize your findings.

> **NSES A** Develop understandings about scientific inquiry.

Standardized Test Practice

MULTIPLE CHOICE
Read the paragraph, then the question that follows. Read the answer choices and choose the best answer to fill in the blank. Write your answer on a separate sheet of paper.

> As children start school, two factors become important in choosing clothing for children. First, children this age have definite likes and dislikes. Second, group identification becomes important and may bring with it a desire to wear clothes like those of classmates.

20. In this passage, group identification means ___.
  a. recognizing others in a group
  b. participating in group activities
  c. a feeling of belonging
  d. losing your identity in a group

> **Test-Taking Tip** In a multiple-choice test, the answers should be specific and precise. Read the question first, then read all the answer choices. Eliminate answers that you know are incorrect.

Emotional and Social Development from Four to Six

Chapter Objectives

After completing this chapter, you will be able to:

- **Identify** a single characteristic that marks the emotional development of four- to six-year-olds.
- **List** five ways to help children reduce worry and tension.
- **Describe** how to help children develop self-confidence.
- **List** three social skills children must learn as they begin school.
- **Identify** seven guidelines for encouraging moral development in children.
- **Describe** three ways to encourage conflict resolution and cooperation in children.

Writing Activity   *Character Analysis*

Looking Back One way to describe a person is by writing a character analysis. A character analysis is a look at a person's traits, feelings, and behaviors. Write a 60- to 80-word character analysis of yourself when you were five years old. It might help to remember a specific event or occasion from your youth.

Writing Tips Begin by spending a few minutes thinking about what you were like when you were five. Then use these tips to write your character analysis:

1. Be specific in describing physical characteristics such as curly hair or big feet.
2. Describe emotional and social characteristics. Did you feel you were not good at soccer? Were you shy or outgoing?
3. Try to make the character analysis interesting. List facts that the reader might not expect.

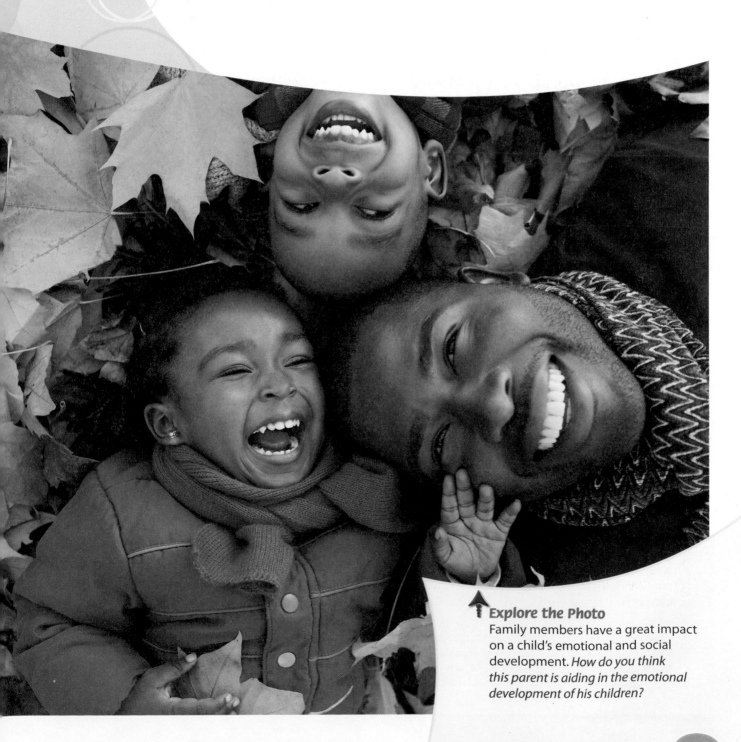

Explore the Photo
Family members have a great impact on a child's emotional and social development. *How do you think this parent is aiding in the emotional development of his children?*

Reading Guide

Before You Read

Identifying Main Points Identifying an author's main points keeps your thinking on-track. As you read, write down the main points for each head or subhead.

Read to Learn
Key Concepts
- **Identify** a single characteristic that marks the emotional development of four- to six-year-olds.
- **List** five ways to help children reduce worry and tension.
- **Describe** how to help children develop self-confidence.

Main Idea
Between the ages of four and six, children grow more independent and express a wide range of emotions. These children become more self-confident as they learn new skills and learn how to make decisions.

Content Vocabulary
◇ tension
◇ self-confidence
◇ initiative

Academic Vocabulary
You will find these words in your reading and on your tests. Use the glossary to look up their definitions if necessary.
- impulsive
- turmoil

Graphic Organizer
As you read, look for ways that parents can help children handle fears. Use a chart like the one shown to help organize your information.

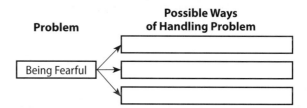

Problem

Possible Ways of Handling Problem

Being Fearful

Graphic Organizer Go to this book's Online Learning Center at **glencoe.com** to print out this graphic organizer.

Academic Standards . . . .

 English Language Arts

NCTE 2 Read literature to build an understanding of the human experience.

 Science

NSES A Develop abilities necessary to do scientific inquiry, understanding about scientific inquiry.

 Social Studies

NCSS I C Culture Apply an understanding of culture as an integrated whole that explains the functions and interactions of traditions, beliefs and values, and behavior patterns.

NCSS V D Individuals, Groups, and Institutions Apply concepts such as role, status, and social class in describing the connections and interactions of individuals and groups in society.

NCTE *National Council of Teachers of English*
NCTM *National Council of Teachers of Mathematics*

NSES *National Science Education Standards*
NCSS *National Council for the Social Studies*

Emotional Patterns

Justin was unusually quiet as he walked to school with his mother. It was his first day. He was both excited and fearful. His new teacher was there to greet them. As his mother talked with the teacher, Justin peered into the classroom and saw two of his friends from preschool. "Can I go and play with Scott and Dakota?" he asked. When the teacher said yes, he walked off. Justin was proud to be old enough for school. He was also glad to share the experience with familiar freinds.

Justin's behavior shows the increase in independence that is common for four- to six-year-olds. This independence is one characteristic that marks most clearly the emotional development for this age group. It is at this age that many children venture out of the home environment to attend preschool, daycare, or kindergarten. Perhaps for the first time, they find themselves with unfamiliar adults and large groups of other children. Each child responds to these challenges differently. There are, however, certain milestones that children in this age group generally attain.

Four Years

Most four-year-olds are still very self-centered. They can be defiant, impatient, loud, and boastful. They might argue and be bossy with other children and even with adults. At other times, four-year-olds may be very loving and affectionate. This is because they still need and seek the approval of parents and other caregivers.

Four-year-olds want to see themselves as separate from their parents or other main caregivers. They want to do things for themselves, such as washing and dressing. They enjoy the feeling of independence that they get from doing these tasks.

The vocabulary and language skills of four-year-olds show clear improvements from the skills of toddlers. At this age, children enjoy testing out the sounds of language and making up nonsense words. Four-year-old Martin, for example, goes around chanting phrases like "Antsy, wantsy, pantsy," and then breaks into hysterical laughter. Children of this age might also try using rude words, just to see how adults will react.

▲ Young Children at Play
Children are hurt easily and often disagree with other children. *What can caregivers do to help children manage these feelings?*

Understanding Success

Danielle and her five-year-old daughter Lori are enrolled in a parent-child art class at the park district. Each week, the teacher introduces them to new materials and techniques to use in their artwork. The first week focused on drawing. Lori likes to draw and works very hard to stay within the lines when coloring her drawings. This is something she has observed her mother do. The next week they began to make little clay pots. Lori had trouble with the process. She could not smooth out the walls of her pot the same way the teacher did. She pushed it away and said she did not like art anymore. Danielle knew that Lori was just frustrated. Danielle wanted to help Lori enjoy the class again.

Write About It Many children Lori's age feel that there is a right and a wrong way to perform tasks. They are afraid to continue if they think they are doing a task wrong. Write a scenario explaining how you might help Lori feel she is succeeding in her art class.

There are many reasons for these changes in the expression of anger. Frustration is a major cause of anger, and a child's tolerance for frustration generally increases with age. Also, some sources of earlier frustration are eliminated as the child's skills improve. Finally, by age six, children have better social skills, which can help them deal with situations that lead to anger. They can usually work in groups, for example, and recognize that some things belong to other people.

Disagreements with other children are the most common cause of anger. Although quarrels are still loud and verbal, five- and six-year-old children begin to conceal and disguise their feelings. Sometimes their methods of revenge are indirect. They may pretend indifference, sneer, or make sly remarks. Often they make exaggerated threats. Occasionally, they take their anger out on a scapegoat, such as a younger sibling, a pet, or even a toy. A *scapegoat* is one that takes the blame for others.

Criticism can also be a cause of anger. Six-year-olds do not like to be criticized. Children who are scolded for doing something wrong may try to punish a parent by breaking yet another rule.

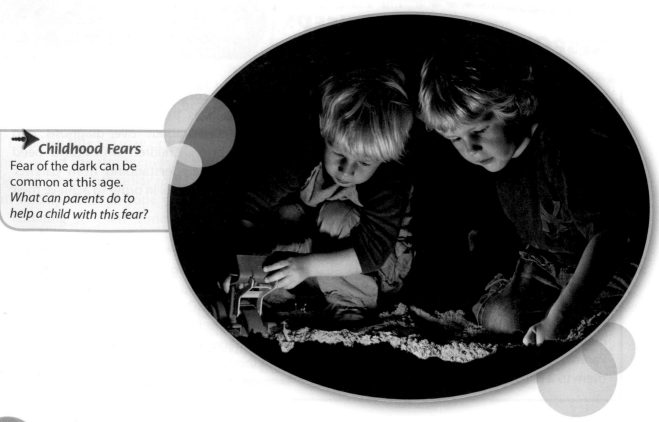

Childhood Fears
Fear of the dark can be common at this age. *What can parents do to help a child with this fear?*

Children vary greatly in how much anger they show and how they show it. Variations depend on a child's temperament and the child's environment. Children tend to imitate the behavior of adults. Parents and other caregivers can teach children self-control by expressing their own anger in appropriate ways.

Fear

Imagination is a major emotional force in children from four to six, and many of their fears center on imaginary dangers. They may be afraid of ghosts or monsters. Many children of this age are afraid of the dark. Some may worry about being left alone or abandoned. Fear of thunder and lightning is also common at this age. Many children fear situations related to school. They may be afraid of being criticized by a teacher or teased by other children. They may even fear that they will not perform as well as the other children.

Here are some ways that caregivers can help children deal with fears:

- **Accept the fear.** Just listening and saying you understand can greatly help a fearful child. Never say that what the child fears does not exist. It is very real to the child.
- **Let the child express the fear without ridicule.** Children this age fear being made fun of. If they worry that they might be ridiculed, they may not be open about their fears.
- **Help the child feel able to face the fear.** Use talking and acting out to help the child learn to face the fearful situation. Reading a book together about another child who dealt with a similar fear might also help.

Sometimes, of course, a child's fear about a certain situation is justified. A bully at school, for example, could be a cause for real concern. In such cases, parents need to take action to deal with the source of the fear and give support and reassurance.

Jealousy

Sibling rivalry is jealousy of brothers and sisters. It is common during this period. Some parents unintentionally make the problem

worse. They may try to improve behavior by comparing one child to another. One father, for example, asked his daughter, "Why can't you be neat like your sister Selena? I never have to tell her to put her toys away." Comparisons such as this are rarely effective. They can actually damage a child's self-esteem and undermine family relationships.

Children at this age sometimes express their feelings of jealousy by tattling, criticizing, or lying. Some may feel jealous and react by boasting.

Parents and other caregivers can help children work through jealous feelings by encouraging cooperation and empathy. It is best to avoid taking sides and to give children a chance to practice working out their own problems. Sibling rivalry tends to fade as children mature and find interests outside the home.

Worry

Children, like people of all ages, experience tension. **Tension** is another word for emotional stress. Children may worry about everything from a fire in their home, to a stranger taking them, to a bully in the neighborhood. Their active imagination contributes to the stress that they experience.

Parents and other caregivers can help preschoolers and kindergartners develop self-confidence in many ways. Four of the best ways to help build self-confidence are showing respect, offering praise, planning activities, and encouraging individuality.

Show Respect

Express confidence in the child's abilities. Offer the child choices whenever possible. Then show respect by going along with the child's decisions. When you make a decision, show respect by explaining your reasons rather than saying, "Because I said so."

Give Praise and Encouragement

Try to catch the child doing something right, and then praise the action or accomplishment.

Be specific, such as "I really appreciate it when you help clear the table after dinner." Children might not know what you are referring to when you use general comments such as, "Good job."

Plan Activities

Select activities that are challenging, but not overwhelming. Be sure the child has the ability to perform a given task to help avoid frustration and failure. Then give the child plenty of time and opportunity to practice. Be sure not to plan too many activities though. Children need downtime to relax and play.

Encourage Individuality

Give boys and girls opportunities to develop a wide range of skills. This can include skills such as making breakfast or learning how to drive screws or pound nails.

Section 14.1   After You Read

Review Key Concepts

1. **Identify** three main emotional differences in children ages four, five, and six.
2. **Explain** the relationship between imagination and fear in the mind of a preschooler.
3. **Describe** how initiative and self-confidence are related.

Practice Academic Skills

 English Language Arts

4. Carefully read the classic children's book *Where the Wild Things Are* by Maurice Sendak. Write an essay discussing how the book deals with common childhood emotions such as anger and fear. Also discuss how the book might build a child's self-confidence.

 Social Studies

5. Follow your teacher's instructions to form into groups. Work with your group to create a skit that shows the emotional behavior of four-, five-, or six-year-old children. As you develop your skit, keep in mind the emotional characteristics of children in your chosen age group. Be sure to use appropriate language in your skit.

 Check Your Answers Check your answers at this book's Online Learning Center at **glencoe.com**.

> **NCTE 2** Read literature to build an understanding of the human experience.

> **NCSS V D** Apply concepts such as role, status, and social class in describing the connections and interactions of individuals and groups in society.

Section 14.2

Social and Moral Development from Four to Six

Reading Guide

Before You Read

Helpful Memory Tools Successful readers use tricks to help them remember. For example, the acronym HOMES is a memory aid where each letter stands for one of the five Great Lakes. As you read the section, look for opportunities to make up your own memory aids.

Read to Learn

Key Concepts

- **List** three social skills children must learn as they begin school.
- **Identify** seven guidelines for encouraging moral development in children.
- **Describe** three ways to encourage conflict resolution and cooperation in children.

Main Idea

From four to six, children become increasingly involved in the outside world. Friends become important and moral values begin to develop. Children learn about teamwork and competition.

Content Vocabulary

◇ peer
◇ moral development
◇ aggressive behavior
◇ competition

 Graphic Organizer Go to this book's Online Learning Center at **glencoe.com** to print out this graphic organizer.

Academic Vocabulary

You will find these words in your reading and on your tests. Use the glossary to look up their definitions if necessary.

■ refine
■ resort

Graphic Organizer

As you read, look for reasons to encourage and discourage competition. Use a chart like the one shown to organize your information.

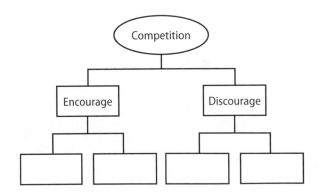

Academic Standards ·

 English Language Arts

NCTE 11 Participate as members of literacy communities.

Social Studies

NCSS V B Individuals, Groups, and Institutions Analyze group and institutional influences on people, events, and elements of culture.

NCTE *National Council of Teachers of English*
NCTM *National Council of Teachers of Mathematics*

NSES *National Science Education Standards*
NCSS *National Council for the Social Studies*

General Social Patterns

Children four through six years of age find themselves in an expanding world. As they begin preschool, kindergarten, and elementary school, they must learn three important social skills: how to interact with new people, how to make friends, and how to work and play in organized groups. Children must also learn how to take direction and accept authority from adults outside the home. Increasingly, young children must determine right and wrong and act accordingly.

A major task of the preschool, kindergarten, and early elementary school years is to develop social skills. As children spend more time outside the home, they need to **refine**, or improve, their skills at getting along with their peers. A **peer** is someone close to one's own age.

Adult authority figures other than parents and main caregivers also gain more importance. Although the rate at which individual children learn social skills varies, there are general patterns common at each age.

Four Years

Four-year-olds form friendships with their playmates. Unlike toddlers, who tend to engage in parallel play, four-year-olds spend more time in cooperative play. They can play in groups of three or four, sharing toys and taking turns. Four-year-olds are often bossy and inconsiderate, however, so fighting may occur.

Although friends are important to four-year-olds, the family is still more important. Children this age actively seek approval by making such remarks as "I'm good at drawing pictures, aren't I?" or "Look how high I can climb!" If things go wrong, they look to parents and other caregivers for comfort.

Five Years

Five-year-olds tend to be more outgoing and talkative than four-year-olds. They can play in groups of five or six, and their play is more complicated. Fights break out less frequently. When they do quarrel, five-year-olds typically resort to name-calling and wild threats.

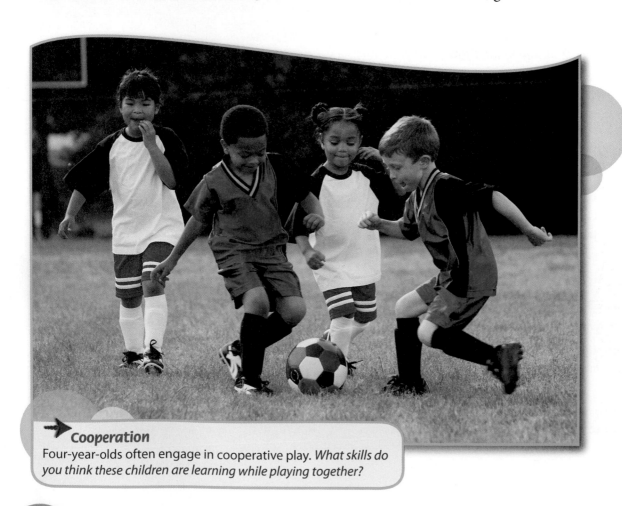

Cooperation
Four-year-olds often engage in cooperative play. *What skills do you think these children are learning while playing together?*

By age five, children have developed more respect for others' belongings. A five-year-old may still try to grab another child's toy, but such behavior is less common.

When children begin school, social acceptance by peers becomes more important. Five-year-olds are concerned about what their friends say and do. They do not want to be thought of as different, and they fear ridicule.

At about this age, some children begin to gossip about other children. Typically they talk about which children they consider to be friends or who has what toys. Gossip indicates what behaviors the children as a group value, and what actions they consider undesirable.

Six Years

The social relations of six-year-olds are often characterized by friction, threats, and stubbornness. Children this age want everything, and they want to do things their own way. They may not want to share their toys. They may be jealous of other children's toys.

Best friends at this age are usually children of the same sex, though six-year-olds play readily in mixed groups. They enjoy group play and organized teams for games. If they tire of playing, however, they will simply drop out of a game. They have no regard for team effort.

What Would You Do?

Handling Family Conflict

The relationship between six-year-old Pam and her family was strained. Nothing seemed to please her. When she screamed and protested after her parents took her television privileges away, they relented. After her parents gave in to her demands, her behavior grew worse. At their wits' end, Pam's parents went to see the school counselor.

"Pam is acting out all the time. How can we get her to change?" they asked. "Perhaps you need to ask what you can do to change the situation," the counselor advised. "Let's begin by looking at your expectations. It is reasonable to expect a six-year-old to follow the family rules or face the consequences. It is not realistic to expect her to be happy about the consequences. You want Pam to learn self-control by accepting the consequences of her actions."

Write About It Imagine that you are one of Pam's parents the day after this meeting. Pam is throwing a temper tantrum because you will not let her go to a friend's house until she has cleaned her room. Write a dialog between you and Pam showing how you would respond to this situation.

New Friendships
By the age of six, children make distinctions between types of friends. *Why are friendships at this age often marked by friction?*

Learning Through PLAY

Play by the Rules

Playing a board game with a four-year-old can be fun, but at the same time very frustrating. Children delight in playing games, though they often create their own set of rules as they go along. Most preschoolers think the world revolves around them. As a child matures, the world seems to get bigger and include more people. Social rules become more important. Playing games allows a child to follow rules. The child learns to take turns and learns that he or she cannot always be the winner. The child is able to see the world from another person's perspective and is able to understand why rules are needed for things to be fair.

Think About It Work with a partner to create a skit in which you are playing a board game. One of you should be a four-year-old and the other the parent. The child keeps trying to change the rules so that she can win. Act out how the parent might respond appropriately.

Family Relationships

Relationships within a family change as a child advances from age four to age six. Four-year-olds feel close ties to home and want to feel important in the family. They are proud that they can help with chores. However, they often quarrel and bicker with their siblings.

Five-year-olds also delight in helping out at home. They now play much better with their brothers and sisters. They are usually protective and kind toward younger siblings.

Six-year-olds do not get along as well with other family members. This is in part because they are more self-centered. Their own feelings and needs come first. Six-year-olds commonly argue with adult family members. They can be rough and impatient with younger brothers and sisters, and may fight with older siblings.

✓ **Reading Check** **Compare** How are six-year-olds' relationships with their families different from those of five-year-olds?

Moral Development

The process of learning to base one's behavior on beliefs about what is right and wrong is called **moral development**. Moral development begins early in life. Toddlers learn the rules their parents and other caregivers set. At that stage, however, they do not understand the reasons for the rules. They just learn that some actions, such as hitting another person, make their caregivers unhappy with them. They do not want to lose love and approval, so they learn to avoid those behaviors.

Preschoolers, on the other hand, are beginning to understand the reasons behind such rules. They are beginning to develop a conscience. A *conscience* is an inner sense of right and wrong that guides people's behavior and helps them make judgments about what is good and bad behavior. The rules that they learn in early childhood form the basis of their developing conscience.

Guidelines for Moral Development

Parents and other caregivers have a responsibility to help children develop a moral sense that will guide their behavior. Here are some suggestions:

- **Set clear standards of behavior.** Tell children, for example, "We do not hit other people. Hitting will hurt them and make them sad." Teaching children the reasons for rules helps them understand why the rules are important.

- **Respond to inappropriate behavior.** When rules are broken, deal with the problem immediately and appropriately. Repeat the rule and the reason for the rule.
- **Talk about mistakes in private.** Six-year-olds, especially, do not like to be criticized. Correcting their behavior in front of others may make them feel humiliated.
- **Understand that children will test the limits.** As children develop a moral awareness, they might try disobeying or refusing to cooperate. This is a sign that they are beginning to understand what is acceptable and what is forbidden behavior.
- **Consider the child's age and abilities.** For example, at preschool, Beth was playing at a shallow table filled with rice and containers. She started tossing the rice into the air and watching it land on the floor. The teacher reminded Beth that she must keep the rice in the table, then handed her a broom and a dustpan to sweep up the mess. Beth's teacher knows that children this age cannot always remember the rules but will learn from the consequences of their actions.
- **It is a lifelong task to learn self-discipline.** It is unfair to expect perfection from children. Instead, help children learn from their mistakes. Always recognize and praise their steps in the right direction.
- **Continue to show love despite misbehavior.** Children need to know that, although you do not like what they did, you continue to love them. Separate the deed from the doer.

Handling Lying

Many children tell tall tales and exaggerate. Young children often confuse stories with reality. These are not deliberate deceptions. Adults can show the child that they know the difference by saying, "I will listen to your story, and then I need to know what really happened."

Parenting Skills

Guide Children's Behavior

Parental guidance makes a major difference in whether children grow up to be happy, well-adjusted adults. Here are some ways to guide children effectively:

- **Build trust.** Respond to their needs lovingly so that they know they can count on you, no matter what.
- **Accentuate the positive.** When you *accentuate* something, you place more emphasis on it. Comment when children show positive behaviors such as kindness and cheerfulness.
- **Build empathy.** Remind children that others have feelings, too.
- **Respect fears and feelings.** Guide children's behavior by offering respect and reassurance.
- **Teach actions and consequences.** Explain that if children angrily throw a toy, and it breaks, it will not be replaced. They will soon avoid actions that have negative consequences.
- **Encourage responsibility.** Assign a daily job. Doing a chore well helps children develop pride in themselves.
- **Guide by example.** Model ways to treat siblings, friends, neighbors, and relatives with kindness and respect.

Take Charge Your child gets angry at the family dog for knocking over his block tower. He kicks the dog, who yelps. What would you say to the child?

Competition

Competition is rivalry with the goal of winning or outperforming others. Not everyone has the same views about the role that competition should play in children's lives. Some say that children benefit from competition because it stimulates individual efforts and promotes higher standards. Competition helps children gain a realistic view of their own abilities in relation to others. It helps children excel and prepares them for the adult world.

Others feel that competition is harmful to children because it instills the idea that success depends on the ability to outdo others. This mindset, they say, can lead to hostile relationships. In addition, they feel competition can discourage initiative in those who rarely win because it points out their inadequacies and lowers their status and self-esteem.

Teamwork and Cooperation

Most preschoolers and kindergartners prefer cooperative play to competitive games. Children can actually engage in both kinds of play. They can play cooperatively in competitive games by working together with their teammates.

Children not playing at a particular time can cheer for their teammates. When they are playing, children can share in the game. For example, in a ball game, each child can have a turn.

Whatever the game, caregivers need to teach children not to compare themselves with others. Show them, instead, how to compare their skills today with their skills in the past. Is Carlos running faster than last month? Children can get a feeling of satisfaction from seeing improvement in their own performance.

Section 14.2   After You Read

Review Key Concepts

1. **Describe** how the nature of play changes between the ages of two and four.
2. **Explain** how parents should respond to a child who is lying.
3. **Identify** ways that competitive games can build cooperation among children.

Practice Academic Skills

 English Language Arts

4. A fable is not just a story. It is a story with a purpose. Fables are short stories designed to teach moral lessons. Write a fable that a four- to six-year-old could understand. Create simple illustrations for your fable. Read your story to a young child. Ask the child: What lesson did you learn?

> **NCTE 11** Participate as members of literacy communities.

 Social Studies

5. Suppose you are part of a group of adults setting up a T-ball league for six-year-olds. Prepare a list of six rules of behavior that the children are to follow. All of the rules must concern appropriate behavior, rather than athletic concerns.

> **NCSS V B** Analyze group and institutional influences on people, events, and elements of culture.

 Check Your Answers Check your answers at this book's Online Learning Center at **glencoe.com**.

Chapter Summary

Children develop increased independence, curiosity, and boldness as they mature from ages four to six. They show emotions such as anger, jealousy, and worry. The rich imagination and fantasy life of preschoolers can lead to fears of ghosts and monsters. As they mature, children learn to express anger with words rather than physical attacks. Children develop an internal sense of right and wrong. They also learn to play both competitive and cooperative games.

Vocabulary Review

1. Write a sentence using two or more of these content and vocabulary terms. The sentence should clearly show how the terms are related.

Content Vocabulary
◇ tension (p. 409)
◇ self-confidence (p. 411)
◇ initiative (p. 411)
◇ peer (p. 414)
◇ moral development (p. 416)
◇ aggressive behavior (p. 419)
◇ competition (p. 420)

Academic Vocabulary
■ impulsive (p. 406)
■ turmoil (p. 406)
■ refine (p. 414)
■ resort (p. 419)

Review Key Concepts

2. Identify a single characteristic that marks the emotional development of four- to six-year-olds.
3. List five ways to help children reduce worry and tension.
4. Describe how to help children develop self-confidence.
5. List three social skills children must learn as they begin school.
6. Identify seven guidelines for encouraging moral development in children.
7. Describe three ways to encourage conflict resolution and cooperation in children.

Critical Thinking

8. Analyze Why might family members experience more friction with a six-year-old than with a younger child?
9. Hypothesize Is it possible for parents to treat all of their children equally at all times? Can they always prevent sibling rivalry? Can they reduce it?
10. Judge Some adults who think competition should be encouraged in children say that it prepares them for the adult world. Do you agree with this point of view? Explain your answer.

Family & Community Connection

11. Friendship Write a definition in your own words of the word *friend*. Then talk with at least two children between the ages of four and five. Ask each child what he or she thinks it means to be a friend. Write a paragraph comparing your definition of the word friend with the children's definitions. Why do you think they are different?

Health Skills

12. Laughter Perhaps you have heard the saying, "Laughter is the best medicine." Laughing can help us relax and get rid of daily tensions. Science has shown that laughter can even improve our health. Conduct research using print or online resources to learn about the health effects of laughter. Then write a one-page report to share what you learn.

Observation Skills

13. Preschoolers and Emotions Preschoolers quickly shift from one emotion to another, often with little or no apparent reason. Some emotions, such as anger, fear, and worry, are typically seen by adults as undesirable.

Procedure Observe two preschoolers with their parents. Watch for the preschoolers to display anger, fear, or worry. Note how the child expressed the emotion and the parent's response.

Analysis Prepare a written report in which you describe the emotion the child displayed and the parent's response. Analyze whether the response appeared to have the desired effect.

NSES A Develop abilities necessary to do scientific inquiry, understandings about scientific inquiry.

Real-World Skills

Problem-Solving

14. Teach Skills You want to design a board game to help your younger nieces and nephews learn social skills. Create an original game out of common materials, such as cardboard and clay. Demonstrate your game to the class and explain the skill it is designed to teach.

Technology Skills

15. Design a Web Page A parents' group is developing a Web site to help parents cope with common problems associated with four- to five-year-olds. Create a Web page listing at least five reasons that children in this age group often have difficulties with anger.

Financial Literacy

16. Playing Together One way to reduce stress is by being physically active. Pick an activity that a family of four might enjoy, such as bicycling or joining a recreation center. Research the cost of this activity. Include, if necessary, membership fees, and buying or renting equipment. Create a chart showing your chosen activity's cost for one year.

 Additional Activities For additional activities, go to this book's Online Learning Center at **glencoe.com**.

Academic Skills

 English Language Arts

17. Research what various child development experts think constitutes *etiquette,* or good manners, in young children. Use this information to create a list of ten etiquette rules that parents can use to guide their preschoolers. Be aware of differences that may occur across different cultures.

> **NCTE 4** Use written language to communicate effectively.

 Mathematics

18. Social Development Child psychologist Erik Erikson believes that four- to six-year-olds learn to cooperate with others, and to lead as well as to follow. A mother is planning a party and wants to encourage all the kids to get to know each other during a variety of games. If there will be 12 children at the party, what are all the sizes of groups possible if each group is the same size?

> **Math Concept** **Common Multiples** Multiples are the products of a given number and various integers.

Starting Hint Divide 12 by 1, 2, 3, 4, 5, and 6. Any dividend without a remainder is a possible group size.

 Math For math help, go to the Math Appendix at the back of the book.

> **NCTM Number and Operations** Compute fluently and make reasonable estimates.

Science

19. Children and Media Many parents restrict their children's exposure to television and movies. For example, parents may limit their children to watching only one hour of television a day, or only allow them to watch movies that are rated G for General Audience.

Procedure Ask 10 parents if they limit their young children's exposure to television or movies. If so, ask them how. Keep track of the types of restrictions.

Analysis Write a report on what you learned. Include a chart summarizing the kinds of restrictions parents placed.

> **NSES A** Develop abilities necessary to do scientific inquiry, understandings about scientific inquiry.

Standardized Test Practice

TIMED WRITING

Because many standardized tests are timed, it is important to develop a good strategy for taking them. Imagine that you have 10 minutes to write an answer to the following question. Read the Test-Taking Tip, and then write your answer.

20. What are some ways in which parents and caregivers can help children deal with sibling rivalry?

> **Test-Taking Tip** Avoid the temptation to immediately begin writing. Start by thinking through your answer and creating an ordered list of your major points. Then begin writing.

Intellectual Development from Four to Six

Chapter Objectives

After completing this chapter, you will be able to:

- **List** eight types of intelligences.
- **Identify** the common element of all theories of intellectual development.
- **Identify** three ways to encourage children's interest in learning.
- **Describe** the link between speech development and physical development.
- **Explain** how parents can help their children adjust to kindergarten.

Writing Activity Humor

Learning to Learn The learning process varies from child to child. Sometimes a learning experience can be humorous. Humor is the ability to see the lighter side of a situation. You can show a sense of humor by laughing during experiences such as:

- Getting caught in the rain without an umbrella on your way to school.
- Shrinking your favorite shirt by washing it in the wrong temperature.
- Misreading a recipe and adding too much pepper.

Mistakes are part of learning. But being able to laugh at your mistakes makes the learning experience fun. Write a story about a time you or someone else had a humorous learning experience.

Writing Tips To write an effective story with humor, follow these steps.

1. If you have trouble thinking of something, try freewriting or brainstorming with a friend to think of a humorous experience.
2. Let your natural humor come through in your writing. Do not try to force the humor.
3. Be sure to explain what you learned from the experience and how humor helped you get through it.

Section **15.1** Brain Development from Four to Six

Section **15.2** Learning from Four to Six

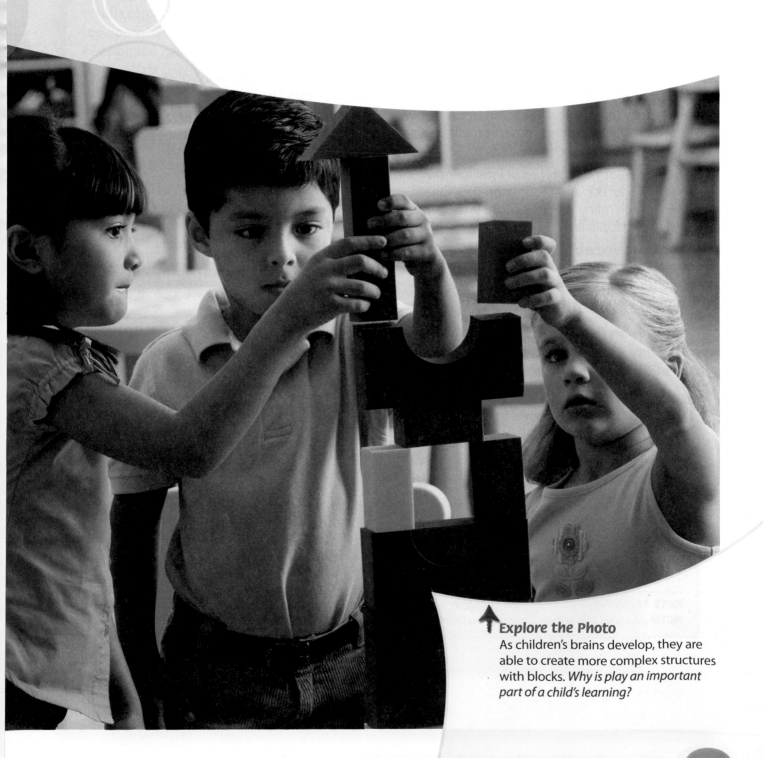

Explore the Photo
As children's brains develop, they are able to create more complex structures with blocks. *Why is play an important part of a child's learning?*

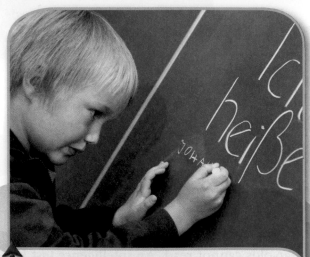

English Language Learners
Intelligence tests must be valid for children whose first language is not English. *Why might a child whose first language is not English have a difficult time with an intelligence test written in English?*

- Factors that have nothing to do with intelligence can influence results. These factors can include whether a child feels ill or stressed on the day of testing. A child's previous experience with the kinds of tasks included in the test also can affect test scores.
- Overall scores, such as IQ scores, do not tell us much about individual strengths and weaknesses. Two people with the same IQ may have very different abilities. It is important for the person giving the test to explain how the child scored on all measures. Some tests are composed of many subtests, each measuring different abilities.

Educators must use intelligence tests with caution. The National Association for the Education of Young Children (NAEYC) is an association dedicated to improving the well-being of children from birth through age eight. NAEYC warns that no decision about a child's placement in school should be based on a single test. Today, schools are more likely to use several techniques to gain an overview of a child's level of development in all areas, not just thinking skills. If the child falls outside the norms of development for his or her age, then an in-depth assessment of skills may be necessary. This will help educators identify problem areas and plan appropriate activities.

Some intelligence tests have been criticized for cultural bias. **Cultural bias** means that many of the test questions favored or gave an advantage to people from one culture over other cultures. Language differences can also affect test results. A child whose first language is not English may not earn as high a score as an equally intelligent child who has learned English from birth. New tests have been designed in response to these criticisms. They have been screened for cultural bias. Children may take them in their native language. The goal is for all children to be assessed fairly.

Multiple Intelligences

In recent years, psychologist Howard Gardner has presented a different way of looking at intelligence. He argues that humans have multiple intelligences. **Multiple intelligences** are abilities in problem solving or creating materials that have value. Gardner has identified eight such intelligences:

- **Linguistic intelligence** involves sensitivity to language, the ability to learn languages, and the ability to use language to accomplish goals. Writers, poets, and lawyers have high linguistic intelligence, according to Gardner.
- **Logical-mathematical intelligence** consists of the ability to analyze problems using logic, perform mathematical operations, and explore issues scientifically. This intelligence is associated with scientific and mathematical thinking and research.
- **Spatial intelligence** involves an understanding of the potential use of space, thinking in three-dimensional terms, and imagining things in clear visual images. Architects and landscape designers are among the careers that rely on this type of intelligence.
- **Musical intelligence** involves skill in performing, composing, and appreciating musical patterns.
- **Bodily-kinesthetic intelligence** has to do with the potential to use one's body to solve problems, and using the mind to coordinate body movements.

- **Interpersonal intelligence** involves the potential to understand the intentions, desires, and motivations of others. This type of intelligence helps teachers, counselors, and religious and political leaders work better with other people.
- **Intrapersonal intelligence** implies the capacity to understand oneself, including fears, hopes, and motivations. According to Gardner, it means having a good working model of ourselves and using it to **regulate**, or control, our actions.
- **Naturalist intelligence** involves recognizing, categorizing, and drawing upon the features of the environment.

Gardner believes that the intelligences usually operate at the same time and balance each other as people develop skills and solve problems. Each person has a blend of intelligences. Gardner believed that deciding how best to take advantage of each person's unique blend is a major challenge.

If caregivers recognize that a child is particularly high in one type of intelligence, they can provide the child with learning opportunities that will build those strengths as well as challenge the child and encourage an interest in learning.

✓ **Reading Check** **Apply** What intelligence is associated with people who know their own strengths and weaknesses?

Figure 15.1 Intellectual Developmental Milestones—Ages 4–6

There are many skills commonly seen in children in this age group. *At what age do children understand about 13,000 words?*

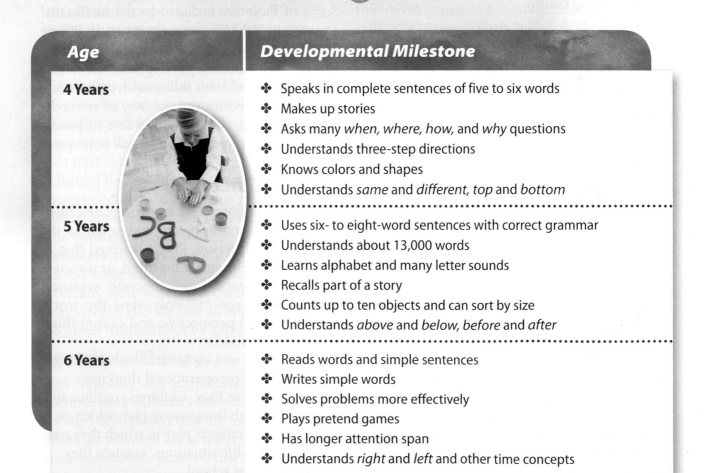

Age	Developmental Milestone
4 Years	❖ Speaks in complete sentences of five to six words ❖ Makes up stories ❖ Asks many *when, where, how,* and *why* questions ❖ Understands three-step directions ❖ Knows colors and shapes ❖ Understands *same* and *different, top* and *bottom*
5 Years	❖ Uses six- to eight-word sentences with correct grammar ❖ Understands about 13,000 words ❖ Learns alphabet and many letter sounds ❖ Recalls part of a story ❖ Counts up to ten objects and can sort by size ❖ Understands *above* and *below, before* and *after*
6 Years	❖ Reads words and simple sentences ❖ Writes simple words ❖ Solves problems more effectively ❖ Plays pretend games ❖ Has longer attention span ❖ Understands *right* and *left* and other time concepts

Help Children Learn

Jorge came home from kindergarten, bursting with excitement about his day. "We have a real bunny at school now," he said. "And Miss Jackson said I can help take care of him! Today I cleaned his cage, and then I filled his water bottle, and then I got to feed him. He has special food to eat, and I gave him some." Jorge thrust a note into his mother's hand. "Look! Mary and I get to feed him every Wednesday! Can I bring some lettuce on those days?"

Four- to six-year-olds are often excited about learning. Parents and caregivers can encourage this enthusiasm in many ways.

Experiences in Everyday Life

Experiences, especially those shared with adults, form the basis for children's learning. Talking with children about their world and what they are doing encourages interests. Positive comments teach vocabulary and encourage feelings of self-worth. These can be as simple as "Wow, the building you are making is so tall. And it has so many windows!"

You can also ask children questions that help them think about their experiences in new ways and focus on the process of their play. Encourage them to organize their thoughts by asking questions like, "How did you do that?" and "What are you going to do next?"

Explanations and suggestions can also be helpful. They must use age-appropriate language, though. You might explain in simple terms why water from a faucet can come out cold or hot. If a child grows frustrated trying to find room to put together a train set, you could suggest removing other toys from the floor to make the job easier.

Asking a child's advice is another effective technique for promoting learning. For example, ask how to fold napkins for a meal and then fold them the way the child suggests.

Trips and activities are important to learning. A ride on a bus, train, or plane can be an adventure that leads a child to discuss what is seen and to ask questions. Nature walks are also fun. Nature walks are free and everyone in the family can learn about the natural world by taking a close look at plants and animals.

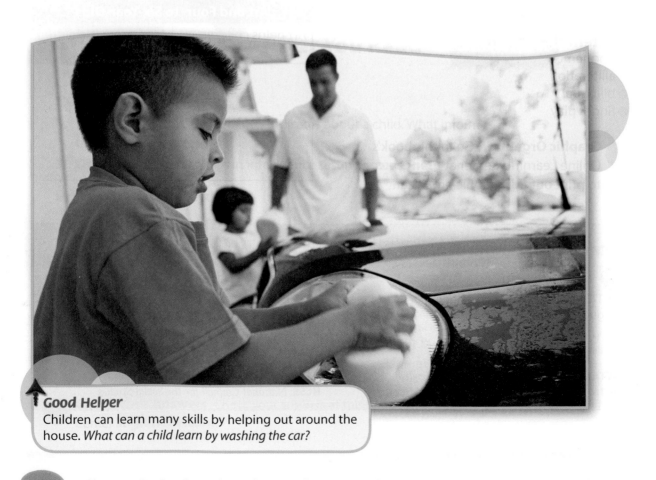

Good Helper
Children can learn many skills by helping out around the house. *What can a child learn by washing the car?*

Helping around the house provides great learning opportunities. Four- to six-year-olds can help sort laundry to be washed into lights and darks. They can also set the table and put their toys away. Helping around the house gives children a sense that they are part of the family and play an important role in it.

Reading

Developing an interest in reading is important because books provide an opportunity to learn about and understand the world. Children who enjoy reading will find learning easier and more fun. Reading to young children regularly helps them associate books with enjoyment at an early age. Reading together can remain part of a daily routine even as children start school and begin learning to read on their own.

An important factor in learning to read is the ability to hear phonemes. A **phoneme** (ˈfō-ˌnēm) is the smallest individual sound in a word, such as the *ou* in *house*. Rhyming words help develop phoneme awareness, so reading rhyming books to children is a good learning activity. When a book becomes familiar, stop from time to time and let the child fill in the sounds and words. When Jessica's mom reads, "Hey diddle, diddle, the cat and the…" Jessica shouts, "Fiddle!"

Another way to develop phoneme awareness is through alliteration. **Alliteration** is the repetition of certain sounds. Many alphabet books provide opportunities to use alliteration because they collect words that begin with the same letter. After children have learned the sound, they can begin to associate the letter with the sound, which is an important step in learning to read. You can also help the child by making associations beyond the book.

Parenting Skills

How Much Television Is Too Much?

From ages four to six, children's brains are rapidly developing. Watching television may affect their brain development. When children watch television, they are missing out on other experiences, like forming relationships, getting exercise, and using their imagination. Children who spend a lot of time watching television are less active. This can lead to weight problems and other health problems.

Researchers suspect that attention deficit disorders and weak problem-solving skills among children are related to watching too much television. Watching more television is associated with poorer academic performance, especially in reading.

While watching television is no substitute for reading or other challenging activities, some programs for children are educational and interactive. For example, many public television programs encourage imaginative play and pose questions for children to answer. There are also educational videos available to help reinforce language or math skills. Parents should restrict children's viewing of programs that depict violence or that contain material that is not appropriate to a child's level of development.

Take Charge What activities would you suggest to a six-year-old instead of watching television? Create a poster titled "Ten Things to Do Instead of Watching Television."

For example, Hayden's mother read "A is for apple and alligator." She then paused and asked "What else starts with A?" Hayden was able to answer "Ants!"

Watching television is not a substitute for reading. Studies have shown that children whose caregivers read to them have an easier time learning to read.

Some research suggests that children who are bilingual find it easier to learn to read. **Bilingual** means being able to speak two languages. Children who are bilingual seem to understand that printed words convey a specific meaning sooner than children who speak only one language. This may give them an edge when learning to read.

Choosing Books

Young children love books and stories. When caregivers encourage this interest, children are more likely to read for pleasure as they grow older. Books are still a fairly inexpensive form of entertainment. There are many different types of books to choose from. This means there is generally something that will appeal to any child.

Most communities have public libraries that lend children's books. In some cases, children can get their own library cards. This symbol of being grown up helps children look forward to going to the library and choosing their own books. Many libraries also offer story time or other programs to help foster a child's interest in reading.

How can you tell which books will appeal to children? The following questions will help you make appropriate choices:

- Are the pictures colorful, interesting, and easy to understand?
- Will the story appeal to the child's interests?
- Does the story include action that will hold the child's attention?
- Will the child understand most of the words?
- Does the book use descriptive language that brings the story to life?
- For younger children, is the story short enough to read in one sitting?
- If you are considering buying the book, is it sturdy enough to stand up to hard use?

What kind of books do four- to six-year-olds like? Many like stories about experiences that are different from their own. Through books, children who live in cities can learn about farm life. Children who live in rural areas can experience subways, apartments, and other aspects of city life.

Children this age also enjoy humor, including funny rhymes and unusual situations. When they giggle over a picture of a horse in a bathtub, they show that they are beginning to separate reality from fantasy.

Art and Music

Art and music help children express their feelings, develop fine motor skills, and express their creativity. Music often provides an emotional outlet for children who do not yet have the words to express what they are feeling.

Creating Artwork

Four- to six-year-olds benefit from working with many different art materials, such as modeling clay, crayons, paper, paste, paint, and scissors. Even buttons or dried macaroni can be strung into a necklace or painted and pasted onto a sheet of construction paper to make a design.

Children should be encouraged to experiment with art materials without being corrected or criticized. What matters to the child is the creative process. You can help children feel proud of their artwork by displaying it and sharing it with others.

THE DEVELOPING BRAIN

Language Builds the Brain

Children between birth and six-years-old are at the ideal age to learn their own first language as well as other languages. Exposure to more than one language rewires the neurons in the still developing brain in such a way that a child's overall language abilities increase greatly.

■ **Science Inquiry** Adults typically do not learn new languages as easily as children. What might explain this?

Learn Through Books
Children love to go to the library and choose their own books. *Why should parents help children make their choices?*

When you talk to children about their artwork, you **foster**, or encourage, a sense of accomplishment. You also help develop their verbal skills. By asking, "How did you make that?" you can help the child find the words to explain it to you. Rather than guessing what a picture represents, ask the child to tell you. Then find specific aspects of the work that you can praise. For example, you might say, "I really like the bright colors you used for the flowers." Or, "That was very creative to use buttons for the wheels."

Composing Music

The rhythm of music intrigues children. Rhythm can be the thud of a ball bouncing on the sidewalk or the sound of footsteps. Children this age become more aware of rhythms and enjoy singing simple, repetitive songs.

Many children are introduced to singing by a finger play. A **finger play** is a song or chant with accompanying hand motions. *The Itsy, Bitsy Spider* and *I'm a Little Teapot* are examples of popular finger plays. Finger play helps children improve their motor skills.

Music is also a great teaching tool. For example, most children learn the alphabet by singing their ABCs. Many children will set other facts to music to help remember them, such as "one plus one is two."

The opportunity to play simple instruments helps develop children's interest in music. Children enjoy using bells, drums, tambourines, or almost anything that makes a noise. There is no need to buy instruments. Old pans, bowls, and mixing spoons work just as well.

✔ **Reading Check** **Explain** Why is it important to talk to children about their art?

Speech Development

By the time they start school, children have gained an extensive knowledge of language just by listening and talking at home. They probably do not know what an adjective is, but they can use adjectives confidently and correctly. As children grow older, their vocabularies increase and the sentences they use become more complex. However, children learn all the basic forms of language almost effortlessly in the preschool years.

Children ages four, five, and six typically show a rapid increase in their vocabulary. A normally developing six-year-old can understand and use approximately 2,500 words. **Articulation**, or distinct speech, improves dramatically in this period as well. By age six, children can correctly say 90 percent of the words they know.

Much of this improvement in speech depends on physical development. Some sounds are more difficult to make than others. The sounds represented by *b, m,* and *p* are produced simply by moving the lips. By three, most children can make these sounds. The *f* and *v* sounds, among others, involve both the lips and the teeth. Children may not master these sounds until age five. The most difficult sounds are those represented by *j, ch, st, pl, th,* and *sl.* They require the smooth coordination of lip, tongue, and throat muscles. Some children may reach six or seven before *pwease* becomes *please.*

Speech Difficulties

Although most children develop good language skills at home, some have problems with spoken language. They may have plenty of opportunities to listen and speak at home, but they may hear and use only a limited number of simple words. Children need to hear language that is specific and rich in detail. They also need to be encouraged to use this language. For example, rather than using the very general verb *go,* encourage children to use a variety of descriptive verbs. The boys *race* across the field. Mom *jogs* every morning. The bugs *creep* down the tree.

Some children have a head start. When parents and other caregivers begin talking to children from the time they are very young, it helps speech development. Describing what a child is seeing and doing builds vocabulary.

Children who do not speak English at home often face challenges when they begin school. They must learn English language skills and, at the same time, keep up with the class. Some schools have classes with bilingual teachers or aides for English language learners.

Children who move from one part of the country to another may also have difficulty because of differences in pronunciation. Some

➤ **Learn with Laughter**
By the age of six, children's language skills have reached the point where they can understand and enjoy a simple joke. *How can telling jokes enhance a child's language skills?*

Learning Through **PLAY**

Playing Grown-Up

Between the ages of two and nine, children often engage in imaginative play, or make believe. This kind of play aids intellectual development in many ways. In imaginative play, children act out imaginary situations. They often imitate what they see in the adult world. After watching an adult bake a cake, a child may pretend to bake a cake for a favorite stuffed animal. After visiting a parent's workplace, a child may play in a pretend office or store.

Children might also use fantasy play by drawing images from stories or films, perhaps acting out an explorer's voyage across the Atlantic Ocean. Most children show an interest in imaginative play at some time. Adults who provide opportunities for imaginative play do children a great favor.

Think About It Imagine that you are caring for your five-year-old niece and six-year-old nephew who want to play detectives. What materials could you provide for children who want to pretend to be detectives?

---

children have physical problems that prevent normal speech. Others may be intellectually or emotionally delayed.

All these situations may cause children to have difficulties at school. They may not be able to understand the teacher or to make themselves understood. As a result, learning becomes harder.

This situation may cause emotional problems as well. Classmates may be mean to a child whose speech is different, even if the difference is just an accent. Teasing and jokes can add to a child's sense of isolation. Whatever the cause, children with speech problems need special help. They should get this help before they begin school.

> ✓ **Reading Check** **Recall** About how many words can a normally developing six-year-old use and understand?

The School Experience

Because children attend school for many years, it is vital that they develop a positive attitude from the start. Parents and caregivers should plan carefully to make the transition, or change, from home to school as smooth as possible.

Preparing for School

Many parents place their children in a preschool so that they can become used to a school setting. In preschool, children learn to pay attention, take turns, sit quietly for a time, and interact with other children.

At age five or six, most children enter kindergarten. The standard for entering the public school system is usually when the child reaches his or her fifth birthday. Most systems have a cutoff date, such as September 1. If a child is five by that date, the child may enter kindergarten.

Many states require that a child have a physical exam before starting school. Parents also have to show that their children have had the immunizations the school requires. For more information on immunizations, see Chapter 20.

In the past, kindergarten was usually only a half-day long. Today, however, full-day kindergarten programs are common. Research has shown that children in full-day kindergarten programs perform better in elementary school. Why do you think this is true?

Readiness

The question of when a child is ready to start school is a difficult one. Should a child of school age who would be among the youngest

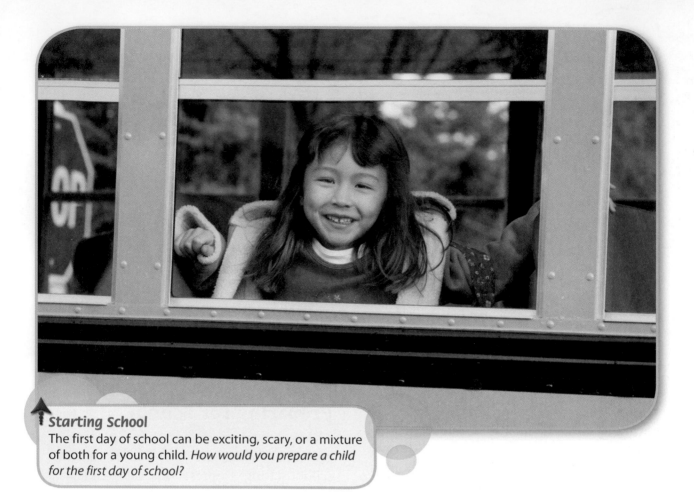

Starting School
The first day of school can be exciting, scary, or a mixture of both for a young child. *How would you prepare a child for the first day of school?*

in the class wait another year before starting school? What about a child who does not seem emotionally ready?

One study showed that even children with high intelligence had emotional problems if they began school before they were ready. Another study, however, suggests that the opposite is true. In this research, children who started later had problems with behavior later in their school careers.

What, then, should a parent do? Many school systems offer screenings to help assess a child's readiness. Parents whose child is enrolled in preschool can talk to the child's preschool teachers. They can judge the child's readiness based on what they have observed.

Parents can also talk with the pediatrician and look for certain signs. A child is ready for school if he or she can do the following.

- **Communicate with Adults** A child must be able to talk to adults other than his or her parents and be understood.
- **Manage Personal Needs** A child should be able to put on and take off his or her coat and shoes, and use the bathroom without help.
- **Complete a Task** A child should be able to complete a task such as finishing a drawing or putting away supplies.
- **Listen Attentively** A child should be able to listen attentively to a story and answer questions about it.

- **Follow Directions and Take Turns** A child must be able to participate in activities and cooperate with classmates.
- **Be Patient** A child should be willing to wait for a request to be met or to have a question answered.

Making the Transition

Starting kindergarten can be a major adjustment for a child. This is true even if the child has gone to preschool. The school is generally bigger than the preschool, and it includes children several years older. A child switching from a half-day preschool to a full-day kindergarten must adjust to the longer hours away from home. Many children entering kindergarten also begin riding a school bus for the first time. Parents can help their children adjust to this new experience in several ways:

- Be sure the child knows his or her full name, address, and telephone number.

- Explain what to expect at school. If possible, visit the school together before the child's first day and meet the teachers. Some schools offer open house or orientation days for new students and their parents.
- Be sure that the child has plenty of rest. It can help to start an earlier bedtime a few weeks before school begins.
- Let the child choose a lunch box or backpack, and pick out the clothes to wear on the first day of school. This will help the child link the new school to feelings of increased independence.
- If possible, arrange to have the child play with future classmates before the first day of school. Seeing people they know helps reassure children in new situations.
- Above all, share positive feelings about school with the child. Tell the child how much fun you had at school as a child.

Section 15.2   After You Read

Review Key Concepts

1. **Give examples** of how parents can encourage a child's interest in reading, art, and music.
2. **Describe** types of school activities that might be challenging for a student with a speech difficulty.
3. **Explain** two steps parents can take to prepare children for kindergarten.

Practice Academic Skills

English Language Arts

4. What challenges might young children whose first language is not English face at school? How can teachers help the child overcome these challenges? Record your ideas in a half-page essay.

NCTE 9 Develop an understanding of diversity in language use across cultures.

Social Studies

5. Think of an experience or activity not mentioned in the chapter that a caregiver could use to teach new skills to a child. Perhaps you remember how you learned a new skill as a child. Describe the activity and explain why you feel it is well-suited to a four- to six-year-old.

 Check Your Answers Check your answers at this book's Online Learning Center at **glencoe.com**.

NCSS IV D Apply concepts, methods, and theories about the study of human growth and development, such as learning, motivation, and behavior.

Kindergarten Teacher

Kindergarten teachers introduce students to concepts they will build on throughout their lives. They teach children how to take turns, share, and treat others with respect. They also build an enthusiasm for learning.

What Does a Kindergarten Teacher Do?

Kindergarten teachers are responsible for planning lessons and activities. They often use hands-on activities, such as making letters out of clay to teach the alphabet. They read books aloud, make learning tools, and even dance, sing, and do artwork. Kindergarteners have a short attention span, so lessons must be interesting and interactive.

Where Do Kindergarten Teachers Work?

Kindergarten teachers work in classrooms in public or private schools. A kindergarten classroom is a bright, colorful place with students' work decorating the walls. Kindergarten teachers work with children individually, in small groups, and as a class.

Preparation and Skills

Education and Training
Kindergarten teachers need to complete a bachelor's degree and an approved teacher-training program. Public school teachers must be licensed to teach.

Aptitudes, Abilities, and Skills
Kindergarten teachers must have patience, creativity, and the ability to motivate children. The ability to recognize children's academic and emotional needs is also important. Teachers should have organizational skills.

Academic Skills
English language arts and math skills are used by kindergarten teachers. They also use science and social studies to teach various lessons.

Explore Careers

Research a teaching career for any grade level. As part of your research, create a list of resources teachers use for curriculum development. Write a paragraph in which you tell whether you think you would like a career in teaching.

 Careers Online For more information on careers, visit the Occupational Outlook Handbook Web site through the link on this book's Online Learning Center at **glencoe.com**.

Chapter Summary

Intelligence tests vary for children of different ages. Gardner identified eight types of intelligence. Piaget's theory says children ages two to seven are in the preoperational period of thinking. Vygotsky and Montessori introduced influential theories of learning. Making reading a regular part of children's lives will encourage them to enjoy books in the future and promote learning. Between ages four and six, children's language skills usually improve rapidly, but some children need help. Children starting school can be helped to prepare for new situations.

Vocabulary Review

1. Create a fill-in-the-blank sentence for each vocabulary term. The sentence should have enough information to determine the missing word.

Content Vocabulary
◇ intelligence quotient (IQ) (p. 427)
◇ cultural bias (p. 428)
◇ multiple intelligences (p. 428)
◇ phoneme (p. 435)
◇ alliteration (p. 435)
◇ bilingual (p. 436)
◇ finger play (p. 437)

Academic Vocabulary
■ regulate (p. 429)
■ oriented (p. 430)
■ foster (p. 437)
■ articulation (p. 437)

Review Key Concepts

2. List eight types of intelligences.
3. Identify the common element of all theories of intellectual development.
4. Identify three ways to encourage children's interest in learning.
5. Describe the link between speech development and physical development.
6. Explain how parents can help their children adjust to kindergarten.

Critical Thinking

7. Predict Choose two types of intelligences. Predict three professions not mentioned that someone high in each intelligence might choose.
8. Apply What are five ways that the parent of an only child could help the child develop his or her interpersonal intelligence?
9. Infer Five-year-olds Sue and Jennifer use make-believe play to have a tea party for their dolls. Give examples of how they might show the other characteristics of preoperational thinking at their tea party.
10. Analyze Determine what intelligences are needed for the following tasks: writing an autobiography, making and selling crafts, writing songs to be used in television commercials, and painting landscapes.

Family & Community Connection

11. Interview a Literacy Worker Work with your teacher to arrange an interview with someone who works in a literacy program. During the interview find out what the program does, how someone gets involved in the program, and who is helped by the program. Create a brochure to promote the program using the information learned during your interview.

Health Skills

12. Research Intellectual Development Use print and online resources to conduct research about intellectual development in children four to six years of age. Research a theory that is not discussed in this chapter. Write a one-page report to share the results of your research. Include a summary of how the theory could be used to help promote learning.

Observation Skills

13. Television and Behavior Scientists have established a link between exposure to visual electronic media (VEM) and violent behavior, even in young children. One source recommends limiting television viewing to one or two hours a day. Another source recommends no more than four hours of television viewing per week.

Procedure Watch two hours of children's television programming. As you watch, keep track of the number of violent incidents you see in the program.

Analysis Use the information you gather to create a graph or chart. Provide recommendations for parents of young children who view television based on your findings.

NCTE 8 Use information resources to gather information and create and communicate knowledge.

Real-World Skills

Problem-Solving Skills

14. Generate Solutions Imagine you are a parenting expert with a magazine column. A parent writes in saying he wants to get his five-year-old son interested in reading, but has trouble getting him to sit still with a book. Write your advice to the parent to be printed in your magazine column.

Technology Skills

15. Create a Presentation Research the experiments that Piaget used to understand preoperational thinking. Choose one experiment to present to the class and explain how it shows preoperational thinking. Use presentation software to present your findings to the class.

Financial Literacy

16. Intelligent Spending Imagine that you have $150 to spend on activities for use at the day care center where you volunteer. You will focus on activities that promote bodily-kinesthetic intelligence for four- to six-year-olds. Go online or to a local educational supply store and create a list of activities and equipment you can purchase.

 Additional Activities For additional activities, go to this book's Online Learning Center at **glencoe.com**.

Academic Skills

 English Language Arts

17. Encourage Learning Imagine that a five-year-old is drawing a picture of her family and where they live. Write a list of five comments you could make or questions you could ask to encourage the child's learning and to promote positive feelings about herself. Write a brief essay in which you explain why you feel these comments or questions would be encouraging.

> **NCTE 4** Use written language to communicate effectively.

 Mathematics

18. Intellectual Development Psychologist Jean Piaget describes this age as intuitive. Children have the ability to perform multiple classification tasks or order objects in a logical sequence. Such an order exists in mathematics and is called the order of operations. Use the order of operations to evaluate this expression:

$$55 - 2 \times (3 + 4) + 15 \times 2 - 4$$

Math Concept **Order of Operations** The order of operations is parentheses, exponents, multiplication and division from left to right, and then addition and subtraction from left to right.

Starting Hint Following the order of operations, complete one step of the problem at a time, starting with the operation in parentheses.

 For math help, go to the Math Appendix at the back of the book.

> **NCTM Number and Operations** Compute fluently and make reasonable estimates.

 Science

19. Research Behavior The developing brain needs stimulation of all five senses: taste, smell, sight, touch, and hearing. Research shows that experiences that stimulate more than one sense at a time are more easily retained in the long-term memory.

Procedure Research why children remember multi-sensory experiences better. Give examples of multi-sensory experiences.

Analysis Create a list of multi-sensory experiences and write a one-page summary of your research findings.

> **NSES C** Develop understanding of the cell; biological evolution; matter, energy, and organization in living systems; and behavior of organisms.

 Standardized Test Practice

TRUE/FALSE

Read the following passage, then answer the question.

> Do you enjoy art, reading, or music? It is quite possible that your interest in these subjects first started when you were between the ages of four and six. At this time, children are exposed to new ideas and activities. These experiences have a significant impact on their growing minds.

20. According to this passage, children between the ages of four and six love music.
  a. True
  b. False

> **Test-Taking Tip** With true/false questions that rely on information given, read the paragraph carefully to make sure you understand it. Read the answer choices. Read the paragraph again before choosing the answer.

Teach New Skills

In this unit you have learned that there are many things parents and caregivers can do to help four- to six-year-olds grow and develop physically, emotionally, socially, and intellectually. In this project, you will interview a child care professional. You will use what you learn to create a brochure that will list activities for caregivers to use to promote growth and development in four- to six-year-olds.

My Journal

If you completed the journal entry from page 379, refer to it to see if your thoughts have changed after reading the unit.

Project Assignment

In this project, you will:
- Choose a person in your community who knows about the growth and development of four- to six-year-olds.
- Write a list of interview questions to ask about activities that will help four- to six-year-olds develop physically, socially, emotionally, and intellectually.
- Arrange and conduct an interview.
- Use what you learned in the interview to create a brochure. The brochure should list activities that will help children develop physically, emotionally, socially, and intellectually.

Child Development Skills Behind the Project

- Identify physical activities appropriate for four- to six-year-olds.
- List activities that will promote emotional and social growth in four- to six-year-olds.
- Describe intellectual activities that will stimulate four- to six-year-olds.

Academic Skills

English Language Arts

NCTE 4 Use written language to communicate effectively.

NCTE 7 Conduct research and gather, evaluate, and synthesize data to communicate discoveries.

Step 1 Choose a Professional to Interview

Listed below are child growth and development experts you may have in your community. Select one of these professionals to contact and interview.
- Preschool teacher
- Kindergarten teacher
- Day care worker
- Pediatrician
- Child psychologist
- Pediatric nurse
- College or high school child development instructor

Step 2 Write Your Interview Questions

Make a list of interview questions to ask the child development professional. Use information from this text and from your own knowledge to write questions about the physical, emotional, social, and intellectual development of four- to six-year-olds.

Writing Skills

★ Use complete sentences.

★ Organize your questions into the four areas of development: physical, emotional, social, and intellectual.

★ Use correct spelling and grammar.

Step 3 Connect to Your Community

Arrange to speak to the professional you chose in Step 1. Use the interview questions you prepared to find out about age-appropriate activities for four- to six-year-olds. Take notes during the interview.

Nonverbal Communication Skills

★ Dress neatly for the interview.

★ Listen attentively.

★ Make eye contact and smile when it is appropriate.

Step 4 Create and Present Your Brochure

Use the Unit Thematic Project Checklist on the right to create your brochure and share it with the other members of your class.

Presentation Skills

★ Organize your presentation by developing an outline.

★ Present your ideas clearly.

★ Be sensitive to the needs of your audience.

Step 5 Evaluate Your Child Development Skills and Academic Skills

Your project will be evaluated based on:

● Content and organization of your information.

● Mechanics—presentation and neatness.

● Speaking and listening skills.

Evaluation Rubric Go to this book's Online Learning Center at **glencoe.com** for a rubric you can use to evaluate your final project.

Unit Thematic Project Checklist

Brochure	✓ Use word processing software to create and illustrate your brochure. ✓ In your brochure, list activities that will help four- to six-year-olds develop physically, emotionally, socially, and intellectually. ✓ Organize the brochure so that activities are easy to locate. ✓ Include the heads: Physical, Emotional, Social, and Intellectual. ✓ Include a title on the front of your brochure. ✓ Add illustrations to your brochure.
Presentation	✓ Make a presentation to your class to share your brochure and discuss what you learned. ✓ Invite the students in your class to ask you any questions they may have. Answer three questions. ✓ When students ask you questions, demonstrate in your answers that you respect their perspectives. ✓ Turn in the notes from your interview and your brochure to your teacher.
Academic Skills	✓ Organize your brochure and presentation so the audience can follow along easily. ✓ Speak clearly and concisely. ✓ Thoughtfully express your ideas.

Unit 6

The Child from Seven to Twelve

Explore the Photo
Independence usually increases as a child gets older. *How can seven- to twelve-year-olds show independence?*

Chapter 16	**Physical Development from Seven to Twelve**
Chapter 17	**Emotional and Social Development from Seven to Twelve**
Chapter 18	**Intellectual Development from Seven to Twelve**

Unit | Thematic Project Preview

Develop an Exercise Program

By completing this unit, you will learn that children ages seven to twelve experience significant changes in their physical, emotional, social, and intellectual growth and development. In your unit thematic project, you can show how getting plenty of exercise plays an important role in these changes.

My Journal

Exercise and Development Write a journal entry about one of the topics below. This will help you prepare for the unit project at the end of the unit.

- Explain why getting regular exercise is important to growth and development.
- Identify exercises that are appropriate for growing children.
- Discuss how lack of physical exercise might affect a growing child physically, emotionally, socially, and intellectually.

Physical Development from Seven to Twelve

Chapter Objectives

After completing this chapter, you will be able to:

- **Describe** the two significant stages that occur between ages seven and twelve.
- **Explain** why children's motor skills improve between the ages of seven and twelve.
- **List** the nine topics in the Dietary Guidelines for Americans.
- **Identify** five areas that contribute to overall physical health and wellness.

Writing Activity Advertisement

Improving Motor Skills To improve their motor skills and learn new skills, many young people take classes. Examples might include ballet, tap dancing, or karate. Choose one type of class that interests you. Use the tips listed below to write an advertisement for the class.

Writing Tips When writing an advertisement, always keep your audience in mind. Otherwise, you will not be able to attract and hold their attention. Here are some tips for writing an advertisement:

1. Write a title and introduction that will grab the reader's attention.
2. Focus on the benefits of your class.
3. Keep your sentences short and simple; avoid using jargon, or terms specific to your activity. People might not know what those words mean.

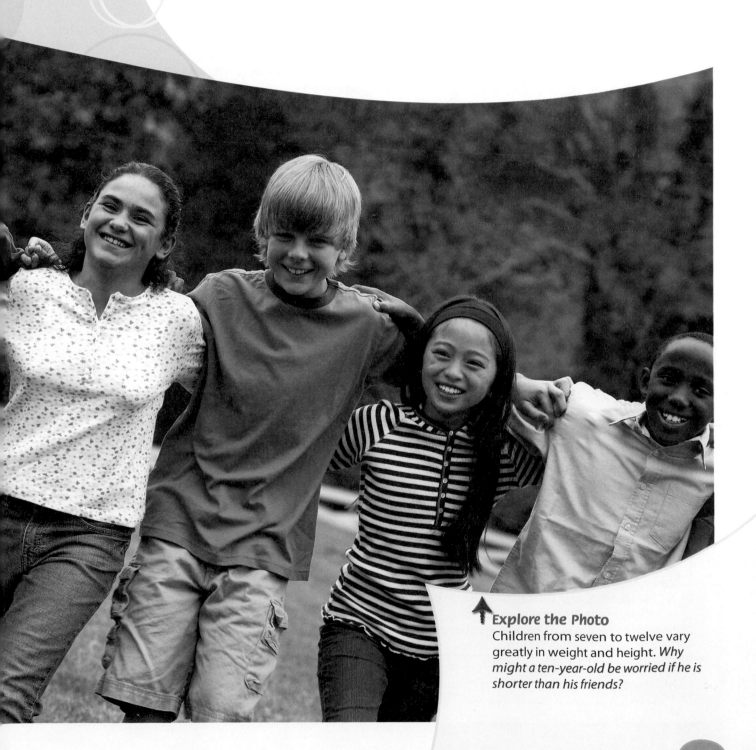

Explore the Photo
Children from seven to twelve vary greatly in weight and height. *Why might a ten-year-old be worried if he is shorter than his friends?*

Section 16.1 Growth and Development from Seven to Twelve

Reading Guide

Before You Read

Two-Column Note-Taking Fold a sheet of paper in half lengthwise. Label the left side "Main Ideas," and the right side "Details." As you read, fill in each side.

Read to Learn

Key Concepts

- **Describe** the two significant stages that occur between ages seven and twelve.
- **Explain** why children's motor skills improve between the ages of seven and twelve.

Main Idea

Children ages seven through twelve go through many changes, ending with puberty. Because of these extensive changes, they often become sensitive about the appearance of their bodies.

Content Vocabulary

◇ growth spurt
◇ puberty
◇ scoliosis
◇ body image
◇ eating disorder
◇ menstruation

Academic Vocabulary

You will find these words in your reading and on your tests. Use the glossary to look up their definitions if necessary.

- profound
- ultimate

Graphic Organizer

As you read, look for three changes that occur in both boys and girls during puberty. Use a diagram like the one shown to help organize your information.

Puberty

 Graphic Organizer Go to this book's Online Learning Center at **glencoe.com** to print out this graphic organizer.

Academic Standards

 English Language Arts

NCTE 5 Use different writing process elements to communicate effectively.

 Mathematics

NCTM Number and Operations Understand numbers, ways of representing numbers, relationships among numbers, and number systems.

 Science

NSES C Develop an understanding of the behavior of organisms.

NCTE *National Council of Teachers of English*
NCTM *National Council of Teachers of Mathematics*

NSES *National Science Education Standards*
NCSS *National Council for the Social Studies*

Growth from Seven to Twelve

From the ages of seven to twelve, children go through a period of **profound**, or overwhelming, physical changes. A sudden spurt of growth adds to their height. Their bodies begin to take on the physical characteristics of adulthood. There are two significant stages during these years: middle childhood and the preteen years. Middle childhood runs from ages seven through ten. During this period, children build on the growth and skills that began in early childhood. Eleven- and twelve-year-olds are in the preteen years. They are just beginning the path to being an adult.

Height and Weight

From the ages of seven to ten, boys and girls grow in height an average of just over two inches (5.1 cm) per year. This is a slower rate of growth than they experienced as preschoolers, toddlers, or infants. The gain in height is usually at a regular pace, but a child can have a growth spurt. A **growth spurt** occurs when a child grows very rapidly in a short period of time. For nine-year-old Ahmad, that meant the pants he bought at the start of the school year were too small by November.

The average rate of growth increases during the preteen years. It is during this time that many children go through puberty. **Puberty** is the set of changes that result in a physically mature body that is able to reproduce. Girls tend to go through puberty a bit earlier than boys.

This means the girls are often taller than the boys in their class at this time. Boys have larger average gains in height between the ages of 12 and 14, when they typically go through puberty. **Figure 16.1** on page 454 shows the average heights of boys and girls from seven- to twelve-years-old.

During this period, growth takes place in different parts of the body at different times. Typically, the hands and the feet are the first to grow, followed by the arms and legs, and then finally the torso. Sometimes one part of the body grows faster than other parts. This can cause embarrassment.

In terms of weight, boys and girls gain an average of about 6½ pounds (2.9 kg) each year during middle childhood. During the preteen years, this increases to about 10½ pounds (4.7 kg) for girls and 9½ pounds (4.3 kg) for boys. Because puberty typically occurs in boys about two years later than girls, boys have a greater annual weight gain than girls after about age twelve.

Growth Spurts
At some point during middle childhood, boys often experience growth spurts. *What other changes do they experience?*

Figure
16.1 **Average Heights and Weights—Ages 7–12**

Children in middle childhood and the preteen years vary greatly in height. *At what ages are the average heights for boys and girls the same?*

| Age | BOYS | | GIRLS | |
---	Height / Inches	Weight / Pounds	Height / Inches	Weight / Pounds
7 years	48	51	47¾	50
8 years	50	56	50½	56
9 years	52½	63	52½	64
10 years	54½	70	54½	72
11 years	56½	79	57½	82
12 years	58¾	89	59½	92

Experts believe that heredity is the most influential factor in determining a child's **ultimate**, or final, height. When parents are considered to be below average in height, it is likely that their children will be short.

Nutrition is an important influence on a child's weight during these years. A child who eats foods low in fat and high in nutrients is less likely to have a weight problem than one who eats fatty foods that are low in nutrients. Physically active children are also less likely to be overweight. **Figure 16.2** offers tips on how to help children enjoy organized sports.

Proportion and Posture

A tall and lean five-year-old typically remains tall and slim through middle childhood. However, as seven- to twelve-year-olds grow, their proportions change. Their legs lengthen, adding height and bringing the head more in proportion to their body. Children also become stronger and develop greater muscle tone in their legs, arms, and torso. Balance and coordination continue to improve.

Some older children and preteens develop a curve of the spine called scoliosis. **Scoliosis** is a sideways curvature of the spine, affecting posture. Scoliosis may be treated with exercise, a brace, or surgery.

Body Image

Some children become sensitive about their body image. **Body image** refers to how a person thinks his or her body looks. Children may become self-conscious about the changing shape of their bodies. Too often, images of thin celebrities and models make children think that they must be thin to be beautiful.

Preteens may experience an unhealthy preoccupation with food and thinness. They see themselves as overweight when they really are not. This, along with other factors, can put preteens at risk for developing an eating disorder. An **eating disorder** is a serious pattern of overeating or restrictive eating. Eating disorders can have a devastating effect on the body and can even lead to death. For more information about eating disorders, see page 462.

Figure

16.2 Organized Sports

Children typically learn team sports in groups and often compete against others. *Why is it more important for children to play for fun than to play to simply win?*

Team sports give children the opportunity to have fun, be physically active, and learn teamwork and other skills. Individual sports, such as swimming, provide some of the same benefits.

Appropriate Sports Children should only play sports for which they have the physical maturity.

Play for Fun Children benefit more when they are encouraged to play for fun and for individual skill development, rather than playing just to win. Look for a coach with this attitude.

Good Sportsmanship Respect for other players and the game should be one of the most important lessons a child learns.

Good Days and Bad Days Prepare children for both failure and success in sports.

Permanent Teeth

Primary teeth are the first set of teeth formed. Most children lose all of their primary teeth between the ages of five and thirteen, and most of the permanent teeth appear at this time, too. Permanent teeth are the second set of teeth formed. There are 32 permanent teeth. As mentioned in Chapter 13, the first permanent teeth to emerge are the set of molars that appear around the age of six. Around age twelve, a second set of molars emerges behind the first set. A third set of molars, called the wisdom teeth, appears later. The last four teeth appear between the ages of 17 and 21.

Puberty

Puberty usually occurs between the ages of nine and sixteen. Researchers believe that the start of puberty is related to heredity as well as nutritional and environmental factors. On average, however, puberty starts at about the age of ten for girls and about one to two years later for boys. Significant physical changes trigger the onset of puberty. The pituitary gland, found in the brain, begins sending out hormones that cause a number of profound physical changes in the body.

In both boys and girls, a significant growth spurt occurs during puberty. Children gain 25 percent of their total adult height through this growth spurt. Hair appears under the arms and in the pubic area for males and females. Sweat and oil glands become more active, and a child can begin to experience body odor and acne.

Boys

In boys, facial hair begins to appear, and the voice deepens during puberty. Sometimes the deepening does not take place smoothly, and a boy's voice may occasionally crack, or change tones. This is due to the growth of the larynx and vocal cords. A boy's shoulders broaden, and his muscles grow larger.

Girls

Girls typically experience more profound changes at puberty. Their breasts begin to enlarge, their waist narrows, and their hips widen. The sexual organs develop and become capable of releasing mature eggs. Most girls begin to have menstrual periods about two years after puberty begins. **Menstruation** is the monthly cycle in which an egg is released and the uterus prepares for a

THE DEVELOPING BRAIN

Fine Motor Skills

Fine motor skills are skills that involve the refined use of small muscles. It is possible to work on one's fine motor skills with activities that teach the brain to control hand and finger movements to a high degree. One such activity is typing. The more a person practices typing, the better his or her fine motor skills will become. This is why learning to type often involves performing routine drills over and over again.

Science Inquiry Typing can help develop fine motor skills. What other activities do you think could help in this development?

possible pregnancy. Girls' menstrual periods may be irregular at first, and not occur every month. Some girls experience discomfort and cramping with menstrual periods.

 Reading Check **Explain** Why are preteen girls often taller than the boys in their class?

Motor Skills

In the years from seven to twelve, a child's motor skills improve greatly. As the body matures, most children experience the following:

- Greater muscle strength
- Faster reaction time for responding to a stimulus, such as catching a ball
- Improved precision in activities such as balancing and aiming
- Greater speed
- Increased flexibility for bending and stretching easily

Thanks to all these more developed skills, children at these ages enjoy active play. Some take lessons to learn to swim and dance, and participate in gymnastics. Team sports are popular. Many children this age will prefer sports that use their improved motor skills, such as skating or bicycling, over simpler activities such as running or jumping.

With the increase in muscular strength comes more muscle control. Hand-eye coordination improves and both gross and fine motor skills become easier and smoother. More complex tasks become possible. For example, catching a baseball is a challenge for a seven-year-old, but a ten-year-old can manage it quite easily. Playing computer games can help children improve their fine motor skills. However, parents should still limit a child's time with computer games due to the impact on brain development.

Fine motor skills development is also evident in children's abilities to play musical instruments, do arts and crafts, and even writing. There is an obvious improvement in handwriting between five and seven years. And by eight, children start writing in script. As with any skill, motor skills improve with practice.

Section 16.1 After You Read

Review Key Concepts

1. **Explain** how a growth spurt affects a child's body during puberty. Why do children sometimes feel awkward at this stage?
2. **Describe** the benefits a child can gain from participating in sports.

Practice Academic Skills

 English Language Skills

3. Pretend you write an advice column for children and teens. Write an encouraging response to a letter from an eleven-year-old boy who is bothered by being the shortest student in his class.

 Mathematics

4. Use the information found in Figure 16.1 to create a line graph showing the average height of boys and girls from ages seven to twelve. Your chart should contain two lines, one for boys and one for girls.

 Check Your Answers Check your answers at this book's Online Learning Center at **glencoe.com**.

> **NCTE 5** Use different writing process elements to communicate effectively.

> **NCTM Number and Operations** Understand numbers, ways of representing numbers, relationships among numbers, and number systems.

Section 16.2 Caring for Children from Seven to Twelve

Reading Guide

Before You Read

Take Breaks It is important to take frequent study breaks. They allow your brain time to process what you have already covered and get ready to remember new information.

Read to Learn

Key Concepts

- **List** the nine topics in the Dietary Guidelines for Americans.
- **Identify** five areas that contribute to overall physical health and wellness.

Main Idea

The Dietary Guidelines for Americans and the USDA's MyPyramid Plan are helpful in meeting nutritional needs. Children need to stay active and learn to take care of their bodies.

Content Vocabulary

◇ fiber
◇ MyPyramid
◇ sedentary activity
◇ sealant
◇ orthodontist

 Graphic Organizer Go to this book's Online Learning Center at **glencoe.com** to print out this graphic organizer.

Academic Vocabulary

You will find these words in your reading and on your tests. Use the glossary to look up their definitions if necessary.

■ capacity
■ suppress

Graphic Organizer

As you read, look for the five food groups included in MyPyramid. Use a chart like the one shown to help organize your information.

MyPyramid
1.
2.
3.
4.
5.

Academic Standards . . . .

 English Language Arts

NCTE 7 Conduct research and gather, evaluate, and synthesize data to communicate discoveries.

Science

NSES A Develop abilities necessary to do scientific inquiry, understanding about scientific inquiry.

 Social Studies

NCSS V F Individuals, Groups, and Institutions Evaluate the role of institutions in furthering both continuity and change.

NCTE *National Council of Teachers of English*
NCTM *National Council of Teachers of Mathematics*

NSES *National Science Education Standards*
NCSS *National Council for the Social Studies*

Nutrition

During middle childhood and the pre-teen years, children experience tremendous physical and emotional growth. Good nutrition from a well-balanced diet is essential for growth, development, learning, and health. Children in this age group require good nutrition to grow, develop, learn in school, and feel their best. Such diets contain essential nutrients and a good balance of carbohydrates, fat, and protein. The Dietary Guidelines for Americans and the U.S. Department of Agriculture's MyPyramid Plan can help ensure that meals and snacks have the variety and amount of food that children need for a healthful diet.

Dietary Guidelines

The Dietary Guidelines for Americans is a useful tool for children and adults. The guidelines present a comprehensive plan for incorporating nutritious foods and physical activity into daily life. They include 41 recommendations, grouped into the following nine topics:

- **Get enough nutrients within your calorie needs.** Everyone needs a certain amount of calories in a day. The amount each child needs will vary based on age, activity level, and current weight.
- **Maintain a healthy weight.** Parents should ask their doctor what a healthy weight range is for their child. Being overweight can cause many health problems both in childhood and later in life.
- **Be physically active every day.** Children and teens need at least one hour of physical activity most or all days of the week. Physical activity has both short-term and long-term health benefits for children.
- **Choose whole grains, fruits, vegetables, and milk.** Foods made from whole grains help form the foundation of a healthy diet. They provide fiber plus many nutrients. **Fiber** is an indigestible plant material that helps the digestive system work properly. Many children fail to get the recommended servings of fruits and vegetables. These foods contain essential vitamins and minerals, fiber, and other substances important for good health. It is important for young children to drink milk every day. It provides vitamins and minerals necessary for the developing bones and body systems.

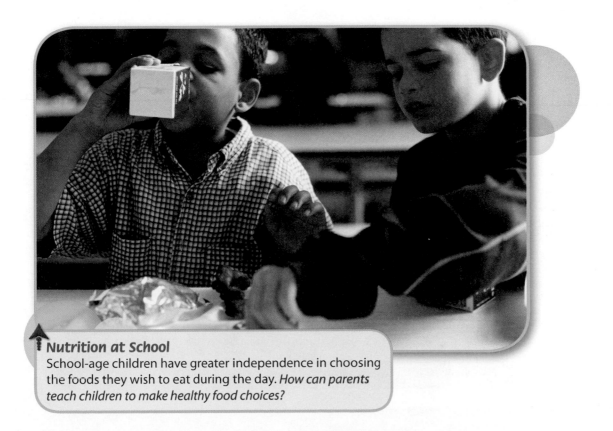

Nutrition at School
School-age children have greater independence in choosing the foods they wish to eat during the day. *How can parents teach children to make healthy food choices?*

- **Limit fats and cholesterol.** You need to eat fats, but only in small amounts. No one needs a diet high in fatty or fried foods and snacks. Most fats that are eaten should come from fish, nuts, and vegetable oils, rather than from red meat sources.
- **Be choosy about carbohydrate foods.** Sugars and starches are carbohydrates. Children should get carbohydrates from sugar that is naturally present in fruit and milk. Foods with added sugar such as candy can lead to tooth decay.
- **Reduce sodium and increase potassium.** Sodium helps control body fluids. However, too much sodium is linked to high blood pressure, heart attack, and stroke. Choose and prepare foods and beverages with little added salt. Potassium is found in many fruits and vegetables.
- **Avoid alcoholic beverages.** Just as the mother should avoid alcohol when pregnant, a child should never be given alcohol. Even a taste can be harmful to a child's developing body.
- **Keep food safe.** Food needs to be properly stored and prepared to help avoid food-borne illness.

MyPyramid

MyPyramid is a guide for healthful eating and active living that was developed by the U.S. Department of Agriculture (USDA). By entering information such as your age, weight, and activity level, the MyPyramid Web site will create a customized plan just for you! It shows how much and what kinds of foods you need each day. It also offers physical activity advice.

MyPyramid is divided into five food groups, plus an oils category. The five food groups include grains, vegetables, fruits, milk, and meat and beans. The meat and beans group is where you get your protein. Eating from all five food groups each day will ensure you get all the nutrients your body needs. This is especially important for children since their bodies are still developing.

Making Food Choices

As children become more independent, they begin to make more of their own food choices. They may make or buy some of their own snacks and meals. Peers or the media may influence these choices, which often take place away from home. For example, Leah can choose from various foods offered at her

MyPyramid
The USDA has developed MyPyramid to provide a guide for healthful eating. *What are three foods included in the milk group?*

MyPyramid
STEPS TO A HEALTHIER YOU

| GRAINS | VEGETABLES | FRUITS | MILK | MEAT & BEANS |

CULTURE MATTERS

Lessons You Can Eat

Martin Luther King Jr. Middle School in Berkeley, California, is home to a program called the Edible Schoolyard. Alice Waters, a chef, had the idea of creating a garden so that students could learn to take care of plants and cook foods they helped grow. Today, students learn how to plant seedlings, identify ripe vegetables, and gather eggs from hens. Establishing a sense of competence is important for students this age. Assigning each student a daily job in the garden enables them to reach goals. Jobs can include activities such as chopping apples to be pressed for their juice. Students learn to take responsibility for their actions.

⭐ **Build Connections** *Do you think these children will be more likely to eat vegetables they have grown rather than ones bought in a store? Explain your answer.*

NCSS V F Individuals, Groups, and Institutions Evaluate the role of institutions in furthering both continuity and change.

school for lunch. When she brings a lunch from home, Leah sometimes trades the fruit from her packed lunch for cookies or chips.

Despite outside influences, family remains the primary influence on a child. Modeling good eating behavior is one of the best ways to teach a child good eating habits. Here are a few specific things that families can do:

- **Eat meals together.** Show by example that healthful eating habits include eating both the right foods and the right amounts.
- **Offer healthy choices.** Serve varied, well-balanced meals that are low in fat, sugar, and salt. Offer appealing choices from all the food groups.
- **Be prepared.** Stock the kitchen with a variety of nutritious foods for snacks.
- **Make treats special.** Limit sweets and deep-fried foods to special occasions.
- **Control portions.** Offer children smaller portions than an adult would eat. Allow and encourage children to stop eating when they feel full.
- **Serve dairy daily.** Make calcium-rich foods and beverages a part of a child's diet to help ensure strong bones.

Starting the Day Right

Breakfast is an important meal for both children and adults. It provides the vital fuel that people need to begin the day. Researchers have found that children who eat breakfast have a greater **capacity**, or ability, for learning and participation. They also have a greater ability to concentrate, especially on tasks that require problem solving and creativity. Skipping breakfast can result in headaches, fatigue, and restless behavior, which interfere with classroom learning.

A healthy breakfast includes two servings from the grain group, one from the dairy group, and one from the fruit group. An example of a nutritious breakfast might include a bowl of cereal and a piece of fruit. National school breakfast programs help provide this nutrition and ensure that all children can begin the school day the right way.

Eating Disorders

Most children go through periods when they rebel against what is served at mealtime. Many children sneak sugary treats from time to time. This is normal behavior. However, a small percentage of children begin to develop eating disorders. There are several types of eating disorders. The three main types include:

- **Anorexia Nervosa** This is an intense fear of weight gain distinguished by starvation techniques and severe weight loss. Symptoms can include fatigue, dizziness, refusal to eat, or excessive exercise.
- **Bulimia** Bulimia involves periods of out-of-control eating followed by purging the body of food, often through vomiting. Symptoms can include fatigue, scars on the hands, laxative use, and going to the bathroom after or during meals.
- **Binge Eating** This disorder includes periods of highly excessive eating, followed by weight gain. Symptoms can include eating to the point of pain, frequent dieting without weight loss, or hiding food.

Researchers believe that some children with eating disorders may be preoccupied with being thin due to a poor body image. Others might see people they admire display eating disorders and want to be like them. Some might have psychological problems, such as depression or low self-esteem. Many strive to please others and feel that food is the only thing they can control in their lives. Children with eating disorders need counseling from a trained professional. Parents should not hesitate to consult a professional if they notice unusual eating patterns or sudden weight gain or loss in their daughter or son. Also encourage children to tell a teacher or school counselor if they notice or suspect a problem in their friends.

✓ **Reading Check** **Analyze** Why is eating breakfast important for children?

Parenting Skills

How Can Parents Help an Overweight Child?

Parents of an overweight child are often concerned about the health and emotional issues their child may face. They may be unsure of how to help. Here are some ways parents can offer support and guidance.

- **Consult with the child's doctor.** Ask for guidance on providing a healthy diet.
- **Focus on health rather than weight.** Do not make losing weight the main issue. Involve the whole family in a healthy eating plan.
- **Make a variety of healthy foods available.** Giving children choices makes them more willing to try new things.
- **Encourage regular physical activity and limit television viewing.** Encourage the child to participate in physical activities he or she enjoys. Be active daily and plan activities the whole family can participate in.
- **Offer unconditional love and support.** Caregivers should make it clear that the child is loved and accepted at any weight.

Take Charge Imagine you are the parent of an overweight child. Write a list of five steps you plan to take to encourage your family to eat a healthier diet.

Sedentary Activities
Television and video games have significantly reduced the amount of physical activity among children. *How can parents encourage children to be more physically active?*

Physical Health and Wellness

Everyone wants to help children be as physically healthy as possible. Being physically active can greatly increase overall health. Establishing healthy habits now will help children be healthier adults. Getting enough sleep, taking care of your body and teeth, and following safety rules are also important.

Physical Fitness

Children today are less likely to walk or ride their bikes to school than were their parents. Many children are less fit than they should be. They run the risk of becoming set in a pattern of inactivity that could result in health problems, especially when they are older.

One reason for the decline in fitness levels is that children spend hours every day in sedentary activities. A **sedentary activity** is an activity that involves little exercise, such as watching television or playing computer and electronic games. The hours children spend in front of a screen take time away from physical activity. Parents and other caregivers make the best role models for healthy living by limiting their own television viewing and their children's time in front of screens, and by joining children in physical activities.

To promote physical fitness, parents should look for a variety of developmentally appropriate activities that their children might enjoy. It is good to include activities that can be continued later in life, such as hiking, biking, swimming, dancing, skating, basketball, or tennis. Children need at least an hour of physical activity each day. Parents who remain physically active are role models for their children.

{ Expert Advice... }

"Physical growth that occurs during this time is more rapid than at any time since infancy. Besides growing bigger and taller, the maturing child begins to develop bodily characteristics that distinguish the male and female adult."

— Virginia K. Molgaard, family life specialist, Iowa State University

Figure 16.3 **Personal Safety from Ages 7–12**

As children spend more time away from home and family, they are exposed to more dangers. *How would you reassure a child who is constantly concerned about personal safety?*

Safe Practice	Examples
Keep doors locked when home alone.	❖ Never open the door to a stranger when home alone, even to someone who is wearing a uniform.
Wear protective gear.	❖ Never engage in sports without the proper protective gear, such as a bike helmet or shin guards.
Know how to get help in an emergency.	❖ Know what constitutes an emergency. ❖ Know how to dial 911 in an emergency. ❖ Practice by playing the "What If?" game. For example: "What if you woke up at night and smelled smoke?"
Pay attention to traffic.	❖ Cross streets at crosswalks only after checking for oncoming cars. ❖ Obey any restrictions concerning which streets may be crossed.
Stay away from strangers.	❖ Never get into a stranger's car or go near a stranger. ❖ Run and scream if you feel threatened.
Walk in groups.	❖ Older children can accompany younger children when they walk to school.
Trust your feelings.	❖ If someone, including an adult, makes you feel afraid or uncomfortable, get away and tell a trusted adult.

Sleep

Most children get busier as they get older. During the evening, school-age children have homework to complete, and perhaps a karate class or a music lesson. Getting to bed on time can be a challenge, but experts recommend enforcing a bedtime for school-age children. The National Sleep Foundation recommends that children this age get from ten to eleven hours of sleep each night. It helps their performance in school, as well as their mood.

Caring for Teeth

By age seven, children may need reminders, but they can brush their own teeth at least twice a day and floss daily. Additional brushings may be needed if very sugary or gummy food is eaten. A dental checkup and cleaning at least once a year is recommended to help prevent tooth decay. Sometimes fluoride treatments are given. Pediatric dentists can help ease fears about visiting the dentist.

Tooth decay occurs when bacteria in the mouth produce acids that break down tooth enamel and expose the softer parts of the tooth. Bacteria produce acids from sugars that a person eats or drinks. As children get older, they have more access to sugary foods and drinks. These have negative health effects and are linked to tooth decay. For these reasons, sugary foods and sweet drinks should always be limited in a child's diet.

To prevent tooth decay, some dentists place a sealant on children's teeth. A **sealant** is a thick plastic coating. Dentists usually place these sealants on permanent molars. Molars are teeth that are especially adapted to grinding food. Sealants have proven to be an effective way to help prevent decay.

Sometimes permanent teeth do not come in straight. This can sometimes cause problems with the way teeth fit together. If so, a dentist may refer the child to an orthodontist. An **orthodontist** is a dental specialist who concentrates on fixing irregularities of the teeth. The orthodontist can determine whether the child would benefit by having braces, separators, or retainers to straighten the teeth.

What Would You Do?

Dealing with Acne

Jerome started going through puberty before his friends. He began feeling self-conscious about his acne. He scrubbed his face every day, but the acne persisted. Finally he decided to ask his parents for help. His father revealed that he, too, had acne as a teen and he knew how it felt to be self-conscious about it. Jerome's dad suggested cleaning his face gently, then using a drying lotion at night. Jerome's mom suggested visiting his doctor to ask about treatments that could help prevent acne from forming. Jerome felt relieved that there might be a way to minimize the problem.

Write About It Write a script of a parent talking with his or her child who has acne. In addition to providing help, be sure the parent explains why the child is having acne at this time of life.

Personal Hygiene

Seven- to ten-year-olds are often unconcerned about good hygiene. This is not because they want to be dirty. They just cannot be bothered to take the time to bathe or shower. They would rather spend their time playing games or reading books. To prevent battles over bathing, there are several things parents or caregivers can do:

- **Focus on the essentials.** Make sure that the child washes hands before eating and after using the bathroom. Brushing teeth should be done daily.
- **Give choices when possible.** Let the child choose between showering and taking a bath. Give a choice of shampoo. Let the child choose the day's outfit. Children, like adults, respond well to having control over decisions that affect them.
- **Send positive messages.** Comment on how refreshing a shower is, or how relaxing and warm a bath feels. This signals to children that bathing and showering bring benefits besides simply getting clean.

The lack of interest in hygiene often changes around age ten. At about this time, the physical changes of puberty increase the need for cleanliness. With puberty, the body produces more sweat, so preteens may develop body odor. In addition to a daily bath or shower, they may need to start using deodorant or antiperspirant. Preteens often need to change into fresh clothes after physical activity. Parents should help preteens make this transition, or change. Sometimes children are unaware of body odor. Parents can help by offering a change of clothes, rather than pointing out the child's smell. Often, preteens will become more interested in choosing their own soap or shampoo, based on the scent.

During puberty, the oil glands in the pores of the skin produce more oil. At times the production can be excessive, resulting in acne and a greasy appearance to the hair. These problems usually go away over time, as the body's production of skin oil goes down. Encourage preteens to remedy the problem. Acne-prone skin should be washed twice a day with warm water and mild soap to help **suppress**, or control, outbreaks. Excessive scrubbing can make acne worse. For extreme cases, there are prescription medications that can be used. Also, shampoo and conditioner are available that are formulated for oily hair.

Checkups and Vaccines

Annual checkups can help prevent illnesses. Before starting fifth grade children typically receive a tetanus and diphtheria booster, and sometimes an MMR booster. MMR stands for measles, mumps, and rubella. A booster is a shot that increases the effectiveness of a previous immunization. Chicken pox and hepatitis B vaccinations are also strongly recommended before the age of thirteen. Children should also receive annual flu shots. This is especially true for children with weak immune systems or chronic lung conditions, such as asthma.

Section 16.2   After You Read

Review Key Concepts
1. **Describe** three eating disorders.
2. **Explain** why plenty of physical activity is vital for seven- to twelve-year-olds. What is the minimum length of time that should be spent on daily exercise?

Practice Academic Skills

 English Language Arts
3. Talk to five adults about what they did between the ages of seven and twelve to stay physically active. Write a paragraph summarizing what you learn. Also discuss which of those activities children still enjoy today and why you think they are still popular.

 Science
4. Conduct research to learn about medical treatments for acne that does not respond to over-the-counter medications. Write a report discussing at least three of the most common treatments. Also discuss any advantages or disadvantages of each type of treatment.

 Check Your Answers Check your answers at this book's Online Learning Center at **glencoe.com**.

> **NCTE 7** Conduct research and gather, evaluate, and synthesize data to communicate discoveries.

> **NSES A** Develop abilities necessary to do scientific inquiry, understanding about scientific inquiry.

Chapter Summary

Most children grow steadily during middle childhood. Some may become sensitive about their body image, which can put them at risk for eating disorders. Good dental hygiene practices are important. The Dietary Guidelines for Americans and the USDA's MyPyramid Plan can be helpful in developing good eating habits and are essential for good health. Increased interest in personal hygiene often begins during the preteen years. Annual checkups and vaccinations help to prevent illnesses.

Vocabulary Review

1. Create multiple-choice test questions for each content and academic vocabulary term.

Content Vocabulary
◇ growth spurt (p. 453)
◇ puberty (p. 453)
◇ scoliosis (p. 454)
◇ body image (p. 454)
◇ eating disorder (p. 454)
◇ menstruation (p. 456)

◇ fiber (p. 459)
◇ MyPyramid (p. 460)
◇ sedentary activity (p. 463)
◇ sealant (p. 465)
◇ orthodontist (p. 465)

Academic Vocabulary
■ profound (p. 453)
■ ultimate (p. 454)
■ capacity (p. 461)
■ suppress (p. 465)

Review Key Concepts

2. Describe the two significant stages that occur between ages seven and twelve.
3. Explain why children's motor skills improve between the ages of seven and twelve.
4. List the nine topics in the Dietary Guidelines for Americans.
5. Identify five areas that contribute to overall physical health and wellness.

Critical Thinking

6. Predict What might happen to a child who is not taught the importance of a balanced diet?
7. Make Inferences Why do you think eating disorders are developing at a younger age?
8. Contrast How are personal hygiene needs different for a preteen and a seven- to ten-year-old?
9. Analyze Why do you think preteens may not get enough sleep?
10. Apply Suppose that you help coach a team of young athletes. How might you educate parents about the importance of being a positive influence at sporting events?

Family & Community Connection

11. Children's Games Choose a cultural group, such as Hispanic or Chinese, to which some people in your community belong. Interview a member of this group or conduct research to learn about games the children in this culture play. Focus on games that involve physical activity. Demonstrate one of the games to your class.

Health Skills

12. Food Intolerances Many people have problems tolerating certain foods. Imagine that you have just learned you have celiac disease. Conduct research to learn about celiac disease and write a report explaining it. Include in the report a list of the foods you cannot eat and a list of foods you can use as substitutes.

Observation Skills

13. Encourage Physical Activity Physical activity can help children remain strong and healthy. It can also help improve their self-image. Parents and teachers can be central in helping children achieve an active lifestyle.

Procedure Observe preteens at a playground. Note how many are engaged in active play or sports. Also note how many are just sitting and talking.

Analysis Write a report in which you discuss the percentage of preteens that were inactive. Then present ideas on how a teacher might encourage these less active children to engage in more physical activity.

> **NCTE 7** Conduct research and gather, evaluate, and synthesize data to communicate discoveries.

Real-World Skills

Problem-Solving	**14. Encourage Good Hygiene** Imagine you are the parent of a 12-year-old boy. You think your son should pay more attention to his personal hygiene. Create a checklist of items to help him remember all the tasks he needs to complete each day. Then write a dialogue in which you present the checklist and explain why his hygiene is important.
Technology Skills	**15. Create a Slide Show** Suppose you need to teach seven-year-olds how to care for their teeth. Use application software to create a slide show that explains how to brush and floss teeth. The slide show should include art and language appropriate for seven-year-olds.
Financial Literacy	**16. Plan Snacks** Imagine that you work at an after-school program for seven- to ten-year-olds. Plan five nutritious snacks for the children. Research the cost of each planned snack. Each snack should cost no more than 50 cents per child. Create a chart listing the snacks and the cost of each.

 Additional Activities For additional activities, go to this book's Online Learning Center at **glencoe.com**.

Academic Skills

English Language Arts

17. Write a Letter Imagine that you are a school nurse. A group of parents is stating that childhood vaccines can cause health problems. Write a letter to the editor of your local newspaper in which you explain why vaccines are safe and vital to the health of children. Conduct research to learn facts to include in your letter.

> **NCTE 7** Conduct research and gather, evaluate, and synthesize data to communicate discoveries.

Mathematics

18. Take a Hike It is often difficult to fit family time into busy lifestyles. A family walk is a great way for parents and children to interact and talk. Suppose a family goes for a 1½ hour hike. According to the trail map, the hike was 2.3 miles round trip. How fast was the family walking?

Math Concept **Rate** A rate is a ratio of two measurements having different kinds of units, such as miles per hour.

Starting Hint Divide the total distance (2.3 miles) by the total time (1½ hours). To convert the fraction to a decimal, first write it as an improper fraction (³⁄₂), then divide the numerator (3) by the denominator (2).

 For math help, go to the Math Appendix at the back of the book.

> **NCTM Algebra** Use mathematical models to represent and understand quantitative relationships.

Science

19. Evaluate a Child's Diet The U.S. Department of Agriculture (USDA) has established guidelines for healthy eating for children. The MyPyramid Web site can provide guidelines based on a person's age, height, weight, and activity level.

Procedure Ask a preteen to keep track of all the food he or she eats for one day.

Analysis Go to the MyPyramid Web site to determine the dietary guidelines for the child. Create a chart that compares the child's diet to these guidelines.

> **NSES F** Students should develop understanding of personal and community health.

Standardized Test Practice

MULTIPLE CHOICE
Carefully read the passage and then answer the question.

> Research has determined that eating trans fat raises low-density lipoprotein (LDL) levels in the blood. This increases the chances of getting coronary heart disease. Manufacturers make trans fat by adding hydrogen to vegetable oil. This increases the shelf life of the oil and stabilizes its flavor.

20. According to this passage, ingesting trans fats can ____.
  a. increase your chances of having diabetes
  b. make you obese
  c. increase your chances of having a heart attack
  d. lead to a vitamin deficiency

> **Test-Taking Tip** If you do not know the answer to a question, first cross off any choices you know are wrong. This will make it easier to evaluate the remaining ones.

Emotional and Social Development from Seven to Twelve

Chapter Objectives

After completing this chapter, you will be able to:

- **Identify** four ways to help ease emotional upsets.
- **Explain** how to help children control and express their anger in socially acceptable ways.
- **List** six ways to help a child develop a sense of competence.
- **Summarize** the four main qualities children look for in friendships.
- **Identify** typical changes that occur in children's attitudes toward their parents.
- **Describe** five ways to help prepare children to make good moral choices.

Writing Activity ✍ *Personal Narrative*

Making Friends Developing new friendships is easy for some people and difficult for others. Some people are naturally shy. Others are outgoing. Some people belong to many clubs and groups. This lets them meet and interact with many people. Other people prefer to spend more time alone. Write a personal narrative about a specific time when you had to make new friends.

Writing Tips To write an effective personal narrative, follow these steps:
1. Test your ideas by talking them through with a friend or by freewriting.
2. Ask yourself questions to fill out details of the narrative.
3. Construct a time line or other graphic organizer for your narrative.

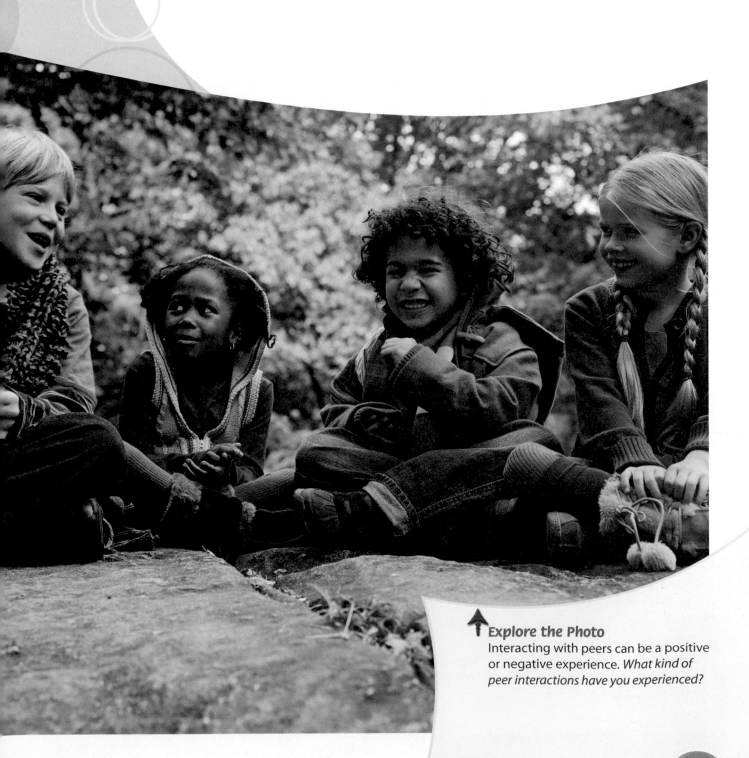

Explore the Photo
Interacting with peers can be a positive or negative experience. *What kind of peer interactions have you experienced?*

Emotional Development from Seven to Twelve

Reading Guide

Before You Read
Guilt-Free Rest If you feel guilty about resting, you create more stress. Your reading skills are more effective if you are relaxed and ready to learn.

Read to Learn
Key Concepts
- **Identify** four ways to help ease emotional upsets.
- **Explain** how to help children control and express their anger in socially acceptable ways.
- **List** six ways to help a child develop a sense of competence.

Main Idea
Children from seven to twelve experience emotional changes. They learn to better control and express emotions. They also develop a sense of self.

Content Vocabulary
◇ anxiety
◇ sense of self
◇ sense of competence
◇ gender identity

 Graphic Organizer Go to this book's Online Learning Center at **glencoe.com** to print out this graphic organizer.

Academic Vocabulary
You will find these words in your reading and on your tests. Use the glossary to look up their definitions if necessary.
- shift
- persevere

Graphic Organizer
As you read, look for four emotions that seven- to twelve-year-olds need help learning to control. Use a web diagram like the one shown to help organize your information.

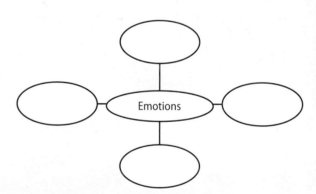

Emotions

Academic Standards . . . .

 English Language Arts

NCTE 12 Use language to accomplish individual purposes.

 Social Studies

NCSS IV D Individual Development and Identity Apply concepts, methods, and theories about the study of human growth and development, such as behavior and personality.

NCTE *National Council of Teachers of English*
NCTM *National Council of Teachers of Mathematics*

NSES *National Science Education Standards*
NCSS *National Council for the Social Studies*

Emotional Changes

Andrea's parents had a hard time describing her to others. When she was seven, Andrea often stayed in her room. By age ten, she had become more outgoing. Her parents were relieved that she was more cheerful and showed more affection. A year later, she became moody and did not want to spend time with her parents at all.

There is nothing unusual about going through an emotional **shift**, or change. Even the multiple shifts that Andrea experienced are normal. They are typical of the changes children go through at this age. Children ages seven to twelve may sometimes feel that they are on an emotional roller coaster. One year they are withdrawn; the next year they are outgoing. One year they feel anxious; the next year they are relaxed. These changes are a normal part of the emotional development that occurs along with physical, social, and intellectual development.

Middle Childhood

Between the ages of seven and ten, children generally progress from negative to positive, or from unhappiness to happiness. Children in this age span are gaining independence and self-confidence.

Age Seven

Seven-year-olds are typically withdrawn and quiet. They tend to stay close to home. Many children this age worry a great deal about all kinds of issues. They may not want to talk about their feelings. Some are particularly sensitive to what others say about them.

Age Eight

Eight-year-olds generally have a more positive attitude than at age seven. They are willing to explore and become curious about new things. They enjoy spending time with friends. They are lively and active. They also are often very dramatic. They might, for example, exaggerate when telling stories or describing their feelings. Parents might need to ask many questions to determine what really happened when an eight-year-old describes it.

Age Nine

Nine-year-olds tend to be absorbed in their thoughts. They can be very harsh about their own failings and even embarrassed by them. Some nine-year-olds keep their feelings hidden and show signs of anxiety and tension. At times, they may become completely absorbed in their own concerns.

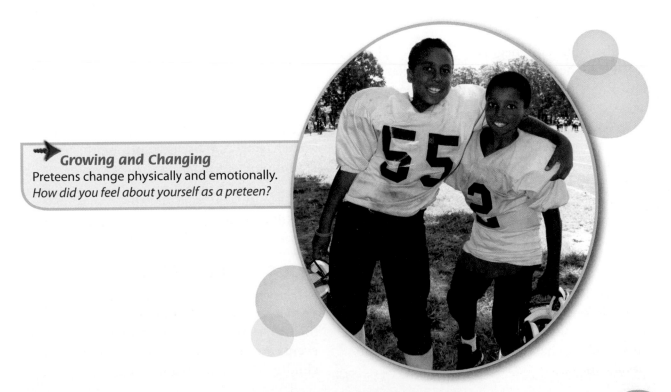

➤ Growing and Changing
Preteens change physically and emotionally.
How did you feel about yourself as a preteen?

Overreacting
Angry outbursts over seemingly minor events are common for preteens. *Why do you think preteens sometimes find it hard to control their anger?*

Age Ten

By age ten, children are usually once again more positive and happy. They have a growing sense of self and increasing feelings of competence. They start to spend more time with their friends. They might make new friends by joining clubs or sports teams. This helps them focus on their strengths rather than their failings.

The Preteen Years

Puberty usually begins around ages eleven or twelve. These are known as the preteen years. The physical changes of puberty, caused by the release of hormones, bring emotional changes as well. Preteens often feel and act awkward. Mood swings can carry them from happiness to sadness—and back again—in just minutes.

Preteens tend to be very absorbed in their own thoughts and concerns. They may pay little attention to people other than their peers. Their peers are extremely important to them. They usually crave group acceptance and become worried if they stand out in any way from their peers. They hate the thought of being different. It is not unusual for preteens to hide their true feelings behind a mask of not caring. This behavior is a sign of growing emotional control.

Living with Children Seven to Twelve

Children ages seven to twelve can be easily upset. The hormones released into the body during puberty can cause emotional changes. Preteens may start feeling the mood swings that are associated with teenagers. A quiet, withdrawn seven-year-old might not be willing to talk about his feelings. An eight-year-old girl, though cheerful, might cling to her mother. An eleven-year-old boy might be experiencing secret fears. Here are some tips to keep minor emotional upsets from becoming major problems:

- **Be patient.** Remember that school-age children still do not have full self-control. When preteens show anger, it is often due to the difficulty they are having adjusting to the changes in their bodies.
- **Avoid taking it personally.** A child who is angry or upset may say nasty things to a parent or caregiver. Remember that children do not usually mean what they say in angry moments.
- **Help the child maintain self-control.** Make sure children understand that their behavior must stay within acceptable limits. Actions that break the rules need to be dealt with. If misbehavior is not serious, talking it through may be enough.
- **Listen attentively.** Ask the child to explain what happened and why. There may have been a valid problem. Help the child express his emotions. Even if there is a valid problem, this does not excuse inappropriately expressed anger. Let the child know that you do not approve of the behavior, and discuss more appropriate options.

✓ **Reading Check** **Recall** At what age do children generally have a sense of self and increased feelings of competence?

Specific Emotions

The emotional life of young children centers on the family. In older children and preteens, the focus shifts to the wider world. People and events outside the family have more impact on children's emotions than before.

Children gradually gain better control of their emotions. They begin expressing emotions in more socially acceptable ways. Socially acceptable ways of expressing emotions do not conflict with society's morals and are approved by most people.

Anger

Children at any age can feel angry and let others know it. Even ten-year-olds, who are typically quite happy, show anger. When they do, though, it usually passes quickly. Depending on temperament and environment, some children become angry more often than others.

Preteens tend to be moody. Anger can erupt at any time. Often the outbursts of anger are eruptions that boil over and pass quickly. A preteen may storm out of a room and slam a door but then return a little while later as if nothing had happened.

Many times, these outbursts have little to do with the event that seemed to trigger them. Courtney, for example, became very angry when her mother asked her to hang up her coat after school. Within minutes, though, she was cheerful. Courtney was really angry because her friends went shopping without her.

By age seven, children generally know that they should express their anger in socially acceptable ways. For example, they should use words to talk about their anger. They should not lash out with violence or words that can hurt others' feelings. They know that they should seek a compromise to settle their differences or turn away from the situation.

On occasion, however, an older child may show aggression. It is important to avoid responding in the same way. Setting a good example is the best method of teaching a child. Here are some additional approaches that may work:

- **Teach the child how to gain self-control.** Counting to ten and taking deep breaths are two ways of helping an angry child learn to calm down.
- **Help the child learn nonaggressive ways to resolve conflicts.** Children who learn how to express their anger appropriately at home will be better equipped to settle conflicts at school. They might have learned this when angry with their siblings.
- **Reward the child for controlling anger.** Saying something like "I'm proud of the way you responded to the teasing," reinforces self-control.

RESPOND TO SPECIAL NEEDS

Generalized Anxiety Disorder

Children and adolescents with generalized anxiety disorder engage in extreme, unrealistic worry about everyday life activities. They worry too much about their academic performance, sporting activities, or even about being on time. These young people are generally very self-conscious, feel tense, and have a strong need for reassurance. They may complain about stomachaches or other discomforts that do not appear to have any physical cause.

Parents or other caregivers who notice repeated symptoms of an anxiety disorder in their child should talk with the child's doctor.

Doctors can help determine whether the symptoms are caused by an anxiety disorder or by some other condition. They can also provide a referral to a mental health professional, if needed.

Critical Thinking There are many anxiety disorders such as separation anxiety and panic disorders. Research one anxiety disorder to learn how it affects children and how it can be treated. Share your findings in a one-page essay.

Envy and Jealousy
Preteens often experience feelings of envy and jealousy. *How can parents help preteens deal with these emotions?*

- **Help the child learn to use unrelated physical activity to work off anger.** Exercise can help relieve stress and make a person feel calmer. Throwing a basketball, running, or walking the family dog are all harmless ways to blow off steam.

Fear and Worry

All children have fears, but the nature of their fears changes. Seven-year-olds may still have some of their earlier fears, such as a fear of the dark. Look for easy solutions such as leaving a light on at night.

By age ten, the fears of earlier years have largely disappeared. However, as childhood fears disappear, new worries may take their place. News reports of terrorism, fatal car accidents, or natural disasters can set off worries in some older children and preteens. They may worry that such events will strike their families. They need to be reassured that adults will take all the steps necessary to protect them.

Other worries that occupy this age group have to do with how others see them. Until the age of ten, most children are concerned mainly with how adults see them. During the preteen years, however, the focus of these fears shifts toward the attitudes of their peers. Parents can help children by teaching self-confidence early on. Remind school-age children of their strengths.

Anxiety

Anxiety is a state of uncertainty and fear, often about an unspecified but seemingly immediate threat. A certain amount of anxiety, especially about specific problems or events, is normal. For example, anxiety about passing a major test or a parent's serious illness is understandable. In these instances, offer the child support and reassurance.

Excessive anxiety, though, can be a sign of an anxiety disorder. People who have an anxiety disorder often worry that something terrible is about to happen. Preteens or teens with an anxiety disorder can develop constant physical symptoms such as tension headaches, nausea, or rapid heartbeat. Parents who suspect an anxiety problem in their child should talk to the child's doctor.

Envy and Jealousy

As older children become more aware of the world around them, they are apt to develop feelings of envy and jealousy. Envy is the feeling of wanting something another person has. It can often lead to a feeling of intense dislike for that person.

"I hate Erica," Kayla told another friend. "She gets everything she wants. Now that her parents bought her a new TV for her bedroom, I'm not going to talk to her anymore."

Jealousy is a complex emotion involving the fear that a loved one might prefer someone else. A seven-year-old might be jealous of a parent's attention to a sibling. A ten-year-old might feel jealous when a best friend spends time with another friend. A preteen, learning to feel comfortable with the opposite sex, might feel jealous of a peer who seems to be at ease and to get all the attention.

At the middle school dance, for example, Nicholas was happy that he found the courage to ask Yasmine to dance, and that she accepted. They had a great time dancing together. His happiness turned to painful jealousy, however, when another boy asked Yasmine to dance and they danced several songs together.

Children between the ages of seven and twelve are often very aware of their changing bodies, absorbed with their feelings, and anxious to fit in with their peers. For these reasons, jealousy is especially common.

✓ **Reading Check** **Define** What is anxiety?

A Sense of Self

One of the most important changes that occurs between the ages of seven and twelve is the development of a sense of self. Your **sense of self** is your idea of who you are, based on your emotions, personality, and the ways you perceive the world. As children grow, they develop the ability to think in more abstract terms. This affects the way they see themselves.

Parenting Skills

Help a Child Work Through a Difficult Situation

All children and adolescents need help sometimes. Children ages seven to twelve become less likely to confide in their parents. They can develop secret fears or worries. Relationships with others become more complex than they were before. More than ever, they need guidance from caring adults to help them figure out how to deal with difficult situations.

❦ **Establish genuine communication.** Accept each child as a unique individual. The child will sense your genuine interest and may become more willing to confide about issues.

❦ **Take their concerns seriously.** Do not belittle or dismiss any fears or worries that cause children emotional distress. Let children know that you are available to talk about anything that is troubling them.

❦ **Put any worries into perspective.** Brandon worried constantly that his mother might die and that he would be left alone. When his mother had to take a plane trip for business, Brandon begged her not to go. His mother reminded him that plane crashes were much less likely than car accidents.

❦ **Try to determine how serious the problem might be.** Be aware of such danger signs as depression, feelings of hopelessness, or increased self-centeredness and lack of concern for others. Consult a professional for help in dealing with the situation.

Take Charge If you were a caregiver of a child who was struggling with working through a difficult situation, do you think the child would benefit from seeing a counselor? Write a letter explaining why or why not.

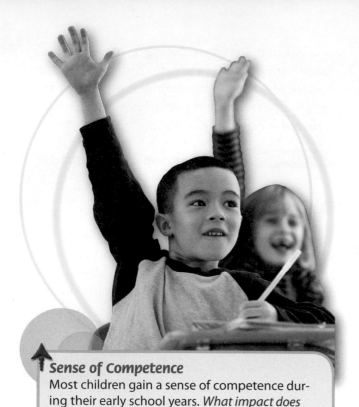

Sense of Competence
Most children gain a sense of competence during their early school years. *What impact does that have on later success in school?*

reasoning on physical traits. "The dog," she said, "has brown eyes and walks like a dog." When a nine-year-old was asked whether she could become her brother, she also answered no but for a different reason. "I'm me and he's him. I can't change in any way because I've got to stay like myself."

Children between the ages of seven and twelve recognize that they have a personality that is uniquely theirs. They see themselves as a mixture of many qualities. Some of those qualities are based on physical appearance, others on talents or abilities. By age ten, children are able to see themselves as being highly skilled in one area and less so in another. By ages eleven and twelve, children also use personal qualities to define themselves. For example, "I'm honest," or "I'm a good friend," or "I can be counted on."

They also see that they behave differently in different situations. Dionte always thought of himself as being friendly and outgoing until he went to a party at his cousin's house. The only person he knew there was his cousin, and he found it hard to talk to anyone else. "How can I be both friendly and shy?" he wondered. As he thought about it, Dionte realized that he is shy around strangers. He also realized that his behavior is influenced by the situation he is in.

Dionte recognized that different people might perceive him in different ways. To people he knows, he seems friendly and outgoing. However, strangers might think of him as quiet or even stuck-up, or conceited. Dionte's ability to understand how others might see him is a good example of his growing thinking skills.

Compare the following answers that were given by a five-year-old and a nine-year-old to a researcher's questions. The researcher asked a five-year-old girl whether she could become the family dog. The girl said no, but based her

THE DEVELOPING BRAIN

Stimulation Builds Competence

Why do some children become more competent at mental tasks than other children the same age? Are those individuals simply smarter than others? Some children do have a genetic inheritance that makes them better equipped to learn than some of their peers. But most people have far more intellectual capacity than they use. Growing up in a stimulating environment and having determination to succeed are two other factors that can lead to success and feelings of competence.

■ **Science Inquiry** A stimulating environment can help a child gain competence. What might explain this?

Sense of Competence

According to theorist Erik Erikson, the early school years mark the stage when children strive to develop a sense of competence. A **sense of competence** is the feeling that one can be successful and meet most challenges. Children gain this feeling by acquiring and improving a wide range of skills. In the classroom, these skills include reading, math, and writing. Outside the classroom, children may develop skills in sports, music, art, or crafts. Erikson believed that as children refine these skills, they see themselves as competent and increase their self-esteem.

A child's feelings about his or her competence can have a real effect on the choices he or she makes and on satisfaction later in life. Children with high self-esteem are more willing to try new things and to **persevere**, or persist, at difficult tasks. In contrast, Erikson believed that those who experience repeated failures and disappointments begin to see themselves as inferior and incompetent. Children's beliefs about their competence can greatly affect their choices and their satisfaction in later life. For these reasons, Erikson said it is essential that children ages seven to twelve experience more successes than failures.

Eleven-year-old Andrew went home to an empty house every day after school. His parents would not let him have friends over. He did not mind this much because he did not have many friends. Unsupervised and with time on his hands, he often got into trouble. One day he was caught shooting a BB gun at cars in a nearby office parking lot and was given a stern warning. About a month later, Andrew scratched, "A loser was here" into the front door of the office building. His way of identifying himself revealed much about his self-esteem.

Sound relationships with peers are an important part of developing a sense of competence. As children grow from seven to twelve, their peers become much more important to them. They begin to let go of their total reliance on parents and start to depend on friends for help and reassurance.

Children ages seven to twelve are going through other changes that prepare them for the learning and mastery that lead to competence. Their brains develop connections that allow their memory to expand. Increased memory allows children to learn and understand more.

There are a variety of ways to help seven- to twelve-year-olds develop a sense of competence:

- **Help children focus on their strengths.** Ask them to make a list of the things that they are good at. Encourage them to develop special skills and talents.

What Would You Do?

Learning to Build Confidence

Margaret, the mother of eleven-year-old Hannah, was surprised at what she was hearing from her daughter's teacher. Mrs. Schwartz said that whenever she asked Hannah to do something, her response was, "I can't."

"I don't understand Hannah," said Margaret. "She seems confident. I know I have high expectations, but she's a bright child. If she gets Bs, I ask why she didn't get As. If she gets an A, I ask why it wasn't an A+, because I know that she could get those grades if she applied herself."

Mrs. Schwartz thought for a moment and said, "Maybe Hannah says she can't because she is becoming afraid of failing to meet others' expectations." She suggested that Margaret rethink the messages she was sending. Hannah might be feeling that nothing she did would ever be good enough to please her mother.

✎ **Write About It** Think about the questions Margaret asks Hannah when she sees her grades. What do you think Hannah would prefer to hear? Rewrite the statements to help build Hannah's self-confidence.

- **Provide opportunities.** Include children in the work of the family. Doing chores can help them learn practical skills and contribute to the family.
- **Encourage learning.** Recognize the importance of learning. Make sure children have a quiet time and place to do homework and practice skills.
- **Establish reachable goals.** Help children break large tasks down into smaller parts. They can focus on accomplishing one part at a time. Eventually, they will see that they have completed the larger goal.
- **Recognize successes.** Look for things children do well, and be specific in praise. "You did a great job of explaining the book's plot in your book report."

- **Focus on the positive.** "You got twelve out of fourteen right on that math test! That's much better than you did on the last test."

Sense of Gender

An important part of a child's growing sense of self is gender identity. **Gender identity** is the awareness of being male or female. It is a complex process that begins in early childhood and is usually firmly fixed by about age four. In middle childhood and early adolescence that identity becomes stronger as children become more aware of their bodies and of gender differences. Between the ages of seven and twelve, children generally:

- Choose to spend more time with others of the same sex. Close friendships at this stage are almost always with children of the same sex.
- Show an increased desire to act and talk like others of the same sex.

- Choose adults of the same sex as their role models. Role models are the people whom children admire and try to pattern their behavior after.
- Begin to explore relationships with the opposite sex late in this stage.

There are many influences on gender identity such as family, other adults, peers, and media. Children begin taking in information about gender identity from birth. You are a role model to any child you meet or interact with. Children observe the behavior of people around them. This lets them learn which feelings and responses are appropriate for their gender. It is important to be aware of this so you can be a better role model for children. No single gender identity fits everyone. You can help children appreciate and develop their positive traits, talents, and qualities. Encourage them to pursue their unique interests.

Section 17.1 — After You Read

Review Key Concepts

1. **Describe** the typical emotional state of a seven-, eight-, nine-, and ten-year-old child.
2. **List** the kinds of fears a ten-year-old might have.
3. **Summarize** two signs of a child's growing sense of self.

Practice Academic Skills

English Language Arts

4. Children who have a high sense of competence are generally more successful in school than children who do not. Write a one-page essay in which you explain why a sense of competence in school-age children is important to future success in life.

> **NCTE 12** Use language to accomplish individual purposes.

Social Studies

5. Observe older children and preteens. Look for typical behaviors that you read about in this chapter. Record the behaviors you observe. Then try to estimate the ages of those you observed. Turn in your notes and estimates.

> **NCSS IV D** Apply concepts, methods, and theories about the study of human growth and development, such as behavior and personality.

 Check Your Answers Check your answers at this book's Online Learning Center at **glencoe.com**.

Section 17.2 Social and Moral Development from Seven to Twelve

Reading Guide

Before You Read

Predict Look at the photos in this section and read their captions. Write one or two sentences predicting what the section will be about.

Read to Learn
Key Concepts
- **Summarize** the four main qualities children look for in friendships.
- **Identify** typical changes that occur in children's attitudes toward their parents.
- **Describe** five ways to help prepare children to make good moral choices.

Main Idea
Relationships become stronger and more complex as children grow. Older children and preteens must learn to deal with peer pressure and accept responsibility for decisions and actions taken.

Content Vocabulary
◇ bullying
◇ peer pressure
◇ conformity

 Graphic Organizer Go to this book's Online Learning Center at **glencoe.com** to print out this graphic organizer.

Academic Vocabulary
You will find these words in your reading and on your tests. Use the glossary to look up their definitions if necessary.
- paramount
- counterproductive

Graphic Organizer
As you read, list guidelines for helping people resolve their differences. Use a chart like the one below to organize your information.

Guidelines for Resolving Conflicts
1.
2.
3.
4.

Academic Standards . . . .

 English Language Arts

NCTE 12 Use language to accomplish individual purposes.

 Social Studies

NCSS IV C Individual Development and Identity Describe the ways family and other group and cultural influences contribute to the development of a sense of self.

NCTE *National Council of Teachers of English*
NCTM *National Council of Teachers of Mathematics*

NSES *National Science Education Standards*
NCSS *National Council for the Social Studies*

Relationships with Peers

As children grow, their friendships get stronger. Because seven- to twelve-year-olds have a sense of self and are better able to communicate their thoughts and feelings, their friendships become more personal. Beginning around age seven or eight, children look for the following qualities in their friendships:

- **Loyalty** Older children value friends who will stand by them when they are in a difficult situation or feeling low.
- **Trustworthiness** Older children need to feel comfortable talking about their inner feelings. They look for friends they can trust. They want friends who will not pass on personal secrets.
- **Kindness and Understanding** Children this age seek friends who will listen and be sympathetic to their feelings, which are often tumultuous.
- **Fun** Most people look for friends whose company they enjoy and with whom they can have a good time.

Children this age still enjoy active, physical play with their friends, but they spend increasing amounts of time simply talking. Preteens who are close friends might spend an afternoon together. Then they go home and call each other and spend an hour or more talking in the evening as well. They might talk about anything from school to peers, or movie stars to personal feelings.

It is development in many areas that brings about these changes. Intellectual growth makes deeper friendships possible. Because they can now think abstractly, older children and preteens can better understand how others see them. At the same time, they can more easily see another person's point of view and feel empathy for him or her. These new skills make it easier to relate to friends in a deeper way.

The physical and emotional changes of puberty also play a role in friendships. Preteens are curious about the changes they are going through. They are trying to figure out the new aspects of their relationships with people of the opposite gender. Talking to their friends helps them explore and think through these issues.

Peer Groups

For older children and preteens, acceptance by peers is closely related to high self-esteem. Children who feel that they fit in are more confident, more likely to make and keep friends, and more likely to succeed at school. Feelings of rejection by peers may negatively affect performance at school and family relationships.

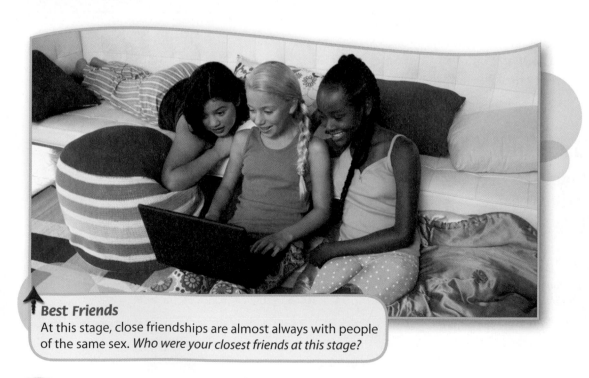

Best Friends
At this stage, close friendships are almost always with people of the same sex. *Who were your closest friends at this stage?*

Learning Through PLAY

Problem Solving

Older children and preteens are learning more about themselves as individuals, as well as about their classmates. During this time, some children experience pressures and problems such as lying, cheating, or bullying. One way to help children work through these problems is to act out typical situations, focusing on ways to prevent and deal with them. Involving children in the problem-solving process helps them develop the skills they will need throughout their lives. Acting out situations and modeling their resolution can give children ideas about how to handle situations if they arise again.

Think About It Imagine that your best friend since childhood has told another friend something personal about you. Now this personal information is being spread around the school. You are very angry. How would you resolve this problem with your friend who betrayed your trust?

Children at this age generally have many peer groups. Peer groups may include classmates, sports teammates, or children who live in the same neighborhood. Adults can help children gain peer acceptance by teaching social skills and encouraging participation in group activities. Children who experience rejection by their peers may need professional counseling to prevent lifelong difficulties.

Making Friends

Tara and Nate were neighbors. They began playing together when they were two years old. When they were six, they played on the same soccer team. At age eight, however, their friendship began to change. Tara began spending more time with her new best friend, Kari, and other girls from school. Nate would pal around with the boys.

The experiences of Tara and Nate show how gender differences become more important as children grow older. Young children play with children of either gender. As children grow older they are more likely to become friends only with children of the same gender. This is true even though puberty makes them more interested in preteens of the opposite gender.

By age twelve, Tara began to see Nate in a whole new way. "I think he's really cute," Tara confided to Kari. "Why don't you tell him?" teased Kari. "Or maybe I will." "Don't you dare," squealed Tara, "I would just die!"

One reason preteens avoid opposite-gender friendships is that such relationships raise questions of being romantically involved. Most eleven- and twelve-year-olds are not ready to take that step. They want to avoid the teasing they may encounter if they have a friend of the opposite gender.

The number of friends children have at this stage varies. Some children have many friends. Some have several friends. And some have just one or two friends. The number of friendships may depend on the child's temperament. Some children enjoy being part of a large group. Others are more private and quiet. These children do not want or need many friends.

Another influence is the child's social environment. Children who are in after-school programs, clubs, or teams have more opportunities to make friends. Therefore, they may naturally have more friends.

There is no set number of friends that children should have. Still, some older children and preteens may "collect" friends. They use the number of friends they have as a way to measure their popularity. Those with fewer friends may feel that they are not liked as well.

Make New Friends
Participating in a variety of activities presents more opportunities to meet people and make friends. *What other factors contribute to a healthy social life?*

In reality, the key to a healthy social life is not how many friends a child has. Whether the child has the social skills for forming and maintaining friendships is what counts. It is important to help and encourage children to build social skills and get involved in activities that interest them.

Resolving Conflicts

The nature of friendship changes as children grow. So too does the nature of conflicts they face. Young children may have conflicts over toys. Older children and preteens have conflicts over more complex issues.

Many conflicts among children arise from envy, jealousy, or gossip. Whitney, for example, heard a rumor that Caitlin had been spreading gossip about her. She confronted Caitlin and accused her of telling lies. Caitlin heatedly denied this, and a shouting match ensued. A crowd of girls soon gathered around them to watch.

Other conflicts may be based on emotional needs. Older children and preteens have a need to belong. Conflicts may arise if they feel excluded from a group or if they think someone is showing them disrespect.

Avoiding Violence

In general, children at this stage should be able to use words to express their anger. Those who received guidance at an earlier age on how to deal with anger are more likely to have self-control. Occasionally, however, anger can lead to aggressive behavior. Preteen boys are more likely than girls to use aggressive behavior to express anger.

If a conflict looks as if it might escalate into violence, others should intervene. Here are some guidelines for helping people in conflict resolve their differences:

- **Set some ground rules.** Establish an agreement to work peacefully toward resolution. Letitia and Emily stepped out of the group around Whitney and Caitlin and tried to calm them down. "Let's get to the bottom of this, but no more yelling or name-calling, okay?"
- **Listen to both sides.** Ask both people to give their side of the story, and listen carefully to what they say. Whitney was less concerned about the silly gossip than about the idea that Caitlin did not respect her. Caitlin was hurt that Whitney did not trust her. "I never said those things. How could you even think I would?" asked Caitlin.
- **Find common ground.** Find something that both people can agree on so that they can move forward. Sometimes this is as simple as deciding to end the disagreement.
- **Reach a solution that is acceptable to both sides.** Win-win solutions, in which both parties gain something they want, are best because both people can feel good about the resolution. At first, Whitney wanted Caitlin to apologize. Caitlin refused, saying

there was nothing to apologize for. Finally, they agreed to apologize to each other for the situation and how it made them feel. "I'm sorry that the rumor made you think I didn't respect you," said Caitlin. "I'm sorry that my reaction made you feel that I don't trust you," said Whitney.

Dealing with Bullies

Bullying means directing aggression or abuse toward another person, usually someone weaker. It can take many forms, including pushing, shoving, or other physical abuse; teasing; spreading rumors; or making offensive comments. Boys are more likely than girls to be bullies and to be the victims of bullies. However, some girls are bullies too.

Bullying can cause both physical and emotional pain for victims. Unfortunately, children who are being bullied often do not tell their parents or other adults. They may fear that telling on a bully will only make the bullying worse. This is often a threat made by the bully.

Parents, teachers, and other caregivers need to be on the lookout for signs of bullying. They should suspect bullying if a child:

- Comes home with cuts, bruises, or torn clothing.
- Frequently loses lunch money or other valuable items.
- Does not want to go to school.
- Becomes unusually moody, withdrawn, and bad tempered.
- Is always anxious and has trouble sleeping.

An adult who suspects that a child is being bullied should question the child in a supportive way. The adult could ask how the child's day went and follow up with questions such as, "What was your favorite activity at school today?" "What was your least favorite thing?"

A child who is being bullied needs to be reassured that it is not his or her fault. Emphasize that no one has the right to bully anyone else. Report the situation to a teacher, principal, or school counselor. Schools usually take the problem of bullying very seriously.

 Reading Check **Explain** What are some typical conflicts among preteens?

Math in Action

The Cost of Child Delinquency

Data collected by the Federal Bureau of Investigation's Uniform Crime Reporting Program show that law enforcement agencies made approximately 253,000 arrests of children younger than 13 in 1997. The highest offense in those arrests was arson, at an alarming rate of 35 percent. How many children younger than 13 were arrested for arson in 1997?

Math Concept **Multiply by Percents** To multiply by percents, change the percent to a fraction with 100 in the denominator. Then change the fraction to a decimal.

Starting Hint Convert 35 percent to a decimal by dividing 35 by 100. Then multiply the result by the total number of arrests.

 For math help, go to the Math Appendix at the back of the book.

NCTM Number and Operations
Understand numbers, ways of representing numbers, relationships among numbers, and number systems.

Family Relationships

There are many changes occurring between the ages of seven and twelve. Therefore, it is no surprise that family relationships change too. Children move from dependence to greater independence. The complex relationships between children and their parents and siblings reflect that transition.

Family situations vary greatly. Some families have two parents in the home. Others have only one. Some children live with a guardian or in a foster home. The main caregiver may be a person other than a parent. It might be a grandparent or other relative. Extended family members, such as a grandparent or aunt, may live with the family.

In many families, both parents work outside the home. This affects how much family time is available. The number and ages of siblings also affect family relationships.

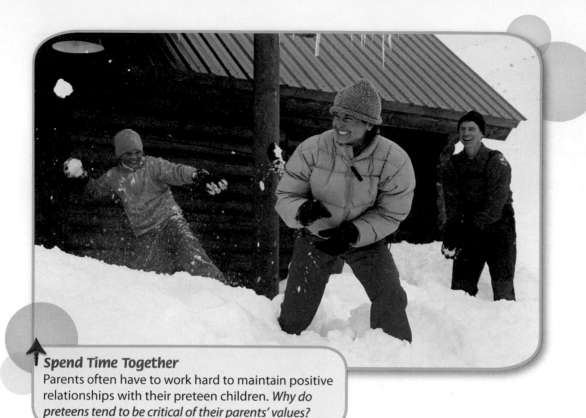

Spend Time Together
Parents often have to work hard to maintain positive relationships with their preteen children. *Why do preteens tend to be critical of their parents' values?*

What Would You Do?

Negative Peer Pressure

Nine-year-old Samantha moved to a new neighborhood. When she first started at her new school, she was concerned about making new friends. Then the group of girls who sat under the trees at recess invited her over to join them. They wanted to be friends with her! At first, being included felt great. After a while, though, the girls started daring each other to steal things. First it was a book from the school library. Then it was lipstick from the drugstore. When Samantha would not steal the lipstick, the girls stopped talking to her. Samantha tried to make new friends but the group of girls spread rumors about Samantha. Soon almost no one in Samantha's class was talking to her.

Write About It Samantha does not know what to do. What options does she have for dealing with the situation? What are the possible outcomes of each? Write a report with your answers to these questions.

Parents

As children grow older, their attitudes toward their parents typically change in the following ways:

- Seven-year-olds depend on their parents, but often challenge parental authority. Tommie is mad that his parents will not let him go out to play until his room is clean. However, he still expects them to feed him dinner an hour later.

- At eight, children tend to cling to their parents. Natalie wants to go shopping with her mother on Saturday instead of playing at her friend Nicole's house.

- By nine, children become wrapped up in their own thoughts and sometimes ignore their parents. Drew's father reminded him three times on Thursday night to take out the trash. Drew was not disobeying; he was preoccupied thinking about his math test and forgot.

- Ten is generally a smooth year. Children are happier and more communicative. Walt and his mother enjoy the drive to and from school everyday. They talk about what Walt is doing at school and with his friends.

- At eleven and twelve, children begin to move away from the direct control and influence of parents. Preteens may become quite critical of their parents' values. The preteen years are often challenging for parents, no matter how healthy the family relationship. Patricia and her parents had a good family relationship. They enjoyed spending Fridays together as a designated "family night." Sometimes they would play games, other times they would watch movies together. However, after Patricia turned eleven, this relationship began to change. Patricia no longer wanted to hang out with her parents. She begged out of family night to go to the movies with her friends instead. She wanted to spend less time at home and more time with her friends. Her parents were disappointed but tried to understand that she needed to build her independence.

Siblings

Starting at age seven, children generally get along well with siblings who are much younger or much older. They are helpful and protective of children under two. They tend to respect and admire siblings in their late teens.

Seven- to twelve-year-olds often have difficult relationships with siblings who are closer to their own age. They tend to judge each other harshly and conflicts are common. Parents and other adults need to help close-in-age siblings develop empathy and a sense of cooperation.

✓ **Reading Check** **Recall** Describe a typical nine-year-old's relationship with his or her parents.

Moral Development

As they spend more time outside the home, children face more decisions about right and wrong. They must make these decisions alone,

Parenting Skills

Teach a Child Tolerance

Prejudice and intolerance are learned from others. Young children are ready to be tolerant of anyone. Parents need to make sure that they stay that way. Tolerance is a moral issue that deals with fairness. Here are some strategies to help parents teach tolerance.

❥ As with any moral behavior, teach by example. Avoid any behavior that signals prejudice.

❥ At work, home, or in public, show that you are willing to get along with anyone who behaves appropriately.

❥ Help children understand and respect the traditions of other cultures or religions. Different does not mean wrong. Teach children that all human beings deserve fair treatment.

❥ Encourage tolerance as a continuous process. Children hear intolerant messages from many outside sources, including the media and peers.

❥ Raise the subject of prejudice anytime the opportunity presents itself. Children are more likely to retain messages about accepting differences if they are repeated.

Take Charge What would you do if your child told a joke that makes fun of a group of people? Write your answer in a half-page essay.

Internet Safety

Internet safety is a concern for parents and children alike. Parents must be aware of what their children are viewing on the Internet. Children must be aware of potential dangers of the Internet. Parents can use software to limit use to appropriate sites. Chat rooms are another concern. Children in this age group may not realize possible dangers and might give out personal information. Keeping the computer in a family area, rather than in a child's room, helps parents monitor use.

Be Prepared There are a number of things parents and their children can do to stay safe while surfing the Internet. Research guidelines for Internet safety for children and teens. Create a poster with the guidelines.

without an adult to guide them. What will they do if a group of classmates teases someone for not being a good athlete? What will they say if a peer dares them to smoke a cigarette or to try drugs? What will they do when a friend asks to cheat off of their homework?

Guidance

Parents, other adults, and older siblings can help prepare children to make the right moral choices in a number of ways. Here are some ways to offer moral guidance.

- **Set a good example.** Modeling moral behavior is the best method of teaching a child to act in a moral way.
- **Support the child's growing conscience.** Sometimes going along with the group may seem like a means to feeling accepted, even if the group is doing something wrong. Children need to be reminded that they will regret doing the wrong thing.
- **Talk about how to handle situations that might occur.** Discussing "what-ifs" ahead

of time can help a child develop coping strategies for difficult situations.

- **Reinforce empathy.** Ask children to put themselves in another person's place. How would they feel if they were the object of their group's teasing? Being able to feel empathy can deter a child from teasing or otherwise harassing someone just to go along with the group.
- **Use the child's sense of fairness.** Children in this age group value fairness. Encourage them to use that sense of fairness to lead them to the right decisions.

Peer Pressure

Children ages eleven and twelve generally become less dependent on their parents. They identify more and more with their peer groups. Being accepted by peers is of **paramount**, or extreme, importance.

Because of this, peer pressure becomes very strong. **Peer pressure** is a social group's influence on the way individuals behave. The desire to be accepted leads preteens to adopt the words, behaviors, habits, and ideas of others in their social group. In their drive for conformity they may dress alike, adopt similar hairstyles, and find other ways to show that they belong. **Conformity** means being like one another.

A child who is different from others in some way can have a hard time during this period. A preteen who likes music that differs from what is currently popular or who dresses differently may be teased by others.

Peer pressure can be a powerful influence on a young person's life. It can be an influence for good or for bad. Those whose friends have positive values are more likely to avoid drugs, alcohol, and other risky behaviors. The urge to go along with dishonest or unethical actions can be equally strong. Older children and preteens are more likely to avoid or resist negative peer pressure if they:

- Join a peer group that shows positive moral values.
- Find others with similar hobbies and interests to spend time with.
- Rely upon their conscience to help make decisions about what is right and wrong.

- Try not to appear upset when teased by peers. People who tease are looking for a reaction. If there is none, they may stop.
- Talk about the problem with a parent or other trusted adult.

Parents and others who work with children can help them avoid the influence of negative peer pressure by giving their love and support.

Taking Responsibility

Children in this age group need to learn that with independence comes responsibility. They need safe opportunities to explore, test, and learn about their new responsibilities. Parents can help in many ways:
- Treat eleven- and twelve-year-olds less like children. Spend time talking and having fun.
- Allow preteens to make low-risk decisions when possible. Preteens need to rebel and test limits. Choosing how to decorate their room is a harmless way to do so.
- Encourage preteens to think through the consequences of their decisions. If they do not do their homework, what will happen to their grades?
- Within reason, let preteens experience the consequences of making bad decisions. Going to bed late means being tired all day. Spending their entire allowance early in the week means having no money at the end of the week.
- Negotiate family rules. Listen to any objections or special needs that a preteen might have. Compromise whenever practical.
- Stick to the family rules. Breaking these rules calls for clear, effective consequences. Physical punishment is counterproductive. **Counterproductive** means something hinders the original goal. Time-out usually does not work with this age group. Grounding and taking away privileges are more effective ways to teach preteens that their behavior has consequences.

Section 17.2 After You Read

Review Key Concepts

1. **List** the ways in which friendships change for seven- and eight-year-olds.
2. **Describe** the factors that contribute to changes in family relationships during this period.
3. **Discuss** the relationship between independence and responsibility.

Practice Academic Skills

English Language Arts

4. Imagine that you are the parent of a preteen who is having a conflict with his or her best friend. Write a conversation you could have with your child and his or her friend to help them resolve their conflict.

> **NCTE 12** Use language to accomplish individual purposes.

Social Studies

5. Imagine that the preteen you mentor has asked for your help. He wants to know how he can use positive peer pressure to his advantage and resist negative peer pressure. Write a letter to him with your answer.

 Check Your Answers Check your answers at this book's Online Learning Center at **glencoe.com**.

> **NCSS IV C** Describe the ways family and other group and cultural influences contribute to the development of a sense of self.

Child life specialists are members of pediatric health care teams who focus on the emotional and social aspects of children who are sick. They help children understand what is happening in the hospital and provide emotional support.

☀ What Does a Child Life Specialist Do?

Child life specialists explain medical procedures in ways that make children feel safe. They offer children age-appropriate toys and teach them how to relax. Child life specialists also provide information to parents and siblings. They plan and host visits from musicians, clowns, and animals while children recuperate.

☀ Where Do Child Life Specialists Work?

Most child life specialists work in hospitals. They might work in emergency rooms or surgical departments. They also sometimes work in neonatal or pediatric intensive care units in children's hospitals.

Preparation and Skills

Education and Training

Child life specialists earn bachelor's degrees, usually in psychology or education. They must also complete an internship, gain work experience, and pass an exam to become certified.

Aptitudes, Abilities, and Skills

A child life specialist must have energy and stamina. They also need the ability to communicate clearly and relate to children. Resourcefulness, emotional stability, and an understanding of family dynamics are helpful.

Academic Skills

English language arts are used to communicate to patients, families, and team members. Social studies skills, such as psychology, are used to better understand patients and families.

Explore Careers

Research other careers that provide aid to children and their families. Choose one career and write a paragraph describing it. Tell whether the career interests you and why.

Careers Online For more information on careers, visit the Occupational Outlook Handbook Web site through the link on this book's Online Learning Center at **glencoe.com**.

Chapter Summary

Emotions play a major role in the development of children. The focus of the child shifts from the home to the larger world. Children must learn to control emotions in socially acceptable ways. Between the ages of seven and twelve, children develop a sense of self. Children with a sense of competence are likely to have high self-esteem and be willing to try new things. Older children's friendships become more personal. Peers become more important, but conflicts are common. As children gain more independence, they need help making moral choices.

Vocabulary Review

1. Use at least six of these content and academic vocabulary terms in a short essay about yourself as a preteen.

Content Vocabulary
◇ anxiety (p. 476)
◇ sense of self (p. 477)
◇ sense of competence (p. 478)
◇ gender identity (p. 480)
◇ bullying (p. 485)
◇ peer pressure (p. 488)
◇ conformity (p. 488)

Academic Vocabulary
■ shift (p. 473)
■ persevere (p. 478)
■ paramount (p. 488)
■ counterproductive (p. 489)

Review Key Concepts

2. Identify four ways to help ease emotional upsets.
3. Explain how to help children control and express their anger in socially acceptable ways.
4. List six ways to help a child develop a sense of competence.
5. Summarize the four main qualities children look for in friendships.
6. Identify typical changes that occur in children's attitudes toward their parents.
7. Describe five ways to help prepare children to make good moral choices.

Critical Thinking

8. Predict How might a child with a good sense of competence be likely to deal with failure?
9. Analyze What social skills do you think a person needs to have in order to make friends?
10. Apply Why might a child be afraid to tell an adult that he or she is being bullied? How can an adult deal with the situation?

Family & Community Connection

11. Interview a School Counselor Many of the issues discussed in this chapter continue to be challenges for teenagers. Arrange to talk with one of your school counselors about the issues he or she typically deals with. Create a list of issues such as bullying, anger, or anxiety. Ask the counselor to rank the items in order of occurrence in the student population. Write a paragraph to summarize the results of your interview.

Health Skills

12. Research Bullying Bullying is a form of harassment that can affect mental, emotional, or physical health. Many preteens are affected by bullying. Adults are also common victims of bullying. Research the laws that govern bullying. This might include bullying at school, in the workplace, or on the Internet. Pay special attention to the rights of the victims. Write a one-page report with your findings.

Observation Skills

13. Observe Children at Play Work with your teacher to arrange to observe children ages seven to twelve playing at a school or park.

Procedure During your observation, keep track of the emotions, such as joy, anger, or anxiety, expressed by individual children.

Analysis Create a table to present the information you collect. Across the top of the table, put fictitious names or numbers for the children observed to maintain confidentiality. Down the side, list the emotions observed. Fill in the corresponding cell of the table with the number of times you observed the emotion in each child. Write a paragraph summarizing your findings.

> **NCSS IV D Individual Development and Identity**
> Apply concepts and methods about the study of human growth and development, such as behavior, perception, and personality.

Real-World Skills

Problem-Solving Skills	**14. Offer Advice** Suppose a friend confides that her twelve-year-old brother is angry all the time and is upsetting the family. The brother seems to have no limits and even throws and breaks things. Write a letter advising your friend how to handle the situation.
Technology Skills	**15. Create a Poster** Use word processing or graphics software to make a poster for a campaign aimed at stopping bullying in schools. Include examples of physical and emotional bullying. Illustrate ways that children can protect themselves from bullies.
Financial Literacy	**16. The Cost of Bullying** Sam was allowed $4.00 each day for lunch at school. Before Sam reported it, bullies took his lunch money every school day for four weeks. How much money did Sam lose to the bullies?

Additional Activities For additional activities, go to this book's Online Learning Center at **glencoe.com**.

Academic Skills

English Language Arts

17. Write a Skit A preteen boy believes a friend has betrayed him by telling a secret. The friend is actually innocent. Write a skit that shows the interaction between the two boys. The behavior of the characters should not be aggressive but should reflect what you have learned about preteens.

> **NCTE 5** Use different writing process elements to communicate effectively.

Mathematics

18. Peer Pressure Decisions Purcell, age 8, and Bethany, age 12, are each asked to compare the lengths of two lines. One line is 8 inches, and the other line is 19 centimeters. Kay, a 13-year-old, tells them that the line measuring 19 centimeters is longer. Bethany agrees with Kay, showing peer conformity. Purcell gives the matter some thought and says he thinks the 8-inch line is longer. Who is correct?

Math Concept **Unit Conversions** Centimeters are a measurement of the metric system, while inches are a measurement in the customary system. To compare measurements, you should convert both numbers to the same system.

Starting Hint 1 inch = 2.5 centimeters. Mulitply 8 inches by 2.5 to convert it to centimeters.

 Math For math help, go to the Math Appendix at the back of the book.

> **NCTM Measurement** Apply appropriate techniques, tools, and formulas to determine measurements.

Science

19. Design a Survey A survey can be a very straightforward way to get information. A survey also can be used to test a hypothesis. An example of a hypothesis is: Children who are in after-school programs, clubs, or teams have more friends than children who do not participate in these activities.

Procedure Design a survey that will test this hypothesis.

Analysis Create a presentation to explain how your survey would test whether the hypothesis is valid or invalid.

> **NSES A** Develop abilities necessary to do scientific inquiry, understandings about scientific inquiry.

Standardized Test Practice

ESSAY
Read the scenario, then write your answer on a separate sheet of paper.

> Researchers have found that teens who witness bullying may feel helpless and guilty for not reporting the incident or standing up to a bully. They have also found that witnessing bullying may influence students to model their own behavior after that of bullies.

20. Do you agree with this research finding? Why or why not? Write your thoughts in a one-page essay.

> **Test-Taking Tip** Before answering an essay question, write down a few notes to help you organize your thoughts. Number your thoughts in the order you will write about them.

18 Intellectual Development from Seven to Twelve

Chapter Objectives

After completing this chapter, you will be able to:

- **Identify** four signs of intellectual development in children ages seven to twelve.
- **Explain** four thinking skills that build a foundation for mastering school work.
- **Describe** three learning methods that are effective for children ages seven to twelve.
- **Identify** characteristics of the middle school experience that make it well suited to preteen learning.
- **Compare and contrast** three types of standardized tests.

Writing Activity Editing

Improving Your Writing Read the Writing Tips below. Then edit the following paragraph.

When editing, you probably will need read through the document several times. For example, you may read through once to check for grammar error and a second time to determine whether the text makes cents.

Writing Tips Good editing can improve almost anyone's writing. Here are some tips that should prove helpful:

1. Read slowly and carefully. Some editors think reading aloud makes it easier to spot problems.
2. Delete any unnecessary words. Extra words can hide the main idea.
3. Make certain the text is well organized. The text should flow naturally from one idea to the next.

Section **18.1** The Developing Brain from Seven to Twelve

Section **18.2** Learning from Seven to Twelve

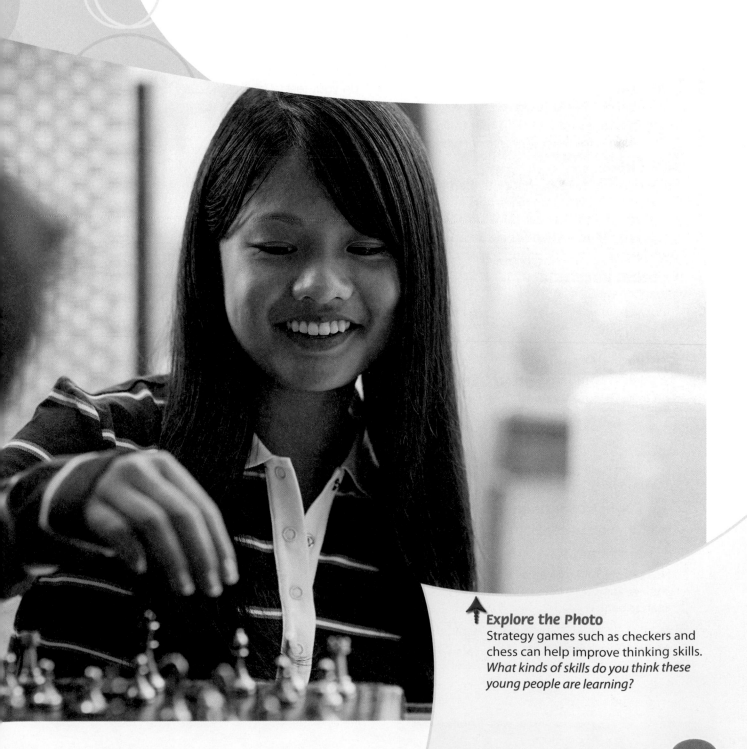

↑ **Explore the Photo**
Strategy games such as checkers and chess can help improve thinking skills. *What kinds of skills do you think these young people are learning?*

Section **18.1** Brain Development from Seven to Twelve

Reading Guide

Before You Read

Create a Table Spend a minute skimming this section. Note that the second part discusses the learning theories of five individuals. As you read, create a table to keep track of these theories.

Read to Learn
Key Concepts
- **Identify** four signs of intellectual development in children ages seven to twelve.
- **Explain** four thinking skills that build a foundation for mastering school work.

Main Idea
From seven to twelve, children's memory improves, they become more curious and idealistic, and they begin thinking abstractly. There are different theories about how children learn.

Content Vocabulary
◇ transitivity
◇ conservation
◇ hypothetical

 Graphic Organizer Go to this book's Online Learning Center at **glencoe.com** to print out this graphic organizer.

Academic Vocabulary
You will find these words in your reading and on your tests. Use the glossary to look up their definitions if necessary.
■ concrete
■ multifaceted

Graphic Organizer
Create a KWL chart like the one shown. Before you begin reading, fill in the first two columns. As you read, fill in the third.

Brain Development in 7- to 12-Year-Olds		
What I Know	What I Want to Know	What I Learned

 Academic Standards . . . .

 English Language Arts

NCTE 3 Apply strategies to interpret texts.

Mathematics

NCTM Data Analysis and Probability Select and use appropriate statistical methods to analyze data.

 Social Studies

NCSS IX A Global Connections Explain how language, art, music, belief systems, and other cultural elements can facilitate global understanding or cause misunderstanding.

NCTE *National Council of Teachers of English*
NCTM *National Council of Teachers of Mathematics*

NSES *National Science Education Standards*
NCSS *National Council for the Social Studies*

Signs of Increased Intellectual Growth

The brain is the center of learning. As children grow from ages seven to twelve, brain development continues to increase their ability to learn. Their intellectual development improves steadily, becoming capable of new ways of thinking. The emotional and intellectual needs of preteens differ from those of younger and older children. Educators created middle schools, or junior highs, in an effort to address these special needs.

Advances in intellectual growth between the ages of seven and twelve are exciting to witness. Learned routines become automatic, so children are able to use their brain power for higher-level learning. Four signs of intellectual development for this age occur in memory, awareness, idealism, and attention span.

Memory

Memory is central to all learning. It is critical to success in school. People use both short-term memory and long-term memory to learn. For example, if you have studied for a test, you have memorized the necessary information. To do so, you brought information into your short-term memory to concentrate on it. You then stored it in your long-term memory. You may forget all about that information until you get to the test. Once there, you recall the information by bringing it back into your short-term memory and answering the question. Then you let it go so that you can recall the answer to the next question.

Improvements in the way the brain functions allow older children and preteens to learn more and to use their knowledge more efficiently. For example, children in this age group generally do not count on their fingers. They can recall and apply basic math operations, such as adding and subtracting, almost automatically. This is because they have done them so many times.

Awareness and Curiosity

Children from age seven to twelve develop a more intense awareness of themselves and those around them. They become better at planning their own behavior. They also get better at understanding their abilities and the abilities of others. Children eight and older begin to recognize another person's point of view and to figure out what that person is thinking. They show more concern about what people think of them.

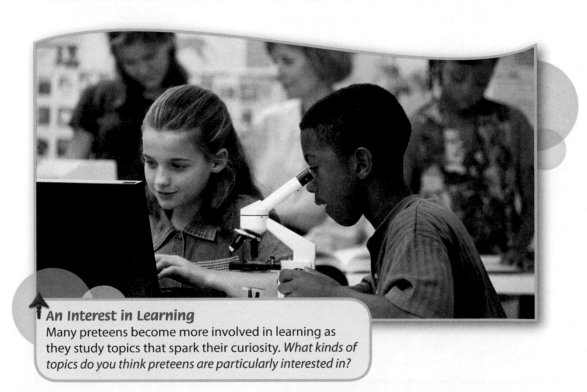

↑ An Interest in Learning
Many preteens become more involved in learning as they study topics that spark their curiosity. *What kinds of topics do you think preteens are particularly interested in?*

In this stage, children begin to think of themselves according to their unique qualities, such as their feelings and beliefs, instead of just their physical features. They are able to strive to achieve a goal because they are learning to control their behavior. At school, they become increasingly independent in their learning. They can determine which learning strategies work best for them. They practice organizing their work so that they can complete long-term projects. Preteens often develop interests that can last a lifetime, such as playing sports, acting in plays, or loving to read.

Idealism and Abstract Thinking

Young children judge whether something is right or wrong by how much pleasure or pain it involves. For example, will they be punished for a particular behavior? Three-year-old Jack knew hitting was wrong only because he was put in time-out for it. Older children and teens adopt moral standards that authority figures, such as parents, will approve of.

By the preteen years, children can recognize complex social problems such as prejudice or crime. However, they do not understand why the problems are difficult to solve. For example, these idealistic children tend to believe that to prevent theft, thieves just need to stop stealing. They cannot yet analyze their ideas to see if they are realistic. Even so, their idealism can help them become involved in improving their world. Parents can encourage preteens to be involved in the community through volunteer work.

Attention Span

For reasons that are not yet understood, at around age twelve, preteens' attention span actually grows shorter. They tend to learn less because they cannot concentrate as long. Their grades may drop at school, and test scores may decline.

✓ **Reading Check** **Recall** How does children's awareness and curiosity change from ages seven to twelve?

CULTURE MATTERS

Analyzing Media Messages

What kind of picture does the media paint of our society and our world? Is it an accurate picture? These questions are the foundation of many media education courses. Some countries, such as Canada and Hungary, require students to take media education courses. Teachers present material from newspapers, magazines, the Internet, films, and television. Teachers show students how to look critically at the media and make comparisons between media outlets. Students then provide real-world examples. Our world is growing more complex. Many people feel that students need to learn how to analyze the media and its messages now more than ever.

Build Connections *What kind of a picture do you think students in a country such as Egypt or China might get of the United States from viewing American movies? Give an example to support your beliefs.*

NCSS IX A Global Connections Explain how language, art, music, belief systems, and other cultural elements can facilitate global understanding or cause misunderstanding.

Figure 18.1 Piaget's Four Periods of Learning

Each of Piaget's four periods of learning build on the previous one. *How are concrete operations different from formal operations?*

Period	Characteristics
Sensorimotor *Birth–2 years*	Children learn through their senses and own actions.
Preoperational *2–7 years*	Children think in terms of their own activities and what they perceive at the moment.
Concrete operations *7–11 years*	Children can think logically but still learn best through experience.
Formal operations *11–Adult*	People are capable of abstract thinking.

Theories About How Children Learn

Questions about how and why thinking skills expand continue to interest child development professionals. Jean Piaget was the earliest researcher to study children scientifically. Piaget's work was followed by some studies that built on his theories, as well as some studies that contradicted his ideas. Some of the best known theories were developed by Lev Vygotsky, Maria Montessori, Howard Gardner, and Robert Sternberg.

Piaget's Theory

As you learned earlier, Jean Piaget proposed a theory to explain how children's thinking skills develop. He divided childhood intellectual development into four stages. Children from ages seven to twelve fall into the last two periods, as shown in **Figure 18.1**.

Concrete Operations Stage

Most children begin to move into Piaget's concrete operations stage at about age seven. Their thinking works effectively on **concrete**, or actual, objects and tasks. They can generalize from their own experiences, but they cannot yet understand abstract ideas. For example, a five-year-old probably could not draw a map of the route from home to a nearby playground visited regularly. An eight-year-old might be able to visualize the neighborhood and draw a rough map. However, a child this age would likely have difficulty imagining what route to take if the usual one was blocked and another had to be found.

During the concrete operations stage, children develop several important thinking skills. These skills include classifying objects, placing objects in a series, extending relationships, and conservation.

Classifying Objects In Piaget's preoperational stage, children as young as three can classify objects, or group them, according to one similar characteristic, such as shape or color. For example, they can find all of the red blocks or all of the square blocks in a set. However, they cannot distinguish the blocks that are both red and square. By age seven, children can usually sort items by two or more different characteristics at the same time.

Can you imagine what it would be like to see the word "learn" as "nrael"? Or, no matter how hard you tried, not to be able to remember how to spell "thought"? Children who have dyslexia must deal with these kinds of problems every day. Dyslexia is a learning disability that makes it hard for children to read and spell. An estimated 3 to 6 percent of school-age children have dyslexia. Researchers believe that dyslexia is a type of brain disorder. People with dyslexia have problems learning to decode written language. Because reading is central to much of learning, these children often do poorly in other subjects, such as social studies and science. Dyslexia is not related to intelligence. People with dyslexia can score high on learning ability tests, as long as the tests do not require them to read.

Critical Thinking Conduct research to learn about one or two of the teaching methods that have been developed to help children with dyslexia. Analyze why you think these methods work. Prepare a presentation to share what you learned and your analysis.

Placing Objects in a Series In the concrete operations stage, children can arrange objects in ascending or descending order, such as from largest to smallest. This requires the ability to compare objects mentally and to make logical connections between what they know and what they are learning.

Extending Relationships Piaget believed that children in this period learn transitivity. **Transitivity** is the concept that a relative relationship between two objects can extend to a third object. For example, if three is greater than two, and two is greater than one, then three must also be greater than one.

Conservation Piaget showed that during the concrete operations stage, children learn the principle of conservation. **Conservation** means that an object has the same characteristics even if there is a change in the way it looks. To test this ability, Piaget showed children of different ages two balls of clay. The balls were of equal size. He then rolled one ball into a long cylinder and asked the children whether one was larger now or if the two pieces of clay were the same size. Younger children thought that the longer piece of clay was larger because it appeared to take up more space. Children age seven and older could see that the amount of clay had not changed just because the shape had changed.

Formal Operations Stage

At about age eleven, children begin to move into Piaget's formal operations stage. They develop the ability to think abstractly and to see different sides of an issue. Abstract thinking shows in a variety of ways, such as:

- Imagining hypothetical situations. **Hypothetical** means involving something that could possibly happen.
- Solving problems by anticipating and preparing for different situations.
- Debating issues.
- Using "if . . . then" formulas to consider what they might decide to do under changing sets of circumstances.
- Recognizing societal problems and understanding the complex reasons for them.

Preteens who begin to show these types of thinking are likely to use them only selectively at first. They will not use them in all situations or at all times. As they gain experience, they will use them more often and with more success.

Piaget felt that the complex, multilevel framework of stages which he proposed was biologically based and universal. Each child experiences the stages in the same order. His ideas deeply influenced several generations of parents and educators. However, other theories arose that offered different views on the way children develop. These theories included children from ages seven to twelve.

Vygotsky's Theory

Vygotsky's theory was that biological development and cultural experience both influenced children's ability to learn. He believed that children learned most, and best, from one another and from adults. Children ages seven to twelve are learning to evaluate themselves and others. This means that the more they interact with other people, the more they will learn. Working together with adults and teachers and receiving their guidance are important. Peer and small-group learning in the classroom are also vital. Social activities such as clubs, team sports, and other events where children can interact and learn from watching and communicating with one another are essential.

Montessori's Theory

In contrast to Vygotsky, Montessori stressed the importance of self-directed learning. She believed that teachers should provide the needed tools for children to learn independently. Teachers should then intrude on the learning experience as little as possible. For seven- to twelve-year-olds, the Montessori classroom might offer a combination of language, history, geography, the sciences, and the arts. However, group lessons are kept to a minimum as teachers allow children to exercise their growing independence by exploring their interests in their own way. Real-life experiences are stressed.

Gardner's Theory

Howard Gardner, who proposed the theory of multiple intelligences, theorized that knowledge is **multifaceted**, or many-sided. For example, a seven-year-old who is at a certain stage in understanding numbers may be at a different stage in visual-spatial development. Educators have supported Gardner's theories because they see their students learning and thinking in different ways every day.

Learning Through PLAY

Children's Museums

Traditional museums are typically filled with historical objects, paintings, and other treasures. Touching these items is usually not allowed. That is one reason children are sometimes less than enthusiastic about visiting museums. Looking at seashells in a case behind glass does not give children the chance to experience them. In special museums designed for children, learning takes place through actual experience. Children might be able to touch a variety of real seashells and feel the differences in texture and size. They might experience how aspects of science work. They can learn through interactive displays. For example, they might learn about gravity and momentum by performing simple experiments with golf balls. Children's museums are based on the belief that children learn best through actual experience.

Think About It Imagine that you work at a children's museum designed to teach young people about the ocean. Think of an exhibit you might create. Describe the exhibit. Then list three things that children could learn from this exhibit.

Section **18.2**

Learning from Seven to Twelve

Reading Guide

Before You Read

Explaining What You Read As you read, pause each time you come to a new heading. Explain what you have just read to an imaginary person who is unfamiliar with the information. This will help you monitor your comprehension.

Read to Learn

Key Concepts

- **Describe** three learning methods that are effective for children ages seven to twelve.
- **Identify** characteristics of the middle school experience that make it well suited to preteen learning.
- **Compare and contrast** three types of standardized tests.

Main Idea

Methods of learning for children in this group include direct learning, peer learning, and independent learning. Middle school provides a needed bridge between elementary and high school. Standardized tests are used to evaluate students' learning abilities, achievements, and aptitudes.

Content Vocabulary

◇ learning method
◇ peer learning
◇ standardized test

Academic Vocabulary

You will find these words in your reading and on your tests. Use the glossary to look up their definitions if necessary.
- integrate
- mandate

Graphic Organizer

As you read, note two advantages and two disadvantages to standardized testing. Use a tree diagram like the one shown to help organize your information.

 Graphic Organizer Go to this book's Online Learning Center at **glencoe.com** to print out this graphic organizer.

Academic Standards · · · · · · · · · · · · · · · · · ·

 English Language Arts

NCTE 5 Use different writing process elements to communicate effectively.

 Social Studies

NCSS IV E Individual Development and Identity Examine the interaction of ethnic, national, or cultural influences in specific situations or events.

NCTE *National Council of Teachers of English*
NCTM *National Council of Teachers of Mathematics*

NSES *National Science Education Standards*
NCSS *National Council for the Social Studies*

Learning Methods

Young children learn skills mainly through imitating older children and adults. Seven- to twelve-year-olds become more capable of abstract thought and of more demanding work. A **learning method** is a way to learn. In order to meet the needs of different children, teachers use a variety of learning methods. Three of the most common methods are direct, peer, and independent learning.

Direct Learning

In their first years in school, children's learning is more activity based. It uses sensory aids such as finger paints, posters, play money, and games. In contrast, language-based, direct learning becomes the more common form of instruction for older children.

Children capable of direct learning can get facts and ideas by listening and reading. For example, the teacher might talk to the class about the Civil War and assign reading in the textbook. The children must pay close attention to the teacher. They also must learn to take notes and read their textbooks on their own. Their progress in mastering these skills is gradual. How well they learn the material can be measured with tests, quizzes, and essays.

Peer Learning

Peer learning is a learning method in which students interact with one another. In peer learning, students work together in pairs, small groups, or as a class on a project or task. One advantage of peer learning is that it provides an environment in which students may feel less awkward about asking questions or expressing confusion. Working on group projects helps students learn to work together cooperatively, to communicate, and to build time- and resource-management skills.

Independent Learning

Teachers should help students build the skills needed for independent learning. Independent learning allows students to work on their own. It also lets them use the information they gather in a variety of challenging ways. It prepares them for long-term assignments common in high school, college, and the working world.

A teacher may, for example, suggest an area of study, such as farming in North America. Students choose a specific topic, perhaps crops of the American desert. Then they will get a week or more to complete the assignment. Students will research and select topics, collect materials, and continue their research, finally preparing a finished assignment.

Direct Learning
Much of what children learn in school is through direct learning. *Do you think an eight-year-old would enjoy activity-based learning or direct learning more? Why?*

Peer Pressure

Middle school is a period of major changes for preteens. They often begin spending more time with their friends with less supervision. To prepare preteens for this freedom, parents should discuss the importance of not going along with friends if their behavior appears to be wrong. Even if the other person is a long-time friend, preteens can stop a friendship that makes them uncomfortable. If necessary, let children know they can make the parent a scapegoat. They might say something like, "My mom won't let me do that," or "My dad always finds out everything I do."

Be Prepared Act out a situation with a partner in which one of you is a preteen and the other is the parent. Have a discussion about what to do if a friend tries to get the preteen involved in an activity that makes him or her feel uncomfortable.

A sixth-grade teacher might give specific directions for each step of the process. Students would complete each step by a designated time to meet the final deadline. Teachers may need to help students allocate their time between steps. Preteens may be given more responsibility in planning their work and meeting their deadlines.

✓ Reading Check **Recall** What is peer learning?

Middle School—A Time of Transition

The typical school day of a fourth grader and a high school freshman are not at all alike. Fourth graders still perform best in the type of classroom setting used with younger children, with one teacher who is almost like a parent.

This teacher leads them through most of their coursework and gives them personal, individual care and guidance. The children know all their classmates and spend most of their time in their familiar classroom surroundings.

On the other hand, high school students rotate from class to class all day with changing teachers and classmates. Their learning environment is more impersonal than elementary school. They are expected to do much of their work independently.

New Independence and Social Skills

The period of time between fourth grade and high school can be very stressful for students as they begin to have new concerns and needs. They become increasingly aware of their changing bodies. At the same time, they are becoming more and more focused on what people think about them. Most are looking for peer acceptance.

They also are more independent. This independence may have led to greater responsibilities at home, though. That may limit personal activities. They are developing social skills, but they are not yet ready for the less personal high school setting.

Effective Middle Schools

Educators often disagree on what is the best education setting for preteens. The main challenge is that preteens want and need more freedom than younger children. However, educators do agree on some approaches to what can be a very stressful age.

Middle school homeroom teachers offer the personal contact that a preteen still needs. They provide someone familiar the students can go to with problems. The best middle schools have a low number of students per teacher or advisor. This might be 10 students to 1 teacher. These schools involve parents and community leaders in their classroom activities. In addition, they **integrate**, or combine, coursework from several classes rather than offering disconnected classes in rigid time frames.

Middle school educators try to personalize the school setting. They also try to provide an environment where students can enjoy being more grown up. Students may be able to choose some of their subjects. They can choose new friends. More challenging academic work can increase their confidence in their ability to learn. All these positive aspects of the middle school can create a comfortable bridge to high school.

The Importance of Parent Involvement

Parents who get involved in their child's education send the message that school counts. Here are some ways parents can be involved:

- **Meet the staff.** Many schools have a back-to-school night for visiting children's classes and meeting the teachers. Teachers describe the curriculum, as well as their expectations and rules.
- **Talk to the teachers personally.** Many schools schedule one-on-one parent-teacher conferences. If the teacher does not request a meeting, the parent can ask for one.
- **Read messages sent by the school.** Teachers and principals often send home important information about the school and activities. They may mail or e-mail the information, or send a note home with the students.

What Would You Do?

A Group Project

Vince, Kirsten, and several of their seventh-grade classmates were working on a project for the science fair. Kirsten and Vince's group was having trouble agreeing on how the project should go. Although Vince and Kirsten were supposed to be working together on a drawing of a single-celled amoeba, Vince was hoarding the markers. Philip, another group member, was trying to slack off and let the others take over. Jared was not letting him get away with it. "Get the scissors and start cutting out the game pieces," he said. Sydney, a bright, hardworking girl who wanted to impress her teacher and classmates, had taken charge of writing an essay for the group. She was worried that Philip's lack of motivation would hurt the group's grade.

Write About It When working in groups, a few members often do most of the work, while others do little. Why do you think this is? Write a paragraph describing what you would do if you were Sydney in the situation that was just described.

Parent Involvement
Involved parents send a message to their children and their children's teachers. *If you were a middle school teacher, what would you think about parents who did not respond to your messages concerning their child?*

- **Review the child's homework.** Parents can judge a child's performance by reviewing homework. Looking at assignments that have been graded helps to identify areas that need improvement.
- **Help out with school activities.** Parents can volunteer to help in the class or for field trips and special activities.
- **Join the parents' group.** Parents can learn about the school and offer constructive suggestions.
- **Talk to the child.** Parents can stay involved simply by talking to their child about school. Encourage students to describe the work they did that day and any important events that took place.

✓ **Reading Check** **List** What are four ways in which parents can be involved in their child's education?

Intellectual Development

Schools often rely on tests to evaluate how well students are developing intellectually and how much knowledge they are gaining. Schools periodically may give standardized tests. A **standardized test** is a test that lets educators see how students are performing intellectually when compared to the thousands of other students who have taken the same test. Many states now **mandate**, or require, that standardized tests be given to students to measure their learning achievement. These tests are also used as an indicator of how well the schools are meeting the learning needs of their students.

Creating Standardized Tests

Standardized tests have a special usefulness in assessing how well children are able to learn, and how much they have learned. Most seven- to twelve-year-olds take standardized tests in one or more grades.

Parenting Skills

Helping with Homework

When children start to have homework, parents and caregivers need to make almost as many adjustments as the child does. They also need to decide just how much help to give. Here are some tips to find the right balance:

- **Avoid doing too much.** Try helping the child think through the assignment and decide how to tackle it.
- **Offer help when it is really needed.** If a child cannot figure out how to do a problem, you may be able to help by showing how to solve a similar one.
- **Supply materials and help with organization.** For example, color-coded folders can help a middle school child organize work by class.
- **Allow time for a break after school.** This gives children a mental break before focusing on studying again.
- **Above all, be there.** It is wonderfully reassuring for a child to have a trusted adult available while doing homework.

Take Charge Imagine you are the parent of a preteen who has asked for help writing a report about Alaska. Write a paragraph describing how you would respond.

Teams of scientists and educators design standardized tests for schools. Along with the tests come exact instructions for giving and scoring them. Before standardized tests are ready for use, they are repeatedly tested with students and revised. This effort guarantees that the tests have three properties that are necessary to make them good tests.

- **Validity** A standardized test is valid when it measures what it is supposed to measure. For example, if a test is supposed to measure reading comprehension, enough time must be given for the students to complete reading the selections and answer the questions.
- **Reliability** Standardized tests must be consistent. The test is reliable if it can be given to the same age group, again and again, with similar results.
- **Practicality** Standardized tests must be practical for schools to be able to use them. They cannot be difficult to give, and they must be quick and relatively easy to score. They must also be affordable.

Kinds of Standardized School Tests

There are many kinds of standardized tests. Three kinds that are given to children ages seven to twelve include tests that measure how well they can learn, how much they have already learned, and what they might have a special ability or interest in learning.

Learning Ability Tests Learning ability tests are designed to help educators predict how well a student might do in a particular learning situation. All the students taking the test answer the same set of questions. Their scores are then compared. Learning ability tests go by several names. They are also called intelligence tests, mental ability tests, scholastic aptitude tests, and academic aptitude tests.

Most tests require students to read questions and write answers. A student with highly developed language skills may earn a higher score than a student with highly developed musical skills. Having a higher IQ on this one test does not mean that the top scoring student is smarter. The second student's learning ability is just different.

Achievement Tests Achievement tests are used to help measure what students have actually learned about a particular topic or subject. Standardized achievement tests are the most prevalent standardized test used in schools. These tests are generally given to students once per school year. Many teachers will give their students practice tests throughout the year. This helps lessen student anxiety when taking the test. These tests give educators a sense of the progress students are making in gaining knowledge. A certain score on these types of tests may be required for graduation.

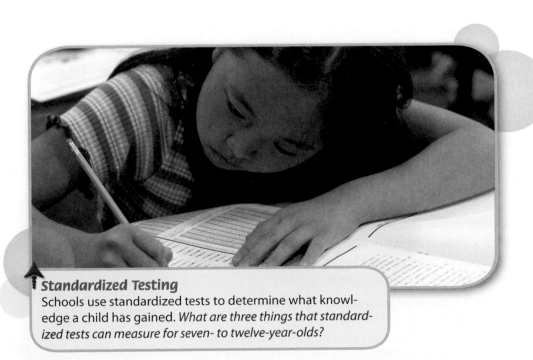

Standardized Testing
Schools use standardized tests to determine what knowledge a child has gained. *What are three things that standardized tests can measure for seven- to twelve-year-olds?*

Aptitude and Interest Tests Aptitude and interest tests offer important measures of people's talents and preferences. A student who scores high in mathematical aptitude might strive to become an engineer or a scientist. Another name for interest tests is interest inventories. Students select what they like best from different groups of ideas, activities, or situations. Patterns in their answers are analyzed to see where their interests are strongest.

Criticism of Standardized Tests

While standardized tests provide useful indicators of how students are developing intellectually, they have important limitations. These tests are estimates that measure only a small sample of a student's abilities or achievements. Even with tests of considerable reliability, scores can vary due to factors such as the age of the test taker and conditions at the test's location. Many critics argue that standardized tests do not accurately assess the intellectual development of minority and disadvantaged students, or English language learners. They feel this is true no matter how culture fair and culture free the test makers claim them to be.

Teachers feel pressured to have their students get high test scores. They are sometimes criticized for teaching only what is going to be on achievement tests, ignoring opportunities to share other important information with students that could enliven their studies.

In spite of the criticism, most educators still feel that standardized testing is needed. Along with teacher tests, it remains the best way to keep informed about what students need and how to best help them develop intellectually.

Section 18.2 **After You Read**

Review Key Concepts

1. **Describe** how a teacher might use direct learning to teach fourth-graders that water boils at 212 degrees Fahrenheit. How might the teacher use peer learning to help students learn the same fact?

2. **Explain** why middle school is considered a time of transition.

3. **Define** what it means for a standardized test to be valid, reliable, and practical.

Practice Academic Skills

 English Language Arts

4. Write a quiz containing five questions. Each question should give an example of one type of learning. The person taking the test must identify each example as direct learning, peer learning, or independent learning. Trade quizzes with your classmates and practice identifying the learning styles.

> **NCTE 5** Use different writing process elements to communicate effectively.

 Social Studies

5. Imagine you are a second grader whose family does not speak English at home. You started learning English in kindergarten, but are still working to catch up to your peers. Write a paragraph describing how this might affect your scores on standardized tests.

 Check Your Answers Check your answers at this book's Online Learning Center at **glencoe.com**.

> **NCSS IV E** Examine the interaction of ethnic, national, or cultural influences in specific situations or events.

Chapter Summary

Children make many advances in their intellectual abilities between the ages of seven and twelve. Children move from the concrete operations stage to the formal operations stage at about age eleven. Piaget, Vygotsky, Montessori, Gardner, and Sternberg developed theories about intellectual development. Direct learning, peer learning, and independent learning are all modes of learning. Middle school programs are specially designed to meet the educational and emotional needs of preteens. Between the ages of seven and twelve, students take standardized tests that are designed to measure intellectual performance and aptitudes.

Vocabulary Review

1. Create multiple-choice test questions for each vocabulary term.

Content Vocabulary

◇ transitivity (p. 500)
◇ conservation (p. 500)
◇ hypothetical (p. 500)
◇ learning method (p. 505)
◇ peer learning (p. 505)
◇ standardized test (p. 508)

Academic Vocabulary

■ concrete (p. 499)
■ multifaceted (p. 501)
■ integrate (p. 506)
■ mandate (p. 508)

Review Key Concepts

2. Identify four signs of intellectual development in children ages seven to twelve.

3. Explain four thinking skills that build a foundation for mastering school work.

4. Describe three learning methods that are effective for children ages seven to twelve.

5. Identify characteristics of the middle school experience that make it well suited to preteen learning.

6. Compare and contrast three types of standardized tests.

Critical Thinking

7. Draw Conclusions Why do you think that children from seven to twelve have a stronger sense of awareness and curiosity?

8. Apply What could a middle school teacher say to help parents become more involved in their child's learning?

9. Analyze What might be some of the causes of math anxiety?

10. Decide Would you rather score high on an achievement test or on an aptitude test in a subject you like? Explain your answer.

Family & Community Connection

11. Tutoring Find out what kinds of tutoring are offered by a local middle school for students having difficulties in a particular subject. Alternatively, find out what kinds of professional tutoring services are available in your community. Summarize what you learn and create a brochure to share the information with other students.

Health Skills

12. Importance of Sleep Not getting adequate sleep can greatly affect students' ability to learn. It also can cause them to do poorly on standardized tests. Conduct research to learn more about the effects of a lack of sleep on learning. Prepare a short presentation to share what you learn. Conclude your presentation with suggestions on how students could get more sleep.

Observation Skills

13. Sternberg's Theory Sternberg divided intelligence into three categories: analytical, creative, and practical.

Procedure Observe seven- to ten-year-olds in at least two different settings. For example, you might observe them in a classroom and on the playground. Keep track of instances in which the children exhibited each of Sternberg's three types of intelligence. Write down a description of exactly how they exhibit a particular type of intelligence.

Analysis Create a table listing Sternberg's three types of intelligence. Under each type, describe the examples you observed. Be specific in your descriptions.

> **NCSS IV D Individual Development and Identity**
> Apply concepts, methods, and theories about the study of human growth and development, such as learning, motivation, and behavior.

Real-World Skills

Interpersonal and Collaborative Skills

14. Work in Teams Follow your teacher's instructions to form into groups of four. Each group should divide into pairs. With your partner, prepare a debate about learning. One pair will argue that Gardner's multiple intelligences theory is more accurate, and the other will argue for Sternberg's intelligence theory. Each group should present their debate to the class.

Technology Skills

15. Analyze Online Practice Tests Some Web sites offer practice tests that claim to help students prepare for standardized tests. Research some of these sites. Then use word processing software to write a report discussing whether you think this is a good use of instructional technology.

Financial Literacy

16. Raising Money Think of a local financial need. Maybe a family has had a house fire or a school needs new playground equipment. Think of an activity that preteens could do to help raise money for this cause. Write a summary of the activity and estimate how much money it might raise.

 Additional Activities For additional activities, go to this book's Online Learning Center at **glencoe.com**.

Academic Skills

English Language Arts

17. Standardized Testing Imagine education without standardized testing. Think about specific parts of education that might change. Write a paragraph describing what your education would be like. Be sure to emphasize the areas that are different from your current education.

> **NCTE 4** Use written language to communicate effectively.

Mathematics

18. Logical Grouping At this age, children develop class logic. This means they can classify unlike objects into logical groups. Previously sorting was based on a perceived attribute such as color. Classify the triangle below in the most detailed and specific classification possible.

Math Concept **Triangle Classification**
Different types of triangles include acute, isosceles, equiangular, right, equilateral, scalene, and obtuse.

Starting Hint The tic marks on each side of the triangle mean they are equal in length. The arcs on all three angles mean the angles are equal. Use the classifications to describe the triangle. Look up definitions for the triangle types if needed.

> For math help, go to the Math Appendix at the back of the book.

> **NCTM Geometry** Use visualization, spatial reasoning, and geometric modeling to solve problems.

Science

19. Math Anxiety Researchers have found that males and females show similar levels of math anxiety in elementary school. However, females show more math anxiety than males in high school and college. Females typically begin to doubt their math abilities around seventh grade.

Procedure Ask 20 people, "Do you think you are good at math?" Half of your respondents should be male and half female. All should be between the ages of 8 and 20.

Analysis Total the number of yes and no responses by age and sex. Write a short analysis of your results.

> **NSES A** Students should develop abilities necessary to do scientific inquiry, understandings about scientific inquiry.

Standardized Test Practice

TRUE/FALSE QUESTIONS
True/false questions have both advantages and disadvantages. One advantage is there are only two possible solutions. A disadvantage is that it is vital to read the question very carefully. The way in which the question is worded is all-important. Read the Test-Taking Tip and then answer the question.

20. Taking a Karate class would help a preteen with bodily-kinesthetic learning
   a. True
   b. False

> **Test-Taking Tip** When answering true/false questions, find out if there is a penalty for guessing. If not, make a guess. You have a 50 percent chance of getting it right.

Unit Thematic Project

Develop an Exercise Program

In this unit, you have learned about the dramatic physical, emotional, social, and intellectual changes experienced by seven- to twelve-year-olds. You have also learned about the important role exercise plays in their growth and development. In this project, you will research exercises appropriate for seven- to twelve-year-olds. You will use what you learn to create an exercise program that will meet the needs of children in this age group.

My Journal

If you completed the journal entry from page 449, refer to it to see if your thoughts have changed after reading the unit.

Project Assignment

In this project, you will:
- Choose exercises appropriate for seven- to twelve-year-olds.
- Research the fitness needs of children in this age group.

Child Development Skills Behind the Project

- Determine the exercises appropriate for seven- to twelve-year-olds.
- Identify ways to meet the fitness needs of seven- to twelve-year-olds.
- Develop an exercise program to meet the needs of this age group.

Academic Skills

 English Language Arts

> **NCTE 4** Use written language to communicate effectively.
>
> **NCTE 8** Use information resources to gather information and create and communicate knowledge.

- Write a list of interview questions that focus on the kinds of exercises appropriate for this age group.
- Identify and interview a professional in the community who is knowledgeable about the fitness needs of children.
- Arrange, take notes, and type the interview.
- Use what you learned in the interview to create an exercise program that will meet the needs of seven- to twelve-year-olds.

Step 1 Choose an Exercise Program to Develop

Fitness affects the growth and development of all areas of life—physical, emotional, social, and intellectual. Choose an exercise program to develop that provides for the needs of seven- to twelve-year-olds. The program should provide both aerobic and strength exercises. Choose one of the following to develop:
- Three one-hour exercise programs.
- Five 30-minute exercise programs.
- Five physically active games that can be played for at least 30 minutes.

Step 2 Research Appropriate Exercises

Fitness needs vary among different groups. Conduct research to learn the fitness needs for seven- to twelve-year-old children. Write a summary of your research.

Research Skills

★ Use information that is corroborated in more than one source.

★ Cite the sources you use; give credit to the author of the information.

Step 3 Connect to Your Community

Identify and arrange to talk with a member of your community who is knowledgeable about the fitness needs of seven- to twelve-year-olds. The community member might be an exercise specialist, medical doctor, nurse, or physical education teacher.

Interviewing Skills

★ Take notes during your talk.

★ Use the knowledge you gained from your research to ask questions so there is a give and take of ideas and information.

★ Listen attentively and use appropriate body language.

Step 4 Develop and Present Your Exercise Program

Use the Unit Thematic Project Checklist on the right to plan and develop your exercise program and make your presentation.

Speaking Skills

★ Speak clearly and concisely.

★ Be sensitive to the needs of your audience.

★ Use standard English to communicate.

Step 5 Evaluate Your Child Development Skills and Academic Skills

Your project will be evaluated based on:
- Content and organization of your information.
- Mechanics—presentation and neatness.
- Speaking and listening skills.

Evaluation Rubric Go to this book's Online Learning Center at **glencoe.com** for a rubric you can use to evaluate your final project.

Unit Thematic Project Checklist

Exercise Program	✓ Use the information from your research and interview to develop an exercise program that fits the category chosen in Step 1.
	✓ Take photos or a video of someone doing your exercise program, or ask volunteers from your class to help you demonstrate some of the exercises in the classroom.
	✓ Show the correct way to perform the exercises for maximum physical benefit and to avoid injury.
	✓ Create an outline to follow when giving your demonstration.
Presentation	✓ Make a presentation to your class to share your demonstration and discuss what you learned.
	✓ Invite the students to ask you questions.
	✓ When students ask you questions, demonstrate in your answers that you respect their perspectives.
	✓ Turn in your research summary, the notes from your interview, and your presentation outline.
Academic Skills	✓ Synthesize data from different resources concisely.
	✓ Organize your presentation so the audience can follow along easily.
	✓ Adapt and modify language to suit different purposes.
	✓ Thoughtfully express your ideas.

Unit 7

Additional Topics of Study

Explore the Photo
The teen years can be both fun and challenging. *How would you describe your teen years?*

Chapter 19 Adolescence

Chapter 20 Children's Health and Safety

Chapter 21 Family Challenges

Chapter 22 Child Care and Early Education

Chapter 23 Careers Working with Children

Unit Thematic Project Preview

Explore Careers in Child Care

After completing this unit, you will learn that there are many career choices for those who wish to work in child care or early childhood learning. In your unit thematic project you can look at some of the options available.

 My Journal

Thoughts on Child Care Write a journal entry about one of the topics below. This will help you prepare for the unit project at the end of the unit.

- Discuss reasons you may or may not be interested in a career in child care or early childhood learning.
- Describe experiences you have had with child care either as a babysitter, or as a child when someone cared for you.

19 Adolescence

Chapter Objectives

After completing this chapter, you will be able to:

- **List** three main areas of change for adolescents.
- **Identify** three ways parents can help adolescents make good nutrition choices.
- **Describe** the four main influences on personal identity development.
- **Identify** the three roles of peers on a teen's social development.
- **List** the major influences on a teen's moral development.
- **Identify** three factors that influence how a student learns in school.
- **Compare and contrast** Piaget and Vygotsky's theories of intellectual development in adolescence.

Writing Activity / Journal Entry

Growing and Changing Many changes occur during the teen years. You change physically, emotionally, socially, morally, and intellectually. Write a journal entry describing some of the changes you have experienced since becoming a teen.

Writing Tips Use these tips to write an effective journal entry:

1. Use freewriting to write whatever comes to mind.
2. Use details to make images clear.
3. Tell how you feel now and how you felt before.

Explore the Photo
During adolescence, teens continue to develop socially. *What kinds of social activities do you enjoy with your friends?*

Physical Development of Adolescents

Reading Guide

Before You Read

Adjust Reading Speed Improve your comprehension by adjusting reading speed to match the difficulty of the text. Reading slower may take longer, but you will understand and remember more.

Read to Learn

Key Concepts

- **List** three main areas of change for adolescents.
- **Identify** three ways parents can help adolescents make good nutrition choices.

Main Idea

During puberty, many physical changes occur. These changes make good hygiene, eating well, exercising, and getting enough sleep especially important.

Content Vocabulary

◇ testosterone
◇ estrogen

Academic Vocabulary

You will find these words in your reading and on your tests. Use the glossary to look up their definitions if necessary.

■ adolescent
■ extracurricular

Graphic Organizer

As you read, list what it means to eat right. Use a diagram similar to the one shown to organize your information.

Eating Right

 Graphic Organizer Go to this book's Online Learning Center at **glencoe.com** to print out this graphic organizer.

Academic Standards . . . .

 English Language Arts

NCTE 12 Use language to accomplish individual purposes.

Mathematics

NCTM Number and Operations Compute fluently and make reasonable estimates.

NCTE *National Council of Teachers of English*
NCTM *National Council of Teachers of Mathematics*

NSES *National Science Education Standards*
NCSS *National Council for the Social Studies*

Physical Development During Adolescence

The term adolescence has a number of meanings. Generally, it refers to the complex time of life when a child begins to mature into an adult. In that sense, the ages of adolescence vary from person to person. It may begin at age 11 or 12. In this chapter, adolescence refers to the teen years, ages 13 to 19.

The teen years are among the most challenging for both the teens and their families. An **adolescent**, or teen, experiences many changes. Three main areas of change include coping with changing emotions, handling new social situations and influences, and using new intellectual abilities. However, the physical changes associated with adolescence are the most obvious signs that a teen is moving toward adulthood.

Adolescence is a time of rapid growth in height and weight. It is also a time of physical changes throughout the body. Both males and females grow taller and become stronger. At the same time, they mature sexually, going through the changes brought on by puberty. While this phase marks the development of sexual characteristics, puberty also includes other kinds of physical changes. Powerful hormones in the body bring on the physical changes of adolescence.

Once the changes of puberty begin, they continue with a rush that can be confusing and even a bit scary. This is especially true when teens or preteens are not prepared. Their only information may come from their friends, who may not be reliable sources. Parents need to prepare their children before puberty begins. Parents should reassure their children that this type of physical growth is normal. A delay in puberty is also usually normal.

Height and Weight

Charts showing average heights are less helpful during this stage because individual growth patterns are so inconsistent. During puberty, it is not unusual for a teen to grow three to five inches (7.6 to 12.7 cm) in height each year for several years. By about age 16, males are often bigger and stronger than most females of the same age. Many teens reach their full adult height by age 16.

To image-conscious teens, size matters. Those who go through puberty early may feel uneasy while at the same time being the object of their peers' envy. Others who mature later may feel that there is something wrong with their bodies. In many sports, players who are larger tend to have an advantage. Cultural expectations also shape teens' feelings about size. In the United States, for example, it is more acceptable to be a small adult female than a small male.

Adolescent Changes Many physical changes take place during adolescence. *How have your height and weight changed during your teen years?*

Males

Between the ages of 11 and 18, a typical male will double his weight from about 75 pounds to 150 pounds (34 kg to 68 kg). In the same time span, he will grow about 14 inches (36 cm) taller.

Eighteen-year-old Mario is average for his age. At nearly 70 inches (178 cm) tall, Mario weighs 150 pounds (68 kg). His shoulders are wider than they were a few years earlier, and he has become noticeably more muscular.

Females

Gina's growth has been typical for an adolescent girl. As an 11-year-old, she was 57 inches (145 cm) tall and weighed 80 pounds (36 kg). By the age of 14, she was slightly smaller than average at 62 inches (157 cm) tall and 105 pounds (48 kg). Now at age 15, she has grown about another 2 inches (5 cm) and has gained 9 more pounds (4 kg).

Girls usually do not grow much taller after about age 15. The average height for females in late adolescence remains just slightly over 5 feet 4 inches. Many girls do, however, gain some additional weight. The average female weighs 125 pounds (57 kg) at age 18. Of course, few teens are exactly average.

Sexual Development

Some of the most significant changes in adolescence are those of sexual development. As teens experience rapid growth spurts, girls develop physically into women and boys grow into men. During this time, teens become capable of sexual reproduction. Girls' bodies release eggs, and boys' begin to produce sperm.

Males

Males, on average, mature sexually about two years later than females. Between the ages of 13 and 15, boys' genitals become larger, and their testes, or testicles, begin to produce sperm. Sperm are the male reproductive cells.

Additional changes are caused by testosterone (tes-'täs-tə-,rōn). **Testosterone** is a hormone produced by the testicles. Testosterone levels in a boy's body begin to rise rapidly at the beginning of puberty. A boy has reached puberty when he experiences ejaculation, the ejecting of semen. Semen is fluid that contains sperm. The first ejaculation often occurs during sleep.

Females

As you learned in Chapter 16, girls generally begin to mature sexually by the age of 11 or 12. As teens, they experience rapid growth. They also go through the outward changes associated with sexual development.

Menstruation begins about two years after breasts begin to develop. The beginning of menstrual periods indicates that a girl's body has increased its production of estrogen. **Estrogen** is a hormone produced by the ovaries. Ovaries are two small glands located next to the uterus, the organ in which a baby develops in a pregnant female. The ovaries also produce eggs, the female reproductive cells.

Usually, an ovary releases one ovum, or egg, every 28 to 32 days. If the ovum is not fertilized

What Would You Do?

Discussing Problems

As they were walking home from school, TJ noticed his brother Jack was angry. When TJ asked him what was wrong, Jack yelled, "Forget it! I don't want to talk about it!" So TJ left him alone for a while. Later that evening, TJ tried to talk to him again. Jack said, "I hate school. I'm never going back. I'm the shortest kid in the class, and I always get picked last for sports. On the field, the other boys yell, 'Hey, Jack, short-stack!' The older boys are always saying they're going to beat me up."

✍ **Write About It** Write a conversation between TJ and Jack. How can TJ help Jack with his problem? What can TJ say or do to help Jack feel better about himself? With a partner, role-play the conversation for the class.

Talk Honestly
During puberty, parents can help to reassure teens about the changes that are happening in their bodies. *How much do parents need to tell young adolescents about their sexuality?*

by male sperm, it dissolves and drains out of the body along with a bloody discharge. This is the menstrual flow. Thus the menstrual cycle is the way the female body discards an unfertilized egg each month and then replaces it with a new one. An average menstrual period lasts from three to seven days.

Some girls experience irregular periods when they first start to menstruate. An erratic menstrual cycle is usually nothing to worry about. In the great majority of cases, a girl's cycle evens out within a year or so. However, if menstrual periods are extremely irregular, or if they are painful or prolonged, she should see a doctor.

Girls entering puberty may experience weight gain. This is normal. The addition of body fat is one of the effects of estrogen. The young teen is becoming a woman, and her body is beginning to round out.

✓ **Reading Check** **Explain** By what age do many teens reach their full adult height?

Health and Wellness

Health and hygiene needs change during adolescence. However, making wise food choices, keeping clean, exercising, and getting enough sleep are still the keys to good health.

With their busy schedules, teens often do not take good care of themselves. It often seems easier to grab a snack than to sit down for a well-balanced meal. Adequate sleep and exercise may also be neglected. Thus, it is not surprising that low self-esteem is common among teens. There is a relationship among these factors. See **Figure 19.1** for tips on improving your self-image while staying healthy.

Nutrition

Puberty and related growth spurts have an impact on nutritional needs. A balanced diet of nutritious foods is needed to fuel growth, as well as normal body processes. Teens typically consume more calories than usual during growth spurts.

Certain vitamins, such as zinc and iron, are especially important during the teen years. Use the MyPyramid Plan to help ensure your body is getting the nutrients it needs to help it stay strong and active during your teen years.

Eating right means avoiding foods high in fat, sugar, and salt, as well as taking sensible portions. Overeating, especially of high-calorie foods, can lead to obesity. Parents can help by making nutritious food choices available, setting a good example, and paying attention to portion sizes.

In the Hasegawa household, for example, bowls of food are not set on the table for family members to help themselves. Instead, Mrs. Hasegawa serves each person a plate of food with reasonable portions. If her children are still hungry, they can ask for seconds.

Figure

19.1 Improving Self-Image

Most people would like to have confidence. *What advice would you give to a friend who wanted to become more confident?*

Choose good nutrition.	The body needs breakfast to get the body and mind going, but it is the most skipped meal. Starting the day with a nutritious breakfast can boost achievement.
Exercise regularly.	Any type of exercise can improve fitness and give a feeling of well being when done regularly.
Think positively.	Everyone has some good features. They might include an interesting face, a strong body, or a great personality. Those who concentrate on their good features instead of real or imagined imperfections stand out for their positive attitude.
Look inside.	It is common to worry about what others think, but the solution is not to just follow the crowd. Having the courage to be an individual makes it easier to see and appreciate the best qualities in others.
Be strong.	Make decisions independently. Teens who have a good self-concept can withstand peer pressure because they believe in themselves. Their strength comes from within, not from what others say about them.

Teens are often "on the go" and find it hard to eat right. But even teens can practice good nutrition. They should make an effort to carry healthful snacks, such as fruit or granola bars, to maintain energy through the day. They should also be sure to drink plenty of water. Some other tips for teens to follow are:

- **Eat slower.** It takes time for your body to feel full. Eating slower can help you eat the right portions of food.
- **Eat breakfast.** It is important for teens to eat a healthy breakfast to get the energy to start their day.
- **Make better choices.** You can still eat out with your friends, but order juice instead of soda. Ask for vegetable toppings on your pizza instead of meat. Order smaller portions instead of upsizing.

Sleep

Everyone needs adequate sleep. The body, especially the brain and nervous system, restores itself during sleep. Teens need at least eight and one-half hours of sleep every night. Unfortunately, most only sleep about seven hours. They tend to go to bed late. Then they find it difficult to get up in the morning. Negative effects of too little sleep can include:

- Difficulty concentrating in school. This can lead to lower grades.
- Becoming irritated more easily and losing emotional control.
- Impaired coordination and slower reaction time. This can affect performance in activities such as sports or driving.
- Decreased resistance to illness.

Many teens enjoy **extracurricular**, or optional, activities such as athletics or clubs that are outside the regular curriculum. Some teens take on too many of these activities though. Some teens have part-time jobs during the school week. Others spend late nights on the computer or watching television. Good choices, time-management skills, and a regular sleep schedule can help teens get the rest they need.

Physical Fitness

A moderate amount of daily exercise is important for everyone, including teens. It builds strong bones and muscles and benefits the heart and blood vessels. Unfortunately, nearly half of Americans between the ages of 12 and 21 do not exercise on a regular basis. Physical inactivity sets the stage for possible obesity and the development of other health problems later in life.

There are many ways teens can add physical activity to their daily routine. Doing so helps the body cope with stress and strengthens muscles, including heart muscles. Physical activity is any activity that gets your body moving. It can be as simple as walking the dog before school or playing ball in the afternoon with friends.

THE DEVELOPING BRAIN

Sleep and the Brain

Scientists have conducted many experiments on sleep deprivation. They keep subjects awake for several days and observe them closely. The frontal cortex of the brain controls speech, memory, and the ability to solve problems. It relies on sleep to function properly. After three days, most people in these studies had difficulty thinking, hearing, or seeing clearly.

Science Inquiry Even though they are nearly adults, teens still need eight and one-half hours of sleep each night to function at their best. What might explain this?

Teens should try and get at least 60 minutes a day of moderate to vigorous physical activity. This can help maintain a healthy weight, increase your flexibility and endurance, and improve your health. Try joining a sport team after school. Or get a friend to join you for regular walks or bike rides. Even helping out with household chores like mowing the lawn can count towards your daily physical activity.

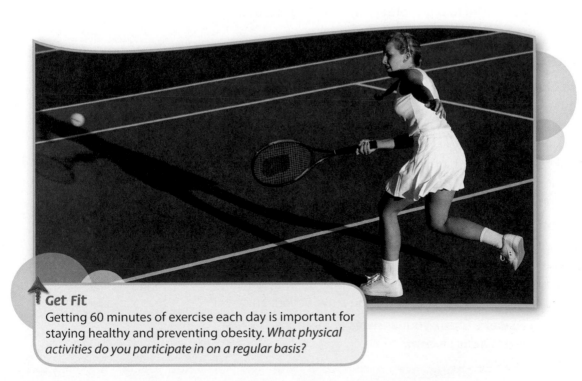

Get Fit
Getting 60 minutes of exercise each day is important for staying healthy and preventing obesity. *What physical activities do you participate in on a regular basis?*

It is often helpful for teens to set a fitness goal. Keeping a fitness log of your daily activity can help to reach your goal. Note the intensity and duration of each activity. Perhaps your goal would be to jog in a 5K charity run. You could begin by running just 15 minutes a day. Gradually increase your time and distance. Be sure to keep track of what you do each day. Use your log to check your progress toward your goal. Once you reach your goal, set a new goal. Reward yourself with something other than food.

Hygiene

Personal cleanliness routines become more important in adolescence. Perspiration odor and oily skin and hair are common problems. Fortunately, most teens care about their appearance and how they are perceived by others. Regular baths or showers remove dirt, sweat, and dead skin cells. Deodorant or antiperspirant helps control body odor. Clean clothes also help present a fresh image. Make sure to wear clean socks every day so that your feet stay healthy.

Teens should use water and a mild soap to wash their face each morning and at night. In addition, you should try to avoid touching your face with your hands throughout the day. Brushing your hair each day and regular shampooing will help keep dirt from building up. Brushing or combing will also help distribute the natural oils in your hair.

Fingernails and toenails should be kept clean and trimmed. Your nails help protect and support the tissues of your fingers and toes. They also add to your overall appearance and image. Just as important to your health and appearance are your teeth. You should brush and floss your teeth every day. Brushing your teeth after eating can help prevent tooth decay and other diseases. Nothing helps make a better first impression than a good-looking smile.

Section 19.1   After You Read

Review Key Concepts

1. **Describe** the roles of estrogen and testosterone.
2. **Explain** why teens need to pay more attention to hygiene than younger children.

Practice Academic Skills

 English Language Arts

3. Follow your teacher's instructions to form into groups. Work with your group to brainstorm answers to the following questions. Write a list of your answers. Between adolescent girls and adolescent boys, who do you think has a more difficult experience in terms of physical changes and development? Why? Compare your group's list of answers with the other groups' lists.

> **NCTE 12** Use language to accomplish individual purposes.

 Mathematics

4. John's weight increased from 75 pounds at age 11 to 150 pounds at age 18. This is an increase of 100 percent. Angie's weight increased from 80 pounds to 125 pounds in the same time. By what percentage did Angie's weight increase? Show how you arrive at your answer.

> **NCTM Number and Operations** Compute fluently and make reasonable estimates.

 Check Your Answers Check your answers at this book's Online Learning Center at **glencoe.com**.

Reading Guide

Before You Read

Be Organized A messy environment can be distracting. To lessen distractions, organize an area where you can read this section comfortably.

Read to Learn

Key Concepts

- **Describe** the four main influences on personal identity development.
- **Identify** the three roles of peers on a teen's social development.
- **List** the major influences on a teen's moral development.

Main Idea

Adolescents must form a personal identity and handle emotional difficulties. They also develop social relationships and a personal value system.

Content Vocabulary

- ◇ personal identity
- ◇ identity crisis
- ◇ depression
- ◇ bipolar disorder
- ◇ morality
- ◇ moral maturity
- ◇ popular culture

Academic Vocabulary

You will find these words in your reading and on your tests. Use the glossary to look up their definitions if necessary.

- ■ stifle
- ■ conviction

Graphic Organizer

As you read, list and describe three emotional difficulties that many teens experience. Use a chart like the one shown to help organize your information.

Emotional Difficulties of Teens	
Difficulty	Description

 Graphic Organizer Go to this book's Online Learning Center at **glencoe.com** to print out this graphic organizer.

Academic Standards . . . .

 English Language Arts

NCTE 12 Use language to accomplish individual purposes.

 Social Studies

NCSS IV C Individual Development and Identity
Describe the ways group and cultural influences contribute to the development of a sense of self.

NCTE *National Council of Teachers of English*
NCTM *National Council of Teachers of Mathematics*

NSES *National Science Education Standards*
NCSS *National Council for the Social Studies*

Emotional Development of Adolescents

As teens move toward adulthood, they work to establish their individuality. They typically become more attached to their friends and less dependent on their families. These and related changes can cause tension between teens and their parents.

Adolescence is the time of life when a person asks, "Who am I?" and tries to answer that question. While it is often a period of confusion, it can also lead to a strong sense of self.

Teens find that their emotions become more powerful and more difficult to control. Emotions can even be frightening. Teens must learn to control their emotions. Sometimes they struggle to do so. When teens' emotions become too overwhelming, they may need the help of friends and family to cope.

Personal Identity

During early adolescence, young teens begin to develop the mental capacity to form ideas and opinions that are theirs alone. They see that these ideas and opinions may differ from those of their family and friends. In this way, they begin to experience a strong personal identity. **Personal identity** is a sense of oneself as a unique individual. Teens begin to understand that their ideas, attitudes, and opinions are what form their personality. At this stage, adolescents are forming the personality that they will present to the world as adults.

As they develop a personal identity, teens grow more concerned with what their peers think of them. Some become self-conscious or self-absorbed. Young teens, in particular, tend to worry about their physical appearance.

Later in adolescence, a teen's sense of personal identity strengthens. Teens become better at understanding others' feelings. Their personalities often show more compassion and responsibility.

Influences on Identity Development

Social and cultural influences strongly affect the formation of a personal identity. These influences include family, peers, media, and the future.

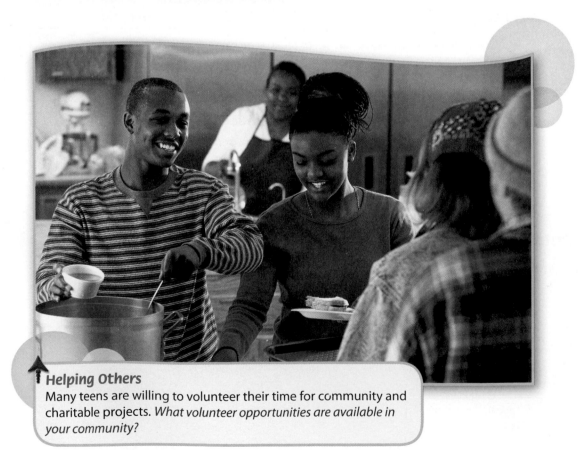

Helping Others
Many teens are willing to volunteer their time for community and charitable projects. *What volunteer opportunities are available in your community?*

Family Even though teens sometimes rebel against parental authority, family continues to be an important influence. Some teens and their parents maintain close emotional ties through this period. Other teens become especially close to another family member, such as a sibling or grandparent.

To parents it may sometimes seem that their teen is rejecting the family's values and beliefs. This may be true in the short term. However, an adult's personal identity usually incorporates much of what he or she learned while growing up.

Peers A teen's classmates and friends are forming their own personal identities. Peer pressure is an especially strong influence for teens. Those in a peer group often adopt the tastes and beliefs of more popular members. More confident teens evaluate those ideas and beliefs, accepting some and rejecting others. In this way, they can form a strong identity that is their own.

Media Popular media can also influence your personal identity. Television, movies, books, advertisements, and music all portray different values and beliefs. It is important to remember that much of what you see in the media is not realistic. The actions of characters in books, movies, and television shows are often exaggerated. These are all created to be entertaining. Advertisements are designed to try and influence you. Be sure to evaluate what the ads are saying and decide for yourself if it is true.

The Future By mid to late adolescence, teens have to start thinking about their lives as adults. By planning for a career or further education, they can start to see themselves as unique and independent individuals in the adult world. Deciding what they want to do or be in the future can affect the choices they make today. A teen who decides he or she wants to be an engineer in the future might join the science club today.

Theories of Identity Development

Many researchers have studied how adolescents form their sense of self. Two leaders in this field of study are Erik Erikson (1902–1994) and James Marcia (b. 1937).

{ **Expert Advice...** }

"During adolescence imagination is boundless. The urge toward self-perfection is at its peak. And with all their self-absorption and personalized dreams of glory, youth are in pursuit of something larger than personal passions, some values or ideals to which they might attach their imaginations."

— Louise J. Kaplan, psychologist and author, *Adolescence*

Erikson's Identity vs. Confusion Erik Erikson noted that even the most well-adjusted adolescent may experience some confusion about identity or sense of self. He and other psychologists considered this normal because adolescence is the time of life when teens strive to discover who they are. Erikson recognized that this confusion can become a serious problem for some teens.

Erikson believed that social and cultural influences have a strong effect on how teens develop a sense of self. He believed that one of the most significant influences is peer pressure. Peer pressure is the influence of friends in the same age group. Erikson held that conforming too rigidly to the attitudes and opinions of one's peers could result in an identity crisis. An **identity crisis** is a confusion about one's personal identity that results from failing to find a strong identity, or sense of self, through personal exploration.

Marcia's Identity Processes James Marcia elaborated on Erikson's theory by offering ways for teens to solve their identity crisis. Marcia believes that there are four paths to a sense of personal identity. Most teens explore more than one of these paths.

On the first path, teens accept the values of their parents and other respected adults without questioning those values. On the second

What Would You Do?

Dealing with Feelings

Cameron grinned and waved his new driver's license as he walked in the house. He had been confident he would pass the test and had planned to drive his friends to a game on the weekend. But when he asked to use the car, his parents said no. They told him he was still too inexperienced to drive the family car without an adult along. Cameron was angry and humiliated. He had bragged to his friends that he would be driving them. He had to call and tell them that his parents would not let him drive. Cameron refused to speak to his parents for two days. He felt they treated him like a child, and he was determined to make sure they understood how upset he was.

🖊 *Write About It* Put yourself in Cameron's parents' place. Why might they have made the decision they did? Write a paragraph in which you explain to Cameron why his parents made their decision.

path, teens are unsure of their values. They are determined to find an identity, but they are still in the process of developing it. On the third path, adolescents have no clear sense of identity and they are not attempting to find one. On the fourth path, adolescents have solidified their values and have developed a sense of identity. These individuals may redefine this identity in adulthood, but they have made choices they are comfortable with for now.

The Push for Independence

Teens naturally want more freedom. Many parents are often reluctant to grant that freedom. Parents want to protect their children from the dangers and disappointments that more freedom brings. As one mother put it, "Aiden can't remember to pick up his dirty socks or take his homework to school. The idea of his roaming around on that motorcycle he wants to buy is very scary. My goal is to keep

him alive and well, even if he hates me for it." Parents want teens to prove they are ready for more independence. Teens do not always see the need to do so.

Teens want to spend more time with friends and less time with family. Parents often want more time with their teens because they know the teens are getting ready to leave home. These opposing positions can lead to friction and arguments at home. Teens' tendency to begin questioning adult wisdom and authority also causes tension. All of these changes in attitudes and actions can cause tension between teens and adults.

The need to move toward independence is a major concern of teens. Understanding the importance of this need can help parents better respond to teens' concerns. Teens typically want to spend more time with their friends without adult supervision. They enjoy practicing adult skills, such as driving, and want to explore the world on their own.

Parents sometimes worry that lack of supervision can lead to reckless or even illegal behavior, sexual activity, and possibly pregnancy. They may also worry about a teen's safety while driving alone. They may worry that a teen with too much freedom will neglect schoolwork. Teens need to experience a reasonable amount of independence. That is how they learn the consequences of their decisions as they transition to young adulthood. When a teen asks for more freedom, parents should consider:

- Has the teen usually been responsible, well behaved, and truthful?
- Do I know and trust the teen's friends and their families?
- Does the teen drive safely and understand all traffic laws?
- Is he or she doing well in school?

If parents answer yes to all of these questions, they should consider increasing a teen's privileges. However, it should be clear that these privileges will be taken away if any serious trouble results. This understanding will be a strong incentive to use the newly won independence in a responsible way. Often, parents and teens can come to agreeable rules by talking about them together.

Handling Emotional Difficulties

Adolescence is a very emotional time of life. Ideally, its pleasures include making new friends, learning new skills, and becoming active at school and possibly in the community. However, life does not always go smoothly. Sometimes the pressures of school, family, social life, and physical changes can be difficult to handle.

Everyone goes through difficult times. For teens, emotional ups and downs are normal. But sometimes significant emotional problems do occur. Recognizing the symptoms of emotional problems in a teen is an important step in preventing those problems from leading to serious consequences.

Depression

Feeling disappointed or sad from time to time is common, but there is an important difference between temporary sadness and true depression. With **depression**, feelings of intense sadness last for long periods of time and prevent a person from leading a normal life. Depression can result from the loss of a loved one, family problems, the break-up of a close friendship, or failure in school. It can also be linked to the accumulation of smaller problems. A teen's feelings of being unable to cope with stressful situations can be unbearable.

Females have a higher risk of depression because of hormonal changes. However, they also are more likely to seek help for depression than males. Some of the warning signs for depression include:

- Feelings of sadness most or all of the time.
- Feelings of emptiness.
- Lack of energy.
- Difficulty concentrating.
- Loss of interest in social activities, school, or activities that were formerly pleasurable.
- Unexpectedly poor grades.
- A change in eating or sleeping habits.

If these warning signs are ignored, there are risks for further consequences. Anyone who sees signs of depression in a teen should act. Friends can tell the teen's parents, school counselor, or other responsible adult. Consulting a family physician or school counselor is a good first step. If the depression persists, the parents should consult a mental health professional.

Feelings of Depression
Teens sometimes sink into depression if their lives are not going the way they want them to. *How can you help a friend who is suffering from depression?*

Anxiety

Many people who suffer from depression also show signs of anxiety. A large number of people, including teens, experience this heightened feeling of uneasiness, fear, or uncertainty. Although there are different types of anxiety, all involve some degree of worry.

Some possible traits of anxiety include fear of social situations, shortness of breath or racing heart, sadness, difficulty sleeping, and panic attacks. Heather, who suffers from anxiety, avoids elevators, crowded areas such as movie theaters, and parties where there will be strangers. She knows being in such places makes her feel faint.

Teens who experience excessive worry should talk to a guidance counselor or doctor about the problem. If anxiety sufferers turn to alcohol or drugs to help cope, they can easily develop substance abuse problems. For information on anxiety disorders, see the Respond to Special Needs feature on page 475.

Bipolar Disorder

Mood swings and other emotional changes are a normal part of growing up. Sometimes, though, mood swings go beyond what is normal for most teens. Some teens exhibit signs of bipolar disorder. A **bipolar disorder** is a psychiatric disorder characterized by extreme changes in mood, from highly energetic to depressed and withdrawn, sometimes fluctuating rapidly. One week they may be manic. Manic means intense experiences of heightened mood. The next week, they are depressed and withdrawn again, causing others to wonder what is going on. These changes could occur over the course of days, weeks, or months.

Bipolar disorder was formerly called manic depression. It can affect people of nearly all ages. It affects males and females about equally. Scientists are not sure what causes the condition, but they think it results mostly from chemical imbalances in the brain.

During the manic phase of bipolar disorder, the individual may experience exaggerated happiness and optimism, racing thoughts and speech, and reckless behavior. When in the

Parenting Skills

Provide Guidance for Teens

There is a hymn titled "Keep Your Eyes on the Prize." The prize in the hymn is equal rights for all. For parents of teens, the prize is a young adult who can successfully live on his or her own. Many teens often struggle for independence. Here are some tips for providing stability and guidance:

- **Talk regularly.** No matter how stubborn teens may appear, most listen to their parents.
- **Discuss specifics.** Try sharing appropriate personal experiences. For example, you may have been required to make a difficult ethical decision at work.
- **Set limits.** Enforce rules about things that are important, such as personal safety. If a teen asks for more freedom, listen carefully and explain your answer.
- **Hold on.** Keep focused on what really matters, such as getting a good education and treating others with respect.

Take Charge Write a paragraph describing what it means to "Keep Your Eyes on the Prize" when helping a teen develop emotionally.

Changing Relationships
Teens often spend more time with friends than with family. *Who do you like to spend time with?*

depressive phase, the individual may have feelings of guilt or worthlessness, a loss of energy, and an inability to take joy in anything.

The cycles of manic behavior and depression can each last for weeks or months, but sometimes they are much shorter in length. The periods of abnormal behavior may be separated by a time when the person acts more normally. Although there is no cure for bipolar disorder, it can be managed with medication and supportive treatment.

✓ **Reading Check** **Explain** What may happen if someone who suffers from anxiety does not seek help?

Social Relationships in Adolescence

During adolescence, teens explore their independence and self-expression through their social relationships with friends. Teens may hang out with their friends, talk to them on the phone, and communicate online. They may do all of these in the same day. Parents may wonder how they find so much to talk about.

At the same time, teens may begin to rebel against the authority of their parents and other adults. Teens may feel that the adults are trying to **stifle**, or discourage, their self-expression.

Peer Influences on Social Development

Peers play an important role in teens' social development. Adolescents become less dependent on parents and other adults. Most teens become more involved with peers.

Peer Groups

There may never be a time in life when the need for acceptance is greater than during adolescence. Not making the volleyball team or not being invited to a classmate's party can be devastating. As teens form their identity, they may place great importance on the acceptance and admiration of their peer group.

During this time, there is a tendency for teens to conform to the ideas and behavior of the group. They may listen to the same music and watch the same television shows. Most teens do not want to stand out as being different. This is especially true in the early teen years. Charlie would go see the latest horror movie with his friends so he would fit in. But at home, he liked to watch romantic comedies.

An adolescent's conformist behavior can upset parents. The parents worry that teens will forget their many years of careful guidance. Such worries are often unfounded. Often, a teen seeks out a peer group that shares some of the same values.

Eating disorders such as anorexia nervosa (anorexia) and bulimia nervosa (bulimia) are psychological disorders. Anorexia is characterized by a refusal to maintain a minimally normal body weight. Bulimia is repeated episodes of binge eating followed by behaviors such as self-induced vomiting.

Eating disorders often start in adolescence. More than 90 percent of cases occur among females. Anorexia and bulimia affect as many as 3 percent of adolescent and young adult females. The incidence of anorexia appears to have increased in recent decades. Compared with adolescents who have normal eating patterns, those who have eating disorders tend to have lower self-esteem and a negative body image. They also have feelings of inadequacy, anxiety, social dysfunction, depression, and moodiness. Eating disorders can cause many severe complications. People who have eating disorders should receive immediate medical and psychological treatment.

Critical Thinking Conduct research to learn more about the medical and psychological treatments available for eating disorders. Compile your findings in a one-page report.

Romantic Involvement

During adolescence, most teens gain experience being part of a couple through dating relationships. Young teens may spend more time thinking about their appearance and how to be noticed than actually dating. The rise and fall of romantic relationships can bring emotions that are difficult to control. However, such experiences give teens a better idea of what to look for in someone to marry.

Close Friends

The most important peers in a teen's life are the close friends with whom teens share their secret dreams and fears. A teen may tell things to a best friend that he or she would never confide to a parent or other adult.

Having at least one close friend helps a teen navigate the trials of adolescence. Because friends are free to speak their minds with one another, adolescents can learn from a close friend how to alter their behavior or ideas. This lets them do so without the fear of rejection present in a larger group. Having a best friend also gives teens someone to talk to when things are worrying or angering them.

Opportunities for Social Interaction

As adolescents move into their middle and late teens, they typically become involved in more social activities. These activities can be both for pleasure and in service of the community.

Having a Good Time

There are many ways teens can have fun. These range from parties and time with friends, to sports and after-school activities. School and community organizations such as student government or the Boys and Girls Clubs provide opportunities for new friendships.

Taking part in such activities is not just enjoyable. It is also a vital part of becoming a well-adjusted person. It may also help discover what career one might pursue. An adult who did not participate in a variety of activities as a teen may have more trouble developing social skills.

Making a Social Contribution

It is also valuable for teens to become involved in activities that aid their communities. Some teens volunteer in hospitals, with charity events, or on environmental projects.

There are always organizations and programs seeking volunteer workers. Groups such as the Family, Career and Community Leaders of America (FCCLA) can give teens opportunities to design and carry out community projects.

 Reading Check **Explain** What are two sources of tension between teens and their families?

Moral Development of Adolescents

Peers, family, community, and the media all play a role as teens develop their own ideas about right and wrong. Moral development guides teens' behavior as it gives them a greater awareness of the rules of society. Some teens test the limits and make unwise choices.

As they leave childhood behind, teens look forward to taking their places in the adult world. Part of the quest for adulthood involves developing morality. **Morality** is a sense of right and wrong that guides decisions and actions.

Morality is based on values. A person's set of values may be referred to as a moral compass. Like the tools that help hikers find their way and avoid getting lost, values give direction to life. They help people make decisions that are right for them and help people avoid losing their way. During adolescence, teens must develop a moral compass to guide them through life.

Moral development is an important part of the maturing process. Teens who develop a reliable moral compass are more likely to make positive decisions. They are less likely to be lured into negative behaviors. Those who do not have a good moral compass are more likely to make poor choices. They may find themselves at odds with society's rules and laws.

Kohlberg's Levels of Moral Development

One of the most prominent theorists on the subject of moral development was psychologist Lawrence Kohlberg (1927–1987). Kohlberg believed that moral development takes place in six stages and that awareness of other people increases at each stage.

At the first stage, the notion of what is right and wrong is quite simple. It is based on the idea of law and order. The individual obeys rules to avoid being punished. He or she does not hit for fear of being hit in return. At Kohlberg's second stage, the level of morality is egocentric. What is right is what benefits the self. In the third stage, the individual seeks to do what is right in order to gain the approval of others.

➤ Moral Compass
As teens develop a strong set of values to guide them, they often join people who share the same values. *Do your friends tend to have the same or different values than you?*

The individual in the fourth stage of moral development seeks to obey the law and fulfill his or her duty. This person recognizes that a safe society must have rules of behavior. The person accepts and agrees to the rules that have been decided by others.

Kohlberg did not believe that all adults reach the fifth stage of moral development. At this stage, the individual better understands the feelings of others. He or she develops a genuine interest in others' welfare. The person becomes more aware of belonging to a family and community, and having social responsibilities. He or she recognizes that moral principles are based on individual values. Moral principles are tied to the need to uphold a system of moral laws for the good of society.

Kohlberg's sixth and highest stage of moral development, in which people are able to recognize and respect other people's points of view, is called **moral maturity**. The individual is concerned about whether the rules of society are just and fair. People at this stage make decisions based on equal respect for all people.

According to Kohlberg, each stage represents a milestone in moral development. Most people who reach the higher stages do so during adolescence and adulthood.

Influences on Moral Development

Moral development is an ongoing process that occurs within the context of a person's family, community, and society as a whole. As teens decide what is important to them and strive to establish their own value system, the positive and negative influence of others grows more important.

Peer Pressure

Peer groups can have a big influence on teens' moral development. Because teens are still discovering who they are and what is important to them, they look to their peers for approval and guidance. Peers also help teens clarify their values by discussing what is important and providing feedback. Positive influence from peers helps teens build stronger **convictions**, or beliefs, and behave according to their values.

Teens who are desperate to become more popular or to gain acceptance can be more open to negative peer pressure. They may look up to peers who break the rules and show little regard for their own well-being or that of others. Instead of condemning immoral or

Media Messages
A popular movie can send messages. *Do you think today's movies are more likely to influence teens positively or negatively? Why?*

illegal conduct, these teens imitate it in the hope of gaining praise and acceptance. This is how many teens get involved in drugs, drinking, sexual activity, shoplifting, and other negative behaviors that they later regret.

Popular Culture

Teens' moral development is also influenced by the popular culture. **Popular culture** is the culture that prevails in modern society. Today, the media tend to dominate popular culture. Television, movies, music, magazines, and advertising all show behaviors and can influence perceptions of right and wrong.

The media sometimes present negative behaviors in ways that may seem glamorous to adolescents. A rock star uses vulgar language. A movie shows violence as an acceptable way to resolve differences. Advertisements for alcohol suggest that people have more fun when they drink. Television programs show rude, immoral, and selfish behavior as amusing and harmless. Teens who are trying to establish their own identities need critical thinking skills to interpret all these messages.

Family and Community

Parents have a responsibility to teach their children moral values and help them develop an accurate moral compass. Schools reinforce the basic values a society needs to function, such as honesty and cooperation. Many families and individuals also draw on their religious faith for moral guidance. Some teens seem to reject the values of their parents, but with time most come to recognize the importance of a system of morality that all can live by. Parents who practice what they preach and live according to their stated values are more likely to have a positive influence.

Open and honest communication within the family helps teens learn values. Parents should discuss core values such as honesty and responsibility within the context of daily life. This can help teens see the role these values play in keeping families and societies functioning. Teens also learn more about values by having more responsibility within the family. As they make their own choices and mistakes, they can learn from each experience.

Dealing with Mood Swings

"I never know what to expect from my fourteen-year-old son," said Yolanda. "One minute, Tyrell is hugging me before he leaves for school and telling me he loves me. The next minute, he's making fun of his sister's singing and telling me I need clothes that don't make me look so much like an old lady. When I confront him about it, he always shrugs and says, 'Mama, you know I was just joking.' He spends a lot of time in the basement alone instead of being with his family."

Write About It How could Tyrell help his family understand and deal with his mood swings? Write a script of a possible conversation between Tyrell and his mother and sister in which Tyrell explains his feelings.

Of course, some teens do break the rules and get into trouble. Parents who know or suspect that a teen is engaging in morally unacceptable behavior need to confront the teen. Even though teens may be reluctant to talk to their parents about such problems, it is their parents' duty to help them change their wrong behavior.

Teens learn moral responsibility within the community too. Every community has expectations and rules to follow. Teens discover that they must follow the rules or suffer the consequences. Gradually, they also recognize the reasons behind rules and laws. As they learn to respect the rules of society, teens become better prepared to live successfully in that society.

Sometimes, despite a family's best efforts, a teen seems determined to pursue immoral and harmful behaviors. In such cases, the family may need to seek outside help. The teen might be more willing to listen to a favorite teacher than to a family member. Some families choose to get assistance from a member of the clergy or a school counselor. Teens with serious behavioral problems may need help from professional counselors. Counseling may include the family as well as the teen.

Linking Behavior to Personal Values

A teen's personal values will guide his or her behavior. Teens who develop strong values are most likely to avoid negative behaviors. Those who give little thought to morals are more likely to have problems. Teens who mature early are most at risk for engaging in negative behavior. They look older than other teens their age, and are often pulled into older peer groups. Unfortunately, their mental and emotional maturity lags behind their physical maturity.

Sexual activity carries many risks for teens, including pregnancy and sexually transmitted infections (STIs). Some STIs can be cured if they are caught early. Others are incurable. Teens who engage in sexual behavior run the risk of serious long-term consequences. Teens who choose abstinence from sexual behavior avoid the risk of STIs.

Other risky behaviors that can have consequences include drug use and crime. Teens who use drugs risk serious damage to their health. Death rates are significantly higher for teens who use drugs than for those who do not. Teen drug users also run the risk of contracting HIV/AIDS because the disease can be transmitted by sharing needles. People who become addicted to drugs also may resort to crime to support their drug habit. By abstaining from premature sexual activity, drugs, and other self-destructive behaviors, teens show they value and respect themselves.

Consider the risks, negative influences, and potential problems teens encounter. It is hardly surprising that parents are concerned about helping teens develop a good moral compass to guide their behavior. Teens who receive careful and caring guidance as they build their value system are most likely to stand up to negative peer pressure and media influences.

Section 19.2 — After You Read

Review Key Concepts

1. **Define** the term *personal identity*. How does it develop during adolescence?

2. **Explain** why teens are likely to conform to the behavior of others in their peer group.

3. **Identify** the risks teens face if they do not have moral values to guide them.

Practice Academic Skills

English Language Arts

4. Give an example of a teen in the media who presents a positive message about moral values. Was it difficult to find a positive example? If so, why? Organize your thoughts in a half-page essay.

> **NCTE 12** Use language to accomplish individual purposes.

Social Studies

5. Observe a group of peers at school. Note how certain group members influence others in the group. In what ways are the teens similar? In what ways are they different? Record your findings in a one-page report.

> **NCSS IV C** Describe the ways group and cultural influences contribute to the development of a sense of self.

Check Your Answers Check your answers at this book's Online Learning Center at **glencoe.com**.

Intellectual Development of Adolescents

Reading Guide

Before You Read

Use Color As you read this section, try using different color pens to take notes. This can help you learn new material and study for tests. You could use red for main ideas, blue for details, and green for examples.

Read to Learn
Key Concepts
- **Identify** three factors that influence how a student learns in school.
- **Compare and contrast** Piaget and Vygotsky's theories of intellectual development in adolescence.

Main Idea
Teens experience great intellectual growth due in part to educational experiences. There are different theories about teen intellectual development.

Content Vocabulary
◇ prefrontal cortex
◇ amygdala
◇ abstract thought

 Graphic Organizer Go to this book's Online Learning Center at **glencoe.com** to print out this graphic organizer.

Academic Vocabulary
You will find these words in your reading and on your tests. Use the glossary to look up their definitions if necessary.
■ sophisticated
■ profound

Graphic Organizer
As you read, list the reasons adolescents experience significant intellectual growth. Use a web diagram like the one shown to organize your information.

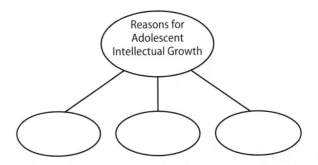

Reasons for Adolescent Intellectual Growth

Academic Standards . . . .

 English Language Arts

NCTE 4 Use written language to communicate effectively.

 Social Studies

NCSS IV D Individual Development and Identity
Apply concepts, methods, and theories about the study of human growth and development, such as learning, motivation, and behavior.

NCTE *National Council of Teachers of English*
NCTM *National Council of Teachers of Mathematics*

NSES *National Science Education Standards*
NCSS *National Council for the Social Studies*

Brain Development in Adolescents

Dramatic advances in brain development come with the physical and emotional changes of the adolescent years. Teens start to think less like children and more like adults as their brains mature. They gain the ability to think in more complex and **sophisticated**, or refined, ways. This ability lets teens do increasingly difficult mental tasks and use better judgment.

In the early teen years, adolescents experience major intellectual growth. One reason for this growth is the physical changes in the brain. Other reasons include gains in education and life experience.

Changes in the Brain

There are brain imaging techniques that allow scientists to observe the changes that occur in brain functioning during adolescence. It is now known that the brain starts to grow again just before puberty. The brain then continues to mature for several years.

The part of the brain that undergoes the most dramatic changes is the prefrontal cortex. The **prefrontal cortex** is the part of the brain that sits just behind the forehead and controls planning, organization, prioritizing, and other complex thought processes. The growth and maturing of the prefrontal cortex makes it possible for teens to reason better and to control their impulses. As teens mature they rely more on the prefrontal cortex and less on impulses.

Until the prefrontal cortex is fully developed, teens tend to rely more on the amygdala (ə-'mig-də-lə). The **amygdala** is the part of the brain that controls fear, joy, and other emotional reactions. Teens have a tendency to use the emotional part of their brain more than the thinking part. This can lead to impulsive actions based primarily on instinct.

Just as in earlier stages of development, the teen brain makes many more new connections than it actually needs. It then goes through a period of consolidation, in which unused connections cease functioning.

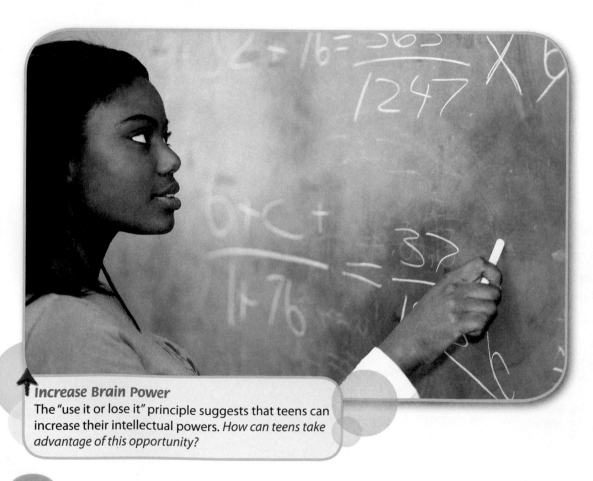

Increase Brain Power
The "use it or lose it" principle suggests that teens can increase their intellectual powers. *How can teens take advantage of this opportunity?*

Brain researchers say this process indicates that the adolescent brain is a work in progress. They suggest that what teens do during this period of development can affect their thinking skills for the rest of their lives. Those who challenge themselves to develop their intellectual powers are more likely to develop strong brain connections and more advanced thinking skills.

Educational Experiences

Even though there are different theories about intellectual development, there can be no doubt that education has a **profound**, or deep, impact on learning. This is true for students of all ages. The school experience is especially important for teens, though. This is because of the changes that take place in the brain at this stage.

Research has identified factors that influence how a student learns in school. Three main factors are the classroom environment, the degree of discipline and guidance at the school, and the involvement of parents.

Classroom Environment

How would you describe the environment in your favorite class? It is not surprising that when the learning environment is positive and stimulating, more learning takes place. Those who know that they will not be criticized for giving a wrong answer in class feel more comfortable participating.

{ **Expert Advice...** }

"Critical thinking skills begin to develop during puberty, and no one is quite sure when these skills stop developing. Children entering the teen life stage are now able to think in gray areas. No longer is everything black and white."

— Denise Witmer, teen development expert and author, *The Everything Parent's Guide to Raising a Successful Child*

SAFE CHILD HEALTHY CHILD

Self-Destructive Behaviors

Adolescence is a time for trying new things. It is not uncommon for teens to experiment with drugs and alcohol. Some try them to fit in. Others do it because they are curious, or as a form of rebellion. Unfortunately, engaging in this kind of behavior can be harmful to one's health and safety. The use of drugs or alcohol can lead to aggressive behavior and health risks, such as seizures and vomiting. Overdosing on drugs or alcohol can be fatal.

Be Prepared Teens will often drive after using alcohol or drugs. Use print or online resources to research the number of auto accidents involving teens and alcohol or drugs. Write a speech to share what you learn with your class.

When students feel at ease in the classroom, they generally have a more positive attitude about school. This usually translates into more learning when compared with similar students who have negative feelings about school.

School Discipline and Guidance

The degree of discipline and guidance in a school also add to the atmosphere of the classroom and the success of the students. Students who respect their teachers are more willing to learn. Less discipline can mean more disorder. This makes it harder for students to focus and learn. A low level of discipline can also lead to misbehavior which disrupts class activities and interferes with learning. Studies have shown that the level of discipline in a school is not related to its size, financial status, or location.

A school with strong discipline generally has close ties to the community. This means more parental involvement. These schools also have high behavioral expectations. With this comes a commitment by all of the school staff to maintain appropriate behavior. In addition, these schools usually have a strong guidance

Figure 19.2

Piaget's Four Periods of Learning

Piaget believed the teen years are part of the formal operations period. *Why is the formal operations period important?*

Period	Characteristics
Sensorimotor *Birth–2 years*	Children learn through their senses and own actions.
Preoperational *2–7 years*	Children think in terms of their own activities and what they perceive at the moment.
Concrete Operations *7–11 years*	Children can think logically but still learn best through experience.
Formal Operations *11–adult*	People are capable of abstract thinking.

program. Guidance counselors should be able to identify and address any problems that would interfere with a student's ability to learn, succeed, or participate in school.

The Role of Parents

Although teens often seem embarrassed by their parents, they generally still want their parents' support. Caring parents do more than simply make sure that their teen goes to school every day and does the required homework. They might ask questions about schoolwork, offer suggestions for completing assignments, assist their children as needed, or attend school functions.

Parents also need to emphasize the importance they place on education. If teens skip school or fail to complete homework, parents need to get to the root of the problem. They can then help the teen find ways to resolve it. Regular attendance and homework are essential parts of a good education. A good education is a key to a fulfilling life.

✓ **Reading Check** **Recall** What does the prefrontal cortex control?

Teen Intellectual Development

Many people have studied the intellectual growth of adolescents. Two leaders in this field of research were Jean Piaget and Lev Vygotsky.

Piaget's Theory

Adolescents have reached the fourth and final stage of Piaget's four main stages of intellectual development. Piaget called this stage the period of formal operations.

As shown in **Figure 19.2**, Piaget said this stage of intellectual growth begins at about age 11 and continues into adulthood. During this period, young people become capable of abstract thought. **Abstract thought** is the capacity to consider "what if" situations, to create sophisticated arguments, and to reason from different points of view.

With their expanding intellectual abilities, young people can organize their thoughts and find solutions to everyday problems. They can also absorb information and apply it to their own lives. Thus they can start making intelligent decisions about their future.

Piaget has had a very strong influence on the field of child psychology. However, some people have criticized his theories. They argue that his four stages present too rigid a picture of intellectual development. Many believe that there are more than four stages throughout a person's life span. Some of Piaget's critics also believe that he underestimated the influence of culture and social interaction on learning. One theorist that felt this was Lev Vygotsky.

Vygotsky's Theory

Vygotsky differed from Piaget in that he placed a stronger emphasis on social interactions. In fact, he saw a clear connection between intellectual development and social interaction. Vygotsky believed that children develop the ability to think by interacting with parents, teachers, and peers. In this way, they learn to think, gain mastery over their environment, and use language.

Vygotsky believed that language is the most important tool for influencing intellectual development. Younger children use it simply to communicate. Adolescents use it as a kind of inner speech to guide what they think and do.

Vygotsky used the term *zone of proximal development* to explain his theory about the role of instruction in a child's learning. The zone of proximal development is the difference between what a child is capable of learning unaided and what the child could learn with the help of a parent or teacher or by working with peers. It is a measure of learning potential. Vygotsky emphasized that only through teamwork with teachers and other students could students meet their potential.

This is put into practice in the classroom when the teacher assigns projects to a group instead of an individual. Also, some teachers offer additional help with assignments outside of the normal classroom hours. In this way, the student can learn from the teacher's expertise.

Section 19.3   **After You Read**

Review Key Concepts

1. **Explain** why the brain of an adolescent is said to be a work in progress.
2. **Define** Vygotsky's term *zone of proximal development*.

Practice Academic Skills

 English Language Arts

3. Consider your classes. Do you feel that you learn better in a small-group setting in which you work with peers? Or do you work better on your own? Write a letter to one of your teachers explaining why you do or do not learn better in small-group settings.

> **NCTE 4** Use written language to communicate effectively.

Social Studies

4. Parents generally have a desire to participate in their child's growth and development. This includes their intellectual development. Conduct research to create a list of actions parents can take to enhance intellectual development in their teen children. Your research might include reading articles on brain development or an interview with a parent educator.

> **NCSS IV D** Apply concepts, methods, and theories about the study of human growth and development, such as learning, motivation, and behavior.

 Check Your Answers Check your answers at this book's Online Learning Center at **glencoe.com**.

Coaches train athletes to improve their skills. America is a nation of sports fans and sports players. Some who participate in amateur sports dream of becoming paid professional coaches. Coaches can work with teams, such as a football or baseball team, or with individual athletes, such as a gymnast or swimmer.

What Does a Coach Do?

Coaches organize athletes and teach them the fundamentals of individual and team sports. They train athletes for competition by holding practice sessions to perform drills that improve the athletes' form, technique, skills, and stamina. Along with refining athletes' individual skills, coaches are responsible for teaching good sportsmanship, a competitive spirit, and teamwork.

Where Do Coaches Work?

Some coaches form businesses to train athletes. Others work for schools, recreation centers, or universities. Some coaches work with individual athletes, while others coach teams in competition.

Preparation and Skills

Education and Training

Education and training requirements for coaches vary greatly by the level and type of sport. Coaching jobs require immense overall knowledge of the sport, usually acquired through years of experience at lower levels.

Aptitudes, Abilities, and Skills

Coaches must have the ability to teach. Energy, physical endurance and strength, and an interest in working with young people are also needed.

Academic Skills

English language arts are used by coaches to communicate with athletes, their families, and other staff. Science skills are used to develop fitness and training routines. Psychology skills can help with motivating the athletes.

Explore Careers

Research related careers such as sports instructors, umpires, trainers, or sports officials. Choose one career and write a paragraph to describe it. Explain whether this career interests you, and why.

 Careers Online For more information on careers, visit the Occupational Outlook Handbook Web site through the link on this book's Online Learning Center at **glencoe.com**.

Chapter Summary

During adolescence, the physical changes that occur due to puberty are completed. It is important for teens to practice good personal hygiene, eat well, exercise, and get enough sleep. An important part of adolescence is establishing a strong personal identity. During the teen years, peers become more important. Social and cultural influences affect moral development. Changes in the brain during adolescence enable teens to reason better and control impulses. In Piaget's stage of formal operations, teens become capable of abstract thought. Vygotsky believed that social interactions are essential for learning. Positive educational experiences contribute to intellectual growth.

Vocabulary Review

1. Use at least six of these content and academic vocabulary terms in a short essay about peer pressure.

Content Vocabulary
◇ testosterone (p. 522)
◇ estrogen (p. 522)
◇ personal identity (p. 528)
◇ identity crisis (p. 529)
◇ depression (p. 531)
◇ bipolar disorder (p. 532)
◇ morality (p. 535)
◇ moral maturity (p. 536)
◇ popular culture (p. 537)
◇ prefrontal cortex (p. 540)
◇ amygdala (p. 540)
◇ abstract thought (p. 542)

Academic Vocabulary
■ adolescent (p. 521)
■ extracurricular (p. 525)
■ stifle (p. 533)
■ conviction (p. 536)
■ sophisticated (p. 540)
■ profound (p. 541)

Review Key Concepts

2. **List** three main areas of change for adolescents.
3. **Identify** three ways parents can help adolescents make good nutrition choices.
4. **Describe** the four main influences on personal identity development.
5. **Identify** the three roles of peers on a teen's social development.
6. **List** the major influences on a teen's moral development.
7. **Identify** three factors that influence how a student learns in school.
8. **Compare and contrast** Piaget and Vygotsky's theories of intellectual development in adolescence.

Critical Thinking

9. **Draw Conclusions** Why can the teen years be both the most difficult and the most rewarding period of life for many people?
10. **Infer** What qualities or characteristics do you think allow some teens to get along well with others while remaining true to their own opinions and beliefs?

Family & Community Connection

11. Interview a School Counselor Interview a school counselor about the frequency of eating disorders among students. Ask for the rate of incidences among males and females, and by age level. Also ask about local resources to help with eating disorders. Compile your information in a chart. Include a paragraph about help that is available to students with eating disorders.

Health Skills

12. Research Sleep Habits Keep track of the number of hours of sleep you get during the next seven days. Are you getting the recommended eight and one-half hours of sleep each night? If not, what changes could you make in your habits? Write a realistic plan of action that would give yourself enough sleep time.

Observation Skills

13. Observe Teaching Styles There are many different teaching methods. A teaching method that works for you may not work for your friend.

Procedure During each of your classes, note how the teacher teaches. Is the class mostly lecture or demonstration? Is there interaction between students and teacher? Are assignments given to groups or individuals?

Analysis Use your notes to create a table that shows the teaching methods used, the subjects of the classes, and the number of teachers who use them. Write a summary of your findings.

> **NCSS IV D Individual Development and Identity**
> Apply concepts, methods, and theories about the study of human growth and development, such as learning, motivation, and behavior.

Real-World Skills

Interpersonal and Collaborative Skills

14. Work in Teams Follow your teachers instructions to form into groups. Brainstorm a list of possible reasons why teens may engage in negative behaviors. Based on one of the reasons, work together to write a dialogue in which you persuade a peer to change her negative actions.

Technology Skills

15. Information Literacy List the advantages and disadvantages of having a close friend. Do the advantages outweigh the disadvantages? Use word processing software to create a report of your findings.

Financial Literacy

16. The Cost of Fitness Choose three types of fitness programs you might enjoy and research the cost of each. For example, you might choose taking classes at a gym or hiking with friends. Be sure to consider the cost of any equipment needed, as well as any membership fees. Create a table to compare the costs and write a paragraph telling which activity you would like to try and why. Is cost the most important factor in your decision?

 Additional Activities For additional activities, go to this book's Online Learning Center at **glencoe.com**.

Academic Skills

 English Language Arts

17. Persuade Your Audience Teens in a peer group often adopt the tastes and beliefs of more popular members. Write a persuasive essay to convince other teens about the potential dangers of blindly following the crowd.

> **NCTE 5** Use different writing process elements to communicate effectively.

 Mathematics

18. Meal Planning To practice budgeting, a mother assigns one day of the week to her teenaged son Bryce to plan and prepare dinner. Bryce is given $20 to spend. He decides to make cheeseburgers and fries. At the store, he finds buns for $2.99, a package of cheese for $3.95, one pound of lean meat for $4.49, lettuce for $1.49, a tomato for $0.75, and a bag of frozen fries for $4.39. Bryce is worried that he will not have enough money. If the tax rate is 7%, how much money will he need total?

Math Concept **Multiplying by Percents** To multiply by percents, change the percent to a fraction with 100 in the denominator. Then change the fraction to a decimal.

Starting Hint Add up the cost of all the items. Then multiply your answer by 7 percent to get the amount of tax. Add the tax to the cost of the items for a total cost.

 For math help, go to the Math Appendix at the back of the book.

> **NCTM Number and Operations** Understand numbers, ways of representing numbers, relationships among numbers, and number systems.

 Science

19. Create a Hypothesis Follow your teachers instructions to form teams of two. Think about this question: Do you think that thin, average, and overweight people eat different portion sizes when compared to one another?

Procedure Work with your partner to create a hypothesis of the eating habits of people for each weight category. At a food court or cafeteria, discreetly observe and take notes on the eating habits of four anonymous people in each weight group.

Analysis Report your findings in a chart. Does your hypothesis seem true? What other possible factors are involved in weight besides portion sizes?

> **NSES A** Students should develop abilities necessary to do scientific inquiry, understandings about scientific inquiry.

Standardized Test Practice

ESSAY

Read the prompt. Then answer the question by writing an essay. Use details and examples to illustrate your points.

According to sleep experts, sometime in late puberty, the teen body secretes the sleep-related hormone melatonin later than before. This means that teens may feel fully alert later into the evening, making it physically more difficult for them to get up in the morning.

20. How might teens best deal with this hormonal change?

> **Test-Taking Tip** Plan your essay before you begin writing. Jot down the main points you want to focus on. Refer to these points as you write.

Chapter Objectives

After completing this chapter, you will be able to:

- **Explain** how regular checkups and immunizations can help prevent illness.
- **Summarize** effective ways to care for a sick child.
- **Outline** the steps to follow in an emergency situation.
- **Describe** appropriate first-aid procedures for three types of bleeding.
- **Compare and contrast** rescue breathing and CPR.

Writing Activity Descriptive Paragraph

Being Sick Spend a few minutes thinking back to a time when you were sick. Were you miserable? Scared? Lonely? Bored? Use these memories to write a descriptive paragraph about yourself during that time.

Writing Tips Descriptive writing is attention-getting. It draws in the reader with details. Use these tips to help you write your descriptive paragraph:

1. Focus on using interesting adjectives and adverbs.
2. Work at painting a picture in the reader's mind.
3. Keep your words varied. Use a thesaurus to come up with appealing synonyms.

Section 20.1 Childhood Illnesses

Section 20.2 Accidents and Emergencies

Explore the Photo
Appropriate safety gear is important at any age. *What messages are parents sending to children when they insist the children wear safety gear?*

Reading Guide

Before You Read

Use a Dictionary Many of the names of diseases are difficult to pronounce. When you encounter a word you cannot pronounce, look it up in a dictionary or other appropriate resource.

Read to Learn
Key Concepts
- **Explain** how regular checkups and immunizations can help prevent illness.
- **Summarize** effective ways to care for a sick child.

Main Idea
Regular checkups and immunizations can help prevent many health problems and diseases. Common childhood illnesses include allergies, asthma, ear infections, colds, and diseases such as chicken pox.

Content Vocabulary
◇ communicable disease
◇ pollen
◇ asthma
◇ contagious

 Graphic Organizer Go to this book's Online Learning Center at **glencoe.com** to print out this graphic organizer.

Academic Vocabulary
You will find these words in your reading and on your tests. Use the glossary to look up their definitions if necessary.
- detection
- sensitivity

Graphic Organizer
As you read, list common childhood illnesses. Use a diagram like the one shown to help organize your information. Add additional lines as needed.

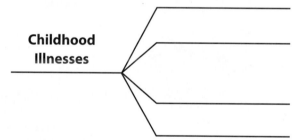

Childhood Illnesses

Academic Standards . . . .

 English Language Arts

NCTE 3 Apply strategies to interpret texts.

Science

NSES F Develop understanding of personal and community health; science in local, national, and global challenges.

NCTE *National Council of Teachers of English*
NCTM *National Council of Teachers of Mathematics*

NSES *National Science Education Standards*
NCSS *National Council for the Social Studies*

➤ **Regular Medical Checkups**
Regular checkups go a long way toward keeping a child healthy. *During what time of a child's life should regular checkups be the most frequent?*

Regular Checkups

Children, like adults, should have regular medical checkups. Early **detection**, or discovery, followed by early treatment may keep a minor condition from becoming serious. Checkups also let parents know that their children are developing normally. Regular checkups and immunizations can help prevent many illnesses.

During their first year, babies should be examined regularly. After the first year, healthy children need checkups less frequently. However, they still need one at least once a year. Because these checkups are so important, many local health departments have free or inexpensive clinics that provide examinations and medical care for children who do not have their own pediatrician.

When a child becomes sick, parents and other caregivers need to know what to do. They need to be able to recognize common childhood illnesses. They also need to distinguish between minor conditions and those that need medical attention.

If a child shows symptoms that cause concern, caregivers should call the child's doctor. In younger children, fever, lack of energy, prolonged diarrhea, constipation, vomiting, or difficulty breathing all warrant a call to the doctor. In older children, symptoms to bring to a doctor's attention include fever, persistent cough, vomiting, severe headache, or dizziness.

Immunizations

To immunize is to protect a person against a particular disease. People can be protected from communicable diseases by being immunized. A **communicable disease** is a disease that is passed from one person to another.

The most common way to immunize people is to administer a vaccine. A vaccine is a small amount of a disease-causing agent that is introduced into the body so that a person can build resistance to it. After getting a vaccine, a person's body produces antibodies. These are substances capable of fighting off germs for the disease. For example, if Monica gets the vaccine for chicken pox at twelve months of age, she will have the antibodies to fight it if she is later exposed to the disease.

Figure 20.1 shows what immunizations a child should receive and when. Parents are responsible for making sure their children get the immunizations they need at the right times. Parents should keep a record of each child's immunizations.

Many states require all children to be immunized for certain diseases before they enter school. Many also require that children in child care centers be immunized. Children under the age of five are the most likely to develop complications from the diseases. Therefore, parents should not wait until their children start elementary school to have them immunized.

Figure 20.1

Schedule of Immunizations

The Centers for Disease Control and Prevention (CDC) establishes schedules for children's immunizations. *How many polio vaccines should a child have received by age 12?*

Vaccine	Birth	1 mo	2 mo	4 mo	6 mo	12 mo	15 mo	18 mo	24 mo	4–6 yrs	11–12 yrs	13–18 yrs
Hepatitis B	HepB #1	HepB #2[b]			HepB #3[b]				HepB[ab]			
Diphtheria, Tetanus, Pertussis (DPT) 4-dose series with boosters			DPT #1	DPT #2	DPT #3	DPT #4				DPT #5	Booster	Booster[c]
H. Influenza type B			HiB #1	HiB #2	HiB #3	HiB #4 [bf]						
Polio			Polio #1	Polio #2	Polio #3[b]					Polio #4		
Measles, Mumps, Rubella						MMR #1[b]				MMR #2	MMR #2[b]	
Varicella (chicken pox)						Varicella[b]			Varicella[bg]			
Pneumococcal			PCV #1	PCV #2	PCV #3	PCV #4[b]			PCV[b]			
Influenza						Influenza (yearly)[d]						
Hepatitis A										Hepatitis A[e]		

Notes:

○ Green shading indicates that if child did not receive a dose of vaccine earlier, she or he can receive it during the period in green.

○ Yellow shading indicates a range of recommended ages.

a If the child did not receive the Hepatitis B vaccine earlier, the three-dose series should be given in this period.

b Can be given any time during this period.

c Tetanus and diphtheria boosters should be repeated every 10 years after this.

d Influenza vaccine is recommended yearly for children older than 6 months who have certain risk factors, including asthma, HIV, and other diseases. The vaccine is also recommended for healthy children between 6 and 23 months of age.

e Hepatitis A vaccine is recommended for children and adolescents who live in high-risk areas or belong to high-risk groups.

f May not be necessary if a certain brand of vaccine was given in the first two doses.

g Second dose should be given before the age of 12.

Note: This information is periodically reviewed and updated. Check the Web site of the Centers for Disease Control and Prevention for the most current information.

Some parents worry that a vaccine could harm their child. In extremely rare cases, a child does have a bad reaction to a vaccine. Parents should discuss these concerns with their child's doctor. In most cases, the chances of getting the disease are much greater than the chances of having a bad reaction to a vaccine.

Common Childhood Conditions

Allergies and asthma are becoming more and more common among children. Most children can live normal lives with these conditions as long as they receive proper medical care.

Allergies

An allergy is an extreme **sensitivity**, or reaction, to one or more common substances. Children may have allergic reactions when they eat or drink certain foods or inhale certain airborne particles. Foods that commonly cause allergic reactions in babies and children include milk, grains, eggs, shellfish, nuts, fruit juices, chocolate, and food additives. Airborne substances that can cause reactions include pollens, dust mites, molds, air pollution, and tobacco smoke. **Pollen** is a powder-like grain that comes from seed plants. Symptoms of an allergic reaction may be mild, such as a rash, a runny nose with clear drainage, or itchy eyes. Some allergic reactions, however, may be serious or even life-threatening. Sometimes, for instance, the air sacs in the lungs may become constricted, cutting the flow of oxygen in the body.

More than one-third of the children in the United States develop some type of allergy. Specific allergies are not inherited, but the tendency to be allergic seems to be. If both parents have allergies, their child has a 70 percent chance of having at least one.

Allergies cannot be cured, but their effects can often be prevented. For example, a child who is allergic to a specific food can avoid that food. One who is allergic to pollens can be encouraged to play indoors during peak pollen periods. A series of allergy tests can determine which specific substances are causing problems so that they can be avoided in the future. Medication or injections are used to control allergies.

SAFE CHILD HEALTHY CHILD

Asthma and Sports

Playing sports helps children keep physically fit and teaches them to be part of a team. However, some parents are tempted to pull their child from a sport when they see that it induces asthma attacks. It is important to know that recent government guidelines indicate keeping fit through exercise and maintaining a healthy weight can help control asthma. While exercise can strengthen the lungs, it also can cause airways to become irritated, leading to constriction and an asthma attack. Fortunately, inhalers can be used to expand the airways. A child with asthma should always have an inhaler available when participating in sports.

Be Prepared Conduct research to learn which sports are less likely to induce asthma attacks. Write a report discussing why some sports are more likely to cause asthma attacks than others. Which sports may be more appropriate for children with asthma?

Asthma

A growing health problem among children in this country is asthma. **Asthma** is a condition that causes the lungs to contract more than they should, narrowing the air passages and making it difficult to breathe. When this contraction of the lungs occurs, it is called an asthma attack.

Asthma attacks can be brought on by an allergic reaction. They may also be caused by a cold or the flu, physical activity, or exposure to cold air, smoke, or other irritants. Signs that a child may be having an asthma attack include coughing, wheezing, rapid breathing, and shortness of breath.

Children with asthma can take medication to open their airways and breathe more easily. A doctor must prescribe the medicine. Some medicines are taken every day to prevent asthma attacks.

Other medications are taken only to relieve an attack when it happens. Older children can be taught to give themselves their medication when they need it.

✓ **Reading Check** **Recall** What signs indicate a possible asthma attack?

Caring for a Sick Child

All children get sick. Caregivers need to recognize the symptoms of common illnesses. Parents should feel free to call the doctor's office. Often, a nurse assesses the symptoms, consults with the doctor, and decides if the child should be seen. **Figure 20.2** provides detailed information about some childhood diseases.

Caring for a sick child may involve little more than keeping the child inside and comfortable for a while. Recovery from many childhood illnesses takes only a few days. It may also be important to keep the child away from other children during the contagious period of an illness. When a child is **contagious**, the child can pass the illness on to someone else. In general, children with a fever should not go to school or to a child care setting.

Children may need medicine to relieve pain or to reduce fever. However, some children who take aspirin develop a serious illness called Reye syndrome. Be sure to use only children's medicines recommended by the doctor, not those meant for adults. Parents should always check with their pediatrician before giving a child any over-the-counter medicine.

Comforting a Sick Child

It is important to maintain a calm and cheerful manner around a child who is sick. Treat the illness matter-of-factly while remembering that the child may need some extra love and attention.

Children who are very ill do not have much energy and may spend a lot of time sleeping. However, children who have only a mild illness and those who are recovering after a serious illness may get restless or easily bored. Quiet play or reading, especially with a caregiver, helps pass the time.

Parenting Skills

Provide Good Nutrition During an Illness

Poor appetite during an illness is normal. If you have had the flu, you probably remember that eating was the last thing on your mind. The same response occurs in babies and children, but their smaller bodies cannot go as long without food and liquids. If illness and poor appetite persist for more than a few days, consult your doctor. Here are some ways to provide the nutrition sick children need:

- **Give the child more liquids.** Children need liquids to avoid dehydration. This is the depletion of needed body fluids. One good liquid is a sugar and mineral (glucose-electrolyte) solution, which can be found in most drugstores.
- **Encourage the child to eat.** Keep offering foods the child likes, a little at a time and as often as possible.
- **Do not force the child to eat.** One or two days of low food intake will not be harmful, as long as the child gets enough liquids.

Take Charge Write a paragraph describing ways to make food and liquids more appealing to a sick child who is not interested in either.

Figure 20.2

Identifying and Treating Diseases

Children often get illnesses such as the common cold. *Which illnesses in this chart require a doctor's attention?*

Disease	Signs	Treatment
Chicken Pox	A red, itchy rash appears first, usually on the head and back. It may spread to cover the entire body. The rash begins as small bumps that look like pimples. These develop into fluid-filled blisters, which break open, leaving sores that become dry, brown scabs. Fever usually rises no higher than 102°F (39°C).	Rest in bed during initial stage. Give acetaminophen to relieve fever. Keep the child cool in loose clothing. Apply calamine lotion to relieve itching, or give cool baths with baking soda or oatmeal added. Usually lasts 7 to 10 days. Marks left on the skin may take 6 to 12 months to fade.
Common Cold	Stuffy or runny nose, sneezing or coughing, mild fever, sore throat, diminished appetite.	Encourage rest and plenty of liquids. Give acetaminophen to reduce fever. Recovery takes 7 to 10 days.
Ear Infection	An infant may pull at the ear and cry. An older child is likely to say that the ear hurts. During the infection, there may be some temporary hearing loss. There is usually a fever.	See a doctor, who may prescribe an antibiotic. For a fever, use cool baths and acetaminophen.
Influenza (Flu)	Sudden onset of fever, chills, shakes, nausea, tiredness, and aching muscles. After a few days, a sore throat and stuffy nose may occur. The disease may last as long as a week.	Encourage rest and plenty of liquids. Doctors may prescribe antiviral medications for certain strains of flu. They may reduce the severity of the symptoms and shorten their duration.
Strep Throat and Scarlet Fever	Sudden onset, with headache, fever, sore throat not accompanied by runny nose or congestion, painful swallowing, white patches on the tonsils, loss of appetite, and fatigue. In scarlet fever, a rash of fine red dots usually appears within 24 hours. The rash is seen first on the neck and upper part of the chest before spreading. When it fades, the skin peels.	See a doctor, who will prescribe antibiotics for a positive throat culture. The child should rest in a warm, well-ventilated room. Throat lozenges and iced drinks can help reduce pain. Patients usually recover in a week. (The rash is the only sign that differentiates scarlet fever from strep throat.)

Children's behavior and needs during illness depend on their age. Infants may sleep much more than usual and tend to want lots of physical comforting. Children between one and three are usually very active and may have trouble staying in bed. Doctors might allow them to play quietly in the house. Older children can often help take care of themselves. They usually enjoy reading books, doing puzzles, or playing games while recovering.

Going to the Hospital

A hospital stay can be a difficult experience for a child. Children may fear that they will never go home, that they will be hurt, or that they will die. They may be frightened by unfamiliar doctors and nurses.

Parents can prepare their child for a hospital stay, unless it is an emergency. They can explain in simple terms what to expect. If possible, parents should take the child to tour the hospital. They may be able to see patient rooms, operating rooms, and recovery rooms. When the child is admitted, these things are already familiar and therefore less frightening.

The Hospital Stay

Hospital staff recognize that children are more at ease and may recover more quickly if a parent stays with them. Some hospitals provide a cot in the child's room so that a parent can sleep nearby. Other hospitals have rooms with space for both the child and a parent. Even when there are no such arrangements, parents can often visit their child any time.

A child may need many tests and forms of treatment. If the child asks, "Will this hurt?" the parent should answer truthfully. Parents may not want to upset the child, but it is more helpful to say something like, "It will hurt for a while, but then you will feel much better. It's all right to cry, if you want."

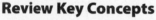

Section 20.1 After You Read

Review Key Concepts

1. **Identify** what antibodies are and what the purpose is behind producing them by vaccination.

2. **Explain** why a sick child should be kept away from other children during the contagious period of a disease.

Practice Academic Skills

 English Language Arts

3. Go to a library and locate a book designed to help children prepare for a hospital stay. Read the book. Write a review discussing how the book attempts to help children and whether you think it is successful.

NCTE 3 Apply strategies to interpret texts.

 Science

4. Conduct research to learn more about polio and the development of the first polio vaccine. Write a report discussing the effects of polio in the years immediately prior to the vaccine. Also discuss the scientists who developed the first vaccine.

NSES F Develop understanding of personal and community health; science in local, national, and global challenges.

 Check Your Answers Check your answers at this book's Online Learning Center at **glencoe.com**.

Reading Guide

Before You Read

Visualizing As you read this section, visualize yourself actually performing the first-aid instructions on a child. This will help you remember the necessary steps.

Read to Learn
Key Concepts
- **Outline** the steps to follow in an emergency situation.
- **Describe** appropriate first-aid procedures for three types of bleeding.
- **Compare and contrast** rescue breathing and CPR.

Main Idea
The steps to take in an emergency depend on several factors. If a child is choking or stops breathing, immediate action is essential.

Content Vocabulary
◇ antiseptic ◇ hives
◇ fracture ◇ shock
◇ sprain ◇ rescue breathing
◇ abdominal thrust ◇ cardiopulmonary
◇ convulsion   resuscitation (CPR)

Graphic Organizer Go to this book's Online Learning Center at **glencoe.com** to print out this graphic organizer.

Academic Vocabulary
You will find these words in your reading and on your tests. Use the glossary to look up their definitions if necessary.
- elevate
- expel

Graphic Organizer
As you read, list the four steps of rescue breathing for small children. Use a chart like the one shown to organize your information.

Four Steps of Rescue Breathing

Academic Standards . . . .

 English Language Arts

NCTE 3 Apply strategies to interpret texts.

 Science

NSES C Develop understanding of the cell; biological evolution; matter, energy, and organization in living systems; and behavior of organisms.

 Social Studies

NCSS V F Individuals, Groups, and Institutions Evaluate the role of institutions in furthering both continuity and change.

NCSS V G Individuals, Groups, and Institutions Analyze the extent to which groups and institutions meet individual needs and promote the common good in contemporary and historical settings.

NCTE *National Council of Teachers of English*
NCTM *National Council of Teachers of Mathematics*

NSES *National Science Education Standards*
NCSS *National Council for the Social Studies*

Safety

A caregiver's most important responsibility is to keep children safe. Young children do not know what can harm them. To keep children safe, caregivers should know what to expect. Each age has different hazards because of different interests and abilities.

The Safe Child, Healthy Child features throughout this textbook highlight some of the dangers. Infants, for example, will chew on almost anything and run the risk of choking. Toddlers are so mobile that they can quickly get into dangerous situations. Safety in and around vehicles is essential for all children.

If you care for children in their own home, you need to plan for the possibility of a fire. Locate all outside doors. Note escape routes from the home. Find out whether the home has smoke detectors and a fire extinguisher. Ask parents to go over their escape plan.

If a fire does occur, the children are your first responsibility. Lead or carry them to safety. Then call the fire department.

Guidelines for Fast Action

Even if you do not spend a great deal of time with children, you should be prepared to act quickly in an emergency. Fast action can make the difference between minor harm and more serious injury. Memorizing the following five steps will help you if an accident occurs:

1. **Stay calm.** A soothing approach helps reassure the child and keeps your thoughts clear.
2. **Evaluate the situation.** Is the injury minor or serious? Can you handle it on your own, or do you need someone else to help?
3. **Provide comfort.** Offer words of comfort, along with treatment, if the injury is minor. If the injury is serious, keep the child warm until help arrives. Do not move the child.
4. **Call for help if necessary.** If you do not know what to do or if the child is seriously injured, call for help. Keep a list of emergency numbers on hand. In many communities, you can get help by calling 911. Know how to contact an ambulance service, the child's doctor, and nearby hospitals. When you call for help, give the child's age, your name, and your relationship to the child, as well as your location's address. Describe the problem clearly and follow instructions.
5. **Give basic first aid.** If you know what to do, provide the necessary treatment. If you are not sure how to handle the injury, keep the child comfortable and wait until help arrives.

✓ **Reading Check** **Analyze** Why do you think toddlers are especially likely to be involved in accidents?

A House Fire
In case of a house fire, your first responsibility is to get everyone to safety. *What are two ways that you can prepare for a fire?*

CULTURE MATTERS

Preventing Infant Death in Australia

Infant mortality refers to the death of children under age one. These deaths are usually caused by genetic diseases, birth defects, or diseases that can be transmitted to others. Infant mortality rates are thought to indicate the overall health of a population. Australian rates of infant death declined sharply in the 20th century. Why?

In the first part of the century, the decline was linked to improvements in sanitation and health education, as well as the use of antibiotics. In the second half of the 20th century, declines were attributed to improved medical technology and campaigns to prevent sudden infant death syndrome (SIDS).

Build Connections *What did Australians do in the second half of the 20th century to reduce infant mortality?*

NCSS V F Individuals, Groups, and Institutions Evaluate the role of institutions in furthering both continuity and change.

First Aid

Following are some general first aid guidelines. Reading about first aid is no substitute, though, for getting hands-on training. If you plan to take care of children, contact the American Red Cross for information about first aid training classes.

Bleeding

Many common injuries involve bleeding. To prevent the spread of disease, child care workers are advised to wear disposable gloves when giving first aid to a bleeding child.

Minor Cuts or Scrapes

Place a clean cloth or gauze pad on the cut and apply firm pressure until the bleeding stops. Then clean the area with mild soap and warm water. Dry the wound, and apply an antiseptic. An **antiseptic** is a substance that prevents or stops the growth of germs. Cover the wound with an adhesive bandage or sterile gauze.

Deep Cuts or Wounds

If a cut or wound seems very deep, or if the bleeding does not stop, seek medical attention immediately. Continue to try to stop the bleeding until help arrives. Do not try to use a tourniquet. This is a bandage that cuts off the blood supply to a part of the body. This could seriously harm the victim.

Nosebleeds

Have the child sit or stand and lean slightly forward over a sink or bowl. Squeeze the lower half of the child's nose with a tissue for about ten minutes. Then release your hold and check to see if a clot has formed and the bleeding has stopped. If not, apply pressure again for ten minutes. If you cannot stop the bleeding, get medical help.

Bumps and Bruises

Minor bruises should be treated for ten minutes with a cold pack or a bag of frozen vegetables. Place a towel between the cold pack and the child's skin. You should **elevate**, or raise, a bruised arm or leg for a while.

A fall resulting in a hard blow to the head can be serious. Seek medical help right away if a child loses consciousness, becomes drowsy or irritable, complains of a headache, or vomits after receiving a blow to the head.

Bicycle Safety Classes

While bike riding is fun, it also raises serious safety concerns. Each year, about 500,000 bicycle accidents require emergency room visits. Children fourteen and under are five times more likely to have injuries than older cyclists. Every child who rides a bike should know and practice safe bike-riding techniques. Some park districts, schools, and bicycle shops offer bicycle safety classes for children of various ages. Learning the rules of the road is very important. Knowing which side of the street to ride on and how to signal to make a turn are just two of these rules. In addition, the bike should be the correct size for the child and the rider should always wear a protective helmet. This helps shield the brain if an accident occurs.

Think About It You often see an eleven-year-old child in your neighborhood riding her bike unsafely. She never wears a helmet and frequently darts into traffic without looking. Write a paragraph describing what you might do to improve this situation.

Fractures and Sprains

A **fracture** is a break or crack in a bone. A **sprain** is an injury caused by sudden, violent stretching of a joint or muscle. Both types of injury may cause pain, swelling, and bruising. It is often difficult to tell a fracture from a sprain without an X-ray.

If you suspect that a child has a fracture or a sprain, do not move the child until you know how serious the injury is. This is especially important if the injury is to the head, neck, or back. Movement can cause further damage. Call for qualified medical help.

For a mild sprain, elevate the injured area and apply cold packs to help reduce swelling. If the pain persists, check with a doctor about further treatment.

Splinters and Thorns

A splinter is a tiny piece of wood, metal, glass, or plastic that becomes embedded in the skin. Thorns are treated like splinters. Although splinters are usually not dangerous, they do hurt and can cause an infection.

If the splinter is sticking out of the skin and is small, you can use tweezers to remove it. Sterilize the tweezers in boiling water or in the flame of a candle or match. Pull evenly on the exposed part of the splinter to remove it. Then put antiseptic and a bandage on the wound.

If a splinter is just under the surface of the skin and is not glass, you can remove it with a sterilized needle and tweezers. Use the needle to break the skin and expose the end of the splinter. Grasp the end of the splinter with the tweezers, and gently pull it out. Clean and cover the wound.

Large, deeply embedded splinters, glass splinters, or those in the eye can be more serious. These should be removed by a medical professional.

{ Expert Advice... }

"With a toddler on the loose, accidents are bound to happen once in a while. One study showed that the typical toddler has three minor bumps or boo-boos a day."

— Heidi Murkoff, Arlene Eisenberg, and Sandee Hathaway, coauthors, *What to Expect: The Toddler Years*

Burns

First aid for burns depends on the cause and how serious the burn is. Most burns are serious because they may cause shock, infection, or scarring. Burns are classified by degrees.

First-Degree Burns

First-degree burns are mild and may turn the skin pink or red. There are no blisters or peeling. First-degree burns may be caused by too much sun, hot objects, hot water, or steam. Put the burned area under cold water or a cold, wet cloth. Then keep it dry and clean. Do not put ointment on the burn.

Second-Degree Burns

Second-degree burns are red and form blisters. They can be caused by too much sun or by hot liquids and flames. If the burned area is small, cover it with a clean, wet cloth and take the child to a doctor. If the burned area is large, cover the child with a blanket or clean sheet and call for emergency help.

Third-Degree Burns

Third-degree burns leave the skin blackened or white. These burns do not always cause pain because nerve endings may have been destroyed. They can be caused by flames, very hot objects, or electricity. Immediate medical care is essential.

Chemical Burns

Some products, such as disinfectants, can burn the skin. These products should always be kept away from children. Always read the directions and cautions on product labels. Should a burn occur, use protective gloves to thoroughly wash off the affected area with cool water. Remove any clothing with the chemical on it, unless the clothing has stuck to the skin. Seek immediate medical attention.

Electrical Burns

These burns may be deep, but appear to be minor. They may leave only a small black dot on the skin. Cool the burn with water. Cover it with a clean, smooth cloth. Lay the child down with legs elevated and head turned to one side to prevent shock. Call emergency services.

Science in Action

Resistance to Antibiotics

Germs are natural-born survivors. When scientists develop antibiotics to kill specific germs, the germs often mutate so that they are immune to the drugs. This mutation has caused many diseases to become more resistant to antibiotics. Conditions such as ear infections and tuberculosis are becoming harder to treat.

Procedure

Conduct research to find out what scientists think is causing this growing resistance. What can be done to reduce it?

Analysis

Analyze what scientists and doctors say can be done to reduce antibiotic resistance. Choose two of these ideas and prepare a presentation to explain the ideas to your class.

NSES C Develop understanding of the cell; biological evolution; matter, energy, and organization in living systems; and behavior of organisms.

Choking

Choking occurs when a person's airway becomes blocked by a piece of food or some other object. Young children are especially prone to choking because they tend to put all kinds of objects, including small toys, into their mouths. If the object is not removed, air will not reach the lungs and the person could die.

A choking child may wheeze or make high-pitched noises or gurgling sounds. An inability to speak, breathe, or cry and a bluish tint to the face are other signs of choking.

If a child is choking, you must act quickly. For a choking infant, follow the steps shown in **Figure 20.3** on page 562. For children older than one and adults, use abdominal thrusts. An **abdominal thrust** is a quick upward thrust with the heel of the hand into the abdomen that forces the air in the lungs to **expel**, or force out, an object caught in the throat. **Figure 20.4** on page 563 illustrates this technique.

The amount of pressure to use depends on the age and size of the choking person. Too much pressure can harm a child. Get training before you use abdominal thrusts.

Convulsions

A **convulsion**, or seizure, is a brief period during which muscles suddenly contract, causing the person to fall and twitch or jerk. Most convulsions last less than five minutes. There are many causes of convulsions. In infants and toddlers, the most common cause is a high fever.

During a convulsion, do not move the child. Move any hard objects out of the way. Do not try to restrain the child or stop the movements. Loosen any tight clothing, especially around the neck. If the child vomits, or if saliva builds up in the mouth, turn the child onto his or her side or stomach to help drain the fluids. Do not attempt to put anything into the child's mouth.

Bring the fever down by applying cool washcloths to the forehead and neck. Once the convulsion is over, give the child acetaminophen. If the seizure lasts more than five minutes, or if the child remains confused or groggy, call emergency services.

Bites and Stings

Many young children suffer bites, mostly from household pets or from other children. It also is common for a child to be stung by an insect such as a bee. The type of treatment depends on the seriousness of the injury and the child's response to the injury.

Figure 20.3 Rescue Technique for Choking Infants

Choking infants require immediate attention. *What is the purpose of giving the infant five quick blows to the back?*

Step 1 Place the infant stomach-down across your forearm, using your thigh or lap for support, and hold the infant's chest in your hand and jaw in your fingers.

Step 2 Point the infant's head downward and give up to five quick, firm blows to the infant's back with the heel of your hand.

If this procedure fails to expel the object that is causing the choking, follow these steps:

Step 3 Turn the infant face up. Lay the infant on your thigh or lap, and support the infant's head with your hand.

Step 4 Using your other hand, place two fingers on the middle of the infant's breastbone just below the nipples. Give up to five quick downward thrusts.

Step 5 Continue giving five back blows followed by five chest thrusts until the object is dislodged or the infant loses consciousness.

If the child loses consciousness or starts to turn blue, immediate cardiopulmonary resuscitation (CPR) is needed. Have someone call 911, and begin CPR if you have been trained. Also, look into the infant's throat. If you can see the object that is causing the choking and think you might be able to grasp it, try to remove it with a finger.

Animal or Human Bites

For a bite that does not break the skin or has a small puncture wound, wash the area with soap and water. Flush with water for several minutes. Apply antibiotic ointment and give acetaminophen for pain relief if necessary.

If the wound is more serious and is actively bleeding, apply pressure to stop the bleeding. Then elevate the area of the bite. If the wound is bleeding heavily and the child cannot move or is too weak to stand, apply pressure to the wound and call emergency services. If the animal that bit the child was a bat, fox, coyote, skunk, or raccoon, call the local health department so that the animal can be caught and tested for rabies. The child must be given shots to prevent the disease after being bitten by an infected animal.

Any bite that punctures the skin carries a risk of infection. Cat bites, in particular, tend to cause infection. The site of a bite should be checked for several days. If the bite becomes infected, medical help is needed.

Insect Stings and Bites

The greatest risks from stings and bites are allergic reactions and infections. Any child known to be allergic to bee stings should be taken to a doctor immediately after being stung. Other symptoms after a sting that require immediate medical attention include wheezing, tightness in the chest, vomiting or dizziness, and heavy perspiration. A severe allergic reaction called *anaphylactic shock* can cause the airway to swell shut and a person to die.

Figure 20.4 Rescue Technique for Choking Children and Adults

Rescue techniques are different depending on whether or not the victim is conscious. *If a victim is unconscious, what should you do first?*

If the victim is standing or sitting:

Step 1 Stand behind the victim and wrap your arms around his or her waist.

Step 2 Make a fist with one hand and place it, with the thumb toward the victim, just above the child's navel. Grasp the fist with your other hand.

Step 3 Thrust your fist upward and inward quickly. Repeat the technique until you dislodge the object.

If the victim is unconscious:

Step 1 Position the victim on his or her back, and look inside the mouth. If you can see the object, use a sweeping motion with your index finger to remove it.

Step 2 If not, kneel over the victim, place the heel of one hand in the middle of the abdomen just above the navel, and place your other hand on top of the first hand.

Step 3 Give five quick thrusts, pressing your hands in and up.

Step 4 Open the victim's mouth again, and sweep the area again to try to remove the blockage.

Step 5 Repeat these steps until the object is expelled or help arrives.

Step 6 If the victim stops breathing, begin CPR if you have been trained in this technique.

Figure 20.5 **Common Household Poisons**

Most poisonings occur when children eat or drink a substance they have found. *What plants should you keep away from children?*

Type of Poison	Examples	Type of Contact
Medicines	Painkillers, stimulants, sleeping pills, aspirin, vitamins, cold medicines	Swallowing
Cleaning Products	Ammonia, automatic dishwashing detergent, laundry detergent, bleach, drain and toilet-bowl cleaner, disinfectant, furniture polish	Swallowing, contact with skin or eyes, inhaling
Personal Care Products	Shampoo, conditioner, soap, nail polish remover, perfume, aftershave lotions, mouthwash, rubbing alcohol	Swallowing, contact with skin or eyes, inhaling
Gardening and Garage Products	Insecticides, fertilizers, rat and mouse poisons, acids, gasoline, paint thinner, charcoal, lighter fluid, antifreeze	Swallowing, contact with skin or eyes, inhaling
Plants	Some wild mushrooms, English ivy, daffodil bulbs, rhubarb leaves, holly berries, poinsettias, poison ivy, poison oak	Swallowing, contact with skin or eyes

You should also seek help if a child is stung in the mouth or breaks out in hives. **Hives** are blisterlike sores caused by an allergic reaction.

You can remove a bee's stinger by scraping it with a blunt-edged object, such as a credit card. Wash the area with soap and water, and apply a cold pack. Watch the site for the next few days for signs of infection.

Ticks are small insects that cling to the skin and may carry diseases. If you find a tick, use tweezers to grasp the tick as close to the skin as possible. Pull the tick off in one smooth motion. Wash the area with soap and water.

Mosquito, ant, and chigger bites are annoying but not usually dangerous. Calamine lotion or a paste of baking soda and water will gener-ally relieve itching. Using witch hazel or rubbing alcohol on the spot may also provide relief.

Poisoning

Children are curious and do not always comprehend danger. Young children tend to put things in their mouth. These factors can lead to poisoning. It is not always easy to tell that a child has been poisoned. The following symptoms may indicate poisoning:

- Inability to track movement with the eyes
- Burns or stains around the mouth
- Strange-smelling breath
- Difficulty breathing
- Unconsciousness
- Fever

- Rash
- Burning or irritation of the eyes or blindness
- Choking, coughing, nausea, dizziness

If you believe a child has swallowed, breathed, or touched poison, call the hospital or a poison control center. Describe the poison, how it was taken, and if the child has vomited. You will also be asked the child's age, weight, and height, and any health problems the child has. Keep the poison's container with you when you call so that you can answer any questions. Follow the directions you receive. Take the container with you if you take the child to the emergency room. **Figure 20.5** gives examples of poisons and lists the ways children usually come into contact with them.

Shock

When a person suffers a severe injury, loses a great deal of blood, or is poisoned, the body may go into shock. **Shock** is a serious medical condition in which important body functions, including breathing and heartbeat, are impaired. Symptoms of shock can include cool, clammy skin; a rapid and weak pulse; shallow breathing; enlarged pupils; or loss of consciousness. Shock must be treated quickly. If you suspect shock, seek medical help. Lay the child down and elevate the feet. Loosen tight clothing, and keep the child warm until help arrives.

✓ **Reading Check** **Recall** What should you do if a child appears to be in shock?

Figure 20.6 Rescue Breathing for Infants and Small Children

If an infant or small child has stopped breathing, it is vital to get air into his or her lungs as quickly as possible. *What steps should you take to open the airway?*

If you determine that a child is not breathing, send someone to call 911 and follow the steps below. If you are alone and no one hears your call for help, continue the following steps for one minute. Then make the 911 call yourself.

Step 1

Place the child face up on a firm surface. Turn the child's head to one side and clear the mouth of any fluid or foreign matter. If there is an object caught in the child's throat, use the procedure for choking described on pages 561–563. You should remove the object only if it is visible and loose.

Step 2

To open the child's airway, lift the child's chin with one hand and push down on the forehead with the other.

Step 3

Take a breath, cover the child's mouth with your mouth, and pinch the nose closed. Keeping the child's chin lifted, give one slow breath. If you see the child's chest rise, remove your mouth and let the child's lungs expel the air. Then repeat the breathing. If the chest does not rise, position the head, as in Step 2, and attempt another breath. If the second breath does not make the chest rise, use the procedure for choking described on pages 561–563.

Step 4

If the child is still not breathing and there are no signs of life, CPR, which combines chest compressions with rescue breathing, should be started immediately.

Rescue Techniques

When a child stops breathing, or when a child's heart stops beating, immediate and correct action is vital. Learning rescue techniques will allow you to respond quickly and possibly save a life.

Rescue Breathing

Rescue breathing is a procedure for forcing air into the lungs of a person who is not breathing. In children, breathing may stop as a result of drowning, choking, serious head injury, poisoning, or other emergency situations. If the brain is deprived of oxygen for five minutes, brain damage may result. Longer periods without oxygen usually result in death.

The technique to use with infants and small children is shown in **Figure 20.6** on page 565. Child care workers should wear gloves and use a protective face mask when using this technique. You can learn more about rescue breathing in a rescue training class.

Cardiopulmonary Resuscitation (CPR)

Cardiopulmonary resuscitation (CPR) combines rescue breathing with chest compressions to restore breathing and circulation. CPR can save the life of a person who has stopped breathing and whose heart has stopped beating. The technique used for infants and children is different from that used for adults. Only people who have received training from a certified instructor can perform CPR. Many communities offer training programs. For information, call your local chapter of the American Red Cross or the American Heart Association.

Section 20.2 After You Read

Review Key Concepts

1. **Identify** the steps you would take to be prepared in case a fire broke out where you were caring for children.
2. **Explain** what you should do if you think a child has been poisoned.
3. **Define** rescue breathing. Under what circumstances would rescue breathing be needed?

Practice Academic Skills

 English Language Arts

4. Locate three different articles containing instructions on how to care for burns. Carefully read each article. Write an analysis in which you choose the article that you think gives the best instructions. Explain why you chose this article as the best.

> **NCTE 3** Apply strategies to interpret texts.

 Social Studies

5. Lead poisoning is a serious problem that can lead to brain damage in children. Conduct research to determine what federal and state governments are doing to reduce lead poisoning in children. Prepare a presentation to share the information you learn with your class.

> **NCSS V G** Analyze the extent to which groups and institutions meet individual needs and promote the common good in contemporary and historical settings.

 Check Your Answers Check your answers at this book's Online Learning Center at **glencoe.com**.

Chapter Summary

Regular checkups allow health problems to be detected early. Immunizations help prevent certain diseases. Children who have allergies and asthma can take steps to avoid the causes and treat the symptoms. Caregivers should know what steps to follow when a child gets sick or injured. The rescue technique to use with a choking victim depends on the person's age. Rescue breathing is needed for someone who stops breathing. If the person does not respond to rescue breathing, CPR should be used.

Vocabulary Review

1. Arrange the vocabulary terms below into groups of related words. Explain why you put the words together.

Content Vocabulary

◇ communicable disease (p. 551)
◇ pollen (p. 553)
◇ asthma (p. 553)
◇ contagious (p. 554)
◇ antiseptic (p. 559)
◇ fracture (p. 560)
◇ sprain (p. 560)

◇ abdominal thrust (p. 561)
◇ convulsion (p. 562)
◇ hives (p. 564)
◇ shock (p. 565)
◇ rescue breathing (p. 566)
◇ cardiopulmonary resuscitation (CPR) (p. 566)

Academic Vocabulary

■ detection (p. 551)
■ sensitivity (p. 553)
■ elevate (p. 559)
■ expel (p. 561)

Review Key Concepts

2. Explain how regular checkups and immunizations can help prevent illness.
3. Summarize effective ways to care for a sick child.
4. Outline the steps to follow in an emergency situation.
5. Describe appropriate first-aid procedures for three types of bleeding.
6. Compare and contrast rescue breathing and CPR.

Critical Thinking

7. Analyze Why do you think infants need more frequent checkups than older children?
8. Draw Conclusions Suppose you are taking a group of children on a campout. As a leader, what safety skills should you have?
9. Predict Imagine you are going to care for two small children. Do you think you would prepare differently now than you would have before reading this chapter? Explain your answer.
10. Apply You have a neighbor who has not been taking her eight-month-old to the doctor for routine checkups. She says it costs too much. What might you say to her to encourage her to take the child?

Family & Community Connection

11. Health and Safety Improvements Interview an adult over age fifty. Ask the person to discuss how concerns about children's health and safety have changed over the years. For example, they might discuss improvements in automobile safety or in immunizations. Also ask them to discuss why they think these changes have occurred. Write a report discussing what you learn.

Health Skills

12. PRICE A series of steps commonly called PRICE (for *protect, rest, ice, compression,* and *elevation*) is commonly used for minor injuries, such as a bruise. Research the steps in PRICE. Then create a poster containing both text and illustrations that explains the procedure.

Observation Skills

13. Hazards in the Home Many parents and grandparents are unaware of the hazards present in their homes. As a child grows from a baby to a toddler, they may not realize how much more mobile the child has become.

Procedure Ask a parent or grandparent of a child from one to three if you may evaluate their home for safety hazards. When you visit, tour the home and identify any potential hazards.

Analysis Write a list of the items you notice along with an explanation of why each is a hazard. Also offer potential solutions.

> **NSES F** Develop understanding of personal and community health; natural and human-induced hazards.

Real-World Skills

Problem-Solving Skills

14. Organize Information Many babysitters may not have the needed information in case of an emergency. Create a form babysitters can take with them and complete when caring for children. Be sure to include space for all the needed information, such as the children's names and ages, and any needed phone numbers.

Technology Skills

15. Write an E-mail When a child stops breathing, immediate action can help save his or her life. Write an e-mail to a friend who babysits explaining how tragedy can be avoided when caregivers know CPR. Explain in your e-mail the options for learning CPR in your community.

Financial Literacy Skills

16. First-Aid Kits Imagine that you have decided to sell home first aid kits. Research what each kit should contain and each item's cost. Create a table listing each item and its cost. Calculate the total. Add 25 percent to this total to obtain a selling price. Then calculate how much you will make on each kit.

 Additional Activities For additional activities, go to this book's Online Learning Center at **glencoe.com**.

Academic Skills

 English Language Arts

17. Bike Safety Poem Write a poem about bicycle safety. Your poem should contain at least four bicycle safety rules. Use words that can be understood by third- and fourth-graders. If possible, make arrangements to read your poem aloud to a group of elementary school children.

> **NCTE 5** Use different writing process elements to communicate effectively.

 Mathematics

18. Automobile Safety The Centers for Disease Control and Prevention reported that in the United States during 2005, 1,451 children ages 16 years and younger died as occupants in motor vehicle crashes, and approximately 203,000 were injured. How many injuries, on average, is that each day?

Math Concept **Mean or Average** The mean is one type of average. The mean is calculated by dividing the sum of a set of terms by the number of terms.

Starting Hint Convert years to days (1 year = 365 days). Then divide the number of days by the total number of injuries. Round your answer to the nearest whole number.

 For math help, go to the Math Appendix at the back of the book.

> **NCTM Number and Operations** Understand numbers, ways of representing numbers, relationships among numbers, and number systems.

 Science

19. Emergency Preparedness When people confront an emergency, they often realize they do not have the information they need. Perhaps the information is as simple as "Where is the fire extinguisher?" or "What is the house's address?"

Procedure Locate at least eight people who have dealt with emergencies. Find out whether or not they have an emergency plan. Ask each, "Was there any needed information that you did not have? What was it?"

Analysis Write a paragraph summarizing the survey's results. Based on this information, how do you think people can better prepare for emergencies?

> **NSES A** Develop abilities necessary to do scientific inquiry, understandings about scientific inquiry.

Standardized Test Practice

ESSAY

Read the essay question. Then write a one-half page answer on a separate sheet of paper.

20. Describe the three degrees of burns. Explain how you would treat each type of burn.

> **Test-Taking Tip** When writing an answer to an essay question, imagine you are traveling down a narrow country road. Beware of any detours or side paths. Stay focused on the question!

21 Family Challenges

Chapter Objectives

After completing this chapter, you will be able to:

- **Describe** how parents can help children cope with stress.
- **List** eight possible causes of stress in children.
- **Identify** nine categories of disabilities.
- **Describe** some of the traits exhibited by gifted children.
- **Identify** four major types of maltreatment.
- **Summarize** common reasons behind abuse and maltreatment.
- **Explain** what can be done to prevent child abuse.

Writing Activity / Persuasive Essay

Crisis Nursery A crisis nursery is a safe place where parents can temporarily leave their children if they are unable to cope with them. Suppose that you feel your neighborhood needs a crisis nursery. Write a persuasive essay to encourage readers to support a local crisis nursery.

Writing Tips When writing a persuasive essay, you are trying to convince the reader to agree with your point of view. Here are some tips to get you started:
1. Write an opening that will capture the reader's attention.
2. Express your view on the topic clearly.
3. Provide specific reasons why the reader should agree with your view.

Section 21.1 Family Stresses

Section 21.2 Children with Special Needs

Section 21.3 Child Abuse and Neglect

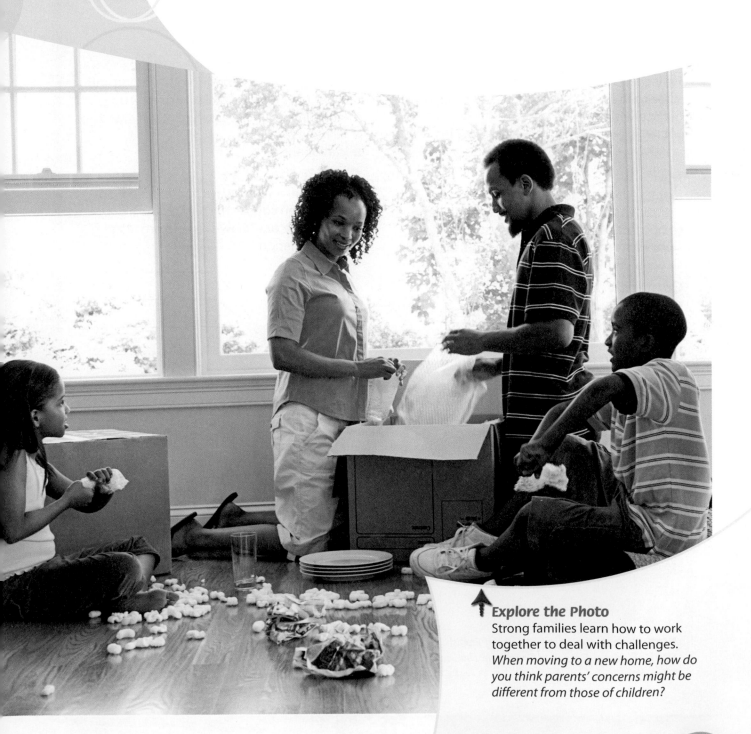

Explore the Photo
Strong families learn how to work together to deal with challenges. *When moving to a new home, how do you think parents' concerns might be different from those of children?*

Section 21.1 Family Stresses

Reading Guide

Before You Read

Preview Preview this section by reading the headings and subheadings. Write one sentence summarizing what you think this section covers. When you are done with the section, reread your sentence and modify it if necessary.

Read to Learn
Key Concepts
- **Describe** how parents can help children cope with stress.
- **List** eight possible causes of stress in children.

Main Idea
Many situations, such as moving, divorce, and difficulties at school, can cause children to become stressed. Adults must watch for signs of stress, including regression, disturbed sleep, and unusual aggression.

Content Vocabulary
◇ regression
◇ situational stress
◇ addiction
◇ support group

 Graphic Organizer Go to this book's Online Learning Center at **glencoe.com** to print out this graphic organizer.

Academic Vocabulary
You will find these words in your reading and on your tests. Use the glossary to look up their definitions if necessary.
- vulnerable
- irrational

Graphic Organizer
As you read, note six ways parents can help their children cope with divorce. Use a diagram like the one shown to help organize your information.

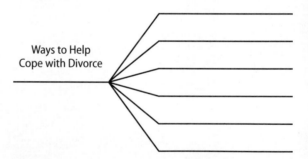

Ways to Help Cope with Divorce

Academic Standards . . . .

 English Language Arts

NCTE 5 Use different writing process elements to communicate effectively.

 Social Studies

NCSS V G Individuals, Groups, and Institutions Analyze the extent to which groups and institutions meet individual needs and promote the common good in contemporary and historical settings.

NCTE *National Council of Teachers of English*
NCTM *National Council of Teachers of Mathematics*

NSES *National Science Education Standards*
NCSS *National Council for the Social Studies*

Children and Stress

Children often can be more **vulnerable**, or helpless, than adults. They may lack an understanding of events, as well as effective coping skills. Parents can help children cope with stress by listening patiently and accepting their feelings of anger, grief, and sadness. Children are often much more aware of parents' worries than their parents realize. It helps when parents are able to admit their own emotions and provide an example of how to cope.

Possible Responses

Children react to stress in a variety of ways, but age is a factor. **Figure 21.1** on page 574 shows typical ways that children of various ages may show stress.

When times are tough, adults should observe children closely for any signs of stress. It is important to be alert for changes in behavior or regression. **Regression** is the temporary backward movement to an earlier stage of development. If a toilet-trained child begins having accidents, for example, it may be a sign of stress.

✓ **Reading Check** **Explain** Why is it important to watch for signs of regression?

Causes of Stress

Situational stress is stress that comes from the environment a child lives in or from certain circumstances and changes. Certain stress factors are a part of every child's life. For example, every child may feel stress when a parent leaves a room. Some of the stress factors that have the greatest impact on a child's daily life include parents' divorce, moving, family financial problems, substance abuse by a family member, illness, or the death of a loved one. The way the parents handle the situation has a huge impact on the child's stress level. One of the worst things a parent or caregiver can do is to say "You shouldn't feel that way." Instead, they should accept the child's feelings. They can then use those feelings as a starting point for trying to offer help.

School

A common cause of situational stress is school. Students can feel the stress of needing to get good grades, peer pressure and fitting in with friends and classmates, and stress from being the target of bullies.

Many children feel they cannot do as well in school as parents and teachers expect. This can lead to feelings of stress. Children may give up

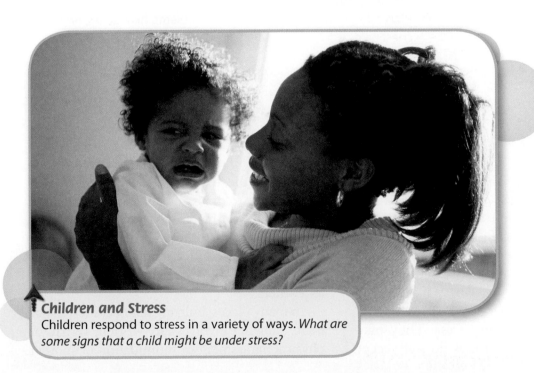

Children and Stress
Children respond to stress in a variety of ways. *What are some signs that a child might be under stress?*

Figure 21.1

Signs of Stress in Children and Teens

Signs of stress vary depending on the age of the child. *How are signs of stress in a small child different from signs of stress in a teen?*

Age	Signs of Stress
Under age 5	❧ Excessive attachment to parents ❧ Fear of being left alone ❧ Increased sensitivity to loud noises ❧ Eating problems ❧ Uncontrollable crying
Ages 5–11	❧ Disturbed sleep ❧ Headache, nausea, or other physical problems ❧ Pretending to be ill to avoid going to school ❧ Fighting ❧ Poor school performance
Ages 11–14	❧ Withdrawing from others ❧ Depression ❧ Aggression ❧ Confusion ❧ Acting out, such as stealing or fighting ❧ Excessive sleeping
Ages 15 and older	❧ Anxiety or panic attacks ❧ Irritability and moodiness ❧ Physical symptoms such as stomach problems, headaches, or chest pain ❧ Sleeping problems ❧ Sadness or depression ❧ Overeating ❧ Drinking alcohol, smoking, or taking drugs

trying. This makes the situation worse. Many young people have test anxiety, or extreme nervousness and tension about being tested. This causes them to perform poorly on tests, increasing the pressure they feel. It is important that children know parents accept them as they are.

Children and teens who see themselves as outsiders often suffer from stress. They may feel worthless if certain groups do not accept them. Even those who are part of a group may feel pressure to dress and act in certain ways. It is the duty of both adults and children to work toward accepting others. When you interact with classmates and friends, focus on their strong points. This will strengthen both you and others.

In many places, bullying has become a major issue. Bullying involves any written, verbal, or physical harassment or intimidation of another person. Schools should not tolerate bullying. Children who are being bullied should report it to a teacher or other adult right away.

Crime

News reports are filled with examples of people hurting others. Most adults would like to keep young people from being exposed to violence. But the reality is that in today's world, this is not possible. Children need to be told that adults are doing everything possible to keep them safe. They also should be taught ways of protecting themselves, such as walking in groups and reporting anything unusual to an adult. Knowing the steps to help keep themselves safe encourages children to feel less stressed and more secure.

Moving

Moving to a new community or a different neighborhood interrupts friendships, affects school performance, and disrupts activities. Moving can be especially difficult for older children because of the importance they place on peer relationships.

Adults can help children by explaining why a move is necessary. Helping in the move can give children a sense of control over the event. For example, children can pack toys and arrange items in a new room. After the move, parents should help their children get involved in activities that allow them to meet others their age. They might sign up for swimming or art lessons, and check out other group opportunities, such as story hour at the library. Gavin's parents signed him up for T-ball and a summer day camp. By the time school started, Gavin already knew several children who would also be in first grade at his new school.

Money

Family money problems can stem from many factors. Unemployment, gambling, shopping addiction, illness and medical bills, and poor money management are just a few. As leaders of the family, parents often set the tone

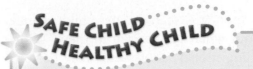

SAFE CHILD HEALTHY CHILD

Depression in Children and Teens

Depression is a brain disorder that leads to intense feelings of sadness and worthlessness. It is not just a temporary feeling of being down that everyone experiences occasionally. At any given time, about 5 percent of adolescents will have symptoms of depression. Here are some signs to watch for:

- Extreme sadness
- Unusual irritability
- Loss of interest in previously enjoyed activities
- Appetite and weight changes
- Fatigue and difficulty sleeping
- Feelings of worthlessness, hopelessness, or self-hatred
- Talk of suicide or a preoccupation with death

If children or teenagers exhibit any of these symptoms, they should be evaluated by a doctor.

Be Prepared Conduct research to learn about the ways in which depression in children and teens is treated. Find out which treatments, or combinations of treatments, appear to be the most effective. Prepare a speech on what you learn. If possible, use presentation software to create a slide show to go with your speech.

for their children's comfort and stress levels. When families are struggling with finances, parents should make a special effort not to argue about money in front of children or take out their worries on them.

Now a young adult, Jane recalls the summer her family spent camping. A few years later she learned that the family's fun adventure had occurred because they were homeless. Because she and her siblings were young and their mother's attitude was positive, the children were spared the stress that might have been expected.

When money is scarce, older children may worry about what will happen to them. Without spending money, adolescents may be concerned about loss of status in their peer group. However, it is important that parents not hide money problems from older children. Parents need to be clear about possible consequences of the problems and the need to budget money.

Divorce

Research has shown that children experience the effects of divorce at the time of the breakup and for decades afterward. Many children of divorced parents face greater fears that their own relationships will fail as they grow up. A child will suffer much less when parents make a joint effort to help him or her adjust to the new family situation. See **Figure 21.2.**

Parents should tell their children together about the divorce and discuss where the children will live. Children often blame themselves for the failure of their parents' marriage. Parents must emphasize that the children did nothing wrong. Parents should remind children of their love for them often.

Some children ask questions. Some cry. Some appear not to react at all when they learn their parents are divorcing. Parents should accept any reaction, including none at all.

Most children want to know how the divorce will affect them. "Where will I live?"

"Can I still go to summer camp?" "Will I go to a new school?" Parents must be honest with children about possible outcomes and involve children in decision making. Parents should never give children false hope that parents might get back together.

Parents should resist the urge to spoil children who are feeling sad. It is also important not to confide in children or place them in the middle of arguments. This unfairly makes them feel that they have to take sides. Children need love from both parents to cope.

Many children show behavior problems after their parents' breakup. Even children who appear happy on the surface may be hiding their pain to keep parents from worrying.

Substance Abuse

Some people develop an addiction to a substance, such as alcohol, cocaine, crack, or prescription drugs. An **addiction** is a dependence on a substance, such as alcohol or drugs. People often feel that they cannot live without the substance. Substance abuse causes serious problems for families.

Some adults who abuse substances hurt their families with words or physical violence. Often they are emotionally unavailable. Some parents lose their jobs because of their addiction, or turn to crime to support their addiction.

Children and Divorce
Children should be able to talk about their feelings, even if they are negative. *What should parents never do to children when the parents are getting divorced?*

Figure 21.2

Helping Children Cope with Divorce

Both parents need to help minimize the impact of divorce and help children adjust to changes. *Why is it important that parents work with the school during a divorce?*

Tip	Examples
Keep things as normal as possible.	Maintain routines, including family mealtimes and rules of behavior.
Maintain ties.	Help children stay in touch with their friends and members of both sides of the family. Encourage visits, calls, and e-mails to help maintain these important relationships.
Create a special place.	If the child must move, help the child personalize his or her space in the new home. Have children keep personal belongings in each parent's home if they go back and forth frequently.
Develop new traditions.	Holiday activities may change. Children may spend holidays with only one parent or with a newly blended family. Invite children to invent new holiday traditions while maintaining some old favorites.
Watch for changes.	Observe changes in the child's behavior, school performance, and temperament. If a child withdraws or shows a major shift in behavior, talk to the pediatrician or a counselor.
Work with the school.	Make the child's teacher aware of the situation. Many schools offer professional resources, referrals, and even lunch groups to help children cope.

Even though family members are aware of a substance abuse problem, they do not always want to admit it. They sometimes help the addict hide the problem or they take on the person's responsibilities. Sometimes they try to rescue the addict, or react so strongly that the focus turns from the addict's behavior to the family member's reaction.

Most addicts become skilled at hiding the evidence of their problem from others. However, they and their families must deal with the problem to get better. Nagging or threatening a substance abuser will not help. Substance abusers will not seek help until they are ready. Usually, this happens when the consequences of the behavior become especially painful, as when they lose their jobs or their families.

In the meantime, family members should take steps to protect themselves. A **support group** is a collection of individuals who work together to explore and accept their feelings. They come to realize that they are not alone with their problems. There are several well-known groups, such as Al-Anon (for the families and friends of alcoholics) and Nar-Anon (for the families and friends of narcotics abusers) available for help.

Anyone who has a friend or family member who is abusing alcohol or drugs can join these groups at no cost. Families can draw on the strength and experience of other people in similar situations. Adolescents might also talk to a school counselor, trusted teacher, or religious leader.

Support Groups
Support groups help friends and family members cope with addictions as well as death of a loved one. *How might you find a group in your community?*

Illness

When a family member is ill, the routines of family life are upset. Children need an honest explanation of what is happening. Of course, it should be geared to their ability to understand. When the illness is minor, children can be reassured that the person should soon be well again. If the illness is serious or the person is dying, adults should tell children the truth in a calm, reassuring way. They might be told, "The doctors are doing everything they can to help Aunt Debbie feel better."

Children sometimes have irrational fears or false beliefs about illness. **Irrational** means lacking reason. Children may worry that they are somehow at fault. They might think that a disease like cancer is contagious. Adults should reassure them that nothing they did caused the illness. Unless the disease is contagious, the child should be assured that no one else in the family will come down with it. A child may also misunderstand what is said. One four-year-old overheard that someone had died in bed. It took her parents days to figure out why she cried wildly at bedtime.

Death

Children's grief, like that of adults, is a complex set of emotions that may include fear, anger, despair, agitation, and guilt. While each child grieves differently, the age of the child influences his or her reaction. Researchers have found that two factors influence their views of death. These two factors are the children's level of development and religious or cultural background. Here are some common reactions by age:

- **Children under three** cannot understand more than a brief separation. They may react to a death in the same way they react to a parent's weeklong vacation.
- **Children ages three to five** think that death is like sleep: you are dead, and then you wake up and are alive again. As a result, they may seem unfeeling when a person dies. They do not understand that death is permanent.
- **Children ages six to nine** may believe that angry words or thoughts caused death. They may fear that other family members will abandon them. Most children this age recognize that death is final, but they may not understand that everyone dies.
- **Preteens** may still feel that the person died because of some bad deed. They may feel angry toward the person who died or toward other family members.

{ **Expert Advice...** }

"Dealing with stressful situations in the family ultimately becomes the responsibility of the family members. If a family is to remain 'strong,' each member needs to recognize stress within the family, its causes, and how to effectively handle it."

— Bryan Adcock, child and family development specialist, University of Missouri

- **Teens** may assume too much responsibility for financial or other family concerns. They understand the finality of death and its impact on the family.

Help Children Cope

By age five, many children have had some contact with death. They may have seen a dead bird or lost a beloved pet, for example. They may not fully understand what has happened, but they will have reactions to the loss. There are a number of ways that parents can help children cope with the loss of a loved one.

- Funerals and memorial services are rituals that allow people to vent feelings and to honor the deceased person. When children want to go, experts believe they should be allowed to attend these services.
- Very young children need simple explanations about death. These might include the loss of functions like eating, sleeping, thinking, or feeling.
- Religion and spiritual beliefs are a source of comfort to many people who have suffered a loss. Beliefs offer explanations and give meaning to life and death. Letting children know that things are the way they are supposed to be, according to the family's faith, can help them feel secure. Parents should let children know that pain is a part of living and that it will lessen in time.

Death of a Parent

The death of a parent is probably the most tragic thing that can happen to a child. A child whose parent dies needs support for an extended period. Many children react with guilt. The child may think, "I wasn't always good when he wanted me to be," or "I wasn't quiet enough when she was sick." Even infants go through a period of excessive crying and searching for a parent who has died.

Parents should reassure children that, no matter what happens, they will always receive loving care. If asked, parents should talk to their children about who would take care of them in the unlikely event of their death. Experts say that children whose parents have died or are dying need three things:

- Someone to meet their emotional and physical needs
- Reassurance that they will always be loved and cared for, no matter what happens
- Explanations that are age-appropriate

Child therapists recommend telling children the truth when death is near. This lets them say goodbye. Children should be allowed to visit the dying parent.

Some people mistakenly believe that it is best to avoid talking about the deceased person. Actually, the opposite is true. When a parent dies, children should be encouraged to express their grief by drawing pictures or talking.

Remembering Loved Ones
A healthy response to a family member's death is to keep memories alive through photos and stories. *What other ideas do you have for keeping memories alive?*

If the child has fears, adults should deal with them. Older children and teens should not be placed in a role with adult responsibilities.

Healthy children sometimes ask, "When will I die?" Often, they simply want to know if they will die. Parents can say that while every living thing dies, most people live a long time. They can also be told that eating healthy foods and wearing seat belts help people live longer.

Suicide

Some people feel overwhelmed by their problems, overcome by depression. They may be irrationally angry at others, and decide that taking their own lives is the solution. Sadly, some of the people who attempt suicide are children and teenagers.

When an adult commits suicide, children who are old enough to understand should be told. Adults can stress that there are many ways of getting help and dealing with problems that are not harmful to anyone.

Anyone who is thinking about suicide should seek help from a parent, friend, doctor, or counselor. Many survivors of a suicide attempt say that they later realized their problems had other solutions. Warning signs of suicide include talking about suicide or giving away possessions. If you know anyone who is doing these things, talk to a school counselor or another adult. Most people who commit suicide are depressed. With modern treatment options, they can find hope again.

Older children and teens who know someone who committed suicide may wonder if they could have done something to prevent it. They may feel betrayed or abandoned. These feelings are a normal part of the grieving process.

Grieving takes time. Talking to a professional counselor can help. Finding a way to accept and express intense feelings is also important. Survivors can do something positive that they believe the person would have wanted them to do.

Section 21.1   After You Read

Review Key Concepts

1. **Explain** why children may be more vulnerable to stress than adults.
2. **Describe** how joining a support group can help a child deal with a stressful situation, such as when a parent abuses alcohol.

Practice Academic Skills

 English Language Arts

3. Imagine you are a 10-year-old child who has just moved to a new town. You do not know anyone and school starts next week. Create a journal entry expressing any fears you might be feeling about the new school and the stress you are feeling.

> **NCTE 5** Use different writing process elements to communicate effectively.

 Social Science

4. Many children face the stress of being bullied at school. Conduct research to determine what schools include in anti-bullying policies. Then work with a partner to create an illustrated poster that explains why bullying is wrong and how to deal with it. Be sure your poster defines the different types of bullying.

> **NCSS V G** Analyze the extent to which groups and institutions meet individual needs and promote the common good in contemporary and historical settings.

 Check Your Answers Check your answers at this book's Online Learning Center at **glencoe.com**.

Reading Guide

Before You Read

Pace Yourself Short blocks of concentrated reading, repeated frequently, are more effective than one long session. Focus on reading for 10 minutes. Take a short break. Then read for another 10 minutes.

Read to Learn
Key Concepts
- **Identify** nine categories of disabilities.
- **Describe** some of the traits exhibited by gifted children.

Main Idea
Children with special needs include those with disabilities and those with special abilities. Parents and teachers must work to meet the educational needs of both groups.

Content Vocabulary
◇ learning disability
◇ dyslexia
◇ ADHD
◇ ADD
◇ mental retardation
◇ type 1 diabetes
◇ asthma
◇ autism
◇ autism spectrum disorders (ASD)
◇ inclusion
◇ gifted

 Graphic Organizer Go to this book's Online Learning Center at **glencoe.com** to print out this graphic organizer.

Academic Vocabulary
You will find these words in your reading and on your tests. Use the glossary to look up their definitions if necessary.
■ profound
■ adaptation

Graphic Organizer
As you read, look for eight common traits of autism or ASD. Use a chart like the one shown to help organize your information.

Traits of Autism and ASD
1.
2.
3.
4.
5.
6.
7.
8.

Academic Standards · · · · · · · · · · · · · · · · ·

 English Language Arts
NCTE 2 Read literature to build an understanding of the human experience.

 Social Studies
NCSS IV H Individual Development and Identity Work independently and cooperatively within groups and institutions to accomplish goals.

NCTE *National Council of Teachers of English*
NCTM *National Council of Teachers of Mathematics*

NSES *National Science Education Standards*
NCSS *National Council for the Social Studies*

Children with Disabilities

Some children have different needs from the average child. They are said to have special needs. These children fall into two categories: children with disabilities and children with special abilities. Children with special abilities are also referred to as gifted children.

Parenting, family life, education, and interaction with the world must undergo adjustment. Both children with disabilities and those who are gifted are sometimes called exceptional children. Most children with physical, mental, or emotional disabilities need special adaptations in some aspect of their lives. Gifted children need additional stimulation.

The attitude of parents and other caregivers has a deep impact on children's futures. Like all children, children with disabilities want to have success and feel good about what they do. The goal is to help children with special needs become as independent as possible by involving them in family and school life.

Types of Disabilities

Disabilities may result from difficulties with mobility, vision, or hearing. Some disabilities affect a child's ability to learn, speak, or express emotions. Some problems are apparent at birth. Others may not be discovered for months or years. Some children have a disability that is clearly apparent. Many have so-called invisible disabilities. These are disabilities that people might not notice right away. Children with a learning disorder, for example, or those with diabetes, have invisible disabilities. Some of the most common types of disabilities, visible and invisible, are described here.

Learning Disabilities

A **learning disability** interferes with a child's ability to learn, listen, think, speak, read, write, spell, or do math. Children with a learning disability often have average or above-average intelligence, but they achieve below their potential because of the difficulties they experience with learning. Learning disabilities result from disorders in the brain and central nervous system. Most learning disabilities are detected in children when standardized testing begins, between the ages of seven and twelve. Early diagnostic testing, followed by intervention is critical to their educational success. Intervention means involvement by professionals using special teaching methods.

A common learning disability is dyslexia. **Dyslexia** is a learning disorder that prevents a child from understanding printed symbols in a normal way. A child with dyslexia may be very intelligent but have trouble processing visual information. Letters and numbers may be reversed or absent, so children with dyslexia may have difficulty with reading, writing, spelling, and math. They may find it hard to understand directions and to **distinguish**, or see a difference in, left from right.

Special Olympics
Programs such as the Special Olympics provide great opportunities for exceptional young people. *What kinds of events do you think might be included in the Special Olympics?*

Mason was thirteen when he started being tired much of the time. He discovered he had type 1 diabetes. Because of his diabetes, Mason faces a number of challenges. The main one is to keep his blood sugar level as even as possible. He pricks his finger several times a day to check his blood sugar level. When Mason's body does not have enough insulin, his blood sugar level is too high. If there is too much insulin, it is too low. Either way, he must adjust the food he eats and the amount of insulin he takes. At first, Mason injected insulin into his body. Now he uses an insulin pump.

The pump places insulin into his blood stream more regularly than injections. Mason also monitors what he eats and exercises regularly. He knows all these activities are necessary to control his diabetes and live an active life.

Critical Thinking Conduct online research to find out at least one way in which scientists are working to find a cure for diabetes. Write a report summarizing what you learn.

Attention Deficit Hyperactive Disorder

ADHD, attention deficit hyperactive disorder, is a behavioral disorder in which children often fail to finish what they start, do not seem to listen, and are easily distracted. These children may always be active and may have trouble staying in their seats. Some have a lack of emotional control. ADHD may be accompanied by learning disabilities. Parents and teachers can learn special teaching methods that may be useful for students with ADHD. Medication is often prescribed for children with ADHD. This practice, though, remains controversial. **ADD**, attention deficit disorder, is similar to ADHD, but does not involve hyperactivity.

Speech and Language Impairments

Speech and language impairments interfere with a child's ability to communicate. A child with a speech disorder may have trouble making certain speech sounds or modulating the volume or quality of the voice. A child with a language disorder may find it difficult to understand and use words correctly. This makes it difficult for the child to express ideas or follow directions.

Some speech and language disorders are associated with hearing impairment, mental retardation, and brain injury. In many cases, though, the cause is not known. Because speech and language are so important to learning in general, it is important that children with these impairments receive help at an early age. Speech-language pathologists can work with teachers and parents to help individual children get effective therapy.

Mental Retardation

Children with **mental retardation** have below-average intelligence and skills. This condition is also known as cognitive impairment or developmental disability. Besides problems with thinking and learning, children with mental retardation may have difficulty paying attention, remembering, communicating, and interacting with others. Levels of mental retardation range from mild to profound, or extreme. There is no cure. Mental retardation may result from a genetic disorder, brain damage, poor prenatal care, or a variety of factors. In many cases, the cause is unknown.

Down syndrome is an example of a genetic disorder resulting in varying degrees of mental retardation. Children with this condition also have distinctive physical features. Fetal alcohol syndrome is a condition that affects children born to some mothers who drank alcohol

Autistic Savants

About 10 percent of people with autism are called autistic savants. Some of these people have a compulsive, or uncontrollable, interest in some narrow activity such as the memorization of sports trivia. Others develop an amazing ability in a certain area, such as music or mathematics. One common mathematical skill among savants is known as calendar calculation. Savants with this ability can mentally calculate the day of the week that any given date fell on, or will fall on, over a span of tens of thousands of years. Scientists do not understand how the brains of autistic savants can do such things.

■ **Science Inquiry** Autistic savants often have astonishing skills in music, art, or performing mathematical calculations. However, they are not good at language skills. Why do you think this is?

during pregnancy. It is another disorder characterized by developmental delays, mental retardation, and physical abnormalities.

Children with mental retardation have lifelong limitations. However, with effective parenting and the right approach to their education, they can experience success. The goal is to help them become as independent as possible. Many are able to learn skills that enable them to live alone or in a group home and to earn a living.

Health Conditions

All children get sick at times. It is often just with a cold or the flu. However, there are some children who have ongoing health conditions. These include conditions such as diabetes and asthma. These can affect their lives in major ways. Parents of children with ongoing conditions should point out that many well-known people with these challenges have led active, productive lives.

Type 1 diabetes is a lifelong condition caused by the body's inability to produce enough insulin. Insulin is a hormone produced by the pancreas. Type 1 diabetes is also called juvenile diabetes. The lack of insulin means that the body cannot control the amount of sugar in the blood. If untreated, type 1 diabetes can result in major damage to body organs, and even death. There is no cure for diabetes. People with type 1 diabetes must take insulin for their entire lives to make up for the body's lack of the hormone. Young people with diabetes often join support groups so that they can talk with others who are managing this disease.

Asthma is a condition that results in sporadic difficulty in breathing and shortness of breath. The airways in the lungs become sore and swollen. More than 50 percent of asthma cases in the United States are caused by allergies. Other causes include irritants such as cigarette smoke, and changes in the weather. The severity of asthma varies greatly from one person to another.

Most people with asthma use a special device called an inhaler to deliver medicine directly to their lungs. This medicine helps open the airways. Some people believe that children with asthma should not participate in sports and other activities. However, with proper control, most children can fully participate in sports. Being in good physical shape also helps keep asthma under control.

Serious Emotional Disturbances

Children with serious emotional disturbances generally have one or more of the following characteristics:

- Inability to learn that cannot be explained by other factors
- Inability to build or maintain satisfactory relationships with others
- Inappropriate behavior or feelings
- General unhappiness or depression
- Irrational fears

Troublesome emotions and behavior may have to do with a child's stage of development. In some cases, though, a child's behavior indicates a more serious problem. Some parents may deny there is a problem and hope the child outgrows it. However, if a serious problem is suspected, the child should be evaluated promptly.

Treatment options include counseling for the child, the parents, or the entire family. Psychiatrists, psychologists, family therapists, and some social workers are trained to help children with emotional difficulties and their families.

Autism and Autism Spectrum Disorders

Autism is a disorder that affects a child's ability to communicate and interact with others. It is one of the most common developmental disorders. Autism affects about four times more boys than girls. It usually appears during the first three years of life.

Autism is one of a group of disorders collectively known as **autism spectrum disorders (ASD)**. Children who have one of these conditions may exhibit many of these symptoms or very few:

- Resistance to change
- Absence of empathy
- Little or no eye contact
- Repetition of words or phrases
- Repetitive movements and play
- Difficulty focusing and inability to remain attentive
- Distress without apparent cause
- Loss of skills already learned

While symptoms of autism and ASD vary widely, parents should seek help if their child does not babble or coo by 12 months, is overly attached to a single toy or object, or becomes withdrawn and unresponsive. Children who are diagnosed early and who receive appropriate therapy do better in the long run.

Hearing and Visual Impairments

Some children with hearing impairments are totally deaf. Others are hard of hearing. This means they can hear some speech with the help of a hearing aid. Communication skills vary. Some children with hearing impairments can speak, but others cannot.

Children with visual impairments may be totally blind or may have very low vision. It can be hard for them to follow traditional classroom instruction since so much teaching is visual.

Physical Disabilities

Physical disabilities take a wide range of forms. They may range from mild to severe involvement. Some may be present at birth. Others may develop over time or result from an injury.

Coping with Physical Disabilities
Children with physical disabilities often must work hard to be able to perform everyday tasks. *How might having a physical disability affect a child's social life at school?*

Normal daily routines that others take for granted can be difficult or impossible for people with disabilities. Children with coordination problems may need assistance with bathing, eating, and getting ready for school. Some children with disabilities need regular physical therapy or specialized equipment. All children with physical disabilities need patient and understanding caregivers who can help them learn how to perform basic activities and enjoy greater independence.

Education of Children with Special Needs

The educational needs of children with disabilities vary. Some can function in a regular classroom and need no special **adaptation**, or adjustment. Others need extra attention but can be placed in a regular classroom. Those with certain disabilities require specialized education in programs designed to meet their specific needs.

Many children receive help from teachers who are specially trained to work with students with learning disabilities. A teacher might give both spoken and written directions, for example, to help children who have trouble with reading. Some students with disabilities have teacher assistants who attend class with them.

Rights of Children with Disabilities

The Individuals with Disabilities Education Act (IDEA) is a federal law. It ensures that children with disabilities receive a free public education that meets their needs. IDEA emphasizes the need for higher academic standards. It also specifies the rights of these children and their parents. These rights include:

- Children have a right to a free public education that meets their needs.
- Parents or caregivers must be notified if a school system plans to evaluate a child or change the child's school arrangement.
- Parents have the right to request that the school evaluate a child.
- Children must be retested at least every three years and their school situation must be reviewed at least every year.
- Children can be tested in the language they know best. Parents must be spoken to in the language they know best.
- Parents can request to see the child's school records.
- The school must draw up an educational program specifically for the child. The plan is called an Individualized Education Plan, or IEP. The child and his or her parents can take part in the process of developing that plan.

▶ Inclusion in the Classroom
Many children with special needs are educated in a regular classroom. *What law ensures that these children receive the education they deserve?*

The law also requires schools to make every effort to practice inclusion. **Inclusion** means placing children with disabilities in regular classrooms while they also receive special education services. This is also referred to as mainstreaming. Education experts believe that inclusion benefits both children with special needs and children without those challenges. It allows them to learn together, develop empathy, and improve communication and social skills.

Classifications of Children Served by IDEA

About 50 percent of American students served by IDEA have been classified as having a specific learning disability, such as dyslexia. Almost 20 percent have a speech or language impairment. Slightly more than 10 percent receive special education services because of mental retardation. About 8 percent have emotional disturbances.

There are also thousands of children who have autism, orthopedic impairments, and hearing and visual impairments. They represent a relatively small percentage of the students receiving special education services. Some children have multiple disabilities.

Raising Children with Disabilities

The responsibilities and demands of raising a child with disabilities or serious health conditions can seem overwhelming. Many parents have difficulty accepting that their child has a disability. They may regret that their child will not be able to do some of the things they imagined. They may feel guilty about devoting more time and energy to the child with special needs. They might fear that they are not giving other family members the time they deserve.

Support for Families

Support groups for parents of children with disabilities can help. Members of these groups share advice and solutions to everyday problems. Members keep each other up to date on research and treatments. They can also help parents meet their children's emotional needs.

What Would You Do?

Family Dilemma

Brooke could hardly wait to tell her family that she had made the volleyball team at her middle school. Then she saw the schedule of games. At least half were on Tuesday nights, the night that her family went to diabetes support group meetings. They had been going for about five years, ever since her sister Melissa was diagnosed with diabetes at age two. Brooke did not mind the meetings. The parents and the kids were broken into separate groups and it was usually fun to go. Their family also worked to raise money for diabetes research. Their group had been the top fundraiser at the annual walk last fall. Brooke was proud of their success, but sometimes it seemed that everything revolved around Melissa's diabetes, including their mealtimes and the foods they ate. "Volleyball isn't going to be much fun if nobody can be there to watch my games," Brooke thought.

✎ **Write About It** Imagine that you are one of Brooke's parents and she discusses this dilemma with you. How would you respond? Write a paragraph describing your response.

Children who get emotional support from their caregivers are more likely to view themselves in a positive light.

In addition to support groups, hundreds of organizations exist to help children with special needs and their families. The child's doctor can often help you find resources. Some financial aid is available for parents who meet certain income guidelines. State funds may offer money for testing and treatment for children with disabilities. Community agencies may also make funds available.

No two children, including children with the same disability, are exactly alike. Some will find it easier to learn self-care skills, such as dressing, bathing, and using toilet facilities, than others. Some may need help with just a few tasks, while others need greater assistance.

Parenting a child with disabilities is just as rewarding and important as parenting any other child. A child with special needs still wants and needs love and support from his parents. Many children with special needs will grow up to be successful, independent adults. These children often just need extra patience. Parents and caregivers who know what they can reasonably expect of a child with disabilities at different ages and stages are more likely to see the child reach his or her full potential.

✓ **Reading Check** **Explain** How does IDEA guarantee parents an active role in their child's education?

Gifted Children

Gifted children show, or have the potential to show, special abilities in one or more areas. Gifted children may present challenges for parents, teachers, and other caregivers. Sometimes it can be difficult to keep them motivated and help them reach their potential. They may find school boring or their talents may be in areas not taught in the classroom.

They might, for example, have a special talent for music, art, mathematics, or language. For a child gifted in mathematics, English or social studies may not be very interesting. Some gifted children are highly creative. They may have the potential to invent new technologies or develop new ways of solving problems.

Parenting Skills

Guiding Gifted Children

Gifted children sometimes become bored with schoolwork. Some gifted children will lose their motivation and stop trying to excel. Here are some tips that parents and caregivers can use to help gifted children reach their potential and still have a happy childhood.

❧ **Provide learning opportunities in and out of school.** If the school has a program for gifted children, find out how to enroll your child. Expose your child to opportunities outside of school as well. If he or she is interested in history, plan trips to museums. Look for classes or camps that might interest your child.

❧ **Do not overload the child.** When planning extracurricular activities, make sure you still allow for downtime. Children need free time to play, read, relieve stress, and to process what they have learned.

❧ **Teach the child social skills.** Gifted children often dislike being labeled. They will sometimes "play dumb" to fit in better with their peers. Teaching them social skills can help them to have more positive experiences and still be themselves.

❧ **Love the child unconditionally.** All children need to know that they are loved and accepted for who they are rather than what they accomplish. Encourage the child to pursue his or her interests but do not force your desires on the child.

Take Charge Suppose a friend told you that their gifted child had become withdrawn and was suddenly getting poor grades in school. Write a letter to your friend with suggestions on how to help motivate her child.

Identify Gifted Children

It is not always easy to identify gifted children. Children who talk and read early, have large vocabularies, and retain information about what they read or observe may be classified as gifted. Such traits do not always show up in gifted individuals, however. Many gifted people even develop language abilities fairly late.

On the other hand, some gifted children can be identified very early in life. They may learn to walk and talk early. Some display advanced skills in writing, coloring, or building. As they grow older, they often have wide-ranging interests and prefer to interact with adults rather than with other children. They might show awareness of serious issues such as world hunger.

Despite their special ability, not all gifted children are high achievers. Some do not have the patience to complete tasks that seem unimportant to them. They may be bored in the classroom, in part because they may be able to perform two or three grades above their actual grade level. They may question classroom procedures or give unexpected answers to questions.

Special Programs

In school districts that offer programs for gifted children, students may be tested to determine if they qualify. These tests sometimes fail to identify all gifted children, however. This is especially true of those who do not perform well in class or who have limited language abilities.

Some gifted students feel isolated and misunderstood. While they benefit from playing with a variety of children, they also need time with other gifted learners. They need stimulation and challenges so that they can make the most of their abilities. They also need to be accepted and to feel good about what makes them different. They need to be valued for themselves, not just for their special abilities.

Section 21.2 After You Read

Review Key Concepts

1. **Describe** how the policy of inclusion benefits both children with disabilities and children without them.
2. **Compare** how the challenges faced by gifted children are similar to those faced by children with disabilities.

Practice Academic Skills

 English Language Arts

3. Many books and magazine articles have been written about individual autistic savants. Locate one and read it. Write a short essay describing this person's unusual ability to someone who has never heard of the term *autistic savant*.

> **NCTE 2** Read literature to build an understanding of the human experience.

 Social Studies

4. Follow your teacher's instructions to form into groups. Imagine you are in the fifth grade and have a new classmate who is either blind or deaf. Write and prepare a skit demonstrating what you could do to make the new classmate feel welcome in your class.

> **NCSS IV H** Work independently and cooperatively within groups and institutions to accomplish goals.

 Check Your Answers Check your answers at this book's Online Learning Center at **glencoe.com**.

Reading Guide

Before You Read

Prepare with a Partner Work with a partner to ask each other questions and then answer them about the topics that will be discussed in this section.

Read to Learn
Key Concepts

- **Identify** four major types of maltreatment.
- **Summarize** common reasons behind abuse and maltreatment.
- **Explain** what can be done to prevent child abuse.

Main Idea

Adults must watch for children who are suffering from maltreatment, such as neglect or physical abuse. Abused children can be helped by improving family communication and providing a safe place to express feelings.

Content Vocabulary

◇ addiction counselor
◇ mandated reporter
◇ crisis nursery

 Graphic Organizer Go to this book's Online Learning Center at **glencoe.com** to print out this graphic organizer.

Academic Vocabulary

You will find these words in your reading and on your tests. Use the glossary to look up their definitions if necessary.

- constructive
- terminate

Graphic Organizer

As you read this section, look for six behaviors that may be seen in adults who are mistreating children. Use a tree diagram like the one shown to help organize your information.

Signs of Adult Behavior that Indicate the Adult May Be Mistreating a Child

---

Academic Standards . . . .

 English Language Arts

NCTE 5 Use different writing process elements to communicate effectively.

🌐 **Social Studies**

NCSS IV I Individual Development and Identity. Examine factors that contribute to and damage one's mental health and analyze issues related to mental health and behavioral disorders in contemporary society.

NCTE *National Council of Teachers of English*
NCTM *National Council of Teachers of Mathematics*

NSES *National Science Education Standards*
NCSS *National Council for the Social Studies*

Maltreatment

Hundreds of thousands of children become the victims of child abuse and neglect each year, often at the hands of their parents. Most victims, however, never come to the attention of authorities. Their abusers may have threatened them with harm if they tell anyone. Victims also may feel intense guilt for things that are not their fault. Emotional and physical scars can last well into adulthood. These scars can affect the overall health of former victims, as well as their future relationships with others.

Forms of Maltreatment

The federal Child Abuse Prevention and Treatment Act (CAPTA) defines maltreatment, and so does each state. Generally speaking, the government recognizes four major types of maltreatment:

- **Physical Abuse** This means intentionally causing an injury to a child. This includes hitting, burning, shaking, or otherwise harming a child.
- **Neglect** Both physical and emotional neglect are possible. Neglect means failing to provide for a child's basic needs, including food, water, a place to live, love, and attention.
- **Sexual Abuse** This category includes any inappropriate sexual behavior with a child, including touching or taking photographs.
- **Emotional and Verbal Abuse** This means rejecting children, blaming them, or constantly scolding them, particularly for problems beyond their control.

Death is the most tragic consequence of maltreatment. More than 1,000 children die in the United States each year because of abuse or neglect. More than half of all victims of child maltreatment are victims of neglect. Neglected children may fail to develop mentally and physically at the same rate as their peers.

Physically abused children may bear physical scars or become permanently disabled. All abused children suffer emotionally. They often feel lonely, unloved, guilty, and unworthy of care and attention. These feelings may last and cause problems in adult relationships.

Signs and Symptoms

When abuse or neglect occurs, there are usually signs in both children and adults. Neglected children are often absent from school, steal food or money, have poor personal hygiene, and lack protective clothing for wet or cold weather.

Risk of Abuse
Children who are abused often feel unloved and lonely. *Why might some children be more at risk for abuse than others?*

Figure
21.3 **Signs of Maltreatment**

Adults such as caregivers and teachers must watch children for these signs of mistreatment. *Can you think of any other signs that a child may be mistreated?*

Signs that children may be receiving mistreatment:	*Signs that adults may be mistreating children:*
❖ Learning problems that cannot be explained ❖ No adult supervision ❖ Withdrawal from others ❖ No desire to go home after school or other activities ❖ Fearfulness, as though waiting for something bad to happen ❖ Changes in school performance or behavior ❖ Untreated medical conditions	❖ Sees the child as bad or worthless ❖ Makes frequent demands that the child cannot achieve ❖ Asks teachers to use physical discipline if the child misbehaves ❖ Denies child's problems in school or at home ❖ Sees the child as a burden ❖ Rarely looks at the child ❖ Over-protective and demands secrecy (in cases of sexual abuse)

Physically abused children may have bruises, broken bones, or burn marks that cannot be explained. This is not always the case, though. Not all physical abuse leaves marks on visible parts of the child's body, such as the face or arms. Some abusers intentionally leave no marks when they hurt children. **Figure 21.3** lists more signs of mistreatment in children and adults.

Consequences

Regardless of the type of abuse a child suffers, there are always consequences to these actions. Children who are sexually abused sometimes run away from home, refuse to participate in physical activities, and exhibit sexual knowledge beyond their normal level of development.

Emotionally abused children often show aggression. They may act inappropriately like an adult (bossing other children), or like a very young child (rocking back and forth).

✓ **Reading Check** **Recall** What is meant by the term *neglect?*

Why Does Abuse Occur?

Children are never responsible for the abuse or harm that others inflict on them. Some children, however, are more at risk of maltreatment than others. Children with physical and mental disabilities are more likely to be abused. Younger children are neglected more often, and they are more likely to die of maltreatment. When children are sexually abused, the abuse most often begins before age seven. Girls are more often the victims of sexual abuse than boys.

Immature mothers who have children at a young age are more likely to abuse children. So are people who live in poverty and have fewer resources to help with child care or other responsibilities. Child abusers may be socially isolated or stressed due to unemployment. However, abuse can occur in households of any income or education level, ethnicity, or religious background. In families with domestic violence, where one parent abuses the other, children are more likely to be hurt as well.

Abusive parents often do not know enough about child development to have reasonable

What Would You Do?

Healing Past Abuse

Miranda is eleven years old. She was nine when she started going to counseling with Dr. Mitchell, a psychologist. She had been abused by her mother from ages six to eight, at which time she went to live with her aunt. She was suffering from anxiety, feelings of guilt, and sleeping problems. Dr. Mitchell helped Miranda recognize that adults, not children, are responsible for healthy parent-child interactions. This helped ease Miranda's feelings of guilt about the abuse. Dr. Mitchell taught Miranda some ways to cope with her sad feelings and established a plan to help her deal with her feelings of anxiety. This plan includes having supportive people to whom she can turn when she feels insecure.

Write About It Imagine that you are Miranda's aunt, with whom she is now living. What would you do to help Miranda cope with her past abuse? Write a list of at least five steps you would take.

expectations. Some expect even very young children to obey them promptly or remember rules given earlier. If abusers get help, they can learn what to expect from children of various ages and how to nurture them.

Studies have shown that a large percentage of child maltreatment cases involve substance abuse. When parents become dependent on alcohol and other drugs, they neglect their children's needs. Substance abusers are often emotionally unavailable and can be violent due to the effects of drugs. They might buy drugs with money that should have been spent on food and other basics for their children.

Many problems, such as mental illness, depression, unemployment, and high stress levels, can go along with substance abuse. So many maltreatment cases involve substance abuse that social service agencies are working hard to manage these cases better. A therapist trained to help substance abusers is called an **addiction counselor**. Addiction counselors are trained to help abusive parents who are also addicted to drugs or alcohol.

Who Abuses Children?

An adult in the home is most often to blame for physical abuse. Statistics indicate that mothers abuse children more often than fathers do. In sexual abuse cases, however, it is most often not a parent, but a relative or a family friend who harms the child, .

People who abuse children often have difficulty controlling their impulses. While many parents feel frustrated when a child is crying or whining, people who abuse children often act without thinking. Abusers often feel depressed, extremely anxious, or overwhelmed. In many cases, they were abused themselves as children and they do not know how to discipline children in a **constructive**, or positive, way. Abuse may come from only one parent. The other parent may deny that it is happening. Sometimes, only one child in a family is targeted for abuse.

✓ **Reading Check** **Describe** What are possible emotional traits of people who abuse children?

Stop Maltreatment

Abuse happens for many reasons. Preventing abuse requires changing the situations in which abuse occurs. Sometimes a parent is too young or immature to handle the challenges of parenthood. Encouraging young people to wait until they are older and more financially stable is important. Parenting classes can help people learn skills for raising children. This helps them avoid feeling overwhelmed. Support groups help stressed parents discuss their emotions and share solutions.

Abusing or neglecting children in any way is illegal. People who work with children, including teachers, doctors, nurses, and counselors, are required by law to report maltreatment if they see evidence of it. A person who is required by law to report maltreatment is called a **mandated reporter**. While others may not have a legal obligation to report abuse, they should contact child protective services agencies as soon as they suspect it.

Every state has a child welfare agency. When an agency hears a report of possible child abuse, it sends someone to investigate. If the child is thought to be in danger, the court may place the child in a foster home. If there is a history of abuse, or if the child has severe injuries, parents may be arrested and charged with crimes. Ultimately, the court may **terminate**, or end, their parental rights and their children may never live with them again.

Putting abusers in prison gives children temporary protection but does not solve the problem. In most cases, abusers receive treatment and counseling to understand the reasons for the abuse and to end it.

Most abusive parents must learn how to care for their children and treat them in loving ways. Several programs are available to help. Members of Parents Anonymous, one of the best-known groups, support each other as they work to change their behavior.

A community may have a crisis nursery. A **crisis nursery** is a child care facility where troubled parents can go to receive short-term, free child care. Many crisis nurseries are open 24 hours a day and provide children with a safe environment. Using a crisis nursery gives parents a chance to cool off and cope with their frustrations, anger, and problems without hurting their children. These facilities often also provide parenting classes, counseling, and job training.

Treatment for Abused Children

Children who have been abused are usually treated through counseling sessions with mental health professionals who have experience with victimized children. Counseling involves helping people make sense of their feelings and behavior, and improving interactions with others. Counselors who work with abused children have many goals, including:

- Protecting children from further harm.
- Improving family communication.
- Encouraging healthy friendships between children and their peers.

Moral Compass
People who work with children are required by law to report maltreatment if they see evidence of it. *Why do you think pediatricians are mandated reporters?*

- Teaching mistreated children to take care of themselves and to make choices that help keep them safe.
- Helping children have realistic expectations of parents who have problems.
- Providing a safe place to express anger, disappointment, and sadness.

Counseling may take many forms. It should always be appropriate for the child's age. Many counselors use techniques that let young children express their feelings about abuse through play.

Each affected person, including the victimized child, the abusers, and other family members, may be involved in individual counseling. Treatment may involve just the child and the nonabusive parent. It also may involve the whole family, with the goal of bringing everyone back together. The abuser must acknowledge responsibility for the abuse and make a commitment to change before the family can be reunited.

Counselors often agree not to tell parents anything without telling the child first. This allows children to feel free to talk to their counselors about anything that worries them. Counselors cannot, however, keep secrets regarding the child's safety from the parents. Counselors will not tell anyone outside the family about what happens in sessions unless the child is in danger or the family requests a release of information.

Many family problems are related to poor parenting skills and lack of knowledge about child development. Classes like the one you are taking give parents and future parents more realistic expectations about children and what it takes to care for them properly. With education, as well as more knowledge about support resources, maltreatment can be prevented. Remember that all parents have to learn parenting skills. A little education and a lot of love can lead to a happy family.

Section 21.3 After You Read

Review Key Concepts

1. **List** five possible signs of abuse in children.
2. **Explain** how substance abuse and child abuse are linked.
3. **Identify** the responsibilities of mandated reporters.

Practice Academic Skills

 English Language Skills

4. Communities have different resources to assist children who are being maltreated. Research local organizations in your area, how to contact them, and what services they offer. Create a brochure that shows the options available to victims of maltreatment and their families.

 Social Studies

5. A National Institute of Justice study showed that maltreated children are more likely to commit violent crimes as adults. Identify one research study supporting this link and one countering it. Write a report analyzing the studies. Explain which one you think is more persuasive.

 Check Your Answers Check your answers at this book's Online Learning Center at **glencoe.com**.

> **NCTE 5** Use different writing process elements to communicate effectively.

> **NCSS IV I** Examine factors that contribute to and damage one's mental health and analyze issue related to mental health and behavioral disorders in contemporary society.

Careers With Children

Camp Counselor

Camps provide experiences that children may not be able to have in their hometowns. There are many different types of camps. There are day camps, week-long camps, and summer camps. Camp counselors are responsible for the health, safety, and well-being of these campers. They help with home-sickness as well as minor injuries.

☼ What Does a Camp Counselor Do?

Camp counselors make sure that campers are safe and have a successful camp experience. A camp counselor may teach horseback riding, lead singing sessions, and toast marshmallows by a fire. They are expected to set a good example, deal with any difficulties that arise, and enforce camp rules.

☼ Where Do Camp Counselors Work?

Some of the different kinds of camps include day camps, overnight camps, religious camps, and camps that serve children with special needs. Many camps are geared toward learning specific sports skills, such as soccer. Some are even aimed at academic skills, such as space camp or computer camp.

Preparation and Skills

Education and Training

Being a camp counselor generally requires someone who is enthusiastic, relates well to children, and understands nature. Some camps may require specific training, licenses, affiliations, or accreditations.

Aptitudes, Abilities, and Skills

Good camp counselors should model good behavior. They need patience and humor, as well as knowledge of the principles of health, safety, and nutrition. Counselors should be able to react to unexpected situations.

Academic Skills

Camp counselors will use English language arts skills to communicate with and teach children. Specialized camps may require counselors to have specific academic skills.

Explore Careers

Think of a skill you have, such as playing baseball or making pottery. Conduct research to learn about a camp where your skill would be useful. Write a paragraph discussing whether you think you would enjoy being a counselor there.

 Careers Online For more information on careers, visit the Occupational Outlook Handbook Web site through the link on this book's Online Learning Center at **glencoe.com**.

Chapter Summary

Most families face difficult situations at times. Children should be told about problems honestly and in a way suited to their age. Some children respond to difficulties by showing signs of stress. When this occurs, children need extra support. Physical, learning, and emotional disabilities can affect children. Early diagnosis and treatment help children with disabilities reach their potential. Federal law requires that public schools meet the needs of children with disabilities. There are four major types of maltreatment. Treatment and counseling can help abusive parents learn to stop patterns of abuse.

Vocabulary Review

1. Write your own definition for each content and academic vocabulary term.

Content Vocabulary
- regression (p. 573)
- situational stress (p. 573)
- addiction (p. 576)
- support group (p. 577)
- learning disability (p. 582)
- dyslexia (p. 582)
- ADHD (p. 583)
- ADD (p. 583)
- mental retardation (p. 583)
- type 1 diabetes (p. 584)
- autism (p. 585)
- autism spectrum disorder (ASD) (p. 585)
- inclusion (p. 587)
- gifted (p. 588)
- addiction counselor (p. 593)
- mandated reporter (p. 593)
- crisis nursery (p. 594)

Academic Vocabulary
- vulnerable (p. 573)
- irrational (p. 578)
- distinguish (p. 582)
- adaptation (p. 586)
- constructive (p. 593)
- terminate (p. 594)

Review Key Concepts

2. Describe how parents can help children cope with stress.
3. List eight possible causes of stress in children.
4. Identify nine categories of disabilities.
5. Describe some of the traits exhibited by gifted children.
6. Identify four major types of maltreatment.
7. Summarize common reasons behind abuse and maltreatment.
8. Explain what can be done to prevent child abuse.

Critical Thinking

9. Apply Imagine that a family moved in next door to you. If you learned the parents were newly divorced, what could you do to help the children, ages seven and ten, adjust to their new situation?
10. Infer Why do you think many families do not consider seeking outside help when they are dealing with a problem?

Family & Community Connection

11. Supporting Families Find out about an organization in your community that provides support for families having difficulties. It may be a crisis nursery, a faith-based organization that provides temporary housing, or something similar. Interview someone from the organization on the services provided. Prepare a speech to share the information you learn about the organization's services.

Health Skills

12. Mandated Reporters Talk with an individual, such as a teacher or counselor, who is a mandated reporter. Ask them to explain the duties of a mandated reporter. Also ask what they watch for when trying to spot abuse. Use what you learn to create a poster describing the duties of mandated reporters.

Observation Skills

13. Dealing with Disabilities Having a physical disability teaches resourcefulness. Disabled people must come up with solutions to performing tasks that others take for granted. For example, a deaf student may need to sit in the front of a classroom.

Procedure Ask a teen with a physical disability if you could spend several hours with him or her. Observe how this person adapts everyday activities to cope with the disability.

Analysis Write one or two paragraphs summarizing any modifications in daily routine this person makes to deal with his or her disability.

NCSS IV D Individual Development and Identity Apply concepts, methods, and theories about the study of human growth and development, such as physical endowment, learning, motivation, behavior, perception, and personality.

Real-World Skills

Problem-Solving

14. Share Concerns Suppose that you babysit a 4-year-old. You are concerned because the child rarely talks and does not seem to understand what you are saying. Write a scenario in which you present your concerns to the child's parent.

Technology Skills

15. Create a Newsletter Imagine that you are in charge of a special Saturday program for gifted students. Use word processing or desktop publishing software to create a monthly newsletter listing upcoming activities for the program. Be creative in your selection of activities.

Financial Literacy

16. Summer Camp Choose one type of disability discussed in this chapter, such as blindness or diabetes. Find a camp designed for children with this disability. Research how much the camp costs and compare it to the cost of a similar camp for children without disabilities.

Additional Activities For additional activities, go to this book's Online Learning Center at **glencoe.com**.

Academic Skills

 English Language Arts

17. A Difficult Beginning Many well-known people grew up in difficult circumstances such as abuse. Research books or magazine articles to learn about one of these individuals. Write an essay discussing what impact you think the person's childhood had on the adult he or she became.

> **NCTE 2** Read literature to build an understanding of the human experience.

 Mathematics

18. Family Challenges Reports show that between 80 and 90 percent of children in homes affected by domestic violence are aware of the abuse and can provide detailed accounts of it. Studies also show that there are about 2.3 million incidents of domestic violence each year. What is the range of the number of children that witnessed those incidents?

Math Concept Range A range is a sequence, series, or scale between limits.

Starting Hint: Convert the percentages to decimals by dividing by 100. Then multiply each decimal by 2.3 million. Order those numbers from least to greatest for your range.

 For math help, go to the Math Appendix at the back of the book.

> **NCTM Number and Operations** Understand numbers, ways of representing numbers, relationships among numbers, and number systems.

 Science

19. Situational Stress As you have learned, situational stress in children is usually caused by events that have a major impact on their lives, such as moving, parents divorcing, a serious illness in the family, or financial difficulties.

Procedure Ask ten children between ages 12 and 15 to state the most stressful event in their lives. Record their responses.

Analysis Combine your results with those of four classmates. Look for any patterns in the responses. Write a summary of your findings.

> **NSES A** Develop understandings about scientific inquiry.

Standardized Test Practice

MULTIPLE CHOICE

Read the passage and then answer the question.

Rett syndrome is a developmental disorder in which children appear to be growing normally and then suddenly quit developing, and even lose skills. Scientists think it is caused by a defective chromosome. Rett syndrome is considered to be one of the autism spectrum disorders.

20. According to this passage, what is the probable cause of Rett syndrome?
a. genetic abnormality
b. poor development skills
c. neglect
d. autism

> **Test-Taking Tip** In multiple choice questions, do not go back and change an answer unless you made an obvious mistake the first time, such as misreading the question.

Chapter Objectives

After completing this chapter, you will be able to:

- **Describe** two types of substitute care for younger children.
- **List** questions a parent should ask when choosing home-based care.
- **Describe** the benefits of having learning centers in early childhood classrooms.
- **Explain** the factors to consider when planning activities.
- **Identify** methods for promoting positive behavior in the classroom.

Writing Activity *Compare and Contrast*

Understanding Child Care Many parents, at some point in time, will need to rely on substitute care for their children. Write a report in which you compare and contrast what you know about in-home child care, such as babysitting, and day-care centers.

Writing Tips Use these tips to write an effective compare-and-contrast report:
1. Choose related items.
2. Organize your paper by comparing subjects or by comparing features.
3. Use appropriate transitions between comparisons and contrasts.

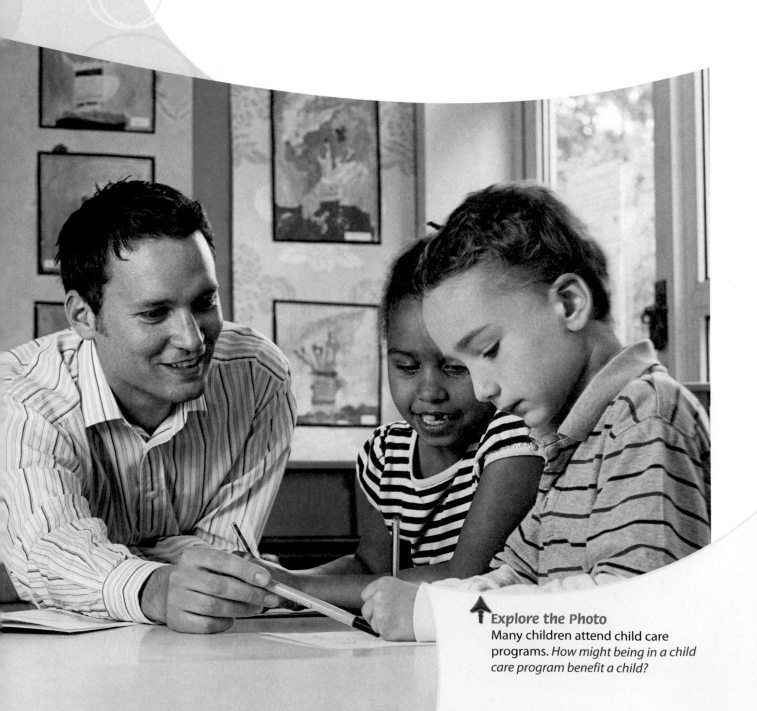

Explore the Photo
Many children attend child care programs. *How might being in a child care program benefit a child?*

Reading Guide

Before You Read

Predict Look at the photos in this section and read their captions. Write one or two sentences predicting what the section will be about.

Read to Learn
Key Concepts
- **Describe** two types of substitute care for younger children.
- **List** questions a parent should ask when choosing home-based care.

Main Idea
Parents who need substitute child care for their children must decide whether home-based care or center-based care is best for the needs of their child.

Content Vocabulary

◇ child care center   ◇ accreditation
◇ in-home care   ◇ play group
◇ family child care   ◇ parent cooperative
◇ nanny   ◇ Head Start
◇ license

Graphic Organizer Go to this book's Online Learning Center at **glencoe.com** to print out this graphic organizer.

Academic Vocabulary
You will find these words in your reading and on your tests. Use the glossary to look up their definitions if necessary.

■ socialize
■ criteria

Graphic Organizer
As you read, look for three types of home-based care. Note characteristics of each one. Use a chart like the one shown to help organize your information. Add additional squares as needed.

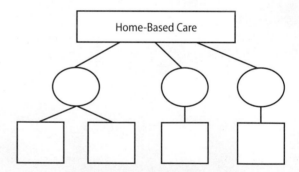

Home-Based Care

Academic Standards . . . .

 English Language Arts

NCTE 4 Use written language to communicate effectively.

 Mathematics

NCTM Data Analysis and Probability Select and use appropriate statistical methods to analyze data.

NCTM Number and Operations Understand numbers, ways of representing numbers, relationships among numbers, and number systems.

NCTE *National Council of Teachers of English*
NCTM *National Council of Teachers of Mathematics*

NSES *National Science Education Standards*
NCSS *National Council for the Social Studies*

Substitute Care

On his way to work each day, Luis takes his son, Alberto, to the Sunny Day Child Care Center. At the end of her workday, Alberto's mother, Elena, comes to get him and brings him home. Luis and Elena, just like millions of other parents, rely on substitute child care.

More and more parents have come to rely on other people to care for their children at least some of the time. Why is there such a demand for substitute care? There are many reasons, including:

- In many two-parent families, both parents work outside the home. When both parents have jobs, their children usually need substitute care.
- Many children live with a single parent who has a full-time job. Parents in this situation need full- or part-time care for their children.
- Some parents who care for a child at home feel that the child could benefit from spending time with a group of other children. They place their child in a child care setting for some time each week.

Types of Substitute Care

Parents who need substitute care have a variety of options. All these options provide the child with physical care and a place to play. Some place greater emphasis than others on education. Substitute care is provided in two general settings. Some services are offered in a home. Others are provided in a child care center. A **child care center** is a facility in which a staff of adults provides care for children.

Home-Based Care

In-home care is provided to many young children from a caregiver who comes to their home. **Family child care** takes place in the caregiver's home. Parents may choose home-based care because they feel a home setting may be easier for their children to adjust to. Home-based care may also be convenient for parents. It may be located close to home and the hours may be more flexible. Some parents like this arrangement because the child care provider is a relative, friend, or neighbor—someone they know and trust.

↑ Providing Child Care
People who run home-based child care programs may be required to get a license from their state. *Why do you think some states insist on licensing for child care providers?*

Home-based care usually involves a smaller group of children than a child care center. For this reason, many parents prefer home-based care for infants or other children who need a lot of individual attention. There are three main types of home-based care.

Care in the Child's Own Home Many parents have their child cared for by someone who comes to their home. In-home care is convenient, but it can be costly. Also, the child may not have a chance to play with other children. Some families hire a nanny. A **nanny** is a person trained to provide child care. The nanny may live with the family or come to the home daily. Although this arrangement is fairly expensive, a nanny can offer reliable and stable care at almost any time of day.

Family Child Care Another option for parents is family child care. In this situation, a child care provider cares for a small group of children in his or her own home. The group often includes the provider's own children. Family child care offers children the comfort of a home setting with opportunities for social interaction. Also, because the group size is small, the child care provider can give the children more individual attention. Family child care usually costs less than in-home care.

Some states require child care providers to have a license. A **license** is a registration with the state that indicates child care providers meet health and safety standards. A license does not indicate the quality of the care provided, however. Some family child care providers go a step further and earn accreditation from a recognized organization such as the National Association for Family Child Care (NAFCC). **Accreditation** means that the child care provider has met strict official standards for quality child care.

Play Groups Some parents and children take part in a play group. A **play group** is an arrangement in which parents take turns caring for one another's children in their own homes. A play group is similar to family child care, but it involves a number of different homes and different caregivers. Most play groups involve no fees because the work is shared. This type of care is best suited for parents who do not work full time but who want their children to have the opportunity to socialize, or participate, with other children.

Center-Based Care

In child care centers, several adults care for one or more groups of children. Centers vary widely in their hours, their fees, and the ages of children they accept. They also differ in the activities, equipment, and play areas provided, and in the training and experience of the staff.

Some child care centers are businesses run for profit. Others are called non-profit organizations. This means that they charge only enough fees to cover expenses. Still others are funded by the city, state, or federal government. Finally, some centers are run by businesses that offer child care as a benefit to their employees or customers.

Each state has an agency that licenses child care centers. A center must meet minimum health and safety requirements to receive a license. The license also limits the number of children a center may accept, depending on space, facilities, and number of people on the staff.

Professionals in the child care field have created a system to recognize centers that meet high standards. Child care centers can choose to join the National Association for the Education of Young Children (NAEYC). This association is dedicated to improving the professional care and education of children from birth through age eight. Members must apply to the association. Accreditation involves a review of the facility's staff, programs, and environment to see if they meet the association's strict **criteria**, or standards. These include strict staff-to-children ratios, as seen in **Figure 22.1**. You will note in this chart that some of the ages overlap. These are general guidelines, but the NAEYC will also take into account the total number of children in a facility to decide the final allowed ratio. A low staff-to-child ratio allows children to get the attention needed to enhance their learning experiences.

Parents can choose from several center-based child care options. These include child care centers, parent cooperatives, preschools, and Head Start centers. Different center-based child care options will meet the needs of different families. See **Figure 22.2** on page 607 for tips on how to make sure your child is doing well in whichever child care you choose.

Child Care Centers Child care centers primarily serve children whose parents work outside the home. The typical center offers children a variety of activities. Some centers emphasize specific learning activities, while others allow more time for informal play. Usually there is a daily routine with time set aside for meals, naps, and indoor and outdoor play. Child care centers may offer half-day or full-day programs. Some child care centers are designed for children two years old and older. Some provide care for infants and young toddlers as well.

Parent Cooperatives A **parent cooperative**, or co-op, is child care that is provided by the parents of the children in the co-op. The parents take turns staffing the co-op, which is usually in a facility other than a home. A preschool teacher or another qualified child care provider may organize the program and guide the parents. A co-op program costs considerably less than a child care center. It may not be an option, however, for families in which both parents work full time.

Figure 22.1 NAEYC Staff-to-Children Guidelines

A low staff-to-child ratio allows children to receive more individualized attention. *How many 13-month-old toddlers could be in a group with two staff persons?*

Ages	Number of Staff	Number of Children
Infants (birth–15 months)	1	4
Toddlers (12–28 months)	1	4
Toddlers (21–36 months)	1	4
Preschoolers (2.5–3 years)	1	9
Preschoolers (4 years)	1	10
Kindergarteners (5 years)	1	12

Preschools Preschools provide educational programs for children ages three to five. They typically offer activities that help children develop in all areas. The staff usually includes one or more teachers as well as a number of assistant teachers. Preschools usually offer half-day sessions from two to five days a week. Some centers offer both child care for younger children and preschool programs for three- to five-year-olds. A growing trend is for children to attend a pre-kindergarten program the year before kindergarten.

Some preschools provide specialized programs that differ from the traditional approach. Montessori preschools, for example, use special learning materials and follow the ideas of Maria Montessori, an Italian educator. See Chapter 15 to learn more about Montessori's theory of learning. Children are encouraged to learn by exploring and experimenting. They are given the freedom to move from one activity to another as they wish. Another example is called High/Scope. This program encourages children to learn through active experiences with people, material, and events rather than through direct teaching.

Head Start Centers **Head Start** is a program that provides locally run child care facilities designed to help lower-income and disadvantaged children from birth to five years of age become ready for school. It is funded by the federal government. Most Head Start centers have half-day sessions. Head Start programs offer a variety of activities. They also provide children with meals, health care, and social services. Parents are expected to be actively involved in the Head Start program.

Care for Older Children

Many parents wonder at what age their children can be left unsupervised. Child care experts advise against leaving children ages twelve and under home alone. This means that many parents and other caregivers need substitute care for their school-age children before and after school and during school holidays, breaks, and summers.

Some children go to the home of a neighbor or relative. Others depend on before- and after-school programs. These may be run by schools or religious or community groups. Such programs offer a safe place where children can have a snack, do their homework, and enjoy supervised activities.

Finding child care for school holidays and summer vacation can be more difficult. Fortunately, parents and other caregivers know in advance when school holidays will occur, so they can make plans well in advance. Often parents take their own vacations from work during the school holidays.

Learning Can Be Fun
Preschool helps to prepare children for kindergarten. *What are some useful skills that children learn in preschool?*

Figure 22.2

Is Your Child Doing Well in Child Care?

Parents want to know if their child is happy and doing well in child care. *What kinds of questions should a parent ask a child care provider?*

Action	Description
Look for bonding.	Children need time to adapt and warm up gradually. After an adjustment period, look for a bond to develop between the child and staff. The child might also develop friendships with the other children depending on his or her age.
Ask for updates.	Sometimes caregivers will answer questions or give feedback at the end of the day or by appointment. Find out how the provider thinks the child is doing. Child care professionals often can give insight about a child's development.
Talk to the child.	Of course, the child is the best source of information if he or she is old enough to talk. Ask questions about activities, meals, and playtime. What is the child learning? Does she or he have fun? With younger children, a reluctance to stay with the caregiver, especially if it lasts beyond the first few minutes, could indicate a problem.
Take time to observe.	Visit the child care center or home. Many allow parents to just drop in. Some centers have a one-way mirror for observation. Some may offer password-protected videos via the Internet. Parents can see how their child acts on a typical day.
Get involved.	If possible, volunteer for special parties or help with field trips. Young children especially are happy to share these occasions with a parent.
Be aware.	Although most child care experiences are positive, be aware of possible warning signs. Listen if a child complains about being bullied, mistreated, or ignored by the staff. Check it out and take any appropriate action. Also be aware of sudden mood changes in the child. If an outgoing toddler suddenly becomes withdrawn or quiet, it could indicate a problem.

Math in Action

Starting Salaries

Tran did an analysis of starting salaries for child care workers in his area. He called three child care centers and was quoted the following salaries: $32,000, $31,800, and $30,850. What is the average salary in his area?

Math Concept **Measures of Central Tendency** The mean, median, and mode are all measures of central tendency because they provide a summary of numerical data in one number. The mean is the same as the average.

Starting Hint To find the mean, add all of the values ($32,000, $31,800, and $30,850) together. Then divide the total by the number of values in the set of data (3).

 For math help, go to the Math Appendix at the back of the book.

NCTM Data Analysis and Probability
Select and use appropriate statistical methods to analyze data.

Few parents can take all of the school holidays off, though. And even fewer can take the whole summer off. They need to find ways to fill the gaps. Here are some suggestions.

- Some parents arrange to share child care with several other families.
- High school and college students on similar school schedules are often available to provide in-home care.
- Some of the programs that offer before- and after-school care also offer care for school holidays. Some also offer some summer programs.
- Museums, zoos, parks and recreation departments, and other community organizations may offer day camps or other programs for longer breaks and summer vacation.

Parents looking for holiday child care should ask the same questions they would ask when looking for any other kind of substitute care. Safety, provider training, and child-to-adult ratios are still very important.

✓ **Reading Check** **Explain** How do preschools differ from child care centers?

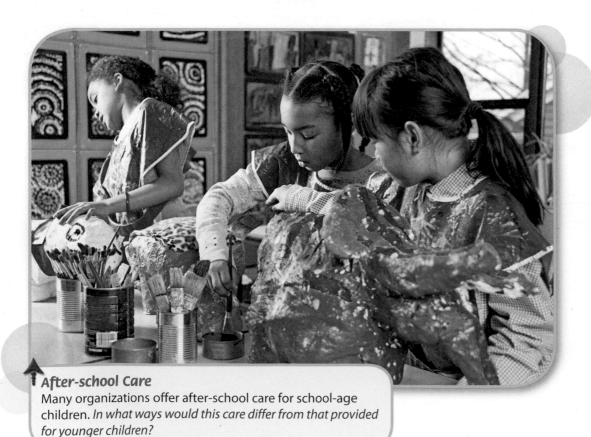

After-school Care
Many organizations offer after-school care for school-age children. *In what ways would this care differ from that provided for younger children?*

Choosing Substitute Child Care

There are many factors to consider when choosing substitute care for a child. Foremost is the quality of care. In addition, the cost, convenience, qualifications of the caregivers, and the facilities and activities provided are all considerations.

What to Look For

When parents start searching for care, it is helpful to use an organized approach. **Figure 22.3** on page 610 provides a list of important considerations when evaluating child care options. The questions are tailored to a child care center, but they could be adapted to other situations as well. Parents should ask some of the questions directly. Other questions require parents to observe the facility and the providers. Because the quality of care has such an impact on a child's well-being and development, it is important to put in the time and effort to find the best choice. Parents will generally visit several child care providers before selecting the best one for their child.

Parents should remember that each child is unique. Therefore, the needs of their child may be different from the needs of another child. A child care center may be perfect for one family but not be right for another. Parents must consider the child's temperament along with that of the caregiver. Does the caregiver's values match the family's values? If a child is not allowed to watch television at home, a child care center with scheduled television time may not be the right choice.

As a child grows, parents may need to make new child care arrangements. Connie put two-year-old Todd in family child care because she liked the idea of a home setting. When Todd turned four, however, she moved him to a preschool program so that he could start to prepare for kindergarten.

A child's behavior also could signal a need to change. If a child suddenly begins to cause trouble at child care, it may be because he or she is bored. Perhaps the activities are no longer interesting or challenging. If a child begins

What Would You Do?

Choosing Child Care

Charlotte and her husband have toured a few child care centers, and she does not feel that any are right for their 18-month-old son, Noah. Charlotte still has doubts about putting Noah in child care. She worries that he will find it hard to make friends or that he will get sick more often if he is with other children. At the same time, she feels that because he is an only child, he needs contact with other children.

Charlotte and her husband arrange to visit another child care center. This experience is more positive. Noah seems to like it there and soon starts playing while the director of the center talks with his parents. The director is able to ease some of Charlotte's fears. Charlotte learns, for example, that the center has a policy that children must stay home when they are sick. Most of all, she notices that the children seem happy.

Write About It Even though the visit to the last child care center was positive, Charlotte and her husband are still not completely comfortable with putting Noah in child care. Write a letter to Charlotte and her husband with suggestions for further steps they might take to help them make their decision.

to cry regularly when being dropped off at child care, this could be a sign that a child no longer feels comfortable in that setting.

Issues Specific to Home-Based Care

Home-based care generally operates on a smaller scale than center-based care and involves fewer caregivers. For these reasons, parents considering home-based care for their children need to ask some additional questions.

- **How many children does the provider care for?** Most experts recommend that a family child care home have no more than six children per adult, including the child care provider's own children. This number should be even lower if infants and

Figure 22.3 Evaluating Child Care

There are many questions parents or other caregivers might ask when evaluating substitute care options. *How could this list be adapted to provide a record of a visit to each facility?*

Aspect of Care	Questions to Consider
Caregiver	❧ Does the number of children per adult meet NAEYC criteria? ❧ What education, training, and experience do providers have? ❧ How long have providers worked at this facility? How often are new providers hired? ❧ What safety and first-aid training do providers have? ❧ How do providers ensure that children are released only to authorized persons? ❧ What arrangements are made if a provider is ill? ❧ Do the providers seem to enjoy caring for the children? Are there joyful interactions between the children and the providers?
Facility	❧ Does the physical space in the facility match NAEYC criteria? ❧ Is the facility licensed or accredited? ❧ Are both indoor and outdoor areas safe, comfortable, and clean? ❧ If meals or snacks are provided, are they nutritious? Are they served in a clean area? ❧ Are sleeping areas separate from noisy areas? ❧ What happens if a parent must pick a child up late? ❧ Does each child have a place for his or her belongings? ❧ Is there a clean diaper-changing area for infants and toddlers? ❧ Are the toilets and sinks clean and easy to reach? Can children reach clean towels, liquid soap, and toilet paper?
Program	❧ Do providers guide children's behavior in appropriate ways? ❧ Are the policies in writing? If so, ask for a copy. ❧ Are rules reasonable for the children's ages? ❧ Are the toys suitable for the children's ages? ❧ Are activities varied and matched to the children's levels? ❧ Do children have time for self-directed free play? ❧ Is there a regular method for the provider to report to parents? ❧ Do the children seem involved and happy? ❧ If you were a child, would you like to spend time here? ❧ What is the policy for sick children?

toddlers are part of the mix. When there are fewer children, each child gets more individual attention. A child care provider working alone should handle no more than two children younger than age two.

- **Is there a back-up plan for illness or vacations?** What happens when the family child care provider must be gone? Are there arrangements for someone to fill in? If not, parents will need to consider a back-up care plan.

- **Who else will be in the home?** Parents need to know who else will be around their children. They should ask about other children, teens, or adults who live in the home. Who are they, what are their backgrounds, and how might they interact with the children?

- **Are there both quiet and active times for children?** Children need a good mix of planned activities and informal play. Children should not simply sit in front of the television much of the day or be left without supervision. Most young children also need scheduled nap times. Often, if a child will not sleep, he or she is allowed to rest quietly with a book.

- **What if there is an emergency?** In most home-based care settings, there is only one adult child care provider. To deal with emergencies—such as an injured child who needs medical attention—the provider should have someone on call who can fill in at short notice.

Consider the Cost

While quality of care is the primary consideration in choosing child care, cost is also an important factor. The cost of child care varies significantly depending on the type of care and where it is located. In some cities, for example, families may pay more than $1,000 per month for a single toddler at a child care center. In general, the least expensive child care option is care provided by family or friends. Nannies are usually the most costly choice. Center-based care is usually more expensive than home-based care, but the cost varies widely from place to place. The age of the child needing care is also a factor. Care of

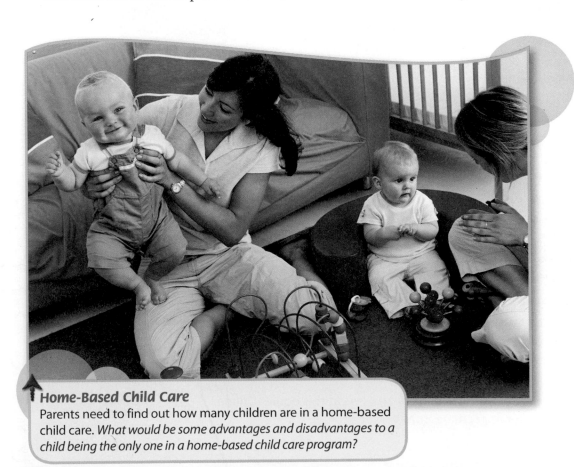

Home-Based Child Care
Parents need to find out how many children are in a home-based child care. *What would be some advantages and disadvantages to a child being the only one in a home-based child care program?*

infants is typically more costly than for pre-schoolers.

No matter what the cost, however, it adds up. Depending on the parents' working hours, children may need substitute care for up to ten hours a day, five days a week.

In two-parent families, when earnings are compared to child care and other job-related costs such as transportation and clothing, it is sometimes less expensive for one parent to stay at home and provide care.

Sources of Information

How can parents locate potential sources of substitute care? Community groups, libraries, and local government agencies can supply listings. Groups such as Child Care Aware, NAEYC, and Nation's Network of Child Care Resource and Referral offer listings for many areas. All three groups have Web sites that provide easy access to their referral services and other information, including helpful information for parents and caregivers and links to other reputable Web sites. Many parents find substitute care by asking friends for referrals.

It is essential that parents visit each home or child care center they are considering before choosing one. This takes time, but it allows them to see the facility and the child care providers firsthand. In fact, taking the child to visit can help a parent see how the child responds to the place and the people, and how the child care providers respond to the child.

Anyone considering a substitute care option should ask for references. Any child care provider should be willing to give the names and phone numbers of parents whose children attend. This is true for a center or a home-based provider.

Children are a precious resource and a responsibility. Parents must do everything possible to ensure their children are receiving quality care.

Section 22.1 — After You Read

Review Key Concepts

1. **List** three reasons parents might need substitute care for their children.
2. **Explain** why it is so important for parents to ask questions of possible substitute child care providers.

Practice Academic Skills

English Language Arts

3. Work with a partner to write an interview between a parent and a director of a child care center. Using the questions in Figure 22.3, decide twelve of the most important questions for the parent to ask. Act out the interview for the class.

NCTE 4 Use written language to communicate effectively.

Mathematics

4. Research the cost of some in-home child care providers and child care centers in your area. Find out their costs to provide care for one two-year-old child. List the names of the providers and their costs in order from least expensive to most expensive.

NCTM Number and Operations Understand numbers, ways of representing numbers, relationships among numbers, and number systems.

Check Your Answers Check your answers at this book's Online Learning Center at **glencoe.com**.

Reading Guide

Before You Read

Prior Knowledge Look over the Key Concepts for this section. Write down what you already know about each concept and what you want to find out by reading the section.

Read to Learn
Key Concepts

- **Describe** the benefits of having learning centers in early childhood classrooms.
- **Explain** the factors to consider when planning activities.
- **Identify** methods for promoting positive behavior in the classroom.

Main Idea

Early childhood classrooms should provide a safe and healthy environment for children. Classrooms should promote positive behavior and plan lessons and activities.

Content Vocabulary

 learning center
◇ circle time
◇ free play
◇ transition

 Graphic Organizer Go to this book's Online Learning Center at **glencoe.com** to print out this graphic organizer.

Academic Vocabulary

You will find these words in your reading and on your tests. Use the glossary to look up their definitions if necessary.

- self-sufficiency
- expectation

Graphic Organizer

As you read, list three precautions child care providers must take to provide a safe environment. Use a fishbone diagram like the one shown to help organize your information.

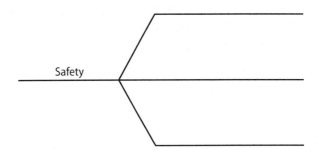

Safety

Academic Standards ·

 English Language Arts

NCTE 12 Use language to accomplish individual purposes.

 Science

NSES F Develop understanding of personal and community health.

 Social Studies

NCSS I A Culture Analyze and explain the ways groups, societies, and cultures address human needs and concerns.

NCTE *National Council of Teachers of English*
NCTM *National Council of Teachers of Mathematics*

NSES *National Science Education Standards*
NCSS *National Council for the Social Studies*

The Early Childhood Classroom

While you are studying child development, you may have an opportunity to visit an early childhood classroom. Perhaps you will observe the children to better understand their development and behavior. You might be a volunteer helping the child care staff. You might also work with children as part of your course work. No matter what your role, you should understand how such programs are organized and the roles, responsibilities, and concerns of the staff. This will help make your experience more rewarding.

If you visit an early childhood classroom, you will notice that it is carefully designed to meet children's varied needs. It takes a special kind of environment to promote the physical, social, emotional, and intellectual development of young children.

First, the classroom environment needs to be child-size. Chairs should allow children to sit with their feet touching the floor. Having shelves within reach allows children to reach and return materials on their own. Posters and other wall decorations should be at the children's eye level. Drinking fountains, sinks, and other facilities should also be accessible.

A child-size environment promotes independence. The children are able to use materials without having to ask adults for help. This helps promote feelings of success and **self-sufficiency**, which is the ability to take care of oneself.

Learning Centers

Early childhood classrooms are often divided into learning centers. A **learning center** is an area designed for certain types of play and learning. Learning centers allow children to make choices. They can explore different areas of knowledge and develop skills through hands-on experiences. **Figure 22.4** on pages 616–617 shows an ideal arrangement of learning centers in an early childhood classroom.

Early childhood educators use guidelines such as these when designing a classroom and setting up learning centers:

- Use low shelves, colored floor coverings, wall decorations, or storage containers to separate learning centers.
- Separate noisy centers from quiet centers.
- Place the art center near a source of water for clean up. The floor should be easy to clean if it gets wet.
- Leave a large, open area for large-group activities, such as dancing or story time.

➤ **Early Childhood Learning**
Learning centers are developed with young children in mind. *How can you tell that this learning center is for young children?*

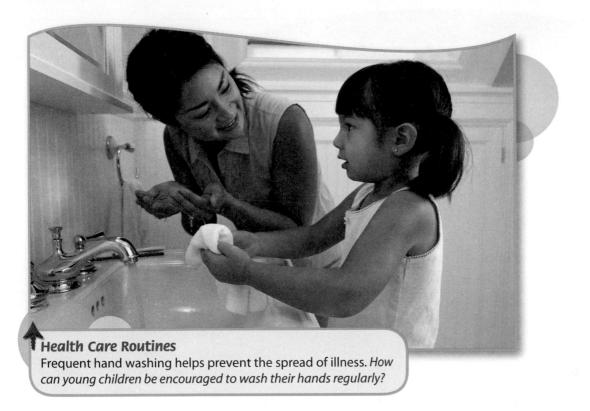

Health Care Routines
Frequent hand washing helps prevent the spread of illness. *How can young children be encouraged to wash their hands regularly?*

Health and Safety

Ensuring the health and safety of the children in the classroom is the most important responsibility of teachers and other child care providers. They must follow health care routines to prevent illness, make sure the environment is safe, and supervise play.

Health Care Routines

Health care routines prevent the spread of illness. Early childhood classrooms usually have strict policies regarding illness and attendance. For example, many early childhood programs do not allow sick children to stay in the classroom. They also ask that sick children be free of fever for at least 24 hours before returning to the classroom.

As children enter the classroom, staff members look for obvious signs of illness, such as a runny nose or fever. Children who are sick or become sick in the classroom will not be allowed to stay with the group. The child's parent or another caregiver will be called to pick the child up. If a major illness, such as chicken pox, occurs, all parents should be notified.

SAFE CHILD HEALTHY CHILD

Food Safety Routines

To prevent cases of food-related illness, child care workers need to follow careful routines when handling food. Their main concerns are to keep eating areas clean and to store foods at safe temperatures.

Eating areas should be thoroughly washed with warm water and food-safe disinfectant both before and after the children eat. The sponges or cloths used to clean these surfaces need to be cleaned and disinfected regularly.

A child care center that serves meals and snacks must follow strict standards when preparing and serving food. Centers that serve food must be licensed and are subject to regular safety and sanitation inspections.

Be Prepared Observe the cafeteria in your own school. Look for things such as cleanliness of the equipment, freshness of the food, and food handling procedures. Write an evaluation of the attention paid to food safety routines.

Figure
22.4

Learning Centers in the Early Childhood Classroom

Early childhood classrooms may have some or all of the learning centers shown here. *What might a child find in the music center?*

1 Block Center

This area may include small and large blocks, building logs, trucks and cars, and people and animal figures. Placing a rug or carpeting on the floor in the block center cuts down on noise.

2 Dramatic Play Center

This area provides children with opportunities for make-believe play. It can include clothes for dressing up, a play kitchen, and materials that can be used to play office or grocery store.

9 Art Center

The art center allows children to be creative and exercise their imaginations through drawing, painting, and working with clay and fabric. It should include paper, scissors, glue, crayons, paints, chalk, clay, and fabric. There should be smocks for children to wear when they work with these materials.

8 Active Play Area

Children exercise their large muscles in the active play area. It can include streamers for tossing; bean bags; areas for climbing, tumbling, and sliding; and a work bench for hammering.

3 Music Center

The music center can include musical instruments such as tambourines, finger cymbals, triangles, and drums. It can also include a piano or keyboard and CDs.

4 Math and Science Center

In this area, children can learn math concepts such as matching, sorting, classifying, and counting. They can also learn about colors, sizes, and shapes. Children can explore their world using science tools such as magnifying glasses, scales, and magnets. Specimens of natural objects, such as rocks, leaves, or a hamster, help children experience the world around them.

5 Computer Center

Children can learn basic computer skills. A wide variety of educational software programs can help children practice specific skills.

6 Language Arts Center

This area includes materials related to speaking, listening, reading, and writing. It should be a quiet area with good lighting and comfortable chairs or pillows.

7 Director's Office

Large, one-way observation windows allow the program director to handle paperwork and meet with parents while viewing the children. Parents might use this observation area to check on their child's progress.

Parents or other caregivers should receive a written copy of the center's health policies. Having the rules in writing helps to prevent misunderstandings about when children should stay home and how illnesses will be handled if they occur when the child is in the classroom.

Careful hand washing is one of the best ways to prevent the spread of illness. Hands need to be washed after using the toilet; after blowing the nose; and before cooking, eating, or playing with materials such as clay. Children should be taught to wash their own hands thoroughly with warm water and soap and to dry them with a clean paper towel.

Child care providers also must wash their own hands often, especially after helping children in the bathroom and before preparing food. This helps protect everyone's health and sets a good example for the children.

Other good health habits that caregivers can teach children include:

- Blowing and wiping their noses and disposing of the tissue.
- Covering their mouths when they cough.
- Using only their own comb, brush, or headwear. They should never use those of another child.
- Avoiding sharing of food and eating utensils.

Safety

To keep children safe, caregivers must create a safe environment, practice and teach safe behaviors, and know what to do in an emergency. A safe environment takes into account the age and developmental levels of the children using it. Playground equipment suitable for preschoolers, for example, could be hazardous for younger children. Older children also should have equipment suitable for their age group.

The classroom and outdoor play areas, and all equipment, should be inspected regularly for possible safety hazards such as uncovered electrical outlets or cords, and broken toys. Toys and equipment should be cleaned regularly to help prevent the spreading of germs and illnesses.

An important part of keeping children safe is to provide close supervision at all times. There should always be an adequate number of adults present to watch the children in each area. If there is an emergency, an adult should stay with the children in the classroom while another adult goes for help.

✓ Reading Check **Explain** What can caregivers do to keep the child care environment safe?

Planning Appropriate Activities

Planning plays an important role in providing appropriate learning experiences for young children. The daily schedule should provide a variety of types of activities. There are several factors to consider when planning the activities. Activities need to provide opportunities in each area of development. Of course, activities also must be appropriate to the age and skill levels of the children, too.

Learning Through Play

Young children learn primarily through play. When planning activities for them, it is important to remember that the more involved the children are and the more realistic their experiences are, the more they learn. For example, reading children a story about a fire truck can help them learn about fire safety and community helpers. However, reading the book becomes a much more powerful learning tool when followed by a trip to the fire station and a chance to climb aboard a real fire truck.

Of course, children cannot go on field trips every day, so care providers need to find other ways to help them experience what they are learning. Children need play experiences that focus on these areas of development:

- Thinking and problem solving
- Movement of large and small muscles
- Creativity, including music, dance, art, and dramatic play
- Relationships with others

Children need a variety of activities that involve different experiences. When several children sit at a table and work on separate puzzles, they are playing individually alongside one another. If they work on the same puzzle, they practice teamwork and getting along with others. Sometimes children play alone, such as when they look at a book by themselves. When the teacher reads the book to the group and they talk about it, they experience the same book in a different way. Children also play in small groups, perhaps dressing up and pretending to be a family. A teacher can guide group music or movement activities. The entire class may also come together at circle time. **Circle time** is when the children share their experiences in show-and-tell or listen to a story together.

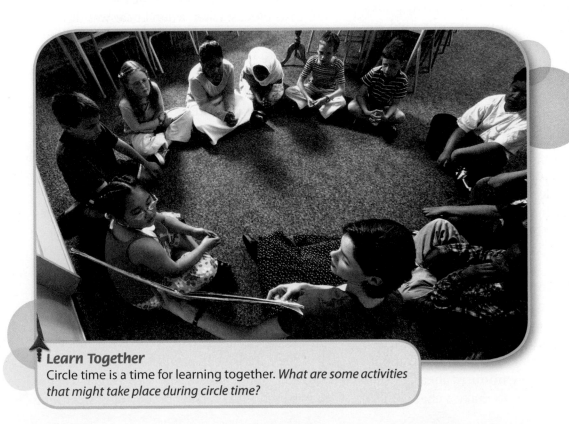

Learn Together
Circle time is a time for learning together. *What are some activities that might take place during circle time?*

Learning Through PLAY

Play in a Montessori School

What is a morning like in a typical child care facility? A child might spend 15 minutes at the science center and then 15 minutes at the language arts center. Then the child might be able to play for 15 minutes in the center of the room. However, all early childhood centers are not structured this way. In a Montessori early childhood room, you would also find learning centers, but they would be called work areas. And children are free to move from area to area at their own will. That is, they do not wait for a caregiver to tell them to move to a different area. The Montessori method of teaching is named after Italian educator Maria Montessori. Her philosophy of education was that when children play purposefully, such as when they play with math manipulatives, they are learning.

Think About It Imagine that you want to put your young son in a child care facility. Would you choose a Montessori school? What questions would you consider to help you make your decision? Write a half-page essay that includes your answer and the reasons behind your decision.

Daily Schedule

The daily schedule is the plan for how children will spend their time in the early childhood classroom. A good schedule for young children features a balance of active and quiet activities and small- and large-group activities. It should also have both teacher-directed and child-selected activities. **Free play** is a time when children can choose any activity they want. Here is a sample schedule for a three-hour session for four-year-olds:

8:30–8:45 Arrival and free play
8:45–9:15 Circle time
9:15–9:45 Learning centers
9:45–10:00 Toilet and hand washing
10:00–10:15 Snack
10:15–10:45 Outdoor play
10:45–11:15 Learning centers
11:15–11:30 Group time and goodbyes

A good daily schedule allows time for transitions. A **transition** is a period during which children move from one activity to the next. During a transition, the children need to finish one activity, put their materials away, and get ready for the next activity. Children should always be warned a few minutes ahead of time that they will soon have to make a change. This helps them mentally prepare for the change and encourages cooperation.

Lucas was happily playing with the blocks. When the teacher said it was time to go wash for snack time, Lucas got upset. He was not finished building his tower and he did not want to leave the blocks. Later, when Lucas was drawing in the art center, the teacher told him he had five minutes to finish his drawing and put the crayons away. Lucas then knew he was almost out of time and happily put the finishing touches on his drawing before cleaning up to leave. The advance warning that it was almost time to go gave Lucas the transition he needed.

Activity Plans

A daily schedule outlines the children's day in general. The lead teacher then plans the specific activities that children will do in the learning centers and during circle time or other group times. There are at least two types of forms that many teachers use to write these plans.

The first form is called the planning chart. This is based on the daily schedule. This form lists the activities that will take place in each learning center during the day. Roger teaches in a preschool and he is preparing a weeklong planning chart based on the daily schedule shown for a three-hour session. His students are currently learning about communities, so he is planning activities for each learning center that relate to this topic in some way. For example, he will have vehicles used by various community workers added to the block center. He will have dress-up clothes for different community members in the dramatic play center. Roger plans to read stories about communities during circle time.

The second form is called an activity plan. This form allows teachers to record detailed information about each planned activity. On this form, teachers include specific information under the following headings:

- Title of the activity
- Objective, or purpose, of the activity
- Type of activity—for a learning center, small group, or large group
- Materials needed
- Procedures
- Evaluation—a recap of the success and challenges with the activity

When Rajee created her activity plan for the following day, it included much more detail than Roger's planning chart. Rajee noted that the children would be making finger puppets to work on their fine motor skills. She noted that the activity would be done with a small group. Rajee also listed that she would need several colors of construction paper, scissors, tape, markers, glitter, glue, and fabric for creating the puppets. She typed up and neatly printed step-by-step instructions for making

Parenting Skills

Choosing Early Childhood Materials

At some point, you may want to donate materials to your child's early childhood classroom. Here are some questions to ask when choosing those materials:

- **Are they safe?** Edges should be rounded rather than sharp. Art materials must be non-toxic.
- **Are they durable?** Materials and equipment should be able to withstand rough use by a group of children.
- **Are they easy to clean?** This is important in the classroom because materials are used by many children.
- **Are they appropriate?** Materials should be appropriate for both boys and girls and for different ages. They should also be free of stereotypes.
- **Are they effective?** Children should be able to learn basic concepts while using the materials.
- **Are they versatile?** Items that have more than one use are usually good choices.
- **Will they hold a child's interest?** Materials should encourage children's active play.
- **Are they enjoyable?** Children should have fun using the materials.

Take Charge *You are buying art materials for a preschool. Identify two items to buy. How well do they meet the guidelines for selection?*

the puppets that she could read to the children. She then left space on her form to complete an evaluation after the project was complete.

The forms teachers use to plan activities are less important than the fact that they make careful plans. Writing plans ahead of time helps teachers think through the appropriateness of each activity. It also provides a list of materials needed so that the activities can be set up before children arrive. Written plans can be filed for future reference and reuse. They are also an excellent way to show parents what their children do each day.

✓ Reading Check) **Explain** Why does a good daily schedule allow time for transitions?

Promoting Positive Behavior

For a classroom to function smoothly, teachers need to promote positive behavior. They must let children know what is expected of them. They must also model good behavior and use positive reinforcement when children

behave appropriately. At the same time, they need strategies for dealing with unacceptable behavior in a safe and nurturing manner. As with other caregivers, teachers must be consistent in maintaining rules.

Setting Classroom Expectations

Teachers should describe **expectations**, or expected behaviors, in positive terms. That is, they should tell the children what they should do instead of what they should not do. Each expectation should also have a clear purpose and be appropriate for the age of the children involved. The younger the child, the shorter the list of expectations should be. Younger children will also not understand all of the reasons for the expectations.

When children are old enough, it is a good idea to involve them in establishing classroom expectations. You might open the discussion by asking what they already know about appropriate behavior at home or in their community. Then they can come up with some of their own ideas for classroom expectations and the reasons why each is necessary. When children are

Positive Behavior
When positive behavior is stressed, children are more likely to be cooperative. *How should teachers describe expected behaviors?*

involved in this process, they feel more ownership in the classroom and they are more likely to meet expectations.

Some classrooms will have expectations that are specific to their facility. For example, "We do not use the back door." But there are many general expectations used by most classrooms. Here are some examples of reasonable expectations for an early childhood classroom:

- **Keep your hands to yourself.** This discourages hitting or pushing.
- **Always walk when you are inside the building.** This helps keep children calmer and prevents accidents and falls.
- **Put things away when you are finished.** This keeps the room well organized. Children are able to find materials when they want them. It also helps prevent tripping over unused toys.
- **Use your inside voice in the classroom.** This helps keep the classroom from being too noisy.
- **Be a friend to others.** This promotes cooperation and builds a pleasant atmosphere.

Using Positive Reinforcement

Children enjoy being recognized and rewarded with attention. They tend to repeat behaviors that are rewarded. To make this technique effective, however, teachers must be sincere in their response to a child's behavior. If they give only automatic or inattentive comments and praise, the children will not see them as rewards. Teachers must also be consistent. If Clay is praised for cleaning up after himself, then Nina and Alexandra should be praised for the same action.

Being a Good Role Model

In the classroom, the teacher's own behavior has a powerful influence on children. Children are more likely to do what their caregivers do. If teachers want the children to use inside voices, then they, too, must use a quiet voice indoors. If teachers want children to treat each other with kindness, they should show kindness to the children and to their coworkers. The teacher told Tyler to put away his materials. The teacher left her

Time-Outs

As a child care provider, Paige knows that one of her tasks is to help children learn what is expected of them. Paige makes sure that the children follow her directions and those of the other adults in charge. "Sometimes," she says, "I have to remind the kids to return from the playground equipment when the five-minute whistle blows. Some of them don't want to come back inside." Paige uses time-outs when children misbehave. She says, "Today one of the children kept poking another child with her paintbrushes. I had to ask her to leave the activity and take a time-out. After a few minutes, I asked her what she needed to do in order to come back. She said that she needed to say 'sorry' to the classmate she poked. She did that, and she was allowed to paint again."

Write About It Not all misbehaviors qualify for a time-out. Think of at least two misbehaviors that you feel do not qualify for a time-out. Write a half-page essay describing the misbehavior and explaining how you would handle it.

papers spread out on the table though. Tyler saw that the teacher did not clean up so he felt he did not really need to either. Remember that actions speak louder than words.

Dealing with Misbehavior

Of course, children will behave in unacceptable ways from time to time. All adults in the classroom need to know in advance how they will handle such situations. The children should also understand what will happen if they misbehave. Cases of misbehavior must be handled consistently in each situation and with each child.

In most cases, a simple statement of what the child should do is an effective way of dealing with misbehavior. If Jesse is using his voice too loudly, for example, he should be reminded of the expectation regarding noise level in the classroom: "Jesse, please use your inside voice. Others can't hear well when you are shouting."

In other situations, a child may be offered a choice of more acceptable activities. If Jackie is not playing well in the block center, she might be told, "Jackie, you may choose to go to the dramatic play center or the art center. You can't stay in the block center because you keep taking Emilio's blocks." Notice that each example includes an explanation of why the child's behavior was unacceptable.

For some types of unacceptable behavior, a stronger response is necessary. Behavior that could hurt other people or damage property must not be permitted at any time. Children who exhibit this type of behavior should receive an immediate and consistent response. One effective approach is to give the child a time-out. This is a set time away from the activity or other children. When a time-out is used, the caregiver should continue to show the child that he or she is cared for but that the actions are not acceptable. For more information about time-outs, see page 79.

{ **Expert Advice...** }

"No school can work well for children if parents and teachers do not act in partnership on behalf of the children's best interests."

— Dorothy H. Cohen, educator and child development specialist

Section 22.2   After You Read

Review Key Concepts

1. **Explain** why child care centers need written policies concerning sick children.
2. **Describe** how writing activity plans can help teachers educate young children.
3. **List** three examples of clearly stated behavior expectations for an early childhood classroom.

Practice Academic Skills

 English Language Arts

4. Think about methods that you might use to teach a group of young children about fire safety. Separate the methods into two groups— active and passive. Create a list for each method to share with the rest of the class.

> **NCTE 12** Use language to accomplish individual purposes.

 Science

5. Imagine that a third grade student visits the child care center where you work. The young student does not understand why everyone washes their hands so often. Write a dialogue between you and the child in which you explain why regular hand washing is important in a child care setting.

> **NSES F** Develop understanding of personal and community health.

 Check Your Answers Check your answers at this book's Online Learning Center at **glencoe.com**.

Chapter Summary

Substitute care for children may be provided in a home- or center-based setting. Home-based care options include in-home care, family child care, and play groups. Center-based care options include child care centers, parent cooperatives, preschools, and Head Start centers. When choosing substitute care, it is important to carefully evaluate choices.

A typical early childhood classroom includes different learning centers. Caregivers' primary duty is for the health and safety of the children in their care. A daily schedule and written plans help ensure good learning experiences. Rules and positive reinforcement help promote appropriate behavior.

Vocabulary Review

1. Write a sentence using two or more of these vocabulary terms. The sentence should clearly show how the terms are related.

Content Vocabulary
◇ child care center (p. 603)
◇ in-home care (p. 603)
◇ family child care (p. 603)
◇ nanny (p. 604)
◇ license (p. 604)
◇ accreditation (p. 604)
◇ play group (p. 604)
◇ parent cooperative (p. 605)
◇ Head Start (p. 606)
◇ learning center (p. 614)
◇ circle time (p. 619)
◇ free play (p. 620)
◇ transition (p. 620)

Academic Vocabulary
■ socialize (p. 604)
■ criteria (p. 605)
■ self-sufficiency (p. 614)
■ expectation (p. 622)

Review Key Concepts

2. Describe two types of substitute care for younger children.
3. List questions a parent should ask when choosing home-based care.
4. Describe the benefits of having learning centers in early childhood classrooms.
5. Explain the factors to consider when planning activities.
6. Identify methods for promoting positive behavior in the classroom.

Critical Thinking

7. Analyze Which five questions would you rank as most important when evaluating substitute child care? Explain your answers.
8. Infer Why do you think it is more effective to tell children what they should do, rather than what they should not do?
9. Examine For young children, play is a learning experience. Provide examples of how children learn through play.
10. Differentiate What is the difference between a child care center that is licensed and one that is accredited?

Chapter 22 Review and Applications

Family & Community Connection

11. Interview a Child Care Worker Interview a home-based or center-based child care worker. Prepare questions ahead of time. Questions should ask for information about how the children interact with one another and with the care providers. Use your notes to create a paper in question and answer format to share with classmates. Be sure to include the ages of the children in your answers.

Health Skills

12. Research Health Issues Use print or online resources to research common health issues that must be dealt with by child care workers. Create a chart in which you list the health issue, how it is spread, and prevention techniques.

Observation Skills

13. Observe a Child Care Center Work with your teacher to arrange a visit to a child care center. You might want to observe at either a Montessori child care center or a traditional child care center.

Procedure During your visit, observe the learning opportunities offered to children in the learning centers or the work areas. Note how the children respond to the learning opportunities offered.

Analysis Organize your notes in a three-column table in which you list the learning center, the learning opportunities offered, and the children's responses to the learning opportunities.

> **NCSS IV D Individual Development and Identity**
> Apply concepts, methods, and theories about the study of human growth and development, such as learning, motivation, behavior, and personality.

Real-World Skills

Interpersonal and Collaborative Skills

14. Work Together Work with a partner to develop a floor plan for a child care center. Your space is 50 feet wide and 100 feet long. Decide what centers to include and how much space to use for each center. Include space for group activities and office space.

Technology Skills

15. Create a Brochure Imagine that you are starting your own home-based child care service. Use word-processing software to create a brochure advertising your service. Be sure to provide information parents will want to know such as the child-to-caregiver provider ratio and learning opportunities.

Financial Literacy

16. Calculate Income Imagine that you care for four children in a home-based child care service and charge $30 a day per child. You pay $80 a week for meals and spend $675 a year on equipment. How much money will you make in a year, if all four children come five days a week?

 Additional Activities For additional activities, go to this book's Online Learning Center at **glencoe.com**.

Academic Skills

English Language Arts

17. Determine Quality Care Several studies have found that the quality of care a child receives plays a major role in his or her development. Conduct research to find the characteristics of quality care provided in early childhood classrooms and to evaluate its effects on child development. Present your findings in a one-page essay.

> **NCTE 7** Conduct research and gather, evaluate, and synthesize data to communicate discoveries.

Mathematics

18. Child Care Costs Early care and education for a four-year-old in a child care center in an urban area averages $5,790 per year. How much would a family have to save weekly to pay for child care?

Math Concept **Multistep Problems** When solving problems with more than one step, think through each step first.

Starting Hint First, convert one year into weeks (52). Then divide the total cost by the number of weeks. Be sure the decimal point is in the correct place in your answer.

 For math help, go to the Math Appendix at the back of the book.

> **NCTM Number and Operations** Compute fluently and make reasonable estimates.

Science

19. Research Computer Use Children are learning to use computers much earlier than in previous years. Many child care centers for young children have computers and encourage the children to use them as part of their daily activities.

Procedure Research the various ways computers are used in early childhood classrooms.

Analysis Write a one-page report that discusses the impact computer use might have on small and large motor skill development.

> **NSES C** Students should develop understanding of the cell; biological evolution; matter, energy, and organization in living systems; and behavior of organisms.

Standardized Test Practice

MULTIPLE CHOICE

Read the passage, then answer the question.

Children enjoy being recognized and rewarded with attention. They tend to repeat behaviors that are rewarded. To make this technique effective, however, teachers must be sincere in their response to a child's behavior. If they give only automatic or inattentive comments and praise, the children will not see them as rewards. Teachers must also be consistent.

20. According to the passage, teachers
   a. must be sincere when rewarding behavior.
   b. should respond to a child's behavior.
   c. must be sincere and consistent when rewarding behavior.
   d. should give automatic praise to children.

> **Test-Taking Tip** Be sure to read the directions carefully. If you are asked to choose the best answer, there may be more than one *correct* answer from which to choose.

Chapter Objectives

After completing this chapter, you will be able to:

- **Describe** three different ways to gain work experience.
- **Identify** factors to consider when evaluating careers.
- **Explain** the relationship between a career goal and a career path.
- **List** six steps involved in a job search.
- **Compare and contrast** job-specific skills and transferable skills.
- **Summarize** an employee's responsibilities when leaving a job.

Writing Activity ✎ *Business Letter*

Volunteering Think of a volunteer position that might interest you, such as being an assistant soccer coach or working in a day care. Write a business letter to the individual in charge of this position explaining why you feel you would be a good choice for this position.

Writing Tips If you are going to succeed in your career, you must be able to create a well-written business letter. Here are some tips to keep in mind:

1. Address the letter to a specific person, if possible.
2. Explain the purpose of the letter clearly.
3. Be brief and to-the-point.

Section 23.1 Preparing for a Career

Section 23.2 Beginning Your Career

Explore the Photo
Large numbers of adults have jobs that involve working directly with children. *Why do you think people might choose these careers?*

Reading Guide

Before You Read

Study New Terms This section contains a variety of terms. Spend a minute skimming the section and reading the definition of each term. As you thoroughly read the section, you will better understand its main points.

Read to Learn
Key Concepts
- **Describe** three different ways to gain work experience.
- **Identify** factors to consider when evaluating careers.
- **Explain** the relationship between a career goal and a career path.

Main Idea
You are most likely to thrive in a career that matches your interests, aptitudes, and abilities. When choosing a career, you should consider factors such as work environment and the required education.

Content Vocabulary
◇ entry-level job ◇ job shadowing
◇ paraprofessional ◇ service learning
◇ professional ◇ work-based learning
◇ entrepreneur ◇ career path
◇ aptitude ◇ career ladder
◇ internship

Academic Vocabulary
You will find these words in your reading and on your tests. Use the glossary to look up their definitions if necessary.
- ability
- visualization

Graphic Organizer
As you read, note the four steps in choosing a career. Use a chart like the one shown to help organize your information.

 Graphic Organizer Go to this book's Online Learning Center at **glencoe.com** to print out this graphic organizer.

Academic Standards •

📖 English Language Arts
NCTE 1 Read texts to acquire new information.

🌐 Social Studies
NCSS I A Culture Analyze and explain the ways groups, societies, and cultures address human needs and concerns.

NCSS I D Culture Compare and analyze societal patterns for preserving and transmitting culture while adapting to environmental or societal change.

NCTE *National Council of Teachers of English*
NCTM *National Council of Teachers of Mathematics*

NSES *National Science Education Standards*
NCSS *National Council for the Social Studies*

Career Options

Choosing a career may seem like a hard decision. There are many jobs to choose from. Where do you begin? Most people start by choosing a career area or career field. This is a group of similar careers. Once they have learned more about the career field, they can choose a specific career to prepare for.

Taking a class in an area of interest is a good way to explore career options. Perhaps you are taking this class because you are interested in working with children. The knowledge and skills gained in this class will help prepare you to make a choice that is right for you.

Working with Children

Those interested in working directly with children often choose careers related to child development or child care. A pediatrician, for example, specializes in medical care for children. In-depth knowledge of child development and medicine are required. A lead teacher in a child care center needs to know about child development to plan appropriate activities and care.

Many careers may not immediately come to mind when you think of working with children. Here are some specialized careers that may interest you:
- Wildlife educator
- Emergency medical technician
- Adoption consultant
- Child development researcher
- Puppeteer
- Occupational therapist
- Play therapist

Look for the Careers with Children features throughout this book for profiles of additional careers that involve working with children.

Levels of Jobs

Within a career area, there are usually jobs available at several levels. These levels depend on the amount of education and training required and the degree of responsibility the job carries.

Entry-Level

An **entry-level job** is the kind of job many people take when they first enter a career area. Most people, however, do not stay at this level. With more experience or education, many move up to jobs with more responsibility. After he received his high school diploma, Russell took an entry-level job at a child care center to explore his interest in helping children. Within a few years, and after earning a degree from a four-year college program, he had moved into a lead teacher position at the center.

Paraprofessional

A **paraprofessional** is someone with some education beyond high school that trains him or her for a certain field. Many paraprofessional jobs require a related degree from a two-year college. An assistant teacher in a preschool, for instance, is a paraprofessional.

Working with Children
People who work with children need to understand child development. *How can an understanding of child development help this teacher do her job?*

Professional

A **professional** has a position that requires at least a degree from a four-year college or technical school in a specific area of study. Many professionals have a more advanced degree, such as a master's degree, and years of experience. Professionals may be in charge of programs or supervise entry-level workers and paraprofessionals. Kindergarten teachers are professionals.

Entrepreneurs

Most people work for someone else. For example, an elementary teacher works for a school district, a toy designer works for a manufacturer. Someone who chooses to be self-employed or to own his or her own business is an **entrepreneur** (ˌän-trə-p(r)ə-ˈnər). An entrepreneur's life can be both exciting and challenging.

Because entrepreneurs have no boss, they get to make the rules, set their own schedules, and make the decisions. However, they also assume all the risks of the business and often end up working very long hours. People who are self-employed must be self-motivated, self-disciplined, good problem solvers, and willing to work hard.

There are many entrepreneurial opportunities related to children. Examples include owning a daycare, writing children's books, or providing entertainment for children's parties. The best entrepreneurs develop businesses around their own personal interests and skills. For example, a children's book author must truly enjoy writing and be able to look at the world from a child's point of view.

Many entrepreneurs start out working for others, and gradually establish their own businesses. After finishing college, a music teacher may work for a public school and then start teaching private lessons. Finally, she might be established enough to open her own studio. Entrepreneurs have the reward of knowing they have succeeded on their own.

Evaluate Interests, Aptitudes, and Abilities

When choosing a career, make sure the job will be a good fit for you. Some careers may sound exciting, but when you look at them more closely, you might realize that they would not be right for you. As you explore various career choices, you need to consider them in light of your own interests and values, aptitudes, and abilities.

Interests and Values

If you work toward a career that does not match your interests, it could set you up for years of unfulfilling work. Your interests might include areas of study that you enjoy, such as psychology or science, or activities that you enjoy, such as photography or music. You also need to consider your values. What is important to you? Do you want a career that pays a high salary? Are you concerned about gaining satisfaction from your work? Are you willing to work weekends or long hours, or is time with family and friends more important?

Aptitudes

An **aptitude** is a natural talent or potential for learning a skill. What kinds of learning come most easily to you? Perhaps you have an aptitude for communicating with young children or learning new computer programs. High school counselors have tests that can help you decide what your aptitudes are. You should consider careers that match your strengths.

Abilities

An **ability** is a skill you have already developed. Identifying what your skills are can help you make career decisions. As you begin to take on more responsibilities, you can expand and improve your abilities. This includes skills specific to career areas that interest you and general skills, such as teamwork or reliability.

Find Career Information

Another important part of career decision making is research. Learning more about areas that interest you will help you narrow your choices. The Career Skills Handbook in the back of this textbook offers valuable tips on career research.

Gather Information

You can gather information from a variety of sources. Online sources, libraries, and people can all be helpful. The Internet can put you in touch with trade and professional organizations, government resources, job listings, and people working in various careers. Most libraries have excellent career information resources. These two government publications are available in print and online:

- *The Occupational Outlook Handbook* gives detailed information on hundreds of jobs.
- *The Occupational Outlook Quarterly* updates information on career trends every three months.

Probably the best way to find out what a career is really like is to talk to people who are in that career. After all, who knows better than a teacher what the day-to-day life of a teacher is like? You can ask school counselors, teachers, relatives, and friends about possible contacts in specific career areas. Most people are happy to share information about their careers.

Career Fair
There are many opportunities for learning more about career areas. *What kinds of questions might these teens ask a potential employer?*

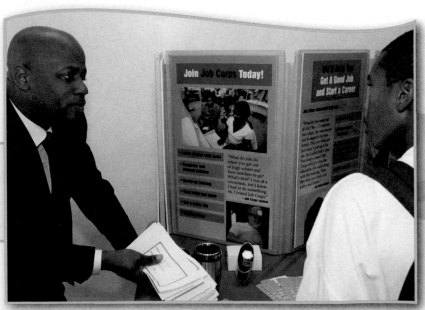

Gain Work Experience

You can learn a lot about a career, and about yourself, by working. Summer work and part-time jobs are good ways to get started. Another way to learn about a job is through an internship. An **internship** is a job in which a person works for little or no pay while gaining experience and receiving supervision. For example, you might get an internship with a coach at a recreational facility such as a YMCA.

You might also be able to arrange to do job shadowing. **Job shadowing** means to observe someone performing his or her job. You would need to contact someone whose career interests you and arrange to spend time at work with that person, following the person around like a shadow. Your guidance counselor may be able to help you make arrangements for job-shadowing experiences. Job shadowing is especially helpful in specialized fields, such as pediatrics, because it allows you to see the variety of skills the professional must have.

Another way to learn about a career is by volunteering. Many organizations, especially those that operate on limited funds, welcome volunteers. The opportunities may be temporary or longer term. Arielle volunteers as a children's storyteller at her local library once a month, while Isaac volunteers as an assistant for children's activities at a city park each weekend. Guidance counselors often have a list of organizations looking for volunteers. Community centers are also a good resource for volunteering opportunities.

Although volunteers are not paid for their work, volunteering offers a great experience. It may even lead to a paying job. One added benefit of volunteering is the satisfaction of helping others in the community. In addition, colleges and employers are impressed by people who make the effort to help out in their community through volunteer work.

Some school programs offer direct work experience. **Service learning** is a school program in which students volunteer in their community as a graduation requirement. **Work-based learning** is a school program that offers students the opportunity to combine in-school and on-the-job learning.

Work experience offers another benefit besides a feel for what it is like to have a job. You may meet people who know someone in the career area that interests you. Supervisors and coworkers may also be willing to serve as references whom a prospective employer can contact for information about your skills and character.

✓ **Reading Check** **Define** What is an ability?

Volunteer Work
You can gain valuable work experience by volunteering. *What are some benefits of getting work experience while you are still in school?*

Evaluate Careers

Knowing where to look for career information is one thing, but then what? There are many factors to consider when choosing a career. Following is a list of some of the most important factors to consider. Can you think of others?

- **Tasks and Responsibilities** What does a worker in this career do? Is the work the same every day or is it varied? Is the pace fast or slow? How much control does an employee have over the work? Is the work mostly physical or mental? Child care workers have a very active work environment. They spend the day playing, leading activities, cleaning spills, and running after children. A child development researcher may spend time observing children but will probably not interact with them. A researcher's job generally involves very little physical activity.

- **Work with People, Information, or Technology** Each career tends to emphasize one area over another. Which do you prefer? A reading teacher works mainly with people. An editor of children's books works mainly with information. A designer of children's clothing works mainly with technology.

- **Work Environment** The work environment is the physical and social surroundings at the workplace. Camp counselors and coaches work outdoors. Nurses and teachers work indoors. Social workers spend a majority of their day in their cars driving to meet different clients in their homes. Some people work alone. Others work in teams. Workers in runaway youth shelters must often deal with children who have psychological or behavioral problems. Child care workers can work in small day care centers; in a private home; or in spacious, well-funded, private nursery schools. Which kind of environment is most appealing to you?

- **Working Hours** Many people work from 9:00 in the morning to 5:00 at night. Many others work different hours. Many social service workers or suicide-prevention hotline workers need to work through the night. Some jobs, like storyteller or magician, require weekend and holiday work. Many jobs require overtime or travel. What is acceptable to you?

- **Aptitudes** Compare the aptitudes needed for a career with your own aptitudes. How well do they match?

- **Education and Training** Although many people gain experience on the job, they need the right education to land that job in the first place. What education and training are required for the careers that interest you? School counselors, libraries, and the Internet offer information about education and training opportunities beyond high school, as well as ways to pay for them.

What Would You Do?

Work or College?

Twenty-year-old Patrick has worked in a drop-in center for runaway and homeless teens for four years. He loves the job. When new clients come in, he makes sure they have a meal, learn their way around the center, and get counseling if needed. Patrick knows that he wants a career that involves helping people, so three years ago he enrolled part-time at a nearby community college and studied for an associate's degree in human services. He will finish his degree in a few months and is considering whether to continue his studies. With a bachelor's degree in social work, he could get a higher-paying job with more responsibility. He could even work as a school social worker or probation officer. On the other hand, it would mean going to college full time and giving up his current job that he enjoys.

Write About It Put yourself in Patrick's position. You must decide whether to keep your job at the drop-in center, which you really enjoy, or continue on in school to get a bachelor's degree in social work. Write a paragraph explaining which decision you would make and why.

- **Salary and Benefits** Income generally increases with training and education. Income also tends to rise as workers gain experience. A first-year paraprofessional can expect to earn less than a coworker with five years in the same job. Many employers offer benefits such as paid holidays, health insurance, retirement plans, and paid vacation time. These benefits are in addition to the regular salary.
- **Career Outlook** What do experts think will happen to this career in the future? Will the demand for the career grow or shrink? Answers to these questions affect how easy it will be to find a job in certain career areas. Many sources estimate future trends for various jobs.

✓ **Reading Check** **Recall** Give examples of three kinds of benefits.

Setting and Achieving Goals

Some people simply take whatever job comes their way. While this approach sometimes works out, it is much smarter to think carefully about the career you would like and then work to achieve it. After all, you will spend most of your waking hours at work. Would it be better if that work were satisfying, challenging, and worthwhile? Establishing career goals can help you achieve this.

Career goals are like a road map to your future. As with other goals, you need both long-term and short-term career goals. If you decide that you want a career as a kindergarten teacher, that is your long-term goal. Getting there will take years and require many smaller achievements. To reach your long-term goal, you will need short-term goals. These are specific actions to achieve in the next few days, months, or year. Without short-term goals, it is less likely that you will achieve your long-term goal.

Lynette's goal was to become a physical therapist. To help achieve that long-term goal, she set a short-term goal of working with children on a daily basis to make certain she would

like that aspect of the career. Through her job as a camp counselor, she met that goal.

There are two basic types of career goals: general and specific. General career goals are goals for the type of work you want to do. Some examples of general career goals are "I want to work with children," or "I want to work outdoors." Specific career goals are goals for the specific job you want. For example, "I want to be a preschool teacher," or "I want to write children's books." If your career goal is too general, you will not know where to start. Make your goal more specific. The more specific and realistic your goals are, the more likely you will be to achieve them.

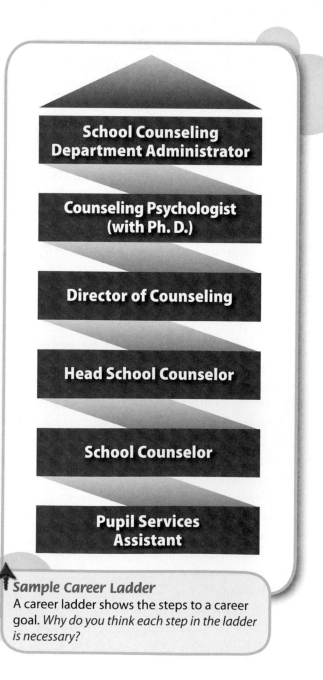

Sample Career Ladder
A career ladder shows the steps to a career goal. *Why do you think each step in the ladder is necessary?*

Setting a Career Path

Once you have chosen a specific career goal, you must look ahead and consider your career path. A **career path** is all of the career moves and job experience that a person gains as he or she works toward a career goal. There are usually many steps to reaching your final career goal.

For a career in social work, for example, you might begin as a caseworker. Caseworkers help clients get the assistance they need. As you gain experience in this position, you might take on more clients and begin to supervise other caseworkers. With more experience and education, such as a master's degree in social work, you could begin supervising other caseworkers. As you learn more on the job and gain more experience, you might be promoted to executive director of your agency.

A **career ladder** is a visualization of your chosen career path. A **visualization** is a mental image. This helps you see where you currently are in reaching your goals. It also helps you decide what your next career step might be.

Modifying Goals

Your career plan is not set in stone. Your goals and the time you spend on them may change over time. You must face your future with an open mind. The motivation to achieve your goals comes from within. If you are not reaching your goals, do not lose motivation. Figure out why you are stuck. You might need to revise your goals to renew your motivation.

The most important thing is to have a plan. Without a plan, you just have an idea or a dream. With a plan, you are moving toward your ultimate career goal, step by step. You will find the career that is right for you.

Section 23.1   After You Read

Review Key Concepts

1. **Explain** why you should evaluate your interests, aptitudes, and abilities when researching careers.
2. **Describe** some of the benefits of gaining work experience through part-time and volunteer work.
3. **Identify** why it is important to have short-term goals.

Practice Academic Skills

 English Language Arts

4. Locate and read at least three different articles on service learning programs and the types of volunteer projects students have worked on. Use what you learn from the articles to write a persuasive essay in support of service learning.

> **NCTE 3** Apply strategies to interpret texts.

 Social Studies

5. Some organizations are devoted to teaching cultural heritages to young people. For example, a summer camp might teach Native American traditions. Research such an organization. Write a brief summary of the skills an individual would need to work for this organization.

> **NCSS I D** Compare and analyze societal patterns for preserving and transmitting culture while adapting to environmental or societal change.

Check Your Answers Check your answers at this book's Online Learning Center at **glencoe.com**.

Reading Guide

Before You Read

Find Answers Before reading this section, write down what you would like to learn about looking for a job. When you are done, determine whether your questions were answered.

Read to Learn
Key Concepts
- **List** six steps involved in a job search.
- **Compare and contrast** job-specific skills and transferable skills.
- **Summarize** an employee's responsibilities when leaving a job.

Main Idea
When looking for a job, it is important to be resourceful. A well-written résumé and cover letter show your professionalism and abilities. Always be prepared when going for a job interview.

Content Vocabulary
◇ networking
◇ job fair
◇ résumé
◇ cover letter
◇ job-specific skills
◇ transferable skills
◇ ethical
◇ lifelong learner
◇ unemployment benefits
◇ COBRA

 Graphic Organizer Go to this book's Online Learning Center at **glencoe.com** to print out this graphic organizer.

Academic Vocabulary
You will find these words in your reading and on your tests. Use the glossary to look up their definitions if necessary.
■ convey
■ legible

Graphic Organizer
As you read this section, look for seven transferable skills, or skills that are useful in any job. Use a web diagram like the one shown to help organize your information.

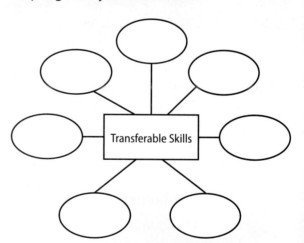

Transferable Skills

Academic Standards . . . .

 English

NCTE 12 Use language to accomplish individual purposes.

 Mathematics

NCTM Number and Operations Understand numbers, ways of representing numbers, relationships among numbers, and number systems.

NCTE *National Council of Teachers of English*
NCTM *National Council of Teachers of Mathematics*

NSES *National Science Education Standards*
NCSS *National Council for the Social Studies*

Look for a Job

A few people find themselves in the right place at the right time and are hired for their dream job. Others are fortunate to have an internship or a part-time job turn into a full-time position. Most people, however, must devote a lot of time and effort to their job search. You should plan to invest time and energy in your own job search. After all, you will be spending many hours at work each week. It is worth the effort to find the right job.

As with all major goals, it is best to break down job hunting into a series of smaller steps. The six steps to secure employment are finding an opening, preparing a résumé, filling out an application, interviewing, following up, and evaluating a job offer. These steps can be accomplished one at a time.

The key to a successful job search is organization. A notebook or computer file used to record names, addresses, and dates is one way many people keep track of their job search. For instance, Will uses his computer to record the dates he responds to newspaper ads, the dates employers contact him, the times and locations of his interviews, and the dates he sends follow-up letters. See the Career Skills handbook at the back of this textbook for more great tips on every step of your job search.

Find Job Openings

The Internet and classified ads from the newspaper are great ways to find job openings, but they are not your only resources. Finding a job often begins with a tip from a friend, relative, or acquaintance. That is why it is a good idea to let people know that you are job hunting. The more people who know that you are looking for a job, the better the chances are that you will find one that is right for you.

For example, Tristan's neighbor has a sister who is a Girl Scout leader. She knows that the organization will be looking for a new staff member soon. Logan's roommate knows of an opening for a teacher at the preschool where his girlfriend works. The practice of using personal and professional contacts to further your career goals is called **networking**. Many people find that networking is the best way to find a job.

Another way to find out about job openings is to attend a job fair. A **job fair** is an event where employers with current or future job openings meet with potential employees. Sometimes community colleges or universities sponsor such events. You may not land the perfect job by attending a job fair, but you will be able to make valuable contacts by meeting some employers.

Computer Resources
A computer can be used to find job openings, locate information about employers, and develop a résumé. *How might you locate information about a potential employer?*

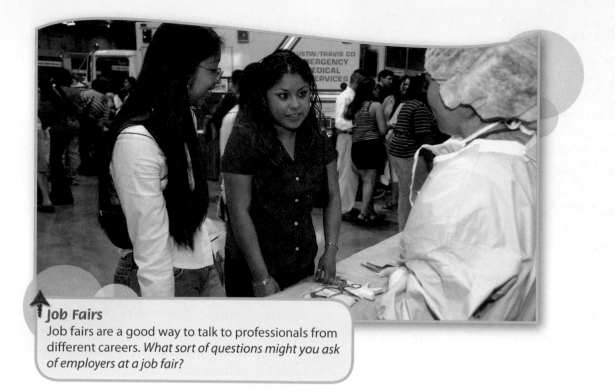

Job Fairs
Job fairs are a good way to talk to professionals from different careers. *What sort of questions might you ask of employers at a job fair?*

Prepare a Résumé

A **résumé** is a concise document that summarizes your career objectives, education, work experience, and accomplishments. It is like a personal advertisement to show prospective employers.

You should create your résumé on a computer. Many word processing programs provide sample résumés with different layouts, typefaces, and designs. Find a sample that fits your needs and customize it with your own information. The résumé in **Figure 23.1** shows the sections that are usually included.

Sections of a Résumé

The first section of the résumé is the objective. It is made up of one or two sentences that state the type of position you are seeking. It should **convey**, or express, a sense of purpose and direction. You should customize the objective for each potential employer or job listing.

In the section on education, list the schools you attended starting with the most recent, along with any degrees, honors, or awards you have received. If you have received several honors or awards, you could list them separately under Honors.

If you do not have much work experience, focus on your skills. If you have done volunteer work, include it. Volunteering shows that you are a responsible and active community member. Also include information about any committees or projects you have worked on. Here are some additional tips for preparing an effective résumé.

- Be concise, keeping the résumé to one page if possible. Two pages is the maximum length.
- Be truthful. Do not misrepresent your work history, accomplishments, or education.
- Use action verbs to describe accomplishments. Words such as achieved, developed, coordinated, produced, led, and conducted are good choices.
- Proofread the document carefully. Have someone else proofread it, too. Poor grammar or misspelled words could cause employers to remove you from consideration.
- Keep it simple. Do not clutter your résumé with pictures, graphics, or a fancy format.
- Ask any references for permission before including their names and contact information. References may be listed on your résumé or on a separate page.
- If an employer requests that your résumé be sent by e-mail, ask for formatting guidelines.

Desiray T. Minter
6412 Elmhurst Drive
Asheville, NC 28810
828.555.1234
DTM@anymail.com

Objective: To work with children as a teacher's assistant in a bilingual education program.

Education: Ashton Community College, Asheville, North Carolina
Associate in Applied Science, Child Development, 2009

Whittier High School, Asheville, North Carolina
High School Diploma, 2006

Skills: Excellent organizational skills
Fluent in Spanish and French
Able to work independently or on a team

Experience:

2006-Present Photography Assistant
Angelface Photography Studio, Asheville, North Carolina
Assist children's photographer with studio sittings; schedule appointments.

2004–2006 Foreign Language Tutor in Spanish and French
Tutored four to five high school students each semester.

2001–2003 Counselor
Far Hills Equestrian Camp, Greenville, North Carolina
Supervised eight campers each session.

Honors: FCCLA State Vice President of STAR Events, 2008
American Legion Award, 2008
National French Honor Society

Membership: Family, Career and Community Leaders of America (FCCLA)
4-H (Chairperson of Horse Leader's Conference)

References available upon request.

Figure 23.2 **Sample Cover Letter**

Cover letters should be short and clearly explain why you think you are well-qualified for the job. *What are the two ways that Desiray suggests Ms. Hansen can reach her?*

6412 Elmhurst Drive
Asheville, North Carolina 28810

June 15, 2009

Ms. Michelle Hansen
Director, Human Resources
School District 184
Asheville, North Carolina 28810

Dear Ms. Hansen:

I am replying to the ad on the Asheville Citizen-Times Web site seeking a teacher's assistant for the Bilingual Education program at the Early Childhood Education Center. I believe that my skills are an excellent match for this position.

As a high school and college student, I enjoyed courses in child development. I have successfully worked with children of all ages—as a camp counselor, tutor, and active member of FCCLA and 4-H. Currently, my job as a photography assistant involves working with preschool and elementary school children.

My other main interest is foreign languages. In 2008, I had the opportunity to participate in a month-long exchange program in Mexico. I speak fluent Spanish and have four years of credit in French. As a language student at Whittier High School, I frequently assisted with special events in an elementary school program for English-language learners.

I am available for an interview any morning of the week. The best time to reach me at home is before noon. My telephone number is 828.555.1234. My e-mail address is DTM@anymail.com. Thank you for your consideration.

Sincerely,

Desiray T. Minter

Desiray T. Minter

Write a Cover Letter

An employer may receive dozens, or even hundreds, of résumés in response to a posted advertisement. A **cover letter** is an introductory letter sent with a résumé. The cover letter is the first thing a potential employer sees, and it can make a powerful impression. An interesting cover letter can set your résumé apart from the rest and result in a request for an interview. **Figure 23.2** shows a sample cover letter.

A cover letter provides an opportunity for you to make a good impression. Your cover letter should highlight your relevant talents and skills, prompt the employer to read the résumé, and ultimately result in an interview. Your cover letter introduces you to the employer and lets you sell yourself. Tell the employer what you can do for the company.

Here are some key points to remember when writing a cover letter:

- Highlight your skills and background but do not repeat everything in the résumé.
- Limit the letter to one page.
- Be sure the letter fits the particular situation. If you are answering an ad, for example, be sure to address the requirements cited in the ad. Always begin the letter with a sentence stating where you heard of the job opening.
- Try to address the letter to an individual rather than "To Whom It May Concern." It is often possible to call the employer to obtain the name of a contact person or the person's title. This information may also be on an employer's Web site.
- End your letter with a request for an interview.
- As with the résumé, make sure your spelling and grammar are flawless.
- Use high-quality white or cream paper. When you sign your name, make certain that it is **legible**, or readable, and signed in black ink.
- Include a cover letter when sending a résumé by e-mail.
- Read and re-read your letter to make sure each sentence is correctly worded and there are no errors in spelling, punctuation, or grammar.

Job Interview

Greg was nervous about going on an interview. Although he had just received a four-year degree in physical education, he still was not sure at what level he wanted to teach. His career counselor at college suggested that he apply for a variety of jobs. That day, Greg was on his way to an interview for an elementary physical education teacher position. He arrived a bit early and went to the school office to check in. The secretary told him to take a seat. The principal called Greg into his office and asked him about his education, his experience, and his desire to teach physical education. Then he took Greg on a tour of the school. Greg told the principal that he hoped to hear from him soon.

Write About It Imagine that you are this school's principal. Write a list of eight specific questions you would ask Greg to determine whether he was a good candidate for this job.

Fill Out an Application

Most employers ask applicants to fill out a job application. An application is a tool that helps employers decide who deserves further consideration. Follow these tips for filling out an application:

- If you have an appointment, arrive on time or a few minutes early.
- Be well groomed and neatly dressed when you go to fill out an application, or to pick up or deliver an application.
- Read and follow the directions on the application carefully. If it is an electronic application, make sure you know how to use the computer before you start.
- Print neatly or type carefully, and answer questions truthfully and as positively as possible. If a question does not apply, write NA, for not applicable, in the space.
- Some applications ask for salary requirements. "Negotiable" is a good response.

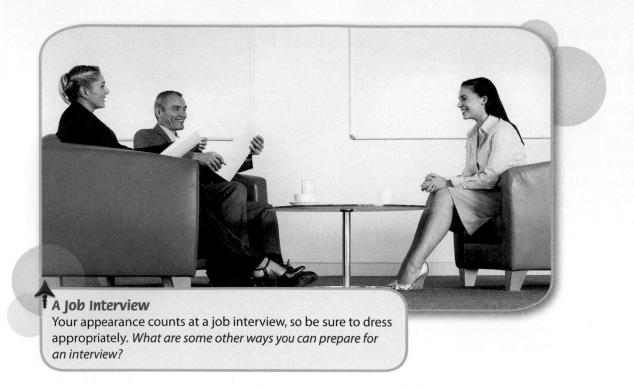

A Job Interview
Your appearance counts at a job interview, so be sure to dress appropriately. *What are some other ways you can prepare for an interview?*

- Bring your job search notebook or printouts from your computer file, and a copy of your résumé. You will need specific information about your educational background and work history. Make sure you bring the name, address, and phone number of your current supervisor to the interview. You will also need to bring personal information such as a driver's license number, your social security number, and former addresses.
- Most applications ask for an availability date. If you are not currently working, write "Immediately". If you have a job and must give notice, write "Upon two weeks' notice".

Interviews

The thought of a job interview makes some people nervous. You are more likely to feel confident if you prepare well for each interview. The interview is your chance to show that you are more than a name on a piece of paper.

If a company is interested in hiring you, it may require you to undergo a drug test or submit to a background check. Many jobs today require this. In many states, people who have drug problems or who have been convicted of a crime against a child will be rejected.

Be Prepared

There are many ways to prepare for an interview. Here are some suggestions to help you:

- **Dress appropriately.** Try to match your outfit to the job. Being well dressed will help you feel confident. Avoid very baggy or tight clothing and keep jewelry to a minimum.
- **Research.** Learn about the company before the interview. Study the employer's Web site. Talk to people who are familiar with the employer.
- **Rehearse.** Practice for the interview with a friend or relative. Remember to keep a positive attitude. You might want to videotape the process and then look for ways you could improve your performance.
- **Arrive early.** Allow for possible traffic delays and arrive a few minutes early. If possible, drive to the location the day before the interview to make sure you know where to go. You can also see how long the journey takes.
- **Greet the interviewer.** Shake the person's hand firmly and make eye contact. Try not to appear anxious or overly eager.
- **Listen carefully.** Pay attention to the questions you are asked. Do not try to change the subject or interrupt the interviewer.

- **Ask appropriate questions.** When the employer asks if you have any questions, focus on the nature of the job, its responsibilities, and the work environment. Try to fill in any gaps in your knowledge about the position. Do not discuss salary and benefits at a first interview unless the interviewer brings it up first.
- **Leave gracefully.** Thank the interviewer and voice your interest in the job as you shake hands to leave.

Common Questions

Knowing the kinds of questions likely to be asked can help you feel more comfortable when preparing for a job interview. Think of replies to these common questions:

- What are your strengths? What are your weaknesses?
- What are your qualifications for this position?
- Why would you like to work for this company or school?
- What do you want to be doing in five years?
- How would a past teacher or employer describe you?
- Why did you leave your last job?
- What rewards are the most important in your career?
- Why did you choose this career?
- How do you work under pressure?
- What two or three accomplishments have given you the most satisfaction?
- What is a major problem you have encountered at school or on the job? How did you deal with it?
- What are some examples of your creativity?
- Have you worked as part of a team? What were the pluses and minuses of the experience?
- Why should we hire you?
- What is the hardest job you have ever done?
- What questions do you have about the job or this company?

Interview Follow-Up

After an interview, it can be hard waiting to find out whether you got the job. Remember that the interviewer might have additional candidates to see before a decision can be made. As you wait, there are tasks you can do to remind the employer of your interest.

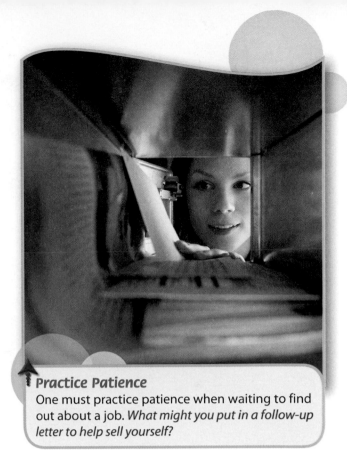

Practice Patience
One must practice patience when waiting to find out about a job. *What might you put in a follow-up letter to help sell yourself?*

Send a Letter

Within 24 hours after an interview, it is appropriate to write a follow-up letter. You can mail your letter or use e-mail. In either case, keep your language formal and businesslike. If more than one person interviewed you, send a separate letter to each. Make sure the letters are different for each person. Here are some points to cover in the letter:

- Refer to information you gathered in the interview. This builds a personal bridge back to the person receiving the letter. It also serves as a reminder and clarification of that information.
- Thank the person for his or her courtesy and time. This shows good manners.
- Turn any concerns or objections that came up during the interview to your advantage.
- Add additional information regarding your qualifications. It is important to sell yourself as the right person for the job.
- If you promised to send any other information, include it with your letter. Prospective employers may request letters of reference, transcripts, or other additional information. Say that you will call to check about the job.

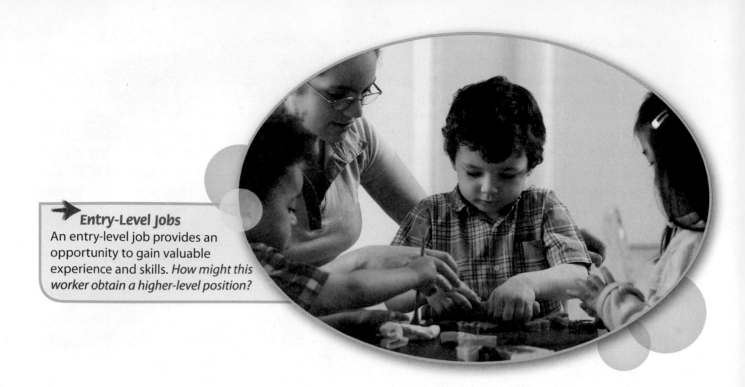

Entry-Level Jobs
An entry-level job provides an opportunity to gain valuable experience and skills. *How might this worker obtain a higher-level position?*

Be Patient

Many job seekers become frustrated with the waiting game they must play after an interview. If the interviewer says that he or she will be in touch within two weeks, you should wait at least that length of time. After that, it is okay to call and politely ask about the status of the application. A good way to approach this situation would be to say, "Could you please tell me what the next step is in the hiring process?" The employer might want you to come in for a second interview, or you might be told that someone else has been hired.

While you might be tempted to ask why you did not get the job, it is better to be gracious in accepting the news. The employer does not have to explain his or her decision. Try to learn from the experience and move on. Reflect on your interview skills so that you learn from this experience. If you felt that some aspects of the interview did not go well, practice improving them for next time.

Evaluate a Job Offer

You might think that the most important factor in deciding whether to accept or reject a job offer is the salary. Compensation is important, but there are other factors to consider.

Perhaps the company is one that could provide a bright future. Many employees have started at entry-level positions simply to "get their foot in the door" at a desirable company or school. If there is potential for advancement, avoid thinking that the job is not good enough. Remember that in the early years of your career, you are building experience and a work history.

When an employer makes a job offer, you do not have to give an answer right away. It is okay to ask for a day to think about the offer. Do not put off the decision for too long. If it is a tough decision, make a list of the pros and cons. The pros are the benefits that go along with the paycheck, such as health insurance and the chance to gain experience. The cons are the disadvantages of the job, such as a long drive or weekend hours.

If you are offered a job but feel that you would want to move on as quickly as possible, it may be best not to take it. Changing jobs frequently does not look good on your résumé. Always be polite when turning down a job offer. You might want to apply for another position with the same employer at another time.

✓ **Reading Check** **Analyze** What is the purpose of a cover letter?

Build Career Skills

Beginning a new job is an exciting time. You will learn new skills and practice those you already have. Whether you are working at a private school or at a children's museum, many of the needed skills will be similar.

Employers expect workers to have two basic types of skills. **Job-specific skills** are the skills or abilities needed to do a specific job. For example, programming a computer is a job-specific skill. **Transferable skills** are general skills used in school and in various types of jobs. Being honest and friendly are examples of transferable skills.

Transferable Skills

Transferable skills are needed for any career you choose. Here are some transferable skills that will help ensure success at any job:

- **Basic skills.** Employees need to have basic skills such as the ability to understand instructions and solve math problems. For many jobs, technology skills, such as using word processing and spreadsheet software, are classified as basic skills.

- **Communication skills.** The way you speak, listen, and write will have an impact on your success in the workplace. Make an effort to speak clearly, listen carefully, and write clearly and concisely.

- **Relationship skills.** Whenever a group of people must work together, there is potential for conflict. Learn to respect differences, work as part of a team, and resolve conflicts before they get out of hand. Good team players are dependable, responsible, and honest.

- **Leadership skills.** Leadership involves making decisions, acting fairly, and supervising and inspiring others. Leaders must be able to set goals and use available resources to get the work done efficiently. Leadership skills are needed for many of the careers that relate to children. After all, children look to the adults in their lives for guidance and leadership.

- **Managing multiple roles.** Throughout your career, you will have many roles. It will be necessary to juggle work, family, social, and community obligations, so learn to prioritize and manage your time.

➤ **Ethical Behavior**
People who work with children must follow ethical practices and strictly obey any rules governing behavior. *Why is it vital that people who work with children always behave ethically?*

- **Learning from performance evaluations.** Wherever you work, you will have periodic performance evaluations. Your supervisor will comment on what you have been doing well and point out areas that need improvement. You may be given, or asked to develop, goals for the following year. Working to improve in these areas should help you advance in your career.

- **Behaving ethically.** Being **ethical** means doing the right thing. In the workplace, it means being honest, following the rules, and reporting violations of the rules. Following ethical practices is particularly important in child care settings. It is essential that parents can trust and rely on the people who care for their children.

Lifelong Learning

To succeed in today's work environment, you must be flexible and willing to change. You should commit to being a lifelong learner. A **lifelong learner** is someone who is willing to learn new information and acquire skills throughout his or her working life. This will help you maintain employment by making you a better worker and a valued employee.

One way to continue learning is with continuing education. Some employers are willing to pay for all or part of the costs. Continuing education can mean attending conferences or workshops, earning credentials through a professional organization, or taking college classes.

✓ **Reading Check** **Explain** Why would an employer want to hire employees committed to lifelong learning?

Leaving a Job

Most people today do not stay in the same job until retirement. In fact, it is highly likely that you will change jobs and perhaps careers a number of times during your working life. You need to know how to make the transition from one job to another as smooth as possible.

It is usually not a good idea to quit one job before you have another one lined up. After all, you do not know how long it will take to find another job and you probably need to keep earning money. As you seek new employment, you should do it on your own time, though. It is unethical to use work time to interview for another job. It is also wrong to use company time to write or print résumés and cover letters, or to contact prospective employers.

Employee's Obligations

When you leave a job, you should make every effort to leave under the best possible circumstances. Follow any established procedures for notifying your employer of your intent to resign. Give as much notice as possible so your employer can find a replacement. A two-week notice is typical. Make sure you express your appreciation for the job opportunity. You may need a reference from your current employer.

Continue to do your job well up to the time you leave. If you are asked to train a replacement, strive to give that person the best possible start. After all, you might work with some of your coworkers in the future. You might even want to return to the same employer later in your career.

Employer's Obligations

Employees do not always leave their jobs because they want to. Employers can terminate employment as well. Some people lose their jobs because they do not perform well. In other cases, such as when business is slow, jobs may be cut through no fault of the employees.

If you lose your job, you may be entitled to claim unemployment benefits. **Unemployment benefits** are funds paid by individual states to unemployed people who are actively seeking employment. Employers are also responsible for paying into the fund that provides for unemployment benefits. Make sure that you clearly understand what benefits you can receive and how long you can receive them. You may not be eligible for unemployment benefits if you simply quit a job.

You may also be able to keep any health insurance that you received through your employer. **COBRA** (Consolidated Omnibus Budget Reconciliation Act) is a law ensuring that former employees can keep the health insurance plan they received through their former employer for up to 18 months. The former employee must pay the entire cost of the premiums.

Ongoing Employability

If you are being laid off or face downsizing, it can make you feel angry or depressed. Try to view it as a career-change opportunity. The company might offer job-search services or help in finding new employment. Go back to the networking and contact lists you created when you searched for this job. Reach out for support from friends, family, and other acquaintances. Consider joining a job-search club. Assess your skills. Upgrade them if needed. Decide the direction you wish to take and move on!

As you move along your career path, be sure to remember the keys to employment success. Commit yourself to excellence. Continue learning. Do all that you can to show that you are reliable, flexible, honest, and responsible. Show that you have what it takes to succeed in the world of work!

Section 23.2 — After You Read

Review Key Concepts

1. **Identify** what a job seeker with little work experience could emphasize on his or her résumé.

2. **Describe** how you can be a lifelong learner.

3. **Explain** why you should continue to do your best after you have resigned.

Practice Academic Skills

 English

4. Follow your teacher's instructions to form into groups of four. Each person in the group writes a description of a job he or she would like to interview for. A second team member conducts a mock interview with this individual. The remaining team members offer suggestions for improving the interview.

> **NCTE 12** Use language to accomplish individual purposes.

 Mathematics

5. Interview at least ten working adults. Ask, "How did you get your current job?" Categorize the responses into five or six groups. Use these categories in creating a bar graph illustrating the different ways these people got their current jobs.

> **NCTM Number and Operations**
> Understand numbers, ways of representing numbers, relationships among numbers, and number systems.

 Check Your Answers Check your answers at this book's Online Learning Center at **glencoe.com**.

Actor in Children's Theatre

Actors in children's theatres present plays that children will enjoy and find meaningful. These actors are artists, and their task is to bring characters to life. Children's theatres are sometimes performed in the round. The actors often interact with the audience.

What Does an Actor in Children's Theatre Do?

Many actors love performing for children because children often respond more candidly to theatre than adults. If children love a play, the performers will know it! Because many children's theatres have small staffs, actors must be resourceful and be able to perform a variety of roles.

Where Do Actors Work?

Many large cities have children's theatres. There are also theatre companies that will travel to different theatres or cities. Because it can be hard to find steady work, many of these actors hold other jobs as well.

Preparation and Skills

Education and Training

Aspiring actors can take small roles in community theatre productions. They can also take acting classes, or pursue a performing arts degree at a college or university. Public speaking is good preparation as well.

Aptitudes, Abilities, and Skills

Actors need to memorize lines and have stamina for rehearsals and performances. They must love to entertain and perform. It is also helpful to have skills such as singing and dancing.

Academic Skills

English language arts are used to memorize lines and speak them well, as well as to take direction. Social studies skills can be helpful in portraying other cultures.

Explore Careers

Conduct research to learn about a children's theatre. Write an advertisement for an actor to perform in a play being performed by this theatre. In the ad, list the specific aptitudes and abilities the actor must have.

 Careers Online For more information on careers, visit the Occupational Outlook Handbook Web site through the link on this book's Online Learning Center at **glencoe.com**.

Chapter Summary

Within career areas, there are various levels of jobs. When choosing a career, consider your interests, aptitudes, and abilities. You can gain work experience through part-time work, internships, volunteering, service learning, and work-based learning. When evaluating careers, there are many factors to consider. Sources of job openings include the Internet, newspapers, other people, and job fairs. Prepare for an interview. Always write a follow-up letter afterward. Transferable skills are needed for success in any workplace.

Vocabulary Review

1. Use these content and academic vocabulary terms to create a crossword puzzle on graph paper. Use the definitions as clues.

Content Vocabulary

◇ entry-level job (p. 631)
◇ paraprofessional (p. 631)
◇ professional (p. 632)
◇ entrepreneur (p. 632)
◇ aptitude (p. 633)
◇ internship (p. 634)
◇ job shadowing (p. 634)
◇ service learning (p. 634)
◇ work-based learning (p. 634)

◇ career path (p. 637)
◇ career ladder (p. 637)
◇ networking (p. 639)
◇ job fair (p. 639)
◇ résumé (p. 640)
◇ cover letter (p. 643)
◇ job-specific skills (p. 647)
◇ transferable skills (p. 647)
◇ ethical (p. 648)
◇ lifelong learner (p. 648)

◇ unemployment benefits (p. 649)
◇ COBRA (p. 649)

Academic Vocabulary

■ ability (p. 633)
■ visualization (p. 637)
■ convey (p. 640)
■ legible (p. 643)

Review Key Concepts

2. **Describe** three different ways to gain work experience.
3. **Identify** factors to consider when evaluating careers.
4. **Explain** the relationship between a career goal and a career path.
5. **List** six steps involved in a job search.
6. **Compare and contrast** job-specific skills and transferable skills.
7. **Summarize** an employee's responsibilities when leaving a job.

Critical Thinking

8. **Infer** Why do you think many employers prefer to interview potential employees who are currently working?
9. **Predict** On her résumé, Zoe falsely stated she was a supervisor at her last job. What do you think might happen as a result of this inaccuracy?
10. **Analyze** In your career, do you think you would prefer to work primarily with people, information, or technology? Explain your choice.

Family & Community Connection

11. Future Job Markets Interview several people who have worked at least ten years in a field you are interested in. Ask them how they think their field will change in the future. Prepare a brief presentation in which you predict the future of this job market based on the information gained in your interviews.

Health Skills

12. Emergency Skills A preschool teacher needs to be prepared for many different emergencies. Use print or online resources to research the kinds of emergency skills a preschool teacher should have. Also find out how they might best obtain the training needed to get these skills. Create an illustrated poster explaining the skills and training needed.

Observation Skills

13. Motivate Children Being a good teacher means more than just knowing the material you are presenting. Good teachers have the ability to motivate children. They make each child want to learn.

Procedure Observe a coach, music instructor, or other adult working with a group of children between the ages of 9 and 12. What does the teacher do to motivate the children?

Analysis Write a paragraph analyzing how the teacher motivated the students. Discuss any additional ways you can think of that the children could have been motivated.

> **NCSS IV D Individual Development and Identity**
> Apply concepts, methods, and theories about the study of human growth and development, such as physical endowment, learning, motivation, behavior, perception, and personality.

Real-World Skills

Problem Solving

14. Make Decisions Suppose you want to become an elementary school teacher. You have just promised to volunteer at an after-school program for children ages 8 to 10. Unexpectedly, a neighbor offers you a part-time job in her infant daycare. What would you do? Why?

Technology Skills

15. Design a Brochure A counselor at a community college who works with students looking for their first professional jobs has asked for your help. Use word processing or desktop publishing software to create an illustrated brochure with tips on preparing for a job interview.

Financial Literacy

16. A Business Wardrobe Conduct research to determine what is generally meant by the term *business casual*. Then determine how much five outfits would cost. Create a table showing the cost and where the outfits would be purchased.

 Additional Activities For additional activities, go to this book's Online Learning Center at **glencoe.com**.

Academic Skills

 English Language Arts

17. Using Transferable Skills Choose two transferable skills, such as communication skills or ethical behavior. Write a scenario showing how you might use these skills in a job in which you are interested. Be specific about how you would apply the skills.

> **NCTE 5** Use different writing process elements to communicate effectively.

 Mathematics

18. How Many Teachers? Out of the 3,954,000 teachers employed in 2006, median annual earnings of kindergarten, elementary, middle, and secondary school teachers ranged from $43,580 to $48,690 in May 2006. The lowest 10 percent earned $28,590 to $33,070. The top 10 percent earned $67,490 to $76,100. How many teachers are in the lowest 10 percent?

Math Concept **Multiplying by Percents**
To multiply by percents, change the percent to a fraction with 100 in the denominator. Then change the fraction to a decimal. For example, $5\% = \frac{5}{100} = 0.05$.

Starting Hint To compute how many teachers made up the lowest 10 percent, multiply the total number of teachers by the percentage.

 For math help, go to the Math Appendix at the back of the book.

> **NCTM Number and Operations** Understand numbers, ways of representing numbers, relationships among numbers, and number systems.

 Science

19. Imagine that you are a preschool teacher who wants to teach simple scientific concepts to your class. Examples might include that warm air rises, or that some objects float in water while others sink.

Procedure Choose a concept you want to teach. Present it to a group of at least three preschoolers in a fun way that they can understand.

Analysis Ask the preschoolers to state what they have learned in their own words. Calculate the percentage who were able to do so.

> **NSES A** Develop understandings about scientific inquiry.

Standardized Test Practice

MATHEMATICS
Many students find test questions involving mathematics intimidating, often because they require a number of steps. Read the test-taking tip and then determine the answer to this question.

20. You teach piano lessons to 12 students each week. Beginning lessons are $20.00 while advanced lessons are $28.00. You have twice as many beginning students as advanced. How much do you make each week?

> **Test-Taking Tip** When answering a math question, it is a good idea to estimate the answer before performing the actual calculations. If your answer is considerably different than your estimate, carefully check it.

Unit Thematic Project

Explore Careers in Child Care

In this unit, you have learned about adolescence, childhood illnesses, challenges that families face, and child care options. You have also learned that there are many different careers within the child care industry. In this project, you will interview and shadow a professional child care worker. You will use what you learn to create a skit that shows a child care worker interacting with children.

 My Journal

If you completed the journal entry from page 517, refer to it to see if your thoughts have changed after reading the unit.

Project Assignment

In this project, you will:
- Choose a type of child care worker that you would like to know more about.
- Write a list of interview questions. Ask about qualifications needed for the job.
- Identify and interview a professional in the community who works in the child care industry.
- Arrange, take notes, and key the interview with your candidate.
- Use what you learned in the interview to create a skit. It should show a child care worker interacting with children.

Child Development Skills Behind the Project

- Evaluate careers available in the area of child care and early learning.
- Identify the qualifications needed for a particular career in child care.
- Describe the ways child care workers interact with children.

Academic Skills

 English Language Arts

> **NCTE 4** Use written language to communicate effectively.
>
> **NCTE 12** Use language to accomplish individual purposes.

Step 1 Choose a Child Care Career that Interests You

The careers below are representative of those typically found in the child care industry. Choose a child care job that you would like to learn more about.
- Center-based child care worker
- Home-based child care worker
- Camp counselor
- After school day care worker
- Preschool teacher
- Pediatrician
- Pediatric nurse

Step 2 Write Your Interview Questions

Make a list of questions you would like to ask about the child care career that interests you. Be sure to ask about the qualifications and education needed for the job and about starting pay for an entry level job.

Writing Skills

★ Use complete sentences.
★ Use correct spelling and grammar.
★ Organize your questions in the order you want to ask them.
★ Write concisely (briefly but completely).

Step 3 Connect to Your Community

Arrange to interview or shadow a member of the community who works in the child care profession you selected in Step 1. Ask the interview questions you wrote in Step 2.

Interview Skills

★ Listen carefully.
★ During the interview, record responses and take notes.
★ If you shadow a professional, take good notes of their interactions but be sure to maintain confidentiality.
★ When you transcribe your notes, write in complete sentences and use correct spelling and grammar.

Step 4 Write and Present Your Skit

Use the Unit Thematic Project Checklist on the right to plan, write, and present a skit sharing what you have learned.

Presentation Skills

★ Act naturally.
★ Use gestures when appropriate.
★ Speak loudly and clearly so the entire audience can hear and understand you.

Step 5 Evaluate Your Child Development Skills and Academic Skills

Your project will be evaluated based on:

● Content and organization of your information.
● Mechanics—presentation and neatness.
● Speaking and listening skills.

Evaluation Rubric Go to this book's Online Learning Center at **glencoe.com** for a rubric you can use to evaluate your final project.

Unit Thematic Project Checklist

Skit	✓ Consider who will play the different roles. You should play the caregiver; ask for one or two volunteers to play the children. ✓ Re-create one of the activities you observed during your shadowing or interview experience in a skit. ✓ Use props to represent the child care setting. ✓ Write a summary at the end of the skit. What did you hope to teach the children? How did you hope to help the children?
Presentation	✓ Make a presentation for the students in your class to share your skit and discuss what you learned. ✓ Invite the students to ask you any questions. Answer three questions. ✓ Demonstrate in your answers that you respect their perspectives. ✓ Turn in the notes from your interview and your skit script.
Academic Skills	✓ Write dialogue between two or more people. ✓ Express your ideas clearly. ✓ Speak clearly and concisely.

Number and Operations

▶ *Understand numbers, ways of representing numbers, relationships among numbers, and number systems*

Fraction, Decimal, and Percent

A percent is a ratio that compares a number to 100. To write a percent as a fraction, drop the percent sign, and use the number as the numerator in a fraction with a denominator of 100. Simplify, if possible. For example, 76% $= \frac{76}{100}$, or $\frac{19}{25}$. To write a fraction as a percent, convert it to an equivalent fraction with a denominator of 100. For example, $\frac{3}{4} = \frac{75}{100}$, or 75%. A fraction can be expressed as a percent by first converting the fraction to a decimal (divide the numerator by the denominator) and then converting the decimal to a percent by moving the decimal point two places to the right.

Comparing Numbers on a Number Line

In order to compare and understand the relationship between real numbers in various forms, it is helpful to use a number line. The zero point on a number line is called the origin; the points to the left of the origin are negative, and those to the right are positive. The number line below shows how numbers in fraction, decimal, percent, and integer form can be compared.

Percents Greater Than 100 and Less Than 1

Percents greater than 100% represent values greater than 1. For example, if the weight of an object is 250% of another, it is 2.5, or $2\frac{1}{2}$, times the weight.

Percents less than 1 represent values less than $\frac{1}{100}$. In other words, 0.1% is one tenth of one percent, which can also be represented in decimal form as 0.001, or in fraction form as $\frac{1}{1,000}$. Similarly, 0.01% is one hundredth of one percent or 0.0001 or $\frac{1}{10,000}$.

Ratio, Rate, and Proportion

A ratio is a comparison of two numbers using division. If a basketball player makes 8 out of 10 free throws, the ratio is written as 8 to 10, 8:10, or $\frac{8}{10}$. Ratios are usually written in simplest form. In simplest form, the ratio "8 out of 10" is 4 to 5, 4:5, or $\frac{4}{5}$. A rate is a ratio of two measurements having different kinds of units—cups per gallon, or miles per hour, for example. When a rate is simplified so that it has a denominator of 1, it is called a unit rate. An example of a unit rate is 9 miles per hour. A proportion is an equation stating that two ratios are equal. $\frac{3}{18} = \frac{13}{78}$ is an example of a proportion. The cross products of a proportion are also equal. $\frac{3}{18} = \frac{13}{78}$ and $3 \times 78 = 18 \times 13$.

Representing Large and Small Numbers

In order to represent large and small numbers, it is important to understand the number system. Our number system is based on 10, and the value of each place is 10 times the value of the place to its right.

The value of a digit is the product of a digit and its place value. For instance, in the number 6,400, the 6 has a value of six thousands and the 4 has a value of four hundreds. A place value chart can help you read numbers. In the chart, each group of three digits is called a period. Commas separate the periods: the ones period, the thousands period, the millions period, and so on. Values to the right of the ones period are decimals. By understanding place value you can write very large numbers like 5 billion and more, and very small numbers that are less than 1, like one-tenth.

Scientific Notation

When dealing with very large numbers like 1,500,000, or very small numbers like 0.000015, it is helpful to keep track of their value by writing the numbers in scientific notation. Powers of 10 with positive exponents are used with a decimal between 1 and 10 to express large numbers. The exponent represents the number of places the decimal point is moved to the right. So, 528,000 is written in scientific notation as 5.28×10^5. Powers of 10 with negative exponents are used with a decimal between 1 and 10 to express small numbers. The exponent represents the number of places the decimal point is moved to the left. The number 0.00047 is expressed as 4.7×10^{-4}.

Factor, Multiple, and Prime Factorization

Two or more numbers that are multiplied to form a product are called factors. Divisibility rules can be used to determine whether 2, 3, 4, 5, 6, 8, 9, or 10 are factors of a given number. Multiples are the products of a given

number and various integers. For example, 8 is a multiple of 4 because $4 \times 2 = 8$. A prime number is a whole number that has exactly two factors: 1 and itself. A composite number is a whole number that has more than two factors. Zero and 1 are neither prime nor composite. A composite number can be expressed as the product of its prime factors. The prime factorization of 40 is $2 \times 2 \times 2 \times 5$, or $2^3 \times 5$. The numbers 2 and 5 are prime numbers.

Integers

A negative number is a number less than zero. Negative numbers like -8, positive numbers like $+6$, and zero are members of the set of integers. Integers can be represented as points on a number line. A set of integers can be written $\{\ldots, -3, -2, -1, 0, 1, 2, 3, \ldots\}$ where $\ldots$ means "continues indefinitely."

Real, Rational, and Irrational Numbers

The real number system is made up of the sets of rational and irrational numbers. Rational numbers are numbers that can be written in the form a/b where a and b are integers and $b \neq 0$. Examples are 0.45, $\frac{1}{2}$, and $\sqrt{36}$. Irrational numbers are non-repeating, non-terminating decimals. Examples are $\sqrt{71}$, π, and $0.020020002\ldots$.

Complex and Imaginary Numbers

A complex number is a mathematical expression with a real number element and an imaginary number element. Imaginary numbers are multiples of i, the "imaginary" square root of -1. Complex numbers are represented by $a + bi$, where a and b are real numbers and i represents the imaginary element. When a quadratic equation does not have a real number solution, the solution can be represented by a complex number. Like real numbers, complex numbers can be added, subtracted, multiplied, and divided.

Vectors and Matrices

A matrix is a set of numbers or elements arranged in rows and columns to form a rectangle. The number of rows is represented by m and the number of columns is represented by n. To describe the number of rows and columns in a matrix, list the number of rows first using the format $m \times n$. Matrix A below is a 3×3 matrix because it has 3 rows and 3 columns. To name an element of a matrix, the letter i is used to denote the row and j is used to denote the column, and the element is labeled in the form $a_{i,j}$. In matrix A below, $a_{3,2}$ is 4.

$$\text{Matrix A} = \begin{pmatrix} 1 & 3 & 5 \\ 0 & 6 & 8 \\ 3 & 4 & 5 \end{pmatrix}$$

A vector is a matrix with only one column or row of elements. A transposed column vector, or a column vector turned on its side, is a row vector. In the example below, row vector b' is the transpose of column vector b.

$$b = \begin{pmatrix} 1 \\ 2 \\ 3 \\ 4 \end{pmatrix}$$

$$b' = (1 \quad 2 \quad 3 \quad 4)$$

▶ Understand meanings of operations and how they relate to one another

Properties of Addition and Multiplication

Properties are statements that are true for any numbers. For example, $3 + 8$ is the same as $8 + 3$ because each expression equals 11. This illustrates the Commutative Property of Addition. Likewise, $3 \times 8 = 8 \times 3$ illustrates the Commutative Property of Multiplication.

When evaluating expressions, it is often helpful to group or associate the numbers. The Associative Property says that the way in which numbers are grouped when added or multiplied does not change the sum or product. The following properties are also true:

- **Additive Identity Property:** When 0 is added to any number, the sum is the number.

- **Multiplicative Identity Property:** When any number is multiplied by 1, the product is the number.

- **Multiplicative Property of Zero:** When any number is multiplied by 0, the product is 0.

Rational Numbers

A number that can be written as a fraction is called a rational number. Terminating and repeating decimals are rational numbers because both can be written as fractions.

Decimals that are neither terminating nor repeating are called irrational numbers because they cannot be written as fractions. Terminating decimals can be converted to fractions by placing the number (without the decimal point) in the numerator. Count the number of places to the right of the decimal point, and in the denominator, place a 1 followed by a number of zeros equal to the number of places that you counted. The fraction can then be reduced to its simplest form.

Writing a Fraction as a Decimal

Any fraction $\frac{a}{b}$, where $b \neq 0$, can be written as a decimal by dividing the numerator by the denominator. So, $\frac{a}{b} = a \div b$. If the division ends, or terminates, when the remainder is zero, the decimal is a terminating decimal. Not all fractions can be written as terminating decimals. Some have a repeating decimal. A bar indicates that the decimal repeats forever. For example, the fraction $\frac{4}{9}$ can be converted to a repeating decimal, $0.\overline{4}$

Adding and Subtracting Like Fractions

Fractions with the same denominator are called like fractions. To add like fractions, add the numerators and write the sum over the denominator. To add mixed numbers with like fractions, add the whole numbers and fractions separately, adding the numerators of the fractions, then simplifying if necessary. The rule for subtracting fractions with like denominators is similar to the rule for adding. The numerators can be subtracted and the difference written over the denominator. Mixed numbers are written as improper fractions before subtracting. These same rules apply to adding or subtracting like algebraic fractions. An algebraic fraction is a fraction that contains one or more variables in the numerator or denominator.

Adding and Subtracting Unlike Fractions

Fractions with different denominators are called unlike fractions. The least common multiple of the denominators is used to rename the fractions with a common denominator. After a common denominator is found, the numerators can then be added or subtracted. To add mixed numbers with unlike fractions, rename the mixed numbers as improper fractions. Then find a common denominator, add the numerators, and simplify the answer.

Multiplying Rational Numbers

To multiply fractions, multiply the numerators and multiply the denominators. If the numerators and denominators have common factors, they can be simplified before multiplication. If the fractions have different signs, then the product will be negative. Mixed numbers can be multiplied in the same manner, after first renaming them as improper fractions. Algebraic fractions may be multiplied using the same method described above.

Dividing Rational Numbers

To divide a number by a rational number (a fraction, for example), multiply the first number by the multiplicative inverse of the second. Two numbers whose product is 1 are called multiplicative inverses, or reciprocals. $\frac{7}{4} \times \frac{4}{7} = 1$. When dividing by a mixed number, first rename it as an improper fraction, and then multiply by its multiplicative inverse. This process of multiplying by a number's reciprocal can also be used when dividing algebraic fractions.

Adding Integers

To add integers with the same sign, add their absolute values. The sum takes the same sign as the addends. An addend is a number that is added to another number (the augend). The equation $-5 + (-2) = -7$ is an example of adding two integers with the same sign. To add integers with different signs, subtract their absolute values. The sum takes the same sign as the addend with the greater absolute value.

Subtracting Integers

The rules for adding integers are extended to the subtraction of integers. To subtract an integer, add its additive inverse. For example, to find the difference $2 - 5$, add the additive inverse of 5 to 2: $2 + (-5) = -3$. The rule for subtracting integers can be used to solve real-world problems and to evaluate algebraic expressions.

Additive Inverse Property

Two numbers with the same absolute value but different signs are called opposites. For example, -4 and 4 are opposites. An integer and its opposite are also called additive inverses. The Additive Inverse Property says that the sum of any number and its additive inverse is zero. The Commutative, Associative, and Identity Properties also apply to integers. These properties help when adding more than two integers.

Absolute Value

In mathematics, when two integers on a number line are on opposite sides of zero, and they are the same distance from zero, they have the same absolute value. The symbol for absolute value is two vertical bars on either side of the number. For example, $|-5| = 5$.

Multiplying Integers

Since multiplication is repeated addition, $3(-7)$ means that -7 is used as an addend 3 times. By the Commutative Property of Multiplication, $3(-7) = -7(3)$. The product of two integers with different signs is always negative. The product of two integers with the same sign is always positive.

Dividing Integers

The quotient of two integers can be found by dividing the numbers using their absolute values. The quotient of two integers with the same sign is positive, and the quotient of two integers with a different sign is negative. $-12 \div (-4) = 3$ and $12 \div (-4) = -3$. The division of integers is used in statistics to find the average, or mean, of a set of data. When finding the mean of a set of numbers, find the sum of the numbers, and then divide by the number in the set.

Adding and Multiplying Vectors and Matrices

In order to add two matrices together, they must have the same number of rows and columns. In matrix addition, the corresponding elements are added to each other. In other words $(a + b)_{ij} = a_{ij} + b_{ij}$. For example,

$$\begin{pmatrix} 1 & 2 \\ 2 & 1 \end{pmatrix} + \begin{pmatrix} 3 & 6 \\ 0 & 1 \end{pmatrix} = \begin{pmatrix} 1+3 & 2+6 \\ 2+0 & 1+1 \end{pmatrix} = \begin{pmatrix} 4 & 8 \\ 2 & 2 \end{pmatrix}$$

Matrix multiplication requires that the number of elements in each row in the first matrix is equal to the number of elements in each column in the second. The elements of the first row of the first matrix are multiplied by the corresponding elements of the first column of the second matrix and then added together to get the first element of the product matrix. To get the second element, the elements in the first row of the first matrix are multiplied by the corresponding elements in the second column of the second matrix then added, and so on, until every row of the first matrix is multiplied by every column of the second. See the example below.

$$\begin{pmatrix} 1 & 2 \\ 3 & 4 \end{pmatrix} \times \begin{pmatrix} 3 & 6 \\ 0 & 1 \end{pmatrix} = \begin{pmatrix} (1\times3)+(2\times0) & (1\times6)+(2\times1) \\ (3\times3)+(4\times0) & (3\times6)+(4\times1) \end{pmatrix} = \begin{pmatrix} 3 & 8 \\ 9 & 22 \end{pmatrix}$$

Vector addition and multiplication are performed in the same way, but there is only one column and one row.

Permutations and Combinations

Permutations and combinations are used to determine the number of possible outcomes in different situations. An arrangement, listing, or pattern in which order is important is called a permutation. The symbol P(6, 3) represents the number of permutations of 6 things taken 3 at a time. For P(6, 3), there are $6 \times 5 \times 4$ or 120 possible outcomes. An arrangement or listing where order is not important is called a combination. The symbol C(10, 5) represents the number of combinations of 10 things taken 5 at a time. For C(10, 5), there are $(10 \times 9 \times 8 \times 7 \times 6) \div (5 \times 4 \times 3 \times 2 \times 1)$ or 252 possible outcomes.

Powers and Exponents

An expression such as $3 \times 3 \times 3 \times 3$ can be written as a power. A power has two parts, a base and an exponent. $3 \times 3 \times 3 \times 3 = 3^4$. The base is the number that is multiplied (3). The exponent tells how many times the base is used as a factor (4 times). Numbers and variables can be written using exponents. For example, $8 \times 8 \times 8 \times m \times m \times m \times m \times m$ can be expressed $8^3 m^5$. Exponents also can be used with place value to express numbers in expanded form. Using this method, 1,462 can be written as $(1 \times 10^3) + (4 \times 10^2) + (6 \times 10^1) + (2 \times 10^0)$.

Squares and Square Roots

The square root of a number is one of two equal factors of a number. Every positive number has both a positive and a negative square root. For example, since $8 \times 8 = 64$, 8 is a square root of 64. Since $(-8) \times (-8) = 64$, −8 is also a square root of 64. The notation $\sqrt{}$ indicates the positive square root, $-\sqrt{}$ indicates the negative square root, and $\pm\sqrt{}$ indicates both square roots. For example, $\sqrt{81} = 9$, $-\sqrt{49} = -7$, and $\pm\sqrt{4} = \pm2$. The square root of a negative number is an imaginary number because any two factors of a negative number must have different signs, and are therefore not equivalent.

Logarithm

A logarithm is the inverse of exponentiation. The logarithm of a number x in base b is equal to the number n. Therefore, $b^n = x$ and $\log_b x = n$. For example, $\log_4(64) = 3$ because $4^3 = 64$. The most commonly used bases for logarithms are 10, the common logarithm; 2, the binary logarithm; and the constant e, the natural logarithm (also called $ln(x)$ instead of $\log_e(x)$). Below is a list of some of the rules of logarithms that are important to understand if you are going to use them.

$$\log_b(xy) = \log_b(x) + \log_b(y)$$
$$\log_b(x/y) = \log_b(x) - \log_b(y)$$
$$\log_b(1/x) = -\log_b(x)$$
$$\log_b(x)y = y\log_b(x)$$

▶ Compute fluently and make reasonable estimates

Estimation by Rounding

When rounding numbers, look at the digit to the right of the place to which you are rounding. If the digit is 5 or greater, round up. If it is less than 5, round down. For example, to round 65,137 to the nearest hundred, look at the number in the tens place. Since 3 is less than 5, round down to 65,100. To round the same number to the nearest ten thousandth, look at the number in the thousandths place. Since it is 5, round up to 70,000.

Finding Equivalent Ratios

Equivalent ratios have the same meaning. Just like finding equivalent fractions, to find an equivalent ratio, multiply or divide both sides by the same number. For example, you can multiply 7 by both sides of the ratio 6:8 to get 42:56. Instead, you can also divide both sides of the same ratio by 2 to get 3:4. Find the simplest form of a ratio by dividing to find equivalent ratios until you can't go any further without going into decimals. So, 160:240 in simplest form is 2:3. To write a ratio in the form *1:n*, divide both sides by the left-hand number. In other words, to change 8:20 to *1:n*, divide both sides by 8 to get 1:2.5.

Front-End Estimation

Front-end estimation can be used to quickly estimate sums and differences before adding or subtracting. To use this technique, add or subtract just the digits of the two highest place values, and replace the other place values with zero. This will give you an estimation of the solution of a problem. For example, $93,471 - 22,825$ can be changed to $93,000 - 22,000$ or $71,000$. This estimate can be compared to your final answer to judge its correctness.

Judging Reasonableness

When solving an equation, it is important to check your work by considering how reasonable your answer is. For example, consider the equation $9\frac{3}{4} \times 4\frac{1}{3}$. Since $9\frac{3}{4}$ is between 9 and 10 and $4\frac{1}{3}$ is between 4 and 5, only values that are between 9×4 or 36 and 10×5 or 50 will be reasonable. You can also use front-end estimation, or you can round and estimate a reasonable answer. In the equation 73×25, you can round and solve to estimate a reasonable answer to be near 70×30 or 2,100.

Algebra

▶ Understand patterns, relations, and functions

Relation
A relation is a generalization comparing sets of ordered pairs for an equation or inequality such as $x = y + 1$ or $x > y$. The first element in each pair, the x values, forms the domain. The second element in each pair, the y values, forms the range.

Function
A function is a special relation in which each member of the domain is paired with exactly one member in the range. Functions may be represented using ordered pairs, tables, or graphs. One way to determine whether a relation is a function is to use the vertical line test. Using an object to represent a vertical line, move the object from left to right across the graph. If, for each value of x in the domain, the object passes through no more than one point on the graph, then the graph represents a function.

Linear and Nonlinear Functions
Linear functions have graphs that are straight lines. These graphs represent constant rates of change. In other words, the slope between any two pairs of points on the graph is the same. Nonlinear functions do not have constant rates of change. The slope changes along these graphs. Therefore, the graphs of nonlinear functions are *not* straight lines. Graphs of curves represent nonlinear functions. The equation for a linear function can be written in the form $y = mx + b$, where m represents the constant rate of change, or the slope. Therefore, you can determine whether a function is linear by looking at the equation. For example, the equation $y = \frac{3}{x}$ is nonlinear because x is in the denominator and the equation cannot be written in the form $y = mx + b$. A nonlinear function does not increase or decrease at a constant rate. You can check this by using a table and finding the increase or decrease in y for each regular increase in x. For example, if for each increase in x by 2, y does not increase or decrease the same amount each time, the function is nonlinear.

Linear Equations in Two Variables
In a linear equation with two variables, such as $y = x - 3$, the variables appear in separate terms and neither variable contains an exponent other than 1. The graphs of all linear equations are straight lines. All points on a line are solutions of the equation that is graphed.

Quadratic and Cubic Functions
A quadratic function is a polynomial equation of the second degree, generally expressed as $ax^2 + bx + c = 0$, where a, b, and c are real numbers and a is not equal to zero. Similarly, a cubic function is a polynomial equation of the third degree, usually expressed as $ax^3 + bx^2 + cx + d = 0$. Quadratic functions can be graphed using an equation or a table of values. For example, to graph $y = 3x^2 + 1$, substitute the values −1, −0.5, 0, 0.5, and 1 for x to yield the point coordinates (−1, 4), (−0.5, 1.75), (0, 1), (0.5, 1.75), and (1, 4).

Plot these points on a coordinate grid and connect the points in the form of a parabola. Cubic functions also can be graphed by making a table of values. The points of a cubic function form a curve. There is one point at which the curve changes from opening upward to opening downward, or vice versa, called the point of inflection.

Slope

Slope is the ratio of the rise, or vertical change, to the run, or horizontal change of a line: slope = rise/run. Slope (m) is the same for any two points on a straight line and can be found by using the coordinates of any two points on the line:

$$m = \frac{y_2 - y_1}{x_2 - x_1}, \text{ where } x_2 \neq x_1$$

Asymptotes

An asymptote is a straight line that a curve approaches but never actually meets or crosses. Theoretically, the asymptote meets the curve at infinity. For example, in the function $f(x) = \frac{1}{x}$, two asymptotes are being approached: the line $y = 0$ and $x = 0$. See the graph of the function below.

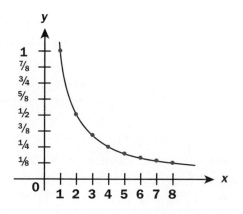

▶ Represent and analyze mathematical situations and structures using algebraic symbols

Variables and Expressions

Algebra is a language of symbols. A variable is a placeholder for a changing value. Any letter, such as x, can be used as a variable. Expressions such as $x + 2$ and $4x$ are algebraic expressions because they represent sums and/or products of variables and numbers. Usually, mathematicians avoid the use of i and e for variables because they have other mathematical meanings ($i = \sqrt{-1}$ and e is used with natural logarithms). To evaluate an algebraic expression, replace the variable or variables with known values, and then solve using order of operations. Translate verbal phrases into algebraic expressions by first defining a variable: Choose a variable and a quantity for the variable to represent. In this way, algebraic expressions can be used to represent real-world situations.

Constant and Coefficient

A constant is a fixed value unlike a variable, which can change. Constants are usually represented by numbers, but they can also be represented by symbols. For example, π is a symbolic representation of the value 3.1415…. A coefficient is a constant by which a variable or other object is multiplied. For example, in the expression $7x^2 + 5x + 9$, the coefficient of x^2 is 7 and the coefficient of x is 5. The number 9 is a constant and not a coefficient.

Monomial and Polynomial

A monomial is a number, a variable, or a product of numbers and/or variables such as 3×4. An algebraic expression that contains one or more monomials is called a polynomial. In a polynomial, there are no terms with variables in the denominator and no terms with variables under a radical sign. Polynomials can be classified by the number of terms contained in the expression. Therefore, a polynomial with two terms is called a binomial ($z^2 - 1$), and a polynomial with three terms is called a trinomial ($2y^3 + 4y^2 - y$). Polynomials also can be classified by their degrees. The degree of a monomial is the sum of the exponents of its variables. The degree of a nonzero constant such as 6 or 10 is 0. The constant 0 has no degree. For example, the monomial $4b^5c^2$ had a degree of 7. The degree of a polynomial is the same as that of the term with the greatest degree. For example, the polynomial $3x^4 - 2y^3 + 4y^2 - y$ has a degree of 4.

Equation

An equation is a mathematical sentence that states that two expressions are equal. The two expressions in an equation are always separated by an equal sign. When solving for a variable in an equation, you must perform the same operations on both sides of the equation in order for the mathematical sentence to remain true.

Solving Equations with Variables

To solve equations with variables on both sides, use the Addition or Subtraction Property of Equality to write an equivalent equation with the variables on the same side. For example, to solve $5x - 8 = 3x$, subtract $3x$ from each side to get $2x - 8 = 0$. Then add 8 to each side to get $2x = 8$. Finally, divide each side by 2 to find that $x = 4$.

Solving Equations with Grouping Symbols

Equations often contain grouping symbols such as parentheses or brackets. The first step in solving these equations is to use the Distributive Property to remove the grouping symbols. For example $5(x + 2) = 25$ can be changed to $5x + 10 = 25$, and then solved to find that $x = 3$.

Some equations have no solution. That is, there is no value of the variable that results in a true sentence. For such an equation, the solution set is called the null or empty set, and is represented by the symbol $\varnothing$ or {}. Other equations may have every number as the solution. An equation that is true for every value of the variable is called the identity.

Inequality

A mathematical sentence that contains the symbols $<$ (less than), $>$ (greater than), $\leq$ (less than or equal to), or $\geq$ (greater than or equal to) is called an inequality. For example, the statement that it is legal to drive 55 miles per hour or slower on a stretch of the highway can be shown by the sentence $s \leq 55$. Inequalities with variables are called open sentences. When a variable is replaced with a number, the inequality may be true or false.

Solving Inequalities

Solving an inequality means finding values for the variable that make the inequality true. Just as with equations, when you add or subtract the same number from each side of an inequality, the inequality remains true. For example, if you add 5 to each side of the inequality $3x < 6$, the resulting inequality $3x + 5 < 11$ is also true. Adding or subtracting the same number from each side of an inequality does not affect the inequality sign. When multiplying or dividing each side of an inequality by the same positive number, the inequality remains true. In such cases, the inequality symbol does not change. When multiplying or dividing each side of an inequality by a negative number, the inequality symbol must be reversed. For example, when dividing each side of the inequality $-4x \geq -8$ by -2, the inequality sign must be changed to $\leq$ for the resulting inequality, $2x \leq 4$, to be true. Since the solutions to an inequality include all rational numbers satisfying it, inequalities have an infinite number of solutions.

Representing Inequalities on a Number Line

The solutions of inequalities can be graphed on a number line. For example, if the solution of an inequality is $x < 5$, start an arrow at 5 on the number line, and continue the arrow to the left to show all values less than 5 as the solution. Put an open circle at 5 to show that the point 5 is *not* included in the graph. Use a closed circle when graphing solutions that are greater than or equal to, or less than or equal to, a number.

Order of Operations

Solving a problem may involve using more than one operation. The answer can depend on the order in which you do the operations. To make sure that there is just one answer to a series of computations, mathematicians have agreed upon an order in which to do the operations. First simplify within the parentheses, often called grouping symbols, and then evaluate any exponents. Then multiply and divide from left to right, and finally add and subtract from left to right.

Parametric Equations

Given an equation with more than one unknown, a statistician can draw conclusions about those unknown quantities through the use of parameters, independent variables that the statistician already knows something about. For example, you can find the velocity of an object if you make some assumptions about distance and time parameters.

Recursive Equations

In recursive equations, every value is determined by the previous value. You must first plug an initial value into the equation to get the first value, and then you can use the first value to determine the next one, and so on. For example, in order to determine what the population of pigeons will be in New York City in three years, you can use an equation with the birth, death, immigration, and emigration rates of the birds. Input the current population size into the equation to determine next year's population size, then repeat until you have calculated the value for which you are looking.

▶ *Use mathematical models to represent and understand quantitative relationships*

Solving Systems of Equations

Two or more equations together are called a system of equations. A system of equations can have one solution, no solution, or infinitely many solutions. One method for solving a system of equations is to graph the equations on the same coordinate plane. The coordinates of the point where the graphs intersect is the solution. In other words, the solution of a system is the ordered pair that is a solution of all equations. A more accurate way to solve a system of two equations is by using a method called substitution. Write both equations in terms of y. Replace y in the first equation with the right side of the second equation. Check the solution by graphing. You can solve a system of three equations using matrix algebra.

Graphing Inequalities
To graph an inequality, first graph the related equation, which is the boundary. All points in the shaded region are solutions of the inequality. If an inequality contains the symbol $\leq$ or $\geq$, then use a solid line to indicate that the boundary is included in the graph. If an inequality contains the symbol $<$ or $>$, then use a dashed line to indicate that the boundary is not included in the graph.

▶ Analyze change in various contexts

Rate of Change
A change in one quantity with respect to another quantity is called the rate of change. Rates of change can be described using slope:

$$\text{slope} = \frac{\text{change in } y}{\text{change in } x}$$

You can find rates of change from an equation, a table, or a graph. A special type of linear equation that describes rate of change is called a direct variation. The graph of a direct variation always passes through the origin and represents a proportional situation. In the equation $y = kx$, k is called the constant of variation. It is the slope, or rate of change. As x increases in value, y increases or decreases at a constant rate k, or y varies directly with x. Another way to say this is that y is directly proportional to x. The direct variation $y = kx$ also can be written as $k = \frac{y}{x}$. In this form, you can see that the ratio of y to x is the same for any corresponding values of y and x.

Slope-Intercept Form
Equations written as $y = mx + b$, where m is the slope and b is the y-intercept, are linear equations in slope-intercept form. For example, the graph of $y = 5x - 6$ is a line that has a slope of 5 and crosses the y-axis at $(0, -6)$. Sometimes you must first write an equation in slope-intercept form before finding the slope and y-intercept. For example, the equation $2x + 3y = 15$ can be expressed in slope-intercept form by subtracting $2x$ from each side and then dividing by 3: $y = -\frac{2}{3}x + 5$, revealing a slope of $-\frac{2}{3}$ and a y-intercept of 5. You can use the slope-intercept form of an equation to graph a line easily. Graph the y-intercept and use the slope to find another point on the line, then connect the two points with a line.

Geometry

▶ *Analyze characteristics and properties of two- and three-dimensional geometric shapes and develop mathematical arguments about geometric relationships*

Angles

Two rays that have the same endpoint form an angle. The common endpoint is called the vertex, and the two rays that make up the angle are called the sides of the angle. The most common unit of measure for angles is the degree. Protractors can be used to measure angles or to draw an angle of a given measure. Angles can be classified by their degree measure. Acute angles have measures less than 90° but greater than 0°. Obtuse angles have measures greater than 90° but less than 180°. Right angles have measures of 90°.

Triangles

A triangle is a figure formed by three line segments that intersect only at their endpoints. The sum of the measures of the angles of a triangle is 180°. Triangles can be classified by their angles. An acute triangle contains all acute angles. An obtuse triangle has one obtuse angle. A right triangle has one right angle. Triangles can also be classified by their sides. A scalene triangle has no congruent sides. An isosceles triangle has at least two congruent sides. In an equilateral triangle all sides are congruent.

Quadrilaterals

A quadrilateral is a closed figure with four sides and four vertices. The segments of a quadrilateral intersect only at their endpoints. Quadrilaterals can be separated into two triangles. Since the sum of the interior angles of all triangles totals 180°, the measures of the interior angles of a quadrilateral equal 360°. Quadrilaterals are classified according to their characteristics, and include trapezoids, parallelograms, rectangles, squares, and rhombuses.

Two-Dimensional Figures

A two-dimensional figure exists within a plane and has only the dimensions of length and width. Examples of two-dimensional figures include circles and polygons. Polygons are figures that have three or more angles, including triangles, quadrilaterals, pentagons, hexagons, and many more. The sum of the angles of any polygon totals at least 180° (triangle), and each additional side adds 180° to the measure of the first three angles. The sum of the angles of a quadrilateral, for example, is 360°. The sum of the angles of a pentagon is 540°.

Three-Dimensional Figures

A plane is a two-dimensional flat surface that extends in all directions. Intersecting planes can form the edges and vertices of three-dimensional figures or solids. A polyhedron is a solid with flat surfaces that are polygons. Polyhedrons are composed of faces, edges, and vertices and are differentiated by their shape and by their number of bases. Skew lines are lines that lie in different planes. They are neither intersecting nor parallel.

Congruence

Figures that have the same size and shape are congruent. The parts of congruent triangles that match are called corresponding parts. Congruence statements are used to identify corresponding parts of congruent triangles. When writing a congruence statement, the letters must be written so that corresponding vertices appear in the same order. Corresponding parts can be used to find the measures of angles and sides in a figure that is congruent to a figure with known measures.

Similarity

If two figures have the same shape but not the same size they are called similar figures. For example, the triangles below are similar, so angles A, B, and C have the same measurements as angles D, E, and F, respectively. However, segments AB, BC, and CA do not have the same measurements as segments DE, EF, and FD, but the measures of the sides are proportional.

For example, $\dfrac{\overline{AB}}{\overline{DE}} = \dfrac{\overline{BC}}{\overline{EF}} = \dfrac{\overline{CA}}{\overline{FD}}$.

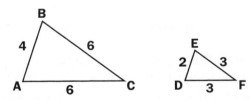

Solid figures are considered to be similar if they have the same shape and their corresponding linear measures are proportional. As with two-dimensional figures, they can be tested for similarity by comparing corresponding measures. If the compared ratios are proportional, then the figures are similar solids. Missing measures of similar solids can also be determined by using proportions.

The Pythagorean Theorem

The sides that are adjacent to a right angle are called legs. The side opposite the right angle is the hypotenuse.

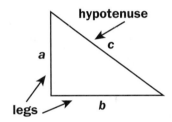

The Pythagorean Theorem describes the relationship between the lengths of the legs a and b and the hypotenuse c. It states that if a triangle is a right triangle, then the square of the length of the hypotenuse is equal to the sum of the squares of the lengths of the legs. In symbols, $c^2 = a^2 + b^2$.

Sine, Cosine, and Tangent Ratios

Trigonometry is the study of the properties of triangles. A trigonometric ratio is a ratio of the lengths of two sides of a right triangle. The most common trigonometric ratios are the sine, cosine, and tangent ratios. These ratios are abbreviated as *sin*, *cos*, and *tan*, respectively.

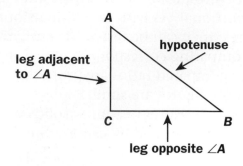

If ∠*A* is an acute angle of a right triangle, then

$$sin\ \angle A = \frac{\text{measure of leg opposite } \angle A}{\text{measure of hypotenuse}},$$

$$cos\ \angle A = \frac{\text{measure of leg adjacent to } \angle A}{\text{measure of hypotenuse}}, \text{ and}$$

$$tan\ \angle A = \frac{\text{measure of leg opposite } \angle A}{\text{measure of leg adjacent to } \angle A}.$$

▶ *Specify locations and describe spatial relationships using coordinate geometry and other representational systems*

Polygons

A polygon is a simple, closed figure formed by three or more line segments. The line segments meet only at their endpoints. The points of intersection are called vertices, and the line segments are called sides. Polygons are classified by the number of sides they have. The diagonals of a polygon divide the polygon into triangles. The number of triangles formed is two less than the number of sides. To find the sum of the measures of the interior angles of any polygon, multiply the number of triangles within the polygon by 180. That is, if *n* equals the number of sides, then (*n* − 2) 180 gives the sum of the measures of the polygon's interior angles.

Cartesian Coordinates

In the Cartesian coordinate system, the *y*-axis extends above and below the origin and the *x*-axis extends to the right and left of the origin, which is the point at which the *x*- and *y*-axes intersect. Numbers below and to the left of the origin are negative. A point graphed on the coordinate grid is said to have an *x*-coordinate and a *y*-coordinate. For example, the point (1,−2) has as its *x*-coordinate the number 1, and has as its *y*-coordinate the number −2. This point is graphed by locating the position on the grid that is 1 unit to the right of the origin and 2 units below the origin.

The *x*-axis and the *y*-axis separate the coordinate plane into four regions, called quadrants. The axes and points located on the axes themselves are not located in any of the quadrants. The quadrants are labeled I to IV, starting in the upper right and proceeding counterclockwise. In quadrant I, both coordinates are positive. In quadrant II, the *x*-coordinate is negative and the *y*-coordinate is positive. In quadrant III, both coordinates are negative. In quadrant IV, the *x*-coordinate is positive and the *y*-coordinate is negative. A coordinate graph can be used to show algebraic relationships among numbers.

▶ *Apply transformations and use symmetry to analyze mathematical situations*

Similar Triangles and Indirect Measurement

Triangles that have the same shape but not necessarily the same dimensions are called similar triangles. Similar triangles have corresponding angles and corresponding sides. Arcs are used to show congruent angles. If two triangles are similar, then the corresponding angles have the same measure, and the corresponding sides are proportional. Therefore, to determine the measures of the sides of similar triangles when some measures are known, proportions can be used.

Transformations

A transformation is a movement of a geometric figure. There are several types of transformations. In a translation, also called a slide, a figure is slid from one position to another without turning it. Every point of the original figure is moved the same distance and in the same direction. In a reflection, also called a flip, a figure is flipped over a line to form a mirror image. Every point of the original figure has a corresponding point on the other side of the line of symmetry. In a rotation, also called a turn, a figure is turned around a fixed point. A figure can be rotated 0°–360° clockwise or counterclockwise. A dilation transforms each line to a parallel line whose length is a fixed multiple of the length of the original line to create a similar figure that will be either larger or smaller.

▶ *Use visualizations, spatial reasoning, and geometric modeling to solve problems*

Two-Dimensional Representations of Three-Dimensional Objects

Three-dimensional objects can be represented in a two-dimensional drawing in order to more easily determine properties such as surface area and volume. When you look at the triangular prism,

you can see the orientation of its three dimensions, length, width, and height. Using the drawing and the formulas for surface area and volume, you can easily calculate these properties.

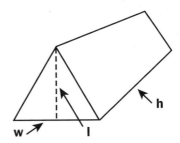

Another way to represent a three-dimensional object in a two-dimensional plane is by using a net, which is the unfolded representation. Imagine cutting the vertices of a box until it is flat then drawing an outline of it. That's a net. Most objects have more than one net, but any one can be measured to determine surface area. Below is a cube and one of its nets.

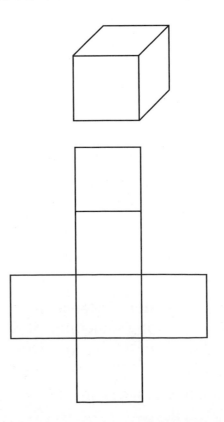

Measurement

▶ *Understand measurable attributes of objects and the units, systems, and processes of measurement*

Customary System
The customary system is the system of weights and measures used in the United States. The main units of weight are ounces, pounds (1 equal to 16 ounces), and tons (1 equal to 2,000 pounds). Length is typically measured in inches, feet (1 equal to 12 inches), yards (1 equal to 3 feet), and miles (1 equal to 5,280 feet), while area is measured in square feet and acres (1 equal to 43,560 square feet). Liquid is measured in cups, pints (1 equal to 2 cups), quarts (1 equal to 2 pints), and gallons (1 equal to 4 quarts). Finally, temperature is measured in degrees Fahrenheit.

Metric System
The metric system is a decimal system of weights and measurements in which the prefixes of the words for the units of measure indicate the relationships between the different measurements. In this system, the main units of weight, or mass, are grams and kilograms. Length is measured in millimeters, centimeters, meters, and kilometers, and the units of area are square millimeters, centimeters, meters, and kilometers. Liquid is typically measured in milliliters and liters, while temperature is in degrees Celsius.

Selecting Units of Measure
When measuring something, it is important to select the appropriate type and size of unit. For example, in the United States it would be appropriate when describing someone's height to use feet and inches. These units of height or length are good to use because they are in the customary system, and they are of appropriate size. In the customary system, use inches, feet, and miles for lengths and perimeters; square inches, feet, and miles for area and surface area; and cups, pints, quarts, gallons or cubic inches and feet (and less commonly miles) for volume. In the metric system use millimeters, centimeters, meters, and kilometers for lengths and perimeters; square units millimeters, centimeters, meters, and kilometers for area and surface area; and milliliters and liters for volume. Finally, always use degrees to measure angles.

▶ *Apply appropriate techniques, tools, and formulas to determine measurements*

Precision and Significant Digits
The precision of measurement is the exactness to which a measurement is made. Precision depends on the smallest unit of measure being used, or the precision unit. One way to record a measure is to estimate to the nearest precision unit. A more precise method is to include all of the digits that are actually measured, plus one estimated digit. The digits recorded, called significant digits, indicate the precision of the measurement. There are special rules for determining significant digits. If a number contains a decimal point, the number of significant digits is found by counting from left to right, starting with the first nonzero digit. If the

number does not contain a decimal point, the number of significant digits is found by counting the digits from left to right, starting with the first digit and ending with the last nonzero digit.

Surface Area

The amount of material needed to cover the surface of a figure is called the surface area. It can be calculated by finding the area of each face and adding them together. To find the surface area of a rectangular prism, for example, the formula $S = 2lw + 2lh + 2wh$ applies. A cylinder, on the other hand, may be unrolled to reveal two circles and a rectangle. Its surface area can be determined by finding the area of the two circles, $2\pi r^2$, and adding it to the area of the rectangle, $2\pi rh$ (the length of the rectangle is the circumference of one of the circles), or $S = 2\pi r^2 + 2\pi rh$. The surface area of a pyramid is measured in a slightly different way because the sides of a pyramid are triangles that intersect at the vertex. These sides are called lateral faces and the height of each is called the slant height. The sum of their areas is the lateral area of a pyramid. The surface area of a square pyramid is the lateral area $\frac{1}{2}bh$ (area of a lateral face) times 4 (number of lateral faces), plus the area of the base. The surface area of a cone is the area of its circular base (πr^2) plus its lateral area (πrl, where l is the slant height).

Volume

Volume is the measure of space occupied by a solid region. To find the volume of a prism, the area of the base is multiplied by the measure of the height, $V = Bh$. A solid containing several prisms can be broken down into its component prisms. Then the volume of each component can be found and the volumes added. The volume of a cylinder can be determined by finding the area of its circular base, πr^2, and then multiplying by the height of the cylinder. A pyramid has one-third the volume of a prism with the same base and height. To find the volume of a pyramid, multiply the area of the base by the pyramid's height, and then divide by 3. Simply stated, the formula for the volume of a pyramid is $V = \frac{1}{3}bh$. A cone is a three-dimensional figure with one circular base and a curved surface connecting the base and the vertex. The volume of a cone is one-third the volume of a cylinder with the same base area and height. Like a pyramid, the formula for the volume of a cone is $V = \frac{1}{3}bh$. More specifically, the formula is $V = \frac{1}{3}\pi r^2 h$.

Upper and Lower Bounds

Upper and lower bounds have to do with the accuracy of a measurement. When a measurement is given, the degree of accuracy is also stated to tell you what the upper and lower bounds of the measurement are. The upper bound is the largest possible value that a measurement could have had before being rounded down, and the lower bound is the lowest possible value it could have had before being rounded up.

Data Analysis and Probability

> ▶ *Formulate questions that can be addressed with data and collect, organize, and display relevant data to answer them*

Histograms

A histogram displays numerical data that have been organized into equal intervals using bars that have the same width and no space between them. While a histogram does not give exact data points, its shape shows the distribution of the data. Histograms also can be used to compare data.

Box-and-Whisker Plot

A box-and-whisker plot displays the measures of central tendency and variation. A box is drawn around the quartile values, and whiskers extend from each quartile to the extreme data points. To make a box plot for a set of data, draw a number line that covers the range of data. Find the median, the extremes, and the upper and lower quartiles. Mark these points on the number line with bullets, then draw a box and the whiskers. The length of a whisker or box shows whether the values of the data in that part are concentrated or spread out.

Scatter Plots

A scatter plot is a graph that shows the relationship between two sets of data. In a scatter plot, two sets of data are graphed as ordered pairs on a coordinate system. Two sets of data can have a positive correlation (as *x* increases, *y* increases), a negative correlation (as *x* increases, *y* decreases), or no correlation (no obvious pattern is shown). Scatter plots can be used to spot trends, draw conclusions, and make predictions about data.

Randomization

The idea of randomization is a very important principle of statistics and the design of experiments. Data must be selected randomly to prevent bias from influencing the results. For example, you want to know the average income of people in your town but you can only use a sample of 100 individuals to make determinations about everyone. If you select 100 individuals who are all doctors, you will have a biased sample. However, if you chose a random sample of 100 people out of the phone book, you are much more likely to accurately represent average income in the town.

Statistics and Parameters

Statistics is a science that involves collecting, analyzing, and presenting data. The data can be collected in various ways—for example through a census or by making physical measurements. The data can then be analyzed by creating summary statistics, which have to do with the distribution of the data sample, including the mean, range, and standard error. They can also be illustrated in tables and graphs, like boxplots, scatter plots, and histograms. The presentation of the data typically involves describing the strength or validity of the data and what they show. For example, an analysis of ancestry of people in a city might tell you something about immigration patterns, unless the data set is very small or biased in some way, in which case it is not likely to be very accurate or useful.

Categorical and Measurement Data

When analyzing data, it is important to understand if the data is qualitative or quantitative. Categorical data is qualitative and measurement, or numerical, data is quantitative. Categorical data describes a quality of something and can be placed into different categories. For example, if you are analyzing the number of students in different grades in a school, each grade is a category. On the other hand, measurement data is continuous, like height, weight, or any other measurable variable. Measurement data can be converted into categorical data if you decide to group the data. Using height as an example, you can group the continuous data set into categories like under 5 feet, 5 feet to 5 feet 5 inches, over 5 feet five inches to 6 feet, and so on.

Univariate and Bivariate Data

In data analysis, a researcher can analyze one variable at a time or look at how multiple variables behave together. Univariate data involves only one variable, for example height in humans. You can measure the height in a population of people then plot the results in a histogram to look at how height is distributed in humans. To summarize univariate data, you can use statistics like the mean, mode, median, range, and standard deviation, which is a measure of variation. When looking at more than one variable at once, you use multivariate data. Bivariate data involves two variables. For example, you can look at height and age in humans together by gathering information on both variables from individuals in a population. You can then plot both variables in a scatter plot, look at how the variables behave in relation to each other, and create an equation that represents the relationship, also called a regression. These equations could help answer questions such as, for example, does height increase with age in humans?

▶ Select and use appropriate statistical methods to analyze data

Measures of Central Tendency

When you have a list of numerical data, it is often helpful to use one or more numbers to represent the whole set. These numbers are called measures of central tendency. Three measures of central tendency are mean, median, and mode. The mean is the sum of the data divided by the number of items in the data set. The median is the middle number of the ordered data (or the mean of the two middle numbers). The mode is the number or numbers that occur most often. These measures of central tendency allow data to be analyzed and better understood.

Measures of Spread

In statistics, measures of spread or variation are used to describe how data are distributed. The range of a set of data is the difference between the greatest and the least values of the data set. The quartiles are the values that divide the data into four equal parts. The median of data separates the set in half. Similarly, the median of the lower half of a set of data is the lower quartile. The median of the upper half of a set of data is the upper quartile. The interquartile range is the difference between the upper quartile and the lower quartile.

Line of Best Fit

When real-life data are collected, the points graphed usually do not form a straight line, but they may approximate a linear relationship. A line of best fit is a line that lies very close to most of the data points. It can be used to predict data. You also can use the equation of the best-fit line to make predictions.

Stem and Leaf Plots

In a stem and leaf plot, numerical data are listed in ascending or descending order. The greatest place value of the data is used for the stems. The next greatest place value forms the leaves. For example, if the least number in a set of data is 8 and the greatest number is 95, draw a vertical line and write the stems from 0 to 9 to the left of the line. Write the leaves to the right of the line, with the corresponding stem. Next, rearrange the leaves so they are ordered from least to greatest. Then include a key or explanation, such as 1|3 = 13. Notice that the stem-and-leaf plot below is like a histogram turned on its side.

```
0|8
1|3 6
2|5 6 9
3|0 2 7 8
4|0 1 4 7 9
5|1 4 5 8
6|1 3 7
7|5 8
8|2 6
9|5
```

Key: **1|3 = 13**

▶ *Develop and evaluate inferences and predictions that are based on data*

Sampling Distribution

The sampling distribution of a population is the distribution that would result if you could take an infinite number of samples from the population, average each, and then average the averages. The more normal the distribution of the population, that is, how closely the distribution follows a bell curve, the more likely the sampling distribution will also follow a normal distribution. Furthermore, the larger the sample, the more likely it will accurately represent the entire population. For instance, you are more likely to gain more representative results from a population of 1,000 with a sample of 100 than with a sample of 2.

Validity

In statistics, validity refers to acquiring results that accurately reflect that which is being measured. In other words, it is important when performing statistical analyses, to ensure that the data are valid in that the sample being analyzed represents the population to the best extent possible. Randomization of data and using appropriate sample sizes are two important aspects of making valid inferences about a population.

▶ Understand and apply basic concepts of probability

Complementary, Mutually Exclusive Events

To understand probability theory, it is important to know if two events are mutually exclusive, or complementary: the occurrence of one event automatically implies the non-occurrence of the other. That is, two complementary events cannot both occur. If you roll a pair of dice, the event of rolling 6 and rolling doubles have an outcome in common (3, 3), so they are not mutually exclusive. If you roll (3, 3), you also roll doubles. However, the events of rolling a 9 and rolling doubles are mutually exclusive because they have no outcomes in common. If you roll a 9, you will not also roll doubles.

Independent and Dependent Events

Determining the probability of a series of events requires that you know whether the events are independent or dependent. An independent event has no influence on the occurrence of subsequent events, whereas, a dependent event does influence subsequent events. The chances that a woman's first child will be a girl are $\frac{1}{2}$, and the chances that her second child will be a girl are also $\frac{1}{2}$ because the two events are independent of each other. However, if there are 7 red marbles in a bag of 15 marbles, the chances that the first marble you pick will be red are $\frac{7}{15}$ and if you indeed pick a red marble and remove it, you have reduced the chances of picking another red marble to $\frac{6}{14}$.

Sample Space

The sample space is the group of all possible outcomes for an event. For example, if you are tossing a single six-sided die, the sample space is {1, 2, 3, 4, 5, 6}. Similarly, you can determine the sample space for the possible outcomes of two events. If you are going to toss a coin twice, the sample space is {(heads, heads), (heads, tails), (tails, heads), (tails, tails)}.

Computing the Probability of a Compound Event

If two events are independent, the outcome of one event does not influence the outcome of the second. For example, if a bag contains 2 blue and 3 red marbles, then the probability of selecting a blue marble, replacing it, and then selecting a red marble is $P(A) \times P(B) = \frac{2}{5} \times \frac{3}{5}$ or $\frac{6}{25}$.

If two events are dependent, the outcome of one event affects the outcome of the second. For example, if a bag contains 2 blue and 3 red marbles, then the probability of selecting a blue and then a red marble without replacing the first marble is $P(A) \times P(B \text{ following } A) = \frac{2}{5} \times \frac{3}{4}$ or $\frac{3}{10}$. Two events that cannot happen at the same time are mutually exclusive. For example, when you roll two number cubes, you cannot roll a sum that is both 5 and even. So, $P(A \text{ or } B) = \frac{4}{36} + \frac{18}{36}$ or $\frac{11}{18}$.

MAKING CAREER CHOICES

A career differs from a job in that it is a series of progressively more responsible jobs in one field or a related field. You will need to learn some special skills to choose a career and to help you in your job search. Choosing a career and identifying career opportunities require careful thought and preparation. To aid you in making important career choices, follow these steps:

STEPS TO MAKING A CAREER DECISION

1. Conduct a self-assessment to determine your:
   - values
   - lifestyle goals
   - interests
   - skills and aptitudes
   - personality
   - work environment preferences
   - relationship preferences

2. Identify possible career choices based on your self-assessment.

3. Gather information on each choice, including future trends.

4. Evaluate your choices based on your self-assessment.

5. Make your decision.

After you make your decision, plan how you will reach your goal. It is best to have short-term, medium-term, and long-term goals. In making your choices, explore the future opportunities in this field or fields over the next several years. What impact will new technology and automation have on job opportunities in the next few years? Remember, if you plan, you make your own career opportunities.

PERSONAL CAREER PORTFOLIO

You will want to create and maintain a personal career portfolio. In it you will keep all the documents you create and receive in your job search:

- Contact list
- Résumé
- Letters of recommendation
- Employer evaluations
- Awards
- Evidence of participation in school, community, and volunteer activities
- Notes about your job search
- Notes made after your interviews

CAREER RESEARCH RESOURCES

In order to gather information on various career opportunities, there are a variety of sources to research:

- **Libraries.** Your school or public library offers good career information resources. Here you will find books, magazines, pamphlets, films, videos, and special reference materials on careers. In particular, the U.S. Department of Labor publishes three reference books that are especially helpful: the *Dictionary of Occupational Titles (DOT)*, which describes about 20,000 jobs and their relationships with data, people, and things; the *Occupational Outlook Handbook (OOH)*, with information on more than 200 occupations; and the *Guide for Occupational Exploration (GOE)*, a reference that organizes the world of work into 12 interest areas that are subdivided into work groups and subgroups.

- **The Internet.** The Internet is becoming a primary source of research on any topic. It is especially helpful in researching careers.

- **Career Consultations.** Career consultation, an informational interview with a professional who works in a career that interests you, provides an opportunity to learn about the day-to-day realities of a career.

- **On-the-Job Experience.** On-the-job experience can be valuable in learning firsthand about a job or career. You can find out if your school has a work-experience program, or look into a company or organization's internship opportunities. Interning gives you direct work experience and often allows you to make valuable contacts for future full-time employment.

THE JOB SEARCH

To aid you in your actual job search, there are various sources to explore. You should contact and research all the sources that might produce a job lead, or information about a job. Keep a contact list as you proceed with your search. Some of these resources include:

- **Networking with family, friends, and acquaintances.** This means contacting people you know personally, including school counselors, former employers, and professional people.

- **Cooperative education and work-experience programs.** Many schools have such programs in which students work part-time on a job related to one of their classes. Many also offer work-experience programs that are not limited to just one career area, such as marketing.

- **Newspaper ads.** Reading the Help Wanted advertisements in your local papers will provide a source of job leads, as well as teach you about the local job market.

- **Employment agencies.** Most cities have two types of employment agencies, public and private. These employment agencies match workers with jobs. Some private agencies may charge a fee, so be sure to know who is expected to pay the fee and what the fee is.

- **Company personnel offices.** Large and medium-sized companies have personnel offices to handle employment matters, including the hiring of new workers. You can check on job openings by contacting the office by telephone or by scheduling a personal visit.

- **Searching the Internet.** Cyberspace offers multiple opportunities for your job search. Web sites, such as Hotjobs.com or Monster.com, provide lists of companies offering employment. There are tens of thousands of career-related Web sites, so the challenge is finding those that have jobs that interest you and that are up-to-date in their listings. Companies that interest you may have a Web site, which will provide valuable information on their benefits and opportunities for employment.

⬤ APPLYING FOR A JOB

When you have contacted the sources of job leads and found some jobs that interest you, the next step is to apply for them. You will need to complete application forms, write letters of application, and prepare your own résumé. Before you apply for a job, you will need to have a work permit if you are under the age of 18 in most states. Some state and federal labor laws designate certain jobs as too dangerous for young workers. Laws also limit the number of hours of work allowed during a day, a week, or the school year. You will also need to have proper documentation, such as a green card if you are not a U.S. citizen.

JOB APPLICATION

You can obtain the job application form directly at the place of business, by requesting it in writing, or over the Internet. It is best if you can fill the form out at home, but some businesses require that you fill it out at the place of work.

Fill out the job application forms neatly and accurately, using standard English, the formal style of speaking and writing you learned in school. You must be truthful and pay attention to detail in filling out the form.

PERSONAL FACT SHEET

To be sure that the answers you write on a job application form are accurate, make a personal fact sheet before filling out the application:

- Your name, home address, and phone number
- Your Social Security number
- The job you are applying for
- The date you can begin work
- The days and hours you can work
- The pay you want
- Whether or not you have been convicted of a crime
- Your education
- Your previous work experience
- Your birth date
- Your driver's license number if you have one
- Your interests and hobbies, and awards you have won
- Your previous work experience, including dates
- Schools you have attended
- Places you have lived
- Accommodations you may need from the employer
- A list of references—people who will tell an employer that you will do a good job, such as relatives, students, former employers, and the like

LETTERS OF RECOMMENDATION

Letters of recommendation are helpful. You can request teachers, counselors, relatives, and other acquaintances who know you well to write these letters. They should be short, to the point, and give a brief overview of your assets. A brief description of any of your important accomplishments or projects should follow. The letter should end with a brief description of your character and work ethic.

LETTER OF APPLICATION

Some employees prefer a letter of application, rather than an application form. This letter is like writing a sales pitch about yourself. You need to tell why you are the best person for the job, what special qualifications you have, and include all the information usually found on an application form. Write the letter in standard English, making certain that it is neat, accurate, and correct.

RÉSUMÉ

The purpose of a résumé is to make an employer want to interview you. A résumé tells prospective employers what you are like and what you can do for them. A good résumé summarizes you at your best in a one- or two-page outline. It should include the following information:

1. **Identification.** Include your name, address, telephone number, and e-mail address.

2. **Objective.** Indicate the type of job you are looking for.

3. **Experience.** List experience related to the specific job for which you are applying. List other work if you have not worked in a related field.

4. **Education.** Include schools attended from high school on, the dates of attendance, and diplomas or degrees earned. You may also include courses related to the job you are applying for.

5. **References.** Include up to three references or indicate that they are available. Always ask people ahead of time if they are willing to be listed as references for you.

A résumé that you put online or send by e-mail is called an *electronic résumé*. Some Web sites allow you to post them on their sites without charge. Employers access these sites to find new employees. Your electronic résumé should follow the guidelines for a regular one. It needs to be accurate. Stress your skills and sell yourself to prospective employers.

COVER LETTER

If you are going to get the job you want, you need to write a great cover letter to accompany your résumé. Think of a cover letter as an introduction: a piece of paper that conveys a smile, a confident hello, and a nice, firm handshake. The cover letter is the first thing a potential employer sees, and it can make a powerful impression. The following are some tips for creating a cover letter that is professional and gets the attention you want:

- **Keep it short.** Your cover letter should be one page, no more.
- **Make it look professional.** These days, you need to type your letter on a computer and print it on a laser printer. Do not use an inkjet printer unless it produces extremely crisp type. Use white or buff-colored paper; anything else will draw the wrong kind of attention. Type your name, address, phone number, and e-mail address at the top of the page.
- **Explain why you are writing.** Start your letter with one sentence describing where you heard of the opening. "Joan Wright suggested I contact you regarding a position in your marketing department," or "I am writing to apply for the position you advertised in the Sun City Journal."
- **Introduce yourself.** Give a short description of your professional abilities and background. Refer to your attached résumé: "As you will see in the attached résumé, I am an experienced editor with a background in newspapers, magazines, and textbooks." Then highlight one or two specific accomplishments.

- **Sell yourself.** Your cover letter should leave the reader thinking, "This person is exactly what we are looking for." Focus on what you can do for the company. Relate your skills to the skills and responsibilities mentioned in the job listing. If the ad mentions solving problems, relate a problem you solved at school or work. If the ad mentions specific skills or knowledge required, mention your mastery of these in your letter. (Also be sure these skills are included on your résumé.)

- **Provide all requested information.** If the Help Wanted ad asked for "salary requirements" or "salary history," include this information in your cover letter. However, you do not have to give specific numbers. It is okay to say, "My wage is in the range of $10 to $15 per hour." If the employer does not ask for salary information, do not offer any.

- **Ask for an interview.** You have sold yourself, now wrap it up. Be confident, but not pushy. "If you agree that I would be an asset to your company, please call me at [insert your phone number]. I am available for an interview at your convenience." Finally, thank the person. "Thank you for your consideration. I look forward to hearing from you soon." Always close with a "Sincerely," followed by your full name and signature.

- **Check for errors.** Read and re-read your letter to make sure each sentence is correctly worded and there are no errors in spelling, punctuation, or grammar. Do not rely on your computer's spell checker or grammar checker. A spell check will not detect if you typed "tot he" instead of "to the." It is a good idea to have someone else read your letter, too. He or she might notice an error you overlooked.

INTERVIEW

Understanding how to best prepare for and follow up on interviews is critical to your career success. At different times in your life, you may interview with a teacher or professor, a prospective employer, a supervisor, or a promotion or tenure committee. Just as having an excellent résumé is vital for opening the door, interview skills are critical for putting your best foot forward and seizing the opportunity to clearly articulate why you are the best person for the job.

RESEARCH THE COMPANY

Your ability to convince an employer that you understand and are interested in the field you are interviewing to enter is important. Show that you have knowledge about the company and the industry. What products or services does the company offer? How is it doing? What is the competition? Use your research to demonstrate your understanding of the company.

PREPARE QUESTIONS FOR THE INTERVIEWER

Prepare interview questions to ask the interviewer. Some examples include:

- "What would my responsibilities be?"
- "Could you describe my work environment?"
- "What are the chances to move up in the company?"
- "Do you offer training?"
- "What can you tell me about the people who work here?"

DRESS APPROPRIATELY

You will never get a second chance to make a good first impression. Nonverbal communication is 90 percent of communication, so dressing appropriately is of the utmost importance. Every job is different, and you should wear clothing that is appropriate for the job for which you are applying. In most situations, you will be safe if you wear clean, pressed, conservative business clothes in neutral colors. Pay special attention to grooming. Keep makeup light and wear very little jewelry. Make certain your nails and hair are clean, trimmed, and neat. Do not carry a large purse, backpack, books, or coat. Simply carry a pad of paper, a pen, and extra copies of your résumé and letters of reference in a small folder.

EXHIBIT GOOD BEHAVIOR

Conduct yourself properly during an interview. Go alone; be courteous and polite to everyone you meet. Relax and focus on your purpose: to make the best possible impression.

- Be on time.
- Be poised and relaxed.
- Avoid nervous habits.
- Avoid littering your speech with verbal clutter such as "you know," "um," and "like."
- Look your interviewer in the eye and speak with confidence.
- Use nonverbal techniques to reinforce your confidence, such as a firm handshake and poised demeanor.
- Convey maturity by exhibiting the ability to tolerate differences of opinion.
- Never call anyone by a first name unless you are asked to do so.
- Know the name, title, and the pronunciation of the interviewer's name.
- Do not sit down until the interviewer does.
- Do not talk too much about your personal life.
- Never bad-mouth your former employers.

BE PREPARED FOR COMMON INTERVIEW QUESTIONS

You can never be sure exactly what will happen at an interview, but you can be prepared for common interview questions. There are some interview questions that are illegal. Interviewers should not ask you about your age, gender, color, race, or religion. Employers should not ask whether you are married or pregnant, or question your health or disabilities.

Take time to think about your answers now. You might even write them down to clarify your thinking. The key to all interview questions is to be honest, and to be positive. Focus your answers on skills and abilities that apply to the job you are seeking. Practice answering the following questions with a friend:

- "Tell me about yourself."
- "Why do you want to work at this company?"
- "What did you like/dislike about your last job?"
- "What is your biggest accomplishment?"
- "What is your greatest strength?"
- "What is your greatest weakness?"
- "Do you prefer to work with others or on your own?"
- "What are your career goals?" or "Where do you see yourself in five years?"
- "Tell me about a time that you had a lot of work to do in a short time. How did you manage the situation?"
- "Have you ever had to work closely with a person you didn't get along with? How did you handle the situation?"

AFTER THE INTERVIEW

Be sure to thank the interviewer after the interview for his or her time and effort. Do not forget to follow up after the interview. Ask, "What is the next step?" If you are told to call in a few days, wait two or three days before calling back.

If the interview went well, the employer may call you to offer you the job. Find out the terms of the job offer, including job title and pay. Decide whether you want the job. If you decide not to accept the job, write a letter of rejection. Be courteous and thank the person for the opportunity and the offer. You may wish to give a brief general reason for not accepting the job. Leave the door open for possible employment in the future.

FOLLOW UP WITH A LETTER

Write a thank-you letter as soon as the interview is over. This shows your good manners, interest, and enthusiasm for the job. It also shows that you are organized. Make the letter neat and courteous. Thank the interviewer. Sell yourself again.

ACCEPTING A NEW JOB

If you decide to take the job, write a letter of acceptance. The letter should include some words of appreciation for the opportunity, written acceptance of the job offer, the terms of employment (salary, hours, benefits), and the starting date. Make sure the letter is neat and correct.

STARTING A NEW JOB

Your first day of work will be busy. Determine what the dress code is and dress appropriately. Learn to do each task assigned properly. Ask for help when you need it. Learn the rules and regulations of the workplace.

You will do some paperwork on your first day. Bring your personal fact sheet with you. You will need to fill out some forms. Form W-4 tells your employer how much money to withhold for taxes. You may also need to fill out Form I-9. This shows that you are allowed to work in the United States. You will need your Social Security number and proof that you are allowed to work in the United States. You can bring your U.S. passport, your Certificate of Naturalization, or your Certificate of U.S. Citizenship. If you are not a permanent resident of the United States, bring your green card. If you are a resident of the United States, you will need to bring your work permit on your first day. If you are under the age of 16 in some states, you need a different kind of work permit.

You might be requested to take a drug test as a requirement for employment in some states. This could be for the safety of you and your coworkers, especially when working with machinery or other equipment.

IMPORTANT SKILLS AND QUALITIES

You will not work alone on a job. You will need to learn skills for getting along and being a team player. There are many good qualities necessary to get along in the workplace. They include being positive, showing sympathy, taking an interest in others, tolerating differences, laughing a little, and showing respect. Your employer may promote you or give you a raise if you show good employability skills.

There are several qualities necessary to be a good employee and get ahead in your job:

- be cooperative
- possess good character
- be responsible
- finish what you start
- work fast but do a good job
- have a strong work ethic
- work well without supervision
- work well with others
- possess initiative
- show enthusiasm for what you do
- be on time
- make the best of your time
- obey company laws and rules
- be honest
- be loyal
- exhibit good health habits

LEAVING A JOB

If you are considering leaving your job or are being laid off, you are facing one of the most difficult aspects in your career. The first step in resigning is to prepare a short resignation letter to offer your supervisor at the conclusion of the meeting you set up with him or her. Keep the letter short and to the point. Express your appreciation for the opportunity you had with the company. Do not try to list all that was wrong with the job.

You want to leave on good terms. Do not forget to ask for a reference. Do not talk about your employer or any of your coworkers. Do not talk negatively about your employer when you apply for a new job.

If you are being laid off or face downsizing, it can make you feel angry or depressed. Try to view it as a career-change opportunity. If possible, negotiate a good severance package. Find out about any benefits you may be entitled to. Perhaps the company will offer job-search services or consultation for finding new employment.

◕ TAKE ACTION!

It is time for action. Remember the networking and contact lists you created when you searched for this job. Reach out for support from friends, family, and other acquaintances. Consider joining a job-search club. Assess your skills. Upgrade them if necessary. Examine your attitude and your vocational choices. Decide the direction you wish to take and move on!

Glossary

How to Use This Glossary

- Content vocabulary terms in this glossary are words that relate to this book's content. They are **highlighted yellow** in your text.

- Words in this glossary that have an asterisk (*) are academic vocabulary terms. They help you understand your school subjects and are used on tests. They are **boldfaced blue** in your text.

- Some of the vocabulary words in this book include pronunciation symbols to help you sound out the words. Use the pronunciation key to help you pronounce the words.

Pronunciation Key		

a . . . . **a**t	**ô** . . . . f**o**rk, **a**ll	**th** . . . **th**in
ā . . . . **a**pe	**oo** . . . w**oo**d, p**u**t	**th** . . . **th**is
ä . . . . f**a**ther	**ōo** . . . f**oo**l	**zh** . . . trea**s**ure
e . . . . **e**nd	**oi** . . . **oi**l	**ə** . . . . **a**go, tak**e**n, penc**i**l, lem**o**n, circ**u**s
ē . . . . m**e**	**ou** . . . **ou**t	
i . . . . **i**t	**u** . . . . **u**p	**'** . . . . indicates primary stress (symbol in front of and *above* letter)
ī . . . . **i**ce	**ū** . . . . **u**se	
o . . . . h**o**t	**ü** . . . . r**u**le	**ˌ** . . . . indicates secondary stress (symbol in front of and *below* letter)
ō . . . . h**o**pe	**u** . . . . p**u**ll	
ȯ . . . . s**a**w	**ŋ** . . . . si**ng**	

abdominal thrust • adequate

abdominal thrust A quick upward thrust with the heel of the hand into the abdomen that forces the air in the lungs to force out an object caught in the throat. (p. 561)

* **ability** A skill you have already developed. (p. 633)

abstinence A deliberate decision to avoid high-risk behaviors, including sexual activity and the use of tobacco, alcohol, and other drugs. (p. 44)

abstract thought The capacity to consider "what if" situations, to create sophisticated arguments, and to reason from different points of view. (p. 542)

* **accommodate** To make room for. (p. 200)

accreditation Official recognition as having met a standard, such as child care provider for quality child care. (p. 604)

* **adaptation** Adjustment; the process of changing to fit new circumstances. (p. 586)

ADD Attention deficit disorder; similar to ADHD, but does not involve hyperactivity. (p. 583)

addiction A dependence on a substance, such as alcohol or drugs. (p. 576)

addiction counselor A therapist trained to help substance abusers. (p. 593)

* **adequate** Sufficient in quantity or quality to meet a need. (p. 332)

ADHD Attention deficit hyperactive disorder; a behavioral disorder in which children often fail to finish what they start, do not seem to listen, and are easily distracted. (p. 583)

* **adolescent** Teen; someone who has reached puberty but is not yet an adult. (p. 521)

age appropriate Something is suitable for the age and individual needs of a child. (p. 274)

* **aggravate** To anger or irritate. (p. 212)

aggressive behavior Hostile, and at times destructive, behavior that people display when faced with conflict. (p. 419)

* **alleviate** Ease, make less severe. (p. 133)

alliteration The repetition of beginning sounds. (p. 435)

alternative birth center A facility that provides a more homelike environment for labor and delivery. (p. 157)

ambidextrous The ability to use both hands with equal skill. (p. 387)

amniocentesis (ˌam-nē-ō-(ˌ)sen-ˈtē-səs) The process of withdrawing a sample of the amniotic fluid surrounding the unborn baby. (p. 113)

amniotic fluid (ˌam-nē-ˈä-tik) The liquid that surrounds and protects the developing baby in the uterus. (p. 100)

amygdala (ə-ˈmig-də-lə) The part of the brain that controls fear, joy, and other emotional reactions. (p. 540)

anecdotal record A report of a child's actions that concentrates on a specific behavior or area of development. (p. 22)

anemia A condition that results from not having enough red blood cells. (p. 130)

* **anesthesia** Drugs that cause a loss of feeling, used for pain relief. (p. 171)

antibody A substance produced by the body to fight off germs. (p. 213)

antiseptic A substance that prevents or stops the growth of germs. (p. 559)

anxiety A state of uncertainty and fear, often about an unspecified but seemingly immediate threat. (p. 476)

Apgar scale A system of rating the physical condition of a newborn baby. (p. 177)

aptitude A natural talent or potential for learning a skill. (p. 633)

articulation The ability to use clear, distinct speech. (pp. 369, 437)

* **assumption** A fact that is taken for granted. (p. 21)

asthma A condition that causes the lungs to contract more than they should, narrowing the air passages and making it difficult to breathe. (p. 553)

attachment A baby's bond to his or her main caregiver. (p. 239)

attention span The length of time a person can concentrate on a task without getting bored. (p. 268)

autism A disorder that affects a child's ability to communicate and interact with others. (p. 585)

autism spectrum disorders (ASD) A group of disorders that includes autism. (p. 585)

autonomy Personal independence and the capacity to make decisions and act on them. (p. 342)

axon The connection between neurons that transmits instructions from the cell body to another neuron. (p. 259)

B

baseline A count made before any steps are taken to try to change a behavior. (p. 22)

bilingual Able to speak two languages. (p. 436)

bilirubin A substance produced by the breakdown of red blood cells. (p. 180)

Glossary

bipolar disorder A psychiatric disorder characterized by extreme changes in mood, from highly energetic to depressed and withdrawn, sometimes fluctuating rapidly. (p. 532)

blended family A family that is formed when a single parent marries another person, who may or may not have children. (p. 63)

body image How a person thinks his or her body looks. (p. 454)

bonding The act of forming emotional ties between parents and child. (p. 180)

bullying Directing aggression or abuse toward another person, usually someone weaker. (p. 485)

*__capacity__ The ability to do or experience something. (p. 461)

cardiopulmonary resuscitation (CPR) A technique that combines rescue breathing with chest compressions to restore breathing and circulation. (p. 566)

career ladder A visualization of your chosen career path. (p. 637)

career path All of the career moves and job experience that a person gains as he or she works toward a career goal. (p. 637)

caregiver A person who takes care of a child. (p. 8)

cause and effect A relationship between events in which one event, the effect, is caused by another event. (p. 245)

cervix The lower part of the uterus. (p. 165)

cesarean birth (si-'zer-ē-ən) Also known as a cesarean section or c-section, it is the delivery of a baby through a surgical incision in the mother's abdomen. (p. 172)

child care center A facility in which a staff of adults provides care for children. (p. 603)

childproof To take steps to protect the child from possible dangers. (p. 275)

chromosome A tiny threadlike structure in the nucleus of every cell. (p. 95)

circle time When the children share their experiences in show-and-tell or listen to a story together. (p. 619)

COBRA (Consolidated Omnibus Budget Reconciliation Act) A law ensuring that former employees can keep the health insurance plan they received through their former employer for up to 18 months. (p. 649)

colic Uncontrollable crying by an otherwise healthy baby. (p. 238)

colostrum (kə-'läs-trəm) A high-calorie, high-protein early breast milk. (p. 181)

communicable disease A disease that is passed from one person to another. (p. 551)

competition Rivalry with the goal of winning or outperforming others. (p. 420)

*__complication__ A problem; something that makes something else more difficult. (p. 155)

*__compressed__ Flattened; pressed together. (p. 156)

concept A general category of objects and information that can also include abstract ideas. (p. 269)

conception The process of the sperm fertilizing the ovum. (p. 95)

*__concrete__ Actual; certain; specific. (p. 499)

confidential adoption An adoption in which the birth parents do not know the names of the adoptive parents. (p. 49)

confidentiality (ˌkän-fə-ˌden(t)shē-'a-lə-tē) The protection of another person's privacy by limiting access to personal information. (p. 25)

conformity Choosing to be like one another. (p. 488)

*__congenital__ Present at birth. (p. 120)

conscience An inner sense of what is right. (p. 74)

conservation When an object has the same characteristics even if there is a change in the way it looks. (p. 500)

consistent Continually the same. (p. 81)

* **constructive** Positive; carefully considered and meant to be helpful. (p. 593)

contagious Transmitted from one person to another, such as touching an infected person. (p. 554)

contraction The tightening and releasing of the muscles of the uterus. This is also a sign of labor. (p. 166)

* **controversial** Causing extremely opposing views. (p. 99)

* **convey** To express or communicate something and make it known. (p. 640)

* **convictions** Firmly held beliefs or opinions. (p. 536)

convulsion A seizure; a brief period during which muscles suddenly contract, causing the person to fall and twitch or jerk. (p. 562)

cooperative play A type of play in which children play and interact with one another. (p. 336)

cord blood The blood left behind in the umbilical cord and placenta following birth. (p. 171)

cortex Part of the brain's cerebrum; its growth permits more complex learning. (p. 259)

* **counterproductive** Producing difficulties or problems instead of helping achieve a goal. (p. 489)

cover letter An introductory letter sent with a résumé. (p. 643)

cradle cap A skin condition known for yellowish, crusty patches on the scalp. (p. 223)

creativity A mental ability that involves using the imagination to produce original ideas. (p. 361)

crisis nursery A child care facility where troubled parents can go to receive short-term, free child care. (p. 594)

* **criteria** Accepted standards. (p. 605)

* **crucial** Essential; very important. (p. 239)

cultural bias An advantage to people from one culture over other cultures. (p. 428)

* **curb** To limit or control something. (p. 213)

custodial parent The parent with whom the child resides. (p. 62)

D

* **decipher** To interpret; to study something until it can be understood. (p. 368)

* **deformity** A defect in normal body structure. (p. 116)

delivery The birth of the baby. (p. 154)

dendrite A branchlike feature at the end of each axon that receives the messages from other neurons. (p. 259)

depression Feelings of intense sadness that last for long periods of time and prevent a person from leading a normal life. (p. 531)

deprivation A lack of the critical needs and encouraging environment that are essential for physical, emotional, and intellectual well-being. (p. 70)

depth perception The ability to perceive objects that are three-dimensional. (p. 201)

* **designate** To specify or choose. (p. 224)

* **detection** Discovery; the act of noticing the existence of something. (p. 551)

* **determined** Reasoned; to bring to light or disclose. (p. 270)

developmental checklist A list of skills children should master, or behaviors they should exhibit at a certain age. (p. 23)

developmental milestone A key skill used to check a child's progress. (p. 195)

Glossary

developmental task The challenge to be met or skill to be acquired in each stage of the human life cycle. (p. 18)

developmentally appropriate Toys, activities, and tasks that are suitable for a child at a specific age. (p. 297)

dexterity The skillful use of the hands and fingers; ease and skill in physical activity. (pp. 299, 386)

diaper rash A condition that includes patches of rough, red, irritated skin in the diaper area. (p. 223)

dilate To widen or open. (p. 170)

directed learning Learning that results from being taught, often by parents, other caregivers, teachers, or older siblings. (p. 356)

dispute Quarrel. (p. 73)

* **distinguish** See or perceive a difference in. (p. 582)

* **distraction** A diversion; something that interferes with concentration. (p. 341)

DNA (deoxyribonucleic acid) The complex molecules that make up genes. (p. 95)

dyslexia A learning disorder that prevents a child from understanding printed symbols in a normal way. (p. 582)

— **E** —

eating disorder A serious pattern of over-eating or restrictive eating. (p. 454)

* **elevate** To raise up. (p. 559)

* **elicit** To bring forth; to produce some sort of reaction or response. (pp. 270, 360)

embryo The developing baby from about the third week of pregnancy through the eighth week. (p. 100)

* **emerge** To appear out of or from behind something. (p. 225)

emotion A feeling response to the world around us. (p. 235)

emotional development The process of learning to recognize and express feelings and to establish a personal identity. (p. 235)

emotional maturity Being responsible enough to consistently put someone else's needs before your own needs. (p. 35)

empathy The ability to understand how another person feels. (p. 330)

enamel The hard, outer coating of teeth. (p. 394)

entrepreneur (ˌänˌtrə-p(r)ə-ˈnər) Someone who chooses to be self-employed or to own his or her own business. (p. 632)

entry-level job The kind of job many people take when they first enter a career area. (p. 631)

environment The people, places, and things that surround and influence a person, including family, home, school, and community. (p. 14)

* **erect** Straight; in an upright position. (p. 384)

* **essential** Necessary; of the highest importance. (p. 48)

estrogen A hormone produced by the ovaries. (p. 522)

ethical Doing the right thing. (p. 648)

* **expectations** Expected behaviors; a standard expected by or of someone. (p. 622)

* **expel** To force out. (p. 561)

extended family A family that includes a parent or parents, at least one child, and other relatives who live with them. (p. 63)

* **extracurricular** Optional; not part of the normal courses of a school or college. (p. 525)

— **F** —

failure to thrive A condition in which babies do not grow and develop properly. (p. 240)

fallopian tube A tube that connects the ovary to the uterus. (p. 93)

family child care Care that takes place in the caregiver's home. (p. 603)

fetal alcohol effects Abnormalities caused by the mother consuming alcohol during pregnancy. (p. 116)

fetal alcohol syndrome (FAS) An incurable condition found in some children of mothers who consumed alcohol during pregnancy. (p. 116)

fetal monitoring The watching of an unborn baby's heart rate for indications of stress. (p. 166)

fetus (ˈfē-təs) The developing baby from around the eighth or ninth week of pregnancy until birth. (p. 101)

fiber An indigestible plant material that helps the digestive system work properly. (p. 459)

fidelity Faithfulness to an obligation, duty, or trust. (p. 50)

fine motor skill A skill that involves the smaller muscles of the body such as those in the fingers. (p. 206)

finger play A song or chant with accompanying hand motions. (p. 437)

fixed expense A payment that generally cannot be changed, such as bills, housing payment, and taxes. (p. 150)

flame-resistant Something that is treated to not burn as quickly as other materials. (p. 314)

flexible expense An expense that can be changed, such as food costs, household items, clothes, and entertainment. (p. 150)

fluoride A substance that strengthens the enamel of teeth to help prevent decay. (p. 394)

fontanel An open space found on the baby's head where the bones are not yet joined. (p. 176)

formula A mixture of milk or milk substitutes, water, and essential nutrients fed to babies. (p. 149)

* foster To encourage the development of something. (p. 437)

foster child A child that comes from a troubled family or difficult circumstances and is placed in the temporary care of another person or family. (p. 64)

fracture A break or crack in a bone. (p. 560)

free play A time when children can choose any activity they want. (p. 620)

frequency count A tally of how often a certain behavior occurs. (p. 22)

* function A job or action for which something is suited or designed. (p. 259)

* fuse To combine; to unite or blend. (p. 176)

* gauge To form a judgment of something uncertain or variable. (p. 336)

gender identity The awareness of being male or female. (p. 480)

gene A unit that determines a human's inherited characteristics. (p. 95)

genome The complete blueprint for the creation of a person. (p. 95)

gestational diabetes A form of diabetes that occurs only during pregnancy. If left untreated, gestational diabetes can cause the baby to be heavier than is normal or healthy. (p. 131)

gifted Showing, or having the potential to show, special abilities in one or more areas. (p. 588)

gross motor skill A skill that involves the large muscles of the body such as those of the legs and shoulders. (p. 206)

Glossary

group identification A feeling of belonging with others. (p. 394)

growth chart A chart that shows the average weight and height of girls and boys at various ages. (p. 198)

growth spurt When a child grows very rapidly in a short period of time. (p. 453)

guidance Using firmness and understanding to help children learn how to behave. (p. 73)

H

hand-eye coordination The ability to move the hands and fingers precisely in relation to what is seen. (p. 207)

* **hazard** Something that is potentially dangerous. (p. 281)

Head Start A program that provides locally run child care facilities designed to help lower-income and disadvantaged children from birth to five years of age become ready for school. (p. 606)

heredity The biological transfer of certain characteristics from earlier generations. (p. 14)

* **hinder** To delay or obstruct the development of someone or something. (p. 243)

hives Blisterlike sores caused by an allergic reaction. (p. 564)

hormone A chemical in the body that controls the changes that occur as teens become sexually mature. (p. 43)

human life cycle A set of stages of human development that each present different challenges to be met or skills to be acquired. (p. 18)

hygiene Personal care and cleanliness. (p. 310)

hypothetical Involving something that could possibly happen. (p. 500)

I

identity crisis A confusion about one's personal identity that results from failing to find a strong identity, or sense of self, through personal exploration. (p. 529)

imaginative play Pretending; seeing or hearing things that might happen but have not happened yet. (p. 272)

imitation Learning by watching and copying others. (p. 356)

immunization A shot of a small amount of a dead or weak disease-carrying germ given so that the body can build up resistance to the disease. (p. 227)

* **impact** A significant effect. (p. 7)

* **impulsive** Having a tendency to act spontaneously without considering the consequences. (p. 406)

* **incident** An action, occurrence, or event. (p. 303)

incidental learning Unplanned learning. (p. 355)

inclusion Placing children with disabilities in regular classrooms while they also receive special education services. (p. 587)

incubator A special enclosed crib where the oxygen supply, temperature, and humidity can be closely controlled. (p. 173)

* **induce** To start; to make the process of labor or a birth begin by a medical intervention. (p. 166)

infertility The inability of a man or woman to contribute to conception. (p. 97)

in-home care Care that is provided to many young children from a caregiver who comes to their home. (p. 603)

initiative The motivation to accomplish more. (p. 411)

* **integrate** To combine; to join together to make something part of a larger whole. (p. 506)

intelligence The ability to interpret and understand everyday situations and to use prior experiences when faced with new situations or problems. (p. 354)

intelligence quotient (IQ) A number obtained by comparing a child's test results to those of other children the same age. (p. 427)

intergenerational Occurring between older and younger age groups. (p. 65)

internship A job in which a person works for little or no pay while gaining experience and receiving supervision. (p. 634)

interpretation The analysis an observer forms and expresses about what was observed. (p. 25)

* **intimacy** A closeness between two people. (p. 43)

* **irrational** Lacking reason. (p. 578)

jaundice (ˈjȯn-dəs) A condition that causes the baby's skin and eyes to look slightly yellow. (p. 180)

job fair An event where employers with current or future job openings meet with potential employees. (p. 639)

job shadowing To observe someone performing his or her job. (p. 634)

job-specific skills The skills or abilities needed to do a specific job. (p. 647)

* **judgment** An opinion. (p. 22)

L

labor The process in which the baby gradually moves out of the uterus and into the vagina to be born. (p. 154)

lactase An enzyme that helps digest lactose. (p. 142)

lactation consultant A professional breast-feeding specialist who shows mothers how to encourage adequate milk produc-

tion and how to position babies properly so that they can nurse. (p. 181)

lactose intolerant Having a condition in which milk products cause symptoms such as abdominal pain and gas. (p. 142)

lanugo Fine, downy hair growing on newborns' foreheads, backs, and shoulders. (p. 177)

* **lead** An example or precedent. (p. 248)

learning center An area designed for certain types of play and learning. (p. 614)

learning disability A condition that interferes with a child's ability to learn, listen, think, speak, read, write, spell, or do math. (p. 582)

learning method A way to learn. (p. 505)

legal guardian A person who is designated by a legal process to assume responsibility for raising a child. (p. 64)

* **legible** Clear enough to be read. (p. 643)

license An official printed document that gives permission, such as one from the state that indicates child care providers meet health and safety standards. (p. 604)

lifelong learner Someone who is willing to learn new information and acquire skills throughout his or her working life. (p. 648)

* **major** Significant; of considerable importance. (p. 180)

* **makeup** Structure or arrangement. (p. 195)

malnutrition Inadequate nutrition. (p. 218)

* **mandate** To require or order. (p. 508)

mandated reporter A person who is required by law to report maltreatment. (p. 594)

manipulate To work with the hands. (p. 280)

Glossary

Glossary

maternity leave Time taken off work by a mother after the birth of a baby. (p. 151)

math readiness The level of knowledge of basic math concepts, such as number recognition, needed for learning math. (p. 366)

menstruation The monthly cycle in which an egg is released and the uterus prepares for a possible pregnancy. (p. 456)

mental retardation Having below-average intelligence and skills. This condition is also known as cognitive impairment or developmental disability. (p. 583)

midwife A professional trained to assist women in childbirth. (p. 155)

miscarriage When the developing baby dies prior to the twentieth week of pregnancy. (p. 106)

model To base a behavior on somebody else; to teach it through example. (p. 245)

* **moral** Ethical; relating to issues of right and wrong. (p. 10)

moral development The process of learning to base one's behavior on beliefs about what is right and wrong. (p. 416)

moral maturity When people are able to recognize and respect other people's points of view. (p. 536)

morality A sense of right and wrong that guides decisions and actions. (p. 535)

* **motivate** To provide a reason to do something. (p. 250)

* **multifaceted** Many-sided; with many qualities or features. (p. 501)

multiple intelligences Abilities in problem solving or creating materials that have value. (p. 428)

myelin (ˈmī-ə-lən) A waxy, protein-based substance that coats axons and helps transmit information from one nerve cell to another. (p. 259)

MyPyramid A guide for healthful eating and active living that was developed by the U.S. Department of Agriculture (USDA). (p. 460)

nanny A person trained to provide child care. (p. 604)

negative reinforcement A response aimed at strengthening desired behavior by removing an unpleasant trigger. (p. 79)

negativism Doing the opposite of what others want. (p. 323)

neonatal period The first month after the baby is born. (p. 180)

networking The practice of using personal and professional contacts to further your career goals. (p. 640)

neural pathway The link between neurons. (p. 257)

neuron A nerve cell. (p. 257)

neuroscience The modern study of the brain. (p. 353)

neurotransmitter (ˌnu̇r-ō-tran(t)s-ˈmi-tər) is a chemical released by the axon. The neurotransmitter acts as a messenger between the neurons. (p. 260)

night terrors A type of sleep disturbance that occurs during the first few hours of sleep, when children are sleeping deeply. (p. 303)

NREM sleep A cycle of sleep in which rapid eye movement does not occur. (p. 333)

nuclear family A family that includes a mother and father and at least one child. (p. 62)

O

object permanence The concept that objects will continue to exist, even when they are out of sight. (p. 271)

objective Something is factual, and leaves aside personal feelings and prejudices. (p. 21)

obstetrician (ˌäb-stə-ˈtri-shən) A doctor who specializes in pregnancy and childbirth. (p. 129)

open adoption An adoption in which the birth parents and adoptive parents know something about each other. (p. 50)

* **oriented** Directed or positioned in a particular way. (p. 430)

orthodontist A dental specialist who concentrates on fixing irregularities of the teeth. (p. 465)

osteoporosis A condition in which bones become fragile and break easily. (p. 139)

ovum An egg cell. (p. 93)

parallel play When children play near, but not actually with, other children. (p. 335)

* **paramount** Of extreme importance or significance. (p. 488)

paraprofessional Someone with some education beyond high school that trains him or her for a certain field. (p. 631)

parent cooperative Also called co-op, it is child care that is provided by the parents of the children in the co-op. (p. 605)

parenting The process of caring for children and helping them grow and develop. (p. 33)

parenting style The way parents and other caregivers care for and discipline children. (p. 72)

paternity The legal identification of a man as the biological father of a child. (p. 48)

paternity leave Time taken off work by the father after a baby's birth. (p. 151)

pediatrician A doctor who specializes in treating children. (p. 149)

peer Someone close to one's own age. (p. 414)

peer learning A learning method in which students observe and interact with one another by working together in pairs, small groups, or as a class on a project or task. (p. 505)

peer pressure A social group's influence on the way individuals behave. (p. 488)

perception The ability to learn from sensory information. (p. 266)

* **perceptive** Observant; quick to understand things. (p. 321)

permanent teeth Teeth that will not be naturally replaced by another set. (p. 384)

* **persevere** To persist steadily in an action or belief. (p. 479)

personal identity A sense of oneself as a unique individual. (p. 528)

* **persuade** To convince; to make somebody believe something. (p. 390)

phobia An unexplainable and illogical fear. (p. 327)

phoneme (ˈfō-ˌnēm) The smallest individual sound in a word, such as the ou in house. (p. 435)

placenta (plə-ˈsen-tə) A tissue that connects the developing baby to the uterus. (p. 100)

play environment A comfortable space free of dangers and with toys that are safe and interesting. (p. 249)

play group An arrangement in which parents take turns caring for one another's children in their own homes. (p. 604)

pollen A powder-like grain that come from seed plants. (p. 553)

* **pollutant** Something that makes the environment dirty. (p. 308)

popular culture The culture that prevails in modern society. (p. 537)

positive reinforcement A response that encourages a particular behavior. (p. 76)

postnatal period The time following the baby's birth. (p. 183)

postpartum depression A condition in which new mothers may feel very sad, cry a lot, have little energy, feel overly anxious about the baby or have little interest in the baby, and, in extreme cases, think of harming the baby. (p. 184)

preeclampsia (ˌprē-i-ˈklam(p)-sē-ə) A condition characterized by high blood pressure and the presence of protein in the mother's urine. (p. 132)

* **predisposition** A tendency to do something or behave in a certain way. (p. 111)

prefrontal cortex The part of the brain that sits just behind the forehead and controls planning, organization, prioritizing, and other complex thought processes. (p. 540)

prenatal development The baby's development during a pregnancy (p. 99)

prepared childbirth A plan for reducing pain and fear during the birth process through education, and the use of breathing and conditioning exercises. (p. 154)

preschooler A child from age three to about age five. (p. 293)

* **pride** Pleasure; a happy satisfied feeling with oneself. (p. 33)

professional Someone with a position that requires at least a degree from a four-year college or technical school in a specific area of study. (p. 632)

* **profound** Overwhelming, very strong, intense; extreme. (pp. 453, 541)

proportion The size relationship between different parts of the body. (p. 200)

* **proportion** Size. (p. 294)

* **prospective** Likely, or expected to happen. (p. 35)

puberty The set of changes that result in a physically mature body that is able to reproduce. (p. 453)

reading readiness Learning the skills necessary for reading, including letter recognition and the understanding that letters of the alphabet combine to form words on a page. (p. 365)

* **receptor** A receiver; a nerve ending that is sensitive to stimuli. (p. 260)

* **refine** To improve something through small changes. (p. 414)

reflex An instinctive, automatic response, such as grasping or sucking. (p. 206)

reflux A condition in which partially digested food rises in the throat. (p. 238)

regression The temporary backward movement to an earlier stage of development. (p. 573)

* **regulate** To control and bring to a desired level. (p. 429)

* **reimbursement** Repayment. (p. 151)

REM sleep A sleep cycle characterized by rapid eye movement. (p. 333)

rescue breathing A procedure for forcing air into the lungs of a person who is not breathing. (p. 566)

* **responsiveness** Reactions, usually strong or favorable, to something. (p. 274)

Rh factor A protein present in most people's red blood cells. A mother's blood is tested for this protein to determine if it is positive or negative in order to protect the fetus. (p. 131)

* **resort** To choose; to turn to something for help, often extreme, in dealing with a problem. (p. 419)

résumé A concise document that summarizes your career objectives, education, work experience, and accomplishments. (p. 640)

* **robust** Thriving, strong, healthy. (p. 132)

rooming-in When the baby remains with the mother in her room during the hospital stay; it can be a full-time or part-time arrangement. (p. 181)

running record A record of everything observed for a set period, such as 15 minutes. (p. 22)

— **S** —

scoliosis A sideways curvature of the spine affecting posture. (p. 454)

sealant A thick plastic coating, often used by dentists on teeth. (p. 465)

* **secure** Safe; untroubled by feelings of fear. (p. 177)

sedentary activity An activity that involves little exercise, such as watching television. (p. 463)

self-centered Thinking about one's own needs and wants and not those of others. (p. 322)

self-concept How people see themselves. (p. 331)

self-confidence Belief in one's own abilities. (p. 411)

self-discipline The ability of children to control their own behavior. (pp. 73, 340)

self-esteem Self-worth; the value people place on themselves. (p. 17)

* **self-sufficiency** The ability to take care of oneself. (p. 614)

sense of competence The feeling that one can be successful and meet most challenges. (p. 478)

sense of self Your idea of who you are, based on your emotions, personality, and the ways you perceive the world. (p. 477)

* **sensitivity** A reaction; ability to be easily damaged or physically irritated. (p. 553)

sensorimotor period Piaget's first stage of learning that lasts from birth to about age two. (p. 270)

sensory integration The process by which the brain combines information taken in through the senses to make a whole. (p. 296)

separation anxiety The fear of being away from parents, familiar caregivers, or the normal environment. (p. 327)

* **sequence** An order of steps. (p. 14)

* **serious** Severe; important enough to require attention. (p. 111)

service learning A school program in which students volunteer in their community as a graduation requirement. (p. 634)

sexuality Your beliefs and values about sexual behavior. (p. 43)

sexually transmitted infection (STI) A disease that is spread from one person to another by sexual contact. (p. 45)

shaken baby syndrome A condition that occurs when someone severely shakes a baby, usually in an effort to make him or her stop crying. (p. 211)

* **shift** To change; to move to a different position. (p. 473)

shock A serious medical condition in which important body functions, including breathing and heartbeat, are impaired. (p. 565)

sibling rivalry The competition between brothers or sisters for parents' affection and attention. (p. 328)

SIDS Sudden infant death syndrome; the sudden, unexpected death of a baby under one year of age with no clear cause. (p. 118)

single-parent family A family that includes either a mother or a father and at least one child. (p. 62)

situational stress Stress that comes from the environment a child lives in or from certain circumstances and changes. (p. 573)

Glossary

* **slat** A flat, narrow strip of wood, such as on the sides of a crib. (p. 147)

sleep deprived Lacking adequate sleep. (p. 332)

social development The process of learning how to interact and express oneself with others. (p. 245)

socialization The process of learning to get along with others. (p. 335)

* **socialize** To participate; to behave in a friendly way to others. (p. 604)

* **sophisticated** Refined; self-confident; complex; advanced. (p. 540)

sperm The male reproductive cell. (p. 93)

sphincter (ˈsfiŋ(k)-tər) **muscles** The muscles that help regulate elimination from the bowels. (p. 311)

* **spontaneous** Unplanned, without external influence. (p. 101)

sprain An injury caused by sudden, violent stretching of a joint or muscle. (p. 560)

* **stable** Unchanging; steady and firm. (p. 183)

standardized test A test that lets educators see how students are performing intellectually when compared to the thousands of other students who have taken the same test. (p. 508)

stem cells Cells capable of producing all types of blood cells. (p. 171)

* **stifle** To suppress, or prevent the development of something. (pp. 362, 533)

stillbirth When the fetus dies after the twentieth week of pregnancy. (p. 106)

* **stimulating environment** An environment in which one has a wide variety of things to see, taste, smell, hear, and touch. (p. 197)

stimulation Any activity that arouses a baby's sense of sight, sound, touch, taste, and smell. (p. 13)

stranger anxiety A fear of unfamiliar people, usually expressed by crying. (p. 247)

stuttering When a person speaks with sporadic repetition or prolonged sounds. (p. 370)

subjective To rely on personal opinions and feelings, rather than facts, to judge an event. (p. 21)

support group A collection of individuals who work together to explore and accept their feelings. (p. 577)

* **suppress** To control; to prevent from happening. (p. 466)

surrogate (ˈsər-ə-ˌgāt) A substitute. A surrogate mother is a woman who becomes pregnant to have a baby for another woman. (p. 98)

symbolic thinking The use of words and numbers to stand for ideas. (p. 272)

synapse (ˈsi-ˌnaps) The tiny gap between the dendrites where messages are transmitted from one neuron to another. (p. 260)

synthetic fibers Fabrics made from chemicals, rather than natural sources. (p. 314)

teething The process of the teeth pushing their way through the gums. (p. 225)

temper tantrum When children release anger or frustration by screaming, crying, kicking, pounding, and sometimes holding their breath. (p. 324)

temperament A person's unique emotional makeup. (p. 240)

* **terminate** To end. (p. 594)

tension Emotional stress. (p. 409)

testosterone (tes-ˈtäs-tə-ˌrōn) A hormone produced by the testicles. (p. 522)

* **theory** A belief; an abstract thought or idea. (p. 13)

time-out When a child is removed from the group, perhaps by being required to sit in a special chair for a short period of time. (pp. 79, 345)

toddler A term that refers to one- and two-year-olds. (p. 293)

toxoplasmosis (ˌtäk-sə-ˌplaz-ˈmō-səs) An infection caused by a parasite. (p. 120)

transferable skills General skills used in school and in various types of jobs. (p. 647)

transition A period during which children move from one activity to the next. (p. 620)

transitivity The concept that a relative relationship between two objects can extend to a third object. (p. 500)

trial-and-error learning Learning that takes place when a child tries several solutions to find one that works. (p. 355)

* **turmoil** A state of extreme confusion or agitation. (p. 406)

type 1 diabetes A lifelong condition caused by the body's inability to produce enough insulin. (p. 584)

typical behavior A way of acting or responding that is common at each stage of childhood. (p. 7)

* **ultimate** Final; coming at the very last. (p. 454)

ultrasound A test that uses sound waves to make a video image of an unborn baby. (p. 112)

umbilical cord A long tube that connects the baby to the placenta. (p. 100)

* **undermine** To weaken or diminish. (p. 392)

unemployment benefits Funds paid by individual states to unemployed people who are actively seeking employment. (p. 649)

* **unstructured** Lacking formal organization. (p. 367)

uterus The organ in a woman's body in which a baby develops during pregnancy. (p. 93)

vaccine A disease-carrying germ that usually is injected in the body to build resistance to a disease. (p. 227)

* **variation** The state of differing from a former state or value. (p. 294)

* **venture** To proceed; to presume or dare to do something. (p. 61)

vernix A thick, white, pasty substance made up of the fetus's old skin cells and the secretions of skin glands. (p. 177)

* **visualization** A mental image; a clear picture of something in the mind. (p. 637)

* **vital** Necessary; extremely important and necessary. (p. 57)

* **vulnerable** Helpless, exposed to harm or damage. (p. 573)

weaning Changing from drinking from the bottle or breast to a cup. (p. 217)

work-based learning A school program that offers students the opportunity to combine in-school and on-the-job learning. (p. 634)

Z

zygote (ˈzī-ˌgōt) The fertilized egg. (p. 99)

Glossary

Index

Aptitudes, choosing career matching, 633
Art, learning through, 436–437
Articulation, 369, 370, 437
Artificial insemination, 98
ASD (autism spectrum disorders), 585
Assertive-democratic parenting, 73
Associations, as sign of intellectual growth, 266
Assumptions, 21
Asthma, 16, 553–554, 584
Attachment, 239–240
Attention
   as encouragement for learning, 275
   in one-to-three year olds, 357
Attention deficit disorder (ADD), 583
Attention deficit hyperactive disorder (ADHD), 407, 583
Attention span, 268
   in infants, 268
   in seven-to-twelve year olds, 498
Australia, preventing infant death in, 559
Austria, children in, 411
Authoritarian parenting, 72
Authority stage (parenthood), 38
Autism, 71, 585
Autism spectrum disorders (ASD), 585
Autistic savants, 584
Autonomy, 342
Awareness, 497–498
Axons, 259, 263, 353

B

Babbling, 277, 278
Baby blues, 184
Baby bottle decay, 295

Baby formula, 149, 214. *See also* Bottle-feeding
Bales, Diane, 365
Bandura, Albert, 15
Barbour, Ann, 440
Baselines, 22
Basic needs, 58
Bathing
   infants, 222–223
   one-to-three year olds, 310
   four-to-six year olds, 394
Bathtub safety, 311
Beds, for one-to-three year olds, 303
Bedwetting, 395
Behavior
   in early childhood classrooms, 622–624
   guiding, 72–77
   inappropriate, dealing with, 77–81
   modeling, 74
   typical, 7, 8
Belittling children, 80
Between Generations (Ellen Galinsky), 38
Bicycle safety, 396, 560
Bilingual children, 436
Bilirubin, 180
Binet, Alfred, 427
Binge drinking, 116
Binge eating, 462
Biological children, 64
Bipolar disorder, 532–533
Birth. *see* Childbirth
Birth centers, 155, 157
Birth certificates, 182
Birth control pills, 94
Birth defects, 106–113
   prevention and diagnosis of, 111–113
   types and causes of, 107–111
Birth plan, 154
Bites, first aid for, 562–564
Biting, by one-to-three year olds, 344

Bleeding, first aid for, 559
Blended families, 63
"Bloody show," 165
Bodily-kinesthetic intelligence, 428, 502
Body image, in seven-to-twelve year olds, 454
Body language, 62
Body shape
   infants, 199
   four-to-six year olds, 384
Body systems
   in embryonic stage, 100
   in fetal stage, 101
Bonding, 181
Bonding with infants, 180–181
   and attachment, 239–240
   preemies, 183
Booster shots, 466
Bottle-feeding, 148, 149, 181, 213–215
Brain, 176
   how the brain works, 259–260
   organization of, 261
   structure of, 257–259
Brain development (in general)
   and bonding with parents, 180–181
   during early childhood, 13
   in embryonic stage, 100
   neural connections, 14
   and nutrition during pregnancy, 137
   (*See also* The Developing Brain)
Brain development (infants), 256–264
   environment for, 196–197
   how the brain becomes organized, 261
   how the brain works, 259–260
   stimulating, 262–264

Index

Positive reinforcement, 76–77, 623

Postnatal period, 179–184
bonding in, 180–181
completing legal documents in, 182
defined, 183
help with feeding in, 181
mother's care in, 183–184
for premature babies, 182–183
rooming-in during, 181–182

Postpartum depression, 183, 184

Posture
in infants, 199
in one-to-three year olds, 294
in four-to-six year olds, 384
in seven-to-twelve year olds, 454

Practical intelligence, 503

Predisposition, genetic, 111

Preeclampsia, 132

Prefrontal cortex, 540

Pregnancy, 95, 126–142
age-related risks during, 35, 36
and alcohol use, 115–116
and caffeine, 117
daily routines during, 135–136
development of baby during. *see* Prenatal development
discomforts of, 132–133
diseases and infections during, 120–122
early signs of, 129
ectopic, 95
embryonic stage, 100
emotional health during, 136–137
and environmental hazards, 119–120
fetal stage, 101–104

germinal stage, 99
and illegal drugs, 118–119
losing a baby, 106–113
medical care during, 129–132
nutrition during, 137–142
options for dealing with, 48–50
physical changes during, 133, 135
and prescription or over-the-counter drugs, 116–117
problems caused by, 47–48
stages of, 99
and tobacco, 118

Premature birth, 118, 173

Premature infants, caring for, 173, 182–183

Premature labor, 166

Prenatal addictions, 118

Prenatal care, 111

Prenatal development, 99–104
and alcohol use, 115–116
and birth defects, 106–113
and caffeine, 117
conception, 93, 95
and diseases and infections of mother, 120–122
and environmental hazards, 119–120
and illegal drugs, 118–119
and prescription or over-the-counter drugs, 116–117
and tobacco, 118

Prenatal tests (for birth defects), 112–113

Preoperational period, 356, 430–431, 499, 542

Prepared childbirth, 154

Preparing for parenthood, 144–152
child care options, 151
childbirth options, 153–157
choosing a pediatrician, 149–150
clothes, equipment, and space, 145–147
feeding decisions, 148, 149
making a budget, 150–152
with other children in the family, 145

Preschoolers, 293

Preschools, 605–606

Prescription drugs, during pregnancy, 116–117

Preteen years, 453, 474, 497. *See also* Seven-to-twelve year olds

Primary (baby) teeth, 225

Privileges, loss of, 79

Problem solving, 483

Professional careers, 632

Profound physical change, 453

Promises to behave, 80

Proportion, 200
in infants, 200
in one-to-three year olds, 294
in seven-to-twelve year olds, 454

Pruning (synapses), 261

Puberty, 453
in seven-to-twelve year olds, 456–457
in adolescents, 521–523

Punishment for misbehaviors, 78–81

R

Rapid eye movement (REM), 333

Reading
for four-to-six year olds, 435–436

Index

Index

Cover: Ariel Skelley/Corbis

Internal: v, 20, 327 Rommel/Masterfile; **vi, 144** Terry Vine/Jupiterimages; **vii, 245** Asia Zimmerman/Getty Images; **viii, 295** McGraw-Hill Companies; **ix, 391, 414** Ariel Skelley/Jupiterimages; **x, 497** Creatas/PunchStock; **xi, 606** Liquidlibrary/Jupiterimages; **xiv, 7** Tom Stewart/Zefa/Corbis; **xvi, 299** Paul Chesley/Getty Images; **xvii, 442** Masterfile; **2–3** Yellow Dog Productions/Getty Images; **4–5** Masterfile; **9** Joos Mind/Getty Images; **10(bl)** Royalty-Free/Corbis; **10(br)** Stockbyte/Alamy; **13** Dann Tardif/Jupiterimages; **14** Camille Tokerud/Getty Images; **16** Ariel Skelley/Jupiterimages; **17, 77** Jose Luis Pelaez/Jupiterimages; **22** Frank Siteman/Mira; **24** Joos Mind/Alamy; **26** Masterfile; **30–31, 487** E. Bernager/Jupiterimages; **33** Photodisc Collection/Getty Images; **34, 267(c)** D. Berry/PhotoLink; **37** Asia Images/Jupiterimages; **39** Helena Inkeri/Getty Images; **40, 181** Purestock/PunchStock; **43** Creatas Images/Jupiterimages; **44** Jupiterimages/Real Latino Images; **45** Comstock Images/Jupiterimages; **48** Karen Kasmauski/Corbis; **57** Jim West/Alamy; **59** BananaStock/Jupiterimages; **61** Digital Vision/Getty Images; **62** SW Productions/Getty Images; **63** BananaStock/Alamy; **66** Getty Images; **69, 462** BananaStock/PunchStock; **70** Mieke Dalle/Getty Images; **72** Image Source/Jupiterimages; **73** Liz Banfield/Jupiterimages; **74, 395** Tom Grill/Corbis; **75, 588** Pixland/Jupiterimages; **76** Brand X Pictures/PunchStock; **78, 343** Masterfile; **79** Laurence Mouton/Photoalto/PictureQuest; **82** Peter Dazeley/Getty Images; **88–89** Ariel Skelley/Masterfile; **90–91** Masterfile; **93** Ryan McVay/Getty Images; **96** Corbis; **98** SuperStock; **99** Dennis Degnan/Corbis; **106** James Darrell/Getty Images; **110** Kevin Winter/Getty Images; **111** Sally Greenhill/Alamy; **115** James Leynse/Corbis; **117** ERproductions/Getty Images; **119** Tanya Constantine/Real Latino Images; **121** McGraw-Hill Companies; **127–128** Karen Knaver/Jupiterimages; **129** Brand X Pictures/PunchStock; **130** Purestock/Getty Images; **131** Blend Images/Jupiterimages; **132** P. Gueritot/Jupiterimages; **134(b)** David P. Hall/Masterfile; **134(c)** Adam Crowley/Getty Images; **134(t)** Anthony-Masterson/Jupiterimages; **136** Ryan McVay/Getty Images; **138(bl)** Comstock/Punchstock; **138(br)** Creatas/PunchStock; **138bc** Creatas/PunchStock; **139(bc)** Comstock/PunchStock; **139(bl)** Comstock/PunchStock; **139(br)** StockFood USA; **140** Brand X Pictures/Jupiterimages; **145, 328** Diane McDonald/Getty Images; **146(bl)** Bananastock/PictureQuest; **146(br)** Corbis/PictureQuest; **146(c)** C Squared Studios/Getty Images; **146(t)** Getty Images; **148** Sarah M. Golonka/Brand X Pictures/Jupiterimages; **149** Keith Brofsky/Getty Images; **151** Guy Bubb/Getty Images; **154** Roger Tully/Getty Images; **156** Masterfile; **158** Ale Ventura/Jupiterimages; **162–163** Masterfile; **165** Getty Images; **167** Ron Chapple/Jupiterimages; **170** Masterfile; **171** Mark Richards; **172** Luca Trovato/Getty Images; **175** Ariel Skelley/Getty Images; **176** Marc Asnin/Corbis; **180** Corbis; **182** Louie Psihoyos/Getty Images; **190–191** Somos/Veer; **192–193** Masterfile; **195** DK & Dennie Cody/Masterfile; **197** Bananastock/PictureQuest; **199** Jerzyworks/Masterfile; **200(tl)** Corbis/PictureQuest; **200(tr)** Penny Gentieu/Jupiterimages; **202** The McGraw-Hill Companies/Jill Braaten, photographer; **203** Comstock Images; **204** Getty Images/Altrendo RR; **205(b)** Peter Griffith/Masterfile; **205(t)** Jupiterimages; **206** Bronwyn Kidd/Getty Images; **209** Bananastock/PictureQuest; **210(bl)** Getty Images; **210(br)** Cade Martin/Age Fotostock; **211(bl)** Jupiterimages/BananaStock/Alamy; **211(br)** Getty Images; **212, 235** Super-Stock; **214** Jose Luis Pelaez Inc/Blend Images; **216** E. Dygas/Getty Images; **218** Masterfile; **219** PhotoAlto/Alamy; **222** Brand X Pictures/PunchStock; **223** Getty Images/Blend Images; **225** Masterfile; **228** Photodisc Collection/Getty Images; **232–233** A. Inden/zefa/Corbis; **236(l)** Corbis; **236(r)** Rebecca Emery/Getty Images; **237(bcl)** Brand X Pictures/PunchStock; **237(bcr)** ICHIRO/Getty Images; **237(bl)** Corbis/PictureQuest; **237(br)** rubberball/Getty Images; **238** Jose Luis Pelaez Inc./MediaBakery; **239** Ron Nickel/Design Pics/Corbis; **240** Keren Su/Getty Images; **241** Andy Cox/Getty Images; **246(bl)** Elyse Lewin/Getty Images; **246(br)** Charles Gullung/Getty Images; **246(cl)** Stockbyte/Getty Images; **246(cr)** Brooke Fasani/Corbis; **246(t)** A. Inden/zefa/Corbis; **246(tcl)** Zoe/zefa/Corbis; **247** Jose Luis Pelaez, Inc./CORBIS; **249** Erik Snyder/Getty Images; **254–255** ELC/Alamy; **257** Masterfile; **262** BananaStock/PunchStock; **263** Brand X Pictures/PunchStock; **266** Creatas Images/Jupiterimages; **267(b)** JGI/Jupiterimages; **267(t)** Jade Lee/Jupiterimages; **268** Rolf Bruderer/Masterfile; **274, 554** Trinette Reed/Brand X Pictures/Jupiterimages; **276** Christina Kennedy/Alamy; **278** Andy Eaves/Alamy;

278 Masterfile; 280 Masterfile; 282 Jose Luis Pelaez/Getty Images; 288–289 Masterfile; 291 Arnaldur Halldorsson/Getty Images; 293 Weng Leng/Jupiterimages; 296 Jupiterimages; 298(b) D. Hurst/Alamy; 298(t) Jamie Grill/Jupiterimages; 302 PunchStock/Brand X Pictures; 304(bl) StockFood USA; 304(br) StockFood USA; 305(bc) StockFood USA; 305(bl) StockFood USA; 305(br) Stock-Food USA; 306 OJO Images/Getty Images; 307 Getty Images; 308 Think-Stock/Jupiterimages; 309 Rommel/Masterfile; 311 LWA/Dann Tardiff/Jupiterimages; 312, 394 BananaStock/Age Fotostock; 313 Ian West/Alamy; 318–319 Creatas Images/PictureQuest; 321 Asia Images Group/Getty Images; 322(bl) Masterfile; 322(br) Masterfile; 323(bc) SW Productions/Getty Images; 323(bl) Lisa Dumont/Alamy; 323(br) Masterfile; 325 Masterfile; 326 Jack Hollinsworth/Getty Images; 329 Masterfile; 330 BananaStock/PunchStock; 331 Robert E. Daemmrich/Getty Images; 335 Anderson Ross/Getty Images; 336 Masterfile; 339 Masterfile; 340 Masterfile; 342 Heidi Beuser/Zefa/Corbis; 344 Masterfile; 346 Masterfile; 35 Comstock Images/Jupiterimages; 350–351 Masterfile; 353 BananaStock/PunchStock; 354 BananaStock/PunchStock; 357 Picture Partners / Alamy; 359 Chad Johnston/Masterfile; 360 Elmar Krenkel/Corbis; 361, 430 Masterfile; 364 Jupiterimages/Brand X/Alamy; 365 Brand X/Jupiterimages; 367 Andrew Errington/Getty Images; 368, 417 ThinkStock/Jupiterimages; 369 Paul Hudson/Getty Images; 371, 621 McGraw-Hill Companies; 378–379 Masterfile; 380–381 Flashfilm/Getty Images; 383 ImageStock/PunchStock; 386(b) PhotoDisc/Getty Images; 386(c) DAJ/Getty Images; 386(t) Jack Star/PhotoLink/Getty Images; 389 Banana Stock; 390 Moodboard/Alamy; 392 DB Images/Alamy; 398 Jupiterimages/BananaStock/Alamy; 402–403 Camille Tokerud/Getty Images; 405, 477 Digital Vision/Getty Images; 406 Yellow Dog Productions/Getty Images; 408 Hannes Hepp/Zefa/Corbis; 410 World Portraits/Age Fotostock; 411 Tim Garcha/Corbis; 415 Masterfile; 418 Kevin Dodge/Masterfile; 419 Myrleen Ferguson Cate/PhotoEdit; 424–425 Jose Luis Pelaez/Getty Images; 427 Masterfile; 428 Insadco Photography/Alamy; 429 Jupiter-images; 434 BananaStock/Punch-Stock; 435, 463 Andersen Ross/Getty Images; 437, 508 David Taylor/Alamy; 438 Masterfile; 440 Don Mason/Jupiterimages; 448–449 Bob Daemmrich/PhotoEdit; 450–451 Ariel Skelley/Getty Images; 453 Estelle Rancurel/Getty Images; 455(b) Brand X Pictures/Jupiterimages; 455(cl) Masterfile; 455(cr) Chris Cole/Getty Images; 455(t) M.T.M. Images/Alamy; 459 Royalty-Free/CORBIS; 461 Edible Schoolyard; 464(b) Blend Images/Alamy; 464(c) Insadco Photography/Alamy; 464(t) Stockbyte; 470–471 John-Francis Bourke/Corbis; 473 David Deas/Getty Images; 474 Masterfile; 476 Grady Reese/Superstock; 478 Corbis; 482 Workbook Stock/Jupiterimages; 484 Jupiterimages; 486 Getty Images; 490 David Mendelsohn/Masterfile; 494–495 Masterfile; 498 Royalty-Free/CORBIS; 502 BananaStock/PunchStock; 505 Pierre Tremblay/Masterfile; 507 Digital Vision/Getty Images; 509 Charles Gupton/Corbis; 516–517 Digital Vision/Alamy; 518–519 Masterfile; 521 Seth Goldfarb/Getty Images; 523 Ebby May/Getty Images; 525 Corbis/Alamy; 528 Brand X Pictures/PunchStock; 531 TetraImage/Alamy; 533 Roy Morsch/Corbis; 536 John Eder/Getty Images; 538 Yellow Dog Productions/Getty Images; 54–55 Stewart Cohen/Blend Images/Corbis; 540 BananaStock/Jupiterimages; 544 Ron Chapple/Jupiterimages; 548–549 Rick Gomez/Masterfile; 551 Dann Tardif/Corbis; 558 Gabe Palmer/Jupiterimages; 559 Royalty-Free/Corbis; 570–571 Jack Hollinsworth/Getty Images; 573 Ruth Jenkinson/Getty Images; 576 ER Productions/Brand X Pictures/Jupiterimages; 578 Holly Harris/Getty Images; 579 Brand X Pictures/Jupiterimages; 582 Jim Cummins/Getty Images; 585 Royalty–Free/Corbis; 586 Pierre Tremblay/Masterfile; 591 Masterfile; 594 Randy Faris/Corbis; 596 Jeff Greenberg/Alamy; 60 Ryan McVay/Getty Images; 600-601 Masterfile; 603 Moodboard/Alamy; 608 Big Cheese Photo/Jupiterimages; 611 BananaStock/Jupiterimages; 614 Alison Wright/Corbis; 615 David Buffington/Blend Images/Jupiterimages; 618 Stephanie Maze/Corbis; 619 Photodisc/Alamy; 622 Sean Justice/Getty Images; 628–629 Anderson Ross/Jupiterimages; 631 Jose Luis Pelaez/Getty Images; 632 James Ross/Getty Images; 633 Jeff Greenberg/Alamy; 634 Stockbyte/Getty Images; 639 Andersen Ross/Getty Images; 640 Bob Daemmrich/PhotoEdit; 644 Corbis/Alamy; 645 Ron Nickel/Design Pics/Corbis; 646 IT Stock Free; 647 Ed Eckstein/Corbis; 650 Robert Holmes/Corbis